THE HIDDEN PLACES OF
SCOTLAND

By James Gracie

For Sandra

Regional Hidden Places

Cambs & Lincolnshire
Chilterns
Cornwall
Derbyshire
Devon
Dorset, Hants & Isle of Wight
East Anglia
Gloucs, Wiltshire & Somerset
Hereford, Worcs & Shropshire
Kent
Lake District & Cumbria
Lancashire & Cheshire
Lincolnshire & Nottinghamshire
Northumberland & Durham
Sussex
Yorkshire

National Hidden Places

England
Ireland
Scotland
Wales

Hidden Inns

East Anglia
Heart of England
Lancashire & Cheshire
North of England
South
South East
Wales
Welsh Borders
West Country
Yorkshire

Country Living Rural Guides

East Anglia
Heart of England
Ireland
North East of England
North West of England
Scotland
South
South East
Wales
West Country

Published by: Travel Publishing Ltd, 7a Apollo House, Calleva Park, Aldermaston, Berks, RG7 8TN

ISBN 1-904-434-11-8

First published 1994, second edition 1997, third edition 1999, fourth edition 2002, fifth edition 2004

Printing by: Scotprint, Haddington

Maps by: © Maps in Minutes ™ (2004)
© Crown Copyright, Ordnance Survey 2004

Editor: James Gracie

Cover Design: Lines & Words, Aldermaston

Cover Photograph: Towards Cairngorm Mountains, Loch Morlich, Highlands © www.britainonview.com

Text Photographs: © www.britainonview.com

Foreword

The Hidden Places series is a collection of easy to use travel guides taking you, in this instance, on a relaxed but informative tour of Scotland - a country which has been inhabited for thousands of years and is rich in history and culture. Scotland is blessed with some of the most impressive mountains in the British Isles and finest coastlines and offshore islands in the world. It is also full of "hidden places", which can enrich the visitor's knowledge of Scottish heritage and provide landscapes that astound the eye with their sheer beauty.

The covers and pages of the 5th edition of *The Hidden Places of Scotland* have been comprehensively redesigned and the new format will ensure that readers can properly appreciate the beautiful scenery and the many wonderful places to visit in Scotland.

The Hidden Places of Scotland contains a wealth of interesting information on the history, the countryside, the towns and villages and hundreds of places of interest. But it also promotes the more secluded and little known visitor attractions and places to stay, eat and drink many of which are easy to miss unless you know exactly where you are going.

We include hotels, bed & breakfasts, restaurants, pubs, bars, teashops and cafes as well as historic houses, museums, gardens, and many other attractions throughout Scotland, all of which are comprehensively indexed. Most places are accompanied by an attractive photograph and are easily located by using the map at the beginning of each chapter. We do not award merit marks or rankings but concentrate on describing the more interesting, unusual or unique features of each place with the aim of making the reader's stay in the local area an enjoyable and stimulating experience.

Whether you are travelling around Scotland on business or for pleasure we do hope that you enjoy reading and using this book. We are always interested in what readers think of places covered (or not covered) in our guides so please do not hesitate to use the reader reaction form provided to give us your considered comments. We also welcome any general comments which will help us improve the guides themselves. Finally if you are planning to visit any other corner of the British Isles we would like to refer you to the list of other *Hidden Places* titles to be found to the rear of the book and to the Travel Publishing website at www.travelpublishing.co.uk.

Travel Publishing

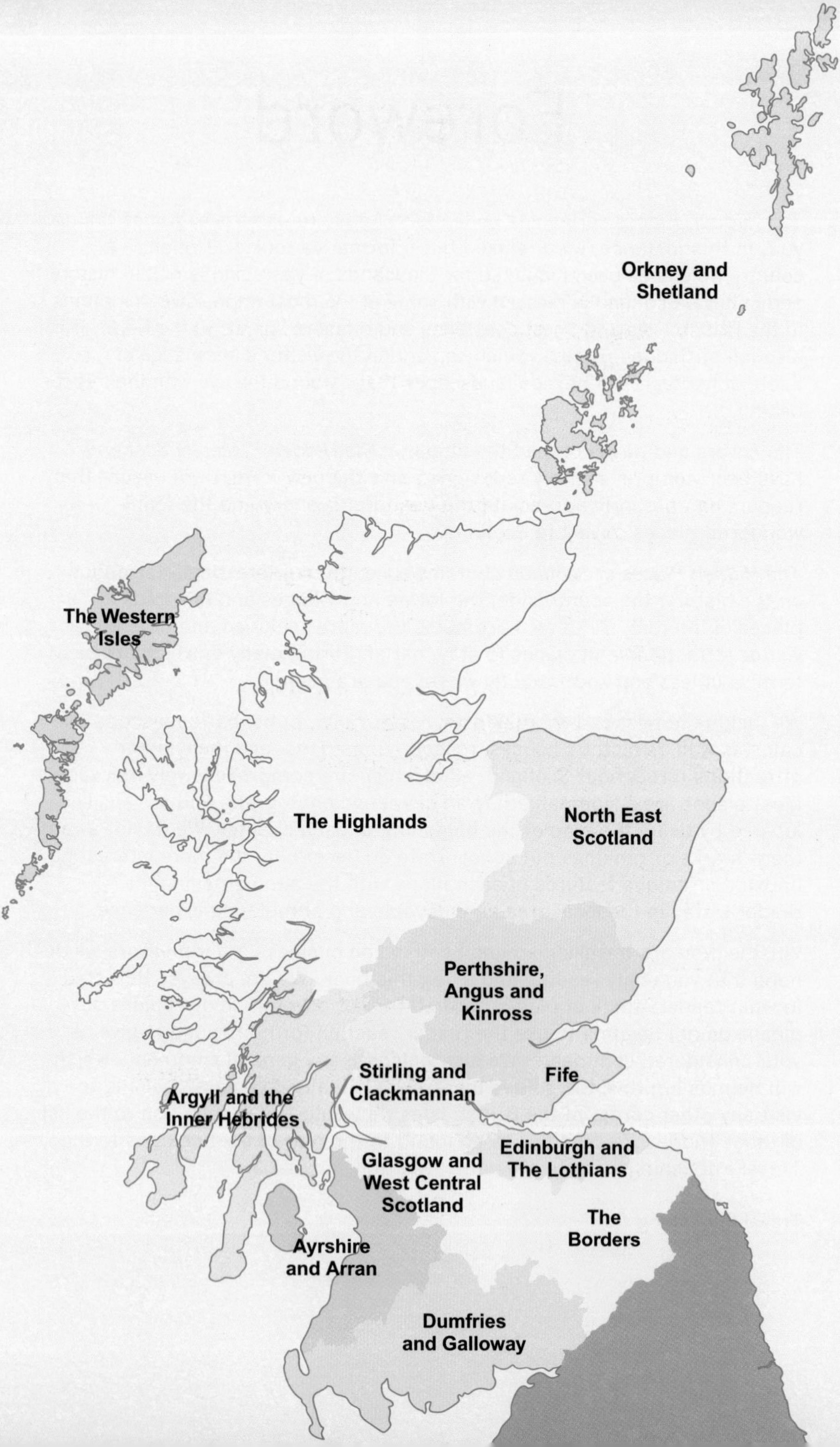
Orkney and Shetland
The Western Isles
The Highlands
North East Scotland
Perthshire, Angus and Kinross
Fife
Stirling and Clackmannan
Argyll and the Inner Hebrides
Edinburgh and The Lothians
Glasgow and West Central Scotland
The Borders
Ayrshire and Arran
Dumfries and Galloway

Contents

The Borders

Of all the regions in Scotland, the Borders has the bloodiest history. It was here, in bygone days, that the constant bickering between Scotland and England boiled over into bloodshed and outright war. This was the land of the reivers, or "moss troopers" - men from both countries who regularly crossed the border and raped, pillaged, burnt and rustled their way into the history books. People nowadays tend to romanticise them, but in fact they were nothing more than upper class thugs, and no one was safe from their activities. They even gave the word "blackmail" to the English language. An old legend that states

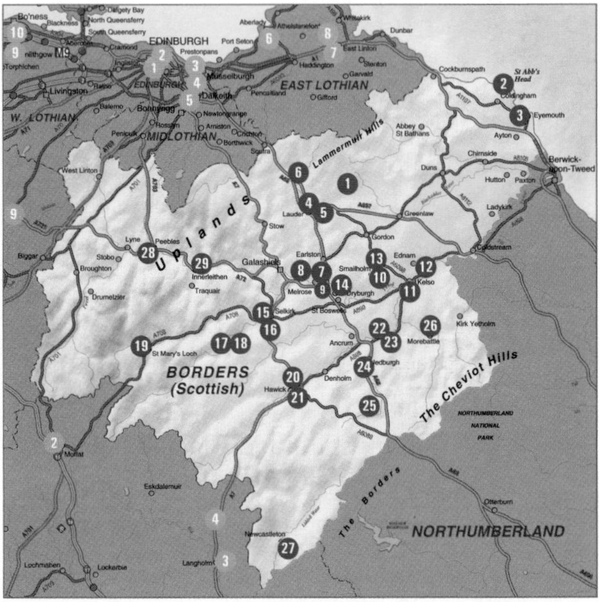

PLACES TO STAY, EAT AND DRINK

Old Thistle Inn, Westruther	1	Pub with Food	p5
St Abbs Head National Nature Reserve	2	Nature Reserve	p7
Ship Hotel, Eyemouth	3	Pub, Food and Accommodation	p8
Thirlestane Castle, Lauder	4	Visitor Attraction	p11
Lauderdale Hotel, Lauder	5	Hotel	p12
The Lodge at Carfraemill, Carfraemill	6	Hotel	p13
Kings Arms Hotel, Melrose	7	Hotel	p16
Fauhope Country House, Gattonside	8	Guest House	p17
Braidwood, Melrose	9	B&B	p18
Smailholm Mains Cottages, Smailholm Mains	10	Self Catering	p19
Oscars, Kelso	11	Bar & Restaurant	p20
Hendersyde Farm Cottages, Kelso	12	Self Catering	p20
Burnbrae Holidays, Nenthorn	13	Self Catering	p21
Dryburgh Abbey Hotel, St. Boswells	14	Hotel	p22
The Place, Selkirk	15	Pub with Food	p23

● Denotes entries in other chapters

that when a male born in the Borders was baptised, his right hand was excluded from the ceremony so that he could use it to kill and maim.

But it was also the land of the Border ballads and tales of high chivalry. Sir Walter Scott, a Borders man, was steeped in them. It was he who, almost single-handedly, invented Scotland's modern image, which depends not on his native heath, but on Highland scenery, skirling bagpipes and kilts. This has not been lost on the hardy Borderers, who know there is more to Scotland than that.

The Borders are not as well known as they should be. People driving north pass through a region that is as beautiful as the Highlands in its own way, and probably has more historical associations than anywhere else in the country. The area stretches from the North Sea in the east to the borders of Dumfriesshire in the west, and contains four former counties – Peeblesshire, Selkirkshire, Roxburghshire and Berwickshire. The scenery is gentler than the Highlands, and the hills are rounded and green, with fertile valleys, quiet villages and cosy market towns to explore. That flat area of Berwickshire known as the Merse, roughly between the Lammermuir Hills and the English border, is one of the most intensely farmed areas in Britain.

There are castles and old houses aplenty, from Floors Castle just outside Kelso, home

The Moor Foot Hills in Winter

PLACES TO STAY, EAT AND DRINK

Queen's Head, Selkirk	16	Pub, Food and Accommodation	p24
Ettrickshaws Country Hotel, Ettrickbridge	17	Hotel	p24
Cross Keys Inn, Ettrickbridge	18	Pub, Food and Accommodation	p25
Tibbie Shiels Inn, St Mary's Loch	19	Pub, Food and Accommodation	p27
Gretel Bar & Restaurant, Hawick	20	Bar & Restaurant	p28
Ellistrin, Hawick	21	Guest House	p29
Hoolets Nest, Mount Hooley	22	B&B and Self Catering	p29
Crailing Old School, Crailing	23	B&B	p30
Meadhon House, Jedburgh	24	B&B	p30
Jedburgh, Camptown	25	Wildlife Park	p31
Templehall Inn, Morebattle	26	Pub, Food and Accommodation	p32
Grapes Hotel, Newcastleton	27	Pub, Restaurant & Accommodation	p34
Glentress Hotel, Peebles	28	Hotel	p35
Corner House Hotel, Innerleithen	29	Hotel	p37

● Denotes entries in other chapters

of the Duke of Roxburgh, to 10th century Traquair House in Peeblesshire, said to be the oldest continually inhabited house in Scotland. Mellerstain too, is worth visiting, as is Paxton, Manderston, Thirlestane and Abbotsford.

But perhaps the area's most beautiful and haunting attractions are its ruined abbeys. Again and again English soldiers attacked them, and again and again, as the Scots crossed the border bent on revenge, the monks quietly got on with rebuilding and repairing them. Now the ruins at Melrose, Kelso, Dryburgh and Jedburgh rest easy under the care of Historic Scotland, and they can be easily visited and appreciated.

The Cheviot Hills

The area's great icon is the River Tweed which, for part of its length, forms the boundary between Scotland and England. Just east of Kelso, the border turns south, and the river is wholly Scottish. Its fame rests on salmon, though not as many are caught nowadays as there used to be. But it is still a river that in some ways defines the region, and most of the larger settlements, from Peebles to Coldstream, are to be found on its banks

The Borders is an area of woodland and forests, and there are plenty of woodland walks. The newly created Tweed Valley Forest Park, between Peebles and Selkirk, is one of the best. At Glentress Forest, a few miles east of Peebles, you can even hire mountain bikes at the Hub car park.

A series of themed trails has recently been laid out which takes you round many Borders attractions. The Ballads Trail (103 miles) takes you to many of the places associated with the Borders ballads; the Poets Trail (118 miles) takes you to places of literary interest; the Berwickshire Car Trail (72 miles) explores the "mysteries of the Merse"; the Sir Walter Scott Trail (66 miles) follows the footsteps of the poet and novelist; the James Hogg Trail (62 miles) takes you to places associated with the writer known as "The Ettrick Shepherd", and the John Buchan Trail (77 miles) looks at places associated with the man who wrote "The Thirty Nine Steps".

If you want to explore the area by bus, a series of leaflets and timetables is published by the Scottish Borders Council giving details of places to visit on or near bus routes. Contact the Transport and Environmental Standards Department. The local tourist board also publish booklets detailing several good walks in the area, plus one on golf courses.

Duns

Berwickshire is an unusual county, in that the town which gave it its name has been within another country since 1482. So Greenlaw, and then in 1853 Duns, was chosen as the county town. It is a quiet, restful place with a wide and gracious market square.

On its outskirts is **Duns Law**, which from the top gives a magnificent view of the surrounding countryside. The Cheviot Hills to the south and the Lammermuir Hills to the north can be seen on a clear day, as can the North Sea, 12 miles away. In 1639 a Covenanting army, which opposed the imposition of bishops on the Scottish church by Charles I, set up camp here under General Leslie, and a **Coventator's Stone** commemorates this. On the west side of Duns Law is a cairn, which marks the original site of the town, now called The Bruntons, or "burnt towns".

It was in old Duns that **John Duns Scotus**, known as the "subtle doctor", was supposed to have been born in about 1265 or 1266. He was a Franciscan monk who became one of the greatest theologians and philosophers of his time. His followers were known as Scotists, and his influence is still felt within the Catholic Church to this day. However, his opponents had another, less flattering, name for them - "Dunses" - from which we get the word "dunce". He eventually died at Cologne in 1308. In 1991 the Pope made him "Venerable", the first step on the ladder to sainthood. In Duns Public Park there is a bronze statue of him and in the grounds of **Duns Castle** the modern Franciscan Order erected a cairn to his memory in 1966 (see also North Uist).

Also in the grounds of Duns Castle is the quaintly named **Hen Poo**, centrepiece for the **Duns Castle Nature Reserve**, owned and run by the Scottish Wildlife Trust. There is a bird hide on the northern shore, and from here you can see mallard ducks, tufted ducks, swans, and coots.

Within the town there is a memorial to a famous man who lived in more recent times. Jim Clark, the racing driver, was born in Fife, but from the age of six lived on a farm near Duns. He was killed in Germany in 1968 and the **Jim Clark Memorial Trophy Room** in Newtown Street is dedicated to his memory. He was world champion in 1963 and 1965, and motor racing enthusiasts from all over the world make the pilgrimage to view the trophies (including the two world championship trophies he won) and mementoes on display. He is buried in Chirnside Parish Church cemetery, about five miles east of Duns.

On the west side of Market Square is the **Tolbooth House**, once the town house of Sir James Cockburn, who owned most of the land surrounding Duns in the 17th century. The local council have recently laid out a town trail, taking you to places of interest. A leaflet is available, linked to plaques at many places within the town.

Old Thistle Inn

Westruther, Berwickshire TD3 6NE
Tel/Fax: 01578 740275
e-mail: mike@struthers355.freeserve.co.uk

The **Old Thistle Inn** is a traditional country pub which dates back to 1721. It stands in a picturesque old village, and retains many original features, such as old, exposed beams. Food is the star here, as the owner, Mike Struthers, is a superb chef.

There is a handsome menu and a chalk board packed with mouth watering dishes, with only the finest and freshest of local produce being used in the kitchens. Or you can enjoy a pint or a single malt in the cosy bar or the beer garden. The Old Thistle Inn is the perfect place for a meal or a drink while visiting the Scottish Borders.

Manderston House lies a mile east of the town and is open to the public. It was built between 1903 and 1905, and was the last great stately home built in Britain. It incorporates a silver staircase that is said to be the only one in the world. Nowadays Manderston is the home of the Palmer family, of the famous Huntly and Palmer biscuit empire, which explains why it houses a large collection of biscuit tins.

East of Duns, at Broomhouse, is the grave of the **Seigneur de la Beaute**, a handsome Frenchman who was warden of the Merse and Teviotdale, murdered in the 16th century by the powerful David Home of Wedderburn, who considered that James V should have made him warden. The seigneur's head was hacked from his body and the rest of him was buried where he fell. The head was subsequently paraded round Duns by David Home.

Around Duns

Abbey St Bathans

7 miles N of Duns on a minor road off the B6355

The pretty village of Abbey St Bathans lies in the valley of the Whiteadder Water, deep within the Lammermuir Hills. It is truly a hidden gem, and sits on the **Southern Upland Way**, the coast-to-coast footpath that transverses Southern Scotland from Portpatrick in the west to Cockburnspath in the east. It was here, in 1170, that Ada, Countess of Dunbar, founded the priory of St Mary, and parts of the priory church have been incorporated into the present **Parish Church**. The tombstone of a former prioress, which touchingly shows her pet dog, is preserved within it. To the south, at **Cockburn Law**, are the ruins of the Iron Age **Edins Hall Broch**, one of the few brochs (a round, fortified stone tower) to be found in Southern Scotland. It is named after Etin, a legendary giant with three heads who is said to have terrorised the area in olden times.

Cockburnspath

13 miles N of Duns just off the A1

The **Parish Church** is partly 14th century, and close by is ruined **Cockburnspath Tower**, dating from the 15th and 16th centuries. In its time it has been owned by the Dunbars, the Homes, the Sinclairs and the Douglases. The village sits close to **Pease Dean**, a Scottish Wildlife Trust reserve. **Pease Bridge** was built in in 1783 and at the time was the highest stone bridge in Europe.

Coldingham

13 miles NE of Duns on the A1107

The village of Coldingham, a mile from the coast, is visited mainly for the remains of **Coldingham Priory**. It was founded in 1098 by King Edgar, son of Malcolm Canmore, and he gifted it to the monks of Durham. It suffered badly during the Scottish Wars of Independence and was finally blown up by Cromwell in 1648. Only the tower and a couple of walls were left standing. In 1854 the remains were restored, and today they are incorporated into the village's parish church.

Four miles NW of the village, on the coast, are the ruins of **Fast Castle**, a former Hume stronghold. They are perched on a cliff top and can be reached via a minor road, though the last few hundred yards must be done on foot. Great care must be taken when visiting, however.

St. Abb's

12 miles NE of Duns, on the B6438

The picturesque fishing village of St Abb's has a small, picturesque harbour. The whole coastline here is rugged and spectacular, one of the most magnificent parts being **St Abb's Head** (National Trust for Scotland - see panel opposite), to the north of the village. The cliffs are over 300 feet high, and are riddled with caves once haunted by smugglers. A monastery for monks and nuns was established on the cliff tops in the 7th

The Harbour at St. Abb's Head

century, and St Ebba, sister of Oswy, King of Northumbria, eventually became a nun here. An old legend recounts that the nuns, instead of living a life of austerity and prayer, spent all their time eating, drinking and gossiping. The whole area is now managed by the National Trust for Scotland and is a National Nature Reserve. Offshore there is one of the best diving sites in the country.

Chirnside

5 miles E of Duns on the B6355

Chirnside sits on a low hill with wonderful views of the surrounding countryside, and nearby is where the Blackadder Water and the Whiteadder Water meet. During World War I the peace of the village was shattered when a Zeppelin bombed it by accident. The **Parish Church** is partly Norman, and an impressive Norman doorway can be seen at its west end. Within the cemetery is the grave of Jim Clark the racing driver. The **Jim Clark Memorial Clock**, with a silhouette of a Lotus racing car on it, stands in the middle of the village.

David Hulme, the 18th century philosopher, though born in Edinburgh, was educated at Chirnside School until he was 12 years old.

Edrom

3 miles E of Duns on a minor road off the A6105

The small village of Edrom has a fine **Parish Church** (Historic Scotland) built in 1732 which incorporates Norman details. Attached to it is the Blackadder Aisle, built for Archbishop Blackadder of Glasgow in

Ship Hotel

Harbour Street, Eyemouth,
Berwickshire TD14 5HT
Tel: 018907 502244

The **Ship Hotel** is a traditional, whitewashed hostelry that sits right on the quayside at Eyemouth, a fishing port that is both historic and picturesque. It is popular with locals (always a good sign!) and tourists alike, and has plenty of olde worlde charm. It is owned and managed by Les Alderman, who recently refurbished the inn to an extremely high standard while retaining many period features that give the place a cosy yet spacious ambience. Value for money combined with modern standards of service means that the Ship Hotel is one of the best hostelries in the area, and if you are visiting this beautiful part of Scotland, it is not to be missed.

The accommodation is superb. The six rooms all have colour television, hair dryers and tea/coffee making facilities, and all are fully en suite. They have been decorated and furnished with the guest in mind, and make comfortable, convenient overnight stopping places if you are travelling north or south. They can also be used as a base for a superb holiday exploring the many charms to be found in this part of the Scottish Borders.

Why not call in at its friendly bar for a relaxing, quiet drink? It is noted for its cosy, welcoming atmosphere - a place to pass the time of day with the friendly locals who will point you in the direction of many beautiful, historical sites in Berwickshire, It is also famous for stocking local real ales from the Hadrian and Borders brewery. Of course, other ales and beers are also available. Plus there is a fine range of spirits (including a range of single malts), wines, liqueurs and soft drinks should you be driving. You could also combine your visit with a wonderfully cooked meal. Being located in a fishing port, seafood predominates, though juicy steaks with all the trimmings, delicious vegetables and chicken are also available. The bar lunches are superb and competitively priced, as are the evening meals. In fact, this is the perfect place to celebrate a happy event, such as an anniversary or birthday! The cuisine is Scottish with some exotic hints, and only the finest and freshest of local produce is used wherever possible.

The full Scottish breakfasts, if you re staying overnight, are hearty and filling - just right to set you up for a day driving or sightseeing. If you prefer something lighter, then Continental breakfasts are also on offer.

Les Alderman is determined to maintain the high standards he has set in the past. For this reason the Ship Inn is a friendly, welcoming place where you will arrive a stranger and leave a friend. So pay it a visit - you are sre of a warm, Scottish welcome!

1499. It contains a tomb and effigy dating from 1553. A burial vault in the graveyard incorporates a Norman arch. The church was gifted to the monks of Coldingham in 1130. In 1499 it was enlarged, and in 1737 partially rebuilt.

Ayton Castle

Hutton

10 miles E of Duns on a minor road off the B6460

Close to the village stands **Hutton Castle**, one time home of Sir William Burrell, shipping magnate and art collector, who donated the Burrell Collection to the city of Glasgow in 1944 (see also Largs). It sits overlooking the River Whiteadder. **Hutton Parish Church** dates from 1835 and has an old bell of 1661.

Ayton

10 miles E of Duns on the B6355

Ayton, a mile or so from the A1, is a pleasant village that sits on the River Eye. Close by is **Ayton Castle**, a fantastic froth of fairy tale pinnacles dating from the 1840s and designed by James Gillespie Graham, a leading Gothic revival architect. It is reckoned to be one of the best examples in the country of that style of architecture called "Scottish Baronial". It is surrounded by a 6000-acre estate, and is open from May - September by appointment. It houses fine paintings, furniture and porcelain.

Eyemouth

12 miles E of Duns on the A1107

Eyemouth is a picturesque little fishing town standing, as the name suggests, at the mouth of the River Eye. The monks of Coldingham Priory founded it as a small fishing port sometime in the 13th century.

Eyemouth

At one time it was a smuggling centre, and some of the harbour-side houses still have old cellars and tunnels where contraband was stored. The centre of the trade was at **Gunsgreen House**, to the south of the harbour. It dates from the 18th century and was designed by James and John Adam. There is a Museum of Smuggling in its basement. Every year in July the **Herring Queen Festival** takes place, when a gaily-bedecked fishing fleet escorts the "Herring Queen" into Eyemouth harbour.

Eyemouth Museum records the history of the town and its fishing industry. Perhaps the most poignant exhibit is a 15-feet long by four feet wide tapestry sewn in 1981 that commemorates "Disaster Day" - October 14, 1881. A great storm wrecked the whole of the town's fishing fleet, and 189 fishermen, 129 from Eyemouth alone, perished in sight of the shore.

Foulden

9 miles E of Duns on the A6105

Foulden Parish Church, at the far end of the village, dates from 1786. Near it is an old **Tithe Barn** (Historic Scotland), dating from medieval times, though restored in the 18th and 19th centuries. "Tithe" means a tenth, and each farmer in the parish was supposed to donate a tenth of his crops to the church, and it was in the barn that it was stored.

Paxton

12 miles E of Duns just off the B6460 and close to the Tweed

Near the village stands **Paxton House**, built in 1758 by Patrick Home, later the 13th Laird of Wedderburn, in anticipation of his marriage to the illegitimate daughter of Frederick the Great of Prussia. Alas, the marriage never took place, though a pair of kid gloves given to Patrick by Frederick's daughter is on display. The house was designed by John and James Adam, with plasterwork by their brother Robert, and it is reckoned to be the finest Palladian mansion in Britain. It houses the finest collection of Chippendale furniture in Scotland, and the art gallery is the largest private gallery in Scotland. It now houses paintings from the National Galleries of Scotland.

It sits in 80 acres of grounds on the banks of the Tweed, with nature trails, woodland walks and a "Paxton Ted" teddy bear trail. From the award-winning red squirrel hide you can catch glimpses of what has become one of Scotland's rarest mammals. In the boathouse on the riverbank is a museum dedicated to salmon net fishing.

Close by is the **Union Suspension Bridge** across the Tweed, connecting Scotland and England. It was built in 1820 by Sir Samuel Browne, who also invented the wrought-iron chain links used in its construction. It is 480 feet long and was Britain's first major suspension bridge to carry vehicular traffic as well as pedestrians.

Ladykirk

7 miles SE of Duns on a minor road off the B6470 and close to the Tweed

The **Parish Church of St Mary** dates from 1500 and is built entirely of stone in case the English ever burnt it. It is supposed to owe its origins to James IV, who had it built in thanksgiving after he was rescued from drowning while trying to cross the Tweed. At the same time he is also supposed to have changed the name of the village from Upsettington to Ladykirk.

Coldstream

12 miles S of Duns on the A697

The town is famous as being the birthplace of the **Coldstream Guards**. It sits on the north bank of the Tweed at a point where the river forms the border between Scotland and England. **Coldstream Bridge**, joining the two countries, was built in 1766, and replaced a ford that had been a natural crossing point for centuries. On the bridge is a plaque that commemorates the fact that Robert Burns entered England by this route in 1787. In the 19th century, Coldstream rivalled Gretna Green as a place for runaway marriages. At the Scottish end of the bridge is the **Old Toll House**, where, in a 13-year period during the 19th century, 1466 marriages were conducted.

General Monk founded the Coldstream Guards in 1659. It is the only regiment in Britain to take its name from a town, and within **Henderson Park** is a memorial stone which commemorates the regiment's foundation. The **Coldstream Museum** in Market Square houses extensive displays on its history. It also has a children's section and a courtyard with fountain and picnic area.

A mile north of the town is **The Hirsel**, home of the Earls of Home since 1611. Sir Alec Douglas Home, the British prime minister, lived here. Though the house isn't open to the public, the grounds can be explored. There is also a small museum, a crafts centre, a gem display and a tearoom.

Fogo

3 miles S of Duns off the B6460

Fogo Church dates from the late 17th century, though parts of it - especially the lower courses of its masonry - date from the 13th century or earlier. On the north wall are traces of built up arches. The church bell dates from 1644, and the picturesque lych gate is now a war memorial. Within the vestry is one of the oldest gravestones in Berwickshire, dating from the 14th century. The church's communion cups are the oldest still in use, and date from 1662. They were presented to the church by George Trotter of Charterhall. On the outside wall of the church are stairs leading to private lofts, where the gentry once worshipped.

Greenlaw

7 miles SW of Duns on the A697

Greenlaw was the county town of Berwickshire from 1696 to 1853, when Duns replaced it. The tower of the **Parish Church** dates from 1712, and was originally a jail. There are many fine buildings within the town, including a town hall built in 1829. Three miles south are the impressive ruins of **Hume Castle**, ancient seat of the Hume family. It was captured by Cromwell in 1651 and partly restored in 1794. The castle sits 600 feet above sea level, and makes an excellent viewpoint.

Lauder

17 miles W of Duns on the A68

To the east of the town is **Thirlestane Castle** (see panel below), which is open to

Thirlestane Castle

Lauder, Berwickshire TD2 6RU
Tel: 01578 722430 Fax: 01578 722761
e-mail: admin@thirlestanecastle.co.uk
website: www.thirlestanecastle.co.uk

Thirlestane, one of the oldest and finest castles in Scotland is set in lovely Border hills at Lauder, 28 miles south of Edinburgh and 68 miles north of Newcastle, on the A68. Built originally as a defensive fort in the 13th century it was re-built in the 16th century as the home of the Maitlands. As the seat of the Earls and Duke of Lauderdale it was enlarged and embellished over the centuries but it still remains home to the Maitland family. The Duke's ghost is said to haunt the castle.

See the Panelled Room and the Library with their defensive walls up to 13' thick. Absorb the atmosphere of the Billiard Room with its fascinating salmon fly screen. Climb the ancient turnpike stair to the Duke's Suite, including the incomparable 17th century plasterwork ceilings. Relish the splendour of the Green Drawing Room and the Ante Drawing Room with their exquisite ceilings and joinery. Meet the Maitlands through the portrait collection in the State Dining Room and discover some of their fascinating treasures. Sink into nostalgia as you enter the Family Nurseries with their unique collection of historic toys. Some are in replica form for children to use and dipping into the dressing up chest can create some memorable moments on a family holiday. Discover the old Kitchens and Laundries, and explore the Border Country Life exhibitions showing domestic, sporting and agricultural life over the centuries.

Lauderdale Hotel

1 Edinburgh Road, Lauder,
Berwickshire TD2 6TW
Tel: 01578 722231 Fax: 01578 718642
e-mail: enquiries@lauderdalehotel.co.uk
website: www.lauderdale-hotel.co.uk

Lauderdale must be one of the most beautiful of the Borders dales. Right at its heart is the old royal burgh of Lauder, famous for its old kirk in the shape of a Greek cross, and for Thirlestane Castle, one of the great Borders houses. And in the town you will find the **Lauderdale Hotel**. Stone-built and well-proportioned, it sits on the Edinburgh Road and is the ideal base for exploring the area. Ten bedrooms are available - one family, three doubles and six twins. All rooms are

non-smoking with full en suite and furnished and decorated to a high standard, with satellite TVs , hospitality trays, direct dial telephones, radio alarm and complimentary toiletries. Extra bedding is available if required.

Comfort and elegance are the watchwords here, though the place, under the careful eye of owner Wilson McKay and manager Jennifer Hogarth, has a friendly, family atmosphere to make you feel relaxed as soon as you cross the threshold. Curl up with a good book in the spacious yet cosy residents' lounge, or watch a video on the wide-screen TV. Or why not listen to the local craic in the traditional Reivers lounge bar, which has a wide range of drinks on offer, You could sample one of the local beers, or perhaps try a glass or wine (even bubbly, if you're celebrating!) or one of the hotel's single malts.

One Edinburgh Road is the hotel's stylish

yet comfortable café bar and bistro. The intimate, yet casual surroundings offer a wide choice of freshly prepared lunches, high teas, suppers and grills. The Leader Restaurant is a small, charming non-smoking restaurant. A full range of both table d'hote and à la carte menus are available. Breakfast is served in true Scottish tradition from either the buffet or tradition breakfast with all the trimmings. You can also enjoy a bar snack, pub lunch or main meal. The food is beautifully cooked, and uses only the finest and freshest of local produce wherever possible. The hotel is open from early morning for breakfast to non residents, lunchtime meals are served from 11am - 3pm and in the evening from 5pm until 8.45pm. Pre-packed meals are always available by prior arrangement. The menus are sure to have something that will appeal to you, and a wide range of vegetarian dishes are always available. Plus, of course, you can choose from an extensive range of fine wines that will complement any cuisine.

There is a large function suite for a party or wedding, and delightful patio gardens to sit in the sun. Group bookings or short break bookings are always welcome, and pre-booked coach parties can be accommodated. There is ample private parking.

The Lauderdale Hotel combines gracious living with a relaxed, casual atmosphere.

the public. It's a flamboyant place, with turrets, pinnacles and towers, giving it the appearance of a French château. It was originally built in the 13th century, but was extended and refurbished in the 16th century for the Maitland family, whose most famous member was John Maitland, Earl and later Duke of Lauderdale. He was a close friend of Charles II and a member of the famous "Cabal Cabinet". So powerful was he that he was soon regarded as the uncrowned king of Scotland. His ghost is said to haunt the castle.

Lauder Parish Church was built in 1673 in the form of a Greek cross and designed by Sir William Bruce. The medieval church formerly stood in the grounds of Thirlestane Castle, and legend states that the Duke had it removed in the

Harvesting, Lauderdale

17th century to improve his view. He instructed a bowman to fire an arrow

The Lodge At Carfraemill

Carfraemill, Lauder, Berwickshire TD2 6RA
Tel: 01578 750750
Fax: 01578 750751
e-mail: enquiries@carfraemill.co.uk
website: www.carfraemill.co.uk

Situated at the junction of the A68 and the A697 north of the small, attractive town of Lauder, **The Lodge at Carfraemill** is one of Scotland's most unusual and distinguished

hotels. It offers the highest standards in a relaxed and informal atmosphere, with its beautiful rooms, its superb food and its friendly service. A team of expert chefs are waiting to prepare exciting and innovative meals for you. Luxurious without being pretentious and traditional without being caught in the past, the hotel offers everyone a warm welcome! Situated on the A68/A697, it makes the ideal overnight stopping place if you're heading to or from Edinburgh!

Brae Lads Gathering, Galashiels

westwards from the castle steps. Wherever the arrow landed the Duke would build a new church. That is why the church now stands within the town of Lauder itself.

Galashiels

Galashiels (known locally as "Gala") sits on the Gala Water, and is a manufacturing town at one time noted for its tweed and woollen mills. As a reflection of this, the motto of the Galashiels Manufacturer's Corporation was "We dye to live and live to die". The **Lochcarron of Scotland Cashmere and Wool Centre** is located within the Waverley Mill in Huddersfield Street, and offers tours which explain the processes involved in the manufacture of woollens and tweeds.

However, the town is very old (the first mention of cloth mills is found in 1588), and every year, in July, it holds the **Brae Lads Gathering**, which celebrates its long history. On the coat of arms of the old burgh appears the words "soor plooms" (sour plums), which refers to an incident in 1337, when some English troops were killed after crossing the border and stealing plums in the town. In 1503, the betrothal of James IV to Margaret Tudor, Henry VII's daughter, took place at the town's old **Mercat Cross**. It's successor dates from 1695.

Old Gala House dates from the 15th century with later additions, and at one time was the town house of the Pringles, Lairds of Gala. It is now a museum and art gallery, and its gardens have recently been re-established, with a pond, spring bulbs and rhododendrons. Exhibitions of local art are sometimes held in the house. In Bank Street are the **Bank Street Gardens**, laid out shortly after World War II. In front of the town's war memorial (described by H.V. Morton as "the most perfect town memorial in the British Isles") is a reminder of the area's bloody past - a bronze statue of a border reiver, armed and on horseback.

Two miles south of the town, on the banks of the Tweed, is **Abbotsford**, the home of **Sir Walter Scott**, writer and lawyer. Scott had it built between 1817 and 1822, and he lived in it until he died. Behind it is the Tweed, and here the monks of Melrose Abbey made a ford across the river, so Scott decided to call it Abbotsford. It is built in the Scottish Baronial style, and is crammed with mementoes and objects that reflected the great man's passion for Scottish history, such as a tumbler on which Burns had etched some verses, a lock of Charles Edward Stuart's hair, and a piece of oatcake found in the pocket of a Highlander killed at Culloden. There is more than a hint of Gothic about the interior, especially the panelled hallway, which contains a carriage clock - still keeping good time - once owned by Marie Antoinette.

The main focus of the house is Scott's austere study, where many of his books were written. A gallery runs round the room, and in one corner is a door with a stairway behind it. Early each morning Scott descended these stairs from his dressing room to write for a few hours before heading for the courthouse in Selkirk.

Perhaps the most poignant room in the house is the dining room. Having returned from a trip abroad in September 1832, Scott knew that his end was near, and called for his bed to be set up at the window so that he could look out towards the Tweed. On September 21 he died. He had never got over the death of his wife in 1826, and at about the same time a publishing firm in which he was a partner went bankrupt. He decided to pay back everything that was owed through writing, even though he still had his duties at Selkirk Sheriff Court to attend to, and it eventually ruined his health. He now lies beside his wife among the ruins of Dryburgh Abbey.

The Southern Upland Way passes through Galashiels, and you can also join the **Tweed Cycle Way**, which passes close by.

Around Galashiels

Clovenfords

3 miles W of Galashiels on the A72

Clovenfords sits about a mile north of the Tweed, and is home to the **School of Casting, Salmon and Trout Fishing**. It offers weekly courses throughout the season. In 1803 William and Dorothy Wordsworth stayed at a local inn while touring the Scottish Borders.

Stow

5 miles N of Galashiels on the A7

Stow (sometimes called Stow-in-Wedale) is a delightful village on the Gala Water. The imposing **St Mary of Wedale Parish Church** has a spire over 140 feet high. To the west of the village are the lonely Moorfoot Hills, and to the east is some further moorland which separates it from Lauderdale. The B6362 leaves Stow and climbs up onto the moorland, reaching a height of 1100 feet before descending through Lauder Common into the small town of Lauder.

Gordon

11 miles NE of Galashiels on the A6089

This pleasant village is the cradle of the Gordon clan, which moved north into Aberdeenshire in the 14th century (see Huntly). The village sits on a crossroads, and to the north are the well-preserved ruins of **Greenknowe Tower**, built in 1581 by James Seton of Touch and his wife Jane Edmonstone. It is a typical L-shaped tower house, built originally as a fortified home. The Pringles, one of the great Borders families, later acquired it.

Mellerstain

10 miles E of Galashiels, on an unmarked road between the A6089 and the B6397

Mellerstain is a grand mansion originally designed by William Adam in the 1720s, with later work by his son Robert. It is one of the grandest Georgian houses in Britain, and holds a collection of fine furniture as well as paintings by Van Dyck, Naismith, Gainsborough and Ramsey. The Italian terraces were laid out in 1909 by Sir Reginald Blomfield, and give excellent views out over a small artificial loch towards the Cheviots.

Melrose

3 miles SE of Galashiels just off the A6091

Melrose sits in the shadow of the triple peaks of the **Eildon Hills**, which have a waymarked path leading to their summits. Legend states that **King Arthur** and his court lie buried beneath one of them. Another legend says that the entrance to the Fairy Kingdom lies among the Eildon Hills, and that Thomas the Rhymer (see

KINGS ARMS HOTEL

High Street, Melrose TD6 9PB
Tel: 01896 822143 Fax: 01896 823812
e-mail: enquiries@kingsarmsmelrose.co.uk
website: www.kingsarmsmelrose.co.uk

The three star **Kings Arms Hotel** is one of the Scottish Borders best loved inns. It sits right at the heart of Melrose, a delightfully picturesque market town that boasts the ruins of one of the finest abbeys in the country. This former coaching inn is over 300 years old, and has now been lovingly restored so that it offers modern standards of service while still retaining period features that make it a place full of character and charm.

The hotel is ideally placed for a host of activities, from golf to fishing and from bird watching to hiking and horse riding. Most can be arranged by the hotel on your behalf. In fact, it was in the hotel that the Melrose Rugby Club once met and founded that branch of rugby called Rugby Sevens, which is now played all over the world.

It is a family run hotel, owned and managed by Georgina and John Fisher and Colin Shepherd. The atmosphere is friendly, welcoming and fun, with value for money and high standards being the watchwords. The seven comfortable bedrooms on offer are all fully en suite, and are decorated and furnished to an extremely high standard, with a traditional Scottish feel to the décor. You're sure of a good night's sleep here! And the courtyard cottage is the perfect place for a self-catering break. It sleeps up to four in double and twin rooms, and has a kitchen and sitting room.

And if you enjoy good food, you've made the right choice if you dine here! The cuisine is traditional Scottish. Over 30 main courses are available, and all are cooked to perfection, using only fresh local produce wherever possible, such as beef, game, fish and locally grown vegetables. The select wine list carries many fine vintages, and there's sure to be a wine that will match your meal to perfection. Lunches are served from noon until 2 pm, and dinners are served between 6.30 pm (6 pm on Sunday) and 9.30 pm on weekdays and 10 pm on Saturdays. All are served either in the cosy, comfortable bar or in the non-smoking family restaurant.

The Kings Arms hotel is also the perfect place to have that quiet, relaxing drink, and indeed it recently won a "Perfect Pub Award" from Green King. There is a fine range of wine, spirits, liqueurs and soft drinks on offer, and the hotel has been recognised by the Campaign for Real Ale for its beers. You have the choice of a public bar - which is popular with the locals - or an elegant cocktail bar.

The staff are friendly and knowledgeable, and are determined that you are going to enjoy your stay at the Kings Arms Hotel. Packed lunches and flasks can be made up by prior arrangement. Holiday packages and special offers can be arranged round particular themes, such as shopping breaks, as Edinburgh, Glasgow, Newcastle and Carlisle are within easy driving distance. Well behaved pets are welcome by prior arrangement, and there is a private car park.

Earlston) used it to visit the magical kingdom for years at a time.

This quiet town, which is on the Southern Upland Way, is mainly visited nowadays to view the ruins of **Melrose Abbey** (Historic Scotland), surely the loveliest of all the Borders abbeys. It was founded in 1136 by David I, and rose to become one of the most important in Scotland. The ruins that the visitor sees nowadays date mainly from the late 14th and early 15th centuries, thanks to the English army of Richard II, which destroyed the earlier buildings. It was here that the heart of Robert the Bruce, Scotland's great hero during the Wars of Independence, was buried. After his death it had been removed and placed in a casket so that Sir James Douglass might take it for burial in the Holy Land. But Sir James was killed, and the casket found its way back to Scotland and Melrose. In the late 1990s, during some restoration work on

Melrose Town and Abbey

the abbey, the lead casket containing his heart was rediscovered and subsequently reburied within the abbey grounds. A plaque in the ground now marks its resting place (see also Dunfermline).

On a bend in the Tweed, two miles from the town, is the site of **Old Melrose**, where, in about AD 650, Celtic monks from Iona established a monastery. It was near here, in about AD 635, that a young shepherd, who was later to become **St Cuthbert**, was born. In AD 651, following a vision in which he saw the soul of St Aidan of Lindisfarne ascending to heaven, he entered the monastery to train as a monk. He eventually became Prior of Lindisfarne, and is now buried in Durham Cathedral. A 62-mile walking route called **St Cuthbert's Way** links Melrose and Lindisfarne.

Close to the abbey ruins is **Priorwood Gardens** (National Trust for Scotland). It specialises in plants which are suitable for drying and arranging, and classes are organised to teach the techniques involved. **Harmony Garden**, also run by the Trust, is close by. It is set around a 19th century house which is not open to the public, and has excellent views of the Eildon Hills. The house and small estate was built by Robert Waugh, a Melrose joiner, in the early 19th century after making his fortune from a Jamaica plantation called "Harmony".

The **100 Aker Wood Visitor Centre** is on the old Melrose to Newstead road, and has woodland walks, a childrens' play area, a coffee shop and car park.

A mile east of Melrose is **Newstead,** where there are the remains of **Trimontium Roman Fort**, covering 15 acres, and named after the three peaks of the Eildons. At its height it housed 1500 Roman soldiers, and supported a large town which covered a further 200 acres. **The Three Hills Roman Heritage Centre**, in the Ormiston Institute in Melrose's Market Square, has displays on what life was like within a Roman fort, as well as artefacts found there. On Thursday afternoons (and Tuesday afternoons in July and August) a guided five mile, four hour walk to the fort leaves from the Centre.

The Scottish Borders is a rugby playing area, and at Melrose that version of the game known as "rugby sevens" was invented.

Earlston

8 miles E of Galashiels on the A68

The small town of Earlston is dominated by **Black Hill**, which gives a good view of the surrounding countryside. One of Scotland's earliest poets, **Thomas Learmont of Earlston,** was born here in about 1220. Also known as Thomas the Rhymer, Thomas of Erceldoune or True Thomas, he attained an almost supernatural status, as he was also a seer who could predict the future. It didn't take much in those days for a man to have the reputation of having mythical and prophetic powers, and

Smailholm Tower

Bannockburn in 1314 and Scotland's defeat by the English at Flodden in 1513. However, like most prophesies, many interpretations can be put on Thomas's.

Smailholm

10 miles E of Galashiels on the B6397

Smailholm Tower (Historic Scotland) seems to grow out of a low, rocky outcrop, and is a four square tower which was once surrounded by a wall. Within it you can see a collection of costumed figures and tapestries connected with Scott's Minstrelsy of the Scottish Borders. Scott, as a child, spent a lot of time with his grandparents at the nearby farm of Sandyknowe, and knew the tower well.

no doubt Thomas's many trips abroad accounted for the stories of him going off to live with the fairies under the Eildon Hills for years at a time. His accurate prophecies included Alexander III's death in 1285, the victory of Bruce over the English at

Kelso

16 miles E of Galashiels on the A698

Kelso is a gracious town with a large, cobbled **Market Square** (said to be the largest in Scotland) that would not look out of place in France or Belgium. Surrounding it are imposing 18th and 19th century buildings, with the supremely elegant **Town House** of 1816, which now houses the tourism information centre, as its centrepiece.

The town sits at the junction of the Tweed and the Teviot. **Kelso Abbey** (Historic Scotland) was founded in 1128, after David I, who had founded the abbey at Selkirk, decided that Kelso was a much better place for it. It was the biggest of the border abbeys, and during a siege by the English under the Earl of Hertford in 1545, it was almost totally destroyed. Now all that remains of the church are the transepts, part of the tower, two nave bays and part of the west end. But the ruins are still dramatic and imposing, and are well worth a visit. A town trail has been laid out which takes you round the town's architectural gems.

The **War Memorial Garden** is in Bridge Street, and formed part of the former abbey grounds. It has helped Kelso to win the Beautiful Scotland and Britain in Bloom competitions on several occasions, and was gifted to the town by the Duke of Roxburgh in 1921.

In July every year the **Kelso Civic Week** takes place, with many events that echo similar ceremonies in other Borders towns. On the banks of the Teviot, three miles south west of the town, once stood the

proud **Royal Burgh of Roxburgh**. This was a thriving walled town in medieval times, but nothing now survives above ground, thanks to the repeated attentions of succeeding English armies. It was one of Scotland's original "four burghs", and received its royal charter in about 1119.

Where the Teviot and the Tweed meet is a high defensive mound, the site of **Roxburgh Castle**. It was during a siege of the castle in 1460 that James II was killed outright when a cannon accidentally blew up in his face. The place has been suggested as yet another possible site for King Arthur's magnificent capital of **Camelot** (see also Ayr). To the west of Kelso, within parkland overlooking the Tweed stands the magnificent Floors Castle, Scotland's largest inhabited castle. It is home to the Duke and Duchess of Roxburgh, and has a huge collection of works of art and furniture.

Kelso

Rennie's Bridge is a handsome, five-arched bridge spanning the Tweed. It was designed by John Rennie the Scottish civil engineer, and was built in 1803 to replace an older bridge destroyed by floods. Rennie based his design for Waterloo Bridge in London on it.

The bridge was the scene of a riot in 1854, when people objected to paying tolls to cross it, even though all the building costs had been met. So bad was it that the Riot Act was read. However, it took another three years before the tolls were withdrawn.

Kelso Race Course hosts national hunt horse racing between September and May.

Ednam

21 miles E of Galashiels on the B6461

The village stands on the Eden Water, a tributary of the Tweed, and was the birthplace of two famous men. The first was **James Thomson**, born in 1700, who wrote the words to *Rule Britannia*, and the other was **Henry Francis Lyte**, born in 1793, who

wrote *Abide with Me*. A memorial to Thomson has been erected at Ferniehill, to the south of the village, and the bridge over the river has a plaque commemorating Henry Francis Lyte.

Dryburgh

7 miles SE of Galashiels off the B6356

The ruins of **Dryburgh Abbey** (Historic Scotland) must be the most romantically situated in all of Scotland, sitting as it does on a loop of the Tweed, surrounding it on three sides. Nothing much remains of the great abbey church, except for the west door and parts of the north and south transepts. However, the other abbey buildings can still be explored. Within the north transept is buried Sir Walter Scott and his wife Charlotte, as well as **Field Marshall Earl Haig of Bemersyde**. He was Commander-in-Chief of the British Expeditionary forces in France and Flanders during World War I.

The Premonstratensian abbey was founded in 1150 by Hugh de Moreville, Constable of Scotland. The site had already been a sacred one, as it was here that **St Modan**, a Celtic monk, set up a monastery in the 6th or 7th century. In 1322, during the Wars of Independence, Edward II's army, after a successful invasion of Scotland, set fire to the place. This was the first of its many sackings. It now forms part of the 55 mile long **Abbeys Cycle Route**, taking in the other three great Borders abbeys of Melrose, Kelso and Jedburgh. A short walk from the abbey is the 31 feet high (including pedestal) **William Wallace Statue**. He spent a lot of time in the Borders hiding from the English in Ettrick

Dryburgh Abbey

Forest. The Earl of Buchan commissioned the statue in 1814.

North of Dryburgh is **Scott's View**, which gives an amazing view of the Eildon Hills. Sir Walter Scott used to ride up to it to get inspiration, and when his funeral cortege was making its way to Dryburgh, the hearse stopped here for a short while. It is best accessed from the A68, where it is signposted from the Leadfoot Viaduct that spans the Tweed.

St. Boswells

7 miles SE of Galashiels on the A68

This village is named after **St Boisil**, who was an abbot of the Celtic monastery at Old Melrose in the 7th century. The centrepiece of the village is its green, which hosts a fair on July 18 (St Boisil's Day) each year. In past times, this fair was one of the largest in the country, and attracted people - especially gypsies - from all over the Borders and beyond.

A mile or so to the east are **Mertoun House and Gardens.** Though the house is not open to the public, the 26-acre gardens can be visited on Saturdays, Sundays and Bank Holiday Mondays. **Mertoun Kirk**, in the grounds of the house, is open on alternate Sundays for church services.

Selkirk

5 miles S of Galashiels on the A7

Once the county town of Selkirkshire, Selkirk is now a quiet royal burgh on the edge of the Ettrick Forest. It was the site of the first abbey in the Borders, which was founded in 1113 by David I. However, 15 years later, before one stone was laid, David moved the monks to Kelso, where the abbey

The Place

73 High Street, Selkirk, Selkirkshire TD7 4BZ
Tel: 01750 23303

The Place is one of the best pubs in the small, picturesque market town of Selkirk. The atmosphere is warm and friendly, the food is great and the drink is marvellous. Here you'll get one of the best pints of Belhaven in the country! A selection of freshly ground coffees from a local supplier are also served. The food is all cooked on the premises from good, fresh local produce with steak pie being a firm favourite with locals and visitors alike. The prices are keen and the clientele ranges from 19 to 90. In fact, there is a popular senior citizens' menu that contains many mouth watering dishes that are sure to please! So if you're in Selkirk, The Place is the place for you!

Queen's Head

28 Westport, Selkirk, Selkirkshire TD7 4D
Tel: 01750 21782

Selkirk is where Sir Walter Scott sat in judgement in the local sheriff court. And if he had been alive today, he would surely have judged the **Queen's Head** to be one of the best inns in the town, if not the whole area! This handsome, whitewashed building is a former coaching inn dating from the 17th century, and retains many original features. It has recently been refurbished, with a small bar, a large lounge (with feature fireplace) and a spacious dining room. Owned and managed by David Easton, it also offers comfortable accommodation. It consists of two self contained flats - one with a double bedroom and bathroom on the ground floor and a large twin/family bedroom, living room and kitchen on the first floor.

The other flat has three bedrooms, two twin, a double/family room, living room and kitchen. The inn's menu is extensive, and caters for most requirements. You can choose from snacks such as jacket potatoes, sandwiches and toasted sandwiches, and the main meals range from chicken supreme to home made steak pie - always a favourite. There is also a senior citizen's menu of two or three courses. So good is the food that the inn recently won a VisitScotland award in its "Best Bar Food" category. David would love you to stay at his friendly hostelry, and will give you a warm Scottish welcome if you do so!

Ettrickshaws Country House Hotel

Ettrickbridge, Selkirkshire TD7 5HW
Tel/Fax: 01750 52229
e-mail: jenny@ettrickshaws.co.uk
website: www.ettrickshaws.co.uk

The Scottish borders is one of the most beautiful regions of Scotland, and is packed with history and heritage. For luxury accommodation in the area, the **Ettrickshaws Country House Hotel** is hard to beat. Formerly a grand country house built in 1891, it is now a stylish and comfortable hotel that offers high standards and friendly service. Though it had a major refurbishment in 1997, many of the house's original features have been retained, including open fires in all the public rooms. The house sits in it own

grounds, and nestles in the shadow of Shaws Hill, which rises to 1500 feet.

The five guest rooms are all fully en suite, and are spacious and elegant. The drawing room, bar and dining room have fine views over lawn and meadow to Rough Law.

Guests can relax, sample fine wines and enjoy fine cuisine that uses only the finest and freshest of local produce wherever possible. Because of its idyllic setting, it makes an ideal venue for house parties, and the whole hotel can sometimes be placed at the disposal of groups. There is trout and salmon fishing on the River Ettrick, which is a short stroll away, and there are also ample opportunities for such pursuits as bird watching and nature study, golfing, sailing, riding, hill walking, cycling and shooting. It makes an excellent base from which to explore the Scottish Borders, yet is close enough to Edinburgh and Glasgow for day trips.

Selkirk Golf Course

was finally built. The Ettrick Water, a tributary of the Tweed, flows to the west of the town, and it is joined a couple of miles out of town by the Yarrow Water. The Vale of Yarrow is very scenic, with the hamlet of **Yarrow** itself, about eight miles west of Selkirk, being very picturesque. Scott's great-grandfather was once minister of **Yarrow Parish Church**.

In Selkirk's High Street, outside the **Old Courthouse** where he presided, there is a statute of Sir Walter Scott, who was sheriff here until his death in 1832. Within the courtroom is an audiovisual display telling of his associations with the area. Another statue in the High Street commemorates **Mungo Park**, the explorer and surgeon, who was born in Yarrow in 1771. The oldest building in the town is **Halliwell's House and Robson Gallery**, where there is a small museum on the ground floor and art gallery on the upper floor. **Robert D. Clapperton Photographic** in Scotts Place is a working museum and photographic archive. Here, the good citizens of Selkirk posed stiffly in Victorian times while having their photograph taken. At the **Selkirk Glass Visitor Centre** at Dunsdalehaugh you can see glass paperweights being made.

In common with many Borders town,

Selkirk has its **Common Riding Ceremony**, held annually in June, when over 500 riders regularly set out to patrol the marches, or boundaries, of the town lands. But the ceremony also commemorates the darkest day in the town's history. In 1513, Selkirk sent 80 of its bravest men to fight alongside James IV at Flodden, taking with them the town flag. The battle was a disaster for Scotland, with the flower of Scottish manhood, including the king himself, being killed. Only one Selkirk man, named Fletcher, returned, without the Selkirk flag but bearing a bloodstained English one, which can be seen in Halliwell's House. A memorial to the fallen can be found outside the Victoria Halls in the High Street.

The **Scottish Borders Archive and Local History Centre** is within St Mary's Mill, and offers research facilities on local history, geography and genealogy, including the records of the old counties of Berwickshire, Selkirkshire, Roxburghshire and Peeblesshire.

Three miles west of the town is **Bowhill**, the Borders home of the Duke of Queensberry and Buccleuch. It is a fine early 19th century mansion, and in its grounds is **Bowhill Little Theatre**, which presents many professional plays. A **James Hogg Exhibition** is housed in a building off the courtyard (see St Mary's Loch). There is also a visitors centre, rural walks, a restored Victorian kitchen and a display of fire engines.

Aikwood Tower, (not open to the public), home of Sir David Steel, was once the home of Michael Scott the legendary wizard. He lived from about 1175 to 1230, and was one of the cleverest men of his age. He was credited with dividing the Eildon Hills (see Melrose) into three, though the Roman name for the hills (Trimontium) shows that they always had three peaks. He was educated at Durham Cathedral School and later Oxford, Paris and Bologna, where he studied mathematics, law and theology. In his day he was known as the "wonder of the world", and his reputation spread all over Europe as a man who had learned everything there was to know in the Christian world.

He is also said to have dabbled in alchemy, and some of the legends attached to him and his so-called "wizardry" (such as his "demon horse" and "demon ship") were no doubt borrowed from the story of Merlin the Magician. He probably died in Italy and was buried there.

St. Mary's Loch

15 miles SW of Galashiels on the A708

The loch is in a truly beautiful setting of rounded, green hills. Both Scott and William Wordsworth have sung its praises, but no words can adequately describe this delightful sheet of water. A narrow spit of land separates it from the smaller **Loch of the Lowes**, with **Tibbie Shiel's Inn**, now an angling hostelry, situated between them. It was opened in 1824, and is named after Isabella Shiels, the woman who ran it until 1878. Her visitor's book is still in existence, and records such names as R.L. Stevenson, Gladstone and Thomas Carlyle. It is a favourite stopping point on the Southern

St. Mary's Loch

Tibbie Shiels Inn

By St Mary's Loch, Near Selkirk,
Selkirkshire TD7 5LH
Tel: 01750 42231 Fax: 01750 42302
e-mail: info@tibbieshielsinn.com
website: www.tibbieshielsinn.com

Tibbie Shiels Inn is one of the most famous inns in Scotland, and its visitors' book includes such famous names as Robert Louis Stevenson, Thomas Carlyle, William Gladstone and Thomas Stoddart the angler and poet. It also has associations with Sir Walter Scott, James Hogg (the "Ettrick Shepherd") and William Wordsworth. Tibbie Shiels was one Isabella Shiels, who, after being widowed in 1824, supported her six children by taking in gentlemen lodgers up until her death in 1878. The inn sits on a narrow tongue of land between the beautiful St Mary's Loch and the Loch o' the Lowes, and is on the Southern Upland Way long distance footpath. The inn has five guest rooms - one twin, two double and two family rooms, all fully en suite and extremely comfortable, with hospitality trays.

The excellent food is served in the bar or non-smoking dining room, which up until 1972 was the old kitchen. Tasty and beautifully cooked lunches, afternoon teas, traditional Scottish high teas, evening meals and packed lunches are available. The menu always features four vegetarian dishes, and the bar serves a wide range of beers, wines and spirits (including over 50 single malts), as well as soft drinks if you are driving. And whisky is not the only spirit you'll find in the bar. It is said that Tibbie Shiels' ghost haunts it! The whole area surrounding the inn is rich in history, heritage and literary associations, and it makes an ideal base from which to explore, or overnight stop as you travel between Moffat and Selkirk.

Upland Way, which passes close by.

James Hogg, nicknamed "The Ettrick Shepherd", was also a frequent visitor. He was born nearby in 1770, and wrote *Confessions of a Justified Sinner*, one of the great books of the 19th century (see Bowhill).

Hawick

Hawick has won the "Beautiful Scotland in Bloom Contest" 16 times, and sits in picturesque Teviotdale. It is the largest town in the Borders, and is famous for the quality of its knitwear, with names like Pringle and Lyle and Scott being known worldwide.

The **Hawick Common Riding** takes place in June each year, and commemorates yet another skirmish between the English and the Scots. This occurred in 1514, when some Hawick men beat off English soldiers camped near the town and captured their banner. A disagreement of a different kind took place in the mid 1990s, when two women riders tried to join what had traditionally been an all-male occasion. Their participation provoked hostile opposition, even from some women. It took a court case to establish that women had the right to join in, though even today some people still tolerate their presence rather than welcome it.

St Mary's Parish Church was built in 1763, and replaced an earlier, 13th century church. The town's oldest building is the 16th century **Drumlanrig's Tower**. In 1570 it survived a raid by English troops which destroyed the rest of Hawick, and was once a typical moated L-shaped Borders tower house before the area between the two "legs" was filled in. At one time it belonged to the Douglases of Drumlanrig, in Dumfriesshire, and it was here that Anna, Duchess of Buccleuch, and wife of the executed Duke of Monmouth, once stayed. The basement was later used as a prison, and finally a wine cellar when it became a hotel. Now the tower has been restored and

Hermitage Castle, Hawick

houses the town's visitor information centre and an exhibition explaining the history of the Borders.

The award-winning **Wilton Lodge Park** sits by the banks of the Teviot, and has 107 acres of riverside walks, gardens, a tropical glasshouse and recreational facilities.

Within it is the **Hawick Museum and Scott Art Gallery**, which explains the history of the town and its industries. The gallery has a collection of 18th and 19th century Scottish paintings, and regularly hosts exhibitions of works by local and national artists. Many of the mills in the town, such as **Peter Scott and Company** in Buccleuch Street and **Wrights of Trowmill** have visitor centres and guided tours. The **Hawick Cashmere Company**, based in Mills in Duke Street, has a viewing gallery and shop. And if Duns has its Jim Clark Memorial Trophy Room, Hawick has its **Jimmy Guthrie Statue**. He was a local TT rider who was world champion in the 1930s. He was killed in 1937 while competing in the German Grand Prix.

Ellistrin

6 Fenwick Park, Hawick,
Roxburghshire TD9 9PA
Tel: 01450 374216 Fax: 01450 373619
e-mail: eileen@ellistrin.com
website: www.ellistrin.co.uk

With three guest rooms - two doubles and a twin - **Ellistrin** is an elegant Victorian mansion that has been converted into a superior guest house within the town of Hawick in the Scottish Borders. All the rooms have en suite facilities, as well as TVs, hospitality tray and hair dryer, and all are immaculately furnished and decorated to make your stay here one to remember. The full Scottish breakfasts, which are carefully prepared using fresh local produce, will set you up for a day's sightseeing, or you can have something lighter if you prefer. This is the perfect base from which to explore the Scottish Borders, and towns such as Edinburgh, Carlisle and Newcastle are within easy reach.

Around Hawick

Denholm

4 miles NE of Hawick on the A698

In 1775 this pleasant village, with its village green, was the birthplace of John Leyden, poet, doctor, linguist and friend of Sir Walter Scott. The **John Leyden Memorial**, which stands on the green, commemorates the great man, who died in 1811 on the island of Java. In 1806 he had settled in Calcutta, where he became assay master to the local mint, and wrote about the local languages. Also born in the village was **Sir James Murray** (1837-1915), who undertook the tremendous task of editing the *New English Dictionary on Historical Principles*, forerunner of the *Oxford English Dictionary*. Two miles east of the village, atop Minto Crags, sits the curiously named **Fatlips Castle**, built in the 16th century for the Lockhart family. It was restored in 1857 and used as a shooting lodge and private museum, though it is now ruinous.

Jedburgh

14 miles NE of Hawick on the A68

The route of the present day A68 was at one time the main route from Edinburgh to England, so Jedburgh saw many armies passing along its streets when Scotland and England were constantly at war with each other. The local's once called the town "Jethart", and it is still remembered in the expression "Jethart justice", meaning hang first and try later, a throwback to the bad

Hoolet's Nest

Mounthooley,
Jedburgh, TD8 6TJ
Tel & Fax: 01835 850764

The **Hoolets Nest** is a superior B&B and self-catering flat attached to a purpose-built bungalow which is surrounded by extensive, colourful gardens, sitting two miles from the historic town of Jedburgh in the Scottish Borders. It boasts a large, comfortable bedroom/living area, a kitchen/dining room and a well-appointed bathroom. Beside the bungalow is a knitwear showroom that sells the very best in Borders knitwear, such as cashmere and lambs wool garments

Crailing Old School

Crailing, By Jedburgh,
Roxburghshire TD8 6TL
Tel: 01835 850382 Fax: 01835 850382
e-mail:jean.player@virgin.net
website: www.crailingoldschool.co.uk

The warmth and friendliness of Scotland is legendary and at the four star **Crailing Old School** you will find plenty of both! The school has been converted into a charming house and gardens offering the best B&B accommodation in the area. It retains many original features while offering high standards and great value for money. Owners Jean and Ray Leach-Player can provide information on the history and visitor attractions in the area. Ideal base for golfing, walking and fishing.

There is a variety of accommodation for up to six guests, including a lodge annex with disabled/ground floor access ten metres from the house. This is fully contained, with twin bedroom, lounge and bathroom. In the house there are three beautifully maintained cosy guest bedrooms. The fully en-suite "Maple" room has a Canadian theme and a king size bed. The "Birdie" has twin beds and "Eagle" a four foot single bed.These two rooms have a private bathroom with separate shower facilities.

The breakfast menu offers a variety of dishes, from a full Scottish to lighter options. Dinners are served by prior arrangement, with a choice of dishes. Special diets can be catered for if prior notice is given. All are served in the spacious yet comfortable dining room. There is also an elegant residents' lounge which, like the dining room, looks out on to breathtaking scenery. Ray is a PGA golf professional, and can offer lessons during your stay as well as advise on the local golf courses. A dog kennel with enclosed run behind the lodge can be made available for your pet by prior arrangement.

Meadhon House

48 Castlegate,Jedburgh TD8 6BB
Tel/Fax: 01835 862504
e-mail: meadhon@aol.com
website: www.meadhon.com

From most of the guest rooms in early 17th century **Meadhon House** you get a magnificent view of Jedburgh's most famous and historic feature - the ruins of the abbey. For this superior B&B - built from warm local stone, and full of character - sits right in the heart of the town, only a short distance from everything the town has to offer. The rooms are all fully en suite, and are spacious, yet cosy. The furnishings and decoration are of an exceptionally high standard, and this, coupled with value for money, makes Meadhon House one of the best establishments in the area. It is owned and managed by Margaret and Brian Poloczek, who are determined to maintain and improve on these high standards.

There is history attached to the house as well. In 1812 a young woman, Miss Cruickshank who had married a Mr Henderson, a writer from Jedburgh, came here as a bride.When she was only 12, Burns wrote two poems about her - "A Rosebud by my Early Walk" and "Beauteous Rosebud, Young and Gay". She died in 1835 and lies buried in Jedburgh Abbey churchyard. The dining room in Meadhon House is named in her honour, and here beautifully cooked Scottish breakfasts are served every morning, or lighter options should you require them. Jedburgh sits right at the heart of the Scottish Borders, and makes an excellent base from which to explore them. And Meadhon House is the ideal place to stay in the town. You'll always get a good Scottish welcome!

Jedburgh

old days of the reivers. It is an attractive small town with gaily-painted houses, especially in the Market Place and the Canongate, and it regularly wins awards in "Beautiful Scotland in Bloom" competitions. **Jedburgh Abbey** (Historic Scotland), on the banks of the Jed Water, was founded in 1138 by David I. It was destroyed nine times by the invading English. Each time, save for the last one, the monks painstakingly rebuilt it. A visitor centre explains its story, with one of its more intriguing exhibits being the "Jedburgh Comb", found during excavations.

Not far from the abbey is **Mary Queen of Scots House**. Here, in October 1566, Mary Stuart stayed when presiding at local courts in the Borders. When Elizabeth I held her in captivity, she declared that she would have preferred to have died in Jedburgh than England. Now it is a museum and visitors centre with displays on the tragic queen's life. **Jedburgh Castle Jail**, in Castlegate,

Jedforest Deer and Farm Park

Mervinslaw Estate, Camptown,
Jedburgh TD8 6PL
Tel: 01835 840364 Fax: 01835 840362
e-mail: hopedate@gtobalnet.co.uk
website: www.aboutscottand.com/jedforest/

The Jedforest Deer and Farm Park is located just off the main A68 Edinburgh to Newcastle road some 5 miles south of Jedburgh. There are magnificent herds of deer and you can find out more about farming today. You can see how they look after the animals and protect the countryside and watch the farm in action on the special demonstration days. In addition explore the farm animals of yesteryear within the large conservation collection of rare breeds of sheep, pigs, cattle, chickens, ducks and others.

There is a coffee shop, barbecue area, picnic area as well as both indoor and outdoor adventure areas. Rangers offer walks through the lovely Scottish Borders' countryside and allow you to discover more about the environment, nature and wildlife.

was a 19th century reform prison which now houses a display about the history of the town. Four miles northeast of Jedburgh are the **Monteviot House Gardens**, which has a pinetum, a herb garden and a riverside garden linked by bridges.

Jedforest Deer and Farm Park (see panel on page 31) is five miles south of Jedburgh on the Mervinslaw Estate, just off the A68. It is a modern working farm with a deer herd and rare breeds. There are also birds of prey demonstrations using eagles, owls and hawks.

Four miles beyond the Farm Park, the A68 reaches the English border at **Carter Bar**, which is 1370 feet above sea level. From here there is a wonderful view northwards, and it almost seems that the whole of Southern Scotland is spread out before you. In the 18th century herds of sheep and cattle were driven over this route towards the markets in the south.

Ancrum

10 miles NE of Hawick on the B6400

Ancrum is a typical Borders village, to the north of which was fought the **Battle of Ancrum Moor** in 1545. It was part of what was known as the "Rough Wooing", when Henry VIII tried to force the Scots into allowing the young Mary Queen of Scots to marry his son Edward. 3000 English and Scottish horsemen under Lord Eure were ambushed by a hastily assembled army of Borderers. During the battle, the Scots horsemen changed sides when they saw that the Borderers were gaining the upper hand, resulting in a total rout.

Two miles east of the village is the 150 feet high **Waterloo Monument**, erected by the Marquis of Lothian between 1817 and 1824 to commemorate the Battle of Waterloo. Though there are stairs within the tower, it is not open to the public. The best way to reach it is to walk from the **Harestanes Countryside Visitor Centre**, which is close by. The Centre has countryside walks, activities and displays, all with a countryside theme, as well as a car park, gift shop and tearoom.

Morebattle

18 miles NE of Hawick on the B6401

This little village sits close to the Kale Water, with the surrounding area once being a hiding place for Covenanters fleeing the persecution of Charles II's troops in the 17th century. To the north of the village is **Linton Church**, which has Norman details, a fine Norman font and a belfry dated 1697. It sits on a low mound of fine sand, which is almost certainly a natural feature. However, a local legend tells a different story. It seems that a young man was once condemned to death for murdering a priest. His two sisters pleaded for his life, saying

they would carry out a specific task to atone for his crime. They would sieve tons of sand, removing all large grains, and from the small grains build a mound on which a church building could stand. The church authorities agreed this, and the women set to work. Eventually, after many years, a mound of sand was created, and a church was indeed built on it.

The ruins of the L-shaped **Cessford Castle**, which surrendered to the English in 1545, lie two miles to the southwest. It was built by the Kerrs in about 1450, and was once one of the most important castles in the Borders.

Kirk Yetholm

22 miles NE of Hawick on the B6352

This village, lying within the Bowmont Valley, is at the northern end of the **Pennine Way**, with St Cuthbert's Way passing close by as well. It, and to a lesser extent its twin village of **Town Yetholm**, were famous at one time as being where the kings and queens of the Scottish gypsies lived. The most famous queen was Esther Faa Blyth, who ruled in the 19th century. In 1898 Charles Faa Blyth, her son, was crowned king at Yetholm. Though the title had lost much of its meaning by this time, the coronation was attended by an estimated 10,000 people. A small cottage is still pointed out as his "palace". **Yetholm Parish Church**, an elegant building with a small tower, was built in 1836. It has a Burgerhuys bell cast in 1643.

Newcastleton

20 miles S of Hawick, on the B6357

Newcastleton, in Liddesdale, is a planned village, founded by the third Duke of Buccleuch in 1793 as a handloom-weaving centre. The **Liddesdale Heritage Centre Museum** is in the old Townfoot Kirk in South Hermitage Street, and has attractive displays about the history of the area and its people.

This is the heartland of the great Borders families of Kerr, Armstrong and Elliots, and was always a place of unrest when Scotland and England were independent countries. The border with England follows the Liddel Water, then, about three miles south of Newcastleton, strikes east along the Kershope Burn for a mile before turning northeast. At **Kershopefoot**, where the Kershope Burn meets the Liddel Water, the Wardens of the Western Marches of both Scotland and England met regularly to settle arguments and seek redress for crimes committed by both sides. A jury of 12 men settled the disputes, with the Scots choosing the six English, and the English choosing the six Scots. However, even these meetings were known to result in violence, and many a Scottish or English warden and his entourage were chased far into their own territory if redress was not forthcoming.

Every year, in July, the village holds the **Newcastleton Traditional Music Festival**, one of the oldest such festivals in Scotland. It was founded in 1970, and has concerts, ceilidhs and competitions.

Five miles north of Newcastleton is the massive bulk of **Hermitage Castle** (Historic Scotland). It dates from the 14th century, and its imposing walls and stout defences reflect the bloody warfare that was common in this area before the union of Scotland and England. It belonged to the de Soulis family, who built the original castle of wood in the mid 13th century. However, in 1320 William de Soulis was found guilty of plotting against Robert the Bruce, and the crown confiscated his lands and property. It later became a Douglas stronghold.

While staying in Jedburgh, Mary Stuart covered the 50 miles between there and Hermitage and back again in one day to visit the Earl of Bothwell, whom she later married. During her journey, she lost a watch, which was recovered in the 19th century.

Grapes Hotel

16 Douglas Square,
Newcastleton TD 9 0QD
Tel: 01387 375245/375680
Fax: 01387 375896
e-mail: info@the-grapes-hotel.com
website: www.the-grapes-hotel.com

Newcastleton is a lovely, stone-built village nestling in the Borders. It was built in 1793 by the Duke of Buccleuch to house handloom weavers, and is now a centre for exploring this beautiful part of Scotland. Situated in the heart of the village in Douglas Square, the **Grapes Hotel** is one of the best hostelries in the Borders, and offers unrivalled food, drink and accommodation. Value for money and high standards of service are the watchwords here, and the establishment has earned itself

a fine reputation for its hospitality and attention to detail. The Grapes is owned and managed by Trevor Cambridge, and he is determined to maintain its high standards and its great reputation!

There are six guest rooms on offer, each one comfortable and tastefully decorated. Two doubles, a single and a twin are fully en suite, while two family rooms share a bathroom and toilet. Each comes with tea/coffee making facilities. The furniture is traditional/modern, and reflects the tradition and history attached to the hotel

There is a fine range of drinks available, including beer, spirits, wines and liqueurs, with, of course, soft drinks always on offer if you're driving. The Nichol Bar is on the ground floor, and has an open air look due to its central glass atrium, that lets light flood in. Bar meals, snacks, teas and coffees are served here. The lounge bar is cosy and warm, and here you can enjoy morning coffee and afternoon teas, as well as snacks and drinks. The Reivers Bar also on the ground floor, is popular with its two pool tables and games facility. The Douglas Room, the upper bar - a relaxing place of low beams where you can have a drink or bar meal. It is also ideal for that special occasion, such as a wedding reception, private party, christening or small business meeting.

The food in the Grapes Hotel is, as you would expect, outstanding. The Vine is our à la carte restaurant, and offers fine cuisine in stylish yet comfortable surroundings. So popular is it that you are advised to book in advance. The highly acclaimed chef uses only the finest and freshest of local produce wherever possible, and many people return again and again to sample the wonderful dishes on the menu. This is the place for that special and romantic meal to celebrate an anniversary, a birthday or some other special occasion

Peebles

High Street, Peebles

Peebles sits on the banks of the River Tweed, and though it looks peaceful enough nowadays, its history is anything but. It was burnt to the ground by the English in 1545, occupied by Cromwell in 1649, and again by Charles Edward Stuart in 1745.

In June each year the Town holds its **Beltane Week**, with the crowning of the Beltane Queen. The ceremony's origins go right back to pagan times, though the present Beltane Week celebrations date only from the 19th century, when they were revived. The Chambers Institute was founded in 1859 by local man William Chambers, who, with his brother Robert, went on to found the great Chambers publishing house in Edinburgh. Within it is the **Tweeddale Museum and Gallery**, where the history of the town is explained. Here you can also see the

GLENTRESS HOTEL

Innreleithen Road, Peebles,
Peebleshire EH45 8NB
Tel: 01721 720100 Fax: 01721 724205
e-mail: enquiries@glentresshotel.co.uk
website: www.glentresshotel.co.uk

The **Glentress Hotel** is situated on the A72, 40 miles from the Scottish border and 25 miles south of Edinburgh. It makes the perfect base from which to explore the area, with its wonderful heritage and scenery, or it can be used as an overnight stop on your way north or south. Short two, three or five day breaks are also available in this superior establishment where high standards of service and value-for-money combine to make your stay a memorable one. It has 12 comfortable and well furnished rooms, decorated to an extremely high standard and all en-suite with televisions and hospitality trays.

The owners, Liz and Bryan Taylor, have created a new menu, mixing some of their own favourites with some traditional standards. Chef Ross Thomson has had many years experience, and brings his own unique skills to the Glentress kitchen, using fresh, local produce to produce menus that meld imagination with tradition. Special diets are catered for, and some dishes are wheat and dairy free.

The Glentress Forest is close to the hotel, and there are many cycle routes and rides within it. The hotel has introduced secure cycle storage and a wash bay. The River Tweed is within walking distance and there are 20 golf courses close by. The Scottish Borders are a hill walkers' paradise, from gentle walks to the more demanding.

extraordinary classical frieze commissioned by William Chambers which is based on parts of the Parthenon Frieze in the British Museum and on the Alexander Frieze commissioned in 1812 by Napoleon Bonaparte. On Innerleithen Road, opposite the Park Hotel, is the unusual **Cornice Ornamental Plasterwork Museum**, dedicated to displaying and explaining ornate plasterwork.

The ruins of the Trinitarian Friary **Cross Kirk** (Historic Scotland), founded in 1261, are to the west of the town. The Trinitarians were a monastic order founded in 1198 by St John of Math, a Frenchman, to redeem captives taken by the Saracens in the Holy Land during the Crusades. The tower of the former **St Andrews Church** still survives just off Neidpath Road. The present **Peebles Parish Church** is an imposing Victorian building at the west end of the High Street, a short distance from the quaintly named **Cuddy Bridge** over the Eddleston Water, a tributary of the Tweed. One of the hidden places of the town is to be found beyond an archway leading from the high street - the **Quadrangle**. Surrounding the town's war memorial are well laid out, colourful gardens.

Around Peebles

Neidpath Castle

1 mile W of Peebles on the A72

Neidpath Castle was built by the Fraser family in the 14th century, and subsequently passed to the Hays when the daughter of Sir Simon Hay, who was killed by the English in the early 14th century, married Gilbert de Hay of Yester. In 1685 the William Douglas, the first Duke of Queensberry, bought it and it remained a Douglas property until 1810, when it passed to the Earl of Wemyss. Sir Walter Scott visited it frequently when his friend, Adam Ferguson, rented it at the end of the 18th century.

It is the epitome of a Scottish tower house, and originally consisted of three great vaulted halls, one above the other (though the top vault was subsequently removed and replaced by a timber roof), reached by winding stone staircases. There is a genuine dungeon below what was the guardroom which prisoners were sometimes lowered into and in many cases forgotten about. Mary Stuart and James VI both visited the castle, reflecting the importance of the Hay family in the 16th century. The castle is privately owned, and is open to the public. Wall hangings depict the tragic life of Mary Stuart.

Kailzie Gardens

3 miles E of Peebles on the B7062

Extending to 14 acres, Kailzie Gardens sit on the banks of the Tweed, surrounded by hills. The main part is contained in an old walled garden, plus there is a 15-acre wild garden with woodland walks. There is also a restaurant, gift shop and 18-hole putting green.

Innerleithen

6 miles E of Peebles on the A72

Innerleithen is a small town which was the

Kailzie Gardens

original for Sir Walter Scott's St Ronan's Well. It used to be a spa town, and the **St. Ronan's Well Interpretive Centre** at Well's Brae explains the history of the wells, whose waters were full of sulphur and other minerals. In the High Street is **Robert Smail's Printing Works** (National Trust for Scotland). This was a genuine print works that still retained many of its original features and fittings when taken over by the Trust in 1987. Now you can see how things were printed at the turn of the century, and even have a go yourself.

Traquair

6 miles SE of Peebles on the B709

Traquair is a small village visited mostly for the magnificent **Traquair House**. It is reputed to be the oldest continuously inhabited house in Scotland, and has its origins in a royal hunting lodge built on the banks of the Tweed in about AD 950. In its time, 27 kings and queens have visited the place, including Alexander I in the 11th century, Edward I of England (known as the "Hammer of the Scots") in the 13th, and Mary Stuart in the 16th. One laird of Traquair fell with his king at Flodden, and in the 18th century the then laird, the fifth Earl of Traquair, supported the Jacobite cause. Charles Edward Stuart visited in 1745, and when he left, the laird closed the **Bear Gates** at the end of the long drive, vowing that they would never be opened again until a Stuart ascended the British throne once more. They have remained closed ever since. Within the house itself are secret passages and priests' holes, as the owners reverted to Roman Catholicism in the early 17th century. It is still the family home of the Maxwell Stuart family.

In 1965 the then laird renovated the brewhouse which lies beneath the private chapel, and the **Traquair House Brewery** now produces a fine range of ales which can be bought in the estate shop. It is said that when Charles Edward Stuart visited, he too enjoyed a glass or two of Traquair Ale.

Drumelzier

8 miles SW of Peebles, on the B712

It is reputed that one of King Arthur's knights lies buried where the Drumelzier Burn joins the Tweed, just north of the village. At Drumelzier Haugh is an old standing stone known as **Merlin's Stone**, and on Tinnis Hill there is a stone circle. At one time **Drumelzier Castle** stood close to the village, but now little remains above ground. In the graveyard of **Drumelzier Parish Church** is an old burial vault of the Tweedies.

Lyne

4 miles W of Peebles on the A72

Lyne Church, perched picturesquely on a hillside above the road, is said to be the smallest parish church in Scotland, and was

built about 1645. It contains a pulpit and two pews reputed to be of Dutch workmanship.

Stobo

5 miles W of Peebles on the B712

Stobo Kirk, one of the oldest and most beautiful in the area, has a Norman tower, nave and chancel, with some later features and additions. **Stobo Castle** is set in some lovely grounds, and is now one of Scotland's leading health farms and spas. Two miles south, along the B712, is the **Dawyck Botanic Garden and Arboretum**, an outpost of the National Botanic Gardens of Scotland in Edinburgh. It sits on the Scrape Burn, a tributary of the Tweed, and houses a unique collection of conifers, rhododendrons and other tree species within its 62 acres.

Broughton

10 miles W of Peebles, on the A701

Broughton is forever associated with the author and Governor-General of Canada, John Buchan, whose most famous work is undoubtedly *The Thirty Nine Steps.* Though born in Perth, his maternal grandparents farmed nearby, and his father, a Free Church minister, married his mother in the village. The old free kirk is now the **John Buchan Centre,** with displays about his life and writings.

West Linton

14 miles NW of Peebles, just off the A702

West Linton is a delightful village, and one of the hidden gems of Peeblesshire. The picturesque **St Andrews Parish Church** of 1781 stands in the middle of the village, and the surrounding gravestones testify to the craftsmanship of the many stone carvers who used to live in the area. The local **Whipman** ceremonies take place in June each year. They originated in 1803, when some local agricultural workers decided to form a benevolent society known as the "Whipmen of Linton". Now the weeklong festivities include honouring the Whipman (meaning a carter) and his Lass. In the centre of the village stands **Lady Gifford's Well**, with a stone carving of 1666 on one of its sides.

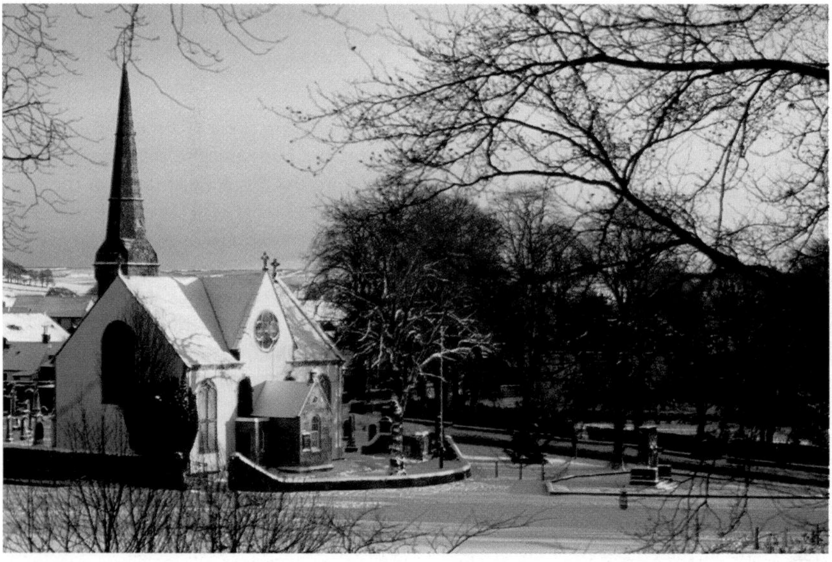

West Linton Church

Dumfries & Galloway

People scurrying north along the M74 rarely turn off at Gretna and head for Dumfries and Galloway, a wonderful area that can match anything in Scotland for beautiful scenery, grandeur and history. There are over 200 miles of coastline, for instance, with small coves, neat fishing ports and wonderful sandy beaches. There are beautiful villages, old abbeys, castles and country roads that meander through soft, verdant scenery or climb up into bleak moorland landscapes that were made for walking. In the fields you will see herds of the region's own indigenous cattle - the Belted Galloways, so called because they have a wide white band running round their bodies.

Then there are the towns. Dumfries is the largest in the area, and is a lovely place, full of old red sandstone buildings and great shopping facilities. It is also where Scotland's national poet, Robert Burns, is buried, and any trip to Scotland should

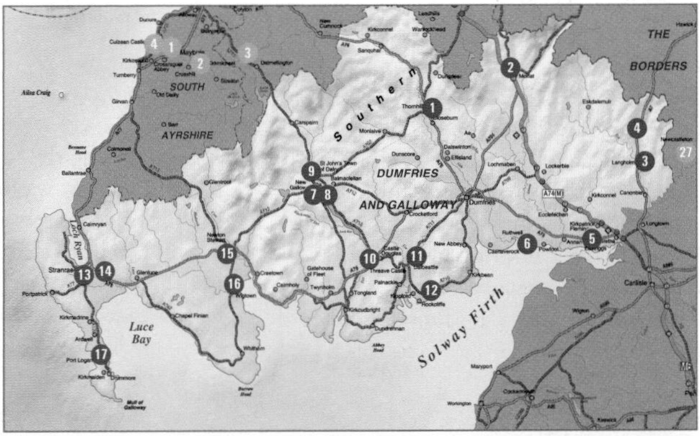

PLACES TO STAY, EAT AND DRINK

● Denotes entries in other chapters

include a visit to St Michael's Kirkyard to see his mausoleum. Kirkcudbright, because of its quality of light, has had an artist's colony since Victorian times, and is a gracious place, full of Regency and Georgian buildings. Stranraer, with its ferries, is a getaway to Northern Ireland, and Lockerbie is forever associated with the disaster of 1988.

Old Blacksmiths Shop, Gretna Green

The area contains three former counties - Dumfriesshire, Kirkcudbrightshire and Wigtownshire, and each one has its own particular charm. You can explore beautiful Nithsdale in Dumfriesshire, for instance, and visit Drumlanrig Castle, one of the homes of the Duke of Queensberry and Buccleuch. Kirkcudbrightshire was the birthplace of John Paul Jones, founder of the American navy, and Wigtownshire was where Christianity was introduced into Scotland.

Surrounding the fertile fields and picturesque towns of coastal Galloway are the high hills and bleak moorland, which cut off Dumfries and Galloway from the rest of Scotland. Because of this, the area was almost independent of Scottish kings in medieval times, and was ruled by a succession of families, from the ancient Lords of Galloway to the mighty Douglases. All have left their mark in stone, such as Devorgilla's Bridge in Dumfries and the mighty Threave Castle, built on an island in the River Dee.

Drystone Walling

Then there are the abbeys, for, like the Borders, this was an area much favoured by medieval monks. At New Abbey is one which gave the word "sweetheart" to the English language; at Glenluce - a word which means "valley of light" - are the wonderful ruins of Glenluce Abbey; and south of Kirkcudbright is Dundrennan, where Mary Stuart - better known as Mary Queen of Scots - spent her last night on Scottish soil. The castles are equally as impressive. Drumlanrig - Threave - Cardoness - Caerlaverock; the names trip off the tongue, and go to the very heart of Scotland's history.

From the middle of August to the end of October each year the area holds its "Gael Force Festival", bringing together musical events, literary festivals, traditional Scottish entertainment, concerts, drama and art. This part of Scotland has a mild climate, and at one time the coastline was nicknamed the "Scottish Riviera". First time visitors are usually surprised to see palm trees flourishing in cottage gardens near the coast, or in the grand, formal gardens such as Logan Botanic Garden in Wigtownshire. But then, Dumfries and Galloway has always been full of surprises.

Dumfries

The Royal Burgh of Dumfries certainly lives up to its nickname of the "Queen of the South". It has a lovely location on the banks of the River Nith, and was once voted the town with the best quality of life in Britain.

The town is forever associated with Scotland's national poet, Robert Burns. Though born in Ayrshire, he died in Dumfries, and lies in the **Burns Mausoleum** within the kirkyard that surrounds **St Michael's Parish Church**, built in the 1740s. Also buried there are his wife, Jean Armour, and five of their family. Burns had a family pew in St Michael's (marked by a plaque), and long after his death his wife was a regular attender. The mausoleum was built in 1815, in Grecian style, and in that year Burns' remains were transferred there. Also in the kirkyard are the graves of many of his friends.

Not far away is Burns Street (formerly called Mill Vennel), where **Burns' House** is situated. He lived here from 1793 until he died in 1796 at the early age of 37. It is open to the public, and though not a grand house, it was nonetheless a substantial building for its day, showing that by the end of his life Burns had achieved some form of financial stability due to his work as an exciseman. On display are letters and manuscripts, the pistol he carried with him on his rounds and the chair in which he sat when he wrote his last poems.

On the west bank of the Nith is the **Robert Burns Centre**, which tells the full story of the poet and his connections with the town. Within it are displays and exhibits, including a model of the Dumfries that Burns would have known in the late 18th century. There is also a cinema.

The history of Dumfries doesn't start with Robert Burns, however. It is an ancient town, and it was here, in 1306, that Robert the Bruce murdered the Red Comyn, a rival contender for the throne of Scotland. The deed took place before the high altar of the Greyfriar's monastery, something that led to him being excommunicated by the Pope. However, this didn't seem to worry the man, as he immediately had himself crowned king of Scotland at Scone in Perthshire in the presence of Scottish bishops, who continued to give him communion. Nothing now remains of the monastery, though the present **Greyfriar's Kirk**, a flamboyant Victorian building in red sandstone, is close to where it stood.

In the High Street stands the **Midsteeple**, built of red sandstone in 1707. It was formerly the town hall and jail, and on its south face is a carving of an ell, an old Scots cloth measurement of about 37 inches. There is also a table of distances from Dumfries to various important Scottish towns. One of the towns however, is in England - Huntingdon. Three successive Scottish kings in medieval times held the earldom of Huntingdon, and it was one of the places where Scottish drovers took cattle to market in the 17th and 18th centuries.

Within the modern **Loreburn Shopping Centre** is a full size model of the world's first true bicycle, invented by Kirkpatrick MacMillan, a Dumfriesshire man (see also Keir). And in Shakespeare Street stands, rather appropriately, the famous **Theatre Royal**, one of the oldest theatres in Scotland, dating from 1792. Burns regularly attended performances. In contrast,

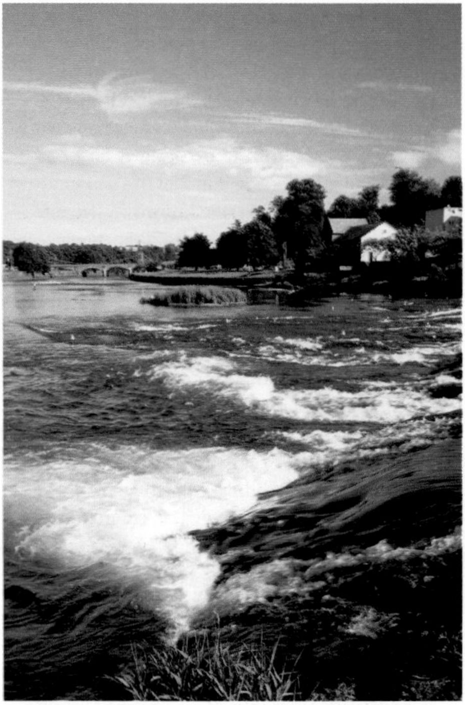

River Nith, Dumfries

Dumfries's newest attraction is **Organised Chaos** on Lockerbie Road. This activity centre has a paint ball arena and purpose-built, all terrain 800 metre track for off-road buggies.

Dumfries proper sits on the east bank of the Nith. On the west, up until it was amalgamated into Dumfries in 1929, was **Maxwelltown**, which was in Kirkcudbrightshire, and had been a separate burgh since 1810. Joining the two towns is **Devorgilla's Bridge**. Though the present bridge dates from 1431, the original structure was built by Devorgilla, Lady of Galloway, in the 13th century. Her husband was John Balliol, who founded Balliol College in Oxford (see also New Abbey).

At the Maxwellton end of the bridge is the **Old Bridge House Museum**, with exhibits and displays illustrating everyday life in the town. Also on the Maxwellton side of the river is **Dumfries Museum**, housed in an 18th century windmill, and with a **Camera Obscura** that gives fascinating views of the town.

On the northern outskirts of the town, but now surrounded by modern housing, are the beautiful remains of **Lincluden College** (Historic Scotland). Built originally in 1164 as a Benedictine nunnery by Uchtred, Lord of Galloway, it was suppressed in the late 14th century by **Archibald the Grim**, third Earl of Douglas, and replaced by a collegiate church. The present ruins date from that time. One of its main features is the elaborate canopied tomb of Princess Margaret, daughter of Robert III. Adjoining the site is the Norman **Lincluden Motte**, which was later terraced and incorporated into a garden.

To the east of the town at Heathhall is the **Dumfries and Galloway Aviation Museum**, run by a group of amateur enthusiasts. It has three floors of display area on an old RAF airfield, and holds a fascinating collection of military aircraft, both propeller and jet driven, as well as engines, memorabilia and photographs. The **Crichton Royal Museum** is within what was Crichton Royal Hospital in Bankend Road, and has health-related artefacts, an operating theatre and a collection of paintings by 19th century hospital patients and stained glass. Close by is the cathedral-like **Crichton Memorial Church**, designed by Sydney Mitchell and built between 1890-1897. For those interested in genealogy, the **Dumfries and Galloway Family History Research Centre** in Glasgow Street must be visited. There are archives, fiches and books about local history and families, though there is a modest fee for the use of the facilities.

The hamlet of **Holywood** sits just off the A76, two miles north of Dumfries. The present **Holywood Parish Church** of 1779 was partly built from the stones of a great medieval abbey, which once stood here, of which nothing now remains above ground. To the west, on the other side of the A76, is a stone circle known as the **Twelve Apostles**, though one massive stone is now missing.

Another writer associated with Dumfries is J.M. Barrie (see also Kirriemuir). Though not born here, he attended **Dumfries Academy**, a handsome building in Academy Street. While at the school, he stayed in a house in George Street, and later admitted that the games of pirates he and his friends played in the garden sloping down to the Nith gave him the idea for Peter Pan and Captain Hook.

Around Dumfries

Dalswinton

6 miles N of Dumfries on a minor road off the A76

The hamlet of Dalswinton is no more than two rows of cottages on either side of the road. But it is an attractive place, built as an estate village. When Robert Burns was living locally at Ellisland Farm, Patrick Millar owned Dalswinton House, in the policies of which (not open to the public) is **Dalswinton Loch**. Patrick encouraged William Symington to experiment with his steam-driven boat on the waters of the loch in the late 18th century, and it is thought that Burns may have been a passenger on one of the sailings.

Ellisland

6 miles N of Dumfries on the A76

Robert Burns brought his family south from Mauchline to Ellisland in June 1788. He leased the farm from Patrick Millar of Dalswinton, but found the soil to be infertile and stony. So much so that by 1791 he gave up the unequal struggle to make a living from it, and moved with his family to Dumfries. It sits in a beautiful spot beside the Nith, and it was this romantic location, which had made Burns lease it in the first place. Here he wrote some of his best poetry, including *Auld Lang Syne* and his masterpiece of the comic/macabre, *Tam o' Shanter*. Burns used to recount that Tam o' Shanter was conceived while walking the banks of the Nith, laughing out loud as he thought up his hero's adventures with the witches. Now the farmhouse houses a lively museum dedicated to his memory. To the north is **Hermitage Cottage**, which Burns used as a place to muse and write poetry.

Ae

8 miles N of Dumfries on a minor road off the A701

The small village of Ae is famous for having the shortest name of any town or village in Britain, and for having the only place name without a consonant in it. It was founded in 1947 to house forestry workers, and is set in a great conifer forest which has some good walks and footpaths.

Closeburn

11 miles N of Dumfries on the A76

Closeburn sits in one of the most beautiful parts of Dumfriesshire - Nithsdale. To the north of the village the wooded dale closes in on either side, with the River Nith tumbling through it. To the south, it gradually opens out into a wide, fertile strath, dotted with green fields and old, whitewashed farms. The **Parish Church of Closeburn** sits some distance away from the village, and is an attractive Victorian building with a slim tower. Fragments of the older church, which date from 1741, can be seen in the kirkyard. **Closeburn Castle** (not open to the public) has been continuously inhabited since the 14th century, when it was built by the Kirkparticks, who were closely associated with Robert 1.

A small road winds up eastwards from just south of Closeburn into the moorland above the village. It makes an interesting drive, and takes you past the small but picturesque **Loch Ettrick**.

Elmarglen Hotel

11 West Morton Street, Thornhill,
Dumfriesshire DG3 5ND
Tel: 01848 330558
e-mail:
elmarglen@dumfriesshire.wanadoo.co.uk

Davy Coltart and Frances Brown would like to welcome you to the **Elmarglen Hotel** in the picturesque village of Thornhill in Dumfriesshire. It sits just off the main street, and is one of the village's secrets. For here you will find great accommodation, good food and even better drink. Between them, Davy and Frances have years of experience in the licensing trade, and have made the hotel one of the most popular in the area, both with tourists and with locals (which is always a good sign). The building itself dates from the late18th century, though the village of Thornhill was laid out and built in the early 1700s by the Duke of Queensberry, who lived in Drumlanrig Castle, a few miles away.

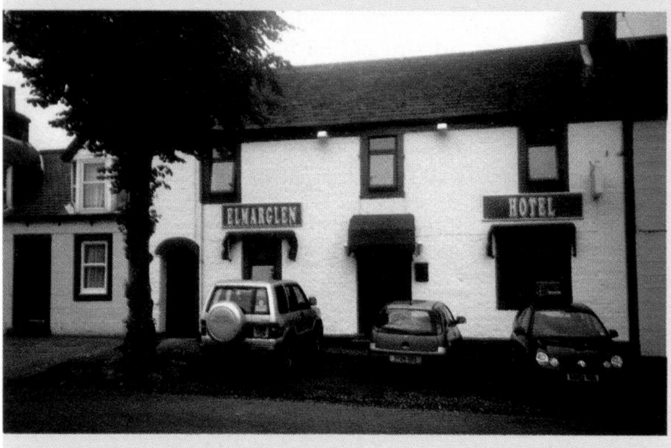

The hotel has five guest rooms on offer, each one comfortable and spacious, and furnished and decorated to a high standard, making this the ideal overnight stopping place or a place for a tasty bar lunch as you travel north or south along the A76 Dumfries-Kilmarnock road. There is ample car parking at the front of the hotel, and to the rear there is a small beer garden, plus a slabbed patio where barbeques are held in the summer months. The floors in the public areas are all wooden or tiled, giving the place a warm, friendly atmosphere. This, coupled with the many framed prints of old Thornhill on the walls, also give an "olde worlde" feel that is sure to please.The cosy, friendly bar on the ground floor is where locals meet to talk, play darts and have a quiet drink. This is the place for the "craic", and the locals will make you feel very welcome if you want to join in. Upstairs there is a lounge and bar which is particularly comfortable, having sofas and furnishings where you can relax in total peace, far away from the bustle of modern life.

The food in the restaurant is always home-cooked, and prepared from good, fresh, local produce and if a favourite dish of yours isn't on the menu, all you have to do is ask, and if it's possible, they will try to provide it. Frances and Davy are always keen to help their guests, and can offer advice on what to see in the area.

Thornhill sits right in the Nith Valley, close to the River Nith. There are great opportunities for many outdoor pursuits and the birthplace of Kirkpartick McMillan, the man who invented the modern bicycle, is at Keir. Ellisland, where Robert Burns lived, is a few miles to the south, and Drumlanrig Castle is only two miles away. At Durisdeer Church are the famous Durisdeer Marbles, a huge funerary monument to the second Duke of Queensberry and his wife.

Thornhill

13 miles N of Dumfries on the A76

This lovely village, with its wide main street and pollarded trees, has a French feel to it, and was laid out in 1714 by the Duke of Queensberry. At the crossroads in the middle of the village is a monument surmounted by a winged horse, a symbol of the Queensberry family. In a field to the west of the village, and close to the bridge over the Nith, is the 15th century **Boatford Cross**, associated with the ferry and ford that preceded the bridge.

Three miles north of the village are the remains of 15th century **Morton Castle**, situated romantically on a tongue of land jutting out into Morton Loch. A castle of some kind has stood here since the 12th century, though the present castle was built by the Douglases.

Drumlanrig Castle

Drumlanrig Castle

16 miles N of Dumfries on a minor road off the A76

Drumlanrig Castle is the Dumfriesshire home of the Duke of Queensberry and Buccleuch. It was built in the 1670s and 80s on the site of an earlier castle, and contains many fine paintings, including works by Gainsborough, Rembrandt and Hans Holbein. In the summer of 2003 it was the scene of a daring burglary when a painting by Leonardo da Vinci worth millions of pounds was stolen from it in broad daylight. Surrounding the castle is a country park and gardens, with some of the outbuildings having been converted into craft workshops.

Durisdeer

19 miles N of Dumfries on a minor road off the A702

The tiny hamlet of Durisdeer consists of a handful of cottages and a **Parish Church** built in 1699. The church is unusual in that it has, attached to it, the former parish school. But it also hides a secret - the wonderful **Durisdeer Marbles**. They are, in fact, an elaborate funerary monument to the second Duke of Queensberry and his wife, who lie buried in the crypt beneath. They were carved in marble by the Flemish sculptor Jan Nost, and are said to be the best of their kind in the country.

Penpont

13 miles N of Dumfries on the A702

This small, attractive village is well worth a visit in the summer months to see the colourful gardens that surround some of the old picturesque cottages. The cathedralesque **Parish Church** is Victorian, and seems far too large for such a small place.

Keir

12 miles N of Dumfries on a minor road off the A702

Keir is no more than a hamlet with a small

church, but it is famous as the birthplace of **Kirkpatrick MacMillan**, inventor of the bicycle. He was born in 1813, and while his brothers all went on to become successful in their careers, Kirkpatrick was content to stay at home and ply the trade of a blacksmith.

Hobbyhorses, which relied on riders pushing themselves forward with their feet, had been around since the early part of the 19th century, but Kirkpatrick Macmillan's bicycle was the first to incorporate revolving pedals (see Dumfries). On June 6 1842 he set out on a 70-mile ride to Glasgow on his bicycle, and was greeted by milling crowd when he arrived there. However, while passing through the Gorbals, he knocked down a young girl, and even though she wasn't badly injured, he was fined five shillings by a Glasgow magistrate, the first recorded case of a cyclist being fined for a traffic offence. However, rumour has it that the magistrate offered to pay the fine out of his own pocket if Kirkpatrick would allow him to have a go on the bicycle.

Tynron

15 miles N of Dumfries on a minor road off the A702

This small, pretty conservation village has only one building dating after 1900. The **Parish Church**, which looks as if it is far too big for such a small place, was built in 1837, and was one of the last in Scotland to be lit by oil lamps. Early in the 20th century a distillery which had a contract to supply the Palace of Westminster was situated here.

Dunscore

8 miles NW of Dumfries on the B729

Dunscore is a small, attractive village with a neat, whitewashed **Parish Church** dating from 1823. When Robert Burns and his family stayed at Ellisland Farm, four miles to the east, they used to worship in its predecessor.

Not far from Dunscore is Lochenhead Farm, birthplace in 1897 of **Jane Haining**, the only British person to have died at Auschwitz during World War II. While still young she joined the Church of Scotland's Jewish Mission Service, and was eventually appointed matron of the Jewish Mission in Budapest in 1932. In 1944 she was arrested, purportedly because she had been listening to BBC broadcasts, but actually because she had been working among the Jews. She was taken to Auschwitz, and on July 17 1944 died there. Her death certificate gave the cause of death as cachexia, a wasting illness sometimes associated with cancer, but there is no doubt she was gassed.

One unusual tale about Dunscore concerns Elspeth Buchan, commonly known as **Mother Buchan**, who founded a religious cult called the Buchanites in Irvine in Ayrshire in the 18th century. She attracted a wide following, claiming she could bestow immortality on a person by breathing on them, and that she herself was immortal. The cult was eventually hounded from Irvine by its magistrates, and it headed south towards Dumfries. In a large field near Dunscore she decided to hold a religious service, and set up a large platform from which to conduct it. However, in the middle of the service the platform collapsed, throwing her and several leading followers to the ground. The sect eventually broke up when Elspeth had the nerve to die a natural death (see also Irvine and Crocketford).

Moniaive

16 miles NW of Dumfries on the A 702

Moniaive, caught in a fold of the hills at the head of Glencairn, through which the Cairn Water flows to join the Nith, must surely be one of the prettiest villages in Dumfriesshire. It is actually two villages, Moniaive itself and Dunreggan, on the other side of the river. Within the village is the **Renwick** Monument, which commemorates a Covenanting martyr who died in 1688.

James Paterson was a painter who was a member of that group known as the "Glasgow Boys". In 1882 he settled in the village with his wife, and lived there until 1906, when he moved to Edinburgh. Several of his paintings show scenes in and around the village.

Three miles east is the great mansion of **Maxwelton House** (not open to the public), formerly known as Glencairn Castle. It was here that Anna Laurie, of **Bonnie Annie Laurie** fame, was born in 1682. The song was written by William Douglas of Fingland, though he later jilted her and joined the Jacobite army. Anna herself went on to marry Alexander Fergusson, 14th Laird of Craigdarroch.

Every September the village hosts the **Scottish Comic Festival**, with displays and exhibitions, as well as talks by cartoonists and comic illustrators.

Wanlockhead

25 miles N of Dumfries on the B797

People are usually surprised to discover that Scotland's highest village isn't in the Highlands, but in the Lowlands. Wanlockhead, in the Lowther Hills, is 1531 feet above sea level, and is a former lead mining village. It is best approached from the A76, passing through one of the most beautiful and majestic glens in Southern Scotland - the **Mennock Pass**. As you drive up, keep your eyes open for a small cross laid flat into the grass on the north side of the road. It commemorates Kate Anderson, a nurse who was killed here in 1925 when she was returning to Sanquhar after attending a patient. She fell off her bicycle in a snowstorm and broke her neck.

In the middle of Wanlockhead you'll find the **Museum of Lead Mining**, which explains all about the industry, and gives you the opportunity to go down the **Lochnell Mine**, a former working mine. The **Miners' Library** is situated on a rise above the Museum, and was founded in 1756 by 35 men. At the height of its popularity it had 3000 books on its shelves. Within the village you'll also find the **Beam Engine**, which used to pump water from one of the mines using, curiously enough, water to power it.

The **Leadhills and Wanlockhead Light Railway** is Britain's highest adhesion railway, reaching 1498 feet above sea level. It was originally built to take refined lead to Scotland's central belt, but finally closed in 1938. Now a length of two-feet gauge track has been reopened between Wanlockhead and its twin village of Leadhills, and trips are available at weekends during the summer.

Lead is not the only metal associated with Wanlockhead. In olden days, this whole area was known as "God's Treasure House in Scotland" because of the gold found there. In fact, the Scottish crown was refashioned for James V in the 16th century from gold mined here. The largest nugget of gold ever discovered in the UK was found close to Wanlockhead. It weighed all of two pounds, and was the size of a cricket ball. Gold panning is still a popular activity in the local streams, and the **UK National Gold Panning Championships** are held here every May.

Sanquhar

28 miles N of Dumfries on the A76

Sanquhar (pronounced San-kar) is a small town in Upper Nithsdale that was created a royal burgh in 1598. The name comes from the language of the ancient Britons, and means "Old Fort". The site of this fort was on a small hill to the north of the town, close to **St Bride's Parish Church**, built in 1824 on the site of a much older church. Within the church is a small collection of stone carvings, including one of St Nicholas and a medieval cross.

The **Sanquhar Tolbooth** was built to the designs of William Adam in 1735 as a town hall, schoolroom and jail, and now houses a small museum. In Main Street is **Sanquhar**

Post Office, dating from 1712, the oldest continuously used post office in the world. The Southern Upland Way passes through the burgh, and the **Sanquhar Historic Walk** takes you round many of the town's attractions and historic sites.

To the south of Sanquhar are the ruins of **Sanquhar Castle**, an old Douglas stronghold. It was here that William Douglas, who wrote the original version of the song *Annie Laurie*, was born in 1672 (see Maxwelton House). The castle was founded in the 11th century, though what you see now dates from much later.

In the 17th century, Sanquhar was a Covenanting stronghold. Charles II had imposed bishops on the Church of Scotland, and the Covenanters took up arms to keep the church Presbyterian. These times were known as the "Killing Times", and many people were executed for following the dictates of their conscience. One of the most militant Covenanters was **Richard Cameron**, who rode into Sanquhar in 1680 and attached what became known as the "**Sanquhar Declaration**" to the Market Cross. This disowned the king, which was effectively treason. Cameron was subsequently killed at the Battle of Airds Moss in the same year (see also Falkland).

One of the more unusual cottage industries in Sanquhar during the 18th century was hand knitting, and the intricate patterns soon made the garments popular throughout the country. Up until the 1950s these patterns had never been published. Now it is possible once more to buy both hand and machine knitted garments made from the distinctive patterns.

A series of plaques on various buildings takes you on a historic walk round the town, with a leaflet being available in the local tourist office.

Eliock House

26 miles N of Dumfries on a side road running parallel to the A76

Set deep in the heart of Nithsdale, Eliock House (not open to the public) was the birthplace in 1560 of **James Crichton**, better known as the "Admirable Crichton". He was the son of the then Lord Advocate of Scotland, and was educated at St Andrews University. He travelled extensively in Europe, where he followed careers in soldiering and lecturing at universities. Though a young man, it is said he could speak twelve languages fluently, and was one of the best swordsmen of his day. However, this didn't prevent him being killed in Mantua in Italy in 1582 while a lecturer at the university there.

The story goes that he was returning from a party one evening when he was set upon by a gang of robbers, and defeated each one in a sword fight. He then realised that one of the robbers was one of his pupils at the university, Vincentio di Gonzaga, son of the Duke of Mantua, ruler of the city. Realising what he had done, he handed Vincentio his sword and asked forgiveness. Vincentio, however, was a nasty piece of work. He took the sword and stabbed the defenceless James through the heart, killing him outright.

Kirkconnel (Upper Nithsdale)

31 miles N of Dumfries on the A76

This former mining village in upper Nithsdale is not to be confused with Kirkconnell House near New Abbey or Kirkconnel graveyard in Annandale. **St Connel's Parish Church** dates from 1729, and is a fine looking building to the west of the village.

High on the hills above the village are the scant remains of an even earlier church, which may date from before the 11th century. Near the present parish is a monument to **Alexander Anderson**, a local poet who wrote under the name of "The Surfaceman". Though born in lowly circumstances, he rose to become chief librarian at Edinburgh University and subsequently the secretary of the Edinburgh Philosophical Union.

Moffat

20 miles NE of Dumfries on the A701

Sheep farming has always been important here, and this is illustrated by the ram that surmounts the Colvin Fountain in the middle of the wide High Street. The town is situated in a fertile bowl surrounded by low green hills, and at one time was a spa, thanks to a mineral spring discovered on its outskirts in the 17th century. By 1827 the sulphurous water was being pumped into the town, and by Victorian times it had become a fashionable place to visit and "take the waters".

View of Moffat

Moffat was the birthplace, in 1882, of **Air Chief Marshal Lord Dowding**, architect of the Battle of Britain. A statue of him can be found in **Station Park**. Though he wasn't born in the town, **John Loudon McAdam**, the great road builder, is buried in the old kirkyard at the south end of the High Street. He lived at Dumcrieff House, outside the town, and died in 1836 (see also Ayr). Though born in Edinburgh, Dorothy

Buccleuch Arms Hotel

High Street, Moffat,
Dumfries & Galloway DG10 9ET
Tel: 01683 220003 Fax: 01683 221291
e-mail: enquiries@buccleucharmshotel.com
website: www.buccleucharmshotel.com

The elegant, whitewashed **Buccleuch Arms Hotel** is situated right in the heart of Moffat, a small market town just off the M74. It has retained many of its Georgian features, and this, coupled with its warm, friendly atmosphere and high standards of service, has made it one of the best hostelries in Dumfriesshire. The 16 en suite rooms are spacious and comfortable, and the food is out of this world. The charcoal grilled steaks from the highest standard of Scottish Beef draw people from all over! The public bar is cosy and inviting, and serves delicious lunches and dinners. This is the ideal stopover as you head north or south along the M74. It is also the ideal base from which to explore this fascinating area of Scotland.

Eskdale Hotel

Market Place, Langholm,
Dumfriesshire DG13 0JH
Tel/Fax: 01387 380357
e-mail: enquiries@eskdalehotel.co.uk
website: www.eskdalehotel.co.uk

The **Eskdale Hotel** is an elegant, stone-built hotel standing in Langholm's Market Place, one of the most attractive towns in the Scottish Borders. A former coaching inn, it is a family-run establishment, owned and managed by Kath and Howard Ashton-Smith. There are 15 recently-modernised, comfortable bedrooms on offer, all of which have en suite bath/shower and toilet facilities. All have colour TV, tea/coffee making facilities, full central heating and phones with Internet access. The furniture and fittings are of an exceptionally high standard, as is the décor.

Food is important in the Eskdale Hotel, with the no-smoking, licensed restaurant offering table d'hôte and à la carte menus that make imaginative use of fresh, local produce guaranteeing you a lunch or dinner that you are sure to remember. Mouth watering bar meals are also available, and there is an extensive wine list.

The hotel boasts two bars, each distinct in character. The main bar is popular with the locals, and here you can join in the "craic" over a pint of ale or a single malt. The Cocktail Bar is the ideal venue for a relaxing evening after a hard day's sightseeing or indulging in one of the many activities available in the area. There is a wide range of beers, ales, ciders, spirits, wines, liqueurs and soft drinks available, and both bar lunches and evening meals are served here as well. The atmosphere is informal, and the staff are friendly and knowledgeable about what to do and see in the area. Good, old fashioned service are the watchwords here. The hotel also caters for wedding receptions, dances and formal dinners, and has function suites to suit most occasions.

Langholm itself is an old, historic town lying in the valley of the River Esk. It is astride the main Edinburgh - Carlisle road, and was the birthplace of Scotland's greatest modern poet, Hugh MacDiarmid. The River Esk and its tributaries provide excellent salmon and trout fishing, with maps and permits being available from the hotel. Other activities include shooting, hill walking, studying wildlife, golf , tennis and bowls. Carlisle is only 21 miles away, and Edinburgh is 77 miles in the other direction. On the last Friday in July the town comes alive with the annual Langholm Common Riding, a ceremony dating back to the 18th century where horsemen patrol the boundaries of the common land surrounding the town. It is a colourful spectacle, and people come from all over to witness it.

Emily Stevenson, better known as the novelist **DE Stevenson**, lived in Moffat, and died there in 1973. She is buried in the local cemetery. The small **Moffat Museum** at The Neuk, Church Gate, charts the history of the town and the people associated with it, including Dowding, McAdam and Stevenson.

The **Black Bull Inn** is one of the oldest in Dumfriesshire, and dates from 1568. Burns was a regular visitor, and Graham of Claverhouse used it as his headquarters while hunting Covenanters in the district. Another hostelry in Moffat that has a claim to fame, albeit a more unusual one, is the **Star Hotel** in the High Street. It is only 20 feet wide, making it the narrowest hotel in Britain. On the other side of the road is the former **Moffat House**, designed by John Adam for the Earl of Hopetoun and dating from 1750s. It too is now a hotel.

Two miles east of the town, on the A708, are **Craiglochan Gardens**, which are open during the summer months. They extend to four acres, and there is a small nursery.

Grey Mare's Tail

28 miles NE of Dumfries just off the A708

The A708 winds northeast from the town, and takes you past St Mary's Loch as you head for Selkirk. About eight miles along the road is a waterfall called The Grey Mare's Tail (National Trust for Scotland), fed by the waters of tiny Loch Skeen, high in the hills. The surrounding area has changed little since the 17th century, when it was a hiding place for Covenanters. It is now a 2,150-acre nature reserve, and is rich in fauna and flora, including a herd of wild goats. During the summer months there is a programme of guided walks starting from the visitor centre.

Tweedswell

26 miles NE of Dumfries, well off the A701

Tweedswell is the source of the Tweed, and sits 1250 feet above sea level. It seems strange that within an area of no more than a few miles, three rivers rise. The Tweed flows east, the Annan flows south, and the Clyde flows north.

Close by is a great hollowed-out area among the hills known as the **Devil's Beeftub**. Here, in olden times, border reivers used to hide their stolen cattle. To the east towers the 2,651 feet high **Hartfell**, supposedly the seat of **Merlin the Magician** in Arthurian days.

Eskdalemuir

23 miles NE of Dumfries on the B709

Eskdalemuir, high in the hills, holds one of Dumfriesshire's hidden gems. The **Samye Ling Centre**, founded in 1967 by two refugee Tibetan abbots, is the largest Tibetan Buddhist monastery in Western Europe. Not only is it a monastery, it is a place where Tibetan culture, customs and art is preserved. To see its colourful Eastern buildings, its flags flying and its prayer wheels revolving in what is a typical Scottish moorland setting, comes as a great surprise. Close by is **Eskdalemuir Observatory**, erected in 1908. In June 1953 it recorded the highest short-term rainfall ever experienced in Scotland - 3.15 inches in half an hour. This represents about 15 per cent of Scotland's average annual rainfall.

Langholm

24 miles NE of Dumfries on the A7

Though within Dumfriesshire, the "muckle toon" of Langholm, in Eskdale, is more of a Borders town than a Dumfries and Galloway one. It was here, in 1892, that Christopher Grieve the poet, better known as **Hugh McDiarmid**, was born (see also Biggar), though it took many years for the people of the town to formally acknowledge his undoubted contribution to Scottish literature. This is Armstrong country, and the **Armstrong Clan Museum** at Lodge Walk in Castleholm traces the history of

Bush Of Ewes

Ewes, Langholm, Dumfriesshire DG13 0HN
Tel: 013873 81241
e-mail: jandsfisher@aol.com

Sitting in a quiet, rural spot in the Ewes Valley you will find the two-star **Bush of Ewes**, a picturesque, stone-built farmhouse offering the best in B&B accommodation. Bush of Ewes is a working farm of 2000 acres with Blackface sheep (Scotland's native breed) and Aberdeen Angus and Limousin suckler cows. Guests are free to stroll round and explore the beautiful countryside, with its inspiring scenery. Or, if they prefer, they can just relax in the comfortable and spacious lounge and let the world go by!

There are three rooms on offer - two twins and a double - and all are welcoming and warm, with central heating and tea/coffee making facilities. The breakfasts, as you would expect on a working farm, are appetising, hearty and filling, with only the freshest of local produce being used. Lighter options are available if you prefer. Evening meals can be provided by prior arrangement, and they reflect the high standards of good, traditional, Scottish home cooking. Packed lunches can also be prepared.

There is plenty of parking space, plus a mature garden where you can relax in the evening, enjoying the pure, fresh air. The farmhouse is situated five miles north of the ancient town of Langholm, in the Scottish Borders, and all around there is history and heritage aplenty. The farmhouse makes the perfect base for exploring the area, or it can be used as an overnight stop as you head north or south.

one of the greatest Borders family. On the last Friday in July the annual **Common Riding Ceremony** is held in the town.

Westerkirk

29 miles NE of Dumfries on the B709

The parish of Westerkirk lies a few miles north west of the Langholm, and it was here that **Thomas Telford** the great civil engineer was born in 1757. Within the parish is the unique **Bentpath Library**, founded in 1792 for the use of the antimony miners who used to work in the nearby Meggat Valley.

Lockerbie

10 miles NE of Dumfries off the M74

This quiet market town in Annandale is remembered for one thing - the **Lockerbie Disaster** of 1988. On the evening of December 21, Pan Am flight 103 exploded in mid air because of a terrorist bomb. Its cockpit crashed into a field at **Tundergarth**, two and a half miles east of the town, and its fuselage crashed into the town itself, killing all the passengers and crew, as well as 11 people on the ground. **Remembrance Garden** is situated within the town cemetery to the west of the motorway on the A709. It is a peaceful spot, though there is still an air of raw emotion about the place, and no one visits without developing a lump in the throat.

On December 6, 1593 the **Battle of Dryfe Sands** took place on the banks of the Dryfe Water north of the town. The two great families in the area - the Maxwells and the Johnstones - were forever fighting and bickering, and eventually they met in battle. The Maxwells, with 2000 men, looked the likeliest victors. However, the Johnstones, with only 400 men, won the day. Over 700 Maxwells were killed.

To the south of the town is **Burnswark**, where two 2nd century Roman siege camps are built on the site of an Iron Age fort.

Hightae

8 miles E of Dumfries on a minor road off the B7020

Rammerscales House is an 18th century manor house (not open to the public) with fine views from its policies. There is a walled garden and a woodland walk.

Lochmaben

8 miles NE of Dumfries on the A709

Lochmaben is a small royal burgh in Annandale. In the vicinity are many small lochs in which is found the vendace, a rare species of fish. Near the Castle Loch stand the scant remains of Lochmaben Castle (Historic Scotland), which originally covered 16 acres. It can only be viewed from the outside. An earlier castle was the home of the Bruce family, Lords of Annandale, and is said to be the birthplace of Robert the Bruce (later Robert 1), though Turnberry in Ayrshire lays a similar, and perhaps more likely, claim.

About three miles to the southwest is Skipmyre, where **William Paterson** was born. He was the driving force behind the ill-fated Darien Scheme of 1698, which sought to establish a Scottish colony in modern day Panama. Many Scots who went to Central America perished there, and it almost bankrupted the country. He was more successful in another venture - he founded the Bank of England in 1694 (see also New Abbey).

Torthorwald

4 miles E of Dumfries on the A709

Within the village, on a narrow road off the A709, is the **Cruck Cottage**, an early 18th century example of a thatched cottage made in the traditional way, with "crucks", or thick, curved wooden supports. They were placed some yards apart within holes in the ground so that they leaned towards each other, forming the shape of an "A". The ruined 14th century **Torthorwald Castle** was once a stronghold of the Carlyle and Kirkpatrick families. In 1544 Lord Carlyle destroyed the castle during a dispute with his relatives.

Caerlaverock

7 miles S of Dumfries on the B725

Think of an old, romantic, turreted medieval castle surrounded by a water-filled moat, and you could be thinking of **Caerlaverock Castle** (Historic Scotland). It was built by the Maxwells, one of the great local families, as their chief seat in the 13th century, and was attacked by Edward I in 1300 during the Wars of Independence. It is

Caerlaverock Castle

triangular in shape, with a turret at two corners and a double turret at the other, where the entrance is located. It was attacked by Covenanters in 1640 and dismantled, though in the early 1600s the then Earl of Nithsdale had some fine courtyard buildings constructed within the walls in the Renaissance style.
Caerlaverock Wildfowl and Wetlands Trust is about three miles west of the castle, and is situated in a 1,350-acre nature reserve. Here a wide variety of wildlife can be observed, including swans and barnacle geese. If you're lucky, you may also come across the extremely rare natterjack toad. There are three observation towers, 20 hides and a wild swan observatory linked by nature trails and screen approaches. There are also picnic areas, a gift shop, refreshments and binocular hire. Some facilities are wheelchair friendly.

The place is on the well signposted **Solway Coast Heritage Trail**, which stretches from Gretna in the east to Stranraer in the west.

Annan

14 miles E of Dumfries, on the A75

The picturesque old Royal Burgh of Annan, even though it is a mile from the sea, was once a thriving seaport, and even had a boat-building yard. **Edward Irving**, the founder of the Catholic Apostolic Church, which thrived on elaborate ceremony and a complicated hierarchy of ministers and priests, was born here in 1792. Four years earlier, **Hugh Clapperton** the explorer had been born in the town. He died in Africa in 1827 in Nigeria while searching for the source of the Niger. His notebooks and diaries have been published under the name *Difficult and Dangerous Roads*. Another Annan man was **Thomas Blacklock**, born in 1721. He was the first blind man to be ordained a minister in the Church of Scotland. **Annan Parish Church** in the High Street, with its stumpy spire, dates from 1786. The place has associations with the Bruce family, who were Lords of Annandale. In Bank Street is the **Historic Resources Centre**, a small museum that puts on a programme of displays and exhibitions.

Haaf Net Fishing is a means of catching fish that stretches back to Viking times, and it is still carried out at the mouth of the River Annan from April to August each year. The fishermen stand chest deep in the water wielding large haaf nets, which are attached to long wooden frames. In 1538 James V granted the haaf net fishermen of Annan a royal charter. In 1992 the rights of the fishermen were challenged in court by the owners of a time-share development further up the river, but the judge took the view that the charter still held good today.

South of the town, at one time, was the **Solway Viaduct**, a railway bridge that connected Dumfriesshire to Cumbria across the Solway Firth. It was opened for passenger trains in 1870, and at the time was the longest railway bridge across water in Britain. In 1881 parts of the bridge were damaged when great ice flows smashed into its stanchions. The then keeper of the bridge, John Welch, plus two colleagues, remained in their cabin on the bridge as the lumps of ice, some as big as 27 yards square, careered into the bridge's supports. At 3.30 in the morning, when disaster seemed imminent, they were ordered to leave. Two lengths of the bridge, one 50 feet long, and one 300 feet long, collapsed into the firth, and 37 girders and 45 pillars were smashed beyond repair. However, unlike the Tay Bridge disaster, there was no loss of life. Finally, in 1934, the bridge was dismantled, and all that is left to see nowadays are the approaches on both shores, and a stump in the middle of the water.

Ruthwell

10 miles SE of Dumfries off the B724

Within the **Parish Church** of 1800 is the famous 18-feet high **Ruthwell Cross**. It dates from about AD 800, when this part of

Scotland was within the Anglo Saxon kingdom of Northumbria. The carvings show scenes from the Gospels, twining vines and verses from an old poem called The Dream of the Rood, at one time thought to have been written by Caedmon of Whitby.

In 1810, the Revd Henry Duncan founded the world's first savings bank in the village, and the small **Savings Bank Museum** (see panel on page 56) has displays and artefacts about the savings bank movement.

Powfoot

13 miles SE of Dumfries on a minor road off the B724

Today Powfoot is a quiet village on the Solway coast. But in the late 19th and early 20th centuries there were plans to make it a grand holiday resort, with hotels, formal gardens, woodland walks, a promenade, a pier, golf courses and bowling greens. The whole plan eventually collapsed, though some of the attractions were actually built. Now the village is famous for its red brick housing and terraces, which look incongruous on the shores of the Solway, but wouldn't look out of place in Lancashire.

Eastriggs

18 miles E of Dumfries on the A75

A huge government works manufacturing explosives and gunpowder once stretched from Longtown in the east to Annan in the west, a total of 11 miles. The **Eastriggs Heritage Project,** in St John's Church on Dunedin Road, traces the lives of the 30,000 workers who manufactured what was known as "The Devil's Porridge".

Savings Bank Museum

Ruthwell, Dumfries DG1 4NN
Tel: 01387 870640
e-mail: Info@savingsbankmuseum.co.uk
website: www.savingsbankmuseum.co.uk

Dr Henry Duncan was an accomplished artist and some of his work is displayed in the museum, but he is best remembered as the man who identified the first fossil footprints in Britain. Minister of the Ruthwell parish church for 50 years, he opened the world's first commercial savings bank in 1810. The museum also houses a large collection of early home savings boxes, coins and bank notes from many parts of the world.Open daily 10am to 1pm and 2pm to 5pm except Sundays and Bank Holidays from 1st October until Easter.

Gretna Green

23 miles E of Dumfries off the M74

This small village, just across the border from England, is the "romance" capital of Britain. In the 18th century it was the first stopping place in Scotland for coaches travelling north, so was the ideal place for English runaways to get married.

In 1754 irregular marriages in England were made illegal, and the legal age at which people could get married without parental consent was set at 21. However, this didn't apply in Scotland, and soon a roaring trade in runaway marriages got underway in the village. The actual border between Scotland and England is the River Sark, and one of the places where marriages took place was the **Old Toll House** (now bypassed by the M74) on the Scottish side of the river. Another place was **Gretna Hall**.

But perhaps the most famous was the **Old Blacksmith's Shop**, built in about 1712. A wedding ceremony in front of the anvil became the popular means of tying the knot, and the Anvil Priests, as they became known, charged anything from a dram of whisky to a guinea to conduct what was a perfectly legal ceremony. By 1856, the number of weddings had dropped, due to what was called the "Lord Brougham Act", which required that at least one of the parties to the marriage had to have been resident in Scotland for the previous 21 days. This act was only repealed in 1979.

However, couples still come from all over the world to get married before the anvil in Gretna Green, though the ceremony is no more than a confirmation of vows taken earlier in the registry office. The Old Blacksmith's Shop is still open, and houses an exhibition on the irregular marriage trade.

Gretna Green was within the **Debatable Lands**, a stretch of land which, as its name implies, was claimed by both Scotland and England. It was therefore a lawless area in the 15th and 16th centuries, as no country could adequately police it. About a mile to

Marriage Room, Gretna Green

the southwest is the **Lochmaben Stone**, a huge rock where representatives from the two countries met to air grievances and seek justice. It is also sometimes known as the "Clochmaben" Stone, Maben being a shadowy figure associated with King Arthur.

Not so long ago, Gretna Green was run down, tacky, and an embarrassing introduction to Scotland for those travelling north. But recent improvements have made it the second most visited tourist attraction in Scotland. Nowadays there are many high quality shops and restaurants in the village. In the nearby village of **Gretna** is the **Gretna Gateway Outlet Village**, a complex of shops selling designer label fashions

Ecclefechan

14 miles E of Dumfries on the B7076

This small village's rather curious name means the church of St Fechan or Fechin, a 7th century Irish saint. Within it you will find **Carlyle's Birthplace** (National Trust for Scotland), where Thomas Carlyle was born in 1795. Called "The Arched House", it was built on the main street by Thomas's father and uncle, who were both master masons. Within it is a collection of memorabilia about the great man.

Dalton

9 miles E of Dumfries on the B7020

This little village has a pretty parish church dating from the late 19th century, though a church has stood on the site since at least the 15th century. Half a mile west, on a minor road, is **Dalton Pottery**, which sells a range of porcelain giftware. Young and old alike can also have fun decorating pots and tiles using ceramic felt-tipped pens, which are fired in a small kiln and ready to take away the same day. You can also throw a pot on a wheel, though you have to return to collect it some time later.

Kirkconnel (Kirtlebridge)

17 mile E of Dumfries off the M74

In the kirkyard of the ruined Kirkconnel Church are said to be the graves of **Fair Helen of Kirkconnel Lee** and her lover **Adam Fleming**. Their story is a romantic one, and a famous ballad was written about it. Helen was loved by two men, Adam Fleming and a man named Bell (whose first name isn't known). Helen found herself drawn towards Adam, and Bell was consumed with jealousy. He therefore decided to kill his rival. He waylaid the couple close to the kirkyard, and pulled out a pistol. As he fired, Helen threw herself in front of her lover, and was killed. There are two versions of the story after this. One says that Adam killed Bell where he stood, and another says he pursued him to Madrid, where he killed him. Either way, he was inconsolable, and joined the army. But he could never forget Helen, and one day he returned to Kirkconnel, lay on her tombstone, and died of a broken heart. He was buried beside her.

It's a poignant tale, but there is no proof that the events actually took place.

Kirkpatrick Fleming

20 miles E of Dumfries off the M74

This pleasant little village is visited mainly to see **Robert the Bruce's Cave**, where the great man is supposed to have seen the spider, though similar claims are made for other caves in both Scotland and Ireland. Sir William Irving hid Robert the Bruce here for three months while he was being hunted by the English.

Canonbie

26 miles E of Dumfries on the B6357

Canonbie means the "town of the canons", because a priory once stood here. The English destroyed it in 1542, and some of the stones may have been used in the building of **Hollows Bridge** across the River Esk, Scotland's second fastest flowing river. This is the heart of the Debatable Lands, and was a safe haven for reivers. Beyond the bridge, and marked by a stone and plaque, is the site of **Gilnockie Castle**, home of

Johnnie Armstrong, one of the greatest reivers of them all. So much of a threat was he to the relationship between Scotland and England that James V hanged him in 1530. The story goes that Johnnie and his men were invited to a great gathering at Carlanrig in Teviotdale where they would meet the king, who promised them safe passage. Taking him at his word, Johnnie and a band of men set out. However, when they got there, James had them all strung up on the spot. Perhaps the most amazing aspect of this tale is that the king was no world-weary warrior, but an 18-year-old lad at the time. Some of the castle's stones also went into building Hollows Bridge.

Standing beside the river is **Hollows Mill**, the last commercial mill in Scotland still to be powered by water. And close by is **Gilnockie Tower**, which dates from the 16th century. Up until 1980 it was a roofless ruin, but now it houses a small museum and Clan Armstrong library.

The **Scots Dyke**, 2 miles south of the village, was erected in the 16th century in an attempt to delineate the boundary between Scotland and England. It consists of a "dyke", or low, earthen wall and an accompanying ditch.

New Abbey

6 miles S of Dumfries on the A710

This attractive little village sits in the shadow of **The Criffel**, a 1,866 feet high hill that can be seen from miles around. Within the village you'll find the beautiful red sandstone ruins of **Sweetheart Abbey** (Historic Scotland), founded in 1273 by Devorgilla, Lady of Galloway in her own right (see also Dumfries). Her husband was John Balliol of Barnard Castle in County Durham, who founded Balliol College in Oxford. After his death she carried his embalmed heart around with her in a small casket, and when she herself died, she was buried along with the heart in front of the abbey's high altar, which has been moved. The Cistercian monks gave the name "Dolce Cor" to the abbey, and thus was born the word "sweetheart". In its graveyard lies William Paterson, founder of the Bank of England (see also Lochmaben).

At the other end of the village is the **New Abbey Corn Mill** (Historic Scotland), dating from the 18th century. It is in full working order, and there are regular demonstrations on how a water powered mill works. The original mill on the site is thought to have belonged to Sweetheart Abbey.

Shambellie House is a large mansion on the outskirts of New Abbey, which houses the **Shambellie House Museum of Costume**, part of the National Museums of Scotland. The house and its collection were given to the National Museums in 1977 by the then owner, Charles Stewart, and most of the costumes, which range from Victorian to the 1930s, are now displayed in appropriate settings.

Kirkbean

10 miles S of Dumfries, on the A710

About two miles south of the village is the estate of **Arbigland**, birthplace in 1747 of the founder of the American navy, **John Paul Jones** (see also Kirkcudbright). The cottage on which he was born is now a small museum. **Kirkbean Parish Church** was built in 1776, and inside is a font presented by the American Navy in 1945. To continue the American theme, **Dr James Craik**, Washington's personal physician, was also born on the estate.

Crocketford

9 miles W of Dumfries, on the A75

It was at Crocketford that the sorry tale of Elspeth Buchan, who founded a religious sect called the Buchanites, came to a macabre end. Part of the sect's beliefs was that Elspeth was immortal, and that she could bestow immortality on others by breathing on them. After having been driven out of Irvine, she and her followers headed south towards Dumfriesshire and settled there. Alas, Elspeth disappointed her followers by dying a natural death, and the sect broke up. But one man, who lived in Crocketford, still believed in her immortality, and that she would rise from the dead. He therefore acquired her body and kept it in a cupboard in his cottage, where it gradually mummified. Every day he would go to the cupboard and open it to see if Elspeth had come alive again, but every time he was disappointed. However, this didn't shake his beliefs, and the body remained in the cottage with him for many years (see also Dunscore and Irvine).

Kirkpatrick Durham

12 miles W of Dumfries on a minor road north of the A75

In Victoria Street is **Moonstone Miniatures**, which has a collection of one-twelfth scale houses ansd shops. Watch out for the barmaid's false teeth and the rats in the bookshop.

Kirkcudbright

Kirkcudbright (pronounced "Kirk-coo-bray") is one of the loveliest small towns in Scotland, and one of its real "hidden places". Its name simply means the kirk of St Cuthbert, as the original church built here was dedicated to that saint. It was an established town by the 11th century, and has been a royal burgh since 1455. It sits close to the mouth of the Dee, and is still a working port with a small fishing fleet.

Kirkcudbright was once the county town of Kirkcudbrightshire, also known as the "Stewartry of Kirkcudbright". It is a place of brightly painted Georgian, Regency and Victorian houses, making it a colourful and interesting place to explore. This part of Galloway has a very mild climate, thanks to the Gulf Stream washing its shores, and this, as well as the quality of light to be found here, encouraged the founding of an artist's colony in the town. On a summer's morning, the edge between light and shadow can be as sharp as a knife, whereas during the day it becomes diffused and soft, and artists have been reaching for their paints and palettes for years to try and capture these two qualities. Even today, straw-hatted artists can still be seen at the harbour side, trying to capture the scene.

It is said that St Cuthbert himself founded the first church here, which was located within the cemetery to the east of the town. Down through the years, gravediggers have often turned up carved stones that belonged to it. Within the graveyard is **Billy Marshall's Grave**. Billy was known as the "King of Galloway Tinkers", and the gravestone states that he died in 1792 aged 120 years. Don't be surprised to see coins lying on top of the gravestone. It's supposed to be an old gypsy custom, whereby a passing gypsy or tinker without money could use the coins to buy food. The money nowadays is usually left by tourists, with the main beneficiaries being local children.

The present **Parish Church** is a grand affair in red sandstone near the centre of the town, and dates from 1838. Parts of a much older church are to be found near the harbour. **Greyfriar's Kirk** is all that is left of a Franciscan monastery that stood here, and dates from the 16th century, though it has been much altered over the years. Within it is the grand tomb of **Sir Thomas MacLellan of Bombie** and his wife Grizzell Maxwell, which was erected in 1597. But the tomb isn't all it seems. The couple's son, in an effort to save money, used effigies from an earlier tomb within what is essentially a Renaissance canopy. The friary is thought to have been founded in 1224 by Alan, Lord of Galloway and father of Devorgilla, who founded Sweetheart Abbey. The kirk sits on a slight rise known as the **Moat Brae**, where Roland, Lord of Galloway in the 12th century, may have had a castle.

Nearby, in Castle Street, are the substantial ruins of **MacLellan's Castle**

(Historic Scotland), built by the same Sir Thomas who lies in the Greyfriar's Kirk. It isn't really a castle, but a grand town house, and Sir Thomas, who was obviously his son's role model where thrift was concerned, used the stones from the friary as building material. Sir Thomas was a local magnate and favourite of the king who became Provost of Kirkcudbright. The castle is open to the public. Watch out for the small room behind the fireplace in the Great Hall. Sir Thomas used to hide himself here and listen to what was being said about him in the Great Hall through a small opening in the wall called the "Laird's Lug".

Walk up the side of the castle into Castle Bank, passing the whitewashed **Harbour Cottage Gallery**, where there are regular exhibitions of work by local artists, and you arrive at the **High Street**. This must be one of the most charming and colourful streets in Scotland. The elegant Georgian and Regency houses - some of them quite substantial - are painted in bright, uncompromising colours, such as yellow, green and pink. **Auchingool House** is the oldest, having been built in 1617 for the McCullochs of Auchengool. **Broughton House**, dating from the 18th century, is now owned by the National Trust for Scotland, and was the home of A.E. Hornel the artist. He was one of the Glasgow Boys, and died in 1933. The house is very much as it was when he lived there. Behind the house is the marvellous **Japanese Gardens**, influenced by trips that Hornel made to that country.

Further along the street is **Greengates Close**, (not open to the public) which was the home of Jessie M. King, another artist. A few yards further on the High Street takes a dog leg to the east, and here stands the early 17th century **Tolbooth**, which has been refurbished and now houses a museum and art gallery telling the story of the artist's colony. The Queen opened it in 1993. This was the former town house and jail, and John Paul Jones, founder of the American navy, was imprisoned here at one time for murder. He got his revenge in later years when he returned to the town aboard an American ship and shelled the nearby **St Mary's Isle**, where the seat of the Earl of Selkirk was located and a medieval priory of nuns once stood. This "isle" is in fact a peninsula, and to confuse matters even further, one of the smaller bays in Kirkcudbright Bay (itself an inlet of the Solway Firth) is called **Manxman's Lake**, one of the few instances in Scotland of a natural stretch of water being called a lake rather than a loch (see also Lake of Menteith, Stenton and Ellon). A walk up St Mary's Wynd beside the Tolbooth and past the modern school takes you to **Castledykes**, where once stood a royal castle. Edward I stayed here, as did Henry VI after his defeat at the Battle of Towton in 1461, and James 1V used it as a staging post on his many pilgrimages to Whithorn. In St Mary's Street, close to where it meets with the High Street, is the **Stewartry Museum**, which has many artefacts and displays on the history of the Stewartry of Kirkcudbright. On the opposite side of the street is the **Town Hall**, where themed painting exhibitions are held every year.

The town also has its literary associations. **Dorothy L. Sayers** set her Lord Peter Wimsey

Broughton House Gardens, Kirkcudbright

whodunit *Five Red Herrings* among the artist's colony. It's not one of her best, as it over-relies on a detailed knowledge of train times between Kirkcudbrightshire and Ayrshire, and of the paints found on an artist's palette. **Ronald Searle** also knew the town, and he based his **St Trinians** innocents on St Trinian's School in Edinburgh, attended by the daughters of Kirkcudbright artist W. Miles Johnston.

Kirkcudbright was where the village scenes in the cult movie **The Wicker Man** were filmed, and indeed many locations in Dumfries and Galloway - and even Ayrshire - stood in for the fictional Summerisles, where the action is supposed to have taken place.

Around Kirkcudbright

Tongland

2 miles N of Kirkcudbright on the A711

The small village of Tongland was once the site of the great **Tongland Abbey**, founded in 1218 by Fergus, Lord of Galloway, and the scant remains - no more than a medieval archway in a piece of preserved wall - can still be seen in the kirkyard. The abbey's most famous inmate was Abbot John Damien, known as the "Frenzied Friar of Tongland", who achieved fame by jumping off the ramparts of Stirling Castle in an attempt to fly like a bird (see also Stirling). Tours are available of **Tongland Power Station**, part of the great Galloway hydroelectric scheme built in the 1930s. Close by is **Tongland Bridge**, a graceful structure across the Dee designed by Thomas Telford and built in 1805.

Loch Ken

9 miles N of Kirkcudbright between the A713 and the A762

Loch Ken is a narrow stretch of water almost nine miles long, and nowhere wider than a mile. It was created in the 1930s as the result of the great Galloway hydroelectric scheme, with the turbines being housed in the power station at Tongland, further down the Dee. Other schemes were constructed at Clatteringshaws and Loch Doon. Loch Ken is a favourite spot for bird watching and sports such as sailing, fishing and water skiing, and round the shores are small nature reserves. Details about using the loch are available from the **Loch Ken Marina,** off the A713 on the eastern shore.

New Galloway

17 miles N of Kirkcudbright on the A762

Though New Galloway is a small village with a population of about 300, it is still a proud royal burgh, and a picturesque place. We are in that part of Kirkcudbrightshire known as the **Glenkens**, an area combining the high drama of lonely moorland with fertile, wooded valleys.

Glenlee Holiday Houses

New Galloway, Kirkcudbrightshire DG7 3SF
Tel: 01644 430212 Fax: 01644 430340
e-mail: agnew@glenlee-holidays.co.uk
website: www.glenlee-holidays.co.uk

Glenlee Estate has been owned by the Agnew family for over 70 years, and lies at the heart of Galloway in an area that is both beautiful and relatively undiscovered. There are five cottages on offer which once formed part of the estate's home farm, but which have now been converted into comfortable and spacious self catering units. All are spacious, comfortable and practical, with a fully equipped kitchen. Water heating is by immersion heater, and each cottage has off-peak Nightstor heaters. The sitting rooms all have TVs and open hearth fires. Linen and towels are not supplied, but can be hired for a small extra charge. Cots and high chairs can also be supplied. The cottages are all grouped round a small courtyard, in a quiet, secluded setting. Chestnut Cottage sleeps four in two bedrooms, a double and a twin. Milhouse sleeps five in a single bedroom, a double and a twin. Tower Cottage sleeps six in a double bedroom, a twin and a bunk, Dairy Cottage sleeps six in a double and two twins, and Bell Cottage sleeps six to seven in a double bedroom, a twin and a twin with an extra Z-bed.

The surrounding area offers opportunities for fishing on Glenlee's stretch of the River Ken, golf at New Galloway, canoeing, sailing and windsurfing on Loch Ken, and walking in the surrounding countryside and on the nearby Southern Upland Way. The towns of Ayr and Dumfries, with their shops, restaurants, bars and leisure facilities are 40 minutes away by car, and there are general stores and post offices in the nearby villages of New Galloway and St John's Town of Dalry.

Kells Churchyard, north of the town, is the grave of a Covenanter, shot in 1685.

Each year in early August New Galloway plays host to the **Scottish Alternative Games**, where sports such as gird and cleek (hoop and stick) racing, hurlin' (throwing) the curlin' stane, flingin' the herd's bunnet and tossin' the sheaf are indulged in.

Balmaclellan

18 miles N of Kirkcudbright off the A712

This attractive little village was the home of **Robert Paterson**, a stonemason who was the model for Old Mortality in Scott's book of the same name. He travelled Scotland cleaning up the monuments and gravestones of the Covenanters, a group of men and women who fought Charles II's attempts to impose bishops on the Church of Scotland. Eventually he left home for good to concentrate on this work, leaving behind a no doubt angry wife and five children. Up to his death in 1800, he continued to travel the country, usually on an old grey pony.

Just outside the village you will find **The Clog and Shoe Workshop**, where 18 styles of footwear are manufactured. Visitors can look round the workshop and see shoes and clogs being made.

St John's Town of Dalry

19 miles N of Kirkcudbright on the A713

St John's Town of Dalry, sometimes known simply as Dalry, lies on the Southern Uplands Way, and is a picturesque Glenkens village with many old cottages. Within the village is a curious chair-shaped stone known as **St John's Stone**. Local tradition says that John the Baptist rested in it. When a reservoir was created at lonely **Lochinvar** near Dalry in 1968, the waters of the loch were raised, covering the scant ruins of a castle owned by the Gordons. This was the home of the famous Young Lochinvar, written about by Scott in his famous lines from *Marmion*:

"O, young Lochinvar is come out of the west,
Through all the wide border his steed was the best..."

A cairn by the loch side, which is reached by a narrow track, records the existence of the castle. It was built using stones from the castle ruins. **Earlston Castle**, overlooking Earlston Loch to the north of the village, was also a Gordon stronghold. It was the birthplace of Catherine Gordon, later Mrs Catherine Stewart, who befriended Burns and encouraged him to write poetry when she lived in Stair Castle in Ayrshire.

Carsphairn

27 miles N of Kirkcudbright on the A713

Close to this quiet village there used to be lead mines. John Loudon MacAdam the roads pioneer, whose father came from near the village, experimented on his revolutionary road surfaces on the A713 north of the village. The **Carsphairn Heritage Centre** has displays and exhibits on the history of the village.

Castle Douglas

9 miles NE of Kirkcudbright off the A75

Castle Douglas is a pleasant town based round what was a small village known as "Carlingwark". It was founded in the 18th century by William Douglas, a local merchant who earned his money trading with Virginia and the West Indies. He wanted to establish a thriving manufacturing town based on the woollen industry, and though he was only partly successful, he did lay the foundations for a charming town, where some of his original 18th century buildings can still be seen. On the edge of the town is **Carlingwark Loch**, which was joined to the River Dee in 1765 by **Carlingwark Lane**, a narrow canal. Marl, a limey clay used as manure, was dug from the bed of the loch and taken down river to the port of Kirkcudbright on barges.

In Market Street is the **Castle Douglas Art Gallery**, gifted to the town in 1938 by the artist Ethel Bristowe. There is a continuing programme of painting, sculpture and craft exhibitions. The **Sulworth Brewery** is in King Street, and here you can see the brewing process from barley to beer, and enjoy a complimentary half pint of Galloway real ale. The **Ken Dee Marches Nature Reserve** follows the woodland and marshes along the River Dee and Loch Ken, north west of the town.

Threave Castle

8 miles N of Kirkcudbright, close to the A75

On an island in the River Dee stand the magnificent ruins of Threave Castle

(Historic Scotland), reached by a small ferry that answers the call of a bell on a jetty on the riverbank. It was built by Archibald Douglas, 3rd Earl of Douglas, known as Archibald the Grim, soon after he became Lord of Galloway in 1369. On his death at Threave in 1400, he was the most powerful man in southern Scotland, and almost independent of the king, Robert III. When James II laid siege to the castle in 1455 to curtail the power of the Douglases, it took two months before the occupants finally surrendered.

Threave Gardens

7 miles NE of Kirkcudbright, on the A75

Threave Gardens and Estate (National Trust for Scotland - see panel below), which surround a house built in 1872 by a Liverpool businessman, were created from scratch, and now house the Trust's School of Practical Gardening. The house itself is open to the public, with its interiors restored to how they would have been in the 1930s. The Maxwell Collection of local bygones is on display within the visitor centre.

Kippford

10 miles NE of Kirkcudbright off the A710

The tides in the Solway Firth are among the fastest in Britain, but this hasn't prevented the picturesque village of Kippford from becoming a great yachting centre. Like its neighbour Rockcliffe, (five miles away, it was once a smuggling village).

Palnackie

10 miles NE of Kirkcudbright on the A711

This small, attractive village on the Urr

Threave Estate

Castle Douglas, Dumfries & Galloway DG7 IRX
Tel: 01556 502575 Fax: 01556 502683
Ranger/natural ist: tel (01556) 502575
e-mail threave@nts.org.uk
website: www.nts.org.uk

Threave Garden is delightful in all seasons and is best known for its spectacular springtime daffodils (nearly 200 varieties), although the herbaceous beds are colourful in summer and trees and heather garden are striking in autumn. The Victorian house is home to the Trust's School of Practical Gardening. The principal rooms in **Threave House** opened to the public for the first time in 2002 and have attracted great interest. The interiors have been restored to their appearance in the 1930s, and from the house visitors can enjoy impressive vistas of the Galloway countryside. Guided walks are available and the Maxwelton Collection of local bygones in the Visitor Centre is on show. There is also a plant Centre.

Threave Estate is a wildfowl refuge and is designated a Special Protection Area for its breeding waders and wintering wildfowl. The important wetlands are designated an Area of Special Scientific Interest. Threave provides a good example of integrated management of the land, taking account of agriculture, forestry and nature conservation. Marked walks include a 2.5 km estate trail through this variety of landscapes, and hides provide good cover to observe bird activity. A Countryside Centre in the old stables highlights nature conservation, forestry and agriculture at Threave.

Water is a mile from the sea, though at one time it was a thriving port. Each year, in summer, it hosts one of the most unusual competitions in Great Britain - the annual **World Flounder Tramping Championships**. People come from all over the world to compete, making it a truly international event. The object is to walk out onto the mud flats south of the village at low tide, feeling for flounders hiding beneath the mud with your toes as you go. The person who collects the largest weight of flounders wins the championship. It may seem a light hearted and eccentric competition, but it has a firm basis in local history, as this was a recognised way of catching fish in in olden times.

The **North Glen Gallery** features glassblowing and interior and exterior design. It is also a good place to get advice on local walks and wildlife. A mile south west is **Orchardton Tower,** the only round tower house in Scotland; it dates from the middle of the 15th century, and was built by John Cairns.

Dalbeattie

11 miles NE of Kirkcudbright on the A711

This small town stands just east of the Water of Urr, which at one time was navigable as far upriver as here. Ships of up to 60 tons could make the four-mile trip from the sea, pulled by teams of horses. Now the "Pool of Dalbeattie" (the name given to the port area) is derelict, and the river has silted up.

Dalbeattie was a planned town, founded in the 1790s as a textile centre. Close by there were easily worked deposits of granite which provided employment as well. In Southwick Road you'll find the **Dalbeattie Museum,** and this has displays and exhibits about the history of the town. It has a particularly fine collection of Victoriana. Within Colliston Park is the **Dalbeattie Granite Garden,** designed by Solway Heritage to celebrate the beauty of the stone and the workers and craftsmen who mined it.

On the west bank of the Urr, about a mile from the town, is all that remains of **Buittle Castle and Bailey,** home to John Balliol, son of Devorgilla, whom Edward I placed on the throne of Scotland as a puppet king. Robert I established a burgh here in 1325, and a recent archaeological dig has revealed that the castle's large bailey may have housed it. A later tower house, the **Old Buittle Tower,** stands close by. It has occasional displays of arms and armour.

On the wall of the former town hall is the Murdoch Memorial to Lt William Murdoch, who was the First Officer aboard the Titanic when it sank in 1912. Through the years he has been unfairly accused of being, among other things, a coward who shot passengers attempting to leave the ship.

He was also accused of not allowing third class passengers near the lifeboats and of accepting bribes from first class passengers to let them board lifeboats to which they were not entitled. The recent film also treated him unfairly, though the witness statements presented at the later official Board of Trade Enquiry cleared him of all these charges. In 1996 his name was finally and officially cleared of any wrongdoing.

Three miles north of Dalbeattie is the **Motte of Urr**, a 12th century motte-hill that is the largest non-industrial man-made hill in Scotland. At its summit at one time would have been a large, wooden castle, supposedly built by William de Berkeley. And five miles south west of the town is **Scree Hill**, with marked walks through forest and woodland to its top, from which there are excellent views.

Rockcliffe

10 miles E of Kirkcudbright on a minor road off the A710

Rockcliffe was at one time a great smuggling centre, but is now a quiet resort sitting on the **Rough Firth**, one of the smallest firths in Scotland. Off the coast is **Rough Island** (National Trust for Scotland), a bird sanctuary. Close to the village is the great **Mote of Mark** (National Trust for Scotland), the site of a prehistoric fort.

There are a number of footpaths connecting Rockcliffe with Kippford, the two-mile long **Jubilee Path** (National Trust for Scotland) being the main one. There is a programme of ranger-guided walks along it in the summer months.

Dundrennan

4 miles SE of Kirkcudbright on the A711

This quiet village is now visited mainly because of the ruins of the once substantial **Dundrennan Abbey** (Historic Scotland). It was founded in 1142 by David I and Fergus, Lord of Galloway, and was where Mary Stuart spent her last night on Scottish soil before sailing for England and her eventual execution. Little of the grand abbey church now remains, though the chapter house and some of the other buildings are well worth seeing, as are some interesting grave slabs.

Twynholm

3 miles NW of Kirkcudbright on the A75

Twynholm is the home village of David Coulthard, and within the **David Coulthard Museum** in Burnbrae you can learn about the racing driver's life. There is also a gift shop and tearoom.

Gatehouse of Fleet

6 miles NW of Kirkcudbright off the A75

This neat little town was the original for

the "Kippletringan" of Scott's Guy Mannering. It sits on the Water of Fleet, about a mile from Fleet Bay, and was at one time a port, thanks to the canalisation of the river in 1823 by a local landowner, Alexander Murray of Cally House. The port area was known as **Port MacAdam,** though the site has now been grassed over. Cally House is now a hotel, though next to it are the **Cally Gardens**, housed in a two and a half acre walled garden.

Gatehouse of Fleet was laid out in the 1760s as a cotton-weaving centre by James Murray of Broughton, and today it remains more or less the way he planned it. He wished to create a great industrial town, though nowadays it is hard to imagine "dark satanic mills" in such an idyllic setting. Within one of the former cotton mills is a museum called the **Mill on the Fleet**, which tells the story of the town's former weaving industry.

It was supposedly in Gatehouse of Fleet, in the **Murray Arms**, that Burns set down the words to *Scots Wha Hae*. About a mile west of the town stands the substantial ruins of 15th century **Cardoness Castle** (Historic Scotland), former home of the McCullochs of Galloway. It stands on a rocky platform above the road, and is open to the public.

Cairnholy

11 miles W of Kirkcudbright off the A75

Cairn Holy (Historic Scotland) comprises two chambered cairns dating from between 2000 and 3000 BC. The most remarkable thing about their construction is how our ancestors managed to raise such huge stones. About a mile north of the cairns are the ruins of **Carsluith Castle**, dating from the 16th century. The castle was built by the Browns of Carsluith.

Creetown

14 miles NW of Kirkcudbright on the A75

Set at the mouth of the River Cree, the neat village of Creetown was once a centre for the mining of granite. Now it is visited chiefly because of the **Creetown Gem Rock Museum**, housed in a former school. It was established in 1971, and since then has amassed a remarkable collection of gemstones and minerals from all over the world. There are also exhibitions on geology and on the formation of our landscapes from earliest times. It even has an "erupting volcano".

The **Creetown Exhibition Centre** in St John's Street has exhibits on local history and wildlife, as well as occasional exhibitions by local artists. Each year in September the **Creetown Country Weekend** takes place, featuring the best in country music.

Stranraer

Sitting at the head of Loch Ryan, and on the edge of the **Rhinns of Galloway**, that hammer shaped peninsula that juts out into the Irish Sea, Stranraer is a royal burgh that is now one of the main Scottish ports for Northern Ireland. It was granted its royal

Building a Stone Wall, near Stranraer

CRAIGNELDER HOTEL

Cairnryan Road, Stranraer,
Wigtownshire DG9 8HA
Tel: 01776 703281 Fax: 01776 705527

The Royal Burgh of Stranraer, in Southwest Scotland, is the country's ferry port for Northern Ireland. It is a pleasant, picturesque town with many narrow, winding streets and small shops. And it is here that you will find the family-friendly **Craignelder Hotel,** which commands an imposing position near to the ferry terminal.

The place has recently been completely refurbished to create a hotel that is stylish and elegant yet friendly, with value-for-money being the watchwords. The building itself is a beautifully proportioned Victorian villa which

was once the home of a sea captain, and it sits within easy walking distance of the ferry terminal itself. It has been converted to give all that is best in Scottish hospitality while retaining many original features. There are eleven guest bedrooms, all fully en suite, with complimentary tea and coffee making facilities and radio and telephone in each one. They have all recently been decorated and furnished to an extremely high standard, and are cosy in winter and cool in summer! And disabled facilities are also available!

The elegant dining room (which gets extremely busy at lunchtimes!) is the place to have that special celebration dinner. Or perhaps you just want to treat yourself! The menu - carefully put together by the resident chef - features traditional Scottish cuisine with some foreign influences. Only the finest and freshest of local produce - game, fish, meat and vegetables - is used to ensure that your meal is a culinary experience not to be forgotten. There are big portions and small prices!

If it's a drink you're after, then the cocktail bar serves a wide range of wines, beers, lagers, spirits and liqueurs. This being Scotland, you should try a dram of superb malt whisky. There are also plenty of soft drinks if you're driving. The place is elegant yet cosy, just right for a relaxing evening. The hotel boasts a comfortable TV lounge where you can also relax.

Stranraer is ideally situated for exploring this area of Dumfries and Galloway. Turnberry, with its championship golf course, is only 40 miles to the north, while the Southern Upland way - Scotland's long distance footpath connecting the west coast to the east coast - starts at the picturesque port of Portpartick, a few miles to the south. At Logan, Ardwell and Castle Kennedy are beautiful gardens, where sub tropical plants such as palm trees flourish in the area's mild weather, caused by the Gulf Stream.

It was in Wigtownshire that Christianity first reached Scotland, and there are still reminders of this to be visited and explored at Whithorn, which is no more than half an hour away from the hotel. Northern Ireland is just one and a half hours away by ferry.

burgh charter in 1617, and is a town of narrow streets and old alleyways.

In the centre of the town is the **Castle of St John**, a tower house which dates from the 16th century. Claverhouse used it as a base while hunting down Covenanters in the area, and it was later used as the town jail. It is now a museum. There is another museum in Stranraer. In the **Old Town Hall** is another museum, which explains the history of the town and the county of Wigtownshire.

North West Castle is now a hotel, but at one time it was the home of **Sir John Ross** (1777-1856), who explored the legendary North West Passage north of Canada, which connects the Atlantic, and the Pacific. He was born near Kirkcolm, son of a minister, and on one of his expeditions he discovered the Boothia Peninsula, mainland America's northernmost point.

On the sea front is the **Princess Victoria Monument,** which commemorates the sinking of the car ferry Princess Victoria on January 31, 1953. It had left Stranraer bound for Larne with 127 passengers and 49 crew, and on leaving the shelter of Loch Ryan encountered a horrific gale. Though lifeboats were launched, it eventually sank with the loss of 134 lives.

Three miles east of Stranraer are the magnificent **Castle Kennedy Gardens**. They cover 75 acres between two small lochs, and are laid out around the ivy-clad ruins of Castle Kennedy, destroyed by fire in 1710. The 2nd Earl of Stair began creating the gardens in 1733, and being a field marshal under the Duke of Marlborough, he used soldiers to construct some of it. Also within the gardens is the relatively modern **Lochinch Castle**, the present home of the Earl and Countess of Stair. It is not open to the public. South of the A75 is Soulseat Loch, where there is good fishing. A narrow peninsula with a few bumps and indentations on it juts out into the water - the site of **Soulseat Abbey**, of which not a stone now remains above ground. It was

Creebridge House Hotel

Minnigaff. Newton Stewart DG8 6NP
Tel: 01671 402121 Fax: 01671 403258
e-mail: info@creebridge.co.uk
website: www.creebridge.co.uk

If you're looking for a family-friendly hotel right in the heart of Bonnie Galloway, then look no further than the **Creebridge House Hotel**. Set near the picturesque market town of Newton Stewart, it has everything for a long or short stay, and is enclosed by three acres of idyllic gardens and mature woodland, but only two minutes walk from the town. It was built in 1760 as the home of the Earl of Galloway, and has been tastefully converted into a hotel while still retaining may original features.

It is owned and managed by Lesley and

David Morby, who have had years of experience in the hotel trade. They have recently refurbished the whole building, and their aim is to create and maintain a hostelry where friendly, efficient service is married to style and value for money - and they have succeeded! This is a truly outstanding hotel, one that you'll come back to again and again. The 20 rooms are all en suite, and furnished and decorated to an extremely high standard. Each one has satellite TV, tea/coffee making facilities with Scottish shortbread, radio alarms and direct dial telephones. You can choose from rooms with a view of the garden, family rooms or luxury four poster rooms.

The Bridges Bar and Brasserie, with its beams and cosy atmosphere, is the ideal place to have a relaxing drink after a day exploring an area of Scotland that is both beautiful and historic. There is a fine selection of malt whiskies, for instance, plus

real ales from a local micro-brewery. And, of course, there are wines, liqueurs and soft drinks if you're driving. The menu mainly features dishes where the emphasis is on fresh, local produce and a daily changing blackboard menu offers many tasty dishes, with seafood predominating in the high season.

The contemporary-style Garden Restaurant is the place to go if you want a meal that is out of this world. As its name implies, it overlooks the hotel gardens, and has an elegant yet informal feel to it. Again, the cuisine reflects fresh, Scottish produce, and it has earned itself an AA Rosette. Vegetarians are also catered for on all the Hotel's menus.

The Creebridge is the ideal venue for a wedding, party or business conference, and Lesley and David will go out of their way to make your occasions run both smoothly and enjoyably.

Dumfries and Galloway is one of Scotland's gems - an area that has history, heritage and beauty aplenty. Small, cosy villages - clean, welcoming market towns - country lanes that cry out to be explored - moorland that makes excellent walking country.

founded for the Premonstratensian Order of canons by Fergus, Lord of Galloway, in 1148 and dedicated to St John the Baptist.

Three miles beyond Castle Kennedy on the A75 is the village of Dunragit, where you'll find **Glenwhan Gardens**, overlooking beautiful Luce Bay. They were started from scratch in 1979, and now cover 12 acres.

Around Stranraer

Cairnryan

5 miles N of Stranraer on the A77

Cairnryan is strung out along the coast of Loch Ryan. Between the main road and the coast is a complex of car parks, piers, jetties and offices, as this small village is the Scottish terminus of the P&O ferries to Larne, Northern Ireland. It was developed as a port during World War II, and had a breaker's yard. It was here that the famous aircraft carrier **HMS Ark Royal** was scrapped.

Glentrool

20 miles NE of Stranraer on a minor road which leaves the A714 at Bargrennan

It was here, close to the lovely but lonely waters of Loch Trool, that Robert I defeated an English army in 1307. His soldiers had hidden themselves in the hills above the loch, and when the English troops went past, they rolled great boulders down on them before attacking. It was a turning point in the Wars of Independence, as up until then Robert had had little success. **Bruce's Stone** above the loch commemorates the event. There is a small visitors centre.

Glenluce

8 miles E of Stranraer off the A75

The attractive little village of Glenluce has been bypassed by the A75, one of the main routes from southern Scotland and Northern England to the Irish ferries at Stranraer and Cairnryan. At one time it was the home of **Alexander Agnew**, nicknamed the "Devil of Luce", who was hanged for blasphemy in the 17th century. A mile to the northwest are the ruins of **Glenluce Abbey** (Historic Scotland), founded in 1192 by Roland, Lord of Galloway. Mary Stuart once visited, as did James 1V and Robert I. **Castle of Park** is an imposing mansion built in about 1590 by Thomas Hay, son of the last abbot of Glenluce.

Immediately after the Reformation, the then Earl of Cassillis, head of the great Kennedy family, claimed the property and lands of Glenluce. He persuaded one of the monks to forge the abbot's signature on a document granting him the lands, then had the monk murdered. He then executed the men who had done the foul deed on his behalf in the name of justice.

Newton Stewart

22 miles E of Stranraer on the A75

The burgh of Newton Stewart sits on the River Cree, close to where it enters Wigtown Bay. It is a pleasant, clean town, which makes the ideal centre for fishing or walking. **Newton Stewart Museum**, in York Road, has displays and exhibits about the

River Cree, Newton Stewart

history of the town and immediate area. In Queen Street you'll find an unusual but internationally known little museum called **Sophie's Puppetstube and Dolls House Museum**, which has 50 beautifully made doll's houses and room settings. The scale is 1:12, and all the exhibits are behind glass. There is also a collection of over 200 exquisitely dressed dolls.

The **Wood of Cree Nature Reserve** is owned and managed by the Royal Society for the Protection of Birds, and lies four miles north of the town on a minor road running parallel to the A714. It has the largest ancient woodland in Southern Scotland, and here you can see redstarts, pied flycatchers, wood warblers and so on. There is a picnic area and nature trails. Six miles west of Newton Stewart is the picturesque village of **Kirkcowan**, which has a church dating from 1834 with external stairs to the gallery.

Wigtown

23 miles E of Stranraer on the A714

This small royal burgh has achieved fame as being **Scotland's Book Town**, and has many bookshops and publishing houses. In the kirkyard of Wigtown Parish Church are the **Martyrs' Graves**. In 1685, during the time of the Covenanters, two women - one aged 18 and one aged 63 - were tied to stakes at the mouth of the River Bladnoch for adhering to the Covenant. Rather than renounce their principles, they drowned as the tide rose over their heads. The spot where the martyrdom took place is marked by the small **Martyrs Monument** on what are now salt marshes (see also Stirling). On a small hill behind the town is another **Covenanters' Monument**, this time a slender column.

One mile west of the town is **Bladnoch Distillery**, Scotland's most southerly whisky distillery. There is a visitor centre, and guided tours are available showing the distilling process.

Four miles west of the town, reached by the B733, is the Bronze Age **Torhouse Stone Circle**. It consists of 19 boulders forming a circle, with three other boulders inside it. It is of a type more commonly found in Aberdeenshire and North East Scotland.

Chapel Finian

16 miles SE of Stranraer on the A747

Beside the road that runs along the western shore of **The Machars**, the name given to that great peninsula that sticks out into the Irish Sea between Luce and Wigtown Bays, you'll find the foundations of a small church. The most interesting thing about them is their great age, as they probably

date from the 10th century. Later on the chapel was probably used as a stopping off point for people making a pilgrimage to Whithorn, 12 miles to the southeast. St Finian of Moville lived during the 6th century, and had founded a great monastic school in Northern Ireland where St Columba studied.

Four miles inland from the chapel, and reached by a minor road off the A7005, is the **Old Place of Mochrum**, on the northern edge of lonely Mochrum Loch. It was built in in the 16th century and restored by the Marquis of Bute.

Whithorn

26 miles SE of Stranraer on the A746

This tiny royal burgh is often called the "Cradle of Scottish Christianity". A century before Columba came to Iona, a monk called **St Ninian** had set up a monastery here. It would have been a typical Celtic foundation, with a high circular bank, or "rath", enclosing an area of monks' cells, workshops and chapels. This monastery was different in one respect, however. The main church was made of stone, not the more common wood, and was painted white. For this reason it was called **Candida Casa**, or "White House". When this part of Scotland was later absorbed into the kingdom of Northumbria, the name was translated into Anglo Saxon as "Hwit Aerne", from which Whithorn is derived.

The place was subsequently an important ecclesiastical and trading centre. In the 12th century Fergus, Lord of Galloway, founded **Whithorn Priory** (Historic Scotland), and its church became the cathedral for the diocese of Galloway. All that is left of the priory church is its nave and crypt, and to the east of the crypt may be seen some scant foundations which may be all that is left of Ninian's original whitewashed church. The cathedral, with its relics of St Ninian, eventually became a place of pilgrimage, and many Scottish monarchs came to pray here.

The town's main street, George Street, is wide and spacious, with many small Georgian, Regency and Victorian houses. **The Pend**, dating from about 1500, is an archway leading to the priory ruins, and above it are the royal arms of Scotland. Close to the priory is the **Priory Museum** (Historic Scotland), with a collection of stones on which are carved early Christian symbols. One of them, the **Latinus Stone**, dates from the 5th century, and may be the earliest carved Christian stone in Scotland. Some years ago, excavations were undertaken at Whithorn, and at the **Whithorn Visitors Centre** you can learn about the excavations and what was found there.

St Ninian's Cave is on the shore three miles southwest of the town. It has incised crosses on its walls, and a legend states that St Ninian himself came to this cave to seek solitude and pray. At Glasserton, two miles west of Whithorn, are the **Woodfall Gardens**, covering three acres within an old walled garden. And at Garlieston, four miles north of the town, are the **Galloway House Gardens**, laid out informally and with walks leading down to the shores of Cruggleton Bay.

Three miles to the southeast is the tiny fishing village of **Isle of Whithorn.** On a headland are the 13th century ruins of the tiny **St Ninian's Chapel**. Though it sits on the mainland, the small area surrounding it may at one time have been an island, giving the village its name. It was probably built for pilgrims to Whithorn Priory who came by sea.

Kirkmadrine

8 miles S of Stranraer on a minor road off the A716

In the porch of what was the tiny parish church of Toskerton are the **Kirkmadrine Stones**, thought to be the oldest inscribed stones in Scotland after those at Whithorn.

They were discovered when the church was being rebuilt and converted into a burial chamber by a local family, the McTaggarts of Ardwell. Parts of the original medieval church have been incorporated into it.

Ardwell

10 miles S of Stranraer on the A716

Ardwell Gardens are grouped round the 18th century Ardwell House. They are a testimony to the mildness of the climate in these parts, and feature a woodland and a formal garden, as well as good views out over Luce Bay.

Port Logan

12 miles S of Stranraer on the B7065

Port Logan is a small fishing village situated on Port Logan Bay. Close by is the **Logan Fish Pond** (see panel below), a remarkable tidal pond famous for its tame sea fish, which can be fed by hand. It was constructed in about 1800 as a source of fresh fish for the tables of nearby Logan House.

If anywhere illustrates the mildness of the climate in this part of Scotland, it is **Logan Botanic Garden**, part of the National Botanic Gardens of Scotland.

Logan Fish Pond

Port Logan, Stranraer
Tel/Fax: 01776 860300
e-mail: ian.whitehead6@btinternet.com
website: www.loganfishpond.co.uk

The first time visitor to **Logan Fish Pond** is often amazed and surprised by what they see. Not until they enter through the original Fish Keepers Cottage and have their first glimpse of the pond below do they have any idea of what this unique and historic attraction holds.

In 1788 Andrew McDouall Laird of Logan decided to create a Fish Larder for storing live sea fish by adapting a natural rock formation in the form of a blow hole, formed during the last ice-age. The work took 12 years and was finished in 1800. Many visitors return year after year and indeed some have been doing so for fifty or sixty years, feeding the fish today as they remember doing as children.

In the springtime, the area around the Pond is a carpet of daffodils, primroses and bluebells and later in the year these are replaced with an abundance of wild flowers, including thrift and sea campion.

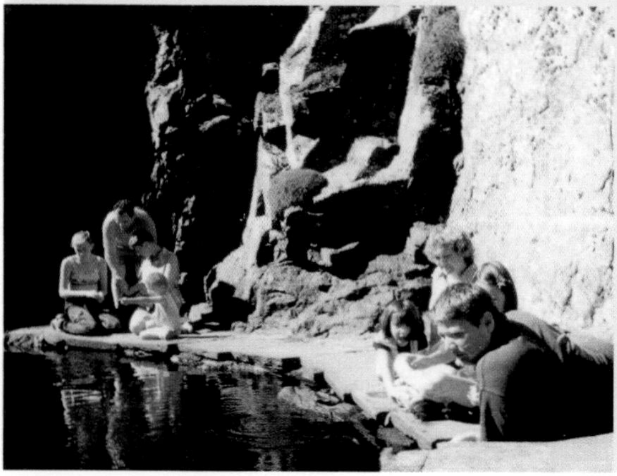

On the rocks next to the Fish Pond is a restored Victorian Bathing Hut which adjoins a Bathing Pool. Recent additions to the original pond include Touch Pools, Cave Aquarium and Gift Shop. Open 1st March to 30th September 12 noon to 5pm and 1st October to 31st October 12 noon to 4pm. Some disabled access.

Here, growing quite freely, are exotic plants and trees such as the tree fern (which can normally only survive in glass houses in Britain), the eucalyptus, palm trees, magnolias and passionflowers. In fact, over 40 per cent of all the plants and trees at Logan come from the Southern hemisphere.

The village achieved national fame when the TV series ***2000 Acres of Sky***, supposedly set on a Hebridean island, was filmed here.

Kirkmaiden

15 miles S of Stranraer on the B7065

Four miles south of Kirkmaiden is the **Mull of Galloway**, Scotland's most southerly point. It comes as a surprise to some people when they learn that places like Durham are further north. The lighthouse was built in 1828 to the designs of Robert Stevenson, and sits on the massive cliffs, 270 feet above the sea.

Portpatrick

6 miles SW of Stranraer on the A77

This lovely little village is at the western end of the Southern Upland Way. At one time it was the main Scottish port for Northern Ireland, but was in such an exposed position that Stranraer eventually took over. It sits round a little harbour that is always busy, and, with its old cottages and craft shops, has become a small holiday resort. On a headland to the south of the village are the ruins of **Dunskey Castle**, built in the early 16th century by the Adair family. The recently re-established **Dunskey Garden and Woodland Walk** is well worth visiting. Every Wednesday afternoon in summer, there are guided tours conducted by the gardener.

Within the village is the ruined **Portpatrick Parish Church**. It was built in the 17th century, and unusually, had a round tower.

Ayrshire & Arran

Ayrshire was at one time Scotland's largest Lowland county. Facing the Firth of Clyde, it is ringed by moorland and hills which slope down to a rich agricultural patchwork of small fields, country lanes, woodland and picturesque villages. The poet Keats, when he made his pilgrimage to the birthplace of Robert Burns in Alloway, compared its scenery to that of Devon.

The county was formerly divided into three parts. Carrick is the most southerly, and it owes a lot to neighbouring Galloway. It is separated from Kyle, a rich dairying area where the native Ayrshire cattle can be seen dotting the fields, by the River Doon. To the north, beyond the River Irvine, is Cunninghame, which at one time was the most industrialised of the three, though it managed this without losing too much of its rural aspect.

Kyle itself was divided by the River Ayr into Kyle Regal and Kyle Stewart, reflecting the fact that one section was ruled directly by the king while the other was ruled by

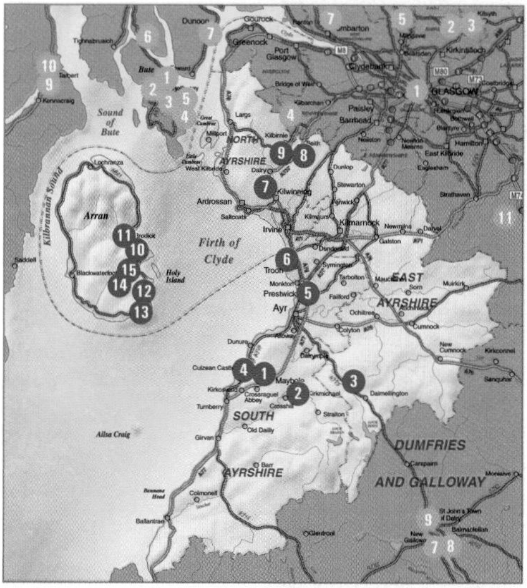

PLACES TO STAY, EAT AND DRINK

Maybole Castle, Maybole	1	Visitor Attraction	p78
Jock's Restaurant and Crafts, Kirkmichael	2	Restaurant	p80
Dunaskin Heritage Centre, Waterside	3	Visitor Attraction	p81
Culzean Castle & Country Park, Maybole	4	Visitor Attraction	p86
Prestwick Old Course Hotel, Prestwick	5	Hotel	p89
Fordell B&B, Barassie	6	B&B	p90
Dalgarven Mill, Dalgarven	7	Visitor Attraction	p101
Shotts Farmhouse, Beith	8	B&B	p102
Anderson's Hotel, Beith	9	Hotel	p103
McLaren & McAlpine Hotels, Brodick	10	Hotel	p105
Dunvegan House, Brodick	11	Guest House	p106
Viewbank House, Whiting Bay	12	Guest House	p107
Breadalbane Hotel, Kildonan	13	Hotel	p108
Dyemill Lodges, Lamlash	14	Self Catering	p109
Pierhead Tavern, Lamlash	15	Pub with Restaurant	p110

● Denotes entries in other chapters

Culzean Castle

high stewards of Scotland, who eventually went on to be kings in their own right.

Ayrshire and Robert Burns, known to all Scottish people as "Rabbie" (never, ever *Robbie!*) are inextricably linked. He was born in Alloway, which nowadays is a well-off suburb of Ayr, and spent the first 29 years of his life in the county before moving south to Dumfriesshire. We know a lot about the man, and all the places in Ayrshire where he lived, drank, courted and visited people are carefully signposted. A full week could easily be spent tootling around the main roads and narrow lanes of the county visiting such towns and villages as Tarbolton, Mauchline, Ayr, Kilmarnock, Irvine, Failford and Kirkoswald. Every year in May the **Burns an' a' That Festival** takes place throughout Ayrshire to celebrate his life and work. Venues include pubs, concert halls, theatres, museums and churches. The most spectacular concert is held out of doors at Culzean Castle.

There are three main towns in the county -

Ayr, Kilmarnock and Irvine. Irvine is the largest, though it was not always so. In the 1960s it was designated a new town, and took an overspill population from Glasgow. Industrial estates were built, factories were opened and new housing established. However, its central core is still worth exploring. Kilmarnock is traditionally the industrial centre, though it is an ancient town, and Ayr was the administrative and commercial capital before Ayrshire ceased to exist as a local government unit in the 1970s.

Up until the 1960s, when more exotic places took over, the Ayrshire coast was Glasgow's holiday playground. Known as the "Costa del Clyde", it attracted thousands of people each year who flocked to such holiday resorts as Troon, Largs, Prestwick, Girvan and Ayr itself. These halcyon days are gone, though it is still a popular place for day trips and for people to retire to, giving it a new nickname - the "Costa Geriatrica". The coastline is also famous for another reason - golf. The first British Open

Brodick Bay, Isle of Arran

Maybole Castle

Maybole, Ayrshire

Maybole Castle is the oldest inhabited house in the town having been built about the middle of the sixteenth century (believed to be around 1560). It was the town house of the Earls of Cassillis who spent most of the winter months in Maybole, and was the largest and finest of the twenty-eight lairds' houses written about by Abercrummie in 1696.It was built in the style of a typical Scottish castle, with square tower and round turrets, and strong enough to protect its occupants from unfriendly neighbours, of whom there were many at that time. The main hall was above vaulted cellars which still remain and above the hall were the sleeping apartments. The retainers' quarters were on the other side of a gateway which gave entrance into the castle yard, built round the well, locally known as "The Pump".

The tower is capped by a lovely little oriel window with heads carved round it which local people wrongly believe represent the heads of Johnnie Faa and his gypsies. The corbels to the roof of the little room at the top of the tower (known as the Countess's Room) are carved with male and female heads and symbols of fertility. The walls are extremely thick (in some places about seven feet) and it must have been a safe retreat in troublesome times when the Earls lived in it, with their own men around them in the small township clustered on the hillside below it.

It was from Maybole Castle that the Earl of Cassillis and his men sallied forth to the fight at Ladycross in December 1601, when young Bargany was killed in the bitter feud between the Cassillis and Bargany families. Locally there is an old tale of the Countess of Cassillis being imprisoned at the top of the tower, after she had allegedly eloped with Johnnie Faa, King of the Gypsies, but while the story is a delightful one, facts disprove it.

As years passed the Earls spent less of their time in Maybole, and gradually the old Castle fell into disrepair and was practically abandoned except for a few old retainers who lived in outbuildings. In 1805 the Earl of Cassillis agreed with the town council that the part sited where the Post Office now stands could be demolished to allow a road to be formed from the foot of the High Street to Duncanland Toll at the bottom of Redbrae. When the old buildings were removed the Earl decided to repair the Castle and in 1812 reroofed it and built some additions. The gardens and park had walls erected round them and from 1812 the Castle has remained as it is now, apart from repairs to the roof following a fire in 1919.

The Historical Society has been very active in promoting Maybole Castle since May-Tag (founded by the Community Council in 1986 as a training company to promote local unemployment) moved out and has said, "The Castle goes from strength to strength and we have a very good relationship with the factor and through him the Estate and Trustee. We are putting together proposals and plans for opening the castle regularly to the public; improving and expanding the display material in the castle; and the future of the castle as a heritage centre".

Golf Championship was held at Prestwick in 1860, and both Troon and Turnberry have regularly hosted the tournament in modern times.

Ayrshire is also a county of castles, from the spectacular Culzean (pronounced "Cull-ane") perched on a cliff top above the sea, to Kelburn near Largs or Dean Castle in Kilmarnock, with its collection of rare musical instruments.

The Ayrshire coalfield used to employ thousands of people, though nowadays not a deep mine remains. But even at its height, the industry never did as much damage to the environment as in, say, South Yorkshire or the Welsh valleys. Now you would never suspect that the industry ever existed, and a day just motoring round the quiet lanes is a relaxing experience in itself.

Twenty miles offshore is the island of Arran, at one time within the county of Bute, but now more associated with Ayrshire. It has been called "Scotland in Miniature", and is a wonderful blend of wild scenery, pastoral views and rocky coastlines. Its history stretches right back into the mists of time, as the many standing stones and ancient burial cairns testify. Also within Bute were two other islands - Great and Little Cumbrae. Little Cumbrae is largely uninhabited, apart from one or two houses, but on Great Cumbrae is the town of Millport, a gem of a holiday resort. Within Millport is another gem - Cumbrae Cathedral, the smallest cathedral in Britain. It is truly one of the hidden places of Scotland.

Maybole

This quiet town is the capital of Carrick, and sits on a hillside about four miles inland from the coast. It was here that Burns's parents, William Burnes (he later changed the name to Burns) and Agnes Broun met in 1756.

In 1562, a famous meeting took place in Maybole between John Knox, the Scottish reformer, and Abbot Quentin Kennedy of nearby Crossraguel Abbey. The purpose of the meeting was to debate the significance and doctrine of the Mass, and it attracted a huge crowd of people, even though it was held in a small room of the house where the provost of the town's collegiate church lived. Forty people from each side were actually allowed in to hear the debate, which lasted for three days. It only broke up - with no conclusion reached - when the town ran out of food to feed the thronging masses round the door. The ruins of **Maybole Collegiate Church** (Historic Scotland) can still be viewed, though they are not open to the public.

There are two "castles" in Maybole. One, now part of the **Town Hall**, was the 17th century town house of the lairds of Blairquhan Castle, about five miles to the east of the town. The other is still referred to as **Maybole Castle**, though it too was a town house, this time for the Earls of Cassillis. There is a curious legend attached to the building. It seems that Lady Jean Hamilton, daughter of the Earl of Haddington, was in love with Sir John Faa of Dunbar (nicknamed "King of the Gypsies"), but was forced against her will to marry John, 6th Earl of Cassillis, head of the Kennedy family. Unwillingly she went to live in Ayrshire, but never forgot her first love. One day when the Earl was away on business, Sir John came with 14 gypsies and carried her away.

However, the Earl returned unexpectedly, and set out in pursuit. He caught Sir John and his men and made his wife watch as he hung them from a tree at Cassillis Castle, his main residence. He then incarcerated his wife in one small room in Maybole Castle, where she spent the rest of her life in one small room making tapestries. A window high in one wall is still pointed out as the room where she was kept, and above it are some carvings of heads, said to be those of Sir John and his gypsies. However, the story is completely untrue, as letters written by both the Earl and his Countess to each other show that they were a close and loving couple.

A few miles west of Maybole, near the farm of Drumshang, is the curiously named **Electric Brae**, on the A719 road between Ayr and Turnberry. Stop your car on the convenient layby at the side of the road, put it out of gear, let off the brake, and be amazed as it rolls uphill. Better still, lay a football on the layby's surface, and watch it roll uphill as well. The phenomenon has nothing to do with electricity, and everything to do with an optical illusion. The surrounding land makes you think that the road rises towards the coast when it fact it descends.

Around Maybole

Kirkmichael

3 miles E of Maybole on the B7045

Like its neighbour Crosshill, Kirkmichael is a former weaving village. However, its roots go deeper into Scottish history. The **Parish Church** dates from 1790, and the picturesque lych-gate from about 1700. Within the kirkyard is the grave of a Covenanter called Gilbert MacAdam, killed in 1686.

Kirkmichael is the scene, every May, of the **Kirkmichael International Guitar Festival**, which draws musicians from all over the world. It covers everything from jazz to pop and country to classical. Huge marquees are erected, and local pubs host impromptu jamming sessions and folk concerts.

Dalmellington

11 miles E of Maybole on the A713

This former mining village sits on the banks of the Doon. Over the last few years, it has exploited its rich heritage, and created some visitor centres and museums that explain the village's industrial past. The **Dunaskin Open Air Museum** (see panel opposite), which covers 110 acres, has many facets, and each one is well worth exploring. The **Dalmellington Iron Works** were first opened in the 1840s, and are now the largest restored Victorian Ironworks in Europe. Other attractions include the **Brickworks** and the **Scottish Industrial Railway Centre**, where steam trains run on a restored track. The **Cathcartson Centre** in the village is housed in weaving cottages dating from the 18th century, and shows how weavers lived long ago.

A couple of miles beyond Dalmellington is a minor road that takes you to lovely **Loch Doon**, surrounded by lonely hills and moorland, and the source of the river that Burns wrote about. It was here, during World War I, that a **School of Aerial Gunnery** was proposed. Millions of pounds were wasted on it before the plans were finally abandoned. When a hydroelectric scheme was built in the 1930s, the water

The Dunaskin Heritage Centre

Dalmellington Road, Waterside, Patna, Ayrshire
Tel: 01292 531144
e-mail: dunaskin@btconnect.com
website: www.dunaskin.co.uk

The Dalmellington Iron Company was founded in 1848, at the height of the Industrial Revolution. At its zenith, the company's eight furnaces worked day and night, providing employment for around 1,400 people, until the last furnace was blown out in 1921. The company produced coal and, later, bricks, up until 1976, when the kilns were finally extinguished. Today, the site has been preserved as Europe's best remaining example of a Victorian Ironworks, with over half its 110 acres listed as a Scheduled Ancient Monument.

Dunaskin is a visitor attraction for all the family. The Dunaskin Experience lets you explore the past as it was actually lived by Ayrshire people. An open air, living museum set amidst beautiful rolling countryside, it follows the story of the people and places of the Doon Valley through the Industrial Revolution, two World Wars and right up to modern times. There's the Mary Gallagher Experience: an audio visual which re-creates Ayrshire life in the 19th and early 20th centuries. For younger children there's the new Furnace Play Tower. Teenagers can interact with our Billy the Brick Computer Quiz.

Everyone will enjoy the delightful walks, including Dunaskin Glen which is a designated Site of Special Scientific Interest. There's a period cottage and industrial machinery. You can even feel what it was like to work in a coal mine. Finally you can break your visit and meet the welcoming staff at Chimneys Restaurant and Coffee Shop and browse in the Gift Shop.

level of the loch was raised. **Loch Doon Castle**, which stood on an island in the loch, was dismantled stone by stone and reassembled on the shore, where it can still be seen.

In the early 14th century it withstood a siege from the English army for four years. When it finally surrendered, its keeper Sir Christopher Seton, who was related to Robert I, was executed at Dumfries.

In the late 1970s it was announced that 32 deep tunnels would be bored in the hills surrounding the loch to store most of Britain's radioactive waste. After many protests by local people, the idea was abandoned.

Crosshill

3 miles SE of Maybole, on the B7023

Crosshill is a former handloom-weaving village established in about 1808, with many small, attractive cottages. Many of the weavers were Irish, attracted to the place by the prospect of work. There are no outstanding buildings, nor does it have much history or legend attached to it. But it is a conservation village with a quiet charm, and well worth visiting because of this alone. Some of the original cottages built by the Irish immigrants in the early 19th century can still be seen in Dalhowan Street.

Straiton

6 miles SE of Maybole on the B741

A narrow road runs south from this lovely village called the **Nick o' the Balloch**. It doesn't go through the Carrick of gentle fields or verdant valleys, but over the wild hills and moorland that make the edges of this area so beautiful, and finally drops down into Glentrool.

Straiton itself sits on the water of Girvan, and has picturesque little cottages facing each other across a main street some with roses growing round the door. The local pub, The Black Bull, dates from 1766, while parts of **St Cuthbert's Parish Church** date back to 1510. Close to the village is **Blairquhan**, a Tudor-Gothic mansion that sits on the site of an earlier tower house. It was once a McWhirter stronghold before passing to the Kennedys, but is now owned by the Hunter Blair family. It is open to the public in summer, and has a fine collection of paintings by the Scottish Colourists. On a hill above the village stands the **Hunter Blair Monument**, built in 1856 to commemorate James Hunter Blair, killed at the Battle of Inkerman.

Many of the scenes in the film *The Match* (also called *The Big Game*) were shot in Straiton, which became the fictional Highland village Inverdoune.

Old Dailly

9 miles S of Maybole on the B734

The ruins of 16th century **Old Dailly Parish Church** stand beside the road. Within the kirkyard are two hefty stones called the **Charter Stones**, which people tried to lift in bygone days during trials of strength.

Buried in the kirkyard is the pre-Raphaelite artist **William Bell Scott**, who was staying at nearby **Penkill Castle** (not open to the public) when he died. Many members of the pre-Raphaelite Brotherhood visited the place, including **Dante Gabriel Rossetti**. Close by is the 17th century **Bargany House**, with its marvellous gardens, once a Kennedy stronghold. The mining village of **New Dailly**, with its T-shaped **New Dailly Parish Church** of 1766 is three miles to the east.

Barr

11 miles S of Maybole on the B734

Tucked in a fold of the Carrick hills, Barr is an idyllic village that was once the site of the wonderfully named **Kirkdandie Fair**. It was the largest annual fair in Southern Scotland during the late 18th and early 19th centuries, and was held on a strip of land where once had stood Kirkdandie Church. Its main claim to fame was the fighting that took place there every year, and it soon became known as the "Donnybrook of Scotland". People even came over from Ireland to participate in the great pitched battles.

Above Barr is the estate of Changue (pronounced "Shang"), to which an old legend is attached. The **Laird of Changue** was a smuggler and distiller of illicit whisky who always penniless. One day, while walking through his estates, Satan appeared and offered him a deal. If he handed over his soul when he died, he would become rich. The laird, who was a young man, agreed, and duly prospered. But as he grew older he began to regret his rashness, and when Satan at last appeared before him to claim his soul - at the same spot where he had appeared all these years before - the laird refused to keep his side of the bargain. Instead he challenged the Devil to fight for it. Drawing a large circle on the ground round both of them, he said that the first person to be forced out of it would be the loser. After a bitter struggle, the laird cut off the end of Satan's tail with his sword, and he jumped out of the circle in pain. The laird had won. Up until the end of the 19th century, a great bare circle on some grassland was shown as the place where all this took place. It's a wonderful story, but no one has ever managed to put a name or date to this mysterious laird.

A small leaflet has been produced which describes some walks that can be taken in the surrounding hills.

Colmonell

19 Miles S of Maybole on the B734

The River Stinchar is the southernmost of Ayrshire's major rivers, and flows through a lovely valley bordered on both sides by high moorland and hills. In this valley, four miles from the sea, sits Colmonell. It's an attractive village of small cottages, with the romantic ruins of **Kirkhill Castle** close by. **Knockdolian Hill**, two miles west, was at one time called the "false Ailsa Craig" because of its resemblance to the volcanic island out in the Firth of Clyde.

Ballantrae

22 miles S of Maybole on the A77

When on a walking tour of Carrick in 1876, R.L. Stevenson spent a night in Ballantrae, a small fishing village. However, dour villagers took exception to his avant-garde clothes and almost ran him out of town. He got his revenge by writing "The Master of Ballantrae", which confused everyone by having no connection with the place whatsoever.

In the churchyard is the **Bargany Aisle**, containing the ornate tomb of Gilbert Kennedy, laird of Bargany and Ardstinchar, who was killed by the Earl of Cassillis (also a Kennedy) in 1601. A bitter feud between the Cassillis and Bargany branches of the Kennedy family had been going on right through the 16th century, with no quarter given or taken. Matters came to a head when the two branches met near Ayr, and Bargany was killed. The power of the Bargany branch was broken forever, and the feud fizzled out. The ruins of **Ardstinchar Castle**, Bargany's main stronghold, can still be seen beside the river.

Glenapp Castle, a few miles south of the village just off the A77, was designed in 1870 by the noted Victorian architect David Bryce for James Hunter, the Deputy Lord Lieutenant of Ayrshire. It is now a luxury hotel surrounded by 30 acres of grounds and gardens.

Lendalfoot

18 miles S of Maybole on the A77

Carleton Castle, now in ruins, was the home of Sir John Carleton, who, legend states, had a neat way of earning a living. He married ladies of wealth then enticed them to **Gamesloup**, a nearby rocky eminence, where he pushed them to their deaths and inherited their wealth. Sir John went through seven or eight wives before meeting the daughter of Kennedy of Culzean. After marrying her, he took her to Gamesloup, but instead of him pushing her over, she pushed him over, and lived happily ever after on his accumulated wealth.

But if it's a gruesome tale you're after, then you should head for **Sawney Bean's Cave** a few miles south of the village, on the shoreline north of Bennane Head, and easily reached by a footpath from a layby on the A77. Here, in the 16th century, lived a family of cannibals led by Sawney Bean, which waylaid strangers, robbed them, and ate their flesh. They evaded capture for many years until a troop of men sent by James VI trapped them in their cave. They were taken to Edinburgh and executed. It's a wonderful story, but no documentary proof has ever been unearthed to prove that it really happened.

Kirkoswald

4 miles SW of Maybole on the A77

It was to Kirkoswald, in 1775, that Burns came for one term to learn surveying. Though his poem Tam o' Shanter is set in Alloway, all the characters in it have their origins in the parish of Kirkoswald, which was where his maternal grandparents came from.

Kirkoswald Parish Church dates from 1777, and was designed by Robert Adam while he was working on Culzean Castle.

Dwight D. Eisenhower worshipped here twice, one of the occasions being when he was president of the United States. Another visitor is not so well known, but the airline he helped to found is. The late Randolph Fields, together with Richard Branson, founded Virgin Airlines. Randolph loved this part of Ayrshire, and when he died in 1997, he left some money for the restoration of the church. A year later his widow presented the church with a small table, on which is a plaque commemorating him.

Old Parish Church of St Oswald lies at the heart of the village. It is a ruin now, but in its kirkyard are the graves of many people associated with Burns, including David Graham of Shanter Farm near Maidens, the real life "Tam o' Shanter". The church also contains one interesting relic - the **Robert the Bruce's Baptismal Font.** Both Lochmaben in Dumfriesshire and Turnberry Castle, within the parish of Kirkoswald, claim to have been the birthplace of Robert the Bruce. Turnberry is the more likely, as it was the ancestral home of the Countess of Carrick, Bruce's mother, and it is known that she was living there at about the time of the birth. The story goes that the baby was premature, and that he was rushed to Crossraguel Abbey for baptism in case he died. The abbey's font was used, and when Crossraguel was abandoned after the Reformation, the people of Kirkoswald rescued the font and put it in their own church.

Within the village you'll also find **Souter Johnnie's Cottage** (National Trust for Scotland). John Davidson was a "souter", or cobbler, and featured in Tam o' Shanter. Now his thatched cottage has been turned into a small museum.

Crossraguel Abbey

2 miles SW of Maybole, on the A77

These romantic ruins (Historic Scotland) sit complacently beside the main Ayr-Stranraer road. They are very well preserved, and give a wonderful idea of the layout of a medieval abbey. Some of the medieval architecture and stone carving, such as that in the chapter house, is well worth seeking out. Duncan, Earl of Carrick, founded it in 1244 for Clunaic monks from Paisley Abbey, though most of what you see nowadays dates from after the 13th century. To the north are the ruins of **Baltersan Castle**, an old fortified 16th century tower house built either for John Kennedy of Pennyglen and his wife Margaret Cathcart or as the residence of Quintin Kennedy, the Abbot of Crossraguel from 1548 until 1564.

Turnberry

7 miles SW of Maybole on the A719

Very little now survives of **Turnberry Castle** where Robert the Bruce is supposed to have been born. The story of how his parents met is an unusual one. The Countess of Carrick was a young widow who saw a knight passing by Turnberry Castle. She immediately became infatuated with him, and had him kidnapped and brought into her presence. He turned out to be Robert de Brus, Lord of Annandale, and she persuaded him to marry her. The result of the marriage was Robert the Bruce, who himself became Earl of Carrick on his mother's death. Because Robert ascended the throne of Scotland as Robert I, the earldom became a royal one, and the present Earl of Carrick is Prince Charles.

Built onto the scant ruins of the castle is **Turnberry Lighthouse**, surrounded on three sides by the championship golf course. The elegant **Turnberry Hotel** is situated south east of the castle, just off the main road, and is one of the premier hotels in Scotland. It even has its own small runway for aircraft. During World Wars I and II, all this area was an airfield, and the runways can still be seen. There is a **War Memorial** on the golf course dedicated to the men of the airfield who died in World War I. It is in the shape of a double Celtic cross, and

Ailsa Golf Course, Turnberry

was erected by the people of Kirkoswald parish in 1923. In 1990 the monument was altered so that the names of the airmen killed during World War II could be added.

Girvan

10 miles SW of Maybole on the A77

This pleasant little town is the main holiday resort in Carrick. It is also a thriving fishing port, with many boats in the harbour at the mouth of the Water of Girvan. Though there is a long, sandy beach, a boating pond and a small funfair in summer the town is a quiet place, overlooked by the bulk of **Byne Hill** to the south. From the top there is a fine view of the Firth of Clyde, and on a clear day the coast of Northern Ireland can be seen. The small **Crauford Monument** above Ardmillan House, on the western side, commemorates Major A.C.B. Crauford, who took part in the capture of the Cape of Good Hope in 1795

Out in the Firth of Clyde the bulk of **Ailsa Craig** rises sheer from the water. It is the plug of an ancient volcano, which is now a bird sanctuary. Trips round it are available from Girvan harbour.

Within the town, in Knockcushan Street, is a small, curious spired building which has been given the nickname of **Auld Stumpy**. It dates from the 18th century, and at one time was attached to the later McMaster Hall, which burnt down in 1939. Behind Knockcushan House, near the harbour, are **Knockcushan Gardens**, the site of a court held by Robert the Bruce in 1328. At the **McKechnie Institute** in Dalrymple Street art exhibitions are sometimes held.

Culzean Castle

4 miles W of Maybole off the A719

Culzean Castle (National Trust for Scotland - see panel on page 86), perched on a cliff above the Firth of Clyde is possibly the most spectacularly sited castle in the country. It was designed by Robert Adam in 1777, and built round an old keep for the 10th Earl of Cassillis. It has some wonderful

Ailsa Craig

Culzean Castle and Country Park

Maybole, South Ayrshire, KA19 8LE
Functions, events and Eisenhower Apartment:
Tel: 01655 884455 Fax 01655 884503
Group/school bookings, ranger service, Country Park information:
Tel: 01655 884400 Fax 01655 884522.
e-mail: culzean@nts.org.uk
website: www.culzeancastle.net

Robert Adam converted a rather ordinary fortified tower house into this elegant bachelor residence for David Kennedy, 10th Earl of Cassillis, between 1777 and 1792. He also built a 'Roman' viaduct and Ruined Arch to add drama to this Italianate castle in its spectacular clifftop setting. Both the exterior stonework and the interior of the castle have been restored by the National Trust for Scotland. It contains a fine collection of paintings and furniture, and a display of weapons in the Armoury. The Circular Saloon has a superb panoramic view over the Firth of Clyde and the beautiful Oval Staircase is Robert Adam's final masterpiece of interior design.

In 1945 the top floor was given to General Eisenhower as a token of Scotland's recognition of his role during World War II. His apartment is now run as a small country house hotel, and an Eisenhower Exhibition in the castle tells something of Ike the man and his visits to Culzean. The Georgian Kitchen gives a glimpse of life below stairs 200 years ago. Educational programmes and tours are available. Through the Clocktower Courtyard, a coach house and stables have been converted into the Castle Shop and Old Stables Coffee House.

The Country Park · Scotland's first country park, created in 1969 and consisting of 563 acres contains a wealth of natural and historical interest. Miles of woodland walks take the visitor to the Deer Park, along the Cliff Walk or to the many restored estate buildings, such as the Ruined Arch and Viaduct, beautiful Camellia House and unique Pagoda. Garden areas include the terraced Fountain Court and the Walled Garden with its redesigned pleasure garden and impressive reconstructed Victorian Vinery. The exciting adventure playground introduces children to the wildlife of the park and makes the Swan Pond a perfect spot for a family picnic.

The Visitor Centre, formerly the Home Farm, is the focus for the main visitor facilities. These include the Home Farm Restaurant, the Home Farm Shop, the Country Park Shop and Plant Centre. The new auditorium and exhibition at the Visitor Centre explain the history of Culzean and the Trust's conservation work, and there are smaller interpretive centres at the Gas House, Ice House and Swan Pond. Three miles of coastline provide panoramic views across the Firth of Clyde and improved facilities have been provided at Croy Shore · 1½ miles of beach · accessed from the A719. The ranger service provides an extensive environmental education service and interpretive programme.

features, such as the Oval Staircase and the Circular Saloon with its views out over the Firth. Surrounding the castle is **Culzean Country Park**, with such attractions as a Walled Garden, the Swan Pond, the Deer Park and the Fountain Court.

In gratitude for his part in World War II, the National Trust for Scotland presented General Eisenhower with the life tenure of a flat in Culzean. Eisenhower accepted, and spent a few golfing holidays there. The **Eisenhower Presentation**, within the castle, explains his connections with the area, and has exhibits about D-Day.

On the shoreline are the **Gasworks**, which at one time produced coal gas to heat and light the castle. At one time a small boat-building yard stood on the shore immediately to the south of the castle, and many fine yachts were built there.

The caves beneath the castle were at one time used by smugglers. A recent archaeological dig unearthed human bones dating form the Bronze Age, showing that the caves have been occupied for thousands of years. However, there is no access to them, as they can be quite dangerous.

Dunure

5 miles NW of Maybole off the A 719

This pretty little fishing village would not look out of place in Cornwall. Arriving by car, you drop down towards it, giving excellent views of its cottages and pub, all grouped round a small harbour. To the south of the village are the ruins of **Dunure Castle**, perched on the coastline. This is the original castle of the Kennedys, and dates mostly from the 14th century. It was here that the famous **Roasting of the Abbot** took place in 1570. The Kennedys were at the height of their powers, and Gilbert Kennedy, 4th Earl of Cassillis, owned most of the land in Carrick. However, he never owned the lands of Crossraguel Abbey, which, at the Reformation, had been placed in the hands of Allan Stewart, commendator, or lay abbot, of the abbey. Gilbert invited Allan to Dunure Castle for a huge feast, and when Allan accepted, had him incarcerated in the Black Vault. He then stripped him and placed him on a spit over a great open fire, turning him occasionally like a side of beef. Eventually Allan signed away the lands, and was released.

But he immediately protested to the king, who ordered Kennedy to pay for the lands. But such was Kennedy's power that he ignored the order.

Ayr

Ayr is the major holiday resort on the Ayrshire coast. It stands at the mouth of the River Ayr, on the south bank, and was formerly the county town of Ayrshire. Always an important place, it was granted its royal charter in the early 1200s, and is the old capital of the Kyle district. Its most distinctive feature is the tall, elegant steeple of its **Town Hall**, built between 1827 and 1832 to the designs of Thomas Hamilton. Seen from the north, it blends beautifully with a cluster of fine Georgian buildings beside the river.

Ayr Racecourse

Bridge over the River Ayr

After the Battle of Bannockburn, Bruce held his first parliament here, in the ancient kirk of St John the Baptist to decide on the royal succession after he died. This kirk is no longer there save for the tower, now called **St John's Tower,** which stands among Edwardian villas near the shore. Oliver Cromwell dismantled the church and used the stone to build **Ayr Citadel,** which has now gone as well, save for a few feet of wall near the river and an arch in a side street. To compensate, he gave the burgh £600 to build a new church, which is now known as the **Auld Parish Kirk,** situated on the banks of the river where a friary once stood. It dates from the mid 1600s, and is a mellow old T-plan building surrounded by old gravestones. Within the lych gate can be seen a couple of mortsafes, which were placed over fresh graves to prevent grave robbing in the early 19th century.

Ayr was the starting off point for Tam o' Shanter's drunken and macabre ride home after spending the evening at an inn, as portrayed in Burns's poem of the same name. In the High Street is the thatched **Tam o' Shanter Inn,** where the ride was supposed to have started. At one time it was a small museum, but now it has thankfully reverted to its original purpose, and you can enjoy a drink within its walls once more.

Robert Burns and Ayr are inseparable. He was born in a village to the south of the town, which has now become a well-heeled suburb, and his influences are everywhere. Off the High Street is the **Auld Brig o' Ayr,** which dates from the 14th century, and down river is the **New Bridge,** dating from 1878. In a poem called "The Twa Brigs" Burns accurately forecast that the Auld Brig would outlast the new one. He was right - the New Bridge of Burns's time was swept away in a flood, to be replaced by the present New Bridge, while the Auld Brig still survives.

Apart from St John's Tower, the oldest building in the town is **Loudoun Hall,** close to the New Bridge. It was built about 1513 as a fine town house for the Campbells of Loudoun, hereditary sheriffs of Ayr. It was due for demolition just after the war, but was saved when its importance was realised. South of Loudoun Hall, in the Sandgate, is **Lady Cathcart's House,** a tenement building which dates from the 17th century. Within it, in 1756, John Loudon McAdam, the roads engineer, was supposed to have been born (see also Moffat).

The bridges of Ayr take you to **Newton upon Ayr** on the north bank of the river, once a separate burgh but now part of the town. Part of its old tolbooth survives as **Newton Tower,** caught in an island in the middle of the street.

The **Belleisle Estate and Gardens** are to the south of the town, with parkland, deer park, aviary and pets corner. Nearby is **Rozelle House Galleries and Gardens.** There are art exhibitions within the mansion house, plus a tearoom and craft shop.

Also south of the town, perched precariously on a cliff top and always seeming to be in imminent danger of collapse, is **Greenan Castle**, a 17th century tower house. It was built in 1603 for John Kennedy of Baltersan and his third wife Florence MacDowell, who owned the lands of Greenan. However, an earlier castle may have stood here, and it may also have been the site of an Iron Age fort. It is typical of many such tower houses in Ayrshire, but some experts believe it has one unique claim to fame - it may mark the real spot where King Arthur's **Camelot** once stood (see also Kelso).

Around Ayr

Prestwick

2 miles N of Ayr town centre, on the A79

Prestwick is one of the oldest towns in Scotland, having been granted its original burgh charter in the 12th century. It was also one of the most popular Clyde Coast holiday resorts until Spain and Florida took over, and still has a long, sandy beach.

To the north of the town is **Prestwick International Airport**, at one time the main transatlantic airport for Glasgow. It is still a busy place, being a favourite starting point for those holidays in warmer climes that eventually saw off Prestwick as a holiday resort. On March 2 1960, the airport had possibly its most famous visitor - **Elvis Presley**. Having been discharged from the American army, his plane touched down at the airport for refuelling when he was returning home from Germany. He stayed at the American air force base (now gone) for just under an hour, and then re-boarded his flight. It was the only time that "The King" ever set foot in Britain. A plaque near the Graceland Bar in the airport commemorates the visit, and people still turn up from all over Europe to pay their respects. In later life, someone asked Elvis what country he would like to visit, and he replied that he would most like to go back to Scotland.

The name Prestwick means "priest's burgh", and the ruins of the ancient **Parish Church of St Nicholas** are near the coastline. At **Kingcase** was a lazar house where Robert the Bruce went to seek a cure for his leprosy. **Bruce's Well** can still be seen there.

Monkton

4 miles N of Ayr on the A79

Traffic between Glasgow and Ayr used to thunder through Monkton, but now it is more or less bypassed. It sits on the edge of Prestwick Airport, and at one time the

PRESTWICK OLD COURSE HOTEL

13 Links Road, Prestwick, Ayrshire KA9 1QG
Tel: 01292 477446 Fax: 01292 478316
e-mail:
enquiries@prestwickoldcoursehotel.com
website: www.prestwickoldcoursehotel.com

Prestwick hosted the first British Open Golf Championship in 1860 and overlooking the 14th and 18th greens of the golf course you'll find **Prestwick Old Course Hotel**, the ideal place to stay while enjoying a golfing break on the Ayrshire coast. Within a 20 minute drive there are at least 20 golf courses - some of them championship class! The hotel has 10 fully en suite rooms, a cosy lounge bar and a restaurant that serves the very best food, all sourced from fresh local produce wherever possible. And it's not only golfers who appreciate the service and comfort of this fine hotel - it is family- friendly, and makes an ideal base from which to explore the Burns Country.

main road cut right across the main runway. This meant that buses and cars were held up every time an aircraft took off or landed - a magnificent site, but time-consuming for people in a hurry. The ruins of 13th century **St Cuthbert's Church** sit at the heart of the village, and at one time the Rev. Thomas Burns, Robert Burns's nephew, was minister here. William Wallace, it is said, once fell asleep in the church, and had a dream in which an old man presented him with a sword and a young woman presented him with a wand. He took it to mean that he must continue his struggle for Scotland's freedom.

To the north of the village is a curious monument known as **MacRae's Monument**. It commemorates James MacRae, Governor of Madras in the early 18th century. He was born in Ochiltree in humble circumstances, his father having died before he was born. He was then brought up by a carpenter called Hugh McGuire, and when MacRae returned from India in 1731 a rich man he bought the Orangefield estate (which stood where part of Prestwick Airport now stands). He also found his old benefactor living in poverty. He bought him an estate at Stair, east of Monkton, and introduced his daughters into polite society, each of them making good marriages, one of them even becoming a countess.

The estate of Ladykirk is to be found a few miles east of Monkton. It was here, in **Ladykirk Chapel**, which has all but vanished, that Robert II (the first Stewart king) married Elizabeth Mure of Rowallan, mother of Robert III.

Troon

6 miles N of Ayr, on the A759

This seaside resort is synonymous with golf, and the British Open has been held here many times. It is a young town, having

Fordell B&B

43 Beach Road, Barassie, Troon,
Ayrshire KA10 6SU
Tel: 01292 313224
e-mail: www.fordell-troon.co.uk

Set right on a road beside Barassie Beach in the pleasant golfing resort of Troon, **Fordell B&B** sets great store by high standards of service and keen prices. The owner, Morag Mathieson, has a wealth of information at her fingertips about the many tourist attractions and historic sites that can be visited in Ayrshire, and any stay here is one that will be remembered for a long time! Troon is right in the Burns Country, and the town is famous for its many championship golf courses. It is also connected to Northern Ireland by modern ferry service.

Fordell is an old, mellow semi-detached Victorian villa built for people who appreciated comfort and coastal living, and, thanks to Morag, it still lives up to those standards. There are two extremely comfortable twin rooms on offer, each with wash hand basins, colour TVs, and tea/coffee making facilities. The warm, inviting residents' lounge has superb views out over the Firth of Clyde to the misty mountains of Arran, which can be reached by ferry from Ardrossan, further up the coast. The beautifully cooked Scottish breakfasts are hearty and filling, though lighter Continental breakfasts are also available. Evening meals are available from a hotel restaurant a few minutes walk away. If you're thinking of a holiday close to the beaches and lovely scenery of Ayrshire, or if you're looking for somewhere to stay overnight, Fordell is the place for you!

Royal Troon Golf Course

been laid out in the early 1800s by the 4th Duke of Portland, who wished to create a harbour from which to export the coal from his Ayrshire coalfields. It formed the western terminus of Scotland's earliest rail line, the **Troon/Kilmarnock Railway**, which was opened in 1812. In 1816 the Duke introduced a steam locomotive onto the line, and it started pulling passenger trains (see also Kilmarnock). The town is now the Scottish terminal for the Scotland/ Ireland Seacat ferry service.

On the shoreline is the **Ballast Bank**, created over the years by ships which discharged their ballast before taking on coal for Ireland. Behind Troon a narrow road climbs up onto the **Dundonald Hills**, from where a magnificent view of the Firth of Clyde can be obtained.

Symington

6 miles N of Ayr off the A77

Symington is a pleasant village of old cottages, though a large estate of council housing on its northern edge has somewhat marred its picturesqueness. At the heart of the village is **Symington Parish Church**, Ayrshire's oldest church still in use. This Norman building, formerly dedicated to the Holy Trinity, was originally built in the early 12th century, and has in its east wall a trio of delightful Norman windows. On a hillside to the west of the village, at a spot called Barnweil, is the Victorian **Barnweil Monument**, looking for all the world like a church tower without a church. This marks the spot where Wallace watched the "barns o' Ayr burn weel" after he set fire to them. Next to it are the scant ruins of **Barnweil Church**, where John Knox once preached. The parish of Barnweil was suppressed in 1673, and the church, which may have been one of the oldest in Ayrshire, gradually became ruinous.

Dundonald

8 miles N of Ayr on the B730

Dundonald Castle (Historic Scotland) sits on a high hill overlooking the village. The hill has been occupied for at least 3,000 years, and has been the site of at least three medieval castles. What you see nowadays are the remains of the third castle, built in the 14th century by Robert II, grandson of Robert the Bruce and the first Stewart king of Scotland, to mark his accession to the throne in 1371. It was here, in his favourite residence, that Robert died in 1390. When Boswell and Dr Johnson visited the castle in 1773 during their Scottish journey, Johnson was much amused by the humble home of "Good King Bob". Since then, the castle has been owned by many families, including the Wallaces and the Cochranes, who later became Earls of Dundonald.

From the top, reached by a metal staircase, are fine views northwards and eastwards over central Ayrshire.

Tarbolton

6 miles NE of Ayr on the B744

When Burns stayed at nearby **Lochlee Farm** (not open to the public) both he and his brother Gilbert looked to Tarbolton for leisure activities. They founded a debating society, which met in a thatched house in the village. This house is now the **Bachelors' Club** (National Trust for Scotland). It was here that Burns also took dancing lessons, something of which his father William did not approve. Round the fireplace in the upper room you'll see a helical pattern drawn in chalk - an old Ayrshire custom to prevent the Devil from entering the house by way of the chimney.

The farm of Lochlee (also known as Lochlea) sat beside a now drained loch to the west of the village, and had poor soil. When Burns's father died in 1784, the family moved to Mossgiel near Mauchline.

Tarbolton Parish Church is an elegant, imposing building of 1821 standing on a low hill.

Mauchline

10 miles NE of Ayr on the A76

When Burns's father died at Lochlee near Tarbolton, the Burns family moved to **Mossgiel Farm** near the village of Mauchline. The farm that Burns knew is no more, but its successor still stands to the north of the village, with its farmhouse looking considerably more prosperous than the one Burns knew. It was in Mauchline that he met Jean Armour, his future wife, and it was here that they first settled down. Their home in Castle Street (which at that time was the main street of the village) now houses the **Burns House Museum**. The red sandstone building actually had four families living in it in the 18th century, but it has now been converted so that various displays and exhibitions can be accommodated. Robert and Jean's apartment has been furnished in much the same way as it would have been in 1788 when they moved in. Across from it, but now a private house, was **Nance Tinnock's Inn**, Burns's favourite drinking place.

Burns lived in Mauchline from 1784 until 1788, when he and his family moved to Dumfriesshire. It was the most productive period in his life, and to his time in Mauchline we owe *To a Mountain Daisy*, *To a Mouse*, *Holy Willie's Prayer* and *The Holy Fair*. But it was also troubled times for him, and while trying to eke a living from the poor soil of Mossgiel, he contemplated emigrating to Jamaica.

The **Parish Church** you see today is not the one that Burns knew. The old Norman church was pulled down and rebuilt in 1826, though the kirkyard still has many graves connected with the poet (including the graves of four of his children). A chart on the church wall explains where each one is. One to look out for is that of **William Fisher**. William was an elder in Mauchline Kirk, and the butt of Burns's satirical poem *Holy Willie's Prayer*, in which he attacks the cant and hypocrisy of the church. Willie asks God's forgiveness for his own, understandable sins, while asking that he severely punish the sins of others. Opposite the church is **Poosie Nansy's Inn**. Though not a great frequenter of this inn, the poet still drank there occasionally, and Burns enthusiasts can still drink there today.

To the north of the village is the **Burns Memorial**, built in 1897. It is a tall building in red sandstone with a small museum inside. From the top, you get good views of the rich agricultural lands of Ayrshire. Beside the memorial, and forming part of it, are some pleasant cottages for old people.

Gavin Hamilton was Burns's friend and landlord, and he stayed in the village. His house can still be seen, and attached to it is the 15th century **Abbot Hunter's Tower**. It looks like a small castle, but was in fact the monastic headquarters of the Ayrshire estates owned by Melrose Abbey.

The **Ballochmyle Viaduct**, to the south of the village, carries the Glasgow to Dumfries line across the River Ayr, and is considered to be one of the finest railway bridges in the world. Work started on it in 1843, and it is still Britain's highest stone and brick railway bridge, being 163 feet above the river. It has three smaller arches at either end, and one long, graceful arch in the middle that spans 181 feet.

The **Ballochmyle** estate, which stood to the south of the village, is no more. Up until recently it was the site of a hospital, but even that has been pulled down. When Burns first came to Mauchline it was owned by the Whitefoords, who had lost everything when a local bank collapsed several years earlier. They eventually sold it to Claud Alexander and his family to pay off their huge debts.

Burns had been used to wandering the Ballochmyle estates, which sit on the banks of the River Ayr, and one day in about 1786 when Burns was strolling along the banks, he saw Miss Wilhelmina Alexander, Claud's sister, and he was so taken by her that he wrote *The Lass o' Ballochmyle*, one of his most famous works, in her honour. He sent it to her, but so angry was she that a humble farmer should write a poem in her honour that she never replied. In later years, however, she cherished the poem.

Failford

7 miles E of Ayr on the B743

Near this little village, in 1786, Burns took his farewell of Highland Mary, who would die soon after in Greenock (see also Greenock and Dunoon). Burns had asked her to accompany him to Jamaica, and she was returning home to prepare for the voyage. The **Failford Monument**, on a slight rise, commemorates this event.

A mile east of Failford, in a field, are the remains of a tumulus known as **King Cole's Grave**. Legend tells us that Old King Cole of nursery rhyme fame was a real person - a British king called Coel or Coilus. In the Dark Ages, he fought a great battle in Ayrshire against the Scots under their king, Fergus. Cole's army was routed, and he fled the battlefield. Eventually he was captured and killed. His supporters later cremated his body and buried it with some pomp at the spot where he died (see also Coylton). The Kyle area of Ayrshire is supposed to be named after him.

The tumulus was opened in 1837, and some cremated bones were discovered. Up until not so long ago the nearby stream was referred to locally as the "Bloody Burn", and one field beside the stream was known as "Deadmen's Holm", as that is where those killed in the battle were supposedly buried. Tales were often told of bits of human bone and armour being turned up by men ploughing the field.

Ochiltree

11 miles E of Ayr on the A70

Ochiltree was the birthplace of yet another Ayrshire writer, **George Douglas Brown**, who was born here in 1869, and went on to write *The House with the Green Shutters*. He wanted to banish the "kailyard school" of writing, which saw Scotland's countryside as being comfortable and innocent, full of couthy, happy people of unquestionable worth. He set his book in the fictional town of "Barbie", which is a thinly disguised Ochiltree, and not many characters in the book have redeeming features. The cottage where he was born (not open to the public) now has green shutters, and is itself known as the "House with the Green Shutters".

Auchinleck

13 miles E of Ayr off the A76

Burns is not the only famous literary person associated with Ayrshire. Though born in Edinburgh, **James Boswell** was the son of a Court of Session judge who lived in **Auchinleck House**, near what became the mining village of Auchinleck. He had the house built in about 1760 as his country seat, and Boswell brought the great Dr Johnson there to meet him when the pair were touring Scotland. They didn't hit it off.

Boswell himself is buried in a small mausoleum attached to **Auchinleck Kirk**, which is no longer used for worship, but instead houses a museum dedicated to the writer and biographer.

Sorn

14 miles E of Ayr on the B743

Sorn is one of the most picturesque villages in the county. It sits on the River Ayr, with an 18th century bridge spanning it, and has many delightful cottages. **Sorn Parish Church** dates from 1658, and the lofts, or galleries, are reached by stairs on the outside of the walls. **Sorn Castle** dates from the 14th century, with later additions. It was built by a branch of the Hamilton family, and James VI once visited on horseback in the depths of winter to attend the wedding of Isobel Hamilton, the daughter of his Treasurer, to Lord Seton. It is open to the public from mid July to early August each year.

Alexander Peden was born at Auchincloich near Sorn in 1626. Known as **Prophet Peden**, he was a Covenanter who held secret conventicles, or prayer meetings, at lonely spots all over central Ayrshire. The whole area abounds with places that have been named after him, such as "Peden's Pulpit" and "Peden's Table". There is even a field called "Preaching Peden".

Cumnock

15 miles E of Ayr off the A76

Cumnock is a small industrial town which was granted its burgh charter in 1509. In the middle of its square sits **Cumnock Old Parish Church**, built in the mid 1800s. It's a foursquare building that seems to sprout transepts, apses and porches in all directions. Two miles west of the town, at Lugar, is **Bello Mill** (not open to the public), birthplace in 1754 of William Murdoch, discoverer of gas lighting. He conducted his experiments in a cave on the banks of the Lugar Water upstream from Bello.

Dumfries House (not open to the public), one mile west of Cumnock, was designed for the 4th Earl of Dumfries in the mid 1700s by John and Robert Adam. It is said that James Armour, Robert Burns's father-in-law, was one of the masons who worked on the building of the house.

Muirkirk

23 miles E of Ayr on the A70

This former mining and iron-working town is surrounded by bleak but lovely moorland. To the west is the site of the **Battle of Airds Moss**, fought in 1680 and marked by a memorial. A Covenanting army was heavily defeated by Government troops. Just south of the town, and along an unmarked road, is a small monument to John Louden McAdam, who owned a tar works in the vicinity. A mile-long canal was dug here in 1789, which served the former iron works.

New Cumnock

18 miles E of Ayr on the A76

It was near here that the **Knockshinnoch Mining Disaster** took place in 1950. 129 miners were trapped underground when a slurry of mud and peat filled some workings that were close to the surface. 116 were eventually brought out alive, and great bravery was shown by the rescuers. A feature film, *The Brave Don't Cry*, was made about the disaster in 1952. To the south of the village is **Glen Afton**, through which flows the Afton Water. A cairn marks the spot where Burns was inspired to write *Flow Gently Sweet Afton.*

Dalrymple

5 miles SE of Ayr on the B7034

In this quiet little village of weavers' cottages Burns first received an education. While staying at Mount Oliphant, he and his brother Gilbert attended the Parish School on alternate weeks. The village sits on the Doon, and has a small **Parish Church** built in 1849. Some people say it was the inspiration for the musical Brigadoon, about a mysterious Scottish village that only appears every 100 years. Alan Jay Lerner, who wrote the words, was looking for a way of turning a German fairy tale about a magical village called *Germelshausen* into a musical, and one day while in Scotland he suddenly happened upon Dalrymple, which sits in a small glen, hidden until you're almost upon it. He immediately thought of locating his musical in Scotland, and called it Brigadoon because there really is a bridge over the River Doon in the village. He also called one of the characters Charlie Dalrymple.

Two miles south, and straight out of a fairy tale as well, is **Cassillis Castle** (not open to the public), the home of the Marquis of Ailsa, head of Clan Kennedy. It is a wonderful concoction of pepper pot turrets and towers built originally in the 15th century but added to throughout the years.

Alloway

2 miles S of Ayr town centre on the B7024

Robert Burns was not the uneducated "ploughman poet" from the peasant classes that his more romantic admirers would have us believe. His father was a tenant farmer, and although not well off, still managed to employ workmen and serving girls on his farm.

Burns himself was a highly educated man for his time, thanks to his far-sighted father. He knew his Classics, he could speak French and some Latin, he could read music, he took dancing lessons, and he could play both the fiddle and, surprisingly, the guitar. When he went to Edinburgh in later life, he was possibly better educated than some of the gentry who patronised him. Two of his sons, James Glencairn Burns and W. Nicol Burns, attained the ranks of Lieutenant Colonel and Colonel respectively in the British Army.

At one time, Alloway was a small country village. Now it forms part of Ayr, and is full of large, impressive houses which illustrate the relative affluence of this part of Ayrshire. It was here, in 1759, that Robert Burns was born in a cottage that his father built with his own hands. Now **Burns Cottage** is a place of pilgrimage, and people come from all over the world to pay their respects. Within the grounds of the cottage is the **Burns Museum**, containing many of his manuscripts, letters and possessions.

Alloway Kirk is where Robert's father, William Burns, is buried, and it was the main setting for the poem Tam o' Shanter. It dates from the early 16th century, but even in Burns's day it was a ruin. Across the road, within some beautiful gardens, is the Grecian **Burns Monument**, built in the 1820s. Inside is a small museum.

Spanning the Doon is the graceful **Brig o'**

Burns Cottage, Alloway

Doon, a single arched bridge dating from the 15th century or possibly earlier. It was across the Brig o' Doon that Tam o' Shanter was chased by witches he disturbed in Alloway Kirk. However, he managed to gain the keystone of the bridge and escaped unharmed (as witches cannot cross running water), even though his horse lost its tail. In Burn's day it lay on the main road south into Carrick, but a newer, wider bridge now carries traffic south.

Across the road from Alloway Kirk is the **Tam o' Shanter Experience**, a visitor centre with two audiovisual shows within its large auditorium. One illustrates Burns's life and times, and the other re-creates what happened to Tam o' Shanter after he left the inn and made his fateful ride south from Ayr.

East of Alloway is **Mount Oliphant Farm** (not open to the public) to which Burns and his family moved when he was seven years old.

St Quivox

2 miles NE of Ayr just off the A77

The tiny **Parish Church** is a small gem of a building. Though altered beyond recognition over the years, its basic fabric is still medieval, and it takes its name from a shadowy Celtic saint called variously St Kevock, St Kennocha, St Kenochis, St Cavocks and St Evox. It was restored by Lord Cathcart of Auchincruive - and no doubt altered to suit Protestant services - in 1595.

To the east is **Oswald Hall** designed by Robert Adam for James Oswald in 1767. It is now a conference centre. The surrounding Auchincruive estate is one of the campuses of the Scottish Agricultural College.

Kilmarnock

Though it is largely an industrial town, Kilmarnock was granted its burgh charter in 1592, so its roots go deep into Scottish history. Legend says it grew up round a church founded by St Marnock, a Celtic saint, in the 7th century. The present **Laigh Kirk** (now called The Laigh West High Kirk) in Bank Street dates from 1802. It has a 17th century steeple (a date stone on it says 1410, but this may refer to an earlier building), and is supposed to stand on the site of this church. In 1801, during a service, 29 people were trampled to deaths when plasterwork started falling off the ceiling of the previous kirk, causing a mad rush for the doors. The town's other old church is the **Old High Kirk**, which dates from the early 1730s.

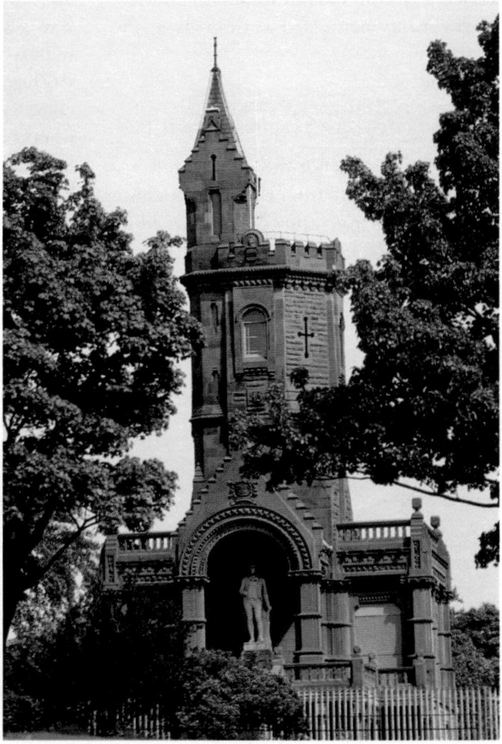

Burns Monument, Kilmarnock

Kilmarnock has many Burns associations, and the first edition of his poems was published in the town, at Star Inn Close (now gone) in 1786. Now a copy is worth thousands of pounds. A stone marking the spot can be found in the small shopping mall. Also in the mall is a stone marking the spot where Covenanting martyr **John Nesbit** was executed in 1683. His grave can be seen in the kirkyard of the Laigh Kirk.

Many of the people mentioned in Burns's poems are buried in the two kirkyards. **Burns Statue**, unveiled in the mid 1990s by the Princess Royal, stands at Kilmarnock Cross. It is the work of Sandy Stoddard, whose other works include the statue of David Hume on Edinburgh's Royal Mile and the sculptured friezes in the Queen's Gallery in Buckingham Palace. In the Kay Park stands another memorial to the poet - **Burns Monument**. Though not now open to the public, it is an impressive red sandstone building.

In truth, Kilmarnock's shopping centre, notably Kilmarnock Cross and King Street, is dull and unattractive, due to uninspired modern developments. But if you go down Cheapside towards Bank Street and the narrow streets round the Laigh Kirk, you get an idea of what the 18th century town looked like. It was in a shop in King Street that Johnnie Walker first started bottling and selling whisky in 1820. The **Johnnie Walker Bottling Plant** in Hill Street is one of the largest plants of its kind in the world. Johnnie Walker himself now lies in the kirk yard of St Andrew's Glencairn Church (no longer used for worship) to the south of the town centre, and his statue can be found in the Strand.

One place not to be missed is the **Dick Institute**, the town's museum, art gallery and library. It is housed in a grand classical building, and has impressive collections connected with geology, archaeology, biology and local history. The gallery is also impressive, with paintings by Corot, Constable, Turner and Kilmarnock's own painter, Robert Colquhoun. The area around the Dick Institute is particularly attractive, with a war memorial, Victorian houses, and the richly decorated façade of the old technical college, now being converted into flats. Across from the Dick Institute is the statue of Kilmarnock's own Dick Whittington - **James Shaw** (known affectionately in the town as "Jimmy Shaw") who became Lord Mayor of London in 1805.

To the north east of the town centre is the town's oldest building, **Dean Castle**. It was the home of the Boyd family, who became Earls of Kilmarnock, and is in fact two castles within a curtain wall - the 14th century Keep and the later Palace. Both are open to the public, and house wonderful collections of tapestries, musical instruments and armour. Surrounding it is **Dean Castle Country Park** with many walks and a small children's zoo.

The Boyd family rose to become the most important family in Scotland in the 1460s, when Sir Robert Boyd became Regent of Scotland. In 1746 the last earl was beheaded in London for fighting alongside Charles Edward Stuart at Culloden, and all his lands and titles were forfeited.

During his trial in London, his young wife, the Countess of Kilmarnock, stayed at the Boyd's other residence in the town - Kilmarnock House (now gone). Daily she walked its grounds, awaiting news of his fate. These grounds are now the **Howard Park**, which has a tree lined avenue known as **Lady's Walk**. The Countess herself died shortly after her husband, and some people say that her ghost still haunts the park (see also Falkirk).

Across from the new sheriff court building near the park is the **Old Sheriff Court** of 1852, an attractive building in neoclassical style. It sits on the site of one of the termini of Scotland's first railway, the Troon/Kilmarnock Railway, built by the Duke of Portland in 1812 (see also Troon).

Two miles west of the town is the **Gatehead Viaduct**, built in 1807 to take the railway over the River Irvine. Though it no longer carries a railway line, it is still Scotland's oldest railway bridge.

Though Elderslie in Renfrewshire seems a likelier location, there are those who claim that **William Wallace** was born at Ellerslie, west of Riccarton, a suburb of Kilmarnock (and named after Sir Richard Wallace, a relation of William). There was certainly a Wallace castle in the area, and young William is known to have had his first skirmish with English troops on the banks of the River Irvine.

In 1862, at Crosshouse, a former mining village west of Kilmarnock, was born **Andrew Fisher**, who rose to become Prime Minister of Australia on three separate occasions.

Around Kilmarnock

Fenwick

4 miles N of Kilmarnock off the A77

Fenwick (pronounced "Fennick") is really two villages - High Fenwick and Laigh Fenwick. They lie on the edge of the Fenwick Moors, which separate the farmlands of Ayrshire from Glasgow and its suburbs, and were originally weaving villages. Some of the cottages still show their weaving origins, with two windows on one side of the door to allow plenty of light to enter the room containing the loom and one window on the other. **Fenwick Parish Church**, which dates from 1643, is an attractive whitewashed building with a Greek cross plan. On one wall hangs the original **Jougs**, where wrongdoers were chained by their necks to the wall.

Two miles south east of the village is the quaintly named, and often photographed, hamlet of **Moscow** (pronounced "Moss-cow" rather than "Moss-coe"), which actually has a burn called the Volga flowing through it. And five miles to the north, off the B764, is **Lochgoin Farm**, which has a small museum commemorating the Covenanters.

Kilmaurs

2 miles NW of Kilmarnock, on the A735

Kilmaurs is a former weaving village, and though only a few fields separate it from Kilmarnock's suburbs, it is still a small, self-contained community with many small cottages. At its centre is the old 17th century **Tolbooth**, still with the jougs attached, which was placed round wrongdoers' necks as a punishment. **St Maurs Glencairn Church** dates from 1888, and replaced an earlier medieval collegiate church. **Glencairn Aisle**, the 16th century burial vault of the Earls of Glencairn, still stands however, and it has an ornate monument inside to the 8th Earl and his family.

John Boyd Orr, first director of the United Nations Food and Agricultural Organisation and Nobel prize-winner, was born in Kilmaurs in 1880.

Stewarton

5 miles N of Kilmarnock on the A735

Stewarton is famous as being the home of bonnet making in Ayrshire. It was the birthplace, in 1739, of **David Dale**, the industrialist and social reformer who founded New Lanark (see also Lanark). The **Parish Church of St Columba** dates originally from 1696, though it has been much altered.

Dunlop

7 miles N of Kilmarnock on the A735

Dunlop is a delightful village of small weavers' cottages. The **Parish Church** dates from 1835, though it has fragments from the earlier church incorporated into the north aisle. In the kirkyard is the ornate early 17th century **Hans Hamilton Tomb**, contained within a small mausoleum. Hamilton was Dunlop's first Protestant minister, and was made Viscount Clandeboyes by James VI. The small **Clandeboyes Hall**, beside the mausoleum, dates from the 17th century, and was the village's first school.

Galston

4 miles E of Kilmarnock on the A71

This pleasant little town in the Irvine Valley has a splendid **Parish Church** dating from 1808. Another church not to be missed is **St Sophia's RC Church**, modelled on the Hagia St Sophia in Istanbul. **Barr Castle** is a solid, 15th century tower house in which John Knox preached in 1556. An ancient game of handball used to be played against its walls by the locals.

To the north of the town are the impressive ruins of **Loudoun Castle**, ancestral home of the Campbells of Loudoun. It was burnt down in 1941, and in its time entertained so lavishly that it was called the "Windsor of Scotland". Three ghosts reputedly haunt it - a Grey Lady, a Phantom Piper and a Benevolent Monk. At one time the great sword of William Wallace was kept within the castle, but it was sold in 1930. Beside its walls is the **Auld Yew Tree**, under which Hugh, 3rd Earl of Loudoun, prepared the draft of the Treaty of Union between Scotland and England.

Loudoun Castle was the birthplace of **Lady Flora Hastings**, who shook the monarchy and government to its core in 1839. Queen Victoria was 20 years old at the time, and had been on the throne for just two years. Lady Flora was a Lady of the Bedchamber who contracted a disease which so swelled her stomach that she appeared pregnant. Gossip raged through the court, and she was shunned, even though doctors whom she consulted confirmed that she wasn't pregnant but ill.

Neither the government nor the Queen did anything to dispel the rumours, and people began to sympathise with the young woman. Soon it was the Queen's turn to be shunned, and she was shocked when people turned their back on her as she proceeded through London by coach. It wasn't until Lady Flora was on her deathbed that a grudging reconciliation took place, though no apology was ever given. She now lies buried in medieval **Loudoun Kirk**, whose ruins can be seen a couple of miles to the west of the castle. It is thought nowadays that Lady Flora may have been suffering from ovarian cancer.

Today the **Loudoun Castle Theme Park** fills the grounds of the castle.

Newmilns

7 miles E of Kilmarnock on the A71

Newmilns is a small lace making and weaving town in the Irvine Valley, which was granted its charter in 1490, making it the oldest inland burgh in Ayrshire. The small crow stepped **Town House** dates from the 1730s, and behind the Loudoun Arms, which itself dates from the 18th century, is **Newmilns Tower**, an early 16th century tower house built by the Campbells of Loudoun.

During the American Civil War, the weavers of Newmilns sent a message of support to Abraham Lincoln, and he in turn sent back an American flag. This was subsequently lost, but in 1949 the American Embassy gave the town a replacement, which is now housed in the early 19th century **Parish Church** in the main street.

Darvel

8 miles E of Kilmarnock, on the A71

Situated in the lovely Irvine Valley, Darvel is a small, attractive town which was laid out in the late 18th and early 19th centuries. Like its neighbour Newmilns, it is a lace making town, the skills having been brought here by the Dutch in the 17th century. It was in Lochfield, near Darvel, that **Sir Alexander Fleming**, the discoverer of penicillin, was born in 1881. To the east of the town is the immense bulk of **Loudoun Hill**, the plug of a former volcano. Both William Wallace and Robert the Bruce fought battles here against the English, in 1297 and 1307 respectively. South of the town is the quaintly named **Distinkhorn**, the highest hill in the area.

Irvine

7 miles W of Kilmarnock on the A71

Irvine is an ancient seaport and royal burgh which, in the 1960s, was designated as Britain's first seaside new town. It is a mixture of old and new, and has many industrial estates surrounding it. However, the historical core has been preserved, though an unattractive and totally unnecessary shopping mall straddling the River Irvine, dominates the whole area. Robert Burns learned flax dressing in Irvine in 1781, and lodged in a house in the cobbled **Glasgow Vennel**. A small museum has been created within both it and the heckling shop behind it.

Irvine has other, more unexpected, literary associations, however. In 1815 the American writer Edgar Allan Poe, spent a couple of months in the town, attending the local school. It is said that part of his lessons was to copy the epitaphs from the tombstones in the kirkyard of the **Parish Kirk**, which may have prepared him for some of the macabre tales he wrote in later life. Irvine was also the birthplace of the writer **John Galt**, a relative of the man who adopted Edgar Allan Poe in the United States. **Alexander MacMillan**, who founded the great publishing house, was also a native of the town.

In the nearby village of **Dreghorn** was born in 1840 yet another famous Ayrshireman - **John Boyd Dunlop**, who invented the pneumatic tyre. **Dreghorn Parish Church**, built in 1780, is unusual in that it is six-sided in plan.

The ruins of **Seagate Castle** date from the early 16th century, and it is said that Mary Stuart lodged here briefly in 1563. Every August the town has its **Marymass Week**, which supposedly commemorates her visit. However, the celebrations probably have more to do with a pre-Reformation religious festival, as the parish church was formerly dedicated to St Mary.

In the 18th century, Irvine saw the founding of perhaps the most unusual religious cult ever seen in Scotland - the Buchanites. Elspet Buchan was the daughter of a publican, and claimed she could bestow immortality on a person by breathing on them, and that she herself was immortal. She attracted a wide following, including a gullible Irvine clergyman, but was hounded, along with her followers, from the town. She eventually died a natural death, and the cult broke up (see also Closeburn and Crocketford).

Down by the harbour side is the **Magnum Leisure Centre**, one of the biggest centres of its kind in Scotland. It has a theatre and concert hall, an indoor bowling green, an ice rink, swimming pool and fitness and coaching areas.

Near the Magnum Centre is one of the three sites of the **Scottish Maritime Museum** (see also Dumbarton and Glasgow). It houses a wide collection of ships, most of which you can board and explore. There's also the

Scottish Maritime Museum, Irvine

Linthouse Engine Works, which houses a vast collection of maritime machinery, such as engines, winding gear and so on. In the Ship worker's Tenement Flat, a typical "room and kitchen" flat dating from the 1920s has been re-created, showing how shipyard workers lived in those days.

Irvine was the setting, in 1839, of the grand **Eglinton Tournament**, organised by the 13th Earl of Eglinton at his home of Eglinton Castle, on the outskirts of the town. Here, a great medieval tournament was to be re-created, with jousting, horse riding and other knightly pursuits for the great and the good, who had promised to come from all over Europe. Alas, the three-day event was a wash out, due to colossal rainstorms. Little remains of the castle, but the grounds have been turned into **Eglinton Country Park**.

Kilwinning

9 miles NW of Kilmarnock on the A737

Though nowadays a continuation of Irvine, Kilwinning was, up until 1975, a separate burgh. The ruins of the great Tironensian **Kilwinning Abbey**, built in the 12th century, still dominate the town centre, though they are not as extensive as those of Ayrshire's other great abbey, Crossraguel. The tower you see nowadays attached to the abbey ruins was built in 1815, and replaced the original medieval one, which fell down the year before. It is here that a competition is held every year called the **Papingo Shoot**, where archers shoot upwards at a target (the papingo) held from a window of the tower. The papingo is usually a wooden pigeon, and such shoots were once common throughout Britain. **Kilwinning Parish Church**, which sits within the ruins of the abbey, was built in 1775. The town is the home of Freemasonry in Scotland.

A few miles out of town, on the A737, is **Dalgarven Mill** (see panel below), dating from about 1620. It is now a museum dedicated to country life in Ayrshire.

Ardrossan, Saltcoats & Stevenston

11 miles W of Kilmarnock on the A78

These towns form a trio of holiday resorts on the Ayrshire coast. Ardrossan is the most industrialised, and is the ferry terminal for Arran. It is a planned town, and its core was laid out in the early 19th century by the

Dalgarven Mill

Dalgarven, Kilwinning KA13 6PL
Tel: 01294 552448
website: www.dalgarvenmill.org.uk

There has been a mill on the site since the 14th century, set up by the monks of Kilwinning Abbey. The present mill was erected in 1640 and rebuilt in 1880 after being damaged by fire. The Garnock waters power a 6 metre diameter breast shot wheel that drives the French millstones through cast iron gearing. With ongoing restoration, it is hoped that demonstration milling will soon be possible.

The 3 storey grain store has been converted to house an extensive collection of Ayrshire farming and domestic memorabilia, much of which has been donated by local people over the years. There is also an exhibition of one of the finest costume collections in private hands, with over 6000 pieces. The items of clothing and a multitude of accessories date between 1775 and 1980. There are delightful walks through unspoilt countryside beside the River Garnock, where an abundance of birds and wildlife can be seen in summer and, in Spring, the wildflower meadow is beautiful. Soak up a farmhouse atmosphere over a light lunch and finish your visit with a browse in the antiques shop.

12th Earl of Eglinton. The ruins of 15th century **Ardrossan Castle**, once a stronghold of the Montgomeries, sit on Castle Hill overlooking the main streets. Cromwell is said to have plundered some of its masonry to build the Citadel at Ayr. The ruins and the land surrounding them were given to the town by the Earl of Eglinton as a public park. The **Obelisk** at the highest point on the hill commemorates a local doctor, Alexander McFadzean, who promoted piped water and gas supplies in the town. At the foot of the hill stands **St Peter in Chains**, designed by Jack Coia, one of Scotland's best-known architects, and built in 1938. It is reckoned to be one of the finest modern churches in Ayrshire.

Just off the coast is **Horse Island**, an RSPB reserve. Though it looks peaceful enough, it has been the scene of many shipwrecks over the years, and many sailors have found themselves marooned on it after their ships struck its submerged reefs. At the **Clyde Marina** is a sculpture park featuring works by the Japanese artist Hideo Furuta, who lives and works in Scotland.

At Saltcoats the **North Ayrshire Museum**, housed in a former church, has an interesting local history collection. A gravestone in the kirkyard may be that of an ancestor of Edgar Allan Poe. The town has a fine beach, and its name is a reminder of the times when salt was produced here from seawater. The small harbour dates from the late 17th century with later alterations, and at low tide fossilised trees can be seen on the harbour floor. It was in Saltcoats, in 1793, that **Betsy Miller**, the only woman ever to have become a registered ship's captain, was born.

Stevenston is a straggling town, with a **High Church** that dates from 1832. It has a good beach, though it is some way from the centre of the town. Nearby, at Ardeer, the British Dynamite Company established a factory in 1873. It later became Nobel's Explosives Company, and in 1926 became part of ICI.

Dalry

11 miles NW of Kilmarnock on the A737

This small industrial town's square is dominated by the **Parish Church of St Margaret,** dating from the 1870s. The name comes from the Gaelic "Dal Righe", meaning the "King's Field", which shows that at one time it must have had royal connections. To the south east of the town is **Blair**, a large mansion centred on what was a typical Scottish tower house. The parkland, which surrounds it, was laid out by William Blair in the 1760s.

Beith

11 miles NW of Kilmarnock off the A737

Beith is a small attractive town in the Garnock Valley. The remains of the **Auld**

Anderson's Hotel

Eglinton Street, Beith, Ayrshire KA15 1AB
Tel: 01505 502034

Looking for superior budget accommodation in the picturesque county of Ayrshire, close to the Burns Country? Then look no further than **Anderson's Hotel**, set within the small town of Beith. It has four extremely comfortable and fully en suite rooms, and dates from the mid 19th century, with many original features. The bar is popular with locals (always a good sign!) and the food - including delicious bar snacks - is out of this world. The hotel makes the ideal base from which to explore Ayrshire, and if you visit, you won't be disappointed!

Kirk date from the late 16th century, while the impressive **High Church** dates from the early 19th century. **Eglinton Street** is the most attractive part of the town, with small, neat two-storey buildings dating from the late 18th and 19th centuries.

Kilbirnie

12 miles NW of Kilmarnock on the A760

Within this small industrial town you'll find the **Barony Parish Church**, dating from the 15th century. Inside is some wonderfully exuberant woodwork from the 17th and 18th centuries, including the extravagant Crawford Loft and the Cunninghame Aisle. In medieval times it was dedicated to St Brendan of Clonfert in Ireland. Standing next to the golf course are the ruins of the **Place of Kilbirnie**, a former castle of the Crawford family dating from the 15th century.

West Kilbride

16 miles NW of Kilmarnock off the A78

West Kilbride is a sedate village of Glasgow commuters, perched above its twin village of **Seamill**, on the coast. **Law Castle** was built in the 15th century for Princess Mary, sister of James III, on her marriage to Thomas Boyd of Kilmarnock, later to be the Earl of Arran. However, the marriage was later annulled and he had to flee the country. His title was eventually given to the Hamilton family. At the hamlet of Portencross, out on a headland beyond Seamill, are the substantial ruins of 14th century **Portencross Castle**, another Boyd stronghold. Also on the headland is **Hunterston Castle** (not open to the public), ancestral home of Clan Hunter, and **Hunterston Nuclear Power Station**.

The Cumbraes

19 miles NW of Kilmarnock, in the Firth of Clyde

These two islands - **Little Cumbrae** and **Great Cumbrae** - were once in the county

Great Cumbrae Island

Largs

of Bute. Little Cumbrae is privately owned, but Great Cumbrae can be visited by a ferry from Largs. The only town on the island is **Millport**, a small, attractive holiday resort with a unique feature - the **Cathedral of the Isles**, Britain's smallest cathedral. It is sometimes referred to as Europe's smallest, but this honour is held by an even smaller cathedral in Greece. Nevertheless it is a real hidden gem, and was completed in 1851 as part of a theological complex funded by the George Boyle, who later became the 6th Earl of Glasgow. Its nave is 40 feet by 20 feet, and can only seat 100 people. It was designed by William Butterfield, who also designed Keble College, Oxford. The ceiling is painted with all the wild flowers found on the island.

On the eastern shore of the island, facing the mainland, is the **University Marine Biological Station**. It is an institution of both Glasgow and London Universities, and offers students research facilities, tuition in diving, and tuition in marine biology. It houses a museum, which is open to the public.

The **Museum of the Cumbraes** can be found in the stables of The Garrison, just off the seafront. There are exhibits and displays on Millport's heyday as one of the Clyde holiday resorts.

Largs

19 miles NW of Kilmarnock on the A78

Largs is the epitome of the Ayrshire seaside town. During the last fortnight in July, hordes of Glaswegians used to descend on places like this for their annual fortnight's holiday. These days are gone, but the towns themselves have adapted, and now cater for retired people and day-trippers.

Largs itself is a lively, attractive place, and is the mainland terminal for the Cumbrae ferry. It was near here that the **Battle of Largs** took place in 1263, when the Scots defeated a force led by King Haakon IV of Norway and finally threw off the Norse yolk (see also Lerwick). A tall thin monument south of the town affectionately known as the **Pencil** commemorates the event. Within the town you'll find **Vikingar!** a museum and interpretation centre that explains the life and travels of the Vikings all these years ago.

Largs Museum, with its local history collection, is also worth a visit, as is the **Skelmorlie Aisle** (Historic Scotland). This sits in the old kirkyard in the centre of the town, and was a transept of the former medieval parish church. Within it is the mausoleum of Sir Robert Montgomery of Skelmorlie and his wife. Built in 1634, it is a Renaissance-style tomb with wonderful stone carving. In the local cemetery is buried **Sir William Burrell**, shipping magnate and millionaire, who gave the Burrell Collection to the city of Glasgow in 1944 (see also Hutton).

Kelburn Castle stands to the south of the town. It is the ancestral home of the Boyles, Earls of Glasgow, and its grounds are now a country park, with gardens, an adventure playground, woodland walks and craft workshops.

Isle of Arran

Arran (13 miles from Ardrossan by ferry) is called "Scotland in Miniature", as it is mountainous in the north, low lying in the middle and rises again towards the south. It is 19 miles long by about ten miles across at its widest, and within its 165 square miles it has history and spectacular scenery aplenty. This is an island of Celtic saints, mysterious standing stones, craft workshops, cairns and old castles. The northern portion can be every bit as spectacular as the Highlands, and for those with the stamina, a climb to the summit of **Goat Fell**, at 2,866 feet the island's highest peak, is a must. The ferry from Ardrossan (a 55 minute crossing) takes you to **Brodick**, a large village and resort strung round Brodick Bay.

Just north of Brodick is the **Arran Brewery**, which has viewing galleries where you can see the brewing process. And at Home Farm, also near Brodick, is **Arran Aromatics**, Scotland's leading producer of body care products and scented candles. Again, you can watch the manufacturing processes from a viewing gallery.

Arran was a Gaelic speaking island up until the early 19th century, though the place names owe as much to the language of the Norsemen who settled here in the 10th and 11th centuries as they do to Gaelic. Dominating Brodick is Goat Fell, with, beneath it, **Brodick Castle** (National Trust for Scotland). This former Hamilton family stronghold (the Hamiltons became the Earls

Dunvegan House

Shore Road, Brodick, Isle of Arran KA27 8AJ
Tel/Fax: 01770 302811
website: www.dunveganhouse-arran.co.uk

Sitting in the Firth of Clyde, Arran has often been called Scotland in miniature, and it is certainly one of the country's most beautiful islands. In Brodick, a small holiday resort and the island's ferry terminal, you will find **Dunvegan House**, a spacious and elegant four-star licensed guesthouse that offers superb accommodation to the discerning tourist. Owned and personally managed by Helen and George McAdam, it sits right on the seafront, between the pier and the centre of the village. It has superb views of Goatfell, Arran's highest mountain, the Ayrshire coastline and Brodick Bay. It is a traditional sandstone building that has been tastefully converted so that it is now one of the best establishments on the island. It has nine

comfortable rooms, eight of which are en suite and the ninth having private facilities. All are individually decorated and furnished, and all have central heating, colour TV, radio/alarm and tea and coffee making facilities.

Renowned for the quality of its food, Helen and George pride themselves on setting and maintaining extremely high standards. Only the finest and freshest of local produce is used wherever possible, and the menus combine flair and imagination with traditional Scottish cuisine. Whether it's the full Scottish breakfast, or the beautifully cooked and presented evening meals, you will be amazed at the high standards of service and the outstanding value for money. The breakfast menu also includes porridge, fruit juice, a selection of yoghurts and cereals, locally smoked kippers, beans on toast or poached, scrambled or boiled eggs. The table d'hôte menu includes such starters as melon and prawn salad, cream of carrot and ginger soup, and crepes filled with mushroom sauce and topped with cheese. The main dishes include Kintyre grilled salmon, Scotch sirloin steak, or chicken with Arran mustard. You can then choose from a selection of sweets or the cheese board. Other menus are available on request. The dining room, with its picture windows, has lovely views out over the bay towards Goatfell, and the lounge, with its small cocktail bar, is the place for a pre dinner drink or just to relax with a book or newspaper. It is smart and elegant yet cosy and welcoming.

Arran is a place where your holiday can be as restful or as energetic as you like. There are wonderful opportunities for hill walking, climbing, golf on one of the island's nine courses, mountain biking, fishing, bird watching and nature study. You can also explore the many historic sites, from Brodick Castle to the prehistoric standing stones, stone circles and old, mysterious cairns. Or you can just relax over a book and watch the world go by away from the bustle of modern life. Helen and George will give you a warm Arran welcome!

of Arran after the title was forfeited by the Boyds of Kilmarnock) sits in a wonderful location, surrounded by mature gardens. There has been a castle of sorts on the site since the Dark Ages, but the present building dates from the 16th century and later. Inside there is a collection of paintings and furniture. On the northern outskirts of the village is the **Isle of Arran Heritage Museum**, which is well worth a visit, as it shows the history of the island's ordinary people. North of Brodick, on the A841 is the beautiful village of **Corrie**, with its whitewashed cottages and its gardens aflame with colour in the summer months.

Lochranza, Isle of Arran

The road from Corrie follows the coast north, then turns north west and goes through the bleak but extremely beautiful **Glen Chalmadale** before bringing you to **Lochranza** ("Loch of the rowan tree

Viewbank House

Golf Course Road, Whiting Bay,
Isle of Arran KA27 8QT
Tel: 01770 700326 Mobile: 07771 783698
e-mail: viewbank@btopenworld.com
website: www.viewbank-arran.co.uk

Built in the 19th century, **Viewbank House** is a former farmhouse that has been converted into an extremely comfortable three-star guest house that offers the very best in hospitality. It is the ideal haven for a relaxing holiday or a getaway break where you can unwind among some wonderful scenery. The beautiful gardens give a superb elevated view out across the Firth of Clyde towards the Ayrshire coast, and a 500 metre stroll along a winding country lane brings you to the shore, where you will find cafés, craft shops, restaurants and bars. Only 200 metres along from Viewbank House is the local Golf Club, where visitors are made very welcome. Viewbank has seven extremely comfortable guest rooms, five fully en suite and two having a shared bathroom and private toilets. Two are on the ground floor, which would suit those with disabilities, and three can be adapted to family or twin bedded rooms. All have hair dryers and hospitality trays. The guest house is open all year round, and has full central heating. The warm, cosy guest lounge is well equipped with television, video, CD player, piano and a selection of games and books.

To make your stay more comfortable, the establishment is completely non-smoking, and well behaved pets are welcome by prior arrangement.

Breadalbane Hotel

Kildonan, Isle of Arran KA27 8SE
Tel/Fax: 01770 820284
e-mail: Yvonne@breadalbanehotel.co.uk
website: www.breadalbanehotel.co.uk

The **Breadalbane Hotel** is a warm and friendly coastal inn with superb views of the islands of Pladda and Ailsa Craig. Situated on the shore road in the quiet village of Kildonan, we attract both locals and visitors alike to enjoy our excellent home cooked meals, real ales and fine whiskies. Our aim is to fulfil the tradition of the village inn, providing quality accommodation, food and drink at a reasonable price.

All our rooms are en suite and finished to a high standard, with colour TV, hair dryer, tea and coffee making facilities and little extras to make your stay more comfortable. All

rooms have central heating and sea views. Our friendly lounge bar is the ideal place to unwind. With its large, open fireplace, it is warm and cosy, even in the depths of winter. As the local "watering hole" there is always a relaxed atmosphere and a varied mix of people. Meals and snacks are served from 12.00 until 21.00. Our extensive menu, with a daily changing specials board, has something to suit everyone's taste. Local produce, including lamb, pork, beef, free range eggs, potatoes and vegetables are used whenever possible. Meals may be eaten in the dining room, bar or sun lounge overlooking the sea.

We also have four superb self-catering flats close to the hotel, and guests staying in them have the full use of the hotel facilities. Flat One is downstairs, and sleeps six in a double room and a room with two sets of bunk beds. It also has a bathroom and an open plan lounge/kitchen area with breakfast bar. Flat Two is also downstairs, and sleeps four in a double and a twin room with bunk beds. It boasts an open plan lounge/dining/kitchen area and a bathroom.

Flat Three is upstairs, and sleeps five in a double room and a room with three single beds. It also has a lounge/dining room, kitchen and bathroom. Flat Four sleeps four in a double room and a twin room with bunk beds. It also has a lounge/dining room, kitchen and bathroom.

For your comfort and convenience, we have tastefully decorated and furnished the flats to an extremely high standard, with TVs, fitted carpets throughout and electric heating in all the rooms. And the kitchens are well equipped to make your stay a pleasure. There is a full-size electric cooker, a fridge and a microwave, and all crockery, cutlery, pans and utensils. All beds have modern duvets with two pillows per person, and all bed linen is included. For an extra small charge, a cot can be hired. Electricity is by £1 coin in the slot meters, and well behaved dogs are welcome.

We pride ourselves on the comfort and high standards we have set in the hotel and the self catering flats. The welcome you get will be warm and friendly, and we are knowledgeable about what to do and see on the lovely island of Arran. We look forward to seeing you at the Breadalbane!

river"). On the shores of this small village are the imposing ruins of **Lochranza Castle** (Historic Scotland), built in the 16th century on the site of an earlier castle. It started life as a hunting lodge for the Scottish kings before passing first to the Campbells and then the Montgomeries, Earls of Eglinton.

At the entrance to the village is the **Isle of Arran Whisky Distillery**, which has guided tours and a visitor centre. In the summer months a small car ferry runs from the Mull of Kintyre to Lochranza, the crossing taking about 35 minutes.

Beyond Lochranza is the small village of **Catacol**, with a row of identical whitewashed cottages known as **The Twelve Apostles**. They were built in the 19th century to accommodate islanders cleared from Glen Catacol in favour of deer. From here you get a good view across to the Mull of Kintyre, which is only four miles away.

Further on, and inland from Machrie Bay, is the wonderful **Auchagallon Stone Circle**, a Bronze Age burial cairn with a circle of stones surrounding it. There are several ancient monuments in the area, including the **Machrie Moor Stone Circle** and the **Moss Farm Road Stone Circle**. The magnificent cliffs at **Drumadoon** stand high above a raised beach, and are spectacular. The **King's Cave** is close to the shore, and is supposed to be the cave where Robert the Bruce saw his spider, (though many other places in Scotland and Ireland make a similar claim). From the village of **Blackwaterfoot**, south of Machrie Bay, a road called **The String** cuts cross the centre of the island towards Brodick. The village of **Shiskine**, on The String, has the lovely **St Molas Church**, with an ancient stone carving of the saint embedded in its wall.

South of Blackwaterfoot the road continues on towards **Lagg**, and if you need convincing about the mildness of the climate hereabouts, the palm trees in the

Dyemill Lodges

Monamhor Glen, Lamlash, Isle of Arran
KA27 8NU
Tel: 01770 600419 Fax: 01770 600130
e-mail: pauldarcher@hotmail.com

Dyemill Lodges are located in the picturesque Monamhor Glen on the island of Arran. The six lodges are set well apart from each other in natural woodland, yet they are only fifteen minutes walk from all the amenities of Lamlash, one of the island's beautiful villages.

The pinewood lodges, all Scandanavian designed, are open between March and October. Each lodge has two bedrooms, a double and a twin, with heating, duvets and linen. A travel cot is available on request. The kitchen is equipped to a high standard, while the living/dining area is comfortable, spacious and inviting. Each lodge has a veranda where you can relax over a refreshing drink on warm summer evenings. Electricity is paid by a £1 coin meter, and there is ample car parking a short distance from the lodges. There is a laundry room on site, and well behaved dogs are welcome by arrangement.

All around Dyemill there are beautiful woodland walks, off-road cycle tracks and picnic areas. If you like observing wildlife, then Arran is a paradise! You may see red squirrels, seals, deer, otters, dolphins and basking sharks as well as a wide variety of birds including golden eagles. There are other activities available close by, such as golf, fishing, bowling, boating and tennis. So whether you're looking for a quiet relaxing holiday where you can recharge your batteries, or one with plenty of outdoor activities, then Dyemill is the place for you!

gardens of the Lagg Inn should do the trick. The **Torrylinn Creamery**, which makes traditional Dunlop cheese in the old fashioned way, has a viewing gallery and shop. Further on the tiny island of **Pladda** can be seen about a mile from the coast before the road turns north once more towards **Whiting Bay**, another small village and holiday resort. At one time it was a fishing port, and it takes its name from the whiting that were caught in the bay. A splendid walk starts from south of the village towards **Glenashdale Falls** and the prehistoric burial cairns known as the **Giant's Graves**.

Beach, Isle of Arran

Lamlash sits on Lamlash Bay. Having the local high school, the hospital and the local government offices, it is the island's capital. In the bay sits the magnificent bulk of **Holy Island**, so called because the Celtic St Molas lived a life of austerity here in the 6th and 7th centuries. Nowadays it has regained its religious significance, as it is home to a Tibetan Buddhist monastery and retreat. Near Lamlash is the factory **Arran Provisions**, the island's biggest employer. It makes a wide range of mustards, jams and preserves, and has a visitor centre and shop.

Glasgow & West Central Scotland

Glasgow and West Central Scotland was at one time Scotland's industrial hub. Heavy engineering, shipbuilding, coal mining and steelworks predominated, providing work for thousands and fortunes for the favoured few. As well as the city of Glasgow, the area takes in the former counties of Dunbartonshire, Renfrewshire and Lanarkshire, which all played their part in Scotland's rich industrial history. But while it is still Scotland's most populous area, and where the bulk of its industry and commerce is located, it is now clean and attractive, with much to do and see.

The scenery can be outstanding, from the upper reaches of the Clyde, with its quiet pastoral scenery and cosy villages surrounded by high, lonely moorland, to the hills above Greenock and of course, the bonnie banks of Loch Lomond. Then there's Glasgow. Once a gritty working class city with an image problem, it has burgeoned into a sophisticated, cosmopolitan city with a lively café society (at least once during a

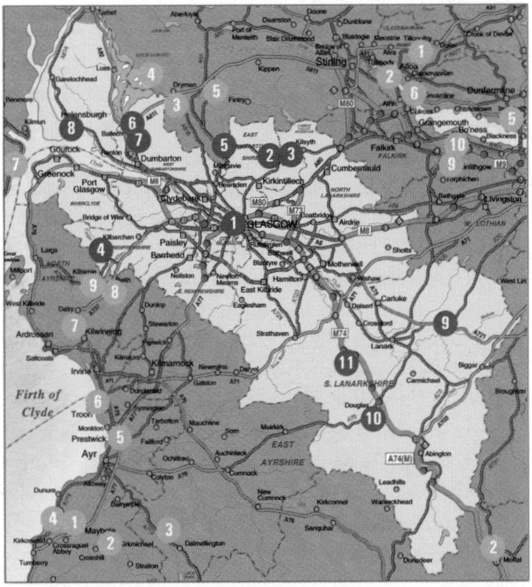

PLACES TO STAY, EAT AND DRINK

The Tall Ship at Glasgow Harbour, Glasgow	1	Visitor Attraction	p114
Eilean B&B, Lennoxtown	2	B&B	p117
The Country Inn, Queenzieburn	3	Pub with Food	p118
Barrs of Cloak, Lochwinnoch	4	Self Catering	p120
The Carbeth Inn, Blanefield	5	Pub with Restaurant	p121
Braeburn Cottage, Balloch	6	B&B	p122
Woodvale B&B/Gowanlea Guest House, Balloch	7	B&B and Guest House	p123
The Hill House, Helensburgh	8	Visitor Attraction	p124
Robertson Arms Hotel, Carnwath	9	Hotel	p132
Kilchoman B&B, Douglas	10	B&B	p134
Fountain Restaurant, Lesmahagow	11	Restaurant	p135

● Denotes entries in other chapters

Cruise Boats on Loch Lomond

visit, do what the locals do - sit at a pavement café sipping coffee while people watch you watching them). There are art galleries and museums galore, bars, shops and shopping malls (it is reckoned to be the second best shopping centre in Britain), award winning restaurants, glitzy hotels, concert halls and nightclubs. It is home to Scottish Opera, The Royal Scottish National Orchestra, Scottish Ballet, and a string of theatres where you can see anything from serious drama to variety shows. It is also one of Britain's best dressed cities, and it is reckoned that there are more Armani and Versace outfits worn here than anywhere else in Britain outside London.

But there is still the quirky Glasgow - the city of fish and chips shops, working men's pubs and street markets, including the raucous Barras, held every Saturday and Sunday in the east end. And the city is ringed by enormous council estates that took the families who used to live in the teeming tenements. It may not be the image of Glasgow that some people would like to project, but they are still there, and in their own way they have as much to do with the city's character as the smart bars, restaurants and trendy city centre apartments built for young professionals.

Glasgow has always been an easy place to get out of. Within half an hour of the city centre you can be admiring the grandeur of bens, glens and lochs, taking it easy in some wonderfully bucolic pastoral scenery, or strolling along a lonely beach, which has a backdrop of magnificent hills.

Loch Lomond is renowned the world over. A train can take you straight to its bonnie banks in just under an hour, and it's a journey thousands of Glaswegians make. We're on the edge of the Highlands here, and indeed the Highland Boundary Fault, which separates the Highland from the Lowlands, passes through the loch.

The River Clyde has traditionally been a working river, its banks once ringing to the sound of shipbuilding. But there is another Clyde, one that isn't so well known. The upper reaches of the river, in rural Lanarkshire, present an altogether different picture. Within the verdant Clyde Valley, you'll find quiet orchards, green fields, woodland, small attractive villages and cosy pubs. The area around Lanark is green and pleasant, with small farms, woodland, low rounded hills and quiet country roads. And the lonely moorland where the river rises has a gaunt but compelling beauty.

The towns also have their attractions. Helensburgh, Gourock and Dumbarton (once the capital of the Kingdom of Strathclyde) sit on the shores of the Firth of Clyde. Hamilton, Paisley, Lanark, Motherwell and East Kilbride are inland towns, and each has its attractions, such as the magnificent Paisley Abbey or the marvellous shopping malls (the largest in Scotland) in East Kilbride. There are certainly towns and areas where the excesses of industry once blighted the

Winter in the Clyde Valley

hardworking and friendly, with a pride in the past and a great faith in the future.

Glasgow

Glasgow has worked hard on its image over the last few years. Gone are the constant references to gang fights, organised crime, drunkenness, ugly industrial townscapes and bad housing. Now people talk of trendy nightspots, restaurants, pavement cafés and art galleries.

The city has changed its image more than once over the years. It started life in early medieval times as a small religious community grouped round a cathedral. In the 17th and 18th centuries it became a city of trade, dealing with the American colonies in such commodities as tobacco and cotton, which made many people very rich indeed. In the 19th century it became a city of industry, with shipyards and heavy engineering works. Now it relies mostly on tourism, the media, service industries and the arts for employment.

The area round the **Cathedral of St Mungo** (Historic Scotland) is where it all started. This was where St Kentigern, or Mungo, established a small church in the 6th century. The present cathedral was founded in the 12th century by David I, and the building shows work from this period onwards. In its crypt is the **Tomb of**

landscape, but these have been cleaned up, and some places, such as Summerlee at Coatbridge, have taken this industrial heritage and turned it into a tourist attraction.

This whole area was once the powerhouse of Scotland. It is not ashamed of the fact, not should it be. Coal was mined here, steel was produced, heavy industry sent smoke pluming into the sky, ships were built, deals were struck and money made. Money is still being made in the area, but now it comes from electronics, banking, tourism, broadcasting and publishing. But the people haven't changed. They have remained

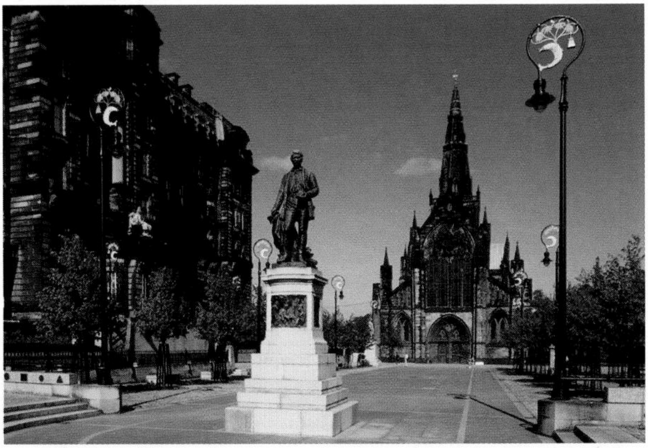

View towards the Cathedral, Glasgow

St Mungo, once a place of pilgrimage, but now visited by pilgrims of a different nature - tourists. The **Blackadder Aisle** is a wonderful piece of architecture added by Bishop Blackadder in about 1500.

Behind the Cathedral, on a hill, is the **Necropolis**, Glasgow's ancient burial ground, and in front of the cathedral is the modern (and looking anything but modern) **St Mungo Museum of Religious Life and Art**. Across from it is Glasgow's oldest house, **Provand's Lordship**, built in 1471 as a manse for the former St Nicholas Hospital.

"The Clyde made Glasgow, and Glasgow made the Clyde", runs an old, but true, saying. In the 17th century, the city was seen as being wholy inland, and the river was so shallow that people could wade across it. But in 1768 a man called John Golborne began canalising and deepening it to allow large ships to sail right up into the city. The **Tall Ship at Glasgow Harbour** (see panel below) at Stobcross Road tells the story of the river and the industries it spawned. The centrepiece is the tall ship itself, the S.V. Glenlee, built in 1896. At Braehead, on the south side of the river, and a few miles downstream, is another museum, which celebrates the Clyde - **Clydebuilt**. It is part of the Scottish Maritime Museum (see also Irvine and Dumbarton), and tells the river's story from the 1700s up to the present day.

Close to the Tall Ship is the **Scottish Exhibition and Conference Centre**, a mammoth complex of halls and auditoriums, including what Glaswegians now refer to as the **Armadillo**, a metal and glass creation whose design owes more than a little to Sydney Opera House. And across the river from it is the city's newest attraction, the **Glasgow Science Centre**. Built on the site of the Glasgow Garden Festival, it is a combination of museum, laboratory and hands-on exhibition area that explores science and discovery, and has four floors featuring over 300 exhibits. The accompanying **Glasgow Tower** (closed for the foreseeable future) is Scotland's tallest freestanding structure at 412 feet, and there's also an **IMAX Theatre**.

Glasgow has always been a city of museums and art galleries, even when it was a city of industry. Like most large cities, its **West End** is where the well off built their mansions, as the prevailing southwesterly winds carried the smells of the city away from them. Here you'll find the **Kelvingrove Art Gallery and Museum** (closed for renovations until 2006), housed in a grand red sandstone building that froths with detail. It has internationally important collections on archaeology, botany, zoology, geology and all the other ologies you can think of. There are Egyptian mummies, fossils, stuffed animals, dinosaur skeletons, clothing and

The Tall Ship at Glasgow Harbour

100 Stobcross Road, Glasgow G3 8QQ
Tel: 0141 222 2513
e-mail: info@thetallship.com
website: www.thetallship.com

Sail through 100 years of maritime history at the **Tall Ship at Glasgow Harbour**. Follow the remarkable restoration of the Glenlee from an abandoned hulk in Seville harbour to her fullyrigged splendour today and learn about the living conditions aboard a deep sea trading ship. Explore the cargo hold where you will see what goods she carried, the deck house where the crew lived, the poop deck and the galley. Also in the harbour is the Pier 17 restaurant, a gift shop and various exhibitions and events. Phone for details.

The Clyde River

the gallery has paintings, furniture and interior design by Mackintosh and Whistler. At the top of Byres Road is the **Glasgow Botanic Gardens**, with at its centre the **Kibble Palace** (closed until 2005), a huge greenhouse with plants from all over the world. Within Victoria Park, further to

uniforms from all over the world, weapons, and a host of other material. The art collection is stunning, and is possibly the most comprehensive civic collection in Europe. While the Kelvingrove is closed, some of the paintings can now be seen in the **McLellan Galleries** in Sauchiehall Street, while some of the exhibits are on display at the **Open Museum** in Nitshill, on the south side of the river.

Across the road from it is the **Glasgow Museum of Transport**, with trains, carriages, motorcars and a marvellous collection of model ships. Perhaps the most striking display is the one on Glasgow's "underground" system. The system forms a simple loop round the city centre and West End, and in the late 70s was upgraded, with orange trains taking the place of the much-loved wood and metal ones. The Glaswegians immediately dubbed it the "Clockwork Orange" and the name has stuck. More properly, it is known as the **Glasgow Subway**, rather than "underground" or "metro".

Also in the West End, just off Byres Road (the area's trendiest street) are the **Hunterian Museum** and the **Hunterian Art Gallery**, which form part of Glasgow University. The museum has fine collections covering geology and numismatics, while

the west, is the **Fossil Grove** (open between April and September only), undoubtedly the city's most ancient attraction. It consists of fragments of an ancient forest over 330 million years old, which was discovered in 1887. They are housed within a small building to protect them.

The heart of Glasgow nowadays is **George Square,** a huge open space in front of the Victorian **City Chambers** (conducted tours available). There are statues galore, and it is a favourite place for city workers to relax in the sun. The City Chambers themselves reflect Glasgow's wealth and confidence in Victorian times, and so opulent are the interiors that they stood in for the Vatican in the film *Heavenly Pursuits*. Round the corner you'll find **Hutcheson's Hall** (National Trust for Scotland), founded in 1641 as a hospice, though the building itself is 18th century. It was designed by David Hamilton, and has a small exhibition about the **Merchant City**, that area that housed the homes and offices of the rich 17th and 18th century merchants who traded with America. Nowadays it is an area of expensive apartment blocks, smart bars, restaurants and pubs. Not far away, in Queen Street, is the **Gallery of Modern Art**, with four floors of work by modern artists such as Peter

Barony North Church, Glasgow

Howson, Beryl Cook and Sean Reid. In Buccleuch Street near Charing Cross, is the **Tenement House** (National Trust for Scotland). Built in the late 19th century, it re-creates the genteel tenement living conditions that were common among Glasgow's lower middle classes in the early 20th century. It is open between March and October.

Glasgow is synonymous with football, and at the redeveloped Hampden Park, on the south side of the Clyde, is the **Scottish Football Museum**. It reveals the sights, sounds and stories of the world's most popular game, and tells how it almost shaped the history of Glasgow in the late 19th and 20th centuries. You can see such things as the oldest football ticket in the world, the Scottish Cup trophy and Kenny Dalglish's 100th Scottish cap.

If you want to wallow in something typically Scottish, then the **College of Piping** in Otago Street has a small museum dedicated to Scotland's national instrument. Within the Caledonian University on Cowcaddens Road, not far away, is the **Heatherbank Museum of Social Work**. It has displays on housing, health and childcare, and looks at how socially excluded people were cared for in the past.

Charles Rennie Mackintosh is the most famous of Glasgow's architects, and was born in 1868. He designed a number of buildings in Glasgow, and there are organised tours taking you to the best of them arranged by the Charles Rennie Mackintosh Society. His most famous building is the **Glasgow School of Art** in Renfrew Street. It is still a working college, though tours are available by appointment. On the south side of the river is the **Scotland Street School**, now a museum dedicated to education. Another school is the **Martyr's Public School** in Parson Street, (no longer used as a school) and it is open to the public. The **Willow Tea Rooms** in Sauchiehall Street still sells traditional Scottish "high teas" amid Mackintosh's designs, and the **Queen's Cross Church** on Garscube Road is now the headquarters of the Charles Rennie Mackintosh Society. At Bellahouston Park, on the south side, is the **House for an Art Lover**, which interprets some of the incomplete designs Mackintosh submitted to a competition in a German magazine. **The Lighthouse**, Scotland's centre for architecture, design and the city, is in Mitchell Lane and has a Mackintosh interpretation centre. It is housed in a Mackintosh-designed building that was once the home of Glasgow's daily newspaper, the Herald. In the Hunterian Art Gallery there is also the **Mackintosh House**, featuring the principal rooms from Mackintosh's own house, together with a collection of designs and watercolours.

Another Glasgow architect, formerly overshadowed by Mackintosh but now more widely known, was Alexander Thomson, known as **"Greek" Thomson** because of the Greek influences in his work (see also Balfron). He lived in the 19th century, and **St Vincent Street Church** was designed by him, as was **Holmwood House** (National Trust for Scotland) in Netherlee Road, south of the river.

Perhaps Glasgow's most famous modern attraction is the **Burrell Collection**, housed in a purpose built complex of galleries in **Pollok Country Park**, south of the river. William Burrell (see also Largs and Hutton Castle) gifted a huge collection of art and historical objects to the city of Glasgow, and now over 8,000 of them are on display. A whole day could be spent going round the collection. Also in the park is **Pollok House** (National Trust for Scotland), a Georgian mansion that houses the Stirling Maxwell collection of decorative arts.

Glasgow Green, a huge area of parkland, near the city's east end, is "Glasgow's lung". It has been common land for centuries, and it was here that Charles Edward Stuart mustered his troops during the Jacobite Uprising when he occupied the city. Now it is the city's largest park, with its centrepiece being the **People's Palace**, a museum which tells the city's own story. On its eastern edge is one of the city's most colourful buildings - **Templeton's Carpet Factory** (now a business centre). It is based on a Venetian design, with walls that incorporate multi-coloured bricks.

Glasgow is Britain's second largest shopping centre, the three main shopping streets being Argyle Street, Sauchiehall Street and Buchanan Street. There are also enormous shopping malls. The **St Enoch Centre** is just off Argyle Street, the **Buchanan Galleries** are at the corner of Buchanan Street and Sauchiehall Street, while the **Braehead Shopping Centre** is south of the river on the city's western fringes, near Renfrew. There's also the **Forge** at Parkhead, in the east end.

Within the city centre there are two exclusive retail developments. **Princes Square**, off Buchanan Street, is a mix of upmarket shops and cafés, while the **Italian Centre** is where you'll find Armani, Versace and other prestige shops.

In Sauchiehall Street is the **Regimental Museum of the Royal Highland Fusiliers**. It is Scotland's second oldest infantry regiment, and was formed in the 1960s when the Highland Light Infantry amalgamated with the Royal Scottish Fusiliers.

Around Glasgow

Kirkintilloch

7 miles NE of Glasgow city centre on the A803

The old burgh of Kirkintilloch sits on the

THE COUNTRY INN

Queenzieburn, Kilsyth G65 GEA
Tel: 01236 822379 Fax: 01236 827569

The pleasant **Country Inn** is housed in a modern yet attractive building, and offers good food and drink at remarkably competitive prices. This is the ideal place to stop off when you are heading north or south, and is just a few miles from the A80 Glasgow/ Stirling road.

The cuisine is a mixture of European and Asian, with some traditional Scottish dishes, and the bar serves a fine range of beers, wines, spirits and liqueurs, with soft drinks should you be driving. It also serves bar meals which are tasty and beautifully cooked. For a relaxing meal or drink, this is the place for you!

Forth and Clyde Canal, which has recently been re-opened after a multi-million pound face lift. It connects the Firth of Clyde and the Firth of Forth, with a further canal, the union Canal, connecting it to Edinburgh. The **Auld Kirk Museum** is housed in the former parish church, which dates from 1644. In **Peel Park** are some Roman remains from the Antonine Wall.

Cumbernauld

12 miles NE of Glasgow off the A80

Cumbernauld is one of Scotland's new towns, and the setting for the 1981 film *Gregory's Girl*. It sits on a hill above the A80, and has an indoor shopping centre. **Palacerigg Country Park** covers 750 acres, and is to the south east of the town. The town was established in the 1950s on what was a bleak upland farm. Though it sits to the north east of Glasgow, Cumbernauld, like Kirkintilloch, was once in a detached part of Dunbartonshire.

Rutherglen

2 miles SE of Glasgow city centre on the A749

This royal burgh is one of the oldest in Scotland, having been granted its royal charter by David I in the 12th century. For a short while the burgh was incorporated into the city of Glasgow, something that was greatly resented by some of its citizens, but it now forms part of South Lanarkshire. A gable of its medieval **Parish Church** survives in the kirkyard of its more modern successor. Robbie Coltrane the actor is a native of the town.

Newton Mearns

7 miles S of Glasgow on the A77

Newton Mearns is a commuter town of smart bungalows and substantial houses. The foursquare Parish Church dates from 1755, and close by is Greenbank House (National Trust for Scotland) surrounded by beautiful gardens. The house is not open to the public.

Clydebank

7 miles W of Glasgow city centre on the A814

Clydebank is a former shipbuilding town, and it was here that the *Queen Mary*, the *Queen Elizabeth* and the *Queen Elizabeth II* were built. The town suffered more damage in proportion to its size than any other British town from air raids in World War II. In early 1941, during the Clydebank Blitz, the centre of the town was flattened, other parts severely damaged and many people were killed. The **Clydebank Museum** at the Town Hall in Dumbarton Road has exhibits devoted to the Blitz, as well as to the former Singer sewing machine factory, which once stood in the town.

Paisley

5 miles W of Glasgow city centre on the A761

Paisley Cathedral

The large town of Paisley is centred on the great Abbey Church of Saints Mary the Virgin, James the Greater of Compostella, Mirin and Milburga, otherwise known as **Paisley Abbey**. It was founded in the 12th century by Walter FitzAlan, first High Steward of Scotland and progenitor of the Stewart dynasty. Within its walls are the tombs of most of the non-royal High Stewards, as well as that of Princess Marjory, daughter of Robert the Bruce, who married Walter, the sixth High Steward, and their grandson Robert III. It can legitimately claim to be the birthplace of the Stewart dynasty, because Robert II, the first Stewart king, was born here in 1316. Marjory had been seriously injured in a riding accident nearby and she was brought to the abbey, where she died soon after giving birth to her son.

The building as you see it now was built from the 12th century onwards, though the bulk dates from the 15th century. The choir was rebuilt in the early 1900s. Within the abbey is a memorial to **John Witherspoon**, a former minister the Laigh Kirk, who signed the American Declaration of Independence. A statue of him can also be found in front of **Paisley University** (see also Gifford).

Another famous Paisley church is the Baptist **Thomas Coats Memorial Church**, sometimes known as the "Baptist Cathedral" because of its size. It was built in 1894 in memory of Thomas Coats of the Coats and Clark thread making firm. The same Thomas Coats gifted the **Coats Observatory** to the town's Philosophical Institution in 1883. It is now open to the public. Adjacent is **Paisley Museum and Art Galleries**, with displays of Paisley shawls and other memorabilia.

Paisley was the birthplace of many famous people. **Tom Conti** the actor was born here, as was **John Byrne** the artist and writer (whose most famous work is undoubtedly the TV series *Tutti Frutti*), **Andrew Neill**, now editor of the Scotsman, **Gerry Rafferty** the singer and **Fulton Mackay** of *Porridge* fame.

At the Corner of Shuttle Street and George Place are the 18th century weaving cottages known as **Sma' Shot Cottages**, housing an interpretation centre which gives an insight into the living conditions of Paisley weaving families in the past. Nearby, in New Street, is **Paisley Arts Centre**, housed in the former Laigh Kirk of 1738.

In the 18th century, the town was famed for its poets, the most famous being Robert Tannahill, who was born in **Tannahill Cottage** in Queen Street in 1774. He was a silk weaver who wrote the words to such beautiful songs as "Jessie the Flower o' Dunblane" and "The Braes o' Gleniffer". The actual braes themselves now form part of the **Gleniffer Braes Country Park**, just outside the town.

BARRS OF CLOAK

by Lochwinnoch, Renfrewshire PA12 4LB
Tel: 0845 2260167
Tel/Fax: 01505 842252 & 843001
e-mail: info@barrs-of-cloak.co.uk
website: www.barrs-of-cloak.co.uk

Barrs of Cloak is set within two acres of natural garden, and has two three-star self catering flats on offer that are comfortable, smart and affordable. The West Flat has a large lounge with dining area, kitchen and open fire, and has a double settee bed and overhead bunk. In addition, there is a separate double bedroom and bathroom. The Studio Flat is open plan, with a double bed being accessed by ladder, while the other two sofa beds fold up to become daytime settees. There is also a bathroom and shower. Both flats come well equipped with TV, radio, video recorder, telephone, hair dryer and shaving points.

Jenny's Well Local Nature Reserve, on the south bank of the White Cart Water, is less than a mile from the centre of the town, and is locked between a council estate and a chemicals factory. For all that, it is a haven for wildlife with some pleasant walks. To the north of Paisley, on the other side of the M8, is **Glasgow International Airport**.

The village of Elderslie, a mile west of the town, is the supposed birthplace of William Wallace, and the **Wallace Memorial** explains his exploits.

Lochwinnoch

16 miles SW of Glasgow on the B786

The **Clyde Muirsheil Regional Park** covers 100 square miles of magnificent countryside from Greenock to Inverkip and down into Ayrshire. It is ideal for walking, cycling, fishing and observing wildlife. There is also sailing on Castle Simple Loch.

Kilbarchan

11 miles SW of Glasgow, off the A761

This is undoubtedly the most picturesque village in Renfrewshire, and is a huddle of old 18th century weaving cottages. **The Weaver's Cottage** (National Trust for Scotland) dates from 1723, and shows what a typical weaver's cottage (complete with working loom) was like.

Renfrew

5 miles W of Glasgow on the A8

The ancient burgh of Renfrew was granted its charter in 1143, making it one of the oldest in Scotland. It was here, in 1164, that the **Battle of Renfrew** took place

Weaver's Cottage, Kilbarchan

between Somerled, Lord of the Isles, and the royal army of Malcolm IV led by Walter FitzAlan, founder of Paisley Abbey. This battle brought the Western Isles fully under the control of the monarchy.

The **Renfrew Community Museum** in Canal Street was opened in 1997 to coincide with the 600th anniversary of the town being granted royal burgh status. It has displays of local history

Bearsden and Milngavie

6 miles NW of Glasgow city centre on the A809 and A81

These two prosperous towns are firmly within Glasgow's inner commuting belt, and are full of large Victorian and Edwardian mansions as well as the more modest bungalows of the 1930s. The **Antonine Wall** (named after Roman Emperor Antoninus Pius) passes close by (see also Falkirk). It was built of turf in the 2nd century to keep out the warring tribesmen of the north, and stretched for 37 miles between the Clyde and the Forth. In Bearsden there are the remains of a **Roman Bathhouse** (see also Falkirk).

Mugdock Country Park sits off the A81 north of Milngavie (pronounced "Mull-guy"), which is the starting point for the 95-mile long **West Highland Way**, which connects the Glasgow conurbation with Fort William.

The Lillie Art Gallery, in Station Road Milngavie, has a collection of 20th century Scottish paintings, including works by the Scottish Colourists and Joan Eardley.

Dumbarton

The town is dominated by **Dumbarton Castle** (Historic Scotland), high on a volcanic plug 240 feet above the Firth of Clyde. It is one of the oldest fortified sites in Britain, and was the capital of the ancient Dark Age kingdom of Strathclyde, which wasn't incorporated into Scotland until the 11th century. The name itself means the "Fort of the Britons", and though

The Carbeth Inn

Stockiemuir Road, Blanefield,
Stirlingshire G63 9AY
Tel: 01360 770002

The **Carbeth Inn** is an old, picturesque coaching inn dating from 1816. It features in Sir Walter Scott's novel *Rob Roy*, as it was where Baillie Nicol Jarvie, a Glasgow magistrate, stayed when travelling to visit him. In the book it is the "halfway house", described as a "most miserable alehouse". Nowdays the inn is certainly not miserable at all! The whole place has an "olde worlde" feel about it, with many period features such as exposed beams and slab floors in the public bar. This is the perfect place to relax with a quiet drink and there is a fine selection of real ales, beers, wines, liqueurs and spirits, including (this being Scotland!) single malts.

At the front of the inn is a popular beer garden that is both colourful and inviting, and there is nothing better on a sunny day than sitting here watching the world go by as you unwind from the stresses of modern life. The inn boasts two non-smoking restaurants, each one reflecting the period atmosphere and history of the building, and each serving wonderful food between 10 am to 9 pm seven days a week. There is no frozen produce used in the kitchens here! Everything - poultry, vegetables, meat and pasta - is all sourced locally, and is fresh and tasty. Try the wide range of baked potatoes, for instance, or the steaks, or the freshly baked home-made pies.

The inn stands in the shadow of the Campsie Hills here, though no more than twelve miles from the centre of Glasgow. It's a pleasant spot and one where you'll surely wish to stop.

Dumbarton Castle

the town is called Dumbarton, the former county is Dunbartonshire, with an "n". The castle now mainly consists of modern barracks, but there is still plenty to see, including a 12th century gateway, a dungeon and a museum. From the top there is a splendid view out over the Firth of Clyde. It was from Dumbarton in 1548 that Mary Queen of Scots set sail for France and her eventual marriage to the Dauphin, Francis. This was considered to be much safer than leaving from an east coast port, as Henry VIII's ships were patrolling the North Sea. The English king had wanted Mary to marry his son Henry, and when the Scottish parliament refused to ratify such an agreement, Henry tried unsuccessfully to force the marriage, a period known as the "Rough Wooing".

The **Denny Tank Museum** in Castle Street forms part of the Scottish Maritime Museum (see also Glasgow and Irvine). It is the oldest experimental water tank in the world, and is the length of a football pitch. It was built in 1882 as part of Denny's shipyard (whose most famous ship was undoubtedly the tea clipper the "Cutty Sark", and it was here that hull shapes were tested in water using carefully crafted models before the ships themselves were built. On display are many of the models built by the craftsmen of the Denny yard.

In Church Street is an old archway called the **College Bow** once part of the long gone Collegiate Church of St Mary.

On the hillside above the town is the beautiful **Overtoun Estate**, with wonderful views over the Firth. It was bequeathed to the people of Dumbarton by Douglas White, a London doctor, in 1939. **Old Kilpatrick**, to the west of the town, is supposed to be the birthplace of St Patrick (though Wales is a likelier location), who was captured by raiders and taken to Ireland in the 4th century.

Around Dumbarton

Balloch

4 miles N of Dumbarton on the A811

This pleasant town sits at the point where the River Leven (at five miles long, Scotland's shortest river) leaves **Loch Lomond** on its way to Dumbarton and the Clyde. The loch is recognised as Scotland's largest and most beautiful sheet of water, covering over 27 square miles. The **Loch Lomond and the Trossachs National Park** was Scotland's first national park, opened in 2002, and **Lomond Shores** at Balloch includes the National Park Gateway.

The loch is at its widest to the south. It gradually narrows and gets deeper as it goes north, and at some points it reaches a depth of over 600 feet, making it the third deepest loch in Scotland. Many songs have been written about this stretch of water, the most famous being the *Bonnie, Bonnie Banks o' Loch Lomond*. It was written by a Jacobite prisoner held in Carlisle Castle who was due to be executed. He is telling a fellow prisoner whose life had been spared that he (the condemned man) will be in Scotland before him because he will take the "low road", i.e., the road of death, while his colleague will take the "high road", or the road of life.

At the nearby village of **Gartocharn** is **Duncryne Hill** (nicknamed "The Dumpling" by locals), where you get a marvellous view, not just of the loch, but also of the surrounding countryside. The **Highland Boundary Fault**, which separates the Lowlands of Scotland from the Highlands, passes through Loch Lomond

from Glen Fruin on the west to Balmaha on the east. The **Balloch Castle Country Park**, north east of Balloch, has lochside walks, gardens and a visitor centre. South from the town you can follow the **Leven Valley Heritage Trail**, taking you down the valley of the Leven to Dumbarton, passing such small industrial towns as **Alexandria** and **Renton**.

In Alexandria is the **Antartex Village Visitor Centre**. It incorporates a factory making sheepskin coats (with factory tours available), a mill shop and a small craft village. Close by is the **Loch Lomond Factory Outlets and Motoring Memories Museum**, housed in a magnificent building where one of Scotland's former makes of car, the "Argyll", was manufactured.

Cardross

4 miles W of Dumbarton on the A814

Geilston Gardens (National Trust for Scotland) surround a late 17th century house (not open to the public) to the east of the town. Also at Cardross is **St Mahew's Chapel**, dating from 1294. It was at Cardross Castle (now gone) that Robert the Bruce died in 1329.

Helensburgh

9 miles W of Dumbarton on the A814

Helensburgh now finds itself within Argyll, though att one time it was in Dunbartonshire. It was founded in the 18th century by Sir James Colquhoun of Luss, and named after his wife Helen. **John Logie Baird**, the inventor of television, was born in this lively holiday resort in 1888. It is one of the ports of call in July and August for the **PS Waverley**, the world's last ocean-going paddle steamer.

In Upper Colquhoun Street you'll find one of Charles Rennie Mackintosh's masterpieces - the **Hill House** (National Trust for Scotland - see panel below). It was commissioned by Walter Blackie, the

The Hill House

Upper Colquhoun Street,
Helensburgh G84 9AJ
Tel: 01436 673900 Fax: 01436 674685
website: www.nts.org.uk

The finest of Charles Rennie Mackintosh's domestic creations, **The Hill House** sits high above the Clyde, commanding fine views over the river estuary. Walter Blackie, director of the well known Glasgow publishers, commissioned not only the house and garden but much of the furniture and all the interior fittings and decorative schemes. Mackintosh's wife, Margaret MacDonald, contributed fabric designs and a unique gesso overmantel. The overall effect is daring, but restrained in its elegance: the result, timeless rooms, as modern today as they must have been in 1904 when the Blackie family moved in.

An information room interprets the special relationship between architect and patron and provides a historical context for Inspirations, a dazzling exhibition in the upper east wing and the gardens. It brings together exceptional pieces of domestic design by great living designers, all of whom, in some way, pay homage to Mackintosh's elegance and invention, Inspiring comparisons may be drawn between the work of Mackintosh, now recognised as one of the geniuses of the early 20th century, and pieces that themselves have become 21st century icons.

The gardens have been restored to their former glory, and reflect features common to Mackintosh's architectural designs, They also contain a kinetic sculpture given to the house by the artist George Rickey.

Glasgow publisher, in 1902, and contains some of Mackintosh's finest work. For not only did he design the building, he also designed the interior decoration, the fittings and most of the furniture. There are also small gardens surrounding the house.

North of Helensburgh is **Glen Fruin**, which has a narrow road that takes you over to Loch Lomond. It was the scene of a battle in 1603 when the MacGregors defeated the Colquhouns with much loss of life.

Luss

11 miles N of Dumbarton off the A82

This beautiful little village - one of the loveliest in Scotland - was once the setting for Scottish Television's soap opera *High Road*, where it was called Glendarroch. It's an estate village built by the Colquhoun family, and sits on the banks of Loch Lomond. On the opposite shore, the mighty bulk of **Ben Lomond** can be seen. It is the most southerly of Scotland's "Munros", or mountains over 3,000 feet, and is a comfortable climb if you're reasonably fit and active. The **Parish Church of St MacKessog** is well worth a visit.

Garelochhead

14 miles NW of Dumbarton off the A814

This old village at the head of the beautiful **Gare Loch** now finds itself in Argyll for administrative purposes. However, along with the picturesque **Rosneath Peninsula**, it was once part of the old county of Dunbartonshire, and it is to Dumbarton that it still looks for shopping and other services. It makes a fine centre for hill walking, bird watching and yachting. At **Cove**, on the Rosneath Peninsula, are the **Linn Botanical Gardens**.

Greenock

Situated on the south bank of the Firth of Clyde, at a point known as **The Tail of the Bank**, Greenock is a bustling industrial town and port. It was the birthplace, in 1736, of **James Watt**, who perfected the steam engine. Hills pile up behind the town, and on the slopes of Lyle Hill is a huge **Cross of Lorraine** mounted on an anchor, which was built in 1946, It commemorates the Free French sailors who lost their lives on the Atlantic during World War II.

Customhouse Quay was the departure point for thousands of Scottish emigrants sailing away to America in the 19th and early 20th centuries. The nearby **Custom House**, built in 1810, reflects the port's importance in bygone days, and it now houses a museum. Another museum is the **McLean Museum and Art Gallery** on Kelly Street, which features exhibits on local history as well as paintings by Courbin, Boudin and the Scottish Colourists.

In Greenock cemetery is the grave of **Highland Mary**, whose real name was Mary Campbell (see also Failford and Dunoon). Burns had met her at a low point in his life in Mauchline, and had asked her to accompany him to the West Indies when he thought of emigrating. However, on a trip home to Dunoon to make arrangements for her departure, she died. She was previously buried in the kirkyard of the former Old West Kirk, but was exhumed and reburied in 1920. When the Old West Kirk, which dated from the late 16th century, was dismantled in 1926, some of its stones were used to build the new **Old West Kirk**, on the Esplanade. It has some wonderful stained glass and woodcarving.

Around Greenock

Port Glasgow

4 miles E of Greenock on the A8

Before the Clyde at Glasgow was canalised and deepened, this town was Glasgow's main port. **Newark Castle** (Historic Scotland) lies close to the riverbank, and dates from the 16th and 17th centuries. It

View of Greenock from Lyle Hill

was built by George Maxwell in the late 15th century, and upgraded to what you see today by its most notorious owner, Sir Patrick Maxwell, in 1597. He was a friend of James VI who murdered two members of his own family and treated his wife so badly that she eventually left him. Up until the 1980s the castle was completely surrounded by shipyards, testament to the importance of this industry to the town at one time.

Two miles west of Port Glasgow is the **Finlaystone Estate**, where the present head of the Clan Macmillan lives. It is open to the public, and features gardens and 140 acres of woodland, which can be explored. Finlaystone House, at the heart of the estate, dates back to the 14th century, though it has been extended over the centuries. It can be visited by special arrangement.

Gourock

2 miles W of Greenock town centre on the A770

This little holiday resort is now more or less a suburb of Greenock, though at one time it was a separate burgh. It is on a most attractive part of the Clyde, opposite Kilcreggan, the Gareloch and the entrance to Loch Long, where the mountains tumble down towards the sea. The Firth of Clyde is a famous yachting area, and the town is the home of the **Royal Gourock Yacht Club**, which is situated near the Promenade. At Cloch Point, four miles to the southwest, is the **Cloch Lighthouse** of 1797, a famous landmark for ships sailing on the Clyde. Between Castle Gardens and Kempock Street in the town is the curiously named **Granny Kempock's Stone**, which dates from prehistoric times. It is shaped like a cloaked figure, and to walk round it is said to bring good luck. The town is the ferry terminal for Dunoon, across the Clyde in Argyll.

Hamilton

Hamilton was once the county town of Lanarkshire, Scotland's most populous and industrialised county. It became a royal burgh in 1548, though it lost this status in 1669. It is very much connected with one of the most important families in Scotland, the Dukes of Hamilton, Scotland's premier dukes. Up until the 1920s, when it was demolished, the immense Hamilton Palace, home to the dukes, was the grandest non-royal residence in Britain. Not a stone now remains of it above ground, though the Hamilton's burial place, the grandiose **Hamilton Mausoleum**, still remains. It is a curious building with an immense dome, and is full of Masonic symbolism. It consists of a chapel above and a crypt below, and was built in the mid 19th century for Alexander, the 10th Duke, who had his ancestors removed from what was left of the old Collegiate Church of Hamilton (now gone) and re-interred in the crypt. When he himself died, he was laid to rest in the sarcophagus of an ancient Egyptian princess, which subsequently reposed in the chapel. The bodies were all removed in 1921, and the place can now be visited. The place was never used as a chapel, however, as it is reckoned to have the longest echo of any building in Britain. One thing to note is that the crypt doors lock from the inside. The reason is simple - once a month a servant was sent from the Palace to dust and clean the coffins. To prevent ghoulish sightseers, she locked herself in.

A two-mile long Grand Avenue once stretched from the palace all the way to **Chatelherault**, a hunting lodge east of the town. Most of the avenue is gone, but Chatelherault survives, having been refurbished in the 1980s in the largest refurbishment project of its time in Britain. It was originally designed by William Adam and dates from the 1730s. The lodge once also housed the Duke's hunting dogs, and was therefore known as the "Dog Kennels". Now it houses a museum and interpretation centre. The lodge got its name because the Dukes of Hamilton were also the Dukes of Chatelherault (the French spelling of the name) near Poitou in France. The title was bestowed in 1548 by Henry II of France in recognition of the part the family played in arranging the marriage of Mary Stuart to his son Francis, the Dauphin. The spelling of the name changed over the years, and Chatellerault gradually became Chatelherault. Surrounding the lodge is **Chatelherault Country Park**, with over ten miles of woodland walks. The ruins of **Cadzow Castle**, the original home of the Hamiltons, and where Mary Stuart once stayed, can be see within the park. There are also the remains of an old **Iron Age Fort** and the **Cadzow Oaks**, which are very old. In a field in front of Chatelherault is a small but famous herd of **White Cattle**.

Hamilton Parish Church, within the town, was designed by William Adam in the early 1730s at the same time as he was designing Chatelherault. It is an elegant building in the shape of a Greek cross, with a cupola over the crossing. The pre-Norman **Netherton Cross** stands at the church entrance, and in the kirkyard is the **Heads Monument**, commemorating four Covenanters beheaded in Edinburgh after the Pentland Rising of 1666. In Almada Street you'll find the town's most prominent landmark - the **County Buildings**. They were built in the 1960s for the then Lanarkshire County Council, and were modelled on the United Nations building in New York. It is one of the few 1960s buildings in Scotland to be listed.

Based on an old 17th century coaching inn once known as the Hamilton Arms is the **Low Parks Museum**, which has displays and memorabilia on local history. It also houses a large display on Lanarkshire's own regiment - the **Cameronians (Scottish Rifles).** Raised as a Covenanting force in the 17th century, it

Chatelherault House and Gardens

chose to disband itself in 1968 rather than amalgamate with another regiment (see also Douglas). Most of the Low Parks, which at one time formed some of Hamilton Palace's parkland, has been given over to a huge retail development that includes a multi-screen cinema.

In the Bent Cemetery is the simple grave of one of Scotland's best-known entertainers, **Sir Harry Lauder**. At one time he worked in the coalmines in Quarter, a mining village near the town (see also Strathaven). Nearby is the plot where the members of the Hamilton family who formerly lay in the Mausoleum are now buried. The10th Duke, who had the Mausoleum built, still lies in his Egyptian sarcophagus.

Hamilton is the start of one of Scotland's ten national tourist routes, the **Clyde Valley Tourist Route**. It follows the Clyde Valley all the way south to Abington on the M74.

Around Hamilton

Airdrie and Coatbridge

7 miles N of Hamilton on the A89

The twin towns of Airdrie and Coatbridge are industrial in character. In Coatbridge, in 1889, was born **John Reith**, first general manager of what was then the British Broadcasting Company. Single-handedly he shaped the character of the organisation. The town is home to the **Summerlee Heritage Centre**, which traces the history of the area's old industries - steel making, coalmining and the manufacture of heavy plant. Tramlines have been laid out in it, and there is a small collection of trams from all over Europe. There is also a short section of the Summerlee branch of the **Monkland Canal** (now closed), which ran from Glasgow to the Lanarkshire coalfields. The canal was built between 1770 and 1794, and at one time was the most profitable in Scotland.

The **Time Capsule** is one of the largest leisure centres in the area. In the **Drumpellier Country Park** there is a visitor centre, butterfly house, formal gardens, golf course and pets' corner.

Motherwell and Wishaw

3 miles E of Hamilton on the A721

The twin towns of Motherwell and Wishaw were, up until 1975, included in the one burgh. They were steel making towns, though the steelworks at Ravenscraig have now gone. The award-winning **Motherwell Heritage Centre** on High Road has a number of exhibitions, and hosts varied activities with a heritage theme. To the west of Motherwell, adjoining the M74, is the 1100 acres of **Strathclyde Country Park**, built on waste ground in the early 70s. Within it there is an international size rowing lake where the rowing events of the 1986 Commonwealth Games were held. On its banks are the remains of a **Roman Bathhouse**. There are guided walks throughout the year, as well as nature trails and a camping and caravanning site. **M&D's Theme Park** is located near the north banks of the loch.

A mile north east of Motherwell is the small industrial village of Carfin, where you will find the **Carfin Pilgrimage Centre and Grotto**, created in the 1920s by Fr. Thomas Nimmo Taylor the local priest and out-of-work miners, and inspired by Lourdes. There are displays and exhibits that help explain the notion of pilgrimage, not just in the Roman Catholic religion, but also in all major religions.

The **Shotts Heritage Centre** is in Benhar Road in Shotts, eight miles to the west of Motherwell and Wishaw. There are displays on the history of this former mining town.

Dalserf

7 miles SE of Hamilton town centre off the A72

Once a sizeable village with inns and a ferry across the Clyde, Dalserf has now shrunk to no more than a few cottages and a church. **Dalserf Parish Church**, with its whitewashed walls, looks more like a house than a place of worship, and dates from 1655, though an ancient chapel dedicated to St Serf stood here before that. The building is a rare survivor of a mid-17th century Scottish church. Most from that period were simply built, with earth floors and a thatched roof. In the 18th and 19th centuries they were usually demolished to make way for something more imposing. Dalserf has lasted because the parish was a poor one, which couldn't afford to rebuild, preferring instead to upgrade whenever it could. In the kirkyard is a pre-Norman "hogs back" grave slab, which was dug up in 1897, and also a memorial to the **Revd John Macmillan**, sometimes called "the last of the Covenanters". He died in 1753.

Stonehouse

6 miles S of Hamilton on the A71

This former weaving village still has rows of 18th and 19th century small weaving cottages. On one side of the main door is a large window, which allows plenty of light into the room, which housed the loom, and on the other is small window, which allowed light to enter the main living quarters.

Patrick Hamilton, Scotland's first Protestant martyr, was born in Stonehouse in about 1503. He was burned at the stake in St Andrews in 1527 (see also St Andrews). The **Alexander Hamilton Memorial Park** was opened in 1925, the gift of a local man. It has a bandstand, which was originally made for the Great Glasgow Exhibition of 1911.

The remains of the Old **St Ninian's Parish Church** are to the north of the village, surrounded by an old kirkyard. A prehistoric burial kist was once dug up in the kirkyard, showing that the site may have had a religious significance long before Christianity came to the area.

Strathaven

7 miles S of Hamilton on the A723

Strathaven (pronounced "Stray-ven") is a real gem of a small town that sits at the heart of Avondale. The ruins of **Strathaven Castle** are all that is left of a once large and powerful 14th century stronghold. It was built by the Douglas family, passed to the Stewarts, and eventually came into the hands of the Hamiltons. A legend says that before the Reformation, a wife of one of the owners was walled up alive in the castle, and when parts of a wall fell down in the 19th century, human bones were found among the rubble. On the edge of the **John Hastie Park** is the **John Hastie Museum**, which has local history collections.

To the west of the town, at Drumclog, was fought the **Battle of Drumclog**, where an army of Covenanters overcame government troops in 1679. A memorial on a minor road off the A71 commemorates the event. At the small village of Sandford, two miles to the south, are the lovely 50-feet high **Spectacle E'e** Falls on the Kype Water, a tributary of the Avon.

East Kilbride

5 miles W of Hamilton on the A726

East Kilbride is the largest and undoubtedly the most successful of Scotland's new towns. Work started on laying it out in 1947 round an old village, and now it has a population of about 70,000. It is renowned for its shopping facilities, and has four shopping malls, **Princes Mall**, the **Plaza**, the **Olympia Centre** and **Centre West**, which together make one of the largest undercover shopping areas in Scotland.

In the Calderwood area of the town is **Hunter House**, birthplace in the 18th century of the Hunter Brothers, pioneering surgeons who worked in both Glasgow and London. The Hunterian Museum in Glasgow is one of their legacies. The house now has a small display and museum about the two men and their lives

On the outskirts of the town is **Calderglen Country Park**, based on Torrance House (not open to the public). It has play areas, nature trails and a children's zoo. To the north of the town is the **James Hamilton Heritage Park**, with a 16-acre boating loch. Behind it is the restored **Mains Castle** (not open to the public), which was built by the Lindsay family in the early 15th century and subsequently sold to the Stuarts of Torrance. Up until the 1970s it was a ruin. Close by is the **Scottish Museum of Country Life**, based around Wester Kittochside Farm, which had been home to the Reid family since the 16th century. In 1992, the last of the family, Margaret Reid, gifted it to the National Trust for Scotland. Run jointly by the National Museums of Scotland and the National Trust, it explains rural life in Scotland throughout the ages, and has a huge collection of farm implements and machinery. The elegant farmhouse of Wester Kittochside, which dates from 1783, is also open to the public.

Eaglesham

9 miles W of Hamilton on the B764

The conservation village of Eaglesham was planned and built by the Earl of Eglinton in the mid 1700s. It is shaped like a huge "A", with the point facing the moorland to the west of the village. Between the two arms of the "A" is a large village green area known as the "Orry", on which once stood a cotton mill. The lovely period cottages and houses in the village make a perfect picture of Scottish rural life, though the village has largely been colonised by commuters from Glasgow. The **Parish Church**, which dates from 1788, has the look of an Alpine church about it, and it is reckoned that while planning Eaglesham the 10th Earl was influenced by villages he had admired in northern Italy.

It was in a field near Eaglesham in 1941 that **Rudolph Hess**, Hitler's deputy, landed after he parachuted (while the plane was upside down) from an ME 110. He was found by a local farmer called David McLean, who took him home and treated him firmly but politely. Hess gave his name as Alfred Horn, but it was soon established that he was Hitler's deputy. He said he was on a secret mission to speak to the Duke of Hamilton, and a map he possessed showed that he had been trying to reach Dungavel House, one of the Duke's hunting lodges near Strathaven.

He was then taken to Maryhill Barracks in Glasgow, where he was sometimes in the custody of Corporal William Ross, who went on to become the Secretary of State for Scotland in the Wilson government. Hess was later moved to Buchanan Castle near Drymen in Stirlingshire, where he was interrogated (see also Drymen).

Bothwell

2 miles NW of Hamilton off the M74

In the centre of this small town is **St Bride's Parish Church**, with a chancel dating from 1398. It was built as part of a collegiate church by Archibald the Grim, 3rd Earl of Douglas, and has a roof made entirely of stone. A year after it was built, it was the scene of a royal wedding when David, son of Robert III, married Archibald the Grim's daughter Marjory. Outside the west end of the Victorian nave is a monument to **Joanna Baillie**, a playwright and poetess born at Bothwell manse in 1762. She was praised by Scott as being one of the finest writers of the 18th century.

On the banks of the Clyde, some distance from the town, are the massive and impressive remains of **Bothwell Castle** (Historic Scotland), which historians have rated as one of the most important secular medieval buildings in Scotland. It was most likely built in the 13th century by Walter de Moravia, who was granted the lands of Bothwell by Alexander II. It later passed to the Douglas family, who rebuilt and strengthened most of it. In the 15th century, when James II overthrew the Douglases, it passed to the crown. Upstream is Bothwell Bridge, scene, in 1679, of the **Battle of Bothwell Bridge** between the Royalist forces of the Duke of Monmouth and a Covenanting army. The Covenanters were heavily defeated, with over 500 being killed and 1,200 taken prisoner. The bridge you see today is basically the same bridge, though much altered and widened. A memorial commemorates the event.

Blantyre

3 miles NW of Hamilton on the A724

Blantyre is a former mining town, which nowadays is visited because of the **David Livingstone Centre** (National Trust for Scotland). Here, at Shuttle Row, was born in 1813 the African explorer and missionary David Livingstone. A great cotton mill stood here, and Shuttle Row was a tenement block that housed some of the workers. The great man was born in a one-room flat, though the whole tenement has now been given over to housing displays and mementos about his life and work.

Lanark

Set above the Clyde Valley near the upper reaches of the Clyde, the ancient royal burgh of Lanark is an historic town that has its roots deep in the heart of Scotland's history. Every year, in June, the town celebrates **Lanimer Day**, which originated as a ceremony of riding the bounds of the burgh.

High on a wall of the 18th century **St Nicholas's Church** is a statue of William Wallace the Scottish freedom fighter. It recalls an event, which took place when the town's castle (now gone) was garrisoned by English troops. Wallace committed some act or other that brought him to the attention of the English sheriff of Lanark, Sir William Hesselrig. He fled, and when Wallace's wife (some versions say girlfriend) refused to divulge where he was, Hesselrig killed her and her household. Wallace later returned and killed the sheriff in revenge. The supposed site of **Wallace's House** is now marked by a plaque near the church.

In the Westport you'll find the **Royal Burgh of Lanark Museum**, which explains the incident, as well as the town's history. Near the centre of the town are the ruins of the original place of worship, **St Kentigern's Church**. In its kirkyard is buried **William Smellie** (pronounced Smillie), the father of modern midwifery, who died in 1763.

On the banks of the Clyde below Lanark lies the village and UNESCO World Heritage Site of **New Lanark**. It was here, in 1785, that David Dale (see also Stewarton) founded a cotton mill and village of 2,500 people that became a model for social reform. Under his son-in-law **Robert Owen**, who was manager, there were good working conditions, decent

River Clyde, New Lanark

homes, fair wages, schools and health care.

The mills were still in production up to 1968, but now the village has been turned into one great museum and interpretation centre. Under the care of the New Lanark Conservation Trust, it has become one of the most popular tourist destinations in Scotland, even though people still live in some of the original tenements and cottages.

Attractions include a **Visitors Centre** (including a Textile Machinery Exhibition and the New Millennium Ride that introduces you to Robert Owen's original vision), the **Millworker's House**, the **Village Store Exhibition** and **Robert Owen's House**. Other buildings have been converted into craft workshops, and there is also a hotel housed in a former mill. A presentation called **Annie McLeod's Story** is shown in what was **Robert Owen's School**, and uses the latest in 3-D technology. The "ghost" of 18th century mill girl Annie Macleod returns to tell the story of her life in the days of Robert Owen. Also in the village is a **Scottish Wildlife Trust Visitors Centre**.

The mills were at one time powered by the Clyde, and close by are the **Falls of Clyde** waterfalls, the most famous being Cora Linn and Bonnington. A hydroelectric scheme now harnesses the power of the water, and the falls are only seen at their most spectacular at certain times of the year.

A few miles north of the town is **Carluke**, which stands above the Clyde Valley. It is noted for its orchards, introduced in medieval times by the monks of Lesmahagow Priory. The bell tower of the former parish church, built in 1715, still stands.

Around Lanark

Biggar

10 miles SE of Lanark on the A702

Biggar is a small, attractive market town that still has its original medieval layout. It sits among the rich agricultural land of South Lanarkshire, and was granted its burgh charter in 1451.

It must have more museums per head of population than any other place in Britain. The **Biggar Gas Works Museum**, housed in the town's former gas works, explains how gas was produced from coal in former times, and the **Moat Park Heritage Centre** has exhibits and displays about the area round the town from when it was formed millions of years ago right up until the present day. **Greenhill Covenanter's House** used to stand at Wiston, 10 miles away, but was transported to Biggar stone by stone, and is now dedicated to the memory of the Covenanters. These were the people who, in the 17th century, resisted the Stuart monarchs' attempts to impose bishops on the Church of Scotland, and sometimes paid with their lives for doing so. The **Gladstone Court Museum** has re-created a Victorian street, with dressmakers, boot makers and even a schoolroom.

The Albion Building houses the **Albion Motors Archives**, which are the records of the Albion Motor Company, started up locally in 1899. It soon grew to be the largest manufacturer of commercial vehicles in the British Empire, and is now part of Leyland DAF. At Brownsbank Cottage, a mile and a half from the town, lived the Scottish poet Christopher Grieve, better known as **Hugh McDiarmid** (see also Langholm). He died in 1978, and his wife Valda continued to live there until her death in 1989. Now it has been restored to exactly how it looked when the poet lived there, and it is home to a writer-in-residence. It can be visited by appointment only.

In Broughton Road is the professionally run **Biggar Puppet Theatre**, which has a Victorian-style theatre seating up to 100 people, plus a museum. Purves Puppets, which owns it, is Scotland's largest puppet company, and regularly presents shows all over Britain.

St Mary's Church was founded in 1546 by Lord Fleming, Chancellor of Scotland. It is a graceful, cruciform building, and was the last church to be built in Scotland before the Reformation.

To the west of the town, just off the M74, are the twin settlements of **Abington** and **Crawford**, which have a number of services, and make ideal stopping off places when heading north or south along the motorway.

Leadhills

18 miles S of Lanark on the B797

Like its neighbour Wanlockhead (which is in Dumfriesshire), Leadhills is a former lead mining village. It has the highest golf course in Scotland, and is full of old 18th and 19th century lead miners' cottages. It forms one terminus for the Leadhills and Wanlockhead Light Railway (see also Wanlockhead). The **Allan Ramsay Library** is the oldest subscription Library in Scotland, and is named after the famous poet born here in 1684 (see also Penicuik). In the graveyard is the grave of **John Taylor**, a lead miner who lived to be 137 years old. Next to the cemetery is a monument to **William Symington**, who was born in the village in 1764. He worked as an engineer in the mines, and was a pioneer of steam propulsion in ships. His paddleboat the *Charlotte Dundas* was launched at Grangemouth in 1802.

Carmichael

4 miles S of Lanark on a minor road west of the A73

The small **Carmichael Parish Church** dates from 1750, and has an interesting laird's loft. One of the past lairds, the Earl of Hyndford, left a sum of money called the Hyndford Mortification to provide the local schoolmasters with a yearly pair of trousers and a supply of whisky. The **Discover Carmichael Visitor Centre** is situated on the Carmichael Estate, and has a display of waxwork models (formerly housed in Edinburgh) that illustrate Scotland's history since the year AD 1000. There are also displays about the history of the Carmichael family, which has owned the lands of Carmichael since the 13th century, and about wind energy.

Douglas

8 miles SW of Lanark on the A70

It was in Douglas, in 1968, that the Cameronians (Scottish Rifles), a proud Scottish regiment, was disbanded (see also Hamilton). The ceremony took place in the grounds of **Castle Dangerous**, ancestral home of the Douglases, of which only a tower now survives. It was here, in 1689, that the regiment was raised by **James, Earl of Angus**. His statue now stands in the village.

The centre of Douglas is a conservation area, with many old cottages and houses. **The Sun Inn** of 1621 was once the village's Tolbooth, where justice was meted out. **Old St Bride's** is the choir of the former parish church dating from the 14th century. Within it are memorials to members of the Douglas family, including Archibald, the 5th Earl of Angus. He was killed at Flodden in 1513, and had the curious nickname of "**Bell the Cat**". There is also a memorial to "the Good Sir James of Douglas", killed by the Moors in Spain while taking Robert the Bruce's heart to the Holy Land for burial. The clock in the

FOUNTAIN RESTAURANT

11 Abbeygreen, Lesmahagow,
Lanarkshire ML11 0ED
Tel: 01555 893237 Fax: 01555 894111
e-mail: the fountain@aol.com
website: www.scotland2000.com/kilchoman

Lesmahagow is an attractive small town standing just off the M74, the main route between Glasgow and England. The **Fountain Restaurant** is one of the best eating places in the district, and takes its name from a Victorian drinking fountain that once stood at the road junction outside its door, though it was removed in the 1930s due to an increase in traffic. The restaurant is housed in the stone-built former church hall of the parish church, which was tastefully refurbished in the 1990s while still retaining some of tis original features. Now it not only offers a restaurant, but a bank, a café and a children's play area. Lesmahagow itself is a former mining village, though its was originally founded by the Tironensian monks of Lesmahagow Priory, whose ruins can be seen beside the parish church.

The Fountains Restaurant food is justly famous throughout the area. The small but comprehensive menu includes such dishes as smoked salmon and trout, Thai oriental fish cakes, breast of chicken and smoked bacon, steak and ale pie, sizzling steaks cooked to your preference, and a range of vegetarian dishes and salads. The drinks and wine list contains a good selection of wines and spirits, and the restaurant also carries a range of soft drinks. If you're travelling on the M74, then the Fountain Restaurant makes the ideal stopping off point for a meal and a welcome break.

clock tower was gifted to the church by Mary Stuart in 1565, and is the oldest working public clock in Scotland.

Crossford

4 miles NW of Lanark on the A72

This lovely little village sits in the heart of the Clyde Valley, on the banks of the river. Above it you'll find the substantial ruins of **Craignethan Castle** (Historic Scotland), where Mary Stuart once stayed. It was built about 1540 by Sir James Hamilton of Finnart, illegitimate son of James Hamilton, 1st Earl of Arran and ancestor of the present Dukes of Hamilton. He was the master of Works to James V, who gave him the lands of Draffan on which the castle was built. However, the king later suspected that Hamilton of Finnart was plotting against him, and had him executed. Sir Walter Scott used the castle as a model for his "Tillietudlem Castle" in *Old Mortality*.

Edinburgh and The Lothians

The Lothians consists of three former counties - East Lothian, Midlothian and West Lothian. It is generally low lying to the north, rising to moorland and hills in the south, with areas of industry to the west and along the coast, and areas of good arable farmland to the east. Being close to Edinburgh, it is the heartland of Scottish history, full of castles, grand houses and churches. It is also a place of quiet, pastoral villages and marvellous scenery. The only towns that could possibly be said to be industrial are Dalkeith, Bo'ness and Bathgate, and even here industry never intruded too much.

Dominating it all is the city of Edinburgh, which probably has more history per square mile than any other comparable city in the world. But it's a compact place, and its suburbs haven't yet gobbled up too much countryside. Behind the city are the Pentland Hills, a lonely area of high moorland stretching south west towards the Lanarkshire boundary, and to the south and south east are the Moorfoot and Lammermuir Hills respectively, which thrust down into the Borders.

East Lothian (formerly "Haddingtonshire") is a farming county, and is a patchwork of fields and woodland dotted all over with small, neat villages. The quiet country lanes cry out to be explored by car, and though there is none of the grandeur of the Highlands here - indeed, the scenery has an almost rural

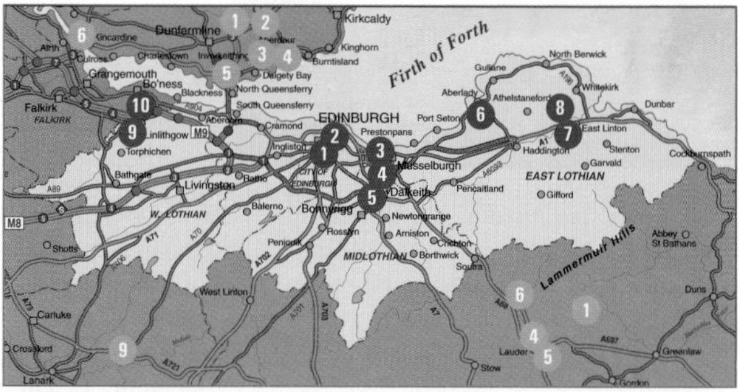

PLACES TO STAY, EAT AND DRINK

Museum of Scotland, Edinburgh	1	Visitor Attraction	p142
The Royal Yacht Britannia, Edinburgh	2	Visitor Attraction	p142
Windsor Park B&B, Musselburgh	3	B&B	p144
Inveresk House, Inveresk Village	4	B&B	p144
Sam's, Dalkeith	5	Pub with Food	p146
Old Aberlady Inn, Aberlady	6	Pub, Restaurant & Accommodation	p151
Crown Hotel, East Linton	7	Pub, Food and Accommodation	p154
Museum of Flight, East Fortune Airfield	8	Visitor Attraction	p155
Thornton B&B, Linlithgow	9	B&B	p157
Bonsyde House Hotel, Bonsyde	10	Hotel	p159

● Denotes entries in other chapters

View of Edinburgh from the Castle

people claim, conceals a mystery that goes to the heart of Christianity.

Before 1975, the county town of West Lothian was Linlithgow. It is an ancient burgh with a royal palace where Mary Stuart, better known as Mary Queen of Scots, was born. West Lothian is more industrial in character than the other two Lothians, and at one time had coal and shale mines, the latter being used to produce oil. Both industries have gone, though the occasional shale spoil heap (called a "bing" hereabouts) can still be seen.

But there are still plenty of tranquil places to be visited, such as Torphichen, with its preceptory of St John, and South Queensferry, in the shadow of the two Forth bridges. A full day could be taken up exploring Linlithgow itself, with its royal palace, medieval church, canal basin and old, stone buildings. Then there are the county's grand houses, such as Hopetoun,

English feel to it - it is still a beautiful area. The county rises to the south, where it meets the Lammermuir Hills, and here the landscape changes, though it never loses it gentle aspect. Haddington is the county town, and is full of old buildings. The main Edinburgh-London railway line bypassed it, so it never developed as a place of industry. The town's main building is the cathedralesque St Mary's Church, the tower of which is sometimes called the "Lamp of the Lothians". A succession of small resorts ring the coastline, though none have been commercialised to any great extent.

Mid Lothian was at one time called "Edinburghshire". Towards the south it meets the Moorfoot Hills, and has a string of small towns sitting like satellites round Edinburgh itself. Coalmining was once important here, though all vestiges of it have now gone. It is home to such places as Dalkeith and Bonnyrigg, which have never been overwhelmed by industry, and the world famous Rosslyn Chapel, which,

Piper at the Highland Games

Newhailes and The Binns, which deserve to be visited and explored.

Edinburgh

Edinburgh, the cultural and administrative capital of Scotland, is one of the great cities of the world. It used to be called the "Athens of the North", and a full week would not be enough to see everything it has to offer the tourist. Whereas Glasgow has worked hard at building a new image, Edinburgh has never needed to do so, though this has led to a certain amount of complacency at times.

With the advent of the Scottish Parliament, the world has rediscovered Edinburgh, and it now has all the feel and buzz of a great capital city once more. It is the sixth most important financial capital in Europe, and both the Church of Scotland and the Scottish law courts have their headquarters here.

The name "Edinburgh" has two possible origins. It either comes from the old Brithonic "eiden burgh", meaning "fortress on the hill slope", or "Edwin's Burgh", from a 7th century Anglo Saxon king of Northumbria who originally built a fort where the castle now stands.

Whatever the explanation, there's no denying that **Edinburgh Castle** (Historic Scotland) is where it all began. It sits on a volcanic plug, with a narrow ridge running east from it on which sits the old town. There has been a fortification on the site for thousands of years, though the first stone castle was probably built by Malcom III in the 11th century, The castle as you see it now dates from all periods, with the oldest part being **St Margaret's Chapel**, which dates from the 12th century. St Margaret was the wife of Malcolm III, and it was thanks to her that the Scottish Church came under the jurisdiction of Rome and swept away the last vestiges of Celtic monasticism. Her son David may have built the chapel in her memory. Every year in August the **Castle Esplanade** hosts the **Edinburgh Military Tattoo**, an extravaganza of military uniforms, marching, music and spectacle that is known the world over. The **Ensign Ewart Tomb** on the esplanade contains the body of Charles Ewart of the 2nd (Scots Greys), who captured the eagle and standard of the French 45th Regiment of the Line at the Battle of Waterloo on 18 June 1815.

Edinburgh Castle

Overlooking the Esplanade and the entrance is the **Half Moon Battery**, built by Regent Morton in the 16th century, and behind it is the **National War Memorial**, designed by Sir Robert Lorimer and converted from an old barracks block between 1924 and 1927. The **King's Lodging** opposite originally dates from the 15th century, and it was here that the monarch had his personal apartments. One of the rooms, **Queen Mary's Room**, is where Mary Stuart gave birth to her son James, who later became James VI of Scotland and I of Britain. There is a curious story about

View of the Castle from Arthur's Seat

this birth. Some people claimed that Mary's baby was stillborn, and that another baby was substituted in its place. At a later date, when the room was being refurbished, workmen are supposed to have found an infant's bones within the walls of the room.

In the **Crown Chamber** can be seen the Scottish crown jewels, known as the **Honours of Scotland**, and the **Stone of Destiny** (see also Dunadd and Scone), supposed to be the pillow on which Jacob slept, and on which the ancient kings of Ireland and Scotland were crowned. It was taken from Scone near Perth by Edward I in 1297, and lay in Westminster Abbey for 700 years. Some people claim, however, that it is merely a copy, and that the monks of Scone gave Edward a worthless drain cover and hid the real one. Others claim that, when the Stone was "liberated" from Westminster Abbey in 1953 by Scottish Nationalists, the perpetrators substituted another stone in its place when it was returned. Whatever is the truth of the matter, there is no doubt that it is a potent symbol of Scottish nationhood. The **National War Museum of Scotland** is also within the castle, and explores military service over the last 400 years.

Leading from Edinburgh Castle down to the **Palace of Holyroodhouse** is the **Royal Mile**, one of the most famous streets in the world. It follows the crest of a ridge that slopes down from the castle, and was the heart of the old Edinburgh. It is actually four streets - Castlehill, Lawnmarket, the High Street and the Canongate, and each one had tall tenements on either side. The city was surprisingly egalitarian in olden days, and the gentry and the poor lived in the same tenement blocks, the rich at the top, the professional classes in the middle, and the poor at the bottom.

The **Scotch Whisky Heritage Centre** on Castlehill tells the story of Scotch, and brings three hundred years of its history to life. You'll learn about how it's made, and every Sunday afternoon there is a tasting session.

Between July and September, Edinburgh plays host to many festivals, the most important being the **Edinburgh International Festival** (with its attendant **Fringe)** in August. The Royal Mile then becomes a colourful open-air theatre, where Fringe performers and buskers take over every inch of pavement to present drama, juggling, classical music, magicians, jazz, piping, folk music and a host of other activities.

Edinburgh has often been called the "medieval Manhatten", as the 16th and 17th century tenement blocks on the Royal Mile went as high as six or seven storeys, due to a lack of building land within the old city. **Gladstone's Land** (National Trust for Scotland), in the Lawnmarket, belonged to Thomas Gledstone, a rich merchant. It was built about 1620, has painted ceilings, and is furnished in the way it would have been in the 17th century. In Lady Stair's House, off the Lawnmarket, you'll find the **Writer's Museum**, with displays on Scotland's trio of

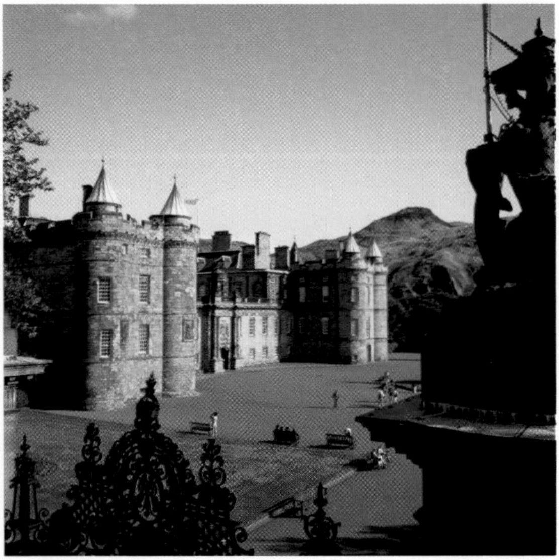

Palace of Holyrood

great writers, Burns, Scott and Stevenson. The house is named after Lady Stair, who owned the house in the 18th century.

The glory of the Royal Mile is **St Giles Cathedral**. Originally the High Kirk of Edinburgh, it was only a cathedral for a short while in the 17th century when the Church of Scotland embraced bishops. It is now the spiritual home of Presbyterianism in Scotland. The first church in Edinburgh was built in the 9th century by monks from Lindisfarne, and St Giles is its direct descendant. It dates mainly from the 15th century, with a magnificent crown steeple, which is, along with the castle, one of Edinburgh's icons. At one time, in the Preston Aisle, an arm bone of St Giles was kept as a holy relic. Attached to the cathedral is the ornate **Thistle Chapel**, designed by Sir Robert Lorimer and built in 1911. It is the home of the **Most Ancient and Noble Order of the Thistle**, founded by James III. One of the delights of the woodcarving is an angel playing the bagpipes. Behind the cathedral is **Parliament House**, where Scotland's parliament met up until the Treaty of Union in 1707. The building itself dates from the late 17th century, though the façade was added in 1829.

Across from the cathedral are the **Edinburgh City Chambers**, home to the city council. It started life as a royal exchange, and was built between 1753 and 1761 to designs by John Adam, brother of the better-known Robert. Though it appears to have only two or three storeys if seen from the Royal Mile, it actually has twelve storeys, which tumble down the slope at the back. Under the Chambers is the **Real Mary King's Close**, a narrow Edinburgh street, which was closed off and built over after the bubonic plague, visited the city in 1645. Conducted tours of this most moving of places are available, though participants are advise to seek out a pub afterwards, as the place is suppose to be haunted. The most moving ghost is said to be that of a young girl, and people still leave gifts for her, such as sweets and dolls.

Further down the Royal Mile is the **Museum of Childhood**, a nostalgic trip down memory lane for most adults. It features toys, games and books, and even medicines such as castor oil. **John Knox House** is almost opposite. It dates from the 15th century, and though there is no real proof that he lived in the house, he may well have died here. Unfortunately, it is closed from spring 2004 until spring 2005 for refurbishment. We're in the **Canongate** now, so called because it is the "gate" or street, of the canons of Holyrood Abbey. At one time Canongate wasn't part of Edinburgh, and the **Canongate Tolbooth** of 1591, which held the council chamber, courtroom and jail for the burgh, is a curious building with a clock that projects out over the pavement. It contains the **Museum of Edinburgh,** which gives an insight into the history of the city itself, and is packed with exhibits from its colourful past.

The **Canongate Church** of 1688 has Dutch influences, and in the kirkyard is buried **Adam Smith**, the famous economist, **Agnes McLehose**, for whom Burns wrote Ae Fond Kiss, and **Robert Fergusson** the poet. He was Burns's hero, and died aged 24 in a madhouse. Burns himself actually paid for the tombstone over his grave. **White Horse Close**, beyond the church, is the most picturesque of Edinburgh's closes, and it was from the White Horse Inn that the London and York coaches left before the days of railways.

The Palace of Holyroodhouse is the Queen's official residence in Scotland. It grew out of the Abbey of Holyrood, of which only the ruined nave remains. Legend says that while out hunting, David I was injured by a stag, and while he grappled with it he found himself grasping, not the stag's antlers, but a holy cross or "rood". As an act of thanksgiving he founded the abbey in 1128 for Augustinian canons. It became a favourite residence for Scottish kings, being much less draughty than the castle up the hill. It was here that Mary Stuart set up court on her return from France in the 16th century, and it was here that the murder of Rizzio, her Italian secretary took place (see also Seton). The picture gallery contains portraits of over 100 Scottish kings. The recently opened **Queen's Gallery** is the first permanent exhibition space for the royal collection of paintings and sculpture in Scotland.

It was designed by Benjamin Tindall Architects, and is housed in the former Holyrood Free Church and Duchess of Gordon's School.

Close to Holyrood is the new **Scottish Parliament Building**, designed by the late Catalan architect Enric Miralles. Officially opened in October 2004 by HM the Queen, it is a controversial building, having cost ten times the original estimate and opened four years late. It's appearance has also divided the nation, with some people loving it and others loathing it. Guided tours are available. In Holyrood Road is **Our Dynamic Earth**, an exhibition and visitors centre that takes you on a journey through the history of the universe, from the beginning of time and on into the future. It features dinosaurs, earthquakes, lava flows and tropical rainstorms.

To the south of the Royal Mile, in Chambers Street behind the old college of Edinburgh University, are the **Royal Museum** and the new **Museum of Scotland** (see panel on page 142). They house internationally important collections relating to natural history, science, the arts and history. One of Edinburgh's hidden gems can be found in the Cowgate - the **Magdalen Chapel** of 1547. Built by the Guild of Hammermen, it contains pre-Reformation stained glass and the tomb of

Edinburgh Military Tattoo

Museum of Scotland

Chambers Street, Edinburgh EH1 1JF
Tel: 0131 247 4422
website: www.nms.ac.uk

The **Museum of Scotland** tells the remarkable story of a remarkable country. From the geological dawn of time to modern day life in Scotland, you'll discover the roots of a nation - a land steeped in fascinating cultures and terrible wars, passionate religion and scientific invention. A land of creative struggle - and occasionally of glorious failure. In a unique and purpose - built new museum, we've gathered together the treasured inheritance and cultural icons which tell Scotland's many stories. The people, the land, the events that have shaped the way we live now. And very probably the way you do too.

If you weren't aware of the extraordinary history and impressive achievements of this small country, then it's time to find out. Because after more than 3,000 million years of Scotland's story, we now have the perfect place in which to celebrate it - the Museum of Scotland. The exhibits include the earliest known fossil reptile found in Bathgate, dating back to 338 million years BC, artefacts from around 8,000 BC when the first settlers arrived and a tiny shrine thought to date from AD 750.

The museum shop sells a wide variety of souvenirs and a café and restaurant ensure that all appetities are catered for. Guides are available and there is a rooftop garden with spectacular views. Open Monday to Saturday 10am-5pm and Sunday 12 noon-5pm.

The Royal Yacht Britannia

Ocean Terminal, Leith, Edinburgh, Scotland
Tel: 0131 555 5566
e-mail: enquiries@tryb.co.uk
website: www.royalyachtbritannia.co.uk

For over forty years **The Royal Yacht *Britannia*** served the Royal Family, travelling over one million miles to become the most famous ship in the world. Travelling to every corner of the globe, in a career spanning 968 royal and official visits, she played a leading role in some of the defining moments of recent history. To Her Majesty The Queen and the Royal Family, *Britannia* proved to be the perfect royal residence for glittering State Visits, official receptions, honeymoons and relaxing family holidays. Since her decomissioning *Britannia* has now made Edinburgh's historic Port of Leith her final home and is open to the public throughout the year. Now owned by The Royal Yacht *Britannia* Trust, a non profit making charity, any proceeds go towards *Britannia's* maintenance.

Your tour of *Britannia* starts in the Visitor Centre on the second floor of Ocean Terminal. Here you can learn about *Britannia's* fascinating history through exhibits and photographs before you collect your complimentary audio handset and step on board *Britannia,* a privilege previously reserved for guests of Her Majesty The Queen and the Royal Family. Starting at the Bridge and finishing at the gleaming Engine Room, come and discover the reality behind life and work on board this Royal Yacht. Viewing five decks, using the lift or stairs for easy access, you will tour *Britannia* at your own pace and enjoy highlights that include the State Dining Room, the Drawing Room, the Sun Lounge, the Wardroom and the Chief Petty Officers' Mess. *Britannia* is furnished with artefacts from The Royal Collection, which are on loan from Her Majesty The Queen.

its founder. Another famous church south of the Royal Mile is **Greyfriars**. Built in 1612, it was here that the National Covenant rejecting bishops in the Church of Scotland was signed in 1638. From this, the adherents of Presbyterianism in the 17th century got the name "Covenanters". In nearby Candlemaker Row is the famous **Greyfriars Bobby** statue. It commemorates a terrier that faithfully kept guard over the grave of John Grey, his former master, who died in 1858. He did this for 4 years, until he too died in 1862.

North of the Royal Mile is Edinburgh's **New Town**. In the late 18th and early 19th centuries the medieval city was overcrowded and unhealthy, so the New Town was laid out in a series of elegant streets and squares to a plan by James Craig. **Princes Street** was one of these streets, and is now the city's main shopping area. It faces **Princes Street Gardens**, created from the drained bed of the old Nor' Loch. Within the new town's Charlotte Square you'll find the **Georgian House** (National Trust for Scotland), which re-creates the interiors found in the New Town when it was being built. At **No. 28 Charlotte Square** is the National Trust for Scotland's headquarters and art gallery. And within the Square gardens each August is held the **Edinburgh Book Festival**. At the west end of the New Town is one of Edinburgh's most spectacular churches - **St Mary's Cathedral**. It was built in Victorian times as the cathedral for the Episcopalian diocese of Edinburgh, and is as large and grand as a medieval cathedral, with three soaring spires that have become Edinburgh landmarks.

The **National Gallery of Scotland** on the Mound, the **Scottish National Portrait Gallery** in Queen Street, the **Dean Gallery** and the **Scottish National Gallery of Modern Art** in Belford Road are all within, or close to, the New Town. A bus service runs between all four. At the east end of Princes Street you'll find **Register House**, where the National Archives of Scotland are stored. It was designed by Robert Adam, with the foundation stone being laid in 1774. Also in Princes Street is Scotland's official memorial to one of its greatest writers, the Gothic **Scott Monument**, which soars to over 200 feet, and offers a marvellous view from the top. It was designed by George Meikle Kemp, and work began in 1840. In August 1846 it opened to the public.

Further north, off Inverleith Row, are the **Royal Botanic Gardens**, 70 acres of greenery and colour surrounded by the bustle of the city. They were founded in 1670 as a "physic garden" at Holyrood, but were transferred here in 1823. And at Leith, up until the 1920s a separate burgh, you'll find the **Royal Yacht Britannia** (see panel opposite) moored at the **Ocean Terminal**, a leisure and entertainment complex. The ship is open to the public. In Pier Place in Newhaven, to the west of Leith, is the **Newhaven Heritage Museum** explaining the history of this former fishing village. It was in Newhaven that the largest fighting ship of its day, the *Great Michael* was built between 1507 and 1513 for James IV's Scottish navy. It is said that the whole fleet, which sailed to America with Columbus in 1492 could fit comfortably into her hull (see also Largo). It was the envy of Europe, and Henry VIII even demanded that it be handed over to him, as it was far too good for the Scots. In charge of the building project was Scotland's Admiral of the Fleet Sir Andrew Wood (see also Largo).

Further to the west, at Corstorphine, are the **Edinburgh Zoological Gardens**, set in 80 acres. The zoo is famous for its penguins, and the daily "penguin parade" (which depends on the weather and the whim of the penguins themselves) is not to be missed.

Craigmillar Castle (Historic Scotland) is on the southeast outskirts of the city. The extensive ruins date from the 14th century, with many later additions. Mary Stuart

Craigmillar Castle

stayed here after her Italian secretay Rizzio was murdered. **Lauriston Castle**, near Davidson's Mains, is also worth visiting. It is set in 30 acres of parkland. One of its owners was the father of **John Napier**, who invented logarithms. It now has a collection of furniture and decorative arts. Napier's own home, Merchiston Tower, is now part of Napier University. The **Royal Observatory** sits on Blackford Hill, south of the city centre, and has displays and exhibits relating to astronomy.

Around Edinburgh

Musselburgh

6 miles E of Edinburgh on the A199

Musselburgh got its name from the beds of mussels that once lay at the mouth of the

Windsor Park B&B

17 Windsor Park, Musselburgh,
Edinburgh EH21 7QL
Tel: 0131 665 2194
e-mail: mary@windsorpark.demon.co.uk

Under the careful eyes of Mary and William Wilson, the **Windsor Park B&B** has become one of the best B&B's in the Edinburgh area. It boasts three comfortable and well furnished rooms, one of which is en suite, and has a friendly, informal atmosphere. You'll be treated as one of the family!

There is a good choice of breakfasts, and evening meals can be arranged by prior notice. This is a great value-for-money establishment with a small but spectacular garden, and if you stay here, you're sure to return again!

Inveresk House

Inveresk Village, East Lothian EH21 7UA
Tel: 0131 665 5855
Fax: 0131 665 0578
e-mail: chute.inveresk@btinternet.com

Dating originally from the 16th century, **Inveresk House** is an historic mansion house located in Scotland's finest conservation village. The public rooms are spacious and furnished in period style as are the three comfortable bedrooms. The décor throughout is stunning and provides a setting for gracious and relaxed living. Breakfasts are hearty, though lighter options are also available. Edinburgh is easily accessible and the countryside surrounding Inveresk Village offers many further attractions.

Inveresk Lodge Gardens

River Esk, on which the town stands. Now it is a dormitory town for Edinburgh. The **Tolbooth** dates from the 1590s, and was built of stones from the former Chapel of Our Lady of Loretto, which in pre-Reformation times was served by a hermit. **Inveresk Lodge Gardens** (National Trust for Scotland), with their terraces and walled garden, illustrates methods and plants that can be used in a home garden. The **Battle of Pinkie**, the last battle fought between Scottish and English national armies, took place near Musselburgh in 1547. The Scots were defeated due to the incompetence of the Earl of Arran, Scotland's commander.

Prestonpans

7 miles E of Edinburgh on the B1348

At the **Battle of Prestonpans** in 1745 the Jacobite army of Charles Edward Stuart defeated a Hanovarian army under Sir John Cope. The whole battle only took 15 minutes, with many of the Hanovarian troops being trapped against a high wall (which can still be seen) surrounding **Prestongrange House**. Contemporary accounts tell of terrified Hanovarian troops trying to scale the wall and drop into the comparative safety of the house's grounds. The Jacobite song *Hey Johnnie Cope* lampoons the English commander, though he wasn't wholly to blame for the defeat.

Port Seton

9 miles E of Edinburgh on the B1348

Port Seton Collegiate Church (Historic Scotland) was built, but never completed, in the 14th century as a church served by a college of priests. It is dedicated to St Mary and the Holy Cross, and has some tombs of the Seton family, as well as fine vaulting. In 1544 it was looted and stripped by the Earl of Hertford and his English army. **Seton Castle** dates from 1790, and was designed by Robert Adam. It replaces the former Seton Palace, one of the grandest Scottish buildings of its time. Mary Stuart visited the Palace after the murder of Rizzio by her second husband, Lord Darnley (see also Edinburgh).

Dalkeith

7 miles SE of Edinburgh on the A68

This pleasant town is nowadays a dormitory for Edinburgh, but at one time was an important market town on the main road south from Edinburgh to England. **Dalkeith Palace** was built around Dalkeith Castle for Anne, Duchess of Monmouth and Buccleuch in the early 18th century. It became known as the "grandest of all classical houses in Scotland", and its grounds are now a country park. **St Nicholas Parish Church** is a large building with, attached to it, the ruins of an old apse in which lie the remains of Anne, who died in 1732. Her husband, James Scott, Duke of Monmouth, was an illegitimate son of Charles II who had defeated a Covenanting army at Bothwell Bridge. However, he later plotted to murder his father, and had himself declared king on June 20 1685. He was defeated at the Battle of Sedgemoor

Sam's

High street, Dalkeith, Midlothian EH22 1AZ
Tel: 0131 663 2515

All are welcome at **Sam's**, a great pub sitting at the top end of Dalkeith's busy High Street. The building is early 19th century, and retains many original period features to give an overall ambience that is both warm and welcoming. The open plan bar/lounge is tastefully and comfortably furnished, with a door leading onto the ever-popular beer garden for those warm summer days. Good food is served here - honest, beautifully cooked "pub grub" at sensible prices. It's the place for a bar lunch or a quiet, relaxing drink!

(the last battle fought on English, rather than British soil) on July 6, and was eventually executed on Tower Hill in London nine days later.

Newtongrange

8 miles SE of Edinburgh on the A7

The monks of Newbattle Abbey started coal mining in the Lothians in the 13th century, so the industry has a long history in the area. The Lady Victoria Colliery in Newtongrange houses the **Scottish Mining Museum**, which tells the story of coal mining in Scotland from those days right up until the present. There is a re-created coalface, as well as the original winding engines and a visitor's centre.

Arniston

9 miles SE of Edinburgh off the A7

Arniston House has been the home of the Dundas family for over 400 years. Both William and John Adam worked on the designs, and it was built between 1726 and the 1750s on the site of an old tower house. The interior detail is wonderful, and there is also a fine collection of paintings by artists such as Raeburn and Ramsay. In the 17th century the Dundas family was one of the most powerful in Scotland, and held many important posts in the Scottish legal system.

Borthwick

11 miles SE of Edinburgh off the A7

Borthwick Castle is a massive castle built by Sir William Borthwick in about 1430 on the site of an earlier tower. It was to this castle that Mary Stuart and Bothwell came after their marriage in 1567. It was a marriage which displeased the Scottish people and 1000 Scottish nobles cornered them there. They demanded that Mary hand over Bothwell for his part in the murder of Lord Darnley, Mary's first husband. However, Bothwell escaped and fled to Dunbar, leaving his wife to the mercy of the nobles. On hearing of his escape, they immediately retired from the Queen's presence, thinking that she had seen through his treachery. However, no sooner had they left her than she tore off her fine gowns and put on breeches and a pageboy's shirt, and made her escape so that she could rejoin her husband.

In 1650 the castle was attacked by Oliver Cromwell's Parliamentarian army, and it was abandoned not long after. In the early 20th century it was restored, and during World War II it was secretly used to store national treasures. It is now a hotel.

The modern **Borthwick Parish Church** has a 15th century aisle with effigies of the first Lord and Lady Borthwick.

Crichton

11 miles SE of Edinburgh on the B6367

Crichton Castle (Historic Scotland) was probably built in the late 14th century by John de Crichton. It consisted of a simple tower house typical of the period, but was added to by his son William, an ambitious and unscrupulous man who became Lord Chancellor of Scotland. During the minority of James II, Archibald the 5th Earl of Douglas was appointed regent, but he died two years after James ascended the throne. Both Crichton and Sir Alexander Livingstone competed to take Archibald's place, fearing that a Douglas might be appointed again.

They invited the 6th Earl of Douglas, who was only 16, to a banquet at Edinburgh Castle, along with his brother and a friend. The head of a black bull was brought to the table, and at this sign the Earl, his brother and their friend were murdered.

The Earl of Bothwell took possession of Crichton in 1581, and immediately transformed it. He demolished the north range and replaced it with an Italianate Renaissance building, which is unique in Scotland. It is now known as Earl Bothwell's Lodging**.**

Crichton Collegiate Church was built in 1449 by William Crichton. **Vogrie Country Park** lies to the north of the castle, and is centred on Vogrie House. It has woodland walks, picnic areas and a golf course.

Soutra

15 miles SE of Edinburgh off the A68

From Soutra, high in the Lammermuir Hills, it is reckoned that you get the best view in Central Scotland. On a clear day you can see the full sweep of the Firth of Forth with Fife beyond, and at least 60 Highland peaks. **Soutra Aisle** is all that remains of a medieval hospital. It was dedicated to the Holy Trinity, and it was here that Augustinian monks looked after travellers, pilgrims and the sick and wounded. A recent archaeological dig uncovered evidence of surgery and the treatment of patients by herbal remedies. Even some pieces of bandage with human tissue still attached to them were recovered.

Rosslyn

7 miles S of Edinburgh on the B7006

Rosslyn (also known as Roslin), according to some people, is the most important place in Christendom. It's all due to **Rosslyn Church**, an extravaganza of a building on which work began in 1446. Its founder was Sir William St Clair, third and last Prince of Orkney, who lived at nearby **Rosslyn Castle**. It is the choir of this unfinished church (still in use) that has both Masonic and Knights Templar associations.

The stone carving in the interior is spectacular, and shows plants that only grow in the New World, even though Columbus hadn't yet sailed across the Atlantic when it was built. There are also pagan carvings of "The Green Man", as well as the famous **Apprentice Pillar**. This was said to have been carved by an apprentice when the master mason working on the church was on the Continent seeking inspiration. When he returned and saw the workmanship, the mason is supposed to have murdered the apprentice in a fit of jealousy.

Legends abound about the church, and much has been written about it lately. One theory says that the writings of Christ lie in its unopened vaults. Another says that the bodies of Knights Templar lie in the unopened crypt, dressed in armour. A third says that the **Holy Grail** is embedded in one of the pillars. And yet another says it is a re-creation of **Solomon's Temple** in Jerusalem.

There's even a theory that the body of Christ himself lies in the vaults. Whatever the truth of the matter, and the theories seem to get wilder and wilder as time goes by, there's no denying that it is one of the most beautiful buildings in Britain. There is certainly an aura about the place that can almost be felt (see also Kilmartin).

Nearby is the **Roslin Glen Country Park**, with woodland walks that go past old gunpowder works.

Penicuik

9 miles S of Edinburgh on the A701

Penicuik was once a mining and paper making town, founded in 1770 by its laird, Sir James Clerk of Penicuik. To the west of the town rise the Pentland Hills, with **Scald Law** being the highest peak at 1,898 feet. In the grounds of Penicuik House stands the **Allan Ramsay Obelisk**, dedicated to the memory of Allan Ramsay, known as the "Pentland Poet" (see also Leadhills). **St Mungo's Parish Church** dates from 1771, and has a 12th century detached belfry. The **Edinburgh Crystal Visitor Centre** at Eastfield has displays and exhibits about the history of crystal and glass making in Scotland, plus factory tours.

Cramond

5 miles W of Edinburgh on a minor road off the A90

Cramond is a charming village of old whitewashed cottages on the banks of the River Almond where it enters the Firth of Forth. The **Parish Church** of 1656, with its medieval tower, sits within the ruins of a **Roman Fort**. The Rev. Robert Walker, who was painted by Raeburn skating on Duddingston Loch in the 18th century, was minister here. At one time, the village was famous for the quality of the nails it manufactured. **Cramond Island** sits one mile offshore, and it is possible to walk to it via a causeway at low tide, though walkers should heed the notices about tide times before setting off.

Ingliston

7 miles W of Edinburgh off the A8

Almost in the shadow of Edinburgh International Airport at Turnhouse is the **Royal Showground**, home each year of the Royal Highland Show, Scotland's premier country and farming fair.

Balerno

7 miles SW of Edinburgh off the A70

Malleny Garden (National Trust for Scotland) is a walled garden extending to three acres and dominated by 400-year-old clipped yew trees. There are herbaceous borders, a fine collection of roses, and it houses the National Bonsai Collection for Scotland. The 17th century house was built in 1635 for Sir James Murray of Kilbaberton.

Ratho

8 miles W of Edinburgh on a minor road off the A8

Ratho sits on the Union Canal, and from the **Edinburgh Canal Centre** canal cruises are available. **Ratho Parish Church** dates from the 12th century, though it has been much restored over the years.

The **Adventure Centre** is billed as the "gateway to adventure", with the National Rock Climbing Centre having 2400 square metres of artificial wall surfaces, the largest

Malleny Gardens, Balerno

climbing arena in the world. One other feature is the Airpark, Europe's largest suspended aerial adventure ropes ride.

South Queensferry

9 miles W of Edinburgh city centre off the A90

South Queensferry is named after St Margaret, husband of Malcolm III, who founded a ferry here in the 11th century to carry pilgrims across the Forth to Dunfermline Abbey and St Andrew's Cathedral. When she herself died she was buried in the abbey and later canonised, with her shrine becoming a place of pilgrimage as well. Now the ferry has been replaced by the **Forth Rail Bridge** and the South **Forth Road Bridge**, two mammoth pieces of civil engineering. The rail bridge was built between 1883 and 1890 to link Edinburgh and Aberdeen, and the road bridge was completed in 1964. In the shadow of the Rail Bridge is the historic **Hawes Inn** of 1683, which features in R.L. Stevenson's *Kidnapped*. Opposite is the slipway from which the former ferry sailed.

The town has a glorious mix of cottages and houses dating from the 16th century onwards. **Plewlands House** (National Trust for Scotland) dates from 1643, and has been converted into private flats. The **Queensferry Museum**, in the High Street, has exhibits and displays on local history. The church of the former **Carmelite Friary** in Rose Lane dates from the 15th century, and is now an Episcopalian church.

Dalmeny House, to the east of the town, overlooks the Firth of Forth. It is the home of the Earls of Roseberry, and was built in the 1820s. There is an excellent collection of tapestries and furniture. **Dalmeny Church** is one of the best-preserved Norman churches in Britain. The south doorway is richly carved, as is the chancel and apse.

Haddington

The royal burgh of Haddington received its royal charter in the 12th century from David I, and is thought to be the birthplace in 1505 of John Knox. At one time it was the fourth largest town in Scotland, and it was in **St Martin's Church**, all that is left of an old nunnery that stood in Nungate outside the town, that the Scottish parliament met to sanction Mary Stuart's marriage to the Dauphin of France. Members of both the French and Scottish nobility attended, and put an end to the English plans to have Mary marry Henry VIII's son Edward.

It is a quiet town of old buildings, including the quite superb cathedralesque **Parish Church of St Mary.** It was formerly collegiate, and dates from the 15th century. It too stood outside the burgh, and when the parliament was meeting at St Martin's, the Scots were laying siege to the town, as it was occupied by the English. Mary of Guise (Mary Stuart's mother) attended the parliament, and when she climbed to the top of St Mary's tower to view the English defences she was shot at. The ruined choir was restored in the early part of the 20th century, and such is the church's size and beauty (it is the longest parish church in Scotland) that some people erroneously refer to it as the church of a former abbey. In the choir is the burial place of **Jane Welsh** (Thomas Carlyle's wife), who was born in the town. The **Lauderdale Aisle**, owned by the Earls of Lauderdale, is unique in that it is a small Episcopalian chapel within a Presbyterian Church. This ecumenicalism continues every year in May with the **Whitekirk and Haddington Pilgrimage**, when people from all the main Christian religions in Scotland walk between the two towns (see also Whitekirk).

St Mary's is one of the few Church of Scotland churches to have a full peel of bells, which were installed in 1999. The 16th century **Nungate Bridge** over the Tyne is behind St Mary's, and is named after the nunnery where the Scottish parliament met.

The writer **Samuel Smiles** was born in

Portrait of King Charles at Lennoxlove House

Haddington in 1812. Though he wrote many books, he is best known for *Self Help*. Alexander II and William the Lion may also have been born here, in a royal castle that has long gone.

The **Town House**, with its graceful spire, was designed by William Adam and built in the late 1740s, though the spire was added in 1831. Close to Haddington is **Lennoxlove**, home to the Dukes of Hamilton since 1946. It houses the death mask of Mary Stuart, which shows her to have been, as many contemporaries observed, an extremely beautiful woman. The origins of the house go back to at least the 13th century, when it was called Lethington Hall, and the home of the Maitland family.

About four miles east of Haddington is **Traprain Law**, from the top of which there are superb views. The summit was occupied from Neolithic times right up until the Dark Ages, and the outline of a fort can clearly be seen. It was the capital of a tribe the Romans called the Votadini, which roughly translated means "the farmers". More Roman finds have been made here, including a horde of Roman silver, than anywhere else in Scotland.

Around Haddington

Gullane

6 miles N of Haddington on the A198

This village sits inland from the Firth of Forth, but has fine views north towards Fife. Nowadays it is a small golfing resort with many large, imposing villas. The British Open is held here regularly, and the course at **Muirfield** is home to the Honourable Company of Edinburgh Golfers. The **Heritage of Golf** exhibition on the West Links Road traces the golfing history of the area.

The ruins of the **St Andrew's Church** can be seen at the west end of the main

Muirfield Golf Course

street. On Gullane Bay, and signposted from the main street, is **Gullane Bents**, one of the best beaches on the Firth of Forth.

Dirleton Castle

Dirleton

6 miles N of Haddington off the A198

The impressive ruins of **Dirleton Castle** (Historic Scotland) dominate this pleasant village. They date to the end of the 13th century, though there have been extensive additions and alterations over the years. The castle was taken by Edward I of England in 1298, but was back in Scottish hands by 1311. It was built by the Norman family of de Vaux, though it has also been owned by the Halyburtons and the Ruthvens. The third Lord Ruthven was implicated in the murder of Mary Stuart's Italian secretary Rizzio in Holyroodhouse. To the west of the castle are some formal terraced gardens.

Aberlady

6 miles N of Haddington on the A198

This pleasant village was the port for Haddington until the bay silted up. The **Aberlady Bay Nature Reserve** covers 1439 acres of foreshore and dunes, and is popular with bird watchers. The village was the home of one of Scotland's most popular historical novelists, **Nigel Tranter**, who died in the year 2000. There is a small cairn to his memory close to Quarry House, where he used to live.

Myreton Motor Museum contains displays of motorcars, cycles and military vehicles. **Aberlady Parish Church** was remodelled in the 19th century, though an interesting 16th century tower still stands. To the east of the village is **Luffness Castle**, once the ancestral home of the Hepburns. It is now a hotel.

Athelstaneford

2 miles NE of Haddington on the B1343

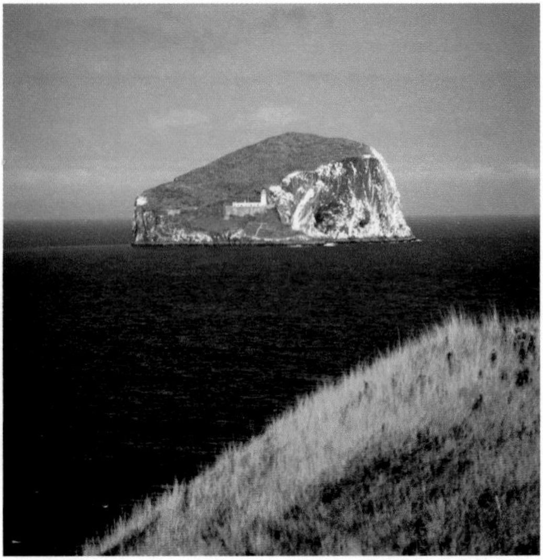

Bass Rock

Athelstaneford has a special place in Scottish history. It was here that the Scottish flag, the **Saltire**, or St Andrew's Cross, was first adopted. Athelstane was a king of Northumbria who fought a combined army of Picts and Scots at Athelstaneford in AD 832. The Pictish leader, Angus mac Fergus, on the day before the battle, saw a huge white cross made of clouds in the sky, and took it as an omen. Athelstane was duly defeated, and a white cross on a blue background was adopted as the flag of Scotland, making it the oldest national flag in Europe.

This is why the Saltire on its own should be white and sky blue, whereas when it is incorporated into the Union Jack the blue darkens. The **National Flag Centre** in the village explains the story of the battle and the flag.

North Berwick

7 miles NE of Haddington on the A198

North Berwick is one of Scotland's best-known holiday and golfing resorts. It is a clean, attractive town, which was granted a royal charter by Robert II in 1373. **North Berwick Law**, a volcanic plug, rises to a height of 613 feet behind the town, and makes a wonderful viewpoint. Two miles off the coast lies the **Bass Rock**, another volcanic plug that broods over the waters of the Firth of Forth. Over 150,000 sea birds nest each year on the 350 feet high cliffs and on other, smaller islands such as Fidra and Craigleith. From the **Scottish Seabird Centre** on a promontory near the old harbour you can use remote controlled cameras which are situated on the islands to study them without disturbing the colonies. There are also powerful telescopes on a viewing deck, a film about Scotland's sea birds, and a café restaurant.

In the 8th century the Bass Rock was home to the hermit **St Baldred**, who evangelised this part of Scotland. In later times it also served as a prison for Jacobites and Covenanters, and there are traces of old fortifications on it.

Also on the promontory are the scant ruins of the **Auld Kirk**, which date from the 12th century onwards. It was finally abandoned in the 17th century due to coastal erosion, and when the Seabird Centre was being built, over 30 well-preserved skeletons from the old graveyard were uncovered, the earliest one dating back to the 7th century. In School Road is the **North Berwick Museum**, housed in a former school, which has displays and memorabilia about local history, wildlife and golf.

In the 16th century the town was supposed to have been the home of a notorious **Witches Coven**, and a well-publicised trial took place in 1595. One of the accusations made was that the witches had caused a terrible storm to rise up when

James VI's ship returned from Denmark with his new bride.

It all started when a poor serving girl called Gelie Duncan was found to have remarkable healing powers, which aroused suspicion. Her master, David Seaton, tried to extract a confession of witchcraft from her using thumbscrews, and when this failed he had her body examined for the "marks of the devil". These were duly found on her throat, and she confessed and was thrown in jail.

On being tortured further, Gelie claimed to be one of 200 witches and warlocks in the town who, at the behest of the Earl of Bothwell, David Seaton's sworn enemy, were trying to harm the king. At Hallowe'en in 1590, Gelie told them, the witches convened at the Auld Kirk, where Satan appeared to them and preached a sermon from the pulpit. King James had all the women identified by Gelie put to death, including one Agnes Sampson and a schoolmaster from Prestonpans called John Fian. Gelie herself was burnt on the Castle Esplanade in Edinburgh.

Though people have subsequently claimed that the Earl of Bothwell dressed up as Satan to take part in the Hallowe'en coven in the kirk, there's little doubt that Gelie made up the stories to save herself from further torture, and many innocent people were executed because of this.

East of North Berwick is **Tantallon Castle** (Historic Scotland). Its substantial and romantic ruins stand on a cliff top above the Firth of Forth, almost opposite the Bass Rock. It was a Douglas stronghold, built in the 14th century by William, 1st Earl of Douglas. Cromwell ordered General Monk to take the castle, and in 1651, after a 12-day siege, he destroyed it.

Whitekirk

7 miles NE of Haddington off the A198

St Mary's Parish Church dates from the 15th century, and is the eastern end of the annual Whitekirk to Haddington Pilgrimage (see also Haddington). However, Whitekirk had been a place of pilgrimage long before this. In pre Reformation times, people came to the village to seek cures at the Well of Our Lady, which used to be located nearby. An account of 1413 relates that over 15,000 people of all nationalities visited yearly. Close to it is the 16th century **Tithe Barn**, built to store the "tithes" (a tithe being a tenth part) given to the church as offerings from the parishioners' agricultural produce.

The place's most famous pilgrim - but one who didn't come seeking a cure - was a young Italian nobleman called **Aeneas Sylvius Piccolomini**. He had set out from Rome in the winter of 1435 as an envoy to the court of James I, and during the sea crossing he was blown off course by a raging gale. Aeneas vowed that if he made it to dry land he would offer thanksgiving at the nearest church dedicated to Our Lady. The boat was eventually shipwrecked between North Berwick and Dunbar, and Aeneas survived. He therefore set out on a ten-mile pilgrimage in a snowstorm to Whitekirk, where he duly offered prayers of thanks. Twenty years later, Aeneas became Pope Pious II.

East Linton

6 miles E of Haddington off the A1

Anyone travelling along the A1 should make a small detour to view this picturesque village. To the east of the village is **Phantassie**, the mansion where **John Rennie** the civil engineer was born. He designed Waterloo, London and Southwark bridges over the Thames.

Preston Mill (National Trust for Scotland) is an old, quaint water mill that has been fully restored to working order. It sits in an idyllic rural spot, and dates from the 18th century, though a mill has stood on the spot for centuries. With its conical roofed kiln and red pantiles, it is a favourite subject for painters and

Crown Hotel

Bridge Street, East Linton,
East Lothian EH40 3AG
Tel: 01620 860335
e-mail: info@thecrowneastlinton.co.uk
website: www,thecrowneastlinton.co.uk

The **Crown Hotel** is an attractive, 18th century stone-built former coaching inn situated at the heart of this attractive village, and combines great value for money with high standards of service and friendliness. There are five comfortable rooms on offer, and the bar is typically Scottish, with period features and a great welcome. The food is all home-cooked, with the produce, especially beef and fish, being fresh and sourced locally. The Crown Hotel is handy for Edinburgh and for the Scottish Museum of Flight, where you can see Concorde.

photographers. Close by is **Phantassie Doocot** (National Trust for Scotland), which belonged to Phantassie House, and could hold 500 birds. Nearby is **Prestonkirk**, a small, attractive church. It was built in 1770, though the 13th century chancel still stands, now used as a mausoleum.

Preston Mill, East Linton

The ruins of **Hailes Castle** lie to the west of East Linton. Its earliest masonry dates from the 13th century, though it was much altered in later years by the Hepburns, who acquired the castle in the 14th century. It was to Hailes Castle that James Hepburn, Earl of Bothwell, brought Mary Stuart after seizing her at Fountainbridge in 1567. He was later to become her third husband.

The **Scottish Museum of Flight** (see panel opposite) is situated at East Fortune, to the north east of the village. Formerly a World War II airfield, it now houses a collection of aircraft, rockets, models and memorabilia. The most famous exhibit is Concorde, brought to the museum in 2004. Another is a Prestwick Pioneer, the only aircraft ever to have been wholly designed and built in Scotland. Also on display are a Soviet MIG, a Blue Streak rocket and a Lightning.

Stenton

7 miles E of Haddington on the B6370

This small conservation village still retains its old **Tron**, on which wool brought to the Stenton Fair by local sheep farmers was weighed. To the south of the village is **Pressmennan Lake**, one of the few lakes, as opposed to lochs, in Scotland (see also Lake of Menteith, Ellon and Kirkcudbright). This one, however, is artificial, created in the early 19th century by the local landowner.

Museum of Flight

East Fortune Airfield, East Lothian, EH39 5LF
Tel: 01620 880308 Fax: 01620 880355
website: www.nms.ac.uk/flight

The **Museum of Flight** is based at East Fortune Airfield, a Scheduled Ancient Monument and one of the most famous sites in world aviation history. It tells the history of East Fortune (established in 1915 as a fighter base to protect Scotland from Zeppelin attacks) and of the Scottish built airship R34 which left East Fortune and flew to Long Island, New York, becoming the first return Transatlantic flight. The Museum collection is housed in the original hangars and restoration work can be seen in progress. A large selection of models, toys and books is on sale in the shop and the Parachute Café serves light refreshments.

The **Pressmennan Forest Trail** runs along its southern shore, and from the highest point you can see Arthur's Seat in Edinburgh and the Bass Rock in the Firth of Forth.

Stenton Kirk is a handsome building designed by the noted architect William Burn in 1829. In Stenton Kirk yard is the **Old Kirk**, dating probably from the 14th century.

Tyninghame

7 miles E of Haddington on the B1407

Tyninghame is a small conservation village, which formerly stood in what are now the grounds of **Tyninghame House** (not open to the public). In 1761 it was moved to its present position by the then Earl of Haddington to improve the view from his house, though the remains of the former parish kirk, dedicated to St Baldred, still stand there.

Dunbar

11 miles E of Haddington on the A1087

The Royal Burgh of Dunbar received its royal charter in 1445. It is a former fishing and whaling port, though its main industries now are brewing and tourism. It was near here, in 1650, that the **Battle of Dunbar** took place between the troops of Cromwell and a Covenanting army under General Leslie. A stone commemorates the event. The ruins of **Dunbar Castle** date back to the 12th century. It was originally built for the Cospatrick family, which later changed its name to Dunbar. It was to Dunbar Castle that Edward II fled after his defeat at Bannockburn. He then boarded a boat for Berwick-upon-Tweed. In 1338 the Countess of Dunbar, known as "Black Agnes", held the castle for five months against an English army before being relieved by a small contingent of Scots. On the orders of the Scottish Parliament, the castle was dismantled after Mary Stuart abdicated.

The old **Town House** dates from about 1620 and houses a small museum on local history and archaeology, though a much newer "attraction" is situated south of the town, near the shore. **Torness Nuclear Power Station** was built in the early 80s, and has a visitor centre that explains how electricity is produced from nuclear power.

John Muir, founder of the American national parks system, was born in Dunbar in 1838. His birthplace in the High Street is now the John Muir Centre. The **John Muir Country Park** is to the north west of the town. Opened in the late 70s, this was the first park of its kind in Scotland, and covers 1760 acres.

Two miles south of the town, off the A1, is **Doonhill Homestead** (Historic Scotland), where once an Anglian hall dating from the 7th - 8th century once stood. It is marked out on the grass, and shows that this area of Scotland was once part of the mighty kingdom of Northumbria.

Garvald

6 miles SE of Haddington off the B6370

This tiny village lies on the northern slopes of the Lammermuir Hills. **Garvald Parish Church** dates partly from the 12th century, and has a sundial dated 1633. South east of the village is the mansion of **Nunraw,** in whose grounds Cistercian monks, who arrived here in 1946, began building the Abbey of Sancta Maria in 1952. It was the first Cistercian monastery in Scotland since the Reformation, and was colonised by monks form Tipperary in Ireland. A Cistercian nunnery, founded by nuns from Haddington, had previously been founded here in about 1158. The mansion is now the abbey's guesthouse.

Gifford

4 miles S of Haddington on the B6369

Gifford was laid out in the 18th century, and is a pretty village with views of the Lammermuir Hills to the south. The whitewashed **Yester Parish Church**, which has Dutch influences, was built in 1708, and has a medieval bell. It was in Gifford that John Witherspoon, the only clergyman to sign the American Declaration of Independence, was born in 1723 (see also Paisley).

Southeast of the village is **Yester House**, designed by James Smith and dating from 1745. The interiors were later restyled by Robert Adam in 1789. Beyond it are the ruins of **Yester Castle**, built by Hugo de Gifford in the late 13th century. He was known as the "Wizard of Yester", and beneath the castle is a chamber known as **Goblin Ha'** where he is supposed to have practised magic and called up goblins and demons. Scott mentions him in *Marmion*.

The narrow road from Gifford up into the Lammermuir Hills is a fine drive, and takes you past Whiteadder reservoir and down into Berwickshire.

Pencaitland

6 miles SW of Haddington on the A6093

The oldest part of **Pencaitland Parish Church** is the Winton Aisle, which dates from the 13th century. Close to the village is the 500-year-old **Winton House**. It was built for the Seton family by the king's master mason, and is famous for its "twisted chimneys". It overlooks the Tyne, and has lovely terraced gardens. **Glenkinchie Distillery**, to the south of the village, has a small exhibition and offers tours showing how whisky is distilled.

Linlithgow

This ancient royal burgh was granted its royal charter in 1138. It is a lovely place, with many historic buildings in its old High Street, and has played a central role in Scotland's history. **Linlithgow Palace** (Historic Scotland), situated on the banks of **Linlithgow Loch**, dates originally from the reign of James I, who ruled in the early 15th century. It replaced an older castle where Edward I once stayed when he invaded Scotland in support of John Balliol's claim to the Scottish throne.

It was a favourite of many Scottish kings and queens, and it was here, in 1512, that James V was born. It was also the birthplace, in 1542, of his daughter, the tragic Mary Stuart. The birth room was most probably the **Queen's Bedchamber** in the northwest tower. Her association with Linlithgow Palace lasted only seven months, as her mother, Mary of Guise, later took her to the more secure Stirling Castle. When Mary Stuart returned from France in 1561 after the death of her husband King Francis II, she only stayed briefly at the castle, and it was allowed to decay.

Cromwell stayed here briefly in 1650 when he invaded Scotland after its parliament had declared Charles II king of Britain. Then, in 1745, Charles Edward

Linlithgow Palace

concrete to replace some of the carvings, and this introduced salts into the structure, which began its decay.

The **Outer Gateway** to the palace still stands, and on it are the coats of arms of the four orders of chivalry to which James V belonged - the Garter of England, the Thistle of Scotland, the Golden Fleece of Burgundy and St Michael of France.

Stuart stayed in the Palace. A year later the troops of the Duke of Cumberland moved in, and when they moved out they left their straw bedding too close to the fires. The whole place caught fire, and soon the whole building was ablaze, leaving it roofless and uninhabitable.

In the castle courtyard is the **King's Fountain**, built between 1536 and 1538 for James V and now being restored to full working order. It is the oldest fountain in Britain, and is in three tiers, with elaborate carving that symbolises his reign, and was badly damaged during the fire. A restoration scheme of the 1930s used

Opposite the Palace is **St Michael's Parish Church**, one of the most important medieval churches in Scotland. It dates from the 15th century, though a church had stood here long before that. Within the church one of the most unusual incidents in Scottish history took place. The church was especially dear to James IV, who worshipped there regularly. In 1514, he had decided to take a large army into England in support of France, which had been invaded by Henry VIII's troops. Most of the Scottish court was against the idea, as was James's wife Margaret, sister of the English king.

Union Canal near Linlithgow

But James held firm, and a few days before he and his army set out, he was at mass in St Michael's Church with his courtiers. A strange man with long, fair hair suddenly appeared in the church dressed in a blue gown tied with a white band and carrying a staff. Pushing aside the courtiers, he approached James and spoke to him. He had been sent "by his mother", he said, to tell James that no good would come of the invasion of England. Furthermore, he was not to meddle with other women.

Some of the courtiers tried to grab him, but before they could the old man made good his escape. Confusion reigned, and people immediately took the man to be a ghost. The reference to his mother, they said, meant that he had been sent by Our Lady (of whom James was especially fond). James took no heed, and marched into England. He, and all the flower of Scottish manhood, was wiped out on the field at Flodden. The "ghost's" prophecy came true.

People nowadays discount the ghost theory, and say that the whole thing had been orchestrated by James's wife with the help of some of the court. The reference to the king's meddling with other women was the Queen's own contribution to the event,

as James was renowned for his philandering.

One of the courtiers was Sir David Lyndsay, Lord Lyon and playwright, who knew all the tricks of the stage, and he may have been involved as well. There is a theory that says that Margaret had been put up to it by her brother Henry VIII, who was totally unprepared for a Scottish invasion, though this is now discounted. All she wanted to do was protect him from his own folly.

It was in Linlithgow that the Earl of Moray, Regent of Scotland, was assassinated in the street by James Hamilton of Bothwellhaugh, who later escaped to France. A plaque on the old **County Buildings** commemorates the event. In Annet House in the High Street is the **Linlithgow Story**, with displays and exhibits explaining the history of the town. There are also herb, fruit tree and flower gardens. At the **Linlithgow Canal Centre** in Manse Road is a small museum dedicated to the Union Canal, which links the Forth and Clyde Canal at Falkirk with Edinburgh. Trips along the canal are also available. **Beecraigs Country Park**, to the south of the town, is set in 913 acres of land near the Bathgate Hills. It has a loch where you can fish, a deer farm and a camping and caravan park.

To the north of the town is the **House of the Binns** (National Trust for Scotland), ancestral home of the Dalyell family, the best known member of which is Tam Dalyell the MP, who still lives there. In 1601 the Edinburgh butter merchant Thomas Dalyell married Janet, daughter of the first Baron Kinloss, and in 1630 he

Bonsyde House Hotel

Bonsyde, By Linlithgow,
West Lothian EH49 7NU
Tel: 01506 842229 Fax: 01506 846233
e-mail: info@bonsydehouse.co.uk

Linlithgow is a historic town, and set on a hillside to the north is the **Bonsyde House Hotel**, which offers the very best in Scottish hospitality. It is an elegant and historic country house with eight stylish en suite bedrooms that are the last word in comfort. Dining in the conservatory restaurant at the Bonsyde is an experience not to be missed, plus there is a wide range of superb bar snacks available. The hotel is close to the M9, and is only a few miles from Edinburgh Airport.

bought the lands of Binns, and set about enlarging the house. What you see now is largely that house.

His son was also Thomas, though he earned an unsavoury reputation as "Bluidie Tam Dalyel", scourge of the Covenanters. He was every inch a king's man, and when Charles I was executed in 1649, he vowed never to cut his hair until there was a king on the throne once more. And indeed, Bloody Tam's portrait in The Binns shows a man with hair flowing down past his shoulders. Tam also helped the Tsar of Russia reorganise the Russian army, and was made a nobleman of Russia. For that reason he also had another nickname - "The Bluidie Muscovite".

Another stately home near Linlithgow is **Hopetoun House**, possibly the grandest "big house" in Scotland. It sits almost on the banks of the Forth, and is home to the Marquis of Linlithgow. It was started in 1699 by the 1st Earl of Hopetoun, ancestor of the present Marquis, and designed by Sir William Bruce with enlargements by William Adam, who introduced the sweeping curves. The inside is spectacular and opulent, with ornate plasterwork, tapestries, furnishings and paintings. Surrounding the house is magnificent parkland extending to 100 acres, with a deer park and spring garden. The main approach to the house is by the Royal Drive, which can only be used by royalty. George IV used it when he visited Scotland in 1822, and Elizabeth II also used it in 1988.

Around Linlithgow

Bo'ness

3 miles N of Linlithgow on the A904

The town's real name is Borrowstoneness, though it is always referred to nowadays by its shortened name. It is an industrial town, and was formerly one of Scotland's leading whaling ports. It was near here that the eastern end of the Antonine Wall terminated. Near the town is the Kinneil Estate, with, at its centre, **Kinneil House**. It was built by the Hamilton family in the 16th and 17th centuries. It isn't open to the public, though it can be viewed from the outside. However, within the house's 17th century stable block is the **Kinneil Museum**, which tells the story of Bo'ness over the last 2000 years. There is also an exhibition called "Rome's Northern Frontier". The ruins of **Kinneil Church** lie near the house, and probably date from the 13th century with later additions. It was accidentally destroyed by fire in 1745 by a troop of dragoons stationed at the house.

The town's main attraction is the **Bo'ness and Kinneil Railway**, which has been developed since 1979 by the Scottish

Railway Preservation Society. There is a Scottish railway exhibition as well as workshops and a working station. Trips on the steam trains, which run, between Bo'ness and Birkhill Station are popular with the public. At Birkhill are the caverns of the former **Birkhill Fireclay Mine**, which can be explored.

Blackness

4 miles NE of Linlithgow on the B903

Blackness Castle (Historic Scotland) must be the most unusually shaped castle in Scotland. It sits on a promontory jutting out into the Firth of Forth, and from the air looks like a huge ship. It was a Crichton stronghold, with the first castle on the site being built in about 1449 by Sir George Crichton, Sheriff of Linlithgow and Admiral of Scotland. However, there is an intriguing but untrue story about how the castle eventually came to look like a ship. By the early 16th century the castle had passed to the Douglases. James V appointed Archibald Douglas as Lord High Admiral of the Scottish fleet, but soon discovered that he had made a mistake, as every time Archibald went to sea he became sea sick.

The young James was enraged, and threatened to dismiss him. Archibald, who was making a fortune out of selling commissions in the navy, wanted to retain his position. So he promised his king that if he was allowed to keep his job, he would build him a ship that the English couldn't sink and on which he would never be sick. Mollified, the king agreed, and Douglas built Blackness Castle. However, a more mundane explanation of its shape is the restricted shape of the site on which it was built.

The castle was subsequently besieged by Cromwell's army in 1650, and was later used as a prison for Covenanters. During the Napoleonic wars, it was again used as a prison, this time for French prisoners-of-war. After that it was used as an ammunition dump, and was finally restored and opened to the public.

Torphichen

3 miles S of Linlithgow on the B792

The Knights of the Order of St John of Jerusalem, or the Knights Hospitallers as they were more commonly called, was a monastic order of soldier monks formed in the 11th century to look after St John's Hospital in Jerusalem, and to offer hospitality and protection to pilgrims travelling to the Holy Land.

Torphichen Preceptory (Historic Scotland) was the Scottish headquarters of the order. It was founded in about 1124, with the lands of Torphichen being given to the monks by David 1. The head of a Knights Hospitaller monastery was called a "preceptor", and for this reason a monastery was always known as a "preceptory". During the Wars of Independence, the then preceptor supported Edward I of England, and after Bannockburn the monks had to flee. However, they later returned.

The only parts left standing of the original preceptory are the transepts and crossing of the monastic church. Above the crossing is a tower, which, no doubt because of the Knights' military role, looks more like a castle than a church tower. Within a small room is a display about the modern Order of St John, which was refounded in 1947 as a separate order in Scotland by George VI. Nowadays it runs old folks homes, mountain rescue units and hospitals in Scotland. Where the nave once stood is now **Torphichen Parish Church**, which dates from 1756, though it incorporates masonry from the earlier building.

Livingston

6 miles S of Linlithgow off the M8

Livingston is one of Scotland's new towns, built round a historic village, which has the **Livingston Parish Church** of 1732. At the 20-acre **Almond Valley Heritage Centre** in Millfield the visitor can find out about local history and the environment, including the Scottish shale industry, which once thrived in West Lothian. There is also an 18th century water mill, a small railway line, a farm, a picnic area and teahouse. The **Almondell and Calderwood Country Park** is three miles east of the town centre, and has woodland and riverside walks. Almondell was originally a private estate, which belonged to the Erskine family, and many items from Kirkhill House, with which it was associated, have been relocated within the park, such as the entrance gates and the astronomical pillar. Calderwood was also a private estate, and belonged to the barons of Torphichen. This area has been deliberately left undeveloped to encourage wildlife. The Oakbank shale bings are a reminder of the shale industry, and have been landscaped. A good view of the surrounding countryside, and even up into Fife, is available from the top.

Mid Calder

8 miles SE of Linlithgow on the B8046

The Kirk of Mid Calder has an apse built in the 16th century. One of the 17th century ministers of the church was Hew Kennedy, who was zealous in his persecution of witches. In 1644 several of them were burnt at the stake.

While staying at **Calder House** (not open to the public) John Knox first administered Holy Communion using the new reformed liturgy. In 1848 the Polish pianist Chopin also stayed here.

Bathgate

6 miles S of Linlithgow on the A89

Bathgate is a substantial industrial town, and was formerly a centre for the shale oil industry. **Sir James Young Simpson**, who introduced chloroform into midwifery, was the son of a Bathgate baker, and he was born here in 1811, as was **James "Paraffin" Young**, who opened the world's first oil refinery in 1850, extracting paraffin from the local shale. **Cairnpapple Hill** (Historic Scotland), to the north of the town, is 1017 feet high, and was the site of a temple built about 2000 - 25000 BC. Fragments of bone and pottery have been found. The view from the top is magnificent, and on a clear day both the Bass Rock in the Firth of Forth and the mountains of Arran in the Firth of Clyde can be seen.

In Mansefield Street is the **Bennie Museum**, which contains collections relating to local history. **Polkemmet Country Park** is four miles west of the town, and has a golf course, a driving range, bowling green and picnic areas. The whole area was owned at one time by the Baillie family, and a mausoleum, built by Robert Baillie, fourth Lord Polkemmet, can still be seen.

Fife

The county of Fife consists of a long peninsula that stretches out eastwards between the Firths of Forth to the south and Tay to the north. It is steeped in history, and for that reason is sometimes referred to as the "Kingdom of Fife". James II once called it a "fringe of gold on a beggar's mantle", meaning that, in his day, it had prosperous coastal towns and a barren interior.

Here, at Dunfermline, was Scotland's capital before Edinburgh took over, and here were small prosperous seaports, which traded with Europe. You can still see the European influence today. Some of the older buildings have a distinctly Low Countries feel to them, and the roofs of the older houses have red pantiles - brought in as ballast from the Netherlands and the Baltic countries - instead of slates. These ports, with names such as Crail, Pittenweem and Anstruther,

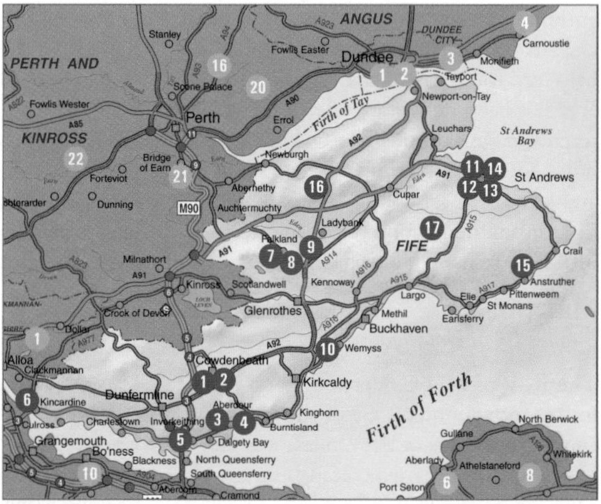

PLACES TO STAY, EAT AND DRINK

The Cross Guns, Cowdenbeath	1	Pub with Food	p166
Wee Jimmy's Bar/Lounge, Cowdenbeath	2	Pub with Food	p166
Cedar Inn, Aberdour	3	Hotel	p167
Forth View Hotel, Hawk Craig Point	4	Hotel	p167
Inverkeithing Museum, Inverkeithing	5	Visitor Attraction	p169
The Unicorn Inn, Kincardine-on-Forth	6	Pub with Restaurant	p173
Falkland Palace & Gardens, Falkland	7	Visitor Attraction	p175
Stag Inn, Falkland	8	Pub with Restaurant	p176
Lomond Hills Hotel & Leisure Centre, Freuchie	9	Hotel	p176
Belvedere Hotel & Restaurant, Coxtool	10	Hotel	p177
Guardbridge Hotel, St Andrews	11	Hotel	p179
The Vine Leaf, St Andrews	12	Restaurant	p179
Pilmour Hotel, St Andrews	13	Hotel	p180
West Park House, St Andrews	14	B&B	p181
Scottish Fisheries Museum, Anstruther	15	Visitor Attraction	p184
The Fernie Castle Hotel, Lethan	16	Hotel	p187
Peat Inn, Peat Inn	17	Pub, Food and Accommodation	p188

● Denotes entries in other chapters

are still there, though now they rely on tourism rather than trade.

Of all the towns on the county's east coast the most famous is surely St Andrews. Seen from a distance, it shimmers with spires and church towers, and is crammed with old buildings and historical associations. It was formerly a place of pilgrimage because of its great cathedral, the impressive ruins of which still overlook the shore. In it were kept the relics of St Andrew, Scotland's national saint, and this made it the country's ecclesiastical capital in pre Reformation days. It was also the seat of an archbishop, and was where Scotland's first university was founded. Even today students can be seen dressed in their traditional red gowns as they scurry to lectures during term time. And the place still attracts pilgrims, though now they come in the name of sport, for the town - or perhaps we should call it small city - is the recognised world home of golf.

View over St Andrews

The county's largest town is Kirkcaldy, famous for the manufacture of linoleum. So much so that people used to say that you could always tell when you were approaching the town by its "queer-like smell". But this royal burgh, which was granted its charter in 1644, is much more that a manufacturing centre, and has many historical associations. At one time it was known as the "Lang Toun", because it appeared to consist of one long street, though it has now spread inland. And it can lay fair claim to being the birthplace of economics, because, in 1728, Adam Smith was born here.

To the west of the county another industry held sway - coal mining. The Fife coalfields used to employ thousands of men, but now it has all but gone, leaving in its wake many small mining villages that are proud and fiercely independent. Dunfermline is the largest town in this area - another Fife royal burgh whose roots go deep into Scotland's history, having been granted its royal charter in 1124. It's abbey, like the cathedral at St Andrews, was once a place of pilgrimage, and is now the resting place of one of Scotland's great heroes, Robert the Bruce. And, like Kirkcaldy, it too has its famous sons. Charles I was born here in 1600, as was, in 1835, Andrew Carnegie the millionaire philanthropist.

Mining has given way to electronics as an employer, and this part of Fife is well and truly part of "silicon glen". But the area hasn't lost its attractiveness, and one of the places that must be visited is Culross, surely one of the loveliest and most historic small towns in Scotland.

Since the opening of the Tay Road Bridge in 1966, the towns and village of northern Fife, such as Newport-on-Tay, Tayport, Leuchars and Wormit, have become dormitory towns for Dundee, across the firth. Even before this people were commuting, thanks to the Tay Rail Bridge,

Dunfermline Abbey and Ruin

founding a Benedictine priory (later to become Dunfermline Abbey) in its place and inviting monks from Durham to serve in it.

Scotland in the 11th century was a small kingdom, perched precariously on the edge of the known world. It was Margaret who brought refinement to the court and made the country think of itself as an integral part of Europe. Under Margaret and Malcolm, who was also a driving force, trade with the continent flourished. Malcolm revelled in this, as though he could neither read nor write, he hankered after refinement and culture, and had only a few years before moved Scotland's capital from Perthshire to Dunfermline to be nearer the Fife ports that traded with Europe. Under Margaret, the centre of power shifted once more - this time to Edinburgh, which later became the nation's capital.

One other innovation is attributed to St Margaret - buttons on the sleeves of men's jackets. She had been disgusted to see that Scottish courtiers - in common with courtiers throughout Europe - wiped their noses on their sleeves, so set about making this habit as uncomfortable as possible.

She died soon after her husband and son were killed in Northumberland in 1093, and was buried in the abbey she had founded. Soon a cult grew up round her, and her burial spot became a place of pilgrimage. In 1250 she was canonised, and even today she is looked upon with reverence in Scotland. The remains of her shrine, destroyed during the Reformation, can still be seen.

Dunfermline Abbey as we see it today is a mixture of dates. The heavily buttressed

opened in 1887 after the first bridge collapsed into the firth in 1879 with much loss of life.

Dunfermline

Now an important industrial town, Dunfermline was at one time the capital of Scotland, and still has many reminders of its past glories. It was here that Malcolm III (known as "Malcolm Canmore", meaning "bighead") and his second queen, later to become **St Margaret of Scotland**, held court in the 11th century.

Malcolm and Margaret's reign was a turning point in Scotland's history. Margaret was the daughter of Edgar Aetheling, heir-apparent to the English throne, and was half Saxon and half Hungarian. When she came to the Scottish court, she was shocked at what she found, and, with her husband's consent, set about changing things. The Scottish church, though nominally subservient to Rome, was still observing the old Celtic rites, which she found abhorrent. So the church was the first thing she changed. A Culdee (from the Irish céli dé, meaning "servants of God") monastery manned by Celtic-Irish priests had previously been established in Dunfermline, and she suppressed it, nave is Norman, and is reminiscent of Durham Cathedral. Beneath it lie the remains of the original church. The choir was rebuilt in the early 19th century as the parish church, and it was during its construction that workmen came across the skeleton of a man. It was lying within a stone coffin and wrapped with gold cloth. It was immediately recognised as that of Robert the Bruce, King of Scots, as the breastbone and ribs had been sawn away. After he died, Bruce's heart had been removed from his body so that it could be taken to the Holy Land (see also Melrose). It was re-interred with due reverence, and now a brass plate beneath the pulpit marks the spot. Around the battlements of the abbey tower are the words "King Robert the Bruce".

The **Dunfermline Abbey and Palace Visitors Centre** (Historic Scotland) tells of the history of the abbey and of the later palace that was built on the site of the monastic buildings. A magnificent 200 feet long buttressed wall is all that now remains of the palace where Charles I was born.

To the west of the abbey is a great mound known as **Malcolm's Tower**, all that remains of Malcolm's fortress. It sits within **Pittencrieff Park** (famous for its peacocks), which was gifted to the town by Andrew Carnegie in 1908. The park had always fascinated him as a boy, though being privately owned at the time, he was always denied access. So when he had the money, he bought it and threw it open to the people of the town. Also in the park is **Pittencrieff House Museum**, based in a 17th century mansion, which has an art gallery and displays on local history.

The **Abbot House Heritage Centre** is housed in a 14th - 16th century house to the north of the abbey in Maygate. It was formerly the Abbot's Lodgings for the great Benedictine monastery, as well as its administrative centre. Poets, kings and bishops visited, and it played its part in some of the great events in Scottish history.

St Margaret's Shrine has been reconstructed with its wall, showing just how rich the interior of the abbey was when it was at the height of its powers. In all, over 1000 years of history can be seen, from the Picts right up until the present day.

Near Chalmers Street Car Park, about a quarter of a mile north of Abbot House, can be found **St Margaret's Cave**, where the pious queen prayed in solitude. A legend has it that Malcolm became suspicious of his wife's unexplained absences from court, and fearing that she had a lover, followed her to the cave one day, where he found her kneeling in prayer.

Andrew Carnegie was, in the 19th century, the richest man in the world. He was born in Dunfermline in 1835, and emigrated with his parents to the United States in 1848. By the 1880s, he had amassed a fortune through iron and steel making, and retired from business in 1901 to distribute his wealth. His humble birthplace in Moodie Street, a former weaver's cottage, is now the central feature of the **Andrew Carnegie Birthplace Museum**. It tells the story of the great man from his humble origins to his death in 1919. In Pittencrief Park, close to the **Louise Carnegie Gates** (named after his wife) is a statue of the great man.

It is not only New York that has a **Carnegie Hall** - Dunfermline has one as well, housing a theatre and concert hall. It can be found in East Port, near the **Dunfermline Museum and Small Gallery** in Viewfield. Here the history of the town is explained, including its time as a centre of manufacture for linen and silk, which continued right up until the 20th century.

To the north of the town, at Lathalmond, is the **Scottish Vintage Bus Museum**, housed in a former Royal Navy Stores depot. It is possibly the largest collection of vintage buses in Britain, and has been open since 1995.

Around Dunfermline

Cowdenbeath

5 miles NE of Dunfermline, off the A909

This small town was at the centre of the Fife coalfields, and though the mines have long gone, it still has the feel of a mining community about it. Its football team has perhaps the most unusual nickname of any senior team in Scotland - the "Blue Brazils". **Racewall Cowdenbeath** has stock car racing every Saturday evening from March to November.

Lochgelly

7 miles NE of Dunfermline on the B981

Lochgelly is a small mining town, famous throughout Scotland at one time for the manufacture of the "Lochgelly", the leather strap used to punish children in school.Near the town is the **Lochore Meadows Country Park**, set in 1200 acres of reclaimed industrial land. The last pits closed here in 1966, with the park being created on the site in the early 70s. The area is now a haven for wildlife.

The Cross Guns

High Street, Cowdenbeath, Fife KY4 8LS
Tel: 01383 514413
e-mail: oldcrossguns@aol.com

Owned and managed by Roseann Lees, **The Cross Guns** in Cowdenbeath is the perfect place for a relaxing drink or a tasty pub lunch. There is a wide range of beers, wines and spirits for the discerning palate, as well as soft drinks should you be driving. Meals are served in the cosy, inviting lounge from noon until 2.30pm Mon-Sat, and use only the finest and freshest local produce wherever possible. Tradition reigns in this friendly hostelry, which is housed in a former railway station. You'll be on the right tracks if you make your way to The Cross Guns!.

Wee Jimmy's Bar/Lounge

High Street, Cowdenbeath KY4 9AE
Tel: 01383 511126 Fax: 01383 610086

If you're looking for a friendly, family-run pub in Fife, then **Wee Jimmy's Bar/Lounge** is the place for you. It is situated in the old town of Cowdenbeath, and has the look and feel of an authentic Scottish hostelry. The inside is cosy and warm, with comfortable seating and old prints on the wall, and is popular with locals and tourists alike.

The pub lunches -always prepared to your own liking - are tasty and filling, and great value for money, A wide range of beers, wines, spirits and - should you be driving - soft drinks - is always available. The atmosphere is authentic Scotland - warm, friendly and welcoming, with live music once a month.

The 260-acre Loch Ore, created as a result of mining subsidence, is stocked with brown trout. It can also be used for water sports.

Saline

6 miles NW of Dunfermline on the B913

The Knockhill Racing Circuit is Scotland's national motor sports centre for cars and motorbikes, and has meetings on most Sundays from April to October.

Aberdour

6 miles E of Dunfermline on the A921

Aberdour is a small coastal burgh that received its charter in 1500. The restored **St Fillan's Church** is partly Norman, and has what is known as a "leper window". This was a window looking on to the high altar through which lepers could see from a private room the mass being celebrated. It is said that Robert the Bruce, himself suffering from leprosy, used the window after his victory at Bannockburn in 1314.

In the late 18th century the church was abandoned, and gradually fell into ruin. However, in 1925 work began on restoring it. The town has two beaches, one of which, **Silver Sands**, has won a European blue flag for its cleanliness. The ruins of **Aberdour**

Castle (Historic Scotland), close to the church, date from the 14th century, later additions being made in the 16th and 17th century. At one time it was owned by James Douglas, 4th Earl of Morton and Regent of Scotland. In 1581 he was executed for his part in the murder of Mary Stuart's second husband, Lord Darnley. The **Aberdour Festival** is held every year at the end of July.

Dalgety Bay

4 miles SE of Dunfermline off the A921

The ivy-clad ruins of **St Bridget's Church**, once the burial place of the Earls of Dunfermline, date from the 12th century. It was near Dalgety Bay that the murder of James Stewart, the **2nd Earl of Moray**, took place, an event which is remembered in one of the best known of Scottish songs, *The Bonnie Earl o' Moray*. Moray was the grandson of Regent Morton, regent of Scotland when Mary Stuart abdicated in favour of her infant son, later to be James VI, and was a popular nobleman, dashing and handsome. But he was always feuding with the Earls of Huntly, one of the great Catholic families of the time, and was implicated in a coup to overthrow James VI, though he probably had no involvement.

But Huntly saw his chance, and armed with a king's warrant and a troop of soldiers, set out to seize the young earl. He eventually found him at his mother's castle at Donibristle, in what is now Dalgety Bay. He demanded that he give himself up, but Moray refused.

The troops therefore set fire to the building. Some men ran out from the front of the castle to distract Huntly's men while Moray ran out the back way, hoping to hide near the shore. Unfortunately, unknown to Moray, his bonnet had caught fire, and the smoke gave him away. He was hacked to death, with Huntly, it is said, striking the fatal blow. When James VI found out about the murder, he feigned outrage, though when the crowds later discovered that Huntly had been armed with a king's warrant, James had to flee to Glasgow to escape its wrath.

It was a death that touched the pulse of the common people of Scotland at a time when the country was in turmoil, not knowing if the Reformation would take hold or whether Roman Catholicism would make a return. Huntly spent a few weeks in Blackness Castle as a punishment, and was then released.

Inchcolm

6 miles SE of Dunfermline, in the Firth of Forth

This small island was at one time known as the "Iona of the East". On it are the substantial ruins of **Inchcolm Abbey** (Historic Scotland), dedicated to St Columba. The story goes that Alexander I, son of Malcolm III and Queen Margaret, was crossing the Forth in 1123 when a storm blew up and the royal party had to seek refuge on the island, which had, for many years, supported a succession of hermits. The hermit of the time shared his meagre provisions with his guests for three days until the storm subsided. When Alexander reached the shore he vowed to build a monastery dedicated to St Columba on the island in thanksgiving for his safe passage, but before he could put his plans into effect he died. His younger brother David I, who succeeded him, founded a priory, which eventually became the Abbey of Inchcolm.

A small stone building to the west of the abbey may have been the original monks' cell, though it has been much restored over the years. The abbey buildings as we see them now date mainly from the 15th century, and represent the most complete medieval abbey in Scotland, with most of the buildings remaining intact.

In the late 18th century, a military hospital was set up on the island to look after wounded sailors from the Russian fleet, which was using the Firth of Forth as a base. In the 20th century it was fortified as part of the United Kingdom's sea defences, and some of these can still be seen. Over 500 troops were stationed on the island, and the first air raid of World War II took place not far away, when German bombers, in 1939, dropped bombs not far from the Forth Rail Bridge.

Inverkeithing

3 miles S of Dunfermline off the A90

Inverkeithing is an ancient royal burgh, which received its royal charter in about 1193. It sits close to the Forth Road and Rail Bridges, and has many old buildings. The **Mercat Cross** is 16th century, and the **Old Town Hall** opposite, with its outside staircase, dates from 1770. Of the 15th century **St Peter's Church**, only the tower remains, as the rest was built in 1826. **Inverkeithing Museum** (see panel below), housed in the hospitum of an old friary, tells the story of Inverkeithing and of **Admiral Sir Samuel Greig**, a local man born in 1735 who entered the service of Tsarina Catherine of Russia in 1764. He largely created the modern Russian navy, manning it initially with Scottish officers.

Near the town, in 1651, was fought the **Battle of Inverkeithing** between a Royalist force under Sir Hector MacLean of Duart and the Parliamentarian forces of Cromwell. The result was a victory for the Parliamentarians, and the death of MacLean. The immediate result of the battle was the plundering of Inverkeithing and Dunfermline, and the long-term result was the ascendancy of Cromwell in Scotland. A small cairn by the roadside opposite **Pitreavy Castle** (not open to the public), erected by the Clan MacLean, commemorates the event.

In the 14th century Pitreavy Castle was owned by Christina Bruce, Robert the Bruce's sister. It later passed to the Kellock family and the Wardlaws, who rebuilt it. From World War II until 1996 a bunker beneath the castle was the naval operations HQ for Scotland.

It is reputedly haunted by three ghosts: the Grey Lady, the Green Lady and a headless Highlander who is said to moan in anguish.

North Queensferry

4 miles S of Dunfermline off the A90

This small town was the northern terminus for the ferry that plied across the Forth from South Queensferry in West Lothian, originally founded by Queen Margaret (hence the town's name) in the 11th century. It sits on a small peninsula, which juts out into the Forth where the river has its narrowest point downstream from the Kincardine Bridge. The **Forth Bridges Visitors Centre** is housed within the Queensferry Lodge Hotel, and tells the story of the two bridges spanning the Forth. There is a magnificent scale model of the Firth of Forth, as well as photographs,

Inverkeithing Museum

The Friary, Queen Street, Inverkeithing, Fife
Tel: 01383 313838
(Fife Council Museums West, Dunfermline)

Inverkeithing Museum is housed in the upper floor of a wonderful 14th century Friary guest house, standing amidst well tended gardens. The gallery is only small but has a lovely collection of local photographs, paintings and artefacts, illustrating the history of the area. Admiral Greig, Inverkeithing's most famous son - the "Father of the Russian Navy", is featured. Open Thursday, Friday, Saturday and Sunday 11am to 12.30 pm and 1pm to 4pm.

Admission is free but access is by stairs only and so is not suitable for the disabled.

Forth Bridge

documents and artefacts. **Deep Sea World** is billed as "Scotland's Aquarium", and takes you on a walk along the "ocean floor", thanks to the world's longest underwater tunnel made of specially toughened glass. Fish swim above and beside you in a specially made sea containing a million gallons of water. As you stand within it you can see sharks, stingrays and electric eels. A special touch pool allows you to touch sharks, sea urchins and anemones.

North Queensferry is the start of the **Fife Coastal Path**, a 78-mile long pathway that eventually takes you through most of the small picturesque towns and villages on the Fife coast, ending at the Tay Bridge on the Firth of Tay.

Charlestown

3 miles SW of Dunfermline on a minor road off the A985

This small village was established in 1756 by Charles Bruce, 5th Earl of Elgin, to exploit the large deposits of limestone in the area, including an easily worked crag facing the sea. It was Scotland's first planned industrial village, though Bruce died before the work was finished. It was finally completed by the 7th Earl (of Elgin Marbles fame). There were 9 kilns here at one time producing lime for building, agriculture and the making of iron and glass. It was a self-sufficient community, with its own harbour, shops and school, and the houses were arranged in the shape of the founder's initials - CE.

The works closed in 1956, having produced in their 200 years of existence over 11 million tons of quicklime. Now guided walks round the complex are available in the summer months thanks to the Charlestown Lime Heritage Trust. Nearby is the village of **Limekilns**, which was once a port for the monks of Dunfermline Abbey.

Culross

7 miles W of Dunfermline on a minor road off the A985

If you wish to see what a Scottish burgh looked like in the 16th, 17th and 18th centuries, then the royal burgh of Culross is the place to do it. It was granted its royal charter in 1592, and though having a

Deep Sea World, North Queensferry

population of no more than a few hundred, it had its own town council and provost up until local government reorganisation in 1975.

It is undoubtedly the most picturesque of Fife's old burghs - a situation that owes more to the town's relative poverty in the 18th, 19th and early 20th centuries than any wish to preserve the past. In the 16th century it was a prosperous port that traded with the Low Countries, but when this trade dried up it sunk into poverty. The council, over the years, didn't have the money to make "improvements" or rebuild the huddle of old houses that form the town's central area. Now it is largely owned by the National Trust or Scotland.

It is a thriving and lively community with most of the quaint crow-step gabled houses occupied. The streets are cobbled, and those around the old **Mercat Cross** (dating from 1588) have a feature known as the "crown o' the causie", a raised portion in the middle where only the wealthy were allowed to walk, while the rest of the townsfolk had to walk on the edges where water and dirt congregated.

The town's main industries were coalmining, salt panning and the making of baking girdles. Coal mining had been introduced by the monks of Culross Abbey at a time when coal was little known about, and wondrous tales spread round Scotland about the "stones that could burn". After the Reformation, the mines were taken over by a man called Sir George Bruce, a descendant of Robert the Bruce. Between 1575 and his death 50 years later he had revolutionised the industry. He even had a tunnel dug under the waters of the Firth of Forth, which was a marvel in its time. It stopped one mile from the coast, where it came up to sea level surrounded by a stone wall to keep the water out. James VI was fascinated by Culross's industry, and paid a visit. Sir George took him on a tour of the mine, and led the unsuspecting king along the tunnel. When he emerged and found himself surrounded on all four sides by water, he panicked, shouting "treason!"

As an offshoot of the mining industry, salt panning became another major industry in the town. It is reckoned that at one time there were 50 saltpans along the coast, all using inferior coal to heat salt water from the sea. Another industry was the making of iron girdles for cooking. Culross blacksmiths are said to have invented these round, flat utensils for frying and cooking after Robert the Bruce, in the 14th century, ordered that each one of his troops be given a flat pan for cooking oatcakes.

Nothing remains of Sir George's mining ventures. However, his home, now called **Culross Palace**, still stands, and is open to the public. Work started on it in 1597, and is a typical residence of its time for someone of Sir George's standing in society. It has splendid kitchen gardens. Along from it is the **Town House**, gifted to the National Trust for Scotland in 1975 when Culross Town Council was wound up. It was

The Gates of the Palace and Garden, Culross

built in 1625 with later additions, and at one time the ground floor was a debtors' prison, while the attic was used as a prison for witches. It now houses the local tourist information centre.

Beside the Mercat Cross is **The Study**. It was built about 1610, and after the Palace, is Culross's grandest house. When the Church of Scotland was Episcopalian, the town formed part of the diocese of Dunblane, and it was here that Bishop Robert Leighton stayed on his visits. The quaint Outlook Tower housed his actual study, hence the name of the house. If you continue past The Study, along Tanhouse Brae and into Kirk Street, you will eventually reach **Culross Abbey**. The choir of the church (restored in 1633) still stands, and is used as the parish church, though the other buildings have either disappeared or are in ruins. It was founded in 1217 by Malcolm, Earl of Fife, and housed a Cistercian order of monks. Off the north transept is the Bruce Vault, where there is an impressive monument to Sir George Bruce, his wife and their eight children.

Culross was the birthplace, in AD 514, of St Kentigern, patron saint of Glasgow. In 1503 Archbishop Blackadder of Glasgow erected a small chapel on the spot where the birth is supposed to have taken place, and its ruins can still be seen to the east of the village. The story goes that he was the son of Thenew (also known as Enoch), a princess of the kingdom of the Lothians. When her father Loth (after which the Lothians was supposedly named) discovered that she was pregnant, he banished her from his kingdom, and she set sail in a boat across the Firth of Forth. She landed at Culross, and here gave birth to her son, who was taken into care by a monk called Serf (later St Serf), who had established a monastic school there. It is now known that St Serf lived in the century following Kentigern's birth, so the story is doubtful.

But Culross's attractions aren't all historical. Close to the town is **Longannet Power Station**, one of Scotland's largest. There are organised tours (which have to be prebooked), and you can see the huge turbine hall from a viewing platform, as well as tour the visitors centre, which shows how coal produces electricity.

Stretching from Longannet past Culross to Combie Point on the shores of the Firth of Forth is the **Torry Bay Local Nature Reserve**, where you can see many species of birds, such as shelduck, greenshank and great crested grebe.

Kincardine on Forth

10 miles W of Dunfermline, on the A985

This small burgh, which received its charter in 1663, sits at the north end of the **Kincardine Bridge**. Up until the Forth Road Bridge opened in 1964, this was the only road crossing of the Forth downstream from Stirling. Opened in 1936, the middle section used to swivel to allow ships to pass up the river.

The town is full of small, old-fashioned cottages with red pantiled roofs, and there are the ruins of the 17th century **Tulliallan Church**. The burgh's **Mercat Cross** dates from the 17th century, and it was in the town, in 1842, that Sir James Dewar, inventor of the vacuum flask was born. To the west of the town is **Tulliallan Castle**, now the main police training college in Scotland.

Kirkcaldy

Kirkcaldy is the largest town in Fife, and is famous for the manufacture of linoleum. At one time it was known as the "Lang Toun", due to the fact that it appeared to stretch out along one main street. It was created a royal burgh in 1644, and one of the famous events held here every year in April is the **Links Market**, reckoned to be the longest street fair in Europe. The town's Esplanade is cordoned off from traffic and taken over by swings, roundabouts, dodgems, carousels, hoopla stalls and all the other attractions of a modern funfair.

The Unicorn Inn

15 Excise street, Kincardine-on-Forth,
Fife FK10 4LN
Tel: 01259 739129
e-mail: info@theunicorn.co.uk
website: www.theunicorn.co.uk

For good food in a smart and friendly ambience, there is no better place than **The Unicorn Inn** in Kincardine-on-Forth. A former 17th century coaching inn, it has now been refurbished to an extremely high standard, and serves excellent food

prepared from only the finest and freshest of ingredients. Fresh beef from the Buccleuch Estates - seafood and smoked salmon from Fort William - and vegetables that are sourced locally - all are served here. Eat in The Grill, where the choice ranges from old favourites such as haddock and hand-cut chips to the best quality Scotch Beef Steaks or Lobster fresh from their tank. The Red Room is ideal for special occassions as the exclusive menu and impressive wine list adds to its allure and elegance.

Within **Kirkcaldy Museum and Art Gallery** is an exhibition devoted to Wemyss Ware, a form of earthenware pottery that was produced in the town by the firm of Robert Heron and Son between 1882 and 1930. It is now much collected, and is possibly the most sought after pottery ever to have been made in Scotland. Its most distinctive feature was its decoration, which was bold, simple and direct. The firing methods caused a lot of waste, which meant that the pottery was always expensive. The museum also houses a local history collection, plus an extensive collection of Scottish paintings.

The ruins of **Ravenscraig Castle** sit on a promontory to the east of the town centre. It was built in the 15th century by James II for his queen, Mary of Gueldres, who died there in 1463. James had a passion for weaponry - especially guns - and had it built so that it could withstand the latest

Ravenscraig Castle, Kirkcaldy

artillery. In 1470 it passed to William Sinclair, Earl of Orkney, who had to give up his earldom and Kirkwall Castle to acquire it. Overlooking the town harbour is the 15th century **Sailor's Walk**, the town's oldest house. The **Old Parish Church** sits at the top of Kirk Wynd, and dates from 1808. However, its tower is medieval.

Beyond Ravenscraig Castle is **Dysart**, which, up until 1930, was a separate burgh. Its harbour area is very picturesque, with whitewashed cottages and houses dating from the 16th, 17th and 18th centuries. At one time this was a salt panning area, and **Pan Ha'** (meaning "Pan Haugh") is a group of particularly fine 17th century buildings with red pantiled roofs. **St Serf's Tower** is the tower of the former parish church, and dates from the 15th century. It looks more like a castle than a tower, and reflects the area's troubled times when English ships prowled the Forth. In Rectory Lane is the **John McDouall Stuart Museum**, dedicated to the life of a locally born explorer who, in 1861-62, made the first return journey across the Australian continent.

Adam Smith, the founder of the science of economics, was born in Kirkcaldy in 1723. He went on to occupy the chair of moral philosophy at Glasgow University, and his famous book, *The Wealth of Nations*, was partly written in his mother's house (now gone) in the town's High Street. Also born in the town were **William Adam** the architect, and his son, **Robert Adam**.

In the town's Abbotshall Kirkyard stands a statue to another person born in Kirkcaldy, but an unusual one. **Marjory Fleming** was a child writer whose nickname was "Pet Marjory". She died in 1811, and yet her writings have intrigued and delighted people down through the ages. She kept a journal, in which she jotted down thoughts, poems and biographical scraps. She was, by all accounts, a "handful", and when her mother gave birth to another girl in 1809, Marjory was sent to live with her aunt in Edinburgh. This is where her writing began, encouraged by her cousin Isa, and she eventually filled three notebooks. Nobody knows what she might have achieved in adulthood, because, one month short of her ninth birthday, and after she had returned to Kirkcaldy, she tragically died of meningitis. Her last piece of writing was a touching poem addressed to her beloved cousin. Her writings were subsequently published, and found great favour with the Victorians, though some frowned on the absolute honesty she displayed when it came to describing her tantrums and innermost thoughts.

Around Kirkcaldy

Glenrothes

5 miles N of Kirkcaldy on the A92

Glenrothes was one of the new towns established in Scotland in the late 1940s. In **Balbirnie Park**, which extends to 416 acres, is a late Neolithic stone circle dating from about 3000 BC. It was moved to its present site when the A92 was widened. The park was created in the estate of Balbirnie House, once owned by the Balfours.

Falkland

10 miles N of Kirkcaldy on the A912

This little royal burgh sits in the shadow of the **Lomond Hills**. There are two distinct peaks - East Lomond, at 1,471 feet, and West Lomond at 1,713 feet, the highest point in Fife. It has quaint old cobbled streets lined with 17th and 18th century cottages, and was a favourite place of the Scottish kings. **Falkland Palace** (National Trust for Scotland - see panel opposite) was built in the 15th century on the site of an earlier castle built by the Earls of Fife. James V later employed stonemasons to turn it into a magnificent Renaissance palace. It was never an important castle like Edinburgh or Holyrood. Rather it was a country retreat for Stuart kings to hunt deer and boar and get away from the affairs of state. James V died in Falkland Palace in 1542, and his daughter Mary Stuart, it is said, spent the best years of her tragic life at Falkland.

Mary was born a few days before James V died, and the story is told that when he was on his deathbed, and told about the birth of a daughter and heir, he exclaimed: "It cam' wi' a lass, and it'll gang wi' a lass!", meaning that the House of Stuart had started with Marjory, daughter of Robert the Bruce, and it would die out with his own daughter. In this prediction, he was both right and wrong. It did die out "wi' a lass", but not Mary Stuart. The last Stuart monarch was Queen Ann, who died in 1715. The Palace is still nominally the property of the monarch, and its chapel, housed in what was the banqueting hall in the South Range, is the only Roman Catholic Church in Britain within royal property.

Both Charles I and Charles II visited Falkland, and it was in the Palace, in 1650, that Charles 1l founded the Scots Guards. His father Charles I had founded a regiment in 1642 called "Argyll's Regiment" to act as his personal bodyguard in Ireland, and this had later merged with nine small regiments to form the Irish Companies. While at Falkland Charles II renamed this regiment The King's Lyfeguard of Foot, and proclaimed it to be his bodyguard. It was later renamed the Scots Guards.

In the East Range can be seen the King's Bedchamber and the Queen's Room, and within the Gatehouse are the Keeper's

Falkland Palace and Gardens

Falkland, Cupar, Fife KY15 7BU
Tel: 01337 857397 Fax: 01337 857980
Tel: shop - 01337 857918
website: www.nts.org.uk

The **Royal Palace of Falkland** was the country residence of Stuart kings and queens when they hunted deer and wild boar in the Fife forest. Mary, Queen of Scots spent some of the happiest days of her tragic life here, 'playing the country girl in the woods and parks'. The Palace was built between 1501 and 1541 by James IV and James V, replacing earlier castle and palace buildings dating from the 12th century, traces of which can still be seen in the grounds. The roofed South Range contains the Chapel Royal, and the East Range the King's Bedchamber and the Queen's Room, both restored by the Trust. The Keeper's Apartments in the Gatehouse are now also on display. The palace contains fine portraits of the Stuart monarchs and two sets of 17th century tapestry hangings.

The garden, designed and built by Percy Cane between 1947 and 1952, contains three herbaceous borders enclosing a wide lawn with many varieties of shrubs and trees. Here also is the original Royal Tennis Court the oldest in Britain still in use, built in 1539. There is also a small herb garden border featuring quotations from John Gerard's book *Herboll* (1597).

Apartments. The gardens were laid out in the mid 20th century, and have magnificent herbaceous borders. Within the gardens is the **Royal Tennis Court**, which dates from the early 16th century, and the oldest in the country still in use. Here "real tennis" is played, with the roofs of the "lean tos" on either side of the court playing an integral part in the game. Tennis is still played here today, and there is a thriving club. The word "real" simply means royal, and it was a favourite sport of kings throughout Europe at one time. It is said that it dates back to at least the 11th century, when monks played it in the cloisters of their abbeys and priories. In the 14th century the Pope banned the playing of the game, but by this time it had become popular among the nobility.

The burgh's **Town Hall**, which dates from 1805, houses an exhibition about the town. Close to it, in the square, is a house with a plaque which commemorates Richard Cameron, a local schoolmaster and Covenanter, who was killed at the Battle of Airds Moss in Ayrshire in 1680 (see also Sanquhar).

Wemyss

4 miles NE of Kirkcaldy on the A955

Below the substantial ruins of **MacDuff Castle**, near the shoreline, are some caves, which have old carvings. They date mainly from between AD 400 to AD 800, though some may go back to before Christ. It has been claimed that there are more carvings

within these caves than in all the other caves in Britain put together. However, due to erosion and subsidence, most of the caves can no longer be entered, though they may be viewed from the shore.

Buckhaven and Methil

7 miles NE of Kirkcaldy on the B931

Buckhaven and Methil constituted one burgh, which was created in 1891. It's motto was Carbone Carbasoque, which means " By Coal and by Sail ", reflecting the fact that it used to export coal. As with other Fife ports, it also had saltpans, and by 1677 three pans were in operation, fuelled by coal. The Methil docks were opened in 1887. In Lower Methil's High Street is the **Methil Heritage Centre**, a lively community museum that explains the history of the area.

Buckhaven, to the west, was never as industrialised as Methil. It was once a fishing port and ferry terminal, and has some old, quaint cottages. In College Street there is the **Buckhaven Museum**, which has displays about the town's industries, including fishing.

Largo

11 miles NE of Kirkcaldy on the A915

There are two Largos - Lower Largo on the shores of the Forth and Upper Largo about half a mile inland, where the **Parish Church**, some parts of which date from the early 17th century, stands. It was here that Scotland's greatest seafarer and one time Admiral of the Fleet, **Sir Andrew Wood**, had his home. He died in 1515, and was buried in the kirkyard. He oversaw the building in Newhaven of the largest and most magnificent fighting ship of its day, the **Great Michael**, flagship of the Scottish fleet (See also Edinburgh). Nothing now remains of Wood's castle but a tower.

Alexander Selkirk was another seafaring man who came from Largo. He was born in 1676, and was the son of a local shoemaker. By all accounts he was a short-tempered, unpleasant man, and while sailing on a ship called the *Cinque Ports* in 1704, he quarrelled with the captain, who put him ashore on the uninhabited island of Juan Fernandez in the Pacific Ocean. He remained there until 1709, when he was rescued. Daniel Defoe, though he never met Selkirk, based his novel *Robinson Crusoe* on his adventures. A statue of Selkirk can be found near the harbour.

Kinghorn

4 miles SW of Kirkcaldy on the A921

This quiet little royal burgh saw one of the most decisive events in Scottish history. At the **Pettycur Crags** to the west of the town Alexander III was killed, throwing Scotland into turmoil. He was the last of the

country's Celtic kings, and had previously married Princess Margaret, daughter of Henry III of England, who had borne him two sons. But Margaret and the sons died; so, at the age of 45, Alexander married again, this time to Yolande, daughter of the Count of Dreux in France, in the hope of continuing the direct royal line.

After a meeting of his nobles at Edinburgh in 1286, Alexander was anxious to return to Queen Yolande, who was staying at Kinghorn Castle. The weather was stormy, and some of his men tried to dissuade him from crossing the Forth. However, he was adamant, and was taken across to Fife. But while riding along the Pettycur Crags, almost in sight of the castle where his wife awaited him, his horse stumbled, sending him over the cliffs to his death. It is said that the spot is haunted by the ghost of Queen Yolande, still waiting for her husband to return to her.

The heir to the Scottish throne was now three-year-old Margaret, known as the "Maid of Norway". She was the daughter of Alexander's own daughter, who had married Eric II of Norway. But while crossing from Norway to Scotland, Margaret also died, leaving the country without an heir. In the resultant vacuum, noblemen jockeyed for position, putting forward many claimants to the throne. Edward I of England was asked to intercede, and he saw his chance. He tried to incorporate Scotland into his own kingdom by installing a puppet king, and thus began the Wars of Independence.

A tall monument at the side of the road, erected in 1886, marks the spot where Alexander was killed.

Burntisland

6 miles SW of Kirkcaldy on the A921

This small royal burgh, called Portus Gratiae, or "Port of Grace" by the Romans, is overlooked by a 632 feet high hill called **The Binn**. It was formerly a port for exporting coal from the Fife coalfields, though its history goes well back beyond this. **St Columba's Parish Church** is a four square building dating from 1592, and is possibly based on a Dutch design. It was the first church built in Scotland after the Reformation which is still in use, and has a wealth of detail inside, including elaborate lofts and pews. The Holy Table sits at the centre of the church, with the pews facing it on four sides, emphasising the "equality of all believers". It is the birthplace of the **Authorised Version of the Bible**, as James VI attended a General Assembly of the Church of Scotland here in 1601, and put forward the proposal for a translation of the Bible into English. The suggestion was enthusiastically received, but it was not until James had assumed the throne of Great Britain that work began.

The **Burntisland Edwardian Fair Museum** is in the High Street, and features displays about Edwardian fairgrounds and local history. Off the coast of the town, in 1633, Charles I lost most of his treasure when his baggage ship, the *Blessing of Burntisland*, foundered and sank. Since then treasure hunters have been trying to find the wreckage.

Rossend Castle, at the western end of the town, was the scene of a bizarre incident concerning Mary Stuart and a love struck French poet who broke into her room to declare his undying love for her. As he had attempted it once before at Holyrood, he was later executed (see also St Andrews).

St Andrews

St Andrews is one of the most important and historic towns in Britain. Perhaps one should call it a city, as it was, in pre Reformation times, Scotland's ecclesiastical capital on account of its huge cathedral, which was Scotland's largest building in medieval times. It is also a university town, and the home of golf.

St Andrews Cathedral (Historic Scotland) was begun by Bishop Arnold in 1160, though the magnificent ruins you see

Guardbridge Hotel

1 Old St Andrews Road, St Andrews,
Fife KY16 0UD
Tel: 01334 839337
e-mail: forbesterris@tiscali.co.uk

Under the careful management of Sheila and Forbes Terris, the **Guardbridge Hotel** is a picturesque and comfortable small hotel with good parking within 3 miles of St Andrews. The bar/lounge with its open log fire and old, local photographs is very welcoming and the restaurant/dining room, which serves beautifully cooked, wholesome meals, has recently been refurbished to a high standard. Upstairs, the three bedrooms are cosy and comfortable. Overlooking a famous Bird Sanctuary and with a Suntrap Beer Garden this is a wonderful Hostelry which combines high standards with keen prices.

nowadays date from many periods. The choir was the first part to be built, and shows both Norman and Gothic details. The nave was completed in the late 13th century, though the great west front was blown down in a gale and had to be rebuilt. The whole building was finally consecrated in July 1318 in the presence of Robert the Bruce. This wasn't the first cathedral on the site. In about 1127 a more modest church was built, a remnant of which still remains. This is **St Rule's Tower** and its attached chancel, to the south of the ruins. From its top, there's a magnificent view of the town.

Legend tells us that St Rule (or Regulus) came from Patras in Greece in the 4th century, carrying with him the bones of St Andrew. He set up a shrine for them on the Fife coast, at what was then called Kilrimont - present day St Andrews. A more likely story is that the bones were brought here by Bishop Acca of Hexham in AD 732. The relics were eventually transferred to the later building, housed in a shrine behind the high altar. St Andrews soon became a place of pilgrimage, with people coming from all over Europe to pray at the shrine.

To the east of the cathedral and outside its precincts are the scant ruins of another church, **St Mary on the Rock**. It seems that when the cathedral was being built, there were still Culdee monks of the old Celtic church at St Andrews, and they refused to join the cathedral priory. In the 13th century they built this church for themselves, which became the first collegiate church in Scotland. However,

The Vine Leaf

South Street, St Andrews,
Fife KY16 9UN
Tel/Fax: 01334 477497
e-mail: vineleaf@tesco.net
website: www.vineleaf/standrews.co.uk

St Andrews is one of the most historic towns in Scotland, and within it you'll fine **The Vine Leaf**, one of Fife's most popular restaurants. Fresh seafood, game, gourmet vegetarian and Scottish beef make up the fixed price two or three course dinner menu which changes regularly. This is an eating place which is extremely popular with the locals (always a good sign!) and you are advised to book in advance. Children are most welcome at this no smoking establishment.

Pilmour Hotel

1 Pilmour Place, St Andrews,
Fife KY16 9HZ
Tel: 01334 473252 Fax: 01334 472252
e-mail: the.pilmourhotel@virgin.net
website: www.pilmourhotel.co.uk

The Pilmour Hotel is housed in an elegant early Victorian town house dating from 1840, and is owned and personally managed by Lennox Harrower and Kenny Phillip, two St Andreans who know the town intimately and have a great love of the place and its traditions. This is an establishment where quality and comfort meet high standards of service and a friendly, inviting atmosphere.

It has six tastefully furnished and decorated guest rooms, each one having spacious en suite facilities, satellite TV, hospitality trays, alarm clocks and hair dryers. Two of the en suite bathrooms have baths as well as showers. The beds are comfortable and cosy, and you're assured of a good night's sleep!

The hotel's lounge is extremely comfortable, and is dedicated to the history of St Andrews, with over 100 black and white photographs and postcards adorning its wall. Lennox and Kenny were assisted in this decoration scheme by golf historian, photographer and artist David Joy, who is a proud fourth generation St Andrean himself. A section of the lounge is dedicated to that great American golfing legend Bobby Jones, who won thirteen major championships between 1923 and 1930, and remains the only player ever to win all four majors in the same year. Golf is king in St Andrews, and the Pilmour Hotel is a two minute walk from the famous Old Course. It can even assist with its guests' personal golfing arrangements.

An extensive dinner and lunch menu is available in the lounge, as well as snacks and sandwiches. The legendary Pilmour breakfasts are served here as well, featuring haggis and locally-produced black pudding. Of course, lighter options are available as well. Close to the lounge is the well-stocked Clubhouse Bar - just right for that relaxing pint of Scottish ale or a fine single malt. It is a favourite place with tourists and locals alike, and there is a friendly, convivial atmosphere. All major sporting events can be enjoyed (and cheered on!) on the large plasma screen that is a feature of the bar.

St Andrews is only an hour's drive from Edinburgh Airport, and Leuchars train station, which is on the main King's Cross - Aberdeen line, is only five miles away. This makes it easily accessible from all parts of the country.

The Pilmour Hotel prides itself on being a small, intimate hotel where quality and value for money take pride of place. The service is excellent, the staff are friendly and knowledgeable, the prices are keen, and you are always sure of a warm welcome when you stay here!

the monks gradually adopted the rites of the Catholic Church, and its priests were soon allowed a place in the cathedral chapter.

St Andrews Castle was the archbishop's residence. It too sits on the coast, and its ruins are sturdy yet picturesque. It was here, in 1546, that **Cardinal David Beaton**, Archbishop of St Andrews, was murdered. In March of that year, George Wishart the Protestant reformer had been burnt at the stake in front of the castle on Beaton's authority, which made him many enemies (see also Dundee and Montrose). In May a group of Fife lairds broke into the castle and murdered him in his bedroom in revenge, hanging the corpse from the window. There then followed a long siege of the castle, during which sappers working for the Earl of Arran dug a tunnel beneath the fortifications to gain entry. These tunnels can still be seen today.

St Andrews Castle

Beaton was not the only Archbishop of St Andrews to have been murdered. The other one was **Archbishop James Sharp**, the Protestant archbishop when the Church of Scotland was Episcopalian. He had embarked upon a savage and bloody persecution of Covenanters, those people who wished the church to remain Presbyterian, and so was a hated man. In May 1679 he was returning to St Andrews from Edinburgh in a coach with his daughter. At Magus Muir, near the city, he was waylaid by Covenanters. Not averse to acts of unspeakable cruelty themselves when it suited them, they stabbed the archbishop to death in front of his daughter.

Nor was Wishart the only Protestant to have been executed in the town. There were others, including **Patrick Hamilton**, who was burnt at the stake in 1528 (see also Stonehouse). The spot is marked by his initials incorporated into the cobbles outside **St Salvator's Church** in North

Street, part of **St Salvator's College**.

It was on August 28 1413 that Pope Benedict XIII issued six papal bulls authorising the founding of the university. At first the classes were held in the cathedral, but this was found to be unsatisfactory. In 1450, therefore, Bishop Kennedy founded St Salvator's College, and classes moved there. In the 16th century two others were founded, **St Leonard's College** and **St Mary's College**. St Leonard's was eventually incorporated into St Salvator's, and a girl's school now stands on the site where it once stood. **St Leonard's Chapel** still exists, however, and the earliest parts date from the 12th century, showing it had been built long before the college came into being.

Bridge over Swilken Burn, Old Course

St Mary's College must be the loveliest of today's colleges. Step through the arch from South Street and you are in a grassed quadrangle surrounded by old, mellow buildings from the 16th century onwards. At the foot of the Stair Tower is **Queen Mary's Thorn**, said to have been planted by Mary Stuart in 1565. She visited the town five times, and possibly lodged at what is now known as **Queen Mary's House** in South Street. It dates from about 1525, and was built by one of the cathedral's canons. Charles II also stayed in it in 1650.

In February 1563 a French poet called Pierre de Châtelard was executed in Market Street. He had accompanied Mary when she returned from France, and swore undying love for her. However, he went too far, twice breaking into Mary's bedroom - once in Holyrood and once at Rossend Castle near Burntisland. He was taken from Burntisland to St Andrews Castle, and there imprisoned. On February 22 he was brought to trial and condemned to death. On the scaffold, he read out a poem called *Hymn to Death*, then cried out "Farewell cruel dame!"

Many people made political capital out of the incidents, saying he had been in the pay of the French, or that Mary had been his mistress. John Knox even claimed that when the poet had said "cruel dame" he had actually meant "cruel mistress", showing that Mary may had been too free with her sexual favours. However, there is little doubt that he was just a foolish young man who had unwisely fallen in love with a queen.

Further along South Street, in front of **Madras College**, one of the town's schools, is all that remains of the **Dominican Friary**. This is the 16th century north transept of the friary church, with some wonderful tracery in its windows. The friary was originally founded in the 13th century by Bishop William Wishart.

Almost across from it is **Holy Trinity Parish Church**. It was founded in the 15th century, though the building as we see it today dates largely from a rebuilding early in the 20th century. The only surviving parts of the medieval building are to be found in the west wall, some pillars and the tower. It contains a memorial to Archbishop Sharp, slain in 1679, though his body no longer rests under it. No doubt it had been removed and disposed of as soon as the Scottish church reverted to Presbyterianism.

At the west end of South Street can be found the **West Port**, one of the original gates into the town. It was built about 1589 on the site of an earlier port. In North Street is the **St Andrews Preservation Trust Museum and Garden**, housed in a charming building dating from the 16th century. It has displays and artefacts illustrating the town's history. The **St Andrews Museum** at Kinburn Park also celebrates the town's heritage.

At the Scores, down near the shore, you'll find the **St Andrews Aquarium**, which not only lets you see lots of fish and animals from sea horses to seals and piranha to sharks, but lets you touch some as well. Also on the Scores is the **Martyr's Monument**, which commemorates the Protestant martyrs who were executed in St Andrews. It is a tall, needle-like monument, erected in 1842. Close by is the **British Golf Museum**, which illustrates the history of a game that Scotland gave to the world, with a particular focus on St Andrews. It has an array of exhibits from over 500 years of golfing history, and gives an insight into "surprising facts and striking feats".

St Andrews and golf are inseparable. The town is still a place of pilgrimage, only today the pilgrims come wearing Pringle sweaters and weighed down by golf bags. **The Royal and Ancient Golf Club** is the world's ruling body on the game (with the exception of the United States), and formulates its rules as well as organising the yearly British Open Championship. The most famous of the town's courses is the **Old Course**, and it is here, in the clubhouse, that the Royal and Ancient has its headquarters.

Two of the greatest names in golf were born in St Andrews - **Tom Morris** and his son, also called Tom. Old Tom was made green keeper at the Old Course in 1865, and was one of the best golfers of his day. His son, however, was even better, and won the Open Championship three times in a row while still a teenager. He eventually died in 1875, aged only 24, some say of a broken heart after his wife died in childbirth. Memorials to both men can be seen in the cathedral graveyard.

Craigton Country Park sits about a mile outside the town to the southwest. It has a small boating loch, miniature railway, aviary, pet's corner, glasshouses, restaurant and café. **Cambo Gardens** is a two and a half acre walled garden within the Cambo estate at Kingsbarns. Cambo has been the home of the Erskine family since 1688, though the present mansion dates from 1881. There is also 70 acres of woodland, which is famous for its snowdrops.

Around St Andrews

Crail

8 miles SE of St Andrews on the A917

Crail is one of the oldest ports in the East Neuk, as this area of Fife is known. It is also possibly the most picturesque, and the small harbour has featured on countless calendars

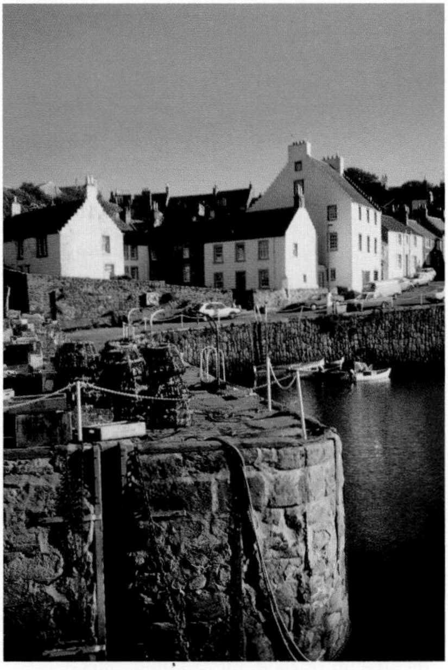

Town and Fishing Dock, Crail

and post cards. Artists flock to the place because of the light and the quaint buildings. The **Tolbooth** dates from the early 16th century, and has Dutch influences. In the Marketgate is the **Crail Museum and Heritage Centre**, which traces the history of the town and its industries.

At Troywood, three miles west of the town, off the B9131, is perhaps the most unusual visitor attraction in Scotland, and certainly one of its true "hidden places". The **Secret Bunker** was Scotland's secret underground command centre, an amazing 24,000 square feet of accommodation on two levels, 100 feet underground and encased in 15 feet thick concrete walls. It was from here that the country was to have been run in the event of a nuclear strike from the Soviet Union. It is entered by an innocent looking farmhouse, and guarded by three tons of blast proof doors. As well as operations rooms and living quarters, it also contains two cinemas and a café. Several similar bunkers were built around the country, and this is one of the largest. It came off the Official Secrets list in 1993 at the end of the Cold War.

Anstruther

9 miles S of St Andrews off the A917

Anstruther (sometimes pronounced "(Ainster") is a former herring fishing port. It comprises two ancient royal burghs, Anstruther Easter and Anstruther Wester, and is a picturesque place full of old white washed cottages with red pantiled roofs and crow stepped gables.

There is a story that, after the English defeated the Spanish Armada in 1588, one of the ships of the Spanish fleet put in at Anstruther and was civilly received by the people of the town. The ship's commander was one Jan Gomez de Midini, and he and his crew were offered hospitality (this at a time when Scotland and England were still

Scottish Fisheries Museum

St. Ayles, Harbourhead, Anstruther,
Fife KY10 3AB
Tel/Fax: 01333 310628
e-mail: info@scottish-fisheries-museum.org
website: www.scottish-fisheries-museum.org

Fishing has always been important to the small villages that fringe the East Neuk of Fife and in the **Scottish Fisheries Museum** you can learn all about the industry, not just in Fife, but throughout Scotland. It is a truly fascinating place, and is housed in buildings dating from the 16th to the 19th centuries. There are displays on many facets of the industry, and a trip round makes a great day out for children and adults alike. It begins by examining a replica dug-out canoe dating from AD 500, created in the museum workshop to illustrate that fishing in Scotland goes back to ancient times. After it was made in 1991, it was tested in Anstruther Harbour, and performed beautifully!

There are many galleries, each one highlighting a facet of the industry. There is an area on whaling, for example, plus a gallery called 'The Herring Market', with a net-loft where nets were repaired, a fish merchant's office, and lively herring lassies gutting and packing the catch. There are also, of course, fishing boats, and you can see and touch the craft that took hardy fishermen out into the seas round Britain in days gone by. One of the most fascinating galleries is the one dedicated to Zulu fishing boats. How did they get their name? What key role did they play in the industry? There is also a tearoom, a room which you can book to enjoy your packed lunch, and a shop, where you can pick up well-crafted souvenirs to remind you of your trip to one of the most interesting and enjoyable museums in Scotland. It is wheelchair friendly, and special themed visits can also be arranged. It makes a memorable day out.

independent countries). A few years later the Spaniard repaid his debt when he discovered fishermen from Anstruther marooned in a foreign port after their boat had been wrecked. He re-equipped them and sent them homewards once more.

Shoreline at Anstruther

Located in 16th century St Ayles House, once a lodging house for the monks from Balmerino Abbey, is the **Scottish Fisheries Museum** (see panel opposite). Here you can follow the fleet with the "herring lassies", explore a typical fishing family's cottage and see skilled craftsmen at work. Also on display are two boats - the Zulu, based on an original African design, and the Reaper, a herring boat. The museum also incorporates the poignant Memorial to Scottish Fishermen Lost at Sea.

Six miles southeast of Anstruther, in the Firth of Forth, is the **Isle of May**. There are ruins of an old priory, and the whole place is now a nature reserve. It was on this island that Scotland's first lighthouse was built in 1635. It was no more than a small stone tower with a brazier atop it, which burnt coal. Trips to the island are available from the pier at Anstruther.

Kilrenny

9 miles S of St Andrews on the A917

Kilrenny Parish Church has a tower dating from the 15th century, though the rest is early 19th century. In the Kirk yard is a mausoleum to the Scotts of Balcomie. There are many picturesque 18th and 19th century cottages, formerly the homes of fishermen.

Pittenweem

9 miles S of St Andrews on the A917

The older houses in this small royal burgh crowd round the picturesque fishing harbour. Like most of the houses in the East Neuk, they are whitewashed with red pantiled roofs and crow step gables. An Augustinian Priory was founded here in 1141, of which very little now remains. The **Parish Church** has a substantial tower (which looks more like a small castle than a piece of ecclesiastical architecture) dating from the 16th century, while the rest is Victorian.

Pittenweem Harbour

St Fillan's Cave is supposed to be where St Fillan, an 8th century missionary to the Picts, used to go for private prayer (see also Tyndrum, Madderty

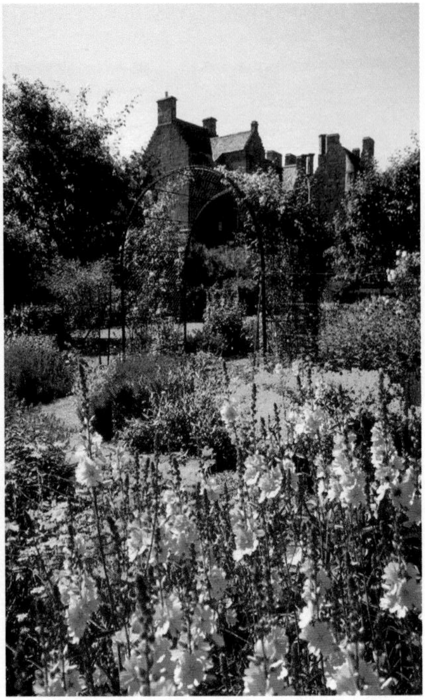

Gardens at Kellie Castle

and St Fillans). It was renovated and re-dedicated in 1935. Pittenweem is one of the few Fife coastal villages still to have a fishing fleet of sorts, though it is much smaller than it used to be. There are also many art galleries and antique shops, a testimony to the popularity of this area with artists and retired people.

Kellie Castle (National Trust for Scotland) dates from the 14th century, and is one of the best examples in the Lowlands of the secular architecture of the time. It contains superb plaster ceilings, murals, painted panelling and furniture designed by Sir Robert Lorimer, who refurbished the place in the late 19th century. There are fine gardens with old roses and herbaceous borders.

St Monans

10 miles S of St Andrews on the A917

This little fishing port's motto is Mare Vivimus, meaning "From the Sea we Have Life" It is famous for the **Parish Church of St Monans**, built by David II, son of Robert the Bruce, in thanksgiving after he survived a shipwreck on the Forth. It stands almost on the shoreline, and is a substantial building consisting of a nave, transepts and stumpy spire atop a tower. The chancel was never built.

Salt panning was once an important industry in the town, and the 18th century **St Monans Windmill** at one time formed part of a small industrial complex, which produced salt from seawater.

Earlsferry and Elie

10 miles S of St Andrews off the A917

These two villages are small holiday resorts surrounding a sandy bay. The older of the two is Earlsferry, which is a royal burgh. It was once the northern terminal for ferries, which plied between it and ports on the south bank of the Forth. The "earl" in its name comes from an incident concerning Macduff, who was a "thane" of the Earl of Fife. He escaped from King Macbeth, took refuge in a cave at Kincraig Point near the town, and was then ferried across the Forth to Dunbar. **Gillespie House**, in Elie, dates

Yachts at Elie Harbour

from the 17th century, and has a fine carved doorway.

At one time an old track called the "Cadgers Road" led from Earlsferry to Falkland, and it was along this that supplies of fresh fish were taken to feed the king when he stayed there.

Cupar

8 miles W of St Andrews on the A91

This small town, sitting on the River Eden, was once the county town of Fife. It is a pleasant place, and well worth strolling round just to see and appreciate its many old buildings. The **Mercat Cross**, topped with a unicorn, was moved from Tarvit Hill to its present location in 1897 to commemorate Queen Victoria's Diamond Jubilee. In Duffus Park is the **Douglas Bader Garden**, designed with the disabled in mind. The **Old Parish Church** dates from 1785, though the tower is medieval.

Hill of Tarvit Mansionhouse (National Trust for Scotland) is a fine Edwardian mansion that lies two miles south of the town, and was designed by Sir Robert Lorimer in 1906. It has French, Scottish and Chippendale furniture, a collection of paintings, an Edwardian laundry and fine gardens. Close by is **Scotstarvit Tower** (Historic Scotland). It was built by the Inglis family around 1487 when they were granted the lands of Tarvit. In 1612 it was bought by Sir John Scott. He was deprived

Hill of Tarvit, Cupar

of his positions in the Scottish judiciary as judge and director of chancery by Cromwell in the 17th century, and retired to Scotstarvit, where he was visited by many eminent men of the time.

A few miles west of Cupar, at Rankeilor Park, is the **Scottish Deer Centre** and **Raptor World**. At the Deer Centre you can see - and even feed - both species of

deer native to Scotland, plus other species from around the world. At the Raptor Centre there are exhibitions about birds of prey such as owls, hawks and falcons, plus there are spectacular flying demonstrations. There is also a small shopping court, an indoor adventure play area and picnic areas.

Ceres

7 miles W of St Andrews on the B939

Ceres is a small picturesque village with a village green and the hump-backed, medieval **Bishop's Bridge**. The memorial by the bridge commemorates the men of the village who followed Bruce to Bannockburn. The **Parish Church** contains some medieval tombs of the Earls of Crawford, and in the **Fife Folk Museum** you can find out about what everyday life was like in Fife in bygone days.

Two miles southwest of Ceres are the ruins of 14th century **Struthers Castle**. It has been owned by the de Ochters, the Keiths, the Lindsays and the Crawfords. At one time the lands belonging to the castle were called "Outhirothistrodyr", from which the word "Struther" comes.

The village's **Bannockburn Monument** was erected in 1914, 600 years after the battle took place, to commemorate the men of Ceres who fell in it. The **Parish Church** was built in 1806 on the site of a much older church. Its most unusual features are the communion tables, which run the full length of the church. Built into a wall on the main street is a curious carving known as **The Provost**.

Newburgh

16 miles W of St Andrews on the A913

This small royal burgh stands on the banks of the Tay. Close to it are the red sandstone ruins of **Lindores Abbey**, founded by David I in 1178 for Tironenisan monks. It was the first abbey in Scotland to be sacked by Protestant sympathisers, 17 years before Scotland officially became a Protestant country. The **Laing Museum** in the High Street has displays on Newburgh's history from medieval burgh to industrial town.

Auchtermuchty

16 miles W of St Andrews on the A91

Auchtermuchty is a typical inland Fife town. It is small and compact, and sits in a fertile area known as the Howe of Fife ("Hollow of Fife"). The **Tolbooth** dates from 1728, and it was here that the TV series *Dr Finlay* was filmed, its town centre being turned into a typical townscape of the 1930s.

Leuchars

4 miles NW of St Andrews, on the A919

Every September, the Royal Air Force puts on the **Leuchars Air Show**, held in one of Scotland's biggest RAF bases. The village is also famous for it's **Parish Church of St Athernase**, said by some to be the second finest Norman church in Britain. The best parts are the finely carved chancel and apse. A bell tower was added to the apse in the 17th century.

Earlshall Castle (not open to the public) was started in 1546 by Sir William Bruce, and completed by his descendant of the same name in 1617. It subsequently fell into disrepair, but was rebuilt in 1891 under the direction of Sir Robert Lorimer.

Tentsmuir Forest, to the north of Leuchars, is a 3,700-acre pine forest planted on sand dunes on the shores of the North Sea and the Firth of Tay. The whole area is rich in wildlife.

Newport-on-Tay

9 miles NW of St Andrews on the A92

This little town sits at the southern end of the Tay Road Bridge, and at **Wormit**, about a mile to the west, is the start of the Tay Rail Bridge. The ruins of **Balmerino Abbey** (National Trust for Scotland) sit five miles to the west. It was founded in 1229 by Queen Ermengarde, widow of William the Lion, king of Scotland, and colonised by Cistercian monks from Melrose. The ruins are not open to the public, but can be viewed from nearby.

Stirlingshire & Clackmannanshire

That area of Scotland between the Firths of Clyde and Forth has always been strategically important. It is often referred to as Scotland's "waist", and before the Kincardine Bridge was built in 1936, the bridge at Stirling was the lowest crossing point of the River Forth. To the west of the town are the Campsie and Kilsyth Hills, and these, along with marshy bogland such as Flanders Moss, formed another natural barrier, so the bridge at Stirling became the gateway to Perthshire and the Highlands.

That's why so many battles have been fought in and around Stirling and Falkirk, including Scotland's most important, the Battle of Bannockburn, which secured Scotland's future as an independent nation. It is also the reason why Stirling Castle was built. It sits sentinel on a great rocky outcrop, with the town of Stirling laid out below it to the west. As a castle, it was almost impregnable, and from its top an approaching army could easily be seen even if it was miles away.

This is an area, which has witnessed great changes over the years due to local government reorganisations. Dunblane, to

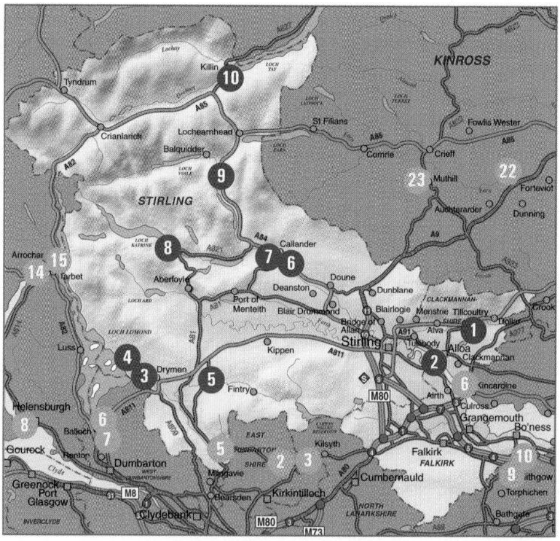

PLACES TO STAY, EAT AND DRINK

The Butterfly Inn, Tillicoultry	1	Pub with Food	p193
Alloa Tower, Alloa	2	Visitor Attraction	p195
Cairneach Milk Bar, Drymen	3	Café	p206
Oak Tree Inn, Balmaha	4	Pub, Restaurant & Accommodation	p207
Pirn Inn, Balfron	5	Pub, Food and Accommodation	p208
Poppies Hotel & Restaurant, Callander	6	Hotel	p209
Crags Hotel, Callander	7	Hotel	p209
Steamship Sir Walter Scott, Loch Katrine	8	Steam Ship Trips	p210
Creagan House, Strathyre	9	Accommodation and Restaurant	p212
Craigard Hotel, Killin	10	Hotel	p212

● Denotes entries in other chapters

Loch Katrine, The Trossachs

the north of Stirling, was at one time in Perthshire, as was Callander and Port of Menteith. For a while, Clackmannanshire ceased to exist (though it remained alive in the hearts of all those born there). Now it has come back, and still proudly proclaims itself to be Scotland's smallest county, with an area of only 55 square miles. It sits in the shelter of the Ochil Hills to the north, which rise to well over 2,000 feet in places, and was a centre for woollens and textiles. The string of "hillfoot villages" at the foot of the Ochils are all picturesque and well worth visiting for this alone.

Around Falkirk and Grangemouth, Stirlingshire is unashamedly industrial. This is the heart of Scotland's petrochemical industry, with great refineries lining the shores of the Forth, which is still tidal at this point. It was also at one time a coal mining area, though the mines have long gone.

Travel northwest from Stirling however, and you enter another world - the Trossachs, one of Scotland's most beautiful areas. Though its hills aren't as high as those of the Grampians or the Cairngorms, and don't have that brooding majesty we tend to associate with Highland scenery, it is still Highland in character. The hills slip down to the wooded banks of lochs such as Loch Katrine, Loch Venachar and the wonderfully named Loch Drunkie, which are among the most picturesque in Scotland, and the skies seem endless and sweeping. The Loch Lomond and Trossachs National Park (see also Balloch) takes in most of the Trossachs in its 720 square miles. It was the country's first national park, opened in 2002.

The town of Stirling is one of the most historic in Scotland, and has played a leading role in shaping the country's destiny. The castle has been fought over countless times by the Scottish and the English, and eventually became a favourite royal residence. Mary Queen of Scots stayed there, and her son, who became James VI, had his coronation in the town's Church of the Holy Rood. Falkirk, though more industrial in character, is also an ancient town, and has witnessed two important battles as Scotland's history was played out.

Boats on Loch

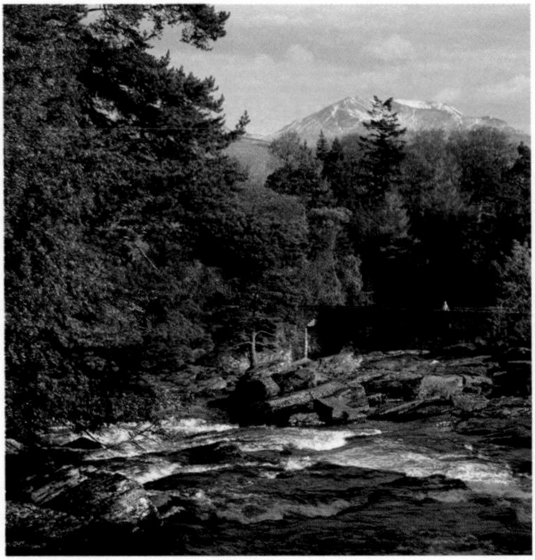

Towards Dochart Bridge, Killin

Alloa, Clackmannanshire's largest town, is also industrial in character, though it too has history aplenty. At one time this was Scotland's brewing capital, though only one brewery now remains.

For those interested in architecture, the place offers some memorable buildings. There are many old, historical buildings in Stirling, including Stirling Castle itself, given a Renaissance makeover by James IV, as well as Dunblane Cathedral, Alloa Tower, the ruins of Camubuskenneth Priory, the Wallace Monument, and both Doune Castle and Castle Campbell

Clackmannan

This small town was granted its burgh charter in 1550. It was once a small port on the Black Devon, a tributary of the Forth, but the river silted up years ago, leaving it high and dry. In the centre of the town is the belfry of the old **Tolbooth**, built by William Menteith in 1592. He was the sheriff of the town, and objected strongly with having to hold felons in his own home, so he built the Tolbooth to hold them instead. Beside it stands the **Mannau Stone**. Legend states that when St Serf came to this part of Scotland in the 6th century to convert it to Christianity, he found the locals worshipping the sea god Mannau, or Mannan, in the form of the stone (known as the "clach mannau"). From this, the town supposedly got its name. Another legend states that the name derives from an incident in the life of Robert the Bruce. It seems that he once rested close to the stone, and on remounting his horse, left his glove lying on it. He ordered one of his servants to return to the "clach" (stone) and retrieve his "mannan" (glove). The stone can still be seen on top of a column close to the Tolbooth and the **Mercat Cross**, which dates from the 1600s.

Clackmannan Tower, built on King's Seat Hill, where once a royal hunting lodge built by David I stood, dates from the 14th century, with later alterations, and was once owned by Robert the Bruce. Though in the care of Historic Scotland, it can only be viewed from the outside at present. Robert Burns visited the area in 1787, and was "knighted" by a direct descendant of Robert the Bruce, a Mrs Bruce, who lived in a mansion house (demolished in 1791) near the castle. She was in her nineties at the time, and a woman of "hospitality and urbanity". She still possessed her ancestor's helmet and two-handed sword, and she used the sword to carry out the ceremony, declaring that she had a better right to confer knighthoods than "some people" (meaning the Hanovarian kings who were on the throne).

Clackmannan's **Parish Church** dates from 1815, though St Serf may have founded the original church in the 6th century. Inside is the beautiful Coronation Window, gifted to the church by its congregation to mark the coronation of

Elizabeth II in 1953. The Queen visited the church specially to view it in 1997, so it seems that the loyalty of at least some Clackmannan people towards the monarchy in London is not in doubt any more.

Two miles north of the town is the **Gartmorn Dam Country Park**. It is centred on the 170 acre Gartmorn Dam, the oldest man made reservoir in Scotland. It was constructed in the early 1700s by John Erskine, 6th Earl of Mar, to power the pumps, which pumped water out of his coal mines around nearby Sauchie. Now a nature reserve, the park is popular with walkers and nature lovers, and the reservoir itself is stocked with brown trout.

Dollar Academy

Around Clackmannan

Tillicoultry

4 miles N of Clackmannan on the A91

Tillicoultry is one of the "hillfoot villages" which relied on water tumbling down from the Ochils to power the mills in which most people were employed. It became a town in 1871, and behind it is the picturesque **Tillicoultry Glen**, whose waters once powered eight mills in the town using a system of lades and channels. Its rather unusual name means, "hill in the back land".

Dollar

5 miles NE of Clackmannan on the A91

Dollar is another "hillfoot village", famous as the home of **Dollar Academy**. This private school (the equivalent of an English public school) was founded in the early 19th century thanks to a bequest of £40,000 by Captain John McNabb, a local herd boy born in 1732 who amassed a fortune before his death in 1802. Eighteen years later the academy had been built,

Castle Campbell, Dollar

though if he came back today he might be puzzled to see his school, for he had intended it to be a school for the children of the poor in Dollar parish. The elegant, colonnaded building was designed by the eminent architect William Playfair, and was opened in 1819.

Within Dollar is the small **Dollar Museum**, which has displays on the history of the village and on the Devon Valley railway. Above the town, and reached through the wooded **Dollar Glen** (National Trust for Scotland), is **Castle Campbell** (National Trust for Scotland). It was one of Clan Campbell's Lowland homes, and was formerly known as "Castle Gloom". Close by are two burns called Care and Sorrow, and even the name Dollar itself is said to derive from "dolour", meaning sadness. It seems strange that such a beautiful spot should have such depressing names. The castle dates essentially from the 15th century, with some later additions. Both John Knox and Mary Stuart have stayed there.

Alva

3 miles NW of Clackmannan on the A91

Alva sits at the foot of the Ochils, and is one of the "hillfoot villages" where weaving and spinning were the main industries. It's name means "rocky plain", as does that of its near neighbour Alloa. To the northeast is the Ochil Hills' highest peak, the 2,363 feet **Ben Cleuch**. At the **Mill Trail Visitor Centre** there are displays and exhibits that explain what life was like in mill factories over the last 150 years. There is also a shop and a café. **The Mill Trail** itself is a signposted route taking you to many mills with retail outlets. **The Ochil Hills Woodland Park** has attractive walks and a visitor centre.

Alva Glen, also called the "Silver Glen", is very picturesque. Silver was once mined here in the 18th century, and **St Serf's Parish Church**, which dates from 1815, has some communion vessels made from local silver. It was the Erskine family that mined the silver, and it was a hit or miss affair. A story is told of one member of the family, Sir John Erskine, showing two of the mines to a friend. "Out of that hole there I earned £50,000," he told him. "And in that hole there I lost it all again."

Menstrie

4 miles NW of Clackmannan on the A91

In **Menstrie Castle**, in 1567, was born **Sir William Alexander**, 1st Earl of Stirling, founder of Nova Scotia, Scotland's only real colony in North America (see also Stirling). The only part of the castle open to the public is the Nova Scotia Commemoration Room, which has displays about the colony. There are also the armorial bearings of the Nova Scotia baronetcies created in Scotland at the beginning of the 17th century, which went on sale at 3,000 Scots merks each. In 1621 Sir William persuaded James VI to create the baronetcies, and when James realised how much money he could make from it, he readily agreed. In 1624, while at Windsor, he began the money making scheme. A year later he was dead, and his son Charles I, not unnaturally, continued the practise.

By the end of 1625 the first 22 titles had been conferred. Even today there are 109 titles still in existence. Sir William died penniless in London in 1644, and now lies buried in the Church of the Holy Rood in Stirling.

Sir Ralph Abercromby, who commanded the British troops at the Battle of Alexandria in 1801, was born in Menstrie in 1734. He died at Alexandria in 1801 of wounds he received during the battle.

Blairlogie

6 miles NW of Clackmannan on the A91

Blairlogie is possibly the most beautiful of the "hillfoot villages", and was the first conservation village in Scotland. It sits in the shadow of the 1373 feet **Dumyat,** which has the remains of a hilltop fort on its summit. The name derives from Dun Maetae, meaning the fort of the Maetae, a Pictish tribe.

Alloa

2 miles W of Clackmannan on the A907

With a population of about 15,000, Alloa is the largest town in Scotland's smallest county. The town sits on the River Forth where it is still tidal, and its name is supposed to mean "rocky plain". It was traditionally an engineering, brewing and glass-making town, though today these industries are less important than they once were.

St Mungo's Parish Church dates from 1817, though it incorporates the 17th century tower of an earlier church. **Alloa Tower** (National Trust for Scotland - see panel below) is all that is left of the ancestral home of the Erskines, one of the most important families in Scotland. They eventually became the Earls of Mar, and as such were (and still are as the Earls of Mar and Kellie) Hereditary Keepers of Stirling Castle. The tower was built for Alexander Erskine, the 3rd Lord Erskine, in the late 15th century, and later remodelled by the 6th Earl of Mar in the 18th century. It has the original oak roof beams, medieval vaulting and a dungeon.

The Erskines were custodians of Mary Stuart during her infancy, and she lived in the tower for a time. James VI, while still a boy, also stayed here. The 6th Earl was an ardent Jacobite, and after the 1715

Alloa Tower

Alloa Park, Alloa,
Clackmannanshire FK10 1PP
Tel: 0 1259 211701 Fax: 0 1259 218744

Alloa Tower, the largest surviving keep in Scotland, dates from the 14th century. It was home to successive generations of the Earls of Mar, who played host to and were guardians of many Scots monarchs. Here, so legend has it, Mary, Queen of Scots was reconciled with Darnley and shortly thereafter granted the 5th Lord Erskine the much coveted earldom in 1565. One tradition holds that Mary's infant son, later James VI and I, died shortly after his birth and was replaced by the baby son of the Earl of Mar.

The Tower has seen six major alterations, the most dramatic being the sweeping Italianate staircase and dome added in the early 1700's by the 6th Earl of Mar. But it still retains original medieval features such as the dungeon, first floor well and magnificent oak roof timbers. Fully restored and furnished to a high standard, the Tower contains a unique collection of family portraits and silver on loan from the present Earl of Mar and Kellie.

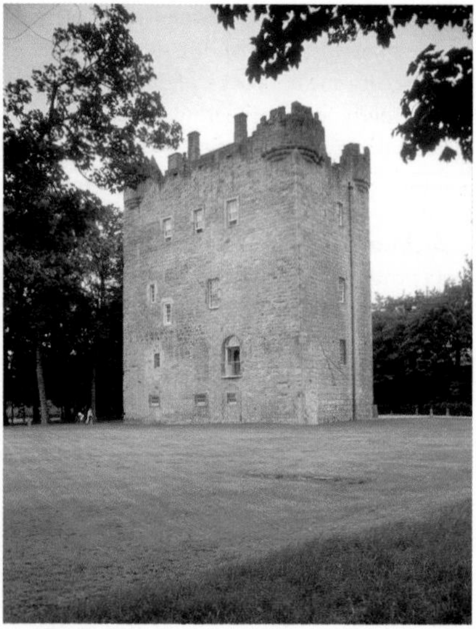

Alloa Tower

Uprising he was sent into exile. The story of the Erskines is told within the tower, and the present Earl has loaned a superb collection of paintings, including works by Raeburn and Kneller.

Alloa Museum and Gallery, in the Speirs Centre in Primrose Street, has exhibits tracing the history of the town.

Tullibody

4 miles W of Clackmannan on the B9140

Legend says that Tullibody was founded by King Kenneth McAlpine, the first king of Scots, who united the kingdoms of Dalriada and the Picts in AD 843. He called it "Tirlbothy", meaning the "oath of the crofts", as he and his followers made an oath there that they would not lay down their arms until their enemies or themselves were killed. A stone once stood at the point where the oath was made.

Tullibody Auld Brig, which spans the River Devon, was built about 1535 by James Spittal, tailor to the royal family (see also Doune). In January 1560 the eastern most arch of the bridge was dismantled by Kirkcaldy of Grange to impede a French army, which was in Scotland in support of Mary of Guise, mother of Mary Stuart and widow of James V. However, the French army dismantled the roof of **Tullibody Auld Kirk** and made a new bridge. In 1697 Thomas Bauchop, a local mason, was commissioned by John, 6th Earl of Mar, to build a new eastern arch.

Robert Dick, the eminent, but self taught, botanist was born in Tullibody in 1811.

Falkirk

Falkirk is Stirlingshire's largest town, and received its burgh charter in 1600. It sits at an important point on the road from Edinburgh to Stirling, and nearby **Stenhousemuir** was once the meeting place of various drove roads coming down from the Highlands. Here great herds of cattle were kept before being sold at "trysts" and taken further south to the markets of Northern England. It has been estimated that over 24,000 head of cattle were sold annually at the three trysts held each year.

The name of the town means the "kirk of mottled stone", a reference to its first stone built medieval church. The present **Old Parish Church** dates from 1810, and incorporates fragments of an earlier church. It's tower dates from 1734. The church was the burial place for many prominent local families, and buried in the churchyard is said to be Sir John de Graeme, who was killed at the Battle of Falkirk fighting in William Wallace's army.

The **Town Steeple** was built in 1814, and was designed by the famous architect David Hamilton. It replaced an earlier building, which dated from the 17th century, and has traditionally been a meeting place for the people of the town. In 1927 the upper portion of the steeple was struck by lightning and had to be rebuilt.

Near Falkirk the two great Lowland canals - the Forth and Clyde and the

Union Canal - meet. Thanks to the Millennium Link Project, they have recently been restored, and the magnificent new 120 feet high **Falkirk Wheel,** which has become a tourist attraction in its own right, carries boats between one canal and the other (which are on different levels), within water filled "gondolas".

Centred on the village of Bonnybridge, two miles west of Falkirk, is the **Bonnybridge Triangle**, so called because there have been more sightings of UFOs and unexplained phenomena in this area than anywhere else in the UK. It all started in 1992 when a cross shaped cluster of lights was seen hovering above a road, and it has continued up until the present day, with mysterious football-sized lights, delta shaped craft and even spaceships with opening doors being seen as well.

Two great battles were fought in or near Falkirk. In 1298 the Scottish army of William Wallace was defeated by the English after his victory at Stirling Bridge the previous year. The superior horsemen and archers of the English won the day, and Wallace became a fugitive, finally being captured in 1305. And in 1746, after its retreat from Derby, the Jacobite forces of Charles Edward Stuart defeated a Hanovarian army.

The town sits on the line of the Antonine Wall, a massive turf wall on a stone base built on the orders of the Roman emperor Antonius Pius just after AD 138 (see also Bearsden and Milngavie). It stretched the 38 miles from the Firth of Clyde at Bowling to the Firth of Forth west of Bo'ness. **Rough Castle** (National Trust for Scotland) five miles from the town, is one of the best preserved of the wall's fortifications. Parts of the wall can be seen in the town's **Callendar Park**, in which you will also find **Callendar House**. This magnificent building, modelled on a French château, has played a major role in Scotland's history. In 1293 Alexander II granted land to one Malcolm de Kalynter, and he may have built a wooden castle. A descendant of Malcolm became involved in plots against David II in 1345, and the estates were forfeited and given to Sir William Livingstone, whose descendants lived there until the 18th century.

The Livingstones were close to Mary Stuart, and the queen visited the estate many times. In 1600 James VI rewarded the family by making them Earls of Linlithgow. But with the rise of the Jacobites, the family's fortunes went into decline. The 5th Earl was forced into exile for siding with the Old Pretender in 1715, and his daughter, Lady Anne married the ill-fated Earl of Kilmarnock, who was beheaded in London for his part in the 1745 Uprising (see also Kilmarnock). A story is told that on the evening before the Battle of Falkirk, the commander of the Hanovarian troops, General Hawley, dined at Callendar House with Lady Anne. He so enjoyed her company that he ignored requests to leave early to be appraised of the Jacobite movements. His troops were soundly beaten the following day.

In 1783 the house and estate was bought by the businessman William Forbes, whose descendants lived there for almost 200 years. It has now been restored by the local council as a heritage centre and museum, with a working Georgian kitchen, printer's and clockmaker's workrooms and a general store. In the Victorian library is an extensive archive of books, documents and photographs on the history of the area, and the Major William Forbes Falkirk exhibition traces the history of the town. The **Park Gallery**, which runs a series of art exhibitions and workshop activities, is also located in Callendar Park.

Around Falkirk

Airth

5 miles N of Falkirk on the A905

It is hard to imagine that a huge royal dockyard founded by James IV was once

The Pineapple

situated close to this small village in the 15th and 16th centuries. Now it is visited because of one of the most unusual buildings in Scotland - **The Pineapple** (National Trust for Scotland) in Dunmore Park. It is a summerhouse, built in 1761, and on top of it is a huge, 45 feet high pineapple made of stone. It is heated using an early form of central heating, as passages and cavities within the stone walls carry hot air through them. It can be rented as a holiday home. Also at Dunmore are 16 acres of gardens.

Parts of the nearby **Airth Castle** (now a hotel) date from the 14th century. An earlier castle stood on the site, and it was here that William Wallace's uncle, a priest, was held prisoner by the English before Wallace rescued him. The castle frontage as seen today dates from 1810, and was designed by David Hamilton.

Close to the castle are the ruins of a 16th century church.

Grangemouth

3 miles E of Falkirk on the A904

Grangemouth is a modern town, and the centre of Scotland's petrochemical industry. It was one of the country's first planned towns, having been established by Sir Laurence Dundas in the late 18th century at the same time as the Forth and Clyde Canal was being dug. His son Thomas continued the work.

On Bo'ness Road is the **Grangemouth Museum**, which traces the history of the town. The **Jupiter Urban Wildlife Garden** is off Wood Street, and was established in 1990 by Zeneca (formerly ICI) and the Scottish Wildlife Trust on a piece of land that was once a railway marshalling yard. Surrounded by industrial buildings and smokestacks, this oasis of green shows how derelict industrial land can be cleaned up and reclaimed for nature. It has four ponds, an area of scrub birch known as The Wilderness, a wildlife plant nursery and a formal wildlife garden, as well as meadows, marshland and reed beds.

Stirling

Stirling is one of the most historic towns in Scotland, having been granted its royal charter in 1226. It sits astride the main route north from the Lowlands at Scotland's narrowest point, which is why it is so strategically important. On a craggy volcanic hill a castle was built, which in medieval times became a royal residence. A settlement was eventually established on the eastern slope of the hill to cater for its needs.

The old town is a mixture of buildings from all periods from the 15th century onwards, and a day could be spent walking about and admiring them. **Stirling Castle** (Historic Scotland) is a mixture of styles and dates. Some form of fortification has no doubt stood here from at last pre-Christian times, and it is one of the many sites in Scotland associated with King

Arthur. It entered recorded history in the early 12th century, when Alexander I dedicated a chapel here. There must also have been a palace of some kind, as Alexander died here in 1124. We next hear of it in 1174, when William the Lion was compelled to hand over various Scottish castles to Henry II of England, Stirling included.

During the Wars of Independence in the 13th and 14th centuries, Stirling Castle played a leading role. By this time it was back in Scottish hands, and Edward I was outraged by the fact that it was the last Lowland castle to hold out against his conquest of the country, and a barrier to further conquest in the north. So, in 1304, he set out to besiege it, and it eventually fell. For the next ten years the English garrisoned it. In 1313 Edward Bruce, brother of Robert I, laid siege to it, and its commander, Sir Philip Mowbray, agreed to surrender if the castle wasn't relieved by June 24 1314.

By this time Edward I was dead, and his son Edward II was on the throne. He didn't want to lose Stirling, so he came north with a great army to relieve it. The Scots met this army at Bannockburn, and secured a great victory - one that sealed Scotland's independence.

All traces of the castle as it was at the time of Bannockburn have long gone. Most now date from the 15th century and later. James III was the first of the Scottish kings to take an interest in its architecture, and built the Great Hall as a meeting place of the Scottish parliament and for great ceremonial occasions. James IV then began building a new palace building in the Renaissance style, with his son James V finishing the work. In 1594 James VI had the Chapel Royal built, and these three buildings represent the most important architectural elements in the castle. It was within the Chapel Royal, on September 9 1543, when she was barely nine months old, that Mary Stuart, known as Mary, Queen of Scots, was crowned in a ceremony that was curiously lacking in pomp or majesty.

A curious tale is told of Stirling Castle. It concerns James IV and John Damien, the Abbot of Tongland in Kirkcudbrightshire, who earned the nickname of the **Frenzied Friar of Tongland** (see also Tongland). He was an Italian, and a learned man, who spent a lot of time at court. In 1507 he convinced James IV that man could fly, and to prove it, he told him that he would jump from the walls of Stirling Castle and soar as free as a bird.

A date was set for the flight to take place, and a bemused James IV and his court assembled on the battlements. Meanwhile, Abbot Damien had told his servants to amass a large collection of feathers from birds, which could fly and construct a large pair of wings from them. However, his servants couldn't collect enough feathers of the right kind in time, so

Stirling Castle

Stone Arch Bridge over the River Forth, Stirling

incorporated some chicken feathers as well. The Abbot duly presented himself on the battlements of the castle with the wings strapped to his back and wrists. No mention is made in contemporary accounts of how the king and the court viewed this unusual sight, but there must have been a few suppressed sniggers.

Damien stood on the battlements, made a short speech, and began flapping his wings. He then jumped - and fell like a stone, landing in the castle midden, on which more than the kitchen scraps were heaped. His fall couldn't have been that far, as all he succeeded in doing was breaking his leg. When he later discovered that his servants had incorporated chicken feathers in the wings, he blamed this for the failure of his flight. The court poet William Dunbar was present at this attempt at the world's first manned flight, and wrote some verses about it.

The **Church of the Holy Rude** on St John Street is Stirling's parish church. It dates from the 15th century, and was built on the site of an earlier place of worship at the command of James IV, who, tradition says, worked alongside the masons during its construction. It is one of the finest medieval churches in Scotland, and has its original oak roof. Within the church, in 1567, the infant James VI was crowned king of Scotland. What isn't generally known is that James (who later became James VI and I of England and Great Britain) had been christened Charles. James was chosen as his "royal" name to continue the tradition of having a "James" on the Scottish throne.

The kirkyard was once the castle's tilting ground, where great tournaments of jousting and horsemanship were held. One of the monuments in the kirkyard is the **Martyr's Monument**, commemorating two women who were drowned for their religious beliefs at Wigtown in 1685 (see also Wigtown). **Lady's Rock** is next to the kirkyard, and was where the ladies of the court sat and watched staged events take place on the fields below. Close by is **Cowane's Hospital**, on which work started in 1639. It is named after John Cowane, who bequeathed funds to establish an almshouse for the unsuccessful merchants, or "decayed guildsmen" of the town. It was later used as a school and an epidemic hospital, and is now a venue for ceilidhs and concerts.

The King's Knot sits beneath the castle and church, on the south side, and is all that is left of a formal garden, originally planted in the 1490s. It is in the shape of an octagonal mound, now grassed over. Near it used to be the **King's Park** (where houses now stand), once a favourite hunting ground for the Scottish kings.

The **Old Town Jail**, down the slope in the city itself, was opened in 1847 to take the prisoners that were formerly held in the

Tolbooth. Now it has been reopened as a tourist attraction, and shows what life was like for prisoners and wardens in the 19th century. You'll also meet a character called Jock Rankin, who was the town's hangman. If, during your visit, a prisoner should try to escape, you should remain calm and follow the advice of the warden!

The intriguingly named **Mar's Wark** is close to the parish church. It was the "wark" (meaning work, or building) of the Earl of Mar, Regent of Scotland and guardian of the young James VI. In 1570 he began building a new palace that would reflect his status and power, and Mar's Wark was the result. In the 18th century it became a military hospital, but soon after fell into disrepair. Now all that is left of the Renaissance building is a façade along the street front.

On the opposite side of the street is **Argyll's Lodging** (Historic Scotland), a Renaissance-style mansion built about 1630 by Sir William Alexander, the founder of Nova Scotia (see also Menstrie). It was further enlarged by the 9th Earl of Argyll in the 1670s, and is possibly the best example of a 17th century town house in Scotland. Most of the rooms have been restored, showing what life would have been like when the Earl lived there.

Stirling is one of the few Scottish towns with parts of its **Town Wall** still standing. It was built in the 1540s as a defence against the English armies of Henry VIII when he was trying to force a marriage between his son Edward and Mary Stuart. The remaining parts stretch along the south side of the town, from near the Old Town Jail to Dumbarton Road. Incorporated into the Thistle Shopping Mall is the 16th century **Bastion**, one of the wall's defensive towers. It contains a vaulted guardroom above an underground chamber, and has a small display about the history of the town. There was no wall to the north of the town, as attacks never came from that quarter, though people who lived there were supposed to build thick, high walls at the backs of their gardens as a defence, and keep them in good repair.

One bloody association with Scotland's past is to be found at the **Beheading Stone**, well to the north of the castle. It was here, in 1425, that James I took his revenge on Murdoch, Duke of Albany, his two sons and the Earl of Lennox his father-in-law by having them beheaded. The Duke's father had controlled Scotland for 18 years while the English held James captive, and he and his cronies had brought the country to its knees by their greed and cruelty. Their lands were forfeited to the crown, and James gave them to his supporters.

The **Tolbooth** sits at the heart of the old town. It was built in 1704 by Sir William Bruce, and was where the town council met and looked after the affairs of the burgh. A courthouse and jail were added in 1809. It is now used as a venue for concerts and rehearsals. The **Mercat Cross**, close to the Tolbooth, has the figure of a unicorn on top, and this is known locally as the "puggy".

Two famous battles have been fought near Stirling. The **Battle of Stirling Bridge** took place in 1297, when William Wallace defeated an English army under John de Warenne, Earl of Surrey, and Hugh de Cressingham. Wallace, who was a guerrilla fighter and a master tactician, used the bridge to divide the English forces - leaving one contingent on each bank - before launching his attack. It was a major set back for Edward I, and he more or less had to start his conquest of the country all over again. The bridge in those days was a wooden one, and the present **Old Stirling Bridge**, which stands at the same spot, was built in the late 15th century. Up until 1831, when **Stirling New Bridge** was built downstream, this was the lowest crossing point of the Forth, which made it one of the most important bridges in Scotland.

The other famous battle was the **Battle of**

Bannockburn, fought to the south of the town in 1314. The actual site of the battle still arouses much debate, but there is no doubt that it was a defining moment in Scotland's history. Edward I had died by this time, and his son Edward II, a much weaker man, was in charge of the English army, which was trying to reach Stirling Castle to relieve it. Robert the Bruce, one of Scotland's great heroes, achieved a stunning victory - one that secured the country's status as an independent nation. **The Bannockburn Heritage Centre** (National Trust for Scotland), on the A872 two miles south of the town, commemorates this victory. There are exhibitions, an audiovisual display and a huge statue of Bruce on his warhorse.

Scotland's other national hero, of course, is William Wallace, and on Abbey Craig, to the east of the town and across the river, is the **National Wallace Monument**. This spectacular tower is 220 feet high, with 246 steps, and from the top you get a panoramic view that takes in the Forth Bridges to the east and Ben Lomond to the west. Here you can learn about the Battle of Stirling Bridge, plus see a re-creation of Wallace's travesty of a trial at Westminster. You can even gaze on his great two-handed broadsword.

The scant ruins of **Cambuskenneth Abbey** (Historic Scotland) also lie on the eastern banks of the Forth. David I founded it as an abbey in 1140 for Augustinian monks, and in 1326 Robert the Bruce held an important parliament here. The detached bell tower of the abbey is more or less complete, though only the foundations of the rest of the buildings survive. James III and his queen, Margaret of Denmark, are buried before the high altar, and a monument marks the spot. In 1488 the king had been assassinated near Bannockburn after his defeat at the Battle of Sauchieburn, where his son, the future James IV, was on the opposing side.

The **Smith Art Gallery and Museum** in Albert Place chronicles Stirling's long history through displays, exhibitions and artefacts. It has a fine collection of paintings, including ones by Naysmith and Sir George Harvey, who painted great works depicting Scottish history. One of the more unusual exhibits in the museum is the world's oldest football.

In the summer of 2002 Stirling was granted city status as part of the Queen's Golden jubilee celebrations.

Around Stirling

Bridge of Allan

2 miles N of Stirling off the M9

Bridge of Allan, which is almost a suburb of Stirling nowadays, was once a small spa town and watering place with a pump room and baths. Now it is chiefly known for being the home of Stirling University, based in the grounds of the **Airthrie Estate**, with its picturesque lake. In 1617, James VI wanted to establish a college or university at Stirling, but it was not until 1967 that his wish came true, when the first 180 students enrolled. Now it has over 3,500 students, and is one of the premier universities in Scotland.

Airthrie was owned by Sir Robert Abercrombie, who was instrumental in setting up the village as a spa, having had the waters of a local spring analysed. In 1844 the estate was bought by a Major Henderson, who developed the town even further. The **Fountain of Ninevah** on Fountain Road was built by him in 1851 to commemorate the archaeological excavations going on at Nineveh at the time. Though healing waters are no longer taken, other, equally interesting, liquids are. **The Bridge of Allan Brewery Company**, a microbrewery in Queens Lane, has tours showing how beer is produced.

Bridge of Allan Parish Church (formerly know as Holy Trinity Church) was built in 1860, and inside it are some furnishings designed by the Glasgow architect Charles Rennie Mackintosh.

Dunblane

5 miles N of Stirling off the M9

Before local government reorganisation, Dunblane (and most of the area north and north west of Stirling) was in Perthshire. This small town, or more properly city, is famous for two things. The first is the horrific shooting that took place here in 1996 when 16 schoolchildren and their teacher were killed in a local school. The second is the **Cathedral Church of St Blane and St Lawrence** (Historic Scotland). It dates mainly from the 13th century, and was built by Bishop Clement, who was elected bishop in 1233. He decided that the only part of the Norman church, which would be left standing, was the tower, though two extra storeys were added to it in the 15th century.

It is not a cathedral in the style of Elgin, St Andrews or any of the great English establishments. Rather it is an intimate church with no side aisles or transepts.

Christianity first came to Dunblane in the 7th century thanks to a Celtic monk called Blane (or Blaan), who was born on Bute in AD 602. He founded a great monastery here, which grew to become very important, and its site is still pointed out just outside the city.

Celtic monasteries were not like the great abbeys or priories built in medieval times. They usually consisted of many small chapels and circular cells (where the monks lived) built of wood or wattle and surrounded by a "rath", or low turf wall. There would also have been storerooms, eating places, kitchens, stables, bakeries, brewing houses and schoolrooms, as most Celtic foundations also acted as schools.

In about 1150 a stone cathedral was built, and a Roman Catholic bishopric established. However, the diocese was a poor one, and the Pope eventually authorised the bishops of Dunkeld and Glasgow to give a fourth of their income to help establish it properly. With this income, Clement managed to build most of the cathedral before his death in 1258.

In the 16th century, with the arrival of Protestantism, only the choir was used for worship, and the nave fell into decay. So too did the city, and it became a small weaving centre. In 1898 the whole building was restored, and in 1914 Sir Robert Lorimer did further work on the choir, with the present choir stalls - one of the glories of the cathedral - being designed by him.

With the coming of the railways, Dunblane became a popular place in which to holiday, and it regained some of its former prosperity. **Dunblane Hydro** was built in 1875 to cash in on the tourist boom, and it is still a luxury hotel to this day.

Within the **Dean's House**, built in 1624 and lived in by Dean James Pearson, is a small museum, which explains the history of the city and its cathedral, and **Bishop Leighton's Library**, housed in a building that dates from 1681, contains over 4,000 books, some of them priceless.

About three miles north east of the town is the site of the **Battle of Sheriffmuir** (see also Callander), one of the deciding battles in the 1715 Jacobite Uprising. It took place on November 13 1715, and was an unusual battle in that the outcome was a stalemate. The Jacobite forces were led by John Erskine, 11th Earl of Mar, and the Government forces by John Campbell, 2nd Duke of Argyll.

Fintry

12 miles SW of Stirling on the B818

This charming village sits on the northern slopes of the **Campsies**, that great range of hills that forms a northern backdrop for the city of Glasgow. There are some fine walks on the hills, which are popular with Glaswegians at weekends and holidays. The village regularly wins awards in the "Best Kept Small Village in Britain" and the "Britain in Bloom" competitions. The **Loup of Fintry**, east of the village, is a fine waterfall caused by the Endrick Water

Loch Venachar

tumbling down a 94-feet high slope.

Culcreuch Castle (now a country house hotel) is a 700-year-old tower house within a large estate that was once owned by the Galbraiths. The last Galbraith chieftain to live there was Robert Galbraith, who fled to Ireland in 1630 after killing a guest in his home. **Carron Valley Reservoir**, to the east of the village, was built in the 19th century to supply Falkirk and Grangemouth with a water supply. It now offers trout fishing (permit required).

Kippen

9 miles W of Stirling on the B822

This attractive little village sits to the south of that expanse of flat land called **Flanders Moss**. It has, in **Kippen Parish Church**, built in 1825, one of the finest post Reformation churches in Scotland. The ruins of the old church, built in 1691, still survive, surrounded by an old graveyard.

In 1891, a man called Duncan Buchanan planted a vineyard in Kippen within a glasshouse, and one of the vines, later to be called the **Kippen Vine**, grew to be the largest in the world. When fully grown, it had an annual crop of over 2000 bunches of table grapes, and in 1958 created a record by producing 2956 bunches. By this time it was enormous, covering an area of 5000 square feet and stretching for 300 feet within four large greenhouses. It became a tourist attraction, and people came from all over Scotland and abroad to see it.

But alas, the vinery closed down in 1964 (when it could also boast the second and third largest vines in the world) and the Kippen Vine was unceremoniously chopped down. The land was later used for housing.

Arnprior

10 miles W of Sterling on the A811

In the early 16th century, a man called John Buchanan, who had styled himself the **King of Kippen**, lived in this small village. One day a party of hunters was returning to Stirling Castle with some venison for James V's court, and passed John's castle. John captured them and confiscated the venison. The hunters told him that the meat was for the king, but John merely replied that if James was King of Scotland, then he was King of Kippen.

The king was duly informed of this, and instead of being angry, found the incident amusing. He and some courtiers rode out from Stirling one day to pay the King of Kippen a visit. He approached John's castle, and demanded that he be allowed to enter. His demand was refused by a guard, who told the king that John Buchanan was at dinner, and could not be disturbed.

James V had a habit of dressing up in peasant's clothes and slipping out of his palaces alone to meet and speak to his subjects and gauge their opinions of their king and country. When he did this, he assumed the guise of the "Guidman of

Ballengeich", Ballengeich being the name of a pathway he always took down from Stirling Castle when in disguise.

He therefore told the guard to tell Buchanan that the Guidman of Ballengeich was at his door, and he humbly requested an audience with the King of Kippen. When informed, John Buchanan knew who his visitor was, and rushed out in trepidation. But James greeted him cordially, and laughed at the escapade of the venison. Buchanan invited the king into his home to dine, and the king agreed. Soon the company was merry, and the king told Buchanan that he could take as much venison as he liked from the royal hunters that passed his door. He also invited the King of Kippen to visit his brother monarch at Stirling any time he liked. The "king" was later killed at the Battle of Pinkie in 1547.

To the east of Kippen, and off the A811, is the village of **Gargunnock**, with a picturesque parish church built in 1774.

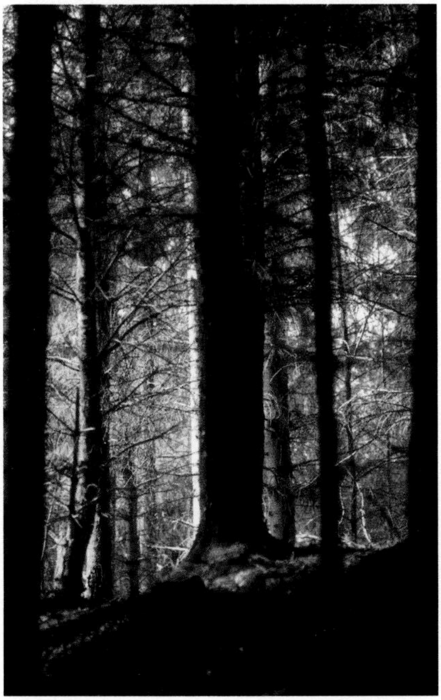

Queen Elizabeth Forest Park, Aberfoyle

Port of Menteith

14 miles W of Stirling on the B8034

This little village sits on the shore of the **Lake of Menteith**, sometimes erroneously called the only lake (as opposed to loch) in Scotland. However, there are several bodies of water in Scotland - some natural, some man made - which are lakes (see also Kirkcudbright, Stenton and Ellon).

But there is no doubting that it is one of Scotland's most beautiful stretches of water. It is only a mile wide by a mile and a half long, with low hills sloping down towards it northern shores. Its name is probably a corruption of Laigh (meaning a flat piece of land) of Menteith, as the land to the south of the lake, Flanders Moss, is flat.

On the island of Inchmahome are the beautiful ruins of **Inchmahome Priory** (Historic Scotland), within which Mary Stuart was kept after the Battle of Pinkie in 1547. Within the re-roofed chapter house are many carved effigies and tombstones. The priory was founded in 1238 by Walter Comyn, Earl of Menteith, for Augustinian canons. In the early 14th century, Robert the Bruce made three separate visits to the place, as the then prior had sworn allegiance to Edward I of England, and no doubt Robert brought pressure to bear on him to change his mind.

On the nearby **Inchtulla** the Menteiths had their castle, and on **Dog Island** the Earl kept his hunting dogs.

The priory can be reached by a small ferry from the jetty at Port of Menteith.

Aberfoyle

17 miles W of Stirling on the A821

Aberfoyle has been called the Gateway to the Trossachs (see also Callander), and sits on the River Forth after it emerges from beautiful Loch Ard. The **Duke's Road** (named after a Duke of Montrose) goes north from the village to the Trossachs proper, and has some good views over Lochs Drunkie and Venachar.

Loch Lomond, Near Balmaha

The **Scottish Wool Centre** is situated within the village, and tells the story of Scottish wool. You can visit the Spinner's Cottage, and have a go at spinning wool into yarn. There are also occasional visits from local shepherds, who put on sheepdog demonstrations. There is also a shop where woollen items - from coats to blankets - can be bought.

It was in Aberfoyle that the famous and mysterious disappearance of the **Rev. Robert Kirk**, minister at Aberfoyle Parish Church, took place. He was born in 1644, and had an abiding interest in fairies, even writing a book called *The Secret Commonwealth of Elves, Fauns and Fairies*.

Legend states that the fairies were none too pleased that Robert had revealed their secrets. In 1692, while walking on Doon Hill, well known in the area as one of the entrances to the fairy realm, Robert disappeared. People claimed that he had been taken to the fairy kingdom, and that one day he would come back, looking no older than he did when he disappeared. To this day, he has not returned. Another legend states that Robert's wife was given the chance of getting her husband back. He would appear, she was told, during Sunday service in the kirk, and she had to throw a knife at him, which should penetrate his flesh. Robert did appear during the service, but his wife couldn't throw the knife, so he disappeared once more.

Robert Kirk was indeed a minister in Aberfoyle in the 17th century, and he did indeed disappear one day while out walking. Did the fairies take him? Or was he the victim of a more earthly crime? No one will ever know - unless he turns up again.

South of Aberfoyle, near the

conservation village of **Gartmore**, is the **Cunninghame Graham Memorial** (National Trust for Scotland). Robert Cunninghame Graham of Ardoch was a Scottish author and politician who died in 1936. The memorial once stood at Castlehill in Dumbarton, but was moved here in 1980.

Drymen

20 miles W of Stirling off the A811

During World War II, **Buchanan Castle** was a military hospital. Its most famous patient was Rudolph Hess, Hitler's deputy, who was kept here after he parachuted into Scotland in 1941 on a secret mission to see the Duke of Hamilton (see also Eaglesham). The castle itself dates from 1855, and was built by the 4th Duke of Montrose after the former castle was destroyed by fire three years previously. It is now partly ruinous, but can be viewed from the outside.

Drymen is on the West Highland Way, the footpath that stretches from Milngavie on the outskirts of Glasgow to Fort William. It is also the gateway to the eastern, and less busy, shores of Loch Lomond, which lie three miles away. The small village of **Balmaha** (also on the West Highland Way) sits on the shore of the loch, and should be visited for the wonderful views it gives of Britain's largest sheet of water. **Balfron**, four miles east of Drymen, is an attractive village with a parish church that dates from 1832. Alexander "Greek" Thomson, the noted architect, was born in Balfron in 1817.

Blair Drummond

6 miles NW of Stirling on the A84

Blair Drummond Safari and Adventure Park is one of the most visited tourist attractions in Scotland. You can tour the 1,500-acre park by car or coach, and see animals such as elephants, lions, zebras, giraffes, white rhino and ostriches in conditions that allow them plenty of

freedom. You can take a boat trip round Chimp Island, watch the sea lion show or glide above the lake on the "Flying Fox".

In the 18th century Blair Drummond was the home of Henry Home, a law lord who sat in the High Court as Lord Kames.

Doune

6 miles NW of Stirling on the A84

The bridge across the River Teith in this picturesque village was built by James Spittal, tailor to James IV (see also Tullibody). Legend has it that he arrived at the ferry that once operated where the bridge now stands without any money, and the ferryman refused to take him across. So, out of spite, he had the bridge built to deprive the ferryman of a livelihood.

Doune Castle (Historic Scotland) is one of the best preserved 14th century castles in Scotland, and was the seat of the Earls of Moray. It stands where the River Ardoch meets the Teith, and was originally built for the Duke of Albany, Regent of Scotland during the minority of James I. Later James had the Duke's son executed for plotting against the crown, and the castle passed to him. It has two main towers connected by a Great Hall with a high wooden ceiling. In 1883 the 14th Earl of Moray restored the castle. It is visited each year by many fans of Monty Python, as some of the scenes in *Monty Python and the Holy Grail* were filmed here.

The village itself gained its burgh charter in 1611, and originally stood close to the castle. In the early 1700s, however, the village and its 17th century **Mercat Cross** were moved to their present position. The village was, at one time, famous as a centre of pistol making. The industry was started in about 1646 by a man called Thomas Cadell, and so accurate and well made were his guns that they soon became prized possessions. By the 18th century Cadell's descendants were all involved in making guns, and began exporting them to the Continent. It is said that the first pistol fired in the American War of Independence was made in Doune.

Deanston

8 miles NW of Stirling on the B8032

Deanston is a village on the banks of the River Teith, built round a cotton mill founded in 1785 by four brothers, one of whom was associated with Sir Richard Arkwright. It passed through several hands before finally closing in 1965. Now the mill houses the **Deanston Distillery**, which makes a range of whiskies, using the same water that once powered the weaving machines. It is not open to the public.

Callander

13 miles NW of Stirling on the A84

This pleasant holiday town stands to the

east of the Trossachs, and has some wonderful walking country on its doorstep. It is home to the **Rob Roy and Trossachs Visitor Centre**, housed in a former church in Ancaster Square, and, as the name suggests, tells the story of both the Trossachs and its most famous son, Rob Roy MacGregor (see also Balquhidder). His real name was Robert MacGregor (1671-1734) and even today people still cannot agree on whether he was a crook, a freedom fighter or the Scottish Robin Hood. The Duke of Montrose confiscated his lands in 1712, and he was imprisoned by the English in the 1720s. He was made famous by two books - Daniel Defoe's *Highland Rogue* and Sir Walter Scott's *Rob Roy*, as well as by the recent film starring Liam Neeson, and Jessica Lange. An earlier film, *Rob Roy the Highland Rogue*, was made in 1953, starring Richard Todd and Glynis Johns.

However, there's no denying that the man was an outstanding leader who could read and write in English and Gaelic, and possessed a large library. It was Sir Walter Scott who made him behave dishonourably at the Battle of Sheriffmuir (see Dunblane), when in fact he acquitted himself with courage and honour fighting for the Jacobites. At his funeral on New Year's Day 1735 people came from all over Scotland to pay their respects.

Steamship Sir Walter Scott

Trossachs Pier, Loch Katrine, by Callander, Stirling FK17 8HZ
Tel: 01877 376315 Fax: 01877 376317
e-mail: gordon@lochkatrine.com
website: www.lochkatrine.com

Loch Katrine is one of the most beautiful lochs in Scotland, and is situated in the heart of the Trossachs, forever associated with the stirring tales of the Highland outlaw, Rob Roy McGregor. The **Steamship Sir Walter Scott** has been magestically sailing Loch Katrine for over a century, offering a unique and spectacular introduction to the history and landscape of the Loch and its environs. It is named after the author who wrote about Rob Roy, and sails past breathtaking scenery.

Two sailings are offered between April and October - one in the morning and one in the afternoon. The longer one, in the morning, leaves from Trossachs Pier at 11am every day (excluding Wednesdays). The cruise lasts one and three quarter hours, and takes you to Stronachlachar, on the west bank, at a leisurely pace as vistas open up before you of wooded banks, blue waters and high hills. You'll pass some historic landmarks on your way, including Ellen's Isle, Silver Strand, Portnellan (one of the burial places of clan McGregor), Royal Cottage and the Factor's Island. This small island was so called because Rob Roy once captured the Duke of Montrose's factor while he was collecting rents and kept him prisoner on the island.

The shorter afternoon sailing take about an hour, and again leaves from Trossachs Pier. There are no stops on this trip but the scenery is just as breathtaking.

When you are cruising these serene waters, it is hard to imagine that the loch is actually the water supply for the city of Glasgow, many miles to the south. The scheme was opened by Queen Victoria in 1859 and was one of the many advanced feats of engineering at the time - and it still functions perfectly.

There is ample coach and car parking on the pier, as well as a tearoom, souvenir shop and bike hire.

Also in Callander is the **Hamilton Toy Museum**, five rooms of model cars, planes, dolls, teddy bears and such TV collectables as Thunderbird, Star Trek and Star Wars figures.

Loch Katrine

23 miles NW of Stirling close to the A821

There is no doubt that Loch Katrine is one of the most beautiful lochs in Scotland. It is surrounded by craggy hills, which in autumn blaze with orange and gold. But the loch as you see it today has more to do with man than nature. In the mid 19th century, the loch became one huge reservoir for the city of Glasgow, and the depth of the water was increased considerably. In 1859 Queen Victoria opened the new reservoir, and 90 million gallons of water a day flowed towards Glasgow, over 30 miles away.

The engineering that made this happen was well ahead of its time, and consisted of tunnels and aqueducts that relied purely on gravity to carry the water towards the city. The engineering surrounding the loch was equally as spectacular. The water from **Loch Arklet**, high in the hills between Lochs Katrine and Lomond, used to flow west into Loch Lomond. By the use of dams, this was changed so that it flowed east into Loch Katrine. The whole scheme was the largest of its kind in the world for many years, and even today, Glasgow still gets its water from Loch Katrine.

The loch was made famous by Sir Walter Scott, who set his poem *The Lady of the Lake* here. And at **Glengyle**, at the western end of the loch, Rob Roy MacGregor was born. It is still a remote place, and cannot be reached by car.

The steamer **Sir Walter Scott** (see panel opposite) has been sailing the waters of the loch from the beginning of the 20th century, and it still does so today. It takes you from the pier at the east end of the loch towards **Stronachlachar,** six miles away. The small islet at Stronachlachan is known as the **Factor's Island**, and recalls one of Rob Roy's exploits. He captured the Duke of Montrose's factor, who was collecting rents in the area, and imprisoned him on the island. He then sent a ransom note to the Duke, but none came. So Rob Roy calmly relieved the man of the £3000 he was carrying and sent him on his way.

This is the heart of the Trossachs (the name translates as "bristly" or "prickly"), and there are other equally as attractive lochs nearby. **Loch Lubnaig**, to the east, is the largest. **Loch Venachar**, **Loch Achray** and **Loch Drunkie** (which can only be reached by a footpath through the forest) are well worth visiting. At the southern end of Loch Lubnaig are the spectacular **Falls of Leny**.

Balquidder

24 miles NW of Stirling on a minor road off the A84

This small village sits to the east of the picturesque **Loch Voil**. It lies in that area of Scotland known as **Breadalbane** ("uplands of Alban", as Alban is the ancient name for Scotland), and in the heart of Clan

Loch Katrine

Creagan House

Strathyre, Callander, Perthshire FK18 8ND
Tel: 01877 384638 Fax: 01877 384319
e-mail: eatandstay@creaganhouse.co.uk
website: www.creaganhouse.co.uk

Strathyre is one of the loveliest areas in Scotland, and it's here that you'll find **Creagan House**, which describes itself as a "restaurant with accommodation". It dates from the 17th century, and its food is superb and renowned throughout the area. Fresh local produce is used wherever possible, some of which comes from local smallholdings, to create The Creagan's innovative and French influenced menus. All five guest rooms are fully en suite, cosy and comfortable. This gem of a place just cannot be missed if you're in "Bonny Strathyre"!

MacGregor country. In the kirkyard of the roofless kirk is **Rob Roy MacGregor's Grave** (see also Callander), plus those of some of his family.

Killin

30 miles NW of Stirling on the A827

Killin sits close to the western end of **Loch Tay**, which stretches for 15 miles north eastwards into Perthshire. The best views of the loch are from the wooded south shore road, though the northern road is wider and straighter.

The **Falls of Dochart**, a series of cascades on the River Dochart, are within the village, and next to them is the **Breadalbane Folklore Centre**, which gives an insight into life and legends of the area.

Craigard Hotel

Main Street, Killin, Perthshire FK21 8UT
Tel: 01567 820285 Fax: 01567 820025
e-mail: craigard.hotel@which.net

In the centre of the small town of Killin you will find the **Craigard Hotel**, a small and friendly hotel. The interior has recently been completely refurbished, making this one of the best establishments in the area. Each of the seven no smoking bedrooms has been given a makeover, with new, modern furniture and those little extras which are appreciated by today's discerning travellers. Each one has a colour TV, tea/coffee making facilities and views of the surrounding hills. The owners, Shelagh and Mike McPartland, are proud of what they have achieved here, and are determined to maintain the high standards and value for money.

In the bar you will find a great choice of drinks, ranging from beers, ales and ciders to liqueurs, wines and spirits, including a great selection of single malts for you to enjoy. The restaurant serves traditional Scottish food, prepared with flair and imagination. Only the finest and freshest of local produce from Scotland's bounteous larder is used wherever possible, ensuring that a meal here is a culinary experience not to be forgotten! The traditional Scottish breakfasts are hearty and filling, though lighter options are available if required. And all around is the magnificent scenery and attractions of Perthshire. Killin itself is small and attractive, and you can visit such tourist attractions as Loch Tay, the Trossachs, Glen Lyon (sometimes called the "loveliest glen in Scotland"), the Falls of Dochart, the Breadalbane Folklore Centre and the "Fair City of Perth" itself.

Three miles north on a minor road are the **Falls of Lochay** on the River Lochay, though care should be taken when approaching them. The **Moirlanich Longhouse** (National Trust for Scotland) on the Glen Lochay road dates from the 19th century, and is a rare surviving example of a Scottish longhouse, where a family and their livestock lived under the one roof. In an adjacent shed is a display of working clothes found in the longhouse, along with displays, which explain the building's history and restoration. The ruins of **Finlarig Castle**, which date from the late 16th century, are to the north of the village. The castle was once a Campbell stronghold, and was built by Black Duncan, one of the most notorious members of the clan. Within its grounds are the remains of a beheading pit and a Campbell mausoleum built in the early 1800s

Loch Dochart

Crianlarich

32 miles NW of Stirling on the A82

The name of this small village comes from the Gaelic for "low pass", and sits on the southern edge of Breadalbane. Surrounding it is some marvellous walking and climbing country, with the West Highland Way passeing close to the village. The twin peaks of Ben More (3,843 feet) and Stobinian (3,821 feet) are to the south east, while the picturesque **Falls of Falloch** (with a small car park close by) lie four miles to the southwest on the A82.

Tyndrum

40 miles NW of Stirling on the A82

This little village has a population of no more than 100 people, and yet it has two railway stations - one on the line from Glasgow to Oban and the other on the line from Glasgow to Fort William. It sits at the head of **Strath Fillan**, which snakes south towards Crianlarich and carrying the West Highland Way. At **Dalrigh**, in 1306, Robert the Bruce was defeated in battle, and nearby was the site of **Strathfillan Priory**, founded by Bruce in 1318. St Fillan was an Irish monk who lived during the 8th century and who founded a monastery in the vicinity (see also Pittenweem, Madderty and St Fillans). It is said that while building the monastery, a wolf attacked and killed one of the oxen used to bring materials to the site. St Fillan then prayed, and a miracle occurred - the wolf took the place of the ox.

Argyll & The Inner Hebrides

Argyll is one of the most diverse and beautiful counties in Scotland. It sits on the western seaboard, where long sea lochs penetrate deep into the interior and mountains tumble down towards fertile glens. Most of the Inner Hebridean islands, such as Mull, Jura and Islay (pronounced Eye-lah) belong to it, and ferries criss-cross the waters between them and the mainland.

"Argyll" itself comes from the Gaelic Earraghaidheal, meaning the "coastline of the Gaels". It can truly claim to be the cradle of Scotland, for this was, at one time, the kingdom of Dalriada, founded by the "Scoti" who originally came from Ireland in the 6th century. Here, at the fortress of Dunadd, they established their capital. From Dunadd, in 843, Kenneth MacAlpin, King of Dalriada,

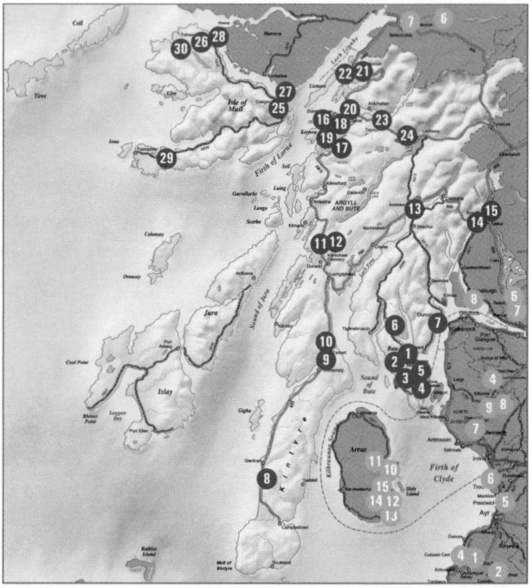

PLACES TO STAY, EAT AND DRINK

Brechin's Brasserie, Rothesay	1	Brasserie	p217
Harbourside Apartments, Rothesay	2	Self Catering	p218
Argyle House, Rothesay	3	B&B	p219
Chandlers, Ascog Bay	4	Hotel	p220
Regent Hotel, Rothesay	5	Hotel	p221
Colintraive Hotel, Colintraive	6	Hotel	p222
Benmore Botanic Garden, Dunoon	7	Visitor Attraction	p224
Hunting Lodge Hotel, Bellochantuy	8	Hotel	p226
Columba Hotel, Tarbert	9	Hotel	p228
Tapestry Tearoom, Tarbert	10	Tea Rooms	p228
Dunchraigaig House, Kilmartin	11	B&B	p231
Kilmartin Hotel, Kilmartin	12	Pub, Food and Accommodation	p231
Inveraray Jail, Inveraray	13	Visitor Attraction	p233
Greenbank Guest House/Restaurant, Arrochar	14	Guest House	p235
Weaver's Restaurant & Gift Shop, Tarbet	15	Restaurant	p236

● Denotes entries in other chapters

Fishing by Loch Ane, Kilchurn Castle

set off towards Scone in Perthshire (taking the Stone of Destiny with him) to claim the throne of the Picts, thus uniting the two great northern kingdoms and creating an embryonic Scotland. In the 11th century two Lowland kingdoms, the Lothians (centred on Edinburgh) and Strathclyde (centred on Dumbarton) were absorbed, and Scotland as we know it today was formed.

The other great Dalriadan centre was at what is now Dunstaffnage, north of Oban. The site is nowadays occupied by Dunstaffnage Castle, one of the most spectacular fortifications on Scotland's western seaboard. And the 12th century Castle Sween, on the shores of Loch Sween, is reckoned to be the oldest stone built castle on the Scottish mainland.

Though it has attractive towns such as Oban, Lochgilphead, Tobermory, Inveraray and Campbeltown, Argyll is sparsely populated. There are few clogged up roads, (though Oban can get very busy in the summer months), and driving is a pleasure. New vistas are constantly being opened up as you drive along roads such as the one from Lochgilphead to Oban, and even on overcast days (which are not unknown in this part of Scotland) they are a constant source of wonder and delight. The climate is mild, thanks to the Gulf Stream, and the place has many fine gardens to explore, such as Ardkinglas, Crarae and Arduaine, some with palm trees and other species you wouldn't expect to thrive so far north.

PLACES TO STAY, EAT AND DRINK

Denotes entries in other chapters

Crofters Cottage, Isle of Mull

Man has lived in Argyll for centuries, and around Kilmartin there are cairns and standing stones built long before the ancient Egyptians built the Pyramids. Iona, off the western tip of Mull, is one of the most sacred places, not just in Scotland, but in all of Christendom. Here St Columba established his great monastery, and from here missionaries set out to convert the northern lands.

St Columba wasn't the first man to bring Christianity to Scotland - that honour goes to St Ninian - but he was the most influential, and we know a lot about his life, thanks to a biography written by St Adamnan, ninth abbot of Iona, almost a hundred years after he died. He told of a man who was all too human - vengeful yet forgiving, impetuous yet thoughtful, arrogant yet unassuming and boastful yet modest. Today Iona is still a place of pilgrimage, though most people now come as tourists to see and admire the later abbey buildings and experience that feeling of calm for which the island is famous.

Argyll is also a place of intriguing legends. When that great order of monastic soldiers called the Knights Templar was suppressed by Pope Clement V in 1307, it was to this part of Scotland, we are told, that their remnants fled. Robert the Bruce, the Scots king, had been excommunicated by the Pope, so Papal authority didn't extend to this part of Europe at the time, and here the warrior monks could settle in peace. Their legacy, some people claim, are the wonderfully carved tombstones with Templar symbols on them found in such places as Kilmichael Glassary and Kilmartin. Legend also says that a troop of Knights Templar from this area helped Robert the Bruce defeat the English at Bannockburn.

The Argyll coastline is rugged and rocky, as are most of the islands, which belong to the county, though there are some marvellous, glistening beaches, which are invariably empty. The largest islands are Mull, Jura and Islay, but there are other hidden gems to be discovered, such as Lismore, Colonsay, Coll, Tiree and Bute. The last mentioned, along with Arran and the Cumbraes, used to form the county of Bute, but local government reorganisation in the 70s shared it out between Argyll and Ayrshire. Local government reorganisation also took Morvern, Sunart and the Ardnamurchan peninsula, north of Mull, from Argyll, and today they form part of the Highlands local government area. But at the same time parts of what were formerly Dunbartonshire, such as the town of Helensburgh and the Rosneath Peninsula, are now within Argyll, although they are dealt with in another section of this book.

That great peninsula known as the Mull of Kintyre, which hangs down into the Atlantic like an arm, is also in Argyll. This is a remote part of Scotland - part of the mainland yet as isolated as any island. Though Glasgow is only 60 miles from

Campbeltown as the crow flies, it takes the average driver three or four hours over twisting, loch-girt roads to reach it. This is the area made famous by Sir Paul McCartney's song, where he sings of "mists rolling in from the sea".

Rothesay

Bute

The island of Bute used to be part of the small county of the same name, which also took in Arran and the Cumbraes. Though it now comes under Argyll, the Highland Boundary Fault passes right through the 175 acre **Loch Fad**, in the heart of the island, which means that the northern part is in the Highlands while the southern part is in the Lowlands. The scenery reflects this, with the north being rugged and relatively uninhabited, while the south is pastoral, with many small farms and settlements.

There are two ferries connecting Bute to the mainland. The main one is from Wemyss Bay in Renfrewshire to Rothesay, while another, smaller one, travels the short

Brechin's Brasserie

2 Bridgend Street, Rothesay,
Isle of Bute PA20 0HU
Tel: 01700 50-2922
e-mail: info@brechins-bute.com
website: www.brechins-bute.com

The yellow and blue frontage of **Brechin's Brasserie** in Rothesay is a welcome sign for all those who appreciate good food served in an informal and welcoming atmosphere. In fact, so good is the food that it has earned a coveted Les Routiers listing, indicating its quality. Owned and managed by Ann and Tim, it serves breakfasts, snacks and hot meals throughout the day and a restaurant menu on Friday and Saturday evenings. It is open all year from Tuesday to Saturday, with Ann supervising the kitchen and Tim looking after the front-of-house.

The produce used in the preparation of the food is always fresh and local, ensuring a dining experience that you will remember for all the right reasons. The coffees - using only fresh, ground beans - are renowned, and include latte, cappuccino and Americano. Why not try one with one of the French pastries and desserts that feature on the menu? Or the delicious filled ciabattas? The lunch menu includes crisp fresh salads, steak and Guinness casserole and Brechin's curry bowl. The evening meals are out of this world and represent great value for money. The main courses include king prawns in a red Thai curry sauce, Tournedos Highlander (fillet of prime Scottish steak with whisky cream sauce), roast rack of Bute lamb and chicken chasseur. Vegetarian options are always available, and there is a fine selection of wines.

Ann and Tim look forward to welcoming you to their brasserie where the atmosphere is informal and friendly and the food and wine is superb.

Harbourside Apartments

Guildford Court, 3 Watergate,
Rothesay, Isle of Bute PA20 9AB
Tel/Fax: 01700 503770
e-mail: ekferguson@btinternet.com

Situated right in the heart of the Royal Burgh of Rothesay are the **Harbourside Apartments**, which offer well furnished and equipped self-catering apartments at very reasonable prices. They are right on the seafront overlooking the marina and pier and have superb views over Rothesay Bay and Harbour to Loch Striven and the Cowal Hills. The Guildford Court building itself is Victorian, and sits on a superb corner site beside the town centre square, which has seating and newly-planted trees. It was converted to apartments from the former Lorne Hotel about 15 years ago. The

apartments sit close to all the amenities of the town - shops, post office, restaurants, bars and tourist and leisure facilities.

The apartments and en-suite rooms are fully furnished and equipped and decorated to a good standard (Visit Scotland 2 star grade) and provide the facilities needed for an enjoyable holiday, short break or overnight stay. They are located on the second and third floors of a 4 storey building.

There are ten units available, of which six are self-catering apartments and four are unserviced en-suite rooms without self catering facilities. Two of the flats sleep two, one sleeps four, two sleep two to four (using convertible settees) and the sixth sleeps four to five. Some are to the back, some overlook Guildford Square and some have fabulous views over the sea towards the Cowal Hills and Loch Striven. Two are studio apartments and the remainder of the flats have either one or two bedrooms, some with bed-settees in the living room.. All have bathrooms with WC, wash hand basin and either bath or shower. The kitchen areas are all equipped with full cooking and food preparation facilities, microwave, fridge, crockery and cutlery.

The en-suite rooms are all on the third floor. One overlooks Guildford Square, the Promenade, and Rothesay Bay shore. The other three have fabulous views over the Rothesay Harbour, Marina and Bay towards the Cowal Hills and Loch Striven. They sleep two in comfort, with either a double bed or two single beds in each room, which also has its own en suite facilities (WC, wash hand basin and shower). TV and full crockery and cutlery is provided. The room price includes a complimentary light breakfast each morning.

The price of apartments and en-suite rooms include all electricity, heating, hot water, TV, bed linen, towels etc. There are no "hidden extras".

The Royal Burgh of Rothesay was once the most popular Clyde Coast holiday resort for Glaswegians, and it has lost none of its charm . There is a wealth of original Victorian and other historic architecture - including Rothesay Castle, Mountstuart House, Ascog Fernery and Rothesay's world famous Victorian toilets. The island of Bute, "Scotland's Unexplored Island" is beautiful and crammed with history and things to do and see. Because of the Gulf Stream, the weather is very mild here, and palm trees flourish quite happily in the award winning gardens along the promenade.

distance between Ardentraive on the Cowal Peninsula and Rhubodach.

The main town is **Rothesay**, an ancient royal burgh that was given its charter in 1401. It is one of the most famous holiday resorts on the Firth of Clyde, and at one time attracted thousands of Glasgow tourists during the "Glasgow Fair", which is always the last two weeks in July. Fine Victorian mansions line the front, built to take Glasgow merchants who would descend on the town, complete with family and servants, for weeks at a time. There were also more modest B&Bs and guest houses that took in the working classes for what was their one and only holiday of the year. It eventually earned the nickname of "Scotland's Madeira", not just because it was on an island, but also because palm trees flourish here due to the influence of the Gulf Stream.

The gentleness of the climate can best be appreciated at **Ardencraig Gardens** in Ardencraig Lane, which were bought by Rothesay Town Council in 1970. They formed part of the original gardens designed by Percy Cane for the owners of Ardencraig House.Every summer it shimmers with colour, and is a popular spot with holidaymakers. Another popular spot is **Canada Hill**, to the south of the town, where there are spectacular views of the Firth of Clyde. From here, people used to watch ships sailing down the Clyde taking Scottish emigrants to a new life in North America, hence its name. On the sea front is a memorial to people who left Rothesay but never returned - the six hundred Bute bowmen who fought alongside William Wallace at the Battle of Falkirk in 1298.

Rothesay Castle (Historic Scotland) is one of the oldest in Scotland. It is a royal castle with an unusual circular curtain wall and a filled moat, and was probably built in the 13th century by Walter, third steward of the royal household. Not long after, the

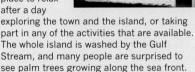

Chandlers

Ascog Bay, Isle of Bute PA20 9ET
Tel: 01700 505577 Fax: 01700 505271
e-mail: info@visitchandlers.com
website: www.visitchandlers.com

Bute is one of the most accessible islands in the Firth of Clyde, and is, surprisingly, no more than an hour and a half from the bustle of Glasgow by train and vehicle ferry. Standing just a couple of miles south of the island's capital, Rothesay, you'll find **Chandlers**, an outstanding hotel with superb views out over the Firth to the Ayrshire coast and beyond. If you're arriving in Scotland via Glasgow or Prestwick Airports, or if you're arriving on the island by ferry, the hotel's Mercedes people carrier can be made available to pick you up.

Once through the door of Chandlers, you know that you are going to be pampered. The

manager individually greets all guests, and welcomes them into the lounge where the sea views from the large bay window will take your breath way. The place is elegant and smart, and here comfort and service take on an entirely new meaning. There is an air of understated luxury here but also of informality, and the staff are friendly, knowledgeable and focused on making your stay as rewarding and as enjoyable as possible. Each of the beautifully appointed, spacious bedrooms are individually furnished and decorated to an exceptional standard, and have TV, video, DVD player, telephone, hair dryer, fresh fruit, bottled water and tissues. Most have stunning vistas out over the waters of the Firth of Clyde. There are well appointed en suite bathrooms, each with bathrobes, a selection of toiletries, cotton wool, shaving mirror, tissues and a selection of luxurious, soft towels.

Food is important in Chandlers. In the spacious restaurant you will be offered a menu that has been carefully and lovingly prepared by the resident chefs, and which meld imagination and flare with fresh local produce. Your palate will be stimulated by the flavours of this gourmet cuisine, which is justly famous throughout the area. And there is a superb collection of fine wines, spirits and liqueurs to add that certain something to an already superb meal. Then, to round it all off, you can have coffee or brandy on the outdoor terrace as you admire the views.

Bute is an island that is rich in history and heritage. Rothesay is an ancient royal burgh with a royal castle that was a favourite of the early Stuarts, and it can still be visited. In addition, there are old ruined chapels to be explored - some dating back to Celtic times - as well as standing stones, stone circles and burial mounds. Plus there is golf, walking, fishing, sailing, and a host of outdoor activities that can be indulged in without leaving the island.

Luxury and comfort are the watchwords at Chandlers. Pay a visit, and you won't be disappointed!

Regent Hotel

23 Battery Place, Rothesay,
Isle of Bute PA20 9DU
Tel/Fax: 01700 502006
e-mail: info@thergent.co.uk
website: www.thergent.co.uk

The three-star **Regent Hotel** was built in 1840 as the home of the Weirs, a local building family. Over the years it has been sympathetically developed with additions in the 1930s and 1970s. The hotel was further refurbished during the 1990s, and now offers a warm, homely reception to guests visiting the lovely island of Bute. It is just five minutes away from the town centre, with commanding views over Rothesay Bay and on to the Kyles of Bute. The accommodation consists of eight rooms - four en suite doubles, an en suite king size twin/double and three singles. All are comfortable and well furnished, with TVs and hospitality trays.

At the à la carte Four Seasons Restaurant, guests can choose from an imaginatively prepared menu,using fresh local produce with a Mediterranean influence. Dishes include Sicilian chicken, Four Seasons pasta, sizzling steaks and a firm Scottish favourite - haggis, neeps and tatties. All are served with a selection of seasonable vegetables.

In Dizzy's Bar you can enjoy a quiet drink, choosing from a wide range of beers, wines and spirits, including single malts. There is a popular twice-weekly cabaret with well known local entertainer Bri W, as well as sessions from local musicians and performers.

The Regent Hotel is close to Rothesay's superb amenities, and the Isle of Bute itself is full of history and heritage. The owners, Wendy and John Thompson, have created a warm, friendly and informal hotel, and you will be sure of a warm Scottish welcome.

Vikings besieged it. King Haakon of Norway took it in 1263, but afterwards was defeated at the Battle of Largs. The Treaty of Perth, signed in 1266, gave Scotland the Inner Hebrides and the island of Bute, and it became a favourite residence of the first Stuart king, Robert II, and his son, Robert III, who may have died there.

It was Robert III who created the dukedom of Rothesay (the first such dukedom in Scotland), and conferred it on his eldest son. Ever since, all royal heirs bear the title, with Prince Charles being the present duke. The whole building was in a ruinous state until 1816, when it was partly rebuilt by the 2nd Marquis of Bute.

In Stuart Street, close to the castle, is the **Bute Museum**, which has displays and artefacts about Rothesay, the Firth of Clyde and the island of Bute itself. The **Church of St Mary** (Historic Scotland), on the southern outskirts of the town, is next to the present High Kirk built in 1796. It dates mainly from the 13th and 14th century, and has two canopied tombs. One contains the effigy of a woman and child, and the other the effigy of a man. It has been recently re-roofed to protect them.

The **Isle of Bute Discovery Centre** is housed in the town's Winter Garden (built in 1924), on the front. It houses an exhibition highlighting life on the island through interactive displays and plasma screens, as well as a cinema/theatre.

But Rothesay has more unusual attractions, such as the **Victorian Toilets** at the end of the pier, which date from 1899. They still work perfectly, and are full of ornate design. They were recently voted the second best place in the world to spend a penny. If you want the best place, you'll have to go to Hong Kong (if you can hang on that long).

Scotland's first long distance island footpath, the 30-mile long **West Island Way**, starts at Kilchattan Bay and finishes at Port Bannatyne. Full details of the trail are available from the Isle of Bute Discovery centre in Rothesay.

Close to Kilchattan Bay, at Kingarth, is **St Blane's Chapel**. The ruins of this Norman structure sit within what was a Celtic monastery, founded by St Blane in the sixth century (see also Dunblane). The whole area shows how such a monastery would have been laid out. The rath, or cashel, a low wall surrounding the monastery, can still be seen, as can the foundations of various beehive cells in which the monks lived. There are two old graveyards - one for men, and one for women.

There are lots of other religious sites on Bute, some dating from the Dark Ages. At **Straad** (a name which tells you that the island once belonged to the Vikings) there are the scant remains of **St Ninian's Chapel**, which may go back at least 1,500 years, and at **Kilmichael** there are the ruins of the old **St Macaille Chapel**.

Mount Stuart House, near the lovely village of **Kerrycroy**, is the ancestral home of the Marquis of Bute. In 1877 a fire destroyed most of the old house, built during the reign of Queen Anne, and the third Marquis employed Robert Rowand Anderson to design the present Victorian Gothic one. It is an immense house, full of treasures, and reflects the history and importance of the family who owned it. When built, it was full of technological wonders. It was the first house in Scotland to be lit by electricity, and the first private house to have a heated indoor swimming pool. Surrounding the house are 300 acres of delightful gardens.

Near Port Bannatyne, north of Rothesay, is **Kames Castle**, dating from the 14th century. Neither it nor its beautiful gardens are open to the public, but they can be viewed from the road. One place, which can be visited, however, is **Ascog Hall Fernery and Garden**, three miles south of Rothesay. It was built about 1870, and has a sunken fern house which houses over 80 sub-tropical fern species. It was awarded the first ever Scottish prize by the Historic Gardens Foundation, which promotes historic gardens and parks throughout the world.

Dunoon

Dunoon is one of the best-known Clyde holiday resorts. It sits opposite the Renfrewshire coast, and an all year ferry connects it to Gourock. Each year in August the town hosts the **Cowal Highland Gathering**, one of the largest in Scotland, where competitors take part in in tossing the caber, throwing the hammer

and other Scottish events.

The **Castle House Museum** is in the Castle Gardens, and has an exhibition entitled "Dunoon and Cowal Past and Present". There are models, artefacts and photographs, which bring the Dunoon of yesteryear to life. There are also furnished Victorian rooms and a shop. The statue of **Highland Mary**, erected in 1896, is close by (see also Failford and Greenock). She was a native of Dunoon, and worked as a maid in a large house near Mauchline in Ayrshire. Burns met her there, and asked her to accompany him to the West Indies when he was thinking of emigrating. She agreed, but on a trip home to Dunoon to make arrangements, she died and was buried in Greenock.

Power Boat Festival, Dunoon

In Hamilton Street is the factory of **Dunoon Ceramics**, which makes mugs and other items. There is a shop, and guided tours of the factory are available to see how the mugs are made and fired. On Tom-a-Mhoid Road, in West Bay, is the **Lamont Memorial**, erected in 1906 to commemorate the massacre of the Lamonts by the Campbells in 1646 (see also Toward).

Three miles north of Dunoon, on the A815, is **Adam's Grave**, the popular name for a 3,500-year-old neolithic burial cairn, which still has two portals and a capstone intact at its entrance. It sits close to the **Holy Loch**, at one time an American nuclear submarine base. It was chosen as a base not just because of its deep water, but because this part of Argyll has a cloud covering for most of the year, thwarting satellite and aerial photography. The Americans left in 1992, taking with them their large American cars and their accents, which were once common in the streets of the town. At Sandbank, on the shores of the loch, is the two-mile long **Ardnadam Heritage Trail**, with a climb up to a viewpoint at Dunan.

At **Hunter's Quay**, between the Holy Loch and Dunoon, is the slipway of yet another vehicle ferry between the Cowal Peninsula and McInroy's Point in Renfrewshire run by Western Ferries.

Around Dunoon

Kilmun

3 miles N of Dunoon on the A880

Kilmun Church was a collegiate church founded in 1442 by Sir Duncan Campbell of Lochawe, ancestor of the present Dukes of Argyll. All that remains is the tower, now roofless. In 1794 a Campbell mausoleum was built close to the present church of St Munn, built in 1841, and in the kirkyard is the grave of **Elizabeth Blackwell**, who, in 1849, was the first woman to graduate in medicine. Born in Bristol in 1821, she studied in Geneva in the United States and at Paris and London. After returning to the United States, she opened (despite intense opposition) the first hospital staffed entirely by women. She died in 1910. Close by is the grave of the **Rev. Alexander Robinson**, a former minister who was deposed after writing *The Saviour in the New Light*, a book that put forward opinions which brought accusations of heresy.

On a hillside is the **Kilmun Arboretum**, extending to 180 acres. First planted in 1930, it has a wide range of trees - some rare - from all over the world, and is maintained by the Forestry Commission, which does research work here.

Benmore

6 miles N of Dunoon off the A815

The **Younger Botanic Garden** (see panel below) is a specialist sector of the Royal Botanic Garden in Edinburgh, and in its 140 acres you can see a wide collection of trees and shrubs from all over the world. There are 250 species of rhododendron, an avenue of giant redwoods from America and a formal garden. Within the Glen Massan Arboretum are some of the tallest trees in Scotland, including a Douglas fir over 178 feet high. From the top of Benmore Hill there is a magnificent view across the Holy Loch to the Firth of Clyde and the Renfrewshire coast.

To the north of Benmore is the seven mile long **Loch Eck**, with the A815 following its eastern shores towards Strachur on Loch Fyne. Near the head of the loch is Tom-a-Chorachasich, a low hill where, legend says, a Viking prince was once slain.

Toward

6 miles S of Dunoon on the A815

The ruins of **Toward Castle** date mainly from the 15th century. It was a stronghold of the Lamonts, who supported the MacDonalds and Charles II in his attempts to impose bishops on the Church of Scotland, while the Campbells were Covenanters, and bitterly opposed to episcopacy.

An episode in 1646 shows just how the Scottish clans took matters into their own hands when dispensing justice. The Campbells laid siege to the castle in that year, and after unsuccessfully trying to blow it up, offered safe passage as far as Dunoon to the Lamonts sheltering within.

The Lamonts duly left the castle, and were immediately rounded up and taken to Tom-a-Mhoid ("Hill of Justice") in Dunoon,

BENMORE BOTANIC GARDEN

Dunoon, Argyll PA23 8QU
Tel: 01369 706261
e-mail: benmore@rbge.org.uk
website: www.rbge.org.uk

A member of the National Botanic Gardens of Scotland, **Benmore Botanic Garden** is famous for its collection of trees and shrubs. Set amid dramatic scenery, the west coast climate provides ideal growing conditions for some of the finest Himalayan rhododendrons. Guided walks are available to discover the secrets of this sensational garden, including the historic formal garden with Puck's Hut and established conifers. There is something of interest all year round and autumn provides a beautiful array of colours. There is a café for refreshments and a shop to buy gifts and plants, whilst various exhibitions and events take place in the Courtyard Gallery. Phone for details.

where 36 clansmen were hung (see also Dunoon). It wasn't just political or religious differences that prompted the massacre. Previously, the Lamonts themselves had slaughtered Campbells at Strachur and attacked and slaughtered the villagers of Kilmun, who were hiding in their church.

Davaar Island, Campbeltown

Campbeltown

Campbeltown has the reputation of being the most isolated town on the British mainland. It sits on the Mull of Kintyre, that great peninsula that hangs down from the main body of Argyll. It received its royal charter in 1700, making it the second youngest royal burgh in Scotland. Though 140 miles from Glasgow by road, it is only 30 miles from Ballycastle in Northern Ireland. It also has the distinction of being the most southerly town in the Scottish Highlands, and is 25 miles further south than Berwick-upon-Tweed.

At one time the main industries were fishing and distilling, but the fishing fleet has gone now, and only three distilleries remain of the 30 or so that once produced over two million gallons of whisky a year. There are conducted tours round **Springbank Distillery**.

The town sits on Campbeltown Loch, which is guarded by the small island of **Davaar**. Within a cave on the island is a famous painting of the Crucifixion by local artist David MacKinnon in 1887. The island can be reached on foot at low tide by a long shingle beach known as The Doirlinn. **Campbeltown Cross**, erected near the harbour, dates from the 14th century. It was used as the mercat cross after the town became a royal burgh. **Campbeltown Heritage Centre** has exhibits and artefacts dealing with the history of the area. In the grounds of Campbeltown Library are the **Lady Linda McCartney Memorial Gardens**, named after the late wife of Sir Paul McCartney, who has a holiday home on Kintyre.

Around Campbeltown

Southend

8 miles S of Campbeltown on the B842

This is the most southerly village in Argyll. It was near here, at **Keil**, that St Columba is supposed to have first set foot on Scottish soil before sailing north towards Iona. In the ancient churchyard at Keil are footprints, which are said to mark the spot. It was near here also that a massacre of 300 MacDonald clansmen under Sir Alasdair MacDonald took place in 1647.

Saddell

9 miles N of Campbeltown on the B842

Saddell Abbey (Historic Scotland) was founded by Somerled, Lord of the Isles in 1148 and completed by his son Reginald, who also founded Iona Abbey and Nunnery. Only scant remains can now be seen, most notably the presbytery and the north transept. As at other places in Argyll, stone carving once flourished here, and no fewer

Hunting Lodge Hotel

Bellochantuy, Argyll PA28 6QE
Tel: 01583 421323 Fax: 01583 421343
e-mail: email@thehuntinglodgehotel,com
website: www.thehuntinglodgehotel.com

Situated on the western shores of the Mull of Kintyre, the **Hunting Lodge Hotel** is a family owned and run hotel that offers fabulous views out over the Atlantic to the islands of Gigha, Islay and Jura. It was once a hunting lodge for the Dukes of Argyll, and many of its original features have been retained, melding

perfectly with all the modern conveniences you would expect from an establishment that puts comfort, luxury and service first. The whole place is elegant and spacious, yet has that informal, family atmosphere that makes a hotel so special.

Great thought has gone into the running of the place, and everything, from the ambience and the food to the guestrooms and the lounges, speaks of careful attention to detail. All the rooms are fully en suite, of course, and all have TV, hospitality trays etc. Family rooms and non smoking rooms are available. The four deluxe rooms have balconies, while the six standard rooms all have sea views. They are beautifully decorated and furnished, while one room has been specially adapted for the disabled.In addition, the hotel has six self-catering cottages conveniently located next to the hotel, ideal for those who enjoy hotel amenities with the independence of self-catering All the cottages are named after islands, and all are well equipped and furnished to give you a memorable holiday. The Craro and the Islay sleeps four - six, the Jura sleeps four, the Sanda sleeps three, the Gigha sleeps two - three and the Cura is a compact studio flat that sleeps two.

As you would expect, the Hunting Lodge is renowned for its food. The Putechan Restaurant is open to residents and non-residents alike from noon until 2.30 pm and from 6.30 pm until 9.30 pm. Every Sunday there is a popular carvery, and at other lunchtimes a bar menu is available that includes home made soup, grilled herring, venison sausage, all-day breakfast, scampi, chicken and steak and ale pie. The evening menu includes such dishes as Border lamb, venison, supreme of chicken, baked cod fillet with Arran mustard, sirloin steak and roast Mediterranean vegetables. Only the finest and freshest of local produce is used wherever possible, and the food is prepared and presented to the highest standards.

A fine range of wines and spirits is also available, including 300 rare and interesting malt whiskies. Why not enjoy a relaxing drink in one of the three magnificent lounges? They all have sea views, and make the perfect place to unwind after a hard day's sightseeing!

The Hunting Lodge is the perfect venue for conferences and weddings, and it even has a licence for holding civil marriage ceremonies. The unusual "rock room" has a natural rock wall, and a ceremony here will be one to remember. And the hotel's own private beach is the perfect place for those photographs that encapsulate the event. The Hunting Lodge is the perfect place to enjoy a holiday that is as restful or as active as you wish - there's so much to see and do on the Mull of Kintyre!

than 11 beautiful grave slabs, each one showing a knight in full armour or a monk, can be seen. **Saddell Castle** (not open to the public) was built in 1508 for the Bishop of Argyll.

Carradale

12 miles N of Campbeltown on the B879

The **Network Carradale Heritage Centre** has displays about fishing, farming and forestry in the area, as well as hands-on activities for children. **Carradale House** dates from the 18th century, but was extended in 1804 for the then owned Richard Campbell. In its grounds are gardens noted for their rhododendrons, of which there are over 100 varieties.

Torrisdale Castle, which has been converted into holiday accommodation, was built in 1815, and has a tannery.

Glenbarr

10 miles N of Campbeltown on the A83

At the **Clan Macalister Centre** in Glenbarr Abbey (not an abbey but a mansion house) are exhibits tracing the history of Clan Macalister as far back as Somerled, Lord of the Isles, nearly 900 years ago. The castle was presented to the clan in 1984 by Angus C. Macalister, 5th Laird of Glenbarr.

Gigha

17 miles NW of Campbeltown off the west coast of Kintyre

This small island, no more than six miles long by two miles wide at its widest is reached by ferry from Tayinloan. The name Gigha (pronounced gee-yah, with a hard "g") comes from the Norse, and means "God's island". It seems to have a climate of its own, and while the rest of Argyll is enveloped in cloud, Gigha is sometimes bathed in sunshine due to the Gulf Stream washing its shores.

The scanty ruins of Kilchattan Church, behind the hotel, date from medieval times. In the kirkyard are some old grave slabs showing knights in armour. One is possibly of Malcolm MacNeill, Laird of Gigha, who died in 1493.

And behind the church, atop the Cnoc A'Charraidh (Hill of the Pillar) is the **Ogham Stone** dating from the time the island formed part of the kingdom of Dalriada. It carries a carving that reads *Fiacal son of Coemgen*, and probably marks a burial.

The 50-acre **Achamore Gardens**, near the ferry port at Ardminish, are open to the public. They were founded by Sir James Horlick, of bedtime drink fame, after he bought the island in 1944. They are famous for their rhododendrons and camellias. In 2001 its inhabitants bought the island.

Tarbert

31 miles N of Campbeltown on the A83

This small fishing port sits at a point where Kintyre is no more than a mile wide. To the east is the small East Loch Tarbert, and to the west is the eight-mile long West Loch Tarbert, where, at **Kennacraig**, ferries leave for Islay and Jura. In 1093 King Magnus Barelegs of Norway is said to have been dragged in his galley across the narrow isthmus, proving to his own satisfaction that the Mull of Kintyre was an island. **An Tairbeart**, to the south of the village, is a heritage centre that tells of the place's history and people. **Tarbert Castle** dates from the late 15th century, and was a royal foundation. It can be reached along a footpath from Harbour Street.

North of the village is Stonefield Castle, built in 1837 and now a hotel. Attached is **Stonefield Castle Garden**, which is open to the public. As with so many gardens in the area, it is famous for its rhododendrons. There are also plants from Chile and New Zealand, and conifers such as the sierra redwood.

Seven miles south of Tarbert is **Skipness Castle** (Historic Scotland), which dates originally from the 13th century. The first historical mention of it is in 1261 when the

Columba Hotel

East Pier Road, Tarbert, Argyll PA29 6UF
Tel/Fax: 01880 820808
e-mail: info@columbahotel,com
website: www.columbahotel.com

Owned and managed by Julie and Kevin Butler, the **Columba Hotel** offers superior accommodation in the small fishing village of Tarbert on the Mull of Kintyre. It is a family run hotel, and overlooks the scenic approach to Tarbert harbour. The hotel boasts ten rooms, all fully en suite, and all having an individual character while still being spacious, comfortable and thoughtfully furnished and decorated. This is the ideal base from which to explore the fabulous Mull of Kintyre with its history and heritage, hill walking, wildlife, horse riding, golf, clay pigeon shooting, mountain biking and so on. And you can sail to some of the wonderful Scottish islands from Kennacraig, just a mile or so to the west.

The hotel serves some of the finest food in Scotland, and the menu features only the finest and freshest of Scottish produce, such as Inveraray venison, Islay lamb, Loch Fyne smoked fish, Gigha cheese and locally grown vegetables. The food is also complemented by a fine range of over 30 wines and 40 single malts. Or why not enjoy a drink in the lounge or bar, which are decorated in themes of fishing and steamers to reflect the village's history.The Columba has a relaxed and informal atmosphere, and makes a great place to recharge your batteries. Julie and Kevin look forward to welcoming you to the Columba Hotel!

Tapestry Tearoom

Argyll House, 1 Harbour Street, Tarbert, Argyll PA29 6UJ
Tel: 01880 820191

The **Tapestry Tearoom** is the place to eat when you're visiting the picturesque fishing village of Tarbert on the Mull of Kintyre. Situated right in the heart of the village, it offers a menu full of mouth watering dishes at affordable prices.

All the food is cooked on the premises from fresh local ingredients wherever possible - no frozen produce here! Even the chips are home-cooked from hand-cut potatoes, and in fact the place is renowned for its crisp, light French fries! The place is popular with both tourists and locals, and people return again and again to sample the hearty meals. Scottish breakfasts are served every day from 9 am to 6 pm, and are very popular. There is a wide range of home-baking to choose from as well, and the place sells everything from a refreshing cup of coffee to steak pie, fish, chips and peas, lasagne, home-made quiche and salads.

The Tapestry Tearoom's baked potatoes are also well worth sampling, and come with a range of tasty fillings. The owners, Isabel and Jim, make sure that high standards are maintained both in the kitchen and in the restaurant area. Isabel has a special interest in making the tearoom special, as she used to work here until she and her husband bought it three years ago, The décor is smart and modern, yet with a homely touch, and everywhere is scrupulously clean.

McSweens owned it, though it later came into the possession of Walter Stewart, Earl of Menteith. It finally came into the possession of the Campbells, and was abandoned in the late 17th century, when a newer, more comfortable house was built close by. The ruins of **Kilbrannan Chapel**, near the foreshore, dates from the 13th century, and were dedicated to St Brendan. Five medieval grave slabs are to be found inside the chapel walls and in the kirkyard. The church replaced an earlier building dedicated to St Columba.

Crinan Canal

Lochgilphead

Lochgilphead, as the name suggests, stands at the head of Loch Gilp, a small inlet of Loch Fyne. It is the main shopping centre for a wide area known as Knapdale, that portion of Argyll from which the long "arm" of the Mull of Kintyre descends. It is an area steeped in history, and though it now seems to be on the edge of things, at one time it was at the crossroads of a great communications network. Ireland was to the southwest, the Isle of Man was to the south, the Hebrides were to the north, the bulk of Scotland itself was to the east, and all could be easily reached by boat.

Kilmory Woodland Park, off the A83, surrounds Kilmory Castle, which has been turned into offices for the local authority. The park contains many rare trees, plus a garden and woodland walks.

The **Crinan Canal** (known as "Scotland's most beautiful shortcut") starts at **Ardrishaig**, a couple of miles south of Lochgiplhead, and skirts the town as it heads across the peninsula towards the village of Crinan on the west coast. In 1795 an Act of Parliament sanctioned the building of a canal between Lochs Gilp and Crinan, and work started in 1794. However, it was beset with problems, and finally opened, albeit in an incomplete form, in 1801. By 1804 it still wasn't complete and had debts of £140,000.

Then, in 1805, some of the canal banks collapsed and had to be rebuilt. It was finally opened in 1809, though in 1815 Thomas Telford, the civil engineer, inspected it and declared that even more work needed doing. In 1817 it reopened, this time to everyone's satisfaction.

It is nine miles long, and has, in this short length, 15 locks. In 1847 it got the royal seal of approval when Queen Victoria sailed its full length as she was making a tour of the Highlands. Perhaps the most unusual craft to have used it were midget submarines during World War II.

Around Lochgilphead

Dunadd

4 miles N of Lochgilphead off the A816

Dunadd (Historic Scotland) is one of the most important historical sites in Scotland. This great rock rises from a flat area of land called Crinan Moss, and is where the ancient kings of **Dalriada** had their royal fort and capital. From here, they ruled a kingdom that took in all of modern day Argyll. It was founded by immigrants from Antrim in present day Northern Ireland in the 5th century, and gradually grew in importance. With them from Ireland they brought that great icon of Scottish nationhood, the Stone of Destiny (see also Scone and Edinburgh).

A climb to the top of Dunadd gives a wonderful view over the surrounding countryside, which is the reason the fort was established here in the first place. Parts of the ramparts can still be seen, and near the top, on a flat outcrop of rock, are some carvings of a boar, a footprint, a bowl and some ogham writing, which may have been connected to the inauguration of the Dalriadan kings.

The kings of Dalriada were special. In those days, kings were looked upon more as great tribal leaders and warriors than as men set apart to rule a kingdom. But one man changed all that - St Columba. His monastery on Iona was within Dalriada, and on that island he conducted the first Christian "coronation" in Britain, though no crowning ceremony took place. In AD 574 he anointed Aidan king of the Dalriadans in a ceremony that relied on Biblical precedents. It also contained an element that is still used in today's coronations, when the assembled crowds shouted out "God Save the King!" in unison. There is no doubt that Aidan sat on the Stone of Destiny during the ceremony.

Though it may now look austere and lonely, Dunadd, in its heyday, would have been a busy place, as excavations have shown that it traded with the kingdoms of present day England and the Continent. When the king was in residence, great flags would have fluttered from the wooden buildings, colourful banners and pennants would have hung from the ramparts and soldiers would have stood guard at its entrance. The River Add, no more than a couple of feet deep nowadays, winds its way round the base of the rock before entering the sea at Loch Crinan. In olden days, before Crinan Moss was drained for agriculture, it would have been navigable right up to the rock itself. Boats would have been tied up at its banks, and there would have been a small township to house the king's retainers. There would also have been storerooms, stables and workshops where jewellery and weapons were crafted, cloth woven and pots made.

The other great kingdom north of the Forth and Clyde was the kingdom of the Picts, and for years it and Dalriada traded, fought, mingled and intermarried. Eventually, in AD 843, because of this intermarriage, Kenneth MacAlpin, king of Dalriada, also inherited the throne of the Picts. By this time the centres of power had moved to the west, so Kenneth MacAlpin set off for Scone in present day Perthshire (taking the Stone of Destiny with him) and established his capital there. Thus was born the kingdom of Scotland, though it would be another 200 years before the kingdoms of the Lowlands - the Angles of the Lothians and the British of Strathclyde - were incorporated as well.

Dunadd survived for a few years after Kenneth left, but it was no longer an important place, and by the 12th century was largely abandoned.

Kilmichael Glassary

4 miles N of Lochgilphead on a minor road off the A816

In common with many other kirkyards in this part of Argyll, the kirkyard of the 19th century **Parish Church** has a fine collection of carved, medieval and later, grave slabs.

The **Cup and Ring Rock** (Historic Scotland) lies within a small fenced off area in the village, and has some ancient cup and ring markings carved into it. No one knows the significance of such carvings, though there are many throughout Scotland.

Kilmartin

8 miles N of Lochgilphead on the A816

The area surrounding Kilmartin is said to be Scotland's richest prehistoric landscape.

Within a six-mile radius of the village over 150 prehistoric and 200 later monuments are to be found. The whole place is awash with standing stones, stone circles, cairns, henges, burial mounds, forts, crannogs, cup and ring markings, castles, carved grave slabs and crosses.

A church has stood in the village for centuries, though the present **Parish Church** was only built in 1835. Within it is a decorated cross that dates from about the 9th century, and within the kirkyard are three further crosses, dating also from the 9th century. Also in the kirkyard is the finest collection of carved medieval grave slabs in Western Scotland. Most date from the 14th or 15th century, though there are some, which might be older. They might come as a surprise to people who imagine Scottish warriors to be wild Highlanders in kilts who brandish broadswords as they dash across the heather. These warriors are dressed in the kind of armour found all over Europe at the time. Only the well-off could have afforded it, and the other carvings on the slabs, such as swords, coats-of-arms and crosses, bear out their aristocratic lineage.

Some people have suggested that the carvings show Knights Templar, those warrior monks whose order was suppressed by Pope Clement V in 1307, egged on by Philip le Bel, king of France, who wanted his hands on the order's fabled treasure.

A great Templar fleet left La Rochelle in France supposedly carrying the treasure, and were never heard from again. Not long before, the Pope had excommunicated Robert the Bruce, and people believe the Templars were heading for Scotland. The

Pope's influence in the country was minimal, and the clergy still gave communion to Bruce. So it would certainly have made sense for the Templars to make for Scotland, bringing their treasure with them. Edward I was forever bemoaning the fact that the Scots seemed to have unlimited funds to defend themselves.

An even more intriguing theory has been put forward that the treasure was in the form of a great secret regarding Jesus, who either survived the crucifixion or married Mary Magdalene. Whatever the truth, many books have been written linking this part of Argyll - and other parts of Scotland - with the Knights Templar (see also Rosslyn).

Behind the church is the **Glebe Cairn**, a circular mound of stones dating from 1500-2000 BC. It forms part of what is known as the linear cemetery, a collection of such cairns, which stretches for a mile along the floor of Kilmartin Glen. The others are **Nether Largie North Cairn**, **Nether Largie Mid Cairn**, **Nether Largie South Cairn** and **Ri Cruin Cairn**. All are accessible by foot. In addition, there is the **Dunchraigaig Cairn**, just off the A816, which doesn't form part of the linear cemetery.

The **Temple Wood Circles**, south of Kilmartin, date from about 3500 BC. There are two of them, with the northern one possibly being used as a solar observatory when agriculture was introduced into the area. Burials were introduced at a later date. The **Nether Largie Standing Stones** are close to the Temple Wood Circle, and the **Ballymeanoch Standing Stones** are to the south of them. Of the seven stones, only six now survive in their original positions.

To the north of Kilmartin are the substantial ruins of **Carnassarie Castle** (Historic Scotland), dating from the 16th century. It was built for John Carswell, Bishop of the Isles, the man who translated Knox's Book of Common Order (his liturgy for the reformed church) into Gaelic. It was the first book ever to be printed in that language.

If you find all these stone circles, cairns, castles, carvings and burial mounds too much to comprehend, then you should visit the award winning **Kilmartin House Museum** next to the church in the village. Using maps, photographs, displays and artefacts it explains the whole chronology of the area from about 7000 BC right up until 1100 AD.

Kilmory

13 miles SW of Lochgilphead on a minor road off the B8025

North of Kilmory, on the shores of Loch Sween, stands the bulky ruins of **Castle Sween**, mainland Scotland's oldest stone castle. It was started by one Suibhne (pronounced "Sween"), ancestor of the MacSweens, over 900 years ago, and in later years became a centre of craftsmanship and artistry. This is shown by the **Kilmory Sculptured Stones**, at the 700-year-old Kilmory Knap chapel, a few miles south west of the castle. There was a thriving settlement here in medieval times, and within the ruins of the chapel is a remarkable collection of carved stones collected from the kirkyard, some going back at least 1000 years. The symbols on them include men in armour, blacksmiths' and woodworkers' tools, swords and crosses. They probably all marked the graves of craftsmen and warriors associated with Castle Sween over the years.

The most spectacular stone is **MacMillan's Cross**, which dates from the 15th century. On one side it shows the Crucifixion, and on the other a hunting scene. There is a Latin inscription that translates, "This is the cross of Alexander MacMillan". Across Loch Sween, at the end of the B8025, is **Keils Chapel**, which has another fine collection of grave slabs.

Kilberry

10 miles SW of Lochgilphead on the B8024

At Kilberry Castle are some late medieval sculptured stones (Historic Scotland), which were gathered from the Kilberry estate.

Kilmarie

On the B8002 10 miles NW of Lochgilphead

If you take the B8002 a few miles north of Kilmartin, you will find yourself on the Craignish Peninsula. Beyond the attractive village of **Ardfern**, a popular haven for yachtsmen is **Kilmarie Old Parish Church**. This roofless ruin, dedicated to St Maelrubha, dates from the 13th century, and contains a wonderful collection of carved grave slabs dating from the 14th and 15th centuries.

Inveraray

Standing on the western shores of Loch Fyne, Inveraray is a perfect example of a planned Scottish town. It was built in the mid 18th century by the 3rd Duke of Argyll, who pulled down his decaying castle and replaced it with a grander one, which would reflect his important position in society. He also wanted to improve the castle's policies, so he had the old township, which stood east of the castle, demolished to give him a view of the loch. He then built a new town to the immediate south. The result is an elegant royal burgh with wide streets and well-proportioned, whitewashed houses. It is actually no bigger than a village, but so well planned is it that it has all the feel of a busy metropolis, and indeed in the summer months tourists flock to it, making it an extremely busy place.

Inveraray Castle sits to the north, and is an elegant, foursquare stately home. With its four turrets - one at each corner of the building - it looks more like a grand French château than a Highland castle, but this was the intention. It was designed to tell the world that the Campbells, Dukes of Argyll, belonged to one of the most powerful families in the land - one which had always supported the Protestant cause and the Hanovarian dynasty against the Jacobites. It was designed by Roger Morris and Robert Mylne, and contains a famous armoury, French tapestries, Scottish and European furniture, and a genealogy room that traces the history of Clan Campbell.

There are two churches within the town - the **Parish Church,** which dates from 1794, and the Episcopalian **Church of All Saints**. The Parish Church was designed by Robert Mylne, and is divided so that services can be held in both English and Gaelic, though this is seldom done nowadays. All Saints Church, which dates from 1886, has a bell tower with the second heaviest ring of ten bells in the world. Each bell is named after a saint, and has the name inscribed on it. Ringers can sometimes be watched in action, and visiting ringers can practise by appointment.

Being the main town for a large area, Inveraray was the place where justice was meted out. **Inveraray Jail** (see panel on page 233) takes you on a trip through Scotland's penal system in the 1800s, and here you can see what the living conditions were like in cells that housed murderers and thieves. There are two prison blocks, one built in 1820 and one in 1848, the latter having more "enlightened" conditions. You can also see the branding irons, thumb screws and whips that passed for justice before the 18th century, and see what life is like in prison today. There is also a courtroom where a tableau, complete with sound, shows how a trial was conducted before a High Court judge.

Within the Arctic Penguin, a three-masted schooner built in 1911, is the **Inveraray Maritime Museum**. Here the maritime history of Scotland's western seaboard is vividly brought to life. There's an on board cinema with an archive of old film, and people can see what conditions were like aboard a ship taking them to a new life in America. Two miles south of the town is the 60-acre **Argyll Wildlife Park**. Here you can walk along woodland paths and try to see such animals as fallow deer, badgers, foxes, wild goats and wallabies.

One of the area's most famous sons was **Neil Munro** (1863-1930), the writer and journalist who wrote the ever-popular Para Handy books. On the A819 through Glen Aray towards Loch Awe is a monument that commemorates him. It stands close to his birthplace at Carnus.

Around Inveraray

Cairndow

6 miles NE of Inveraray across the loch on the A83

This small village stands at the western end of Glen Kinglas, on the shores of Loch Fyne. Within the Arkinglas Estate is the 25-acre **Arkinglas Woodland Garden**. High annual rainfall, a mild climate and light, sandy soil have created the right conditions for a collection of coniferous trees. The Callander family established the collection in about 1875, and it has seven champion trees that are either the tallest or widest in Britain. There is also one of the best collections of rhododendrons in the country.

At Clachan Farm near Arkinglas you'll find the **Clachan Farm Woodland Walks**, which allow you to see many species of native tree, such as oak, hazel and birch. The walks vary from a few hundred yards in length to two and a half miles.

Inveraray Castle

Strachur

4 miles S of Inveraray across the loch on the A815

Strachur sits on the shores of Long Fyne, on the opposite bank from Inveraray. **Strachur Smithy** has now been restored as a small museum and craft shop, and has some original tools and implements used by blacksmiths and farriers. **Glenbranter**, which was once owned by Sir Harry Lauder, has three short walks through mature woodlands. In the kirkyard at Strachur is buried **Sir Fitzroy MacLean**, diplomat and spy, who died in 1996, and said to be the inspiration for Ian Fleming's James Bond.

Lachlan Castle (not open to the public), ancestral home of the MacLachlans, lies six miles south of Strachur on the B8000. Nine miles south of the castle, still on the B8000, is **Otter Ferry**. As the name implies, this village was once the eastern terminal of a ferry that crossed Loch Fyne, but it is long gone. The word "otter" comes from the Gaelic "oitir", meaning a gravel bank, and has nothing to do with the animal.

A single lane track, the **Ballochandrain**, leaves Otter Ferry and rises to over 1000 feet, with some wonderful views towards the Inner Hebrides.

South of Otter ferry is the small, peaceful clachan of Kilfinan. The ruined **St Finan's Chapel,** dedicated to St Finian, a 6th century Irish saint, dates from about the 12th century and has some old burial stones. Five miles further on at Millhouse is a turn off to the right along an unmarked road for **Portavadie**, where the Portavadie-Tarbert ferry will take you onto the Mull of Kintyre (summer only). If you turn left at the same junction and head north again, you pass through **Tighnabruaich** on the Kyles of Bute, and eventually arrive at **Glendaruel**, the site of a battle in about 1110 between Vikings and native Gaels, in which the Vikings were defeated. The road hugs the shoreline most of the way, and gives some wonderful views of sea and hill.

Arrochar

13 miles E of Inveraray on the A83

Arrochar sits at the head of Loch Long. Two miles to the west is the small village of **Tarbet**, which sits on the shores of Loch Lomond. It sometimes surprises people who don't know the area that Britain's largest sheet of fresh water is so close to the sea. From the jetty at Tarbet small ships offer cruises on the loch.

Some of Argyll's finest mountains are to be found close by, such as **Ben Narnain** (3,036 feet) and **Ben Ime** (3,318 feet). This area could fairly claim to be the homeland of Scottish mountaineering, as the first mountaineering club in the country, the Cobbler Club, was established here in 1865. The road westwards towards Inveraray climbs up past the 2,891 feet Ben Arthur, better known as **The Cobbler,** and over the wonderfully named **Rest and Be Thankful** above Glen Croe until it drops down again through Glen Kinglas to the shores of Loch Fyne. It is a wonderful drive, with the floor of Glen Croe several hundred feet below the road at some points.

Near the Jubilee Well in Arrochar are the **Cruach Tairbeirt Walks**. These

Weaver's Restaurant & Gift Shop

Tarbet, Loch Lomond G83 7DN
Tel/Fax: 01301 702685
e-mail: weaversrestaurant@hotmail.com

Situated on the banks of beautiful Loch Lomond, 1¼ miles north of Tarbet on the A82, the **Weaver's Restaurant & Gift Shop** is housed in an old croft and weaver's cottage that dates from the 1700s. The tartan-themed restaurant serves teas, coffees and delicious, mouth-watering, home-cooked meals that are great value for money. Next door is a wonderful craft shop - just right for those souvenirs of your visit to Scotland. Weaving is a feature here, and you can buy kilts, scarves, blankets, sweaters and a host of other goods with that distinctly Scottish touch. Call in if you're passing!

footpaths (totalling just over a mile and a half in length) give some wonderful views over Loch Lomond and Loch Long. Though well surfaced, they are quite steep in some places.

Auchindrain

5 miles S of Inveraray on the A83

Auchindrain Township is an original West Highland village, which has been brought back to life as an outdoor museum and interpretation centre. Once common throughout the Highlands, many of these settlements were abandoned at the time of the Clearances, while others were abandoned as people headed for the cities to find work. Queen Victoria visited Auchindrain in 1875 when it was inhabited, and you can now see what she saw. Most of the cottages and other buildings have been restored and furnished to explain the living conditions of the Highlanders in past centuries. The visitor centre also has displays on West Highland life, showing many farming and household implements.

Crarae

10 miles S of Inveraray on the A83

Crarae Garden is one of the finest woodland gardens in Scotland. Rare trees and exotic shrubs thrive in the mild climate, and over 400 species of rhododendron and azaleas provide a colourful display in spring and summer, with a fine collection of deciduous trees adding colour and fire to autumn. There are sheltered woodland walks and a spectacular gorge. The Scottish Clan Garden features a selection of plants associated with various Argyll clans.

Crarae Garden

Islay

35 miles SW of Inveraray in the Atlantic Ocean

Clan Donald made Islay the centre of their vast Lordship of the Isles, which at one time was almost a separate kingdom, beyond the reach of Scottish monarchs. It is a truly beautiful island, with a range of hills to the east rising to 1500 feet, and low, fertile farmland. It is famous for its distilleries, with over four million gallons of whisky being produced each year. Most of them have tours explaining the distilling process, and offer a dram at the end of it. An Islay malt has a peaty taste all of its own, due to the grain being dried over peat fires.

Kilchiaran Bay, Islay

On islands in **Loch Finlaggan**, west of **Port Askaig** (where there is a ferry to Feolin Ferry on Jura and West Loch Tarbert on the Mull of Kintyre) you will find the ruins of the medieval centre of the Lordship of the Isles, with a visitor centre close by. Ancient burial slabs are thought to mark the graves of important women and children, as the chiefs themselves would have been buried on Iona. Close to Port Askaig itself are the **Bunnahabhain** and the **Caol Ila** distilleries.

To the east of **Port Ellen** (which also has a ferry to Tarbert) are the distilleries of **Lagavulin, Laphroaig** and **Ardbeg**. The ruins of **Dunyveg Castle**, a MacDonald stronghold, sit near Lagavulin. At one time it was owned by a man called Coll Ciotach, or "left handed Coll". While he was away on business, the castle was captured by his enemies the Campbells, and his men taken prisoner. They then waited for Coll to return so that they could overpower him. But one of the prisoners was Coll's personal piper, and when he saw his master approach the castle, he alerted him by playing a warning tune. Coll escaped, but the piper had his right hand cut off, and never again could play the pipes. It's a wonderful story, though whether it is true or not is another matter, as the legend is also associated with other castles in Argyll, notably Duntroon.

At Ardbeg is the **Kildalton Cross and Chapel**. The incised cross dates from the 9th century, and is one of the finest in Scotland. Keeping on a religious theme, **Bowmore**, on the A874 beside the shores of Loch Indaal, has one of only two round churches in Scotland. It was built in 1767 by Daniel Campbell, who reckoned that, having no corners, the devil could not hide anywhere within it. **Bowmore Distillery** - the oldest (founded in 1779) and one of the most famous on the island - can be visited. North of Bowmore, near Bridgend, is an Iron Age fort with the wonderful name of **Dun Nosebridge** (Landrover trips can be arranged to visit and view it), and to the southwest of the village, at the tip of the Mull of Oa (pronounced "oh"), is the **American Monument**, which commemorates the 266 American sailors lost when *Tuscania* sank after being torpedoed in 1918 and the Otranto was wrecked. Many of the bodies were washed up at the foot of the cliff here.

On the opposite side of the loch is a peninsula called the Rhinns of Islay, and it is here that you will find the **Bruichladdich Distillery**, which, in 2003, found itself under surveillance by American intelligence agents as the whisky distilling process is similar to the one used in making certain kinds of chemical weapons. At **Port Charlotte** is the **Islay Natural History Trust**. It has a wildlife information centre, and provides information on the natural history and wildlife of Islay. Also in the village is the **Museum of Islay Life**, which tells of everyday life on the island through the ages. Continue past Port Charlotte on the A874 and you will come to **Portnahaven**. About four miles from the village, and situated on the west side of the Portnahaven to Kilchiaran road, is the **Cultoon Stone Circle**. Not all the stones have survived, but three are still standing and twelve have fallen over at the point where they once stood. The ruins of **Kilchiaran Chapel**, on the west coast of the Rhinns can be reached by car via a narrow track. Though its fabric is basically medieval, its origins go right back to the time of St Columba, who founded it in honour of his friend St Ciaran. Further north is the **Kilchoman Church and Cross**, accessed by another narrow track, which leaves the B8018 and goes past Loch Gorm. The cross dates from the 15th century, and was erected by "Thomas, son of Patrick". The church replaces a medieval building, which once stood here, but has been boarded up, and is in a bad state of repair.

Jura

24 miles W of Inveraray in the Atlantic Ocean

Jura is an island of peat bogs, mists and mountains, notably the **Paps of Jura**, to the south. The highest mountain in the range, at over 2,500 feet, is **Ben an Oir**, though **Ben Shaintaidh** and **Ben a' Chaolais** aren't far behind.

The island's only road, the A846, takes you from **Feolin Ferry,** where there is a ferry to Islay, north along the east coast, where most of the island's population lives. You will pass **Jura House Garden**, with its collection of Australian and New Zealand plants. They thrive in this mild and virtually frost and snow free environment. **Craighouse**, with its distillery, is the island's capital. Behind the parish church of 1776 is a room with some old photographs and artefacts of life on Jura through the ages. A few miles south of the village are the ruins of **Clag Castle**, reputed to be an old MacDonald prison.

A mile or so north of Craighouse is the ruined **Chapel of St Earnadail**. St Earnadail was a disciple of St Columba, and the story goes that he wanted to be buried on Jura when he died. When asked where on the island, he replied that a cloud of mist would guide the mourners to the right spot. On his death, a cloud of mist duly appeared and settled where the ruins now stand.

The road then takes you north to **Ardlussa**, where it peters out. Within the old burial ground is the tombstone of **Mary MacCrain**, who died in 1856, aged 128. They seem to have been long-lived on Jura, for the stone goes on to say that she was a descendant of Gillouir MacCrain, "*who kept one hundred and eighty Christmases in his own house, and died during the reign of Charles 1*".

Just under a mile off Jura's north cost is the small island of **Scarba**. It has been uninhabited since the 1960s, though in the

Looking towards the Paps of Jura

late 18th century it managed to support 50 people. It rises to a height of 1473 feet, and has many Iron Age sites on its west coast. On the east coast are the ruins of **Cille Mhoire an Caibel**, surrounded by an old graveyard. Many miracles were supposed to have taken place within the kirk in early medieval times.

Between Jura and Scarba, in the Gulf of Corryvreckan, is the notorious **Corryvreckan** whirlpool. The name comes from the Gaelic Coire Bhreacain, meaning "speckled cauldron", and it is best viewed from the safety of the cliff tops on Jura (even though you have to walk about five miles from just beyond Ardlussa to get there) as it has sent many boats to the bottom. It is caused by the combination of an immense pillar of rock rising from the seabed and a tidal race, and the best time to see it is when a spring tide is running westward against a west wind. The sound of it can sometimes be heard at Ardfern on the mainland, over seven miles away.

Legend tells us that the whirlpool's name has a different derivation. A Norwegian prince called Breachkan was visiting the Scottish islands, and fell in love with a beautiful princess, a daughter of the Lord of the Isles. Her father disapproved of the young man, but declared that he could marry his daughter providing he could moor his galley in the whirlpool for three days.

Breachkan agreed to the challenge, and had three cables made - one of hemp, one of wool and one from the hair of virgins. He then sailed into the Gulf of Corryvreckan, and while there was a slack tide, moored his boat in the whirlpool. The tides changed, and the whirlpool became a raging monster. The hemp cable snapped on the first day and the wool one snapped on the second. But Breachkan wasn't worried, for he knew that the one made from virgins' hair would keep him safe.

But on the third day it too snapped, sending the prince to his death. It seems that some of the virgins from whom the hair had come were not as innocent as they had made out.

Oban

Seeing Oban nowadays, it is hard to imagine that in the18th century this bustling holiday resort was no more than a village, with a handful of cottages built round a small bay. It got its burgh charter in 1820, but even then it was an unimportant place. With the coming of the railway in 1880, the town blossomed as people discovered its charms. Great Victorian and Edwardian villas were built by prosperous Glasgow merchants, and local people began to open hotels, guest houses and B&Bs.

Now it is the capital of the Western Highlands, and known as the "Gateway to the Western Isles". It has two cathedrals, the Roman Catholic **Cathedral of St**

Woodside Hotel

Teedale Street, Oban, Argyll PA34 5DD
Tel: 01631 562184

The **Woodside Hotel** is set within the middle of the picturesque town of Oban, "gateway to the islands". The building, which dates from the mid 1800s,is of local stone and presents a blaze of colour when the hanging baskets are up. All the nine guest rooms are en suite, with TVs and hospitality trays in each one. Value for money are the watchwords here, though the owner, Marie Lynch, who came here from Dublin, is determined to maintain the high standards of friendly service for which the place is renowned. The traditional bar is a favourite with the locals (always a good sign), and there is also a large, modern lounge with a huge glass water feature behind the bar and where musical evenings are a regular feature.

Braeside Guest House

Kilmore, By Oban, Argyll PA34 4QR
Tel: 01631 770243 Fax: 01631 770343
e-mail: Braeside.Guesthouse@virgin.net
website:
http://braesideguesthouse.ieasysite.com

Three miles south of Oban on the A816 is the small village of Kilmore, and it is here, among the hills of Argyll, that you will find a delightful guesthouse called the **Braeside Guest House**. It is owned and managed by Cherry and Jon Freeman, who have created an establishment that combines value for money, high standards of service and that real "home from home" feeling that everyone appreciates. It has three coveted stars from VisitScotland and is four star rated by the AA, which means that you will get the best of accommodation, the best of service and a welcome that is warm and friendly.This superior establishment is non smoking, and boasts five spacious guest rooms - one twin with en suite, one triple with en suite (three single beds), three doubles, all en suite and one having a king-sized bed. All are equipped with colour TV, radio/alarm, direct dial telephone and hospitality tray. Hair dryers are also available. The decoration and furniture is of a very high standard, making them both comfortable and welcoming. All are on ground level.

Braeside is open all year, and has a restricted hotel license. The guest house serves excellent three-course dinners that are home-cooked and reflect the great culinary traditions of Scotland. Only the finest and freshest of local produce is used wherever possible, and there is a good selection of wines to accompany your meal, as well as an extensive range of single malt whiskies.

There is a spacious and bright guests' lounge/dining room on the ground floor, and you can access the house at all times of the day and night. Well behaved children over ten years old are more than welcome, and there is plenty of car parking space.

The guest house is the perfect base from which to explore the historic county of Argyll. It sits in beautiful countryside, with views of Loch Feochan, the hills of Mullach ban and Craeg Mhor. Oban, the "gateway to the Isles", is only three miles to the north, and from there you can catch a ferry to Mull, Lismore, Colonsay, Coll, Tiree, Barra and South Uist. Iona, forever associated with St Columba, is also in easy reach.

The opportunities to see and study wildlife are endless, and there is also a great range of outdoor pursuits that you can take part in. Golf - hill walking - fishing - mountain biking - shooting - all are available within a short distance of the guest house. And the historic sites are endless, from the cairns and standing stones of Kilmartin to the south to industrial archaeology sites at Inverawe and Bonawe. Dunadd - once the capital of the ancient kingdom of Dalriada can also be climbed and explored.

Columba, built in 1930 of granite and the town's largest church, and the Episcopalian Cathedral Church of St John the Divine in George Street, built in the 19th century but never fully completed.

Dominating the town is **McCaig's Folly**, a vast coliseum of a building that was begun in 1897. To call it a folly is a misnomer, because the man who built it, Oban banker John Stuart McCaig, wanted to establish a museum and art gallery inside it, but he died before it was completed. As the town had a lot of unemployed people at the time, he also wanted to create work for them. In his will he left money for a series of large statues of himself and his family to be erected around the parapet, but these were never carried out.

The oldest building in Oban is **Dunollie Castle**, the ruins of which can be seen on the northern outskirts of the town beyond the Corran Esplanade. It was built on a site that has been fortified since the Dark Ages, and was a MacDougall stronghold. It was finally abandoned as a dwelling house in the early 1700s, when a new McDougall mansion was built. It soon became a quarry for the people of the area. **Armaddy Castle Garden,** eight miles south of Oban off the B844 road for Seil Island, is another of the local gardens that benefit from the area's mild climate.

The pier is where most of the ferries leave for the Western Isles. From here you can sail for Lismore, Mull, Coll, Tiree, Colonsay, Barra and South Uist, and one of the joys of Oban is sitting on the pier watching the graceful ferries entering and leaving Oban Bay. Sheltering the bay is the small rocky island of **Kerrera**, which can be reached by passenger ferry from a point

Glenbervie Guest House

Dalriach Road, Oban, Argyll PA34 5JD
Tel: 01631 564770 Fax: 01631 566723
e-mail: glenbervie@lineone.com

The four star **Glenbervie** is recognised as one of Oban's premier guest houses, and enjoys a glorious setting with views over Oban Bay to Kerrera and Mull. It is only five minutes walk from all the amenities of Oban town centre, and boasts eight guest rooms - six doubles and two singles, all either en suite or with private facilities. TVs and hospitality trays are provided in this friendly, welcoming establishment. A stay at Glenbervie will be long remembered for all the right reasons!

Thornloe Guest House

Albert Road, Oban, Argyll PA34 5JD
Tel/Fax: 01631 562879
e-mail: thornloeoban@aol.com
website: www.thornloeoban.co.uk

Thornloe Guest House has recently been transformed into one of the finest four star B&Bs in Oban, thanks to the hard work of its proprietors, Alan and Val Bichener. Of its eight comfortable guest rooms, seven are fully en suite, with the other one having private facilities. Sitting above the town, it has views out towards Mull which are spectacular. The traditional Scottish breakfasts are hearty and filling, with lighter options also available. The décor in all the rooms is immaculate and stylish, making a stay here a memorable experience!

about two miles south of Oban. At the south end of the island are the ruins of 16th century **Gylen Castle**, another former MacDougall stronghold. It was built by Duncan MacDougall, brother (or son) of the clan chief, Dougal McDougall. It was sacked by a Covenanting army under General Leslie in 1647, and slaughtered all the inhabitants.

The **Oban Distillery** in Stafford Street produces a whisky that is one of the six "classic malts" of Scotland, and has tours showing the distillery at work. The whisky is a lightly peated malt, and the tour includes a free dram.

The **Oban Rare Breeds Farm Park** at Glencruitten has, in addition to rare breeds, a pets corner, a woodland walk, tearoom and shop. And at Upper Soroba is the **Oban Zoological World**, a small family-run zoo specialising in small mammals and reptiles.

The Bay, Oban

Around Oban

Connel Bridge

4 miles NE of Oban off the A828

Connel Bridge was at one time a railway bridge. Now it carries the A828 to Ballachulish and beyond over the entrance to Loch Etive, which stretches inland for

over 16 miles. The entrance to this sea loch is very shallow, and when the tide ebbs, the water pours out of the loch into the Firth of Lorne over the **Falls of Lora**.

Dunstaffnage

3 miles N of Oban off the A85

On a promontory sticking out into Ardmuchnish Bay, in the Firth of Lorne, is the substantial **Dunstaffnage Castle** (Historic Scotland). Seen from the east, it has a glorious setting, with the island of Lismore and the hills of Morvern behind it. It was originally built in the 13th century by Ewan MacDougall on the site of a Dalriadan royal fort and settlement, though the castle as seen today dates from all periods up to the 19th century. In 1309 the castle fell into the hands of Robert the Bruce, and he gave it to the Stewarts. In 1470 Colin Campbell, the first Earl of Argyll, was created hereditary captain, or keeper of Dunstaffnage.

In 1363 a dark deed was carried out here. The then Stewart owner was set upon outside the castle and murdered by a troop of MacDougalls, who still considered the castle theirs. The troop then attacked the castle, and it fell into their hands once more. A few months later a force of men sent by David II, Robert the Bruce's son, retook it.

The castle's resident ghost is called the **Ell Maid**, and sometimes on stormy nights she can be heard wandering through the ruins, her footsteps clanging off the stone as if shod in iron. If she is heard laughing, it means that there will be good news for the castle. If she shrieks and sobs, it means the opposite.

Dunstaffnage Chapel sits outside the castle, and also dates from the 13th century. It is unusual in that chapels were usually within the defensive walls of a castle. A small burial aisle for the Campbells of Dunstaffnage forms an eastern extension.

Benderloch

8 miles N of Oban on the A828

The **Oban Seal and Marine Centre** is Scotland's leading marine animal rescue centre, and it looks after dozens of seal pups that have been injured or orphaned before returning them back into the wild.

Barcaldine Castle has associations with the Appin murder and the Massacre of Glencoe. There are secret passages and a bottle dungeon, and the castle is said to be haunted by a Blue Lady.

Kinlochlaich Gardens

11 miles N of Oban on the A828

This old walled garden was created in 1790 by John Campbell. It sits on the shores of Loch Linnhe, in an area known as Appin,

The Pierhouse Hotel

Port Appin, Appin, Argyll PA38 4DE
Tel: 10631 730302 Fax: 01631 730400
e-mail: pierhouse@btinternet.com
website: www.pierhousehotel.co.uk

Hidden at the end of a twisty, single track off the A828 is the small village of Port Appin, the mainland terminal for a small passenger ferry to the lovely island of Lismore. As far as the eye can see is the boundless beauty of Argyll - high hills, endless skies and blue water. The air is pure and the light is sharp and clear, making this a favourite haunt for artists and writers.

Near the pier you will find the picturesque **Pierhouse Hotel**, a place where excellence comes as standard and value for money are always the watchwords. It is owned and personally managed by Liz and David Hamblin, who are determined to maintain and improve on these standards so that you, the guest, have a stay you will never forget. The hotel started life as the residence of the pier master, and then became a private residence, holiday home and tearoom. It was then granted a licence, and in 1992 a purpose-built hotel block was added. Now it is one of the best hostelries in the area, offering superb accommodation and wonderful food.

The accommodation has been carefully thought out and consists of twelve rooms, all individually furnished and decorated to an exceptional standard, and all having individually controlled central heating and heated towel rails. There are ten double/twin rooms with en suite shower, and two four-poster rooms with bathroom en suite. All have remote control colour TVs, direct dial telephones, tea/coffee making facilities, local sparkling mineral waters and hair dryer, as well as complimentary toiletries.

The no-smoking restaurant can seat up to 60 in absolute comfort, and has panoramic views out over Loch Linnhe towards Lismore and the Morvern Hills. The food, as you would expect, concentrates on locally caught seafood and game. In fact, why not sit on the hotel's terrace on a warm summer afternoon watching the fisherman land the wonderful prawns, scallops, salmon, oysters and mussels that will be gracing the hotel's menu that very evening? The chef is Rita Thomson, who is renowned for the excellence of the dishes she prepares, and who personally oversees the buying of the produce for her kitchen. To complement the food, there is a select range of wines to choose from. Plus there is also a fine range of spirits, liqueurs, beers and soft drinks.

The Pierhouse Hotel is the ideal base from which to explore one of the most historic and beautiful areas of Scotland. A leisurely stroll from the hotel will take you to the Clach Thoull, meaning "hole in the rock", a naturally formed stone arch and the impressive Castle Stalker. There is wildlife to see - otters, eagles, deer and seals, and many activities, such as sailing, walking, cycling and golf.

and it has one of Scotland's largest plant and nursery centres.

Duimneil House Garden

10 miles N of Oban on a minor road off the A828

The garden has a fine display of rhododendrons, shrubs and trees, plus a garden centre. Teas and coffees are available.

Ardchattan

8 miles NE of Oban on a minor road on the north shore of Loch Etive

Ardchattan Priory (Historic Scotland) was built in about 1230 by Duncan McDougall for the Valliscaulian order of monks. The ruins of the church can still be seen, though the rest of the priory was incorporated into Ardchattan House in the 17th century by John Campbell, who took over the priory at the Reformation. There are some old grave slabs which mark McDougall graves. **Ardchattan Priory Garden** is open to the public, and has herbaceous borders, roses, a rockery and a wild flower meadow.

Loch Etive, Taynuilt

Taynuilt

9 miles E of Oban on the A85

Taynuilt lies close to the shores of Loch Etive. Nearby, at Inverawe, is the **Bonawe Furnace**, which dates from 1753.

The Robins Nest Tea Room

Main Street, Taynuilt, Argyll PA35 1JE
Tel: 01866 822429 Fax: 01866 822255
e-mail: murray_sim@btinternet.com
website: www.robinsnesttearoom.co.uk

Located in the heart of this lovely village, **The Robins Nest Tea Room** offers the very best in home baking. The bright and airy room is stylishly decorated and has pine floor and furniture, fresh flowers and an open fire in cooler weather.

The home-made bread, freshly baked cakes and scones are all expertly prepared daily by Maireadh Sim and her friendly staff, as are the excellent pancakes, soups and snack lunches.

The tea room is open daily from spring to the end of October between 10am and 5pm, and during the winter from 10am to 4.30pm. Thursday to Sunday.

The Robins Nest makes an ideal place to stop when combined with a cruise on Loch Etive, generally regarded as one of Scotlands loveliest lochs. The on board commentary will guide you through the glorious mountain country, rich in history and legend.

Ironworking was carried out here for over 100 years, and the furnace made many of the cannonballs used by Nelson's navy. In 1805 the workers erected a statue to Nelson, the first in Britain, and it can still be seen today near Muchairn Church.

At Barguillean Farm you will find **Barguillean's Angus Garden**, established in 1957. It extends to nine acres, and is on the shores of Loch Angus. It was created in memory of Angus Macdonald, a journalist who was killed in Cyprus in 1956.

Loch Awe

16 miles E of Oban on the A85

If you take the road east from Dunstaffnage Castle, passing near the shores of Loch Etive and going through the Pass of Brander, you will come to Scotland's longest loch, Loch Awe. This is its northern shore, and it snakes southwest for a distance of nearly twenty-five and a half miles until it almost reaches Kilmartin. Near the village of Lochawe are the impressive ruins of **Kilchurn Castle** (Historic Scotland), right on the shores of the loch. It was home to a cadet branch of the Campbells, which was eventually elevated to the peerage as the Earls of Breadalbane. It was originally built in the 15th century, though what you see now dates from later periods as well.

St Conan's Kirk, also on the banks of the loch, is reckoned to be one of the most beautiful churches in Scotland, though it dates only from the 1880s, with later additions. It was built by Walter Douglas Campbell, brother to an Earl of Breadalbane, who had built a mansion house nearby. Not only did he commission it, he designed it and also did some of the woodwork. But this church proved too small for him, so in 1907 he began extending it. He died in 1914 before he could complete it, and it was finally finished in its present state in 1930. It has a superb chancel, an ambulatory, a nave with a south aisle, various chapels, and, curiously for a small church, cloisters.

The waters of Loch Cruachan, high on Ben Cruachan above Loch Awe have been harnessed for one of the most ambitious hydroelectric schemes in Scotland. Not only does the **Cruachan Power Station** (see panel opposite) produce electricity from the waters of Loch Cruachan tumbling through pipes towards its turbines and then into Loch Awe; it can actually pump 120 tons of water a second from Loch Awe back up the pipes towards Loch Cruachan by putting its turbines into reverse. This it does during the night, using the excess electricity produced by conventional power stations. In this way, power is stored so that it can be released when demand is high, and it was the first station in the world to use the technology. Now it is used all over the world.

The turbine halls are in huge artificial caves beneath the mountain, and tours are available taking you round one of the wonders of civil engineering in Scotland - one that can produce enough electricity to supply a city the size of Edinburgh.

Kilchurn Castle, Loch Awe

Cruachan Visitor Centre

Dalmally, Argyll PA33 1AN
Tel: 01866 822618 Fax: 01866 822509
e-mail: visit.cruachan@scottishpower.com
website: www.scottishpower.com

Hidden deep within the mountain of Ben Cruachan on the shores of Loch Awe is Cruachan Power Station. Here, a short distance from Oban, you can discover one of the hidden wonders of the Highlands. A power station buried one kilometre below ground. At its centre lies a massive cavern, high enough to house the Tower of London! Here enormous turbines convert the power of water into electricity, available to you in your home at the flick of a switch. Take an unforgettable journey into Ben Cruachan and find out how power is generated. Experienced guides will lead you along a tunnel cut from solid rock. A coach will transport you into a different world, a place so warm that sub-tropical plants grow.

Find the nerve centre of the station and understand how the power of water from Loch Awe is harnessed to provide a rapid response to sharp rises in demand for electricity such as at mealtimes. A generator can go from standstill to an output of 100,000 kilowatts in two minutes to provide as much electricity as necessary.

Back on the surface, the visitor centre has many things to see and do. The Exhibition includes touch screens and demonstrates the way in which power will continue to be generated in the future. To finish off, there is a lochside cafeteria and gift shop. Open Easter to mid November 9.30am-5pm; August 9,30am-6pm.

Kilmelford

11 miles S of Oban on the A816

To the west of this little village, near the shores of Loch Melfort, there was once a gunpowder mill, one of the many small industries that once dotted Argyll. In the kirkyard of the small **Parish Church** of 1785 are some gravestones marking the burial places of people killed while making the "black porridge".

Arduaine

15 miles S of Oban on the A816

The 50-acre **Arduaine Gardens** (National Trust for Scotland) are situated on a south-facing slope overlooking Asknish Bay. They are another testimony to the mildness of the climate on Argyll's coast, and have a wonderful collection of rhododendrons. There are also great trees, herbaceous borders and a diversity of plants from all over the world.

Ardanaiseig Garden

14 miles E of Oban on a minor road off the B845 on the banks of Loch Awe

Ardanaiseig is a large garden, which specialises in fruit and vegetables. There is also a large herbaceous border. The garden is closed from January to mid February each year.

Dalavich

13 miles SE of Oban on a minor road off the B845 on the banks of Loch Awe

If you follow the B845 south from Taynuilt, then turn onto a minor road near Kilchrenan, you will eventually reach the **Dalavich Oakwood Trail**. It is a two-mile long walk laid out by the Forestry Commission, with not only oaks, but also alder, hazel, downy birch and juniper. There are also small sites where 18th and 19th century charcoal burners produced charcoal for the Bonawe Iron Furnace near Taynuilt.

INNER HEBRIDES

Seil and Luing

9 miles S of Oban on the B844

These two islands are known as the "slate isles" due to the amount of slate that was quarried here at one time. Seil is a genuine island, but is connected to the mainland by the **Bridge Across the Atlantic**, designed by Thomas Telford and built in 1792. It is more properly called the Clachan Bridge, with the channel below being no more than a few yards wide.

It got its nickname because at one time it was the only bridge in Scotland to connect an island with the mainland. Now the more recent Skye Bridge dwarfs it. On the west side of the bridge, on the island itself, is a late 17th century inn called the Tigh na Truish, or "House of Trousers". This recalls the aftermath of the Jacobite Uprising, when the wearing of the kilt was forbidden. The islanders, before crossing onto the mainland by the ferry, which preceded the bridge, would change out of their kilts here and into trousers.

On the west coast of the island is the village of **Ellenabeich**, with, facing it, the small island of Easdale. Ellenabeich was itself an island at one time, but the narrow channel separating it from the mainland was gradually filled up with waste from the local slate quarries. One of the biggest quarries was right on the shoreline, with its floor 80 feet below the water line. It was separated from the sea by a wall of rock, and during a great storm, the wall was breached, and the quarry filled with water. Now it is used as a harbour for small craft.

An Cala Garden dates from the 1930s, and is behind a row of cottages that was turned into one home. There are meandering streams, terracing built from the local slate, and wide lawns. A 15 feet high wall of grey brick protects the garden from the worst of the gales that occasionally blow in from the Atlantic.

One of the cottages in the village has been turned into a **Heritage Centre** with a number of displays connected with the slate industry. Offshore lies the small island of **Easdale,** connected to Ellenabeich by a small passenger ferry. This too was a centre of slate quarrying, and one of the small cottages has been turned into the **Easdale Island Folk Museum**.

On Seil's southern tip is the small ferry port of **Cuan**, where a ferry plies backwards and forwards to Luing, to the south. This is a larger island than Seil, though is more sparsely populated. Here too slate quarrying was the main industry.

Lismore

7 miles N of Oban, in Loch Linnhe

Lismore is a small island, no more than a mile and a half wide at its widest and nine miles long. It's name means "great garden", and it is a low-lying, fertile island connected to Oban by a daily ferry. The main village and ferry terminal is **Achnacroish,** though a smaller pedestrian ferry plies between Port Appin on the mainland and the north of the island in summer. In the village is the **Commann Eachdraidh Lios Mor**, an old cottage that re-creates the living conditions in the Lismore of yesteryear.

Lismore, before the Reformation, was the centre of the diocese of Argyll. **Lismore Cathedral** stood at **Kilmoluaig,** near the small village of Clachan. It was destroyed just after the Reformation, but the choir walls were later lowered and incorporated into the present church in 1749. The site had been a Christian one for centuries, and was where St Moluag set up a small monastery in AD 564.

Lismore was a prized island even in those days, and it seems that St Moluag and another Celtic saint, St Mulhac, had a quarrel about who should found a monastery there. They finally agreed to a race across from the mainland in separate boats, with the first one touching the soil of

Eilean Musile Lighthouse, Lismore

Lismore being allowed to establish a monastery. As the boats were approaching the shore, Moluag realised that he was going to lose, so took a dagger, cut off one of his fingers and threw it onto the beach. As he was the first to touch the soil of the island, he was allowed to build his monastery. This was supposed to have taken place at Tirefour, where there are the remains of a broch now called **Tirefour Castle**, whose walls still stand to a height of 16 feet.

On the west coast of the island, facing the tiny Bernera Island, are the ruins of **Achadun Castle**, where the Bishops of Argyll lived up until the 16th century, and further up the coast are the ruins of **Coeffin Castle**, built by the MacDougalls in the 13th century.

The highest point on the island, at a mere 412 feet, is **Barr Morr** (meaning "big tip"), but from the top there is a wonderful panoramic view in all directions.

Mull

8 miles W of Oban, in the Atlantic Ocean

The island of Mull, with over 300 miles of coastline and 120 miles of roads, is the second largest island in the Inner Hebrides. It is also one of the most beautiful, and has the added advantage of being easy to reach, as a car ferry plies all day between the pier at **Craignure** and Oban.

Its name comes from the Gaelic Meall, meaning a rounded hill. It is steeped in history, and was known to the Romans and Greeks. Even Ptolemy wrote about it, calling it *Maleus*. The highest peak, at 3,140 feet, is **Ben More**, the only Munro (a Scottish mountain above 3,000 feet) in any of the Scottish islands.

Torosay Castle & Gardens

Craignure, Isle of Mull PA65 6AY
Tel: 01680 812421
e-mail: torosay@aol.com

Torosay Castle and Gardens is a beautiful Victorian house surrounded by 12 acres of spectacular gardens. You are free to wander around the principal rooms of the house and browse through family scrapbooks and memorabilia. Outside is an important collection of Italian statues, formal terraces and a variety of plant collections and garden settings, including a Japanese Garden with an impressive sea view. As this is a working farm, children will be fascinated with the herd of Highland Cattle and you can round off with a visit to Mull Weavers to see a demonstration on traditional dobby looms. Tearoom, shop and free parking available. Open April to mid October 10.30am-5pm. Gardens open all year.

Highland Cottage Hotel

Breadalbane Street, Tobermory, Isle of Mull,
Argyll PA75 6PD
Tel: 01688 302030 Fax: 01688 302727
e-mail: davidend@highlandcottage.co.uk
website: www.highlandcottage.co.uk

The Highland Cottage Hotel in Tobermory calls itself "a small hotel of quality" and this is no ideal boast. It sits in the heart of this attractive small town, in the heart of its conservation area, and has a fine reputation for the quality of its accommodation, its food, its drink and its warm welcome. Owned and managed by the husband and wife team of Josephine and David Currie, it prides itself on being a place that combines quiet elegance, high standards and that home-from-home feel that makes all the difference to your stay.

Be prepared to be pampered here as you unwind away from the pressures of modern life. Be prepared to dine on some of the best food on the island in the unstuffy, spacious

dining room. Be prepared to sample a fine range of single malts or a freshly brewed coffee as you relax in one of the sumptuous lounges.

And be prepared for bedrooms that are individually decorated and furnished. Each one has an island theme, special touches that remind you of home, and all have en suite facilities. Most also boast antiques, four poster beds and top quality bed bases and mattresses. You're sure of a great night's sleep here after a hard day's sightseeing on an island that offers so much to the discerning tourist.

And in the evening, why not relax in the spacious dining room and sample food that is simply out of this world? Josephine is an award-winning cook, and she likes nothing better than preparing dishes that combine imagination, flair and the experience to bring flavours together that are memorable. But for all that, they still retain that "down to earth" characteristic that marks out truly great cooking. She uses only the finest and freshest of local produce wherever possible, and of course, because Tobermory is on the coast, seafood is a speciality. Josephine holds two AA rosettes, as well as the prestigious RAC and VisitScotland award. For two years running she has held the Mull and Iona Food festival "Chef of the Year". To complement your meal, why not chose a bottle of wine from the hotel's small but select cellar? Someone will always be on hand to help you choose. Plus there is a fine range of single malt whiskies, including Mull's own Tobermory malt.

There is so much to do and see on Mull, and the hotel is the ideal base from which to explore it. The views are absolutely stunning, and the wildlife - from deer, otters and foxes to birds such as falcons, herons and eagles. And don't forget a trip to Iona of Staffa!

The island is home to 816 (yes - someone counted them!) species of plants and trees, including 56 varieties of ferns, 247 varieties of seaweed, 22 species of orchid and 1,787 species of fungi. This diversity has made it popular with botanists, who visit the island throughout the year.

And its wildlife is just as diverse. You can see birds of prey such as golden eagles, polecats, mountain hares, badgers, pine martens, adders, slow worms, otters and red squirrels. And the lonely coastal cliffs are home to wild goats. Take a sea trip and you can see bottlenose dolphins, porpoises, seals and even Minke whales.

Close to Craignure is **Torosay Castle** (see panel on page 249), with its fine gardens. The **Mull and West Higland Railway**, a one and a quarter mile long narrow gauge line, connects the castle with the pier. Also in the vicinity is **Duart Castle**, perched on the cliffs above Duart Point. It is the ancestral home of the MacLeans, and still houses the clan chief. It was confiscated after Culloden, as the MacLeans had fought alongside Charles Edward Stuart, but in 1911 the 26th MacLean chief, Sir Fitzroy MacLean, bought it back and restored it.

Some MacLean chieftains were unsavoury characters. The 11th chief so detested his wife, a sister of the Earl of Argyll, that he had her tied up and marooned on a rocky island below the castle that flooded at each high tide. She was eventually drowned and washed away, and the "distraught" husband reported her sad death to the Earl.

The Earl immediately invited him to his castle in Inveraray, and when the chief got there, he discovered his wife alive and well. A fisherman had rescued her, though nothing was said during the chief's visit. They eventually went home together, and still nothing was said. By this time the chief was terrified, as he knew that retribution would eventually come. But before it did the wife died naturally, and the chief heaved a sigh of

MullRail

Old Pier Station, Craignure, PA65 6AY
Tel: 01680 812494/812567
Fax: 01680 300595
e-mail: mullrail@dee-emm.co.uk
website: www.mullrail.co.uk

In 1975, the owners of Torosay Castle on Mull decided to open the castle to visitors. They solved the problem of getting the people from the ferry pier to the castle grounds by building a narrow gauge railway - the **MullRail** Railway. It was officially opened in 1984, and 20 years later, it is still as popular as ever with tourists disembarking from the ferry at Craignure, only a 40 minute sail from Oban. In fact, it could be said that no visit to Mull is complete without a trip on the railway! The route it takes is partly along an old driveway, once an overgrown and neglected jungle, but after much hard work by many people - mostly volunteers - the ground was prepared for the track to be laid, which included crossing a deep bog and blasting through rock.

The locomotive and the rolling stock are a joy as they are perfect miniatures of engineering, and carry passengers along a route boasting wonderful scenery. The place names along the way are absolutely delightful - Oliver's rock - Big Bob's Ditch - Wakeful's Leap - Skeleton Gulch - Nightshade Straight - each name chosen to highlight a particular incident that took place when the track was being laid. And the wildlife you can see is superb. Occasionally otters can be seen in the sea, and there are many different birds and wild flowers to be admired as you sit and let the world go past. Whether you're young or old, you'll be captivated by a trip on Mull's own railway line, home of the Balamory Express!

Tobermory Hotel

Tobermory, Isle of Mull, Argyll PA75 6NT
Tel: 01688 302091 Fax: 01688 302254
e-mail: tobhotel@tinyworld.co.uk
website: www.thetobermoryhotel.com

Tobermory, the capital of Mull, is the ideal centre from which to explore Mull with its peaceful glens, amazing wildlife and beautiful beaches - or take a boat trip and go whale watching. The **Tobermory Hotel** is one of the best on the island, and was once a row of fishermen's cottages set right on Tobermory Bay. It is a truly delightful hostelry, and entirely family run, famous for its high standards of service, its friendly welcome and its home-from-home feeling. It has views out over the harbour (where, legend tells us, a ship from the Spanish Armada now lies) towards Calve Island and the Morvern hills.

Owned and managed by Andi and Ian Stevens, it has sixteen extremely comfortable and spacious rooms, fifteen of which are fully en suite. All display an attention to detail that is hard to match, with a colour TV, tea and coffee making facilities and a hair dryer. One room on the ground floor is wheelchair friendly, making it the ideal hotel for the disabled. Children are more than welcome, and cots - and even toys - are available. The staff are recruited locally, and both Andi and Ian take a pride in the standards of service they have managed to attain. They are friendly, always willing to be of service, and knowledgeable about what to see and do on the island.

The Water's Edge restaurant is a must if you appreciate good food. It is cosy, intimate and welcoming, with an AA rosette. Under its resident chef Helen Swinbanks it has earned an enviable reputation for its cuisine. She has managed to combine experience with flair to produce a menu that is imaginative while still retaining traditional methods of preparation. All the produce used in the cooking is sourced locally where possible. For instance, the bread comes from a local bakery, the fish comes from local waters and the vegetables and salad leaves are grown in Glengorm Gardens on the island. The meat is all produced on the island, including wild venison. The dinner menu contains such delights as Tobermory Bay mussels in white wine, garlic ansd shallots, monkfish wrapped in smoked bacon on a bed of sautéed potatoes, Sgriob-ruadh pork loin stuffed with apricots and rosemary, and honey roast duck. There is also an excellent wine list that is sure to contain something that complements your meal admirably. Dinner at the Water's Edge is a true culinary experience!

The beautifully decorated and furnished lounges make the ideal place to relax after a hard day's sightseeing in the area. There is a grand selection of single malts to choose from should you require a drink, plus a wide range of beers, cognacs, ciders and liqueurs.

relief. He married again, and she too died. So he married a third time, his new wife bearing him a son and heir He eventually had to go to Edinburgh on business. While there, he was murdered in mysterious circumstances and for no apparent reason. Retribution had come at last.

Tobermory Harbour

Further along the coast from Craignure, on the A849, is **Fishnish Pier**, where a ferry connects the island to Lochaline on the mainland, across the Sound of Mull. At **Salen** the road becomes the A848, and if you turn southwest along the B8035 you can visit **Macquarie's Mausoleum**, where lies Major General Macquarie, Governor General of New South Wales between 1809 and 1820, and sometimes called the "Father of Australia". **Mackinnon's Cave**, on the shoreline at Salen, can only be reached at ebb tide, and great care should be taken if you visit. The cave goes hundreds of feet into the cliff face, and you'll need a torch if you want to explore it.

Eight miles further along the A849 you'll come to **Tobermory**, the island's capital. Its name means "Mary's Well", and it is an attractive small burgh with many brightly painted houses and buildings fronting Tobermory Bay. It is the setting for the popular children's TV programme

Mill Cottage

Bunessan, Isle of Mull, Argyll PA67 6DG
Tel: 01681 700440

Mill Cottage is one of the best self catering cottages on the beautiful island of Mull. It stands on a quiet position and has its own fenced garden with a small burn running through. It is whitewashed and traditionally built of stone, sleeping up to six people in three extremely comfortable and spacious bedrooms. Upstairs there is a double bedroom and a twin bedroom, each with a wash hand basin, and downstairs is another double bedded room, a bathroom with WC, an over-bath shower and another WC. The living room has a TV and a multi-fuel fire surrounded by a beautiful stone fireplace, and there are also electrical storage heaters. Fuel for the fire is provided, as is electricity, bed linen and towels. A single-storey extension houses a well-appointed kitchen/diner, with washing machine, dish washer and separate freezer.

The cottage sits a couple of minute's walk away from the village shops and the licensed hotel in Bunessan, and just a short drive away are some wonderful eating places. Mill Cottage makes an excellent base from which to explore Mull. The ferry to Iona is just a few miles to the west, and all round there are wonderful views out over the water. Mull itself has plenty of shell-sand and rocky beaches just waiting to be discovered and there are plenty of activities to take part in such as golf, sailing, fishing, diving, hill walking and observing the wildlife.

Druimard Country House And Restaurant

Druimard, Dervaig, Isle of Mull,
Argyll PA75 6QW
Tel/Fax: 01688 400345
e-mail: druimard.hote@virgin.net
website: www.ruimard.co.uk

Mull is one of the most beautiful of the Inner Hebridean islands. And at Dervaig, eight miles southwest of Tobermory, you'll find the **Druimard Country House and Restaurant,** which offers superb accommodation and first class food. Owned and managed by husband and wife team Louise and Will Palmer, it has earned an enviable reputation for its high standards, friendly service and outstanding value for money. The atmosphere is relaxing

and peaceful and the tranquil setting is sure to recharge your batteries away from the bustle of modern life.

Druimard can accommodate fourteen guests in seven spacious yet cosy bedrooms, each one individually furnished and decorated, and having colour TV, video, tea/coffee making facilities, direct dial telephone and individually controlled central heating. The residents' lounge commands glorious views out over the glen, as does the conservatory, which is the ideal place to enjoy a relaxing pre- or after-dinner drink. There are plenty of armchairs and sofas in which to relax, and an abundant supply of videos, books and magazines, plus tourism leaflets and brochures to help you enjoy and appreciate your stay on Mull. Well behaved children are more than welcome, and a special high tea for them can be laid on every evening at 5.30 pm in the conservatory. Or you can order half portions for them in the restaurant if you pre book. The Druimard is also a "pet friendly" establishment, and dogs are allowed in the guest bedrooms and grounds but please keep them on a lead while outside the hotel!

The restaurant is justly famous for its superb food. All the produce is fresh and local wherever possible, with salmon, venison and Aberdeen Angus beef regularly on the menu. Why not try locally smoked venison with poached leeks, balsamic syrup and Parmesan wafers, served with Glengorm baby leaves? Or Terrine of marbled salmon? Wild mushroom soup with cream and sauté of wild mushrooms? Locally dived king scallops with smoked bacon and leeks? These imaginative dishes combine various flavours to create a memorable dining experience.

The opportunities to enjoy yourself on Mull are endless. You can go hill walking, sailing, fishing, mountain biking or pony trekking, or take a boat trip to see minky whales, seals, porpoises and dolphins. Or you can explore the island's amazing historical sites, and take a trip over to Iona. Even theatre-lovers are catered for, as Dervaig has the smallest professional theatre in Britain, which puts on a regular programme of plays each year. And if that wasn't enough, it's situated in the grounds of the hotel!

Balamory. **Mull Museum** is situated in Glengorm Road, and has displays explaining the history of the island. In Main Street is the headquarters of the **Hebridean Whale and Dolphin Trust**, a research, education and conservation charity. There is a small visitors centre with displays on whales and dolphins.

At the bottom of Tobermory Bay lies the famous wreck of the **San Juan de Sicilia**, (though some say it was the *Florida*) part of the Spanish Armada fleet. Fleeing in 1588 from the English ships, she weighed anchor in the bay to take on provisions. Having done so, she weighed anchor without paying for them. Donald McLean of Duart boarded the ship and blew it up, and she sank. Stories started circulating that she had 30 million gold ducats aboard her, and though some items were recovered, successive dives to locate the ducats failed. She now lies completely covered in silt, and it is unlikely that anything will ever be recovered from her again (see also Fort William).

The narrow B8073 rises up from Tobermory and passes through **Dervaig** before reaching **Calgary**, on Calgary Bay. In 1883 a member of the Royal Canadian Mounted Police visited Calgary, and was so impressed by the scenery that he named a city in Canada after it.

Dervaig is home to the 38-seat Little Mull Theatre. Though it is tiny, it is a proper professional theatre that puts on a season of plays every year. At the **Old Byre Heritage Centre**, which is close to the village, Mull's visitors can learn about the island's history and heritage through 25 tableaux. There are also displays on natural history and a half hour film. At Ardrioch Farm is **Discover Mull**, where you can see golden eagles, otters, deer, brochs, volcanic dykes and standing stones.

The road continues along the shores of **Loch Tuath**, giving views across to the island of **Ulva**, visited by Boswell and Johnson in 1773. At Ulva Ferry on the island is the small **Ulva Heritage Centre**, housed in a restored thatched cottage. The road then joins the B8035, which, if you turn right, takes you along the beautiful **Loch na Keal** to the A849 once more. At **Bunessan** is the **Ross of Mull Historical Centre**, which explains the local history of the area. At the end of the A849 is **Fionnphort**, the ferry terminal for Iona. Before crossing, a visit to the **Columba Centre** should prepare you for what you'll find on the island.

Iona

36 miles W of Oban off the coast of Mull

No cars are allowed on Iona (National Trust for Scotland), though it is so small (no more than three miles long by a mile and a half wide) that everything on it can easily be visited on foot. It is one of the most sacred spots in Europe (and unfortunately, during the summer months, one of the busiest), and was where **St Columba** set up his monastery in AD 563. From here, he evangelised the Highlands, converting the Picts to Christianity using a mixture of saintliness, righteous anger and perseverance.

Columba's monastery would have been built of wood and wattle, and little now survives of it apart from some of the cashel, or surrounding wall. The present **Iona Abbey**, on the site of the original monastery, was founded in 1203 by Reginald, son of Somerled, Lord of the Isles, though the present building is early 16th century. It was a Benedictine foundation, and later became a cathedral. By the 18th century it was roofless, and the cloisters and other buildings were in ruins. In the 20th century they were restored by the Rev George MacLeod, a Church of Scotland minister who went on to found the **Iona Community**.

Beside the cathedral is the **Reilig Odhrain**, or St Oran's Cemetery. Within it is the **Ridge of the Chiefs**, which is supposed to contain the bodies of many West Highland chiefs who were buried here in medieval times. Close by is the **Ridge of the Kings**, where, it is claimed, no less than

St. Ronans Beach, Iona

48 Scottish, eight Norwegian and four Irish kings lie buried, including Macbeth. However, modern historians now doubt if any kings are buried there at all apart from some from Dalriada. They say that the claims were a "marketing exercise" by the monks to enhance their abbey. One man who does lie within the cemetery is **John Smith** the politician, who was buried there in 1994. **St Oran's Chapel**, near the cemetery, was built as a funeral chapel in the 12th century by one of the Lords of the Isles.

The ruins of **St Mary's Nunnery** are near the jetty, and date from the 13th century. It too was founded by Reginald, and he placed his sister Beatrice in charge as prioress. A small museum has been established in the **Chapel of St Ronan** close to the ruins.

Along the front of the abbey church Oran's Cemetery, goes past the front of the abbey church. Just west of the cathedral is the **Tor Ab**, a low mound on which St Columba's cell may have been situated. Of the many crosses on the island, the best are the 10th century **St Martin's Cross**, outside the main abbey door, and the 16th century **MacLean's Cross**.

In the former parish church manse (designed by Telford) is the **Iona Heritage Centre**, which traces the history of the people who have lived on the island throughout the years.

Staffa

34 miles W of Oban in the Atlantic Ocean

Staffa (National Trust for Scotland) can be reached by excursion boats from Oban. The most remarkable feature on this small uninhabited island is **Fingal's Cave**, which was visited in August 1829 by the composer Felix Mendelssohn. Though he found Edinburgh delightful, he was less enamoured of the Highlands, which he declared to be full of "fog and foul weather". When he made the boat trip to see the cave, he was violently seasick and called the cave "odious". However, it later inspired one of his most famous works, the **Hebrides Overture**. The cliffs are formed from hexagonal columns of basalt that look like wooden staves, some over 50 feet high. The Vikings therefore named the island *Stafi Øy* (Stave Island) from which it got its modern name.

Boat trips to the island are available from Mull and Iona.

Colonsay and Oronsay

40 miles SW of Oban in the Atlantic Ocean

The twin islands of Colonsay and Oronsay are separated by an expanse of sand called **The Strand** which can be walked across at low tide. Colonsay is the bigger of the two, and has a ferry service connecting its main village of **Scalasaig** to Oban.

It is a beautiful island, full of rocky or sandy coves and areas of fertile ground. Perhaps the most beautiful part is **Kiloran Valley**, which is sheltered and warm, and where **Colonsay House**, built in 1722 (not open to the public), stands. It is said that the builder, Malcolm MacNeil, used stones from an old chapel, which stood close by. Its gardens are open to the public.

Oronsay is famous for the substantial ruins of **Oronsay Priory**, perhaps the most important monastic ruins in the west of Scotland after Iona. Tradition gives us two founders. The first is St Oran, companion to St Columba, who is said to have founded it in AD 563. The second is St Columba himself. When he left Ireland, the story goes, he alighted first on Colonsay, and then crossed over to Oronsay, where he established a small monastery. However, he had made a vow that he would never settle where he could still see the coastline of Ireland. He could from Oronsay, so eventually moved on to Iona.

Staffa

John, Lord of the Isles, founded the present priory in the early 14th century, inviting Augustinian canons from Holyrood Abbey in Edinburgh to live within it. The church is 15th century, and the well-preserved cloisters date from the 16th century. A series of large carved grave slabs can be seen within the Prior's House, and in the graveyard is the early 16th century **Oronsay Cross**, intricately carved, and carrying the words *Colinus, son of Christinus MacDuffie*. Another cross can be found east of the Prior's Chapel, with a carving of St John the Evangelist carved at its head.

Coll and Tiree

50 miles W of Oban in the Atlantic Ocean

These two islands, lying beyond Mull, can be reached by ferry from Oban. They are generally low lying, and can be explored by car in a few hours. The ferry first stops at **Arinagiour**, Coll's main village before going on to **Scarinish** on Tiree.

Robert the Bruce granted Coll to Angus Og of Islay, and it was Angus who was responsible for building the 15th century **Breachacha Castle** (not open to the public) to the south of the island. It was in Coll that an incident called the **Great Exodus** took place. In 1856 the southern part of the island, which was the most fertile, was sold to one John Lorne Stewart. In spite of protests from the crofters who farmed there, he raised their rents to a level they could not afford. So the tenants took matters into their own hands. Overnight, they all left their crofts and moved north to the less hospitable lands owned by the Campbells, where the rents were reasonable. Thus Lorne Stewart was left with no rent income whatsoever, and there was nothing he could do about it.

Tiree means the "land of corn", as it is one of the most fertile of the Inner Hebridean islands. It is sometimes called Tir fo Thuinn, meaning the "land beneath the waves", because of its relative flatness. Its highest peaks are **Ben Hynish** (460 feet) and **Ben Hough** (387 feet).

Tiree has the reputation of being the sunniest place in Britain, though this is tempered by the fact that it is also the windiest. Near Vaul to the north east of the island is a curious marked stone called the **Ringing Stone**, which, when struck, makes a clanging noise. Legend says if it is ever broken the island will disappear beneath the Atlantic. At Sandaig is the tiny **Sandaig Museum**, housed in a restored thatched cottage.

Perthshire, Angus and Kinross

The two counties of Perthshire and Angus straddle the Highland Boundary Fault, which separates the Highlands from the Lowlands, while Kinross, once Scotland's second smallest county, is wholly Lowland in character. So there is a wide variety of scenery within them, from mountains, glens and lochs to quiet, intensely cultivated fields and picturesque villages.

Perthshire is a wholly inland county, a place of agriculture, high hills and Highland lochs. It is the county of Loch Rannoch and Loch Tummel, and of possibly the loneliest railway station in Britain, Rannoch station, with its access road petering out into the bleak expanse of Rannoch Moor. It is also the county of the Gleneagles Hotel, one of

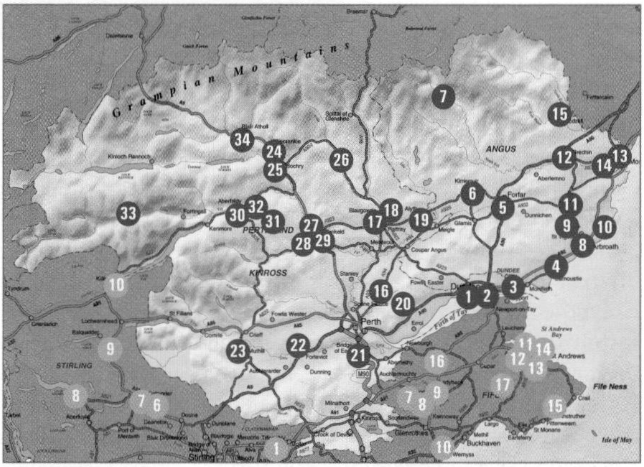

PLACES TO STAY, EAT AND DRINK

Aberlaw Guest House, Dundee	1	Guest House p261
Mills Observatory, Dundee	2	Visitor Attraction p263
Brook House, Broughty Ferry	3	B&B p263
The Old Manor, Panbride	4	B&B and Self Catering p264
Queen St. Tavern, Forfar	5	Pub with Food p266
Starkey's Restaurant, Kirriemuir	6	Restaurant p266
Glen Clova Hotel, Glen Clova	7	Hotel p267
Hotel Seaforth, Arbroath	8	Hotel p268
Colliston Inn, Colliston	9	Pub with Restaurant p268
But 'n' Ben, Auchmithie	10	Restaurant p269
The Star Inn, Friockheim	11	Pub with Food p269
Brown Horse Hotel and Restaurant, Brechin	12	Hotel p270
Murray Lodge Hotel, Montrose	13	Hotel p272
Montrose Basin Wildlife Centre, Rossie Braes	14	Nature Reserve p272
Lettochbeg Guest House, Edzell	15	Guest House p273
MacDonald Arms, Balbeggie	16	Pub, Restaurant & Accommodation p278
Kintrae House Hotel, Blairgowrie	17	Hotel p279

● Denotes entries in other chapters

Britain's most luxurious, and of rich farmland surrounding Perth itself. Blairgowrie is the centre of Scotland's fruit growing industry - fruit that once fed the Dundee jam makers.

River Tay

The A9 north from Perth towards the Drumochter Pass passes through deeply wooded glens, and skirts such historic towns and villages as Dunkeld, Pitlochry and Blair Atholl. In fact, Perthshire likes to call itself the "Big Tree Country", as it has some of the most remarkable woodlands anywhere in Europe.

Perth is a city, and before local government reorganisation in the 70s, had a lord provost, one of only six places in Scotland that could claim that distinction, the others being Edinburgh, Glasgow, Dundee, Aberdeen and Elgin. No legal document has ever specifically taken that honour away from it, so it remains a city still. It is often referred to as the "Fair City of Perth", and this is no idle description. It may be in the Lowlands, but it was never scarred by the industrial developments of the 19th century, as other places in Scotland were. It remains a confident, attractive place with many fine buildings and a good quality of life.

Angus has a coastline that takes in high cliffs and sandy beaches. The coastal towns are famous. Carnoustie, where the British Open is sometimes held; Montrose and its almost land-locked basin where wildfowl can be seen; and of course Arbroath, with

PLACES TO STAY, EAT AND DRINK

Ericht Holiday Lodges, Blairgowrie	18	Self Catering	p279
Burnside Inn, Alyth	19	Pub with Food	p280
Fingask Castle Cottages, Rait	20	Self Catering	p280
River Edge Lodges, Bridge of Earn	21	Self Catering	p281
Duncrub Holidays, Daireoch	22	Self Catering	p282
Drummond Castle Gardens, Muthill	23	Visitor Attraction	p283
The Poplars & Poppies Cottage, Pitlochry	24	B&B and Self Catering	p285
Buttonboss Lodge, Pitlochry	25	B&B	p285
Balknakilly Highland Cottages, Kirkmichael	26	Self Catering	p286
The Pend, Dunkeld	27	B&B	p288
The Taybank, Dunkeld	28	Pub, Food and Accommodation	p288
Royal Dunkeld Hotel, Dunkeld	28	Hotel	p289
Black Watch Inn, Aberfeldy	30	Pub, Restaurant & Accommodation	p290
Drumcroy Lodges, Mains of Murthly	31	Self Catering	p291
Spirit of Wood, Mains of Murthly	32	Wooden Items	p292
Innerwick Estate, Glen Lyon	33	Self Catering	p293
Vale of Atholl Cottages/Restaurant, Blair Atholl	34	Self Catering	p295

Denotes entries in other chapters

the ruins of an abbey where one of the momentous documents in Scottish history was signed - the Declaration of Arbroath. And inland, the glens of Angus, such as Glen Prosen, Glen Clova and Glen Doll, are particularly beautiful as they wind their way into the foothills of the Cairngorms.

Soldier's Leap, Killiecrankie

Dundee is its largest settlement. It is a city of industry, and sits on the north bank of the Firth of Tay. At one time it was one of the powerhouses of Scotland, relying on its three traditional industries of jute, jam and journalism. But it is an ancient place as well, and its roots go deep into Scottish history. One of Scotland's famous historical characters, John Graham of Claverhouse, adopted its name when he became1st Viscount Dundee.

He was a man who was loved by some and loathed by others in 17th century Scotland. To the Covenanters he was Bloody Clavers, a ruthless and cruel persecutor of those opposed to the introduction of bishops into the Church of Scotland. To the Jacobites he was Bonnie Dundee, a dashing and gallant supporter of the Stuarts who was killed fighting for his king at Killiecrankie in 1689.

Kinross sits to the south east of Perthshire. It sits in a great saucer shaped depression with, at its heart, Loch Leven. The main industry is farming, and the gentle countryside, ringed by hills, is well worth exploring if only for the sense of "getting away from it all" it gives. Loch Leven is famous for its fishing, and Vane Farm Nature Reserve was the first educational nature reserve in Europe.

Everywhere in Perthshire, Angus and Kinross there is history. The medieval cathedrals at Dunkeld and Brechin, and the impressive ruins of Arbroath Abbey, are well worth exploring. In AD 685, at Nechtansmere, a Pictish army under King Nechtan defeated the Northumbrians. The Battle of Killiecrankie in 1689 was the first of the Jacobite battles in Scotland. At Scone, outside Perth, was where Scottish kings were crowned as they sat on the Stone of Destiny; at Blair Atholl the Duke of Atholl keeps the only private army in Britain; and Glamis Castle was the childhood home of the late Queen Mother. Mary Stuart was

Tourists at Glamis Castle

held captive in a castle on an island in Loch Leven, and made a daring escape from it.

At Crook of Devon in Kinross a coven was discovered in 1662, with the witches being put on trial and subsequently executed. At Scotlandwell we have yet another place of pilgrimage. A friary once stood here, along with a holy well, and people came from all over Scotland seeking cures for their illnesses. The well is still there, and the waters may still be drunk.

Then there are the literary associations. J.M. Barrie was born at Kirriemuir, and Violet Jacob was born near Montrose. The Dundee publisher D.C. Thomson has given us a host of comic characters that have delighted children (and adults) for years, such as Desperate Dan, Beryl the Peril, Denis the Menace, Lord Snooty, The Bash Street Kids and Oor Wullie.

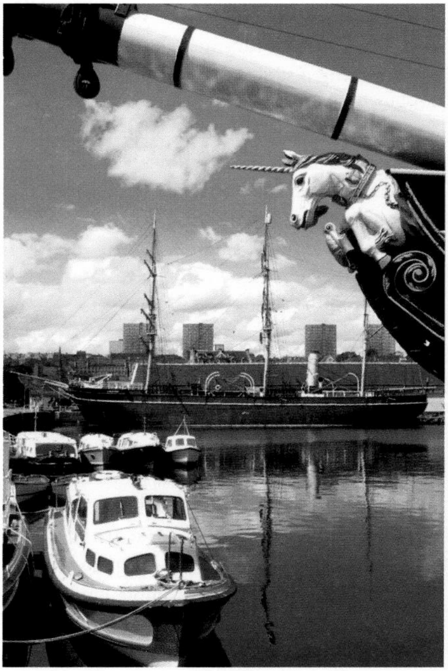

Discovery & Unicorn, Dundee

Dundee

Dundee is Scotland's fourth largest city, and sits on the banks of the Firth of Tay. It is a manufacturing town, at one time famous for the "three Js" of jam, jute and journalism. It also brims with history and heritage, and was granted royal burgh status in the 12th century, when it was one of the largest and wealthiest towns in Scotland. **Dundee Law** (571 feet) looms over the city, and from its summit there is a superb view south towards the Tay Bridges and Fife.

It is joined to Fife by two bridges across the Tay, the **Tay Road Bridge**, opened in 1966, and the **Tay Rail Bridge**, opened in 1887. The road bridge opened up a huge area of north Fife to commuters wishing to work in Dundee, and making it the main shopping centre for the area as well. The

rail bridge replaced an earlier bridge, built in 1878. On the evening of December 28 1879, during a violent westerly gale, this bridge collapsed while a train was crossing it. The 75 train passengers perished.

One of Dundee's best-known sons, **William Topaz McGonagall**, later wrote a poem to commemorate the disaster, which has became almost as famous as the disaster itself:

Beautiful Railway Bridge of the Silv'ry Tay!
Alas! I am very sorry to say
That ninety lives have been taken away
On the last Sabbath day of 1879,
Which will be remember'd for a very long time.

It has been called, rather unfairly perhaps, "the worst poem ever written". However, perhaps we should not judge it so harshly. McGonagall was a simple handloom weaver whose formal education stopped when he was seven years old, and he was trying to put into words the horror he felt at the tragedy.

He was born in Edinburgh in 1830, the son of Irish immigrants, and came to Dundee with his parents after having lived in Paisley and Glasgow. In 1877, he took to writing poetry, having felt "a strange kind of feeling stealing over me", and then wrote until he died in September 1902.

The **Old Steeple** of St Mary's Church, in the heart of the city, dates from the 15th century, and is reckoned to be one of the finest in the country. The rest of the building dates from the 18th and 19th centuries, and was once divided into four separate churches. Until the 1980s, when they finally amalgamated, there were still three churches within the building - the Steeple Church, Old St Paul's and St David's.

Another reminder of Dundee's past is the **Wishart Arch** in the Cowgate. It is one of the city's old gateways, and from its top, George Wishart the religious reformer preached to plague victims during the plague of 1544 (see also Montrose and St Andrews).

RSS Discovery, Captain Scott's ship, was built in Dundee and launched in 1901. It now forms the centrepiece of **Discovery Point & RSS Discovery**, at Discovery Quay. It was one of the last wooden three-masted ships to be built in Britain, and the first to be built solely for scientific research. You can explore the ship, "travel" to Antarctica in the Polarama Gallery and find out about one of the greatest stories of exploration and courage ever told.

At City Quay you'll find **HM Frigate Unicorn**, the oldest British-built ship still afloat. It was built at Chatham in 1824 for the Royal Navy, and carried 46 guns. The ship re-creates the conditions on board a wooden sailing ship during Nelson's time, with officers' quarters, cannons, and the cramped conditions within which the crew lived.

In 1999, **The Verdant Works**, in West Henderson's Wynd, was voted Europe's top industrial museum. Jute was once a staple industry in Dundee, employing over 40,000 people. Here, in a former jute mill, you are taken on a tour of the trade, from its beginnings in India to the end product in all its forms. You will see the processes involved in jute manufacture, you'll see the original machinery, and you'll see the living conditions of people both rich and poor who earned their living from the trade. There are interactive displays, film shows, and a guided tour.

Sensation is Dundee's science centre. Located in the Greenmarket, it is a place where "science is brought to life" using specially designed interactive exhibits. Here you can find out how a dog sees the world, how to use your senses to discover where you are, and why things taste good or bad. The **Mills Observatory** (see panel opposite), in Balgay Park a mile west of the city centre and accessed from Glamis Road, also deals with matters scientific. It is Britain's only full time public observatory,

Mills Observatory

Glamis Road, Balgay Park, Dundee DD2 2UB
Tel: 01382 435967 Fax: 01382 435962
e-mail: mills.observatory@dundeecity.gov.uk
website: www.dundeecity.gov.uk

Mills Observatory, housed in a classically styled sandstone building, is the UK's only full time public observatory. Here you can see the stars and planets for yourself through an impressive Victorian telescope and look at safe projected images of the sun. The planetarium has an artificial night sky giving you the chance to view constellations and planets. More can be learnt through the changing displays, audio and visual presentations and an interactive computer. The shop offers a range of gifts and educational items. Admission to the observatory is free.

and houses a 25mm Cooke telescope. It also has a small planetarium and display area.

The **McManus Galleries** are housed within a Gothic building in Albert Square, and contain many 18th and 19th century Scottish paintings. There is also a museum of more than local interest, with a particularly fine collection of artefacts from Ancient Egypt. The **Dundee Contemporary Arts Centre** in the Nethergate specialises in contemporary art and film, and has galleries, cinemas and workshops.

To the east of the city is **Broughty Ferry**, once called the "richest square mile in Europe" because of the many fine mansions built there by jute barons. The **Broughty Ferry Museum** is at Castle Green, and housed within a 15th century castle built by the Earl of Angus in the late 15th century as a defence against marauding English ships. It has displays on local history, and tells the story of Dundee's former whaling fleet, at one time Britain's largest. If you visit Broughty Ferry at New Year, you can see the annual **N'erday Dook** ("New Year's Day Dip") held on January 1, when swimmers enter the waters of the Firth of Tay. The dip is usually done for charity, and it is not unknown for bystanders to be wrapped up in warm woollens, scarves and gloves as the swimmers enter the water dressed only in swimsuits.

Dudhope Castle, at Dudhope Park in Dundee, dates originally from the 13th century, and was once the home of the Scrymageour family, hereditary constables of Dundee. The present building dates from the late 16th century. In its time it has also been a woollen mill and a barracks. It now forms part of the University of Abertay and is not open to the public, though it can be viewed

Brook House

86 Brook Street, Broughty Ferry,
Angus DD5 1DQ
Tel: 01382 779166

With four fully en suite rooms, **Brook House** is one of the best B&B establishments in Broughty Ferry. It is owned and run by Julie Cromar, who brings a wealth of experience to looking after and cosseting guests. The breakfasts here are justly famous, as they are filling and hearty, and represent the very best in Scottish hospitality. Dating from 1923, the building is modern and smart inside while still retaining some original features. The rooms are smart and airy, and extremely comfortable. But for all these plus points, the value-for-money tariffs at Brook House will pleasantly surprise you!

from the outside. And at the junction of Claypotts Road and Arbroath Road is the wonderfully named **Claypotts Castle** (Historic Scotland), built between 1569 and 1588 by John Strachan. It can be viewed by prior appointment with Historic Scotland.

On the Coupar Angus Road is the **Camperdown Wildlife Centre**, with a fine collection of Scottish and European wildlife, including brown bears, Scottish wildcats, wolves and bats. To the west of the city, on the north bank of the Tay, is the **Carse of Gowrie**, one of the most fertile areas of Scotland.

Around Dundee

Monifieth

6 miles E of Dundee on the A930

This little holiday resort sits at the entrance to the Firth of Tay, and has some good sandy beaches. Its golf courses were used in the qualifying rounds of the British Open. At one time it was an important Pictish settlement, and some Pictish stones were once discovered at **St Rule's Church** that are now in The National Museum of Scotland in Edinburgh.

Carnoustie

11 miles E of Dundee on the A930

Golf is king in Carnoustie. This small holiday resort on the North Sea coast hosted the British Open Championships in 1931 and 1999, and is a favourite destination for golfing holidays.

But it has other attractions. **Barry Mill** (National Trust for Scotland) is a 19th century working corn mill. You can see the large water wheel turning, and also find out how corn is ground. There is an exhibition explaining the historical role of the mill, as well as a walkway along the mill lade. Three miles north west of the town are the **Carlungie and Ardestie Souterrains** (Historic Scotland), underground earth houses dating from the 1st century AD.

Balgray

4 miles N of Dundee off the A90

Four miles north of the city centre, near Balgray, is the **Tealing Souterrain**, an underground dwelling dating from about AD100. It was accidentally discovered in 1871, and consists of a curved passage about 78 feet long and seven feet wide with a stone floor.

Fowlis Easter

6 miles W of Dundee on a minor road off the A923

This small village has one of the finest small churches in Scotland. The **Parish**

Church of St Marnan dates from about 1453, and still has part of its rood screen, as well as medieval paintings and a sacrament house that is reckoned to be the finest in Scotland. Lord Gray built it in 1453 on the site of an earlier church, which was dedicated to St. Marnock in 1242.

This early church was originally built by a lady of the local Mortimer family whose husband was in the holy Land fighting in the Crusades.

Glamis Castle

Glamis

10 miles N of Dundee on the A94

Glamis Castle is famous as being the childhood home of the late Queen Mother and the birthplace of her daughter, the late Princess Margaret. The lands of Glamis (pronounced "Glams") were given to Sir John Lyon in 1372 by Robert II, the first Stewart king and grandson of Robert the Bruce, and still belongs to the family, who are now the Earls of Strathmore and Kinghorne. In 1376 Sir John married Robert's daughter, Princess Joanna, and the castle has had royal connections ever since. The present castle was built in the 17th century to resemble a French château, though fragments of an earlier 14th century castle still survive in the tower.

Shakespeare's *Macbeth* is set in Glamis, and Duncan's Hall, the oldest part of the castle, is said to have been built on the spot where Macbeth murdered Duncan, though history tells us that Duncan most probably died in battle near Elgin. It may even be that Shakespeare visited Glamis, as he and his troupe of actors were sent to Aberdeen by Elizabeth I to perform before James VI.

Tragedy seems to stalk Glamis Castle. In 1540 Lady Glamis was burnt as a witch in Edinburgh and for plotting to murder James V, and the crown seized the lands. She was later found to have been innocent of all the charges, and the lands were restored to her son. It has the reputation of being one of the most haunted castles in Scotland. There is a Grey Lady who haunts the chapel, a Black Page, and a window which looks out from a room that doesn't appear to exist. Legend has it that in the room, which might be within the thickness of the walls of the castle, one of the Lords of Glamis and the Earl of Crawford played cards with the devil, and were sealed up because of it.

Within the village of Glamis, at Kirkwynd, is the **Angus Folk Museum** (National Trust for Scotland), housed in a row of 18th century stone cottages. It contains one of the finest folk collections in Scotland, including a restored 19th century hearse, and shows how the people of rural Angus lived in times past.

Forfar

13 miles N of Dundee on the A932

Once the county town of Angus, Forfar is now a small royal burgh and market town. It gives its name to one of Scotland's culinary delights - the **Forfar Bridie**. It has meat and vegetables within a pastry crust, and used to be popular with the farm workers of Angus, as it was a self-contained

Queen St. Tavern

45a Queen St., Forfar, Angus DD8 3AL
Tel: 01307 462722 Fax: 01307 467067
e-mail: SandPmilne@aol.com

Hidden away off Forfar's main street is the **Queen St. Tavern**, one of the best hostelries in this lovely old market town. Owned and managed by Steve and Pam Milne, the tavern is a picturesque stone building dating from the 19th century, with many original features. The atmosphere is warm and cosy, with a great bar/lounge and a dining room to the rear where superb food is served. You can have full bar lunches, snacks and sandwiches. Evening meals are served Fri/Sat and Sundays. There is also a great selection of drinks (including a fine wine list) both alcoholic and non-alcoholic to accompany your meal.

and easily portable meal.

To get an insight into the town's history and industries, you should visit the **Meffan Museum and Art Gallery** in West High Street, built in 1898 after a daughter of a former provost left a sum of money to the town. During the Dark Ages this part of Scotland was inhabited by the Picts, who, as far as we know, had no alphabet. However, they were expert carvers, and in the museum is a superb display of carved stones. You can also walk down an old cobbled street and peer into shops and workshops. A more unusual display is one about witchcraft in Angus.

Five miles east of Forfar is **Balgavies Loch**, a Scottish Wildlife Trust reserve, where you can see great crested grebe, whooping swans, cormorant and other birds. Keys to the hide are available from the ranger at the Montrose Basin Wildlife Centre.

The ruins of **Restenneth Priory** (Historic Scotland) sit about a mile and a half from the town, on the B9113. It was founded by David I for Augustinian canons on the site of a much earlier church, and its square tower has some of the earliest Norman work in Scotland. It was sacked by Edward I, but under the patronage of Robert the Bruce it soon regained its importance. Prince Robert, one of Bruce's sons, is buried here.

Kirriemuir

15 miles N of Dundee on the A926

At 9 Brechin Road is **JM Barrie's Birthplace** (National Trust for Scotland). The creator of *Peter Pan* (first performed in 1904) was born here in 1860, the son of a

Starkey's Restaurant

1 - 5 Glengate, Kirriemuir, Angus DD8 4HD
Tel: 01571 572523

Tucked away in one of the oldest parts of Kirriemuir is **Starky's Restaurant**, which serves some of he best food in town. It can seat up to 30 people in absolute comfort, and is cosy, spotless and welcoming. You can order teas, coffees, snacks and a wide range of hot meals. The cuisine is simple and unpretentious, but always delicious! Try the home made steak pie, for instance, a dish which has become famous throughout the town. It is hearty and filling! The owner and chef, Elizabeth McGinty, wants to maintain the high standards she has set, and looks forward to welcoming you to her establishment!

handloom weaver, and the building's outside washhouse was his first theatre. He was a bright child, attending both Glasgow Academy and Dumfries Academy (see also Dumfries) before going on to Edinburgh University. He also wrote many stories and novels, setting them in a small town called "Thrums", which is a thinly disguised Kirriemuir.

In 1930 Barrie donated a **Camera Obscura** (National Trust for Scotland) to the town, one of only three such cameras in the country. It is situated within the cricket pavilion on top of Kirriemuir Hill, and is open to the public. The **Kirriemuir Aviation Museum** has a private collection of World War II memorabilia, and is situated at Bellies Brae.

Kirriemuir is the gateway to many of the beautiful Angus glens, and in the **Gateway to the Glens Museum** in the High Street you can find out about life in the glens and in Kirriemuir itself before setting out to explore them. The B955 takes you into **Glen Clova**. At the head of the glen it forms a loop, so you can travel along one side of the glen and return along the other for part of the way. A minor road at the Clova Hotel takes you up onto lonely **Glen Doll** before it peters out among the high peaks of the Cairgorms. At Dykehead you can turn off the B955 onto a minor road for **Glen Prosen** and follow it as it winds deep into the glen. A cairn close to Dykehead commemorates the Antarctic explorers Robert Falcon Scott and Edward Adrian Wilson. Wilson was born in Cheltenham, the son of a doctor, but lived in Glen Prosen, and it was here that some of the Antarctic expedition was planned. He died along with Scott in Antarctica in March 1912.

Glen Isla is the southernmost of the Angus glens, and you can follow it for all of

its length along the B951, which eventually takes you onto the A93 at Glenshee and up to Braemar if you wish. You will pass the **Loch of Lintrathan**, which is noted for its bird life. A couple of miles further up the glen a minor road takes you to lonely **Backwater Reservoir** and its dam.

Dunnichen

13 miles NE of Dundee on minor road off the B9128

Close to the village was fought, in AD 685, the **Battle of Nechtansmere** between the Picts, under King Nechtan, and the Northumbrians. It was a turning point in early Scottish history, as Northumbria was aggressively trying to extend its boundaries, and had already taken the Lothians and Fife. The Northumbrians, under King Ecgfrith, were roundly beaten, and Ecgfrith himself was killed. At the crossroads in the village is a cairn, which commemorates the battle. Some people claim to have seen a ghostly re-enactment of the fighting take place in modern times. The "mere", or loch, which gave its name to the battle, was drained many years ago.

The picturesque village of **Letham**, which is close by, was founded in 1788 by George Dempster, the local landowner, as a settlement for farm workers who had been forced to leave the land because of farming reforms. It became a centre of weaving and spinning, though the introduction of power looms in nearby towns killed it off.

Arbroath

15 miles NE of Dundee on the A92

The ancient town of Arbroath is special to all Scots. It was here, in 1320, that the

nobles of Scotland met and signed **Declaration of Arbroath**, which stated that the country was an independent kingdom, and not beholden to England. It was sent to the Pope in Rome, and in it, they claimed that they weren't fighting for glory, riches or honour, but for freedom. They also, in no uncertain terms, claimed that they would remain loyal to their king, Robert the Bruce, only as long as he defended Scotland against the English. It was a momentous declaration to make in those far off days, when unswerving loyalty to a sovereign was expected at all times.

The Declaration was drawn up in **Arbroath Abbey** (Historic Scotland), the ruins of which still stand within the town, and sometimes a re-enactment of the signing is held there. A Visitor Centre tells the story of the abbey and the Declaration.

The abbey ruins date from the 12th century and later, and are of warm red sandstone. It was founded in 1176 by William the Lion for the Tironensian order of monks, and dedicated to St Thomas of Canterbury. Portions of the great abbey church remain, including the south transept, with its great rose window. In 1951 the abbey was the temporary home of the Stone of Destiny after it was removed from Westminster Abbey by students with Nationalist sympathies.

The award winning **Arbroath Museum**, at Ladyloan, is housed in the elegant signal tower for the Bellrock Lighthouse, and brings Arbroath's maritime and social history alive through a series of models, sounds and even smells.

Arbroath has had a harbour at the "Fit o' the Toon" (Foot of the Town) since at least

the 14th century, and it supported a great fishing fleet. The town gave its name to that delicacy called the **Arbroath Smokie** (a smoked haddock) though the supposed origins of the smokie are to be found not in the town, but in **Auchmithie**, a fishing village four miles to the north. The story goes that long ago it was the practice to store fish in the lofts of the fishermen's cottages. One day, a cottage burned down, and the resultant smoked fish was found to be delicious. Not only that - it preserved them.

The **Cliffs Nature Trail** winds for one and a half miles along the red sandstone cliffs towards Carlinheugh Bay. There is plenty of birdlife to see, as well as fascinating rock formations. The town is also a holiday resort, and at West Link Parks is **Kerr's Miniature Railway**, always a favourite with holidaymakers. It is open during the summer months, and is Scotland's oldest miniature railway. It runs for over 400 yards alongside the main Aberdeen to Edinburgh line.

St Vigeans

17 miles NE of Dundee on minor road off the A92

When the 12th century **Parish Church of St Vigeans** was being rebuilt in the 19th century, 32 sculptured Pictish stones were discovered. They are now housed in the **St Vigeans Museum**, a cottage close to the small knoll where the church stands.

St Fechan, or St Vigean, was an Irish saint who died in about AD 664. The village of Ecclefechan in Dumfriesshire is also named after him.

Aberlemno

18 miles NE of Dundee on a minor road off the B9134

Within the village are the Pictish **Aberlemno Sculptured Stones** (Historic Scotland). One is situated in the kirkyard of the parish church, and the others are within a stone enclosure near the roadside north of the church. The one in the kirkyard shows a fine cross on one side surrounded by intertwining serpents and water horses, and a typical Pictish hunting scene on the other. It dates from the 8th or 9th century. The other two have crosses, angels, and battle or hunting scenes.

Brechin

22 miles NE of Dundee off the A90

If the possession of a cathedral makes a town a city, then Brechin is indeed a city, even though it has a population of only 6,000. **Brechin Cathedral** dates from the 12th century, though most of what we see today is 13th century and later. It was the successor to a Celtic church which stood on the site, and which had been endowed by the queen of Kenneth II, king of Scots between AD 971 and AD 995. It soon became the premier

church for Angus, though by the 11th century Roman Catholic clergy had succeeded the Culdee priests.

In 1806 the nave, aisles and west front were remodelled, and between 1901 and 1902 were restored to their original design. Adjacent to the cathedral, and now forming part of its fabric, is an 11th century **Round Tower**. These towers are common in Ireland, though this is the only one of two to have survived in Scotland (see also Abernethy). It was used as a place of refuge for the priests of the church during troubled times. The south wall of the chapel is all that remains of the **Maison Dieu** almshouses founded in 1267 by Lord William de Brechin.

In St Ninian's Square is **Brechin Museum**, which has exhibits and displays about the cathedral, the ancient city crafts and local archaeology. **Brechin Castle** is the seat of the Earls of Dalhousie, and within the **Brechin Castle Centre** are a garden centre, walks and a model farm. There is also **Pictavia**, an exhibition that explains about the enigmatic Picts, who occupied this part of Scotland for centuries. Their name means the "painted people", and they fought the Romans, the Vikings and the Anglo Saxons. The various tribes eventually amalgamated, forming a powerful kingdom, which ultimately united with the kingdom of the Scots of Dalriada in AD 843.

At Menmuir, near the town, are the White and Brown **Caterthuns**, on which are the well-preserved remains of Iron Age forts. The hills also give good views across the surrounding countryside.

The **Caledonian Railway** runs on Sundays during the summer, when passengers can travel between the Victorian Brechin Station on Park Road and the nearby Bridge of Dun. The railway has seven steam engines and eight diesels, and is run by the Brechin Railway Preservation Society.

To the north west of Brechin is **Glen Lethnot**, one of the beautiful Angus glens. Flowing through it is the West Water, and near the head of the glen is an old trail that takes you over the Clash of Wirren into Glen Esk. Illicit distillers used this as a route in days gone by, who hid their casks in the corries among the hills. For this reason it became known as the **Whisky Trail**.

Montrose

27 miles NE of Dundee on the A92

Montrose is an ancient royal burgh, which received its charter in the early 12th century. It sits on a small spit of land between the North Sea and a shallow tidal basin called the Montrose Basin, which is famous for its bird life. The **Montrose Basin Wildlife Centre** (see panel on page 272) is visited by thousands of bird watchers every year who come to see the many migrant and resident birds.

At the old Montrose Air Station, where some of the Battle of Britain pilots trained, is the **Montrose Air Station Museum**. In 1912, the government planned 12 such air stations, to be operated by the Royal Flying Corps, later called the Royal Air Force. Montrose was the first, and became

Montrose Basin Nature Reserve

Murray Lodge Hotel

2-8 Murray Street, Montrose,
Angus DD10 8LP
Tel: 01674 678880 Fax: 01674 678877
e-mail: laharris@waitrose.com

Situated within what was a late 18th century linen mill, the three star and AA-recommended **Murray Lodge Hotel** is a superior licensed establishment that offers 12 fully en suite rooms that are beautifully furnished and decorated. Each one has a remote control colour TV, direct dial phone, study desk, tourist information pack and hospitality tray. The residents lounge is comfortable and welcoming, and the hotels quiet charm and elegance adds to its overall warmth. This is the place to have a quiet aperitif before dinner. The dining room can seat 24 people in absolute comfort, and it is here that beautifully cooked and presented breakfasts and dinners are served.

The cuisine is traditional, and presented with care and flair. Vegetarian and other diets can be catered for. There is a selection of wines to choose from, and there is sure to be one that will match your meal perfectly. There is also a wide range of beers, spirits, liqueurs and soft drinks.

In the Coffee Mill - the hotel's own coffee shop - you can order light lunches, coffees and afternoon teas. The owner Lesley-Anne Harris, and her staff in the hotel are friendly, approachable and knowledgeable about the attractions in and around Montrose, and will give you a hearty Scottish welcome.

Montrose Basin Wildlife Centre

Rossie Braes, Montrose, Angus DD10 9TJ
Tel: 01674 676336 Fax: 01674 678773
e-mail: webmaster@montrosebasin.org.uk
website: www.montrosebasin.org.uk

Montrose Basin is the 750 hectare enclosed estuary of the South Esk river. Virtually untouched by industrial development and pollution, the Basin provides a rich feeding ground for thousands of resident and migrant birds. The daily tidal cycle and passing seasons, each with its own characteristic pattern of birds - winter and summer visitors and passage migrants - ensure something new and different every month of the year. From here you might see eider ducks, pink footed and greylag geese, otters and much more. Magnificent views of the wildlife can be seen through high powered telescopes and binoculars, whilst television cameras bring the wildlife right into the centre! Unique displays show how a tidal basin works and the routes taken by the migrating birds. There are lots of buttons to press, boxes to open, touch tables and microscopes - ideal for children - and there is a fully equipped classromm for children to enjoy a range of educational activities. A nearby hide provides a closer view of the wildlife and the shop is stocked with a range of unusual and exciting gifts. Open 1st April to 31st October, daily 10.30am-5pm and 1st November to 31st March, daily 10.30am-4pm.

operational in 1913. Now it houses a small collection of aircraft, plus mementoes, documents and photographs related to flying.

To the west of the town, beyond the Basin, is the **House of Dun** (National Trust for Scotland). It was designed by William Adam in 1730 for David Erskine, Lord Dun, and contains good plasterwork, sumptuous furnishings and a collection of embroidery carried out by Lady Augusta Kennedy-Erskine, natural daughter of William IV by his mistress Mrs Jordan.

Montrose was adopted as the title of the Graham family when it was ennobled, and the most famous member was James Graham, 5th Earl and 1st Marquis of Montrose. He was born in 1612, and succeeded to the earldom in 1625. At first he was a Covenanter, then changed sides. He was made Lieutenant-General of Scotland by the king, and unsuccessfully tried to invade Scotland with an army. He later went to the Highlands in disguise to raise a Royalist army. During a succession of skirmishes, he defeated the Covenanting army due to his brilliant leadership and almost reckless courage. Charles's defeat at Naseby, however, left him powerless, and his forces were eventually soundly beaten at Philiphaugh in 1645. Afterwards he fled to the Continent but returned in 1650 in support of Charles II. Charles, however, disowned him and he was hanged.

Though not born in Montrose, George Wishart the religious reformer has close associations with the town. He attended the grammar school here in the 1520s, and went on to Aberdeen University. He later returned and taught at the grammar school, where he used the Greek translation of the bible while teaching his pupils. For this he was accused of heresy, and he had to flee to England. In 1546 he was burnt at the stake in St Andrews on the orders of Cardinal Beaton (see also Dundee and St Andrews).

Edzell

27 miles NE of Dundee on the B966

The ruins of **Edzell Castle** (Historic Scotland) date from the early 16th century. It was a seat of the Lindsays, and reckoned to be the finest castle in Angus. It clearly shows that life in a Scottish castle was not the cold, draughty experience that people imagine from seeing bare, ruined walls. They could be places of refinement and comfort, and at Edzell we have evidence of this.

The gardens were especially tasteful and elegant, and were laid out in 1604 by Sir David Lindsay, though he died in 1610 before they could be completed. The walled garden has been described as an "Italian Renaissance garden in Scotland", and featured heraldic imagery and an array of carved panels representing deities, the liberal arts and the cardinal virtues.

The castle was added to in 1553 when

David Lindsay, 9th Earl of Crawford and a judge, built the west range. In 1562 Mary Stuart spent two nights here, and held a meeting of her Privy Council.

In 1715 the Jacobite Lindsays sold the castle to the Earl of Panmure, who were also Jacobite sympathisers, so that they could raise a Jacobite regiment. After the rebellion the castle and lands were forfeited to the crown and sold to an English company, which went bankrupt in 1732. The castle gradually became ruinous, and in the 1930's the gardens were restored to their former glory. The summerhouse contains examples of the carved panelling that was in the castle in its heyday.

One of the delights of Edzell village is the **Dalhousie Arch**, erected in 1887 over a road into the village as a memorial to 13th Earl of Dalhousie and his wife, who died within a few hours of each other.

Edzell is the gateway to **Glen Esk**. It is the longest and most northerly of the glens, and you can drive the 19 miles to Invermark Lodge, close to Loch Lee, where the road peters out. Along the way you can stop at the **Glen Esk Folk Museum**, which traces the life of the people of the glen from about 1800 to the present day.

Kinross

Once the main town in the county of Kinross, this small burgh now sits quietly on the shores of Loch Leven. The opening of the M90 motorway has put it within half an hour of Edinburgh, and over the last fifteen years it has expanded to become a peaceful haven for commuters.

The town's **Tolbooth** dates from the 17th century, and on the **Mercat Cross** are the "Jougs", an iron collar placed round the neck of wrongdoers. **Kinross House** dates from the late 17th century, and was built for Sir William Bruce, Charles II's surveyor and master of works, who was responsible for the fabric of the Palace of Holyrood in Edinburgh. It is an elegant Palladian mansion with wonderful formal gardens that are sometimes open to the public. The story goes that it was intended as a home for the ill-fated James VII, then Duke of York, in anticipation of the fact that he might not succeed to the throne.

Loch Leven is one of Scotland's most famous lochs, not because of its size (it covers no more than 3,250 acres) or its spectacular beauty, but because of its wonderful trout fishing. Though this has gone into decline in recent years, the trout are still highly prized for their delicate pink flesh, caused by the small fresh water shellfish on which they feed. The whole loch is a National Nature Reserve, and on the south shore of the loch, close to the B9097, is the **Vane Farm Nature Reserve**, administered by the Royal Society for the Protection of Birds. It hosts a programme of events throughout the year, and was the first educational nature reserve in Europe.

The loch has two islands. On **St Serf's Island** a small Augustinian priory once stood, though all that remains are the scant walls of the chapel and the remains of a small priory and chapel. It replaced a Celtic monastery founded by Brude, the last Pictish king, in the 9th century. In 1150 an Augustinian priory was founded on the site, and staffed by monks from St Andrews. One of the priors was Andrew of Wynton, author of the *Orygynale Cronykil* ("Original Chronicle"), which was a history of Scotland.

On the other island are the ruins of **Lochleven Castle** (Historic Scotland). From June 1567 until May 1568 Mary Stuart was held prisoner here, having been seized in Edinburgh for her supposed part in the murder of her husband Lord Darnley. She was 25 years old at the time, and married to Bothwell, who was also implicated in Darnley's murder. While kept prisoner in the castle, she was constantly being asked to abdicate and divorce Bothwell, but this she refused to do, as she was already pregnant by him. Shortly after she arrived on the island, she gave birth to stillborn twins, and eventually signed the deeds. But it was not her stay on the island that made the castle famous; rather it was the way she escaped.

The castle was owned by the Dowager Lady Douglas, mother of Mary's half brother the Earl of Moray, who became regent when Mary abdicated. Both she and her other sons Sir William and George Douglas looked after Mary during her imprisonment. But George gradually fell under Mary's spell, and hatched various plans for her to escape. All failed, and he was eventually banished from the island.

But someone else had also fallen under Mary's spell - 16 year old Willie Douglas, who was thought to be the illegitimate son of Sir William, and who was kept as a page. After the various attempts at escape, Mary was being held in the third storey of the main tower, above the Great Hall where the Douglas family dined. One evening young Willie "accidentally" dropped a napkin over the castle keys, which his father had placed on the table while dining. On picking up the napkin, he picked up the keys as well.

As the meal progressed, Mary and one of her attendants crept out of her room and made for the main doorway, where Willie met them. He unlocked the door, and they both slipped out. He then locked the door behind him and threw the keys into the water before rowing the two women ashore. There they were met by George Douglas, Lord Seton and a troop of loyal soldiers, and taken to the safety of Niddrie Castle.

In those days, the loch was much bigger than it is now, and the water came right up to the doors of the castle. Between 1826 and 1836 it was partially drained, reducing its size by a quarter, and the keys were recovered from the mud. Nowadays, trips to the island leave from the pier at Kinross.

Within the town are the premises of Todd and Duncan, where a small exhibition called **Cashmere at Lochleven** traces the history of this luxury cloth. The **Scottish Raptor Centre** at Turfhills has falconry courses and flying displays. Close to Kinross every year in July is held Scotland's biggest outdoor rock festival, **T in the Park**.

Around Kinross

Milnathort

2 miles N of Kinross off the M90

Milnathort is a small, former wool-manufacturing town. To the east are the impressive ruins of 15th century **Burleigh Castle**, built of warm red stone, which was a stronghold of the Balfour family.

There is an interesting story attached to the castle. In 1707 the heir to the castle fell in love with a servant girl, which so displeased his father that he sent him abroad. However, he declared his undying love for her, and swore that if she married someone else while he was away, he would kill him when he returned.

After a year or so he returned, only to find that she had married a schoolmaster. True to his word, he shot him dead. He then fled, but was captured and sentenced to death. However, he escaped the gallows by changing places with his sister and donning her clothes. He later fought in the Jacobite army during the 1715 Uprising. For this, his castle and lands were taken from the family and given to the Irwins.

Scotlandwell

5 miles E of Kinross, on the A911

Scotlandwell takes its name from the springs that bubble up to the surface in this part of the county, which is on the western slopes of the Lomond Hills. In the early 13th century the Bishop of St Andrews set up a hospice here, and his successor gave it to the "Red Friars", or "Trinitarians", a monastic order that had originally been founded to raise money for the release of captives in the Holy Land during the Crusades. They exploited the springs, and established a **Holy Well**. Soon it became a place of pilgrimage, bringing huge revenue to the monks.

The local landowners, the Arnots of **Arnot Tower,** the ruins of which can still be seen, gazed enviously at the wealth of the Trinitarians, and decided to "muscle in" on the venture. They placed younger sons of the family within the order as fifth columnists, and when enough of them were in place, they occupied the friary and ejected those friars who weren't Arnots. They established Archibald Arnot, the Laird of Arnot's second son, as minister (the name given to the head of the friary), and began creaming off the vast wealth. At the Reformation, the lands and income of the friary were given to them, and the takeover was complete.

Today, the holy well still exists. In 1858 the Laird of Arnot commissioned David Bryce to turn it into a memorial to his wife Henrietta, and this is what can be seen today. The friary has completely disappeared, though a small plaque in the graveyard marks the spot where it once stood.

At Portmoak near Scotlandwell there's the **Scottish Gliding Centre**, where the adventurous can try an "air experience flight".

Crook of Devon

5 miles W of Kinross on the A977

This small village has twice won an award for being the "best kept village in Kinross". It seems quiet enough now, but in the 1660s it achieved notoriety as a centre of witchcraft. A coven of witches had been "discovered" in the area, and in 1662 three women were tried and sentenced to be strangled to death and their bodies burnt at a "place called Lamblaires". A few weeks later four women and one man were executed in the same manner, and not long after two women were tried, one of them escaping death because of her age. The other was burnt at the stake.

By this time the other members of the "coven" had fled from the area. But in July two further women were put on trial, one of whom was executed and the other, called Christian Grieve, acquitted. The acquittal was looked upon as an affront by the local people - especially the clergy - and she was retried and eventually executed.

There is no doubt that the trials were a travesty, and that many old scores were settled by naming people - especially old women - as witches. It was also not unknown in Scotland at that time for the accused, knowing their fate was sealed, to get their own back on the accusers by naming them as witches and warlocks as well. Thus Scotland seemed to be awash with devil worship, when in fact true Satanism was almost non-existent.

Today Lamblaires is a small grassy knoll in a field adjoining the village. It looks peaceful enough, and nothing reminds you of the horrible stranglings and burnings that took place there.

Perth

The "Fair City" of Perth sits on the Tay, and in medieval times was the meeting place of Scottish kings and parliaments. Though a large place by Scottish standards, having a population of about 45,000, it's location away from the Central Belt ensured that it never succumbed to the intense industrialisation that many other towns experienced. But it did succumb to the ravages of modernisation, and many of the ancient buildings that played a part in Scotland's story have been swept away.

The city centre lies between two large open spaces, the **North Inch** and the **South Inch,** and is filled with elegant 18th and 19th century buildings. Up until the local government reorganisations of the mid 70s, it had a lord provost, and was truly a city. However, the city status was never taken away from it, and though it no longer has a lord provost, it remains a city to this day. It even has **St Ninian's Cathedral**, which dates from the 19th century. Perth has played a large part in the history of Scotland.

James I chose it as his capital, and if he hadn't been murdered in the city in 1437, it might have been Scotland's capital to this day. The story of James's murder has been embellished over the years, but the facts are simple. He was an unpopular monarch,

Perth

and when he was staying in the city's Dominican Friary (now gone), he was attacked by a group of nobles under the Earl of Atholl, who hoped to claim the crown. James tried to make his escape through a sewer which ran beneath his room, but was caught and stabbed to death. An embellishment to the story is that one of his Queen's ladies-in-waiting stuck her arm through the boltholes of the door as a bar to prevent the entry of the assassins. However, it is probably a later invention.

In the centre of the city is **St John's Kirk**, one of the finest medieval kirks in Scotland. From this church, the city took its earlier name of St Johnstoune, which is remembered in the name of the local football team. It was consecrated in 1243, though the earliest part of what you see nowadays, the choir, dates from the 15th century, with the tower being added in 1511. It has some Renaissance glass, and it was here, in May 1559, that John Knox first preached after his exile on Europe. It more or less launched the Reformation in Scotland.

After the Reformation of 1560, the building was divided into three churches, with three distinct congregations. It wasn't until the early 20th century that the church housed one congregation again. The architect for the scheme was Sir Robert Lorimer, and the furnishings in the nave are mostly his work.

In Balhousie Castle in Hay Street you'll find the **Black Watch Regimental Museum**. Raised in 1725 to patrol or "watch" the Highlands after the first Jacobite Uprising, it is now the senior Highland regiment (see also Aberfeldy). The **Perth Museum and Art Gallery** is in George Street, and is one of the oldest in Britain. It houses material whose scope goes beyond the city and its immediate area, as well as a collection of fine paintings and sculpture. The **Fergusson Gallery** in Marshall Place is dedicated to the painter JD Fergusson (1874-1961), who, along with Peploe, Cadell and Hunter formed a group called the Scottish Colourists. The gallery opened in 1992 in a former waterworks of 1832.

In 1928 Sir Walter Scott's novel *The Fair Maid of Perth* was published, the heroine of which was Catherine Glover, daughter of Simon Glover, who lived in Curfew Row. It was set in the 14th century, and tells of how Catherine, a woman noted for her piety and beauty, was sought after by all the young men of the city. The Duke of Rothesay, son of Robert III, also admired her, though his intentions were not honourable. He was thwarted by Hal Gow, who came upon the Duke and his men trying to enter Catherine's house in the dead of night.

The ensuing skirmish resulted in one of the Duke's retainers having his hand hacked off by Hal before they fled in disarray. Catherine slept through it all, though Hal wakened her father and showed him the severed hand. The story ends happily when

Hal subsequently marries Catherine. The present **Fair Maid's House** (not open to the public) doesn't go back as far as the 14th century. However, it is over 300 years old, and incorporates some medieval walls, which may have belonged to the original house that stood on the site. In 1867 Bizet wrote his opera *The Fair Maid of Perth*, based on Scott's book, and the story became even more popular.

Cherrybank Gardens is an 18-acre garden on the western edge of the city. It incorporates the National Heather Collection, which has over 900 varieties of heather. **Kinnoull Hill**, to the east of Perth, rises to a height of 729 feet above the Tay. If you are reasonably fit, you can walk to the summit, where there is a folly, and get some wonderful views across the Tay and down over the Carse of Gowrie.

Scone Palace

Around Perth

Scone Palace

2 miles N of Perth off the A93

Historically and culturally, Scone (pronounced "Scoon") is one of the most important places in Scotland. When Kenneth MacAlpin, king of Dalriada, also became king of the Picts in AD 843, he quit his capital at Dunadd and moved to Scone. This was the beginning of the kingdom of Scotland.

Scone Abbey, (now gone) was built by Alexander I in the 12th century for the Augustinians, and was totally destroyed after the Reformation. Outside of it, on the **Moot Hill** (which can still be seen) the Scottish kings were crowned sitting on the Stone of Destiny (see also Dunadd and Edinburgh). A replica of the stone is to be found at the summit, along with a small chapel. The last king to be crowned at Scone was Charles II in 1651. This stone is also called Jacob's Pillow, and is supposed to have been the pillow on which the Biblical Jacob slept, though the present one, housed in Edinburgh, was almost

certainly quarried in Perthshire. However, there are those who say that when Edward I seized the stone in 1296, he was given a worthless copy by the monks of the abbey.

Scone Palace itself is the home of the Earls of Mansfield, and dates from the early 19th century. It has collections of fine furniture, porcelain and needlework.

Stanley

6 miles N of Perth on the B9099

The picturesque small village of Stanley sits on the River Tay, and is a former mill village. Sir Richard Arkwright had an interest in the mills here, the first of which was founded in 1786. Three large mills were built in the 1820s, powered by seven waterwheels. Four miles away are the ruins of 13th century **Kinclaven Castle**, once a favourite residence of Alexander II, who had built it. William Wallace captured the castle from the English in 1297.

Meikleour

10 miles N of Perth on A984

The **Meikleour Hedge,** just outside the village on the A93, is the world's largest. It borders the road for over 600 yards, and is now over 100 feet high. It is of pure beech, and was supposed to have been planted in 1745 by Jean Mercer and her husband Robert Murray Nairne, who died in battle at Culloden. Jean immediately left the area, and the hedge was allowed to grow unattended for many years.

Blairgowrie

14 miles N of Perth on the A93

This trim town, along with its sister village of **Rattray**, is noted as the centre of a

Burnside Inn

Mill Street, Alyth, Perthshire PH11 8PJ
Tel: 01828 633356 Fax: 01828 633864

The **Burnside Inn** is an attractive hostelry on a quiet street close to the town square, that offers a warm welcome to those looking for a relaxing drink or a beautifully cooked, hearty pub lunch. The inside is very spacious and boasts a public bar, a lounge bar and a dining room. Owners Marjorie and Stephen Irvine originate from Glasgow and have been here for 18 months. With the invaluable help of their daughter, they offer a warm welcome to locals and tourists alike.

The inn is open daily and lunches are served between 12noon and 2.30pm (except Monday and Tuesday). A pool table is available and there is live music every other Saturday night.

raspberry and strawberry growing area. It sits on the Ericht, a tributary of the Tay, and the riverside is very attractive. **Cargill's Visitor Centre**, housed in a former corn mill, sits on its banks, and has Scotland's largest water wheel.

The **Cateran Trail** is named after medieval brigands from beyond Braemar who used to descend on Perthshire to wreak havoc and steal cattle. It is a 60-mile long circular route centred on Blairgowrie, and uses existing footpaths and minor roads to take you on a tour of the area. It has been designed to take about five or six days to complete, with stops every 12 or 13 miles, and takes in parts of Angus as well as Perthshire.

Craighall Castle, the earliest parts of which date from the 16th century, are perched on a cliff above the Elricht. Sir Walter Scott visited it, and he used it as a model for Tullyveolan in his book *Waverley*.

Fingask Castle Cottages

Rait, Perthshire PH2 7SA
Tel: 01821 670777 Fax: 01821 670755
e-mail: gill@fingaskcastle.com
website: www.fingaskcastle.com

Set in 130 acres of one of Scotland's great gardens, **Fingask Castle** self-catering cottages offer excellent accommodation in a rural, woodland setting within easy reach of the cities of Perth and Dundee. It is an ideal base for touring, strolling around the castle grounds or relaxing in front of a log fire. There are five attractive cottages of varying size from 2-6 bedrooms some of which are en-suite. Each cottage has parking space, garden furniture, central heating, log fire, TV/video/DVD, pay phone, books, games, bath with separate shower, dishwasher, washing machine, fully equipped kitchen etc....Included in the price are electricity, heating, logs, towels and bedding. The cottages combine comfort with keen prices.

River Edge Lodges

Back Street, Bridge of Earn,
Perthshire PH2 9AB
Tel: 01738 812370 Fax: 01738 813161
e-mail: info@riveredgelodges.com
website: www.riveredgelodges.com

In the small, attractive village of Bridge of Earn are the **River Edge Lodges**, situated in secluded grounds and offering superior self-catering accommodation. The lodges are of cedar, and have either one, two or three bedrooms. They are all very well appointed, with fully-equipped kitchens, bathrooms with bath and shower and full heating throughout. Situated on the banks of the River Earn, this is the ideal place to have a relaxing family holiday while still being close to all the amenities of Perth. There is plenty of scope for a wide variety of activities, including golf, fishing, walking and pony trekking.

Coupar Angus

12 miles NE of Perth on the A94

Situated in Strathmore, Coupar Angus is a small town, which was given its burgh charter in 1607. The scant remains of **Coupar Angus Abbey**, founded by David I for the Cistercians in 1164, stand in the kirkyard. At one time it was the wealthiest Cistercian abbey in Scotland. The town's **Tolbooth** dates from 1702, and was used as a courthouse and prison.

Errol

8 miles E of Perth on a minor road off the A90

Set in the Carse of Gowrie, a narrow stretch of fertile land bordering the northern shore of the Firth of Tay, Errol is a peaceful village with a large **Parish Church** of 1831, which is sometimes called the "cathedral of the Carse". It gives its name to an earldom, which means that there is an "Earl of Errol" (see Slains Castle). A leaflet is available which gives details of most of the old kirkyards and kirks in the Carse.

Elcho

3 miles SE of Perth on a minor road

Elcho Castle (Historic Scotland) was the ancient seat of the Earls of Wemyss. The present castle was built by Sir John Wemyss, who died in 1572, in the 16th century on the site of an earlier fortification dating from the 13th century.

By about 1780, the castle had been abandoned, and it gradually became ruinous. It was re-roofed in 1830.

Abernethy

6 miles SE of Perth on the A913

The 75 feet high **Abernethy Round Tower** (Historic Scotland) is one of only two round towers in Scotland (see also Brechin). It dates from the end of the 11th century, and was used as a place of refuge for priests during times of trouble. At the foot of the tower is a carved Pictish stone.

In 1072 Malcolm III met William the Conquerer here and knelt in submission, acknowledging him as his overlord. The **Abernethy Museum**, founded in the year 2000, explains the village's history, and is house in an 18th century building.

Forteviot

6 miles SW of Perth on the B935

This little village was at one time the capital of a Pictish kingdom. In a field to the north of the River Earn stood the **Dupplin Cross**, erected, it is thought, in the 9th century by King Constantine I, son of Kenneth I, Scotland's first king. It was taken to the National Museum of Scotland in 1998 for restoration, after which it was housed in St Serf's Church in Dunning.

Dunning

8 miles SW of Perth on the B934

This quiet village is mainly visited because of **St Serf's Parish Church**, with its fine early 13th century tower. The original church was probably built by Gilbert, Earl of Strathearn, in about 1200. It now houses the Dupplin Cross. A couple of miles outside the village, near the road, is a monument topped with a cross which marks the spot where, according to its inscription, **Maggie Wall**, a witch, was burned in 1657. It is the only memorial to a witch in Scotland, though no record has ever been found about the trial or execution of someone called Maggie Wall. The whole thing - including who actually built the cairn - remains a mystery.

Auchterarder

12 miles SW of Perth on the A824

Situated a couple of miles north of the Gleneagles Hotel, Auchterarder is a small royal burgh with a long main street. It has been bypassed by the busy A9, and retains a quiet charm. At **Auchterarder Heritage**, within the local tourist office in the High Street, there are displays about local history.

About three miles west of the town, near the A823, is the cruciform **Tullibardine Chapel** (Historic Scotland), one of the few finished collegiate chapels in Scotland that have remained unaltered over the years. It was founded by Sir David Murray of Tullibardine, ancestor of the Dukes of Atholl, in 1446.

Muthill

15 miles SW of Perth on the A822

Within the village are the ruins of the former **Muthill Parish Church** (Historic Scotland), which date mainly from the early 15th century, though the tower was probably built in the 12th century. A settlement of Culdee priests existed here before the church was built.

Three miles east of Muthill, at **Innerpeffray**, is **Innerpeffray Library**, one of the oldest libraries in Scotland. It was founded in 1691 by David Drummond, brother-in-law of the Marquis of Montrose, and is housed in a building specially built for it in 1750. It contains many rare books, such as a copy of the 16th century Treacle Bible, so called because the translation of Jeremiah chapter 8 verse 22 reads, "Is there not triacle (treacle) at Gilead". There is also a 1508 *Ship of Fools*, a medieval satire written by a German writer called Simon Brant. Before moving to its present building it was housed in **Innerpeffray Chapel**, (Historic Scotland), built in 1508 by Sir John Drummond of Innerpeffray as a collegiate church.

Drummond Castle Gardens

Muthill, Crieff, Perthshire PH5 2AA
Tel: 01764 681257 Fax: 01764 681550
e-mail: info@drummondcastle.sol.co.uk
website: www.drummondcastlegardens.co.uk

Described as one of the finest formal gardens in Europe, **Drummond Castle Gardens** were first laid out in the early 17th century by John Drummond, the 2nd Earl of Perth and include a JohnMylne sundial erected in 1630. The gardens were renewed in the 1950's by Phyllis Astor, preserving features such as the ancient yew hedges and the copper beech trees planted by Queen Victoria to commemorate her visit in 1842. Open Easter weekend and then May to October 2pm-6pm. The castle is not open to the public.

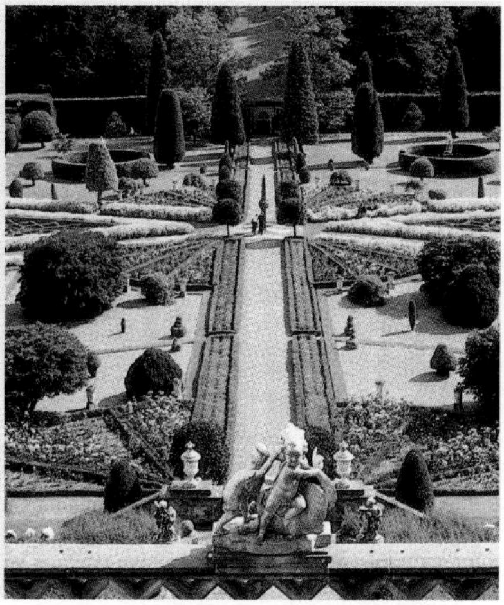

To the west of the village you'll find **Drummond Castle Gardens** (see panel above), one of Perthshire's hidden jewels. They were first laid out in the 17th century, improved and terraced in the 19th, and replanted in the middle of the 20th. In 1842, Queen Victoria visited, and planted some copper beech trees, which can still be seen.

To the east of the village are the sites of two Roman signal stations - the **Ardunie Signal Station** and the **Muir O'Fauld Signal Station**. They were two of a series of such stations running between Ardoch and the Tay, and date to the 1st century AD.

Hunting Tower

2 miles W of Perth on the A85

Huntingtower (Historic Scotland) is a restored 15th century tower house once owned by the Ruthvens, Earls of Gowrie. In 1582 the famous "Raid of Ruthven" took place here, when the Earl and his friend the Earl of Mar tried to kidnap the young King James VI.

Fowlis Wester

12 miles W of Perth on a minor road off the A85

The **Parish Church of St Bean** sits on a spot where a church has stood since at least the eighth century. The present one dates from the 15th century, and is dedicated to an 8th century Irish saint who preached in the area. A ten-foot high cross slab with Pictish carvings stands within the church, as does a smaller one as well. A replica of the larger one stands on the village green. Also in the church is a fragment of the McBean tartan, taken to the moon by American astronaut Alan Bean, who was the lunar module pilot on Apollo 12 during the second mission to the moon in November 1969, and the fourth man to walk on its surface.

Crieff

15 miles W of Perth on the A85

This inland holiday resort is the "capital" of that area of Scotland known as Strathearn. It sits at the beginning of Glen Turret, within which are the picturesque **Falls Of Turret**. At the **Crieff Visitor Centre** on Muthill Road you can see paperweights, pottery and miniature animal sculptures. The **Glenturret Distillery** at the Hosh, home of the famous "Grouse Experience", is Scotland's oldest, and tours (with a dram at the end) are available.

The 3,480 feet high **Ben Choznie,** eight miles north west of Crieff, has been described as the "most boring Munro in Scotland". It can be climbed via a route leaving the car park at Loch Turret dam.

Madderty

10 miles W of Perth off the A85

To the north east of this village is the site of **Inchaffray Abbey**, of which nothing now remains apart from a low mound. The name means "island of the smooth waters", as at one time the mound was an island within a small loch.

The abbot of Inchaffray was the keeper of a holy relic called the Arm of St Fillan, and at the Battle of Bannockburn he paraded it before the Scottish troops to bring good fortune (see also St Fillans, Tyndrum and Pittenweem).

Comrie

21 miles W of Perth on the A85

This village is often called the "earthquake capital of Scotland", as it sits right on the Highland Boundary Fault. James Melville, writing in his diary in July 1597, mentions an earth tremor, though the first fully recorded one was in 1788. In 1839 a major one took place. **The Earthquake House**, built in 1874, houses an array of instruments to measure the tremors. North of the village, in Glen Lednock, is the **De'ils Cauldron Waterfall,** overlooked by a monument to Henry Dundas, 1st Viscount Melville (1742-1811). The village was the "Best Large Village" in the 2001 Britain in Bloom contest.

St Fillans

26 miles W of Perth on the A85

St Fillans stands at the eastern end of Loch Earn, where the River Earn exits on its way to join the Firth of Tay, and is a gateway to the new Loch Lomond and Trossachs National Park. It is named after the Irish missionary St Fillan (see also Pittenweem, Tyndrum and Madderty). Two relics of the saint - his bell and his pastoral staff - are now housed within the National Museum of Scotland. At the top of **Dunfillan Hill** (600 feet) is a rock known as **St Fillan's Chair**. To the southwest, overlooking Loch Earn, is **Ben Vorlich** (3,224 feet).

Pitlochry

This well-known Scottish town is one of the best touring bases in Scotland. It is said to be at the geographical heart of the country, and as such, it is as far from the sea as it is possible to be in Scotland. It was the 2003 winner as the "best small country town" in the Britain in Bloom contest.

Though not a large town, it is full of hotels and guesthouses, and makes a good stopping off point for those travelling further north. But it has its own attractions, not least of which is the marvellous scenery surrounding it. The B8019, the famous **Road to the Isles**, goes west towards Loch Tummel, whose waters have been harnessed for electricity, and is particularly beautiful. It passes the **Forestry Commission Visitor Centre**, which interprets the wildlife of the area. From the **Queen's View** there is a magnificent view west towards Loch Tummel and beyond. Queen Victoria stopped at this point during her

Queens View, Loch Tummel

Dancers and Piper at the Pitlochry Games

Highland tour in 1866 and praised the view, though it is said that it was Mary Stuart who originally gave the place its name when she visited in 1564.

Loch Faskally is close to Pitlochry, and is a man-made loch. It is still a lovely stretch of water, and forms part of the Tummel hydroelectric scheme. At the **Pitlochry Visitor Centre**, near the dam, there is the famous **Salmon Ladder**, which allows salmon to enter the loch from the River Tummel below. There is a viewing gallery, which allows you to watch the salmon, and displays about how electricity is produced from flowing water. Beside the loch is a picnic area, with an archway called the **Clunie Arch**. It is the exact dimensions of the tunnel that brings the waters from Loch Tummel to the Clunie Power Station.

The Poplars & Poppies Cottage

27 Low Oakfield , Pitlochry,
Perthshire PH16 5DS
Tel: 01796 472129
e-mail: gwtait@btopenworld.com

Owned and run by Janice and Gerry Tait, **The Poplars** is a superb stone-built Victorian villa which has been converted to offer first class B&B accommodation. There are seven en suite rooms retaining many of their original features while still offering all that is best in modern comfort and conveniences. In the grounds is Poppies - a self-catering cottage which sleeps six in absolute comfort. The Poplars is only a stroll away from the shops and restaurants of the picturesque town of Pitlochry.

Buttonboss Lodge

Atholl Road, Pitlochry, Perthshire PH16 5BX
Tel/Fax: 01796 472065 or
Tel 01796 473000
e-mail: colin@buttonboss.fsnet.co.uk
website: www.smoothhound.co.uk/hotels/buttonbo.html

You're assured of a warm and friendly welcome at **Buttonboss Lodge**, a wonderful B&B in Pitlochry, one of the most picturesque villages in Perthshire. There are eight guest bedrooms - seven en suite and one with private facilities, and all are cosy, comfortable and decorated to an extremely high standard. A self-catering bungalow is also available nearby, and it shares the same high standards as the B&B itself. The dining room is smart and spacious, and the owners, Marleen and Colin Mackay, are renowned for their friendliness and their in depth knowledge of what to see in the area.

Balnakilly Highland Cottages And Log Cabins

Kirkmichael, Perthshire PH10 7NB
Tel/Fax: 01250 881356
e-mail: balnakilly@hotmail.com
website: www.balnakillyestate.co.uk

Set in the most beautiful part of Perthshire, near the village of Kirkmichael, you will find the **Balnakilly Highland Cottages and Log Cabins**. They are within the 1,500 acre Balnakilly Estate, so offer privacy, comfort and superb facilities at a price that is surprisingly reasonable. The climate here is drier and sunnier than in most areas of Scotland, and is ideal if you enjoy history, heritage, wildlife and outdoor activities.

The estate offers two traditional stone cottages, four log cabins, one farmhouse and an elegant Norwegian timber house, offering the choice of modern or traditional. Each one is warm in winter and cool in summer, and are furnished to an extremely high standard so that your stay is comfortable and enjoyable. All properties have colour TV, and many have added features like open fires.

Loch Cottage has two bedrooms, a dining room and a sitting room, bathroom and kitchen, and can sleep up to five people in absolute comfort. Strathview Farmhouse, as its name implies, has superb views. There are three double bedrooms that can sleep up to seven, a sitting room, dining room, kitchen and bathroom. The kitchen comes with an Aga cooker (worked by gas), a dishwasher and a washing machine. The farmhouse also has part central heating, and there is a garage, stables and a garden.

Rowan Lodge offers the highest possible standards of accommodation. There is a spacious lounge, a telephone, a dining room, kitchen and toilet downstairs, and three comfortable bedrooms with balconies and bathroom upstairs. It boasts a fully automatic heating system plus a wood burning stove. The kitchen has an automatic dishwasher and washing machine.

The log cabins each have living/kitchen/dining rooms with modern fitments. Each has two bedrooms, one with a double bed and the other with twin beds. The open patios are sun traps, and sitting outside in the evening is one of the pleasures of the cabins. They are full insulated throughout, and are ideal for winter as well as summer use.

Downies, clean covers and pillows are provided free of charge, and linen, such as sheets, pillow cases and towels can also be provided at a small fee. Well behaved pets are welcome, though there is a small charge.

The **Edradour Distillery,** situated among the hills to the east of Pitlochry, is Scotland's smallest, and possibly its most picturesque distillery. It was established in 1837 and produces handcrafted malt using only local barley. Conducted tours, finished off with a tasting, are available. Bell's **Blair Atholl Distillery** is the oldest working distillery in Scotland, and is also in Pitlochry.

Another place not to be missed is the **Pitlochry Festival Theatre**. It was founded in 1951, and presented its first plays in a tent. It continued like this until 1981, when a purpose-built theatre was opened at Port-na-Craig on the banks of the Tummel. It presents a varied programme of professional plays every summer, and is one of Scotland's most popular venues.

The A924 going east from Pitlochry takes you up into some marvellous scenery. It reaches a height of 1,260 feet before dropping down into Kirkmichael and then on to Bridge of Cally. On the way, at Enochdhu, you will pass **Kindrogan**, a Victorian country house where the Scottish Field Studies Association offer residential courses on Scotland's natural history.

There are many fine guided walks in the area, some organised by such bodies as National Trust for Scotland, the Scottish Wildlife Trust and the Forestry Commission. A small booklet about them is available.

Around Pitlochry

Spittal of Glenshee

13 miles NE of Pitlochry on the A93

As the name suggests, a small medieval hospital, or "spittal", once stood close to this village, which lies in the heart of the Grampian Mountains at a height of 1,125 feet. It sits on the main road north from Perth to Braemar, and surrounding it is some marvellous scenery. The Glenshee skiing area (Britain's largest) lies six miles north of the village, and is dealt with in the North East Scotland section of this guidebook. The **Devil's Elbow** on the A93 lies about five miles north. A combination of steep inclines and double bends made it a notorious place for accidents in days gone by, though it has been much improved. At **Cairnwell** the road reaches a height of 2,199 feet, making it the highest public road in Britain. During the winter months the road can be blocked by snow for weeks on end.

Dunkeld

11 miles S of Pitlochry off the A9

Though it has all the appearance of an attractive town, Dunkeld is in fact a small cathedral city. **Dunkeld Cathedral** sits on the banks of the Tay, and consists of a ruined nave and a restored chancel, which is now used as the parish church.

For a short period Dunkeld was the ecclesiastical capital of Scotland. Kenneth 1, when he ascended the throne as the first king of Scots in AD 843, established his capital at Scone, near Perth, and brought relics of St Columba with him, no doubt because Iona was too vulnerable to Viking attack. He placed them in the church of a Celtic monastery set up at Dunkeld, which

Farming at Strath Barn, Dunkeld

The Pend

5 Brae Street, Dunkeld, Perthshire PH8 0BA
Tel: 01350 727586 Fax: 01350 727173
e-mail: molly@thepend.sol.co.uk
website: www.thepend.com

Housed in an elegant building of c.1840, **The Pend** offers three comfortable and well furnished rooms to discerning guests. In the 2003 edition of *Which Good Hotel Guide* it gained an award as the best B&B in Scotland. Evening meals are available, and as it is *Taste of Scotland* accredited, the food in the combined sitting/dining room is superb. The Pend is close to the centre of this small cathedral town. Well behaved pets are welcome. It makes the ideal base for exploring this beautiful part of Scotland, or the perfect stopping off place when heading north or south.

in AD 865 was the seat of the chief Scottish bishop, though St Andrews took over in the middle of the 10th century.

The cathedral as we see it nowadays dates from many periods. The choir (the present parish church) was built mainly in the early 14th century, while the nave (now ruined) was built in the early 15th century. Within the church is the tomb of Alexander Stewart, son of Robert II and known as the Wolf of Badenoch, the man who sacked Elgin Cathedral in the 14th century after a disagreement with the Bishop of Moray (see also Elgin and Fortrose).

In 1689 the town was the scene of the **Battle of Dunkeld**, when Jacobite forces were defeated by a force of Cameronians under **William Cleland**. This was an unusual battle, as the fighting and gunfire took place in the streets and buildings of the town, and not in open countryside. William Cleland was fatally wounded

The Taybank

Tay Terrace, Dunkeld, Perthshire PH8 0AQ
Tel: 01350 727340 Fax: 01350 727979
e-mail: admin@thetaybank.com
website: www.thetaybank.com

Music and value for money are the keywords at **The Taybank** inn, which offers five comfortable guest rooms at remarkably reasonable prices. There is a music bar downstairs with spontaneous sessions, and upstairs in the Music Gallery on some weekday evenings there are music learning sessions. On Friday evening a folk club meets, complementing the music theme. When the weather is warm, you can relax in the riverside garden with a drink from the bar. Food is traditional and hearty, though lighter options are available. This is the ideal base from which to explore the area, or to stay overnight as you pass north or south along the A9.

The Hermitage, Dunkeld

during the encounter, and now lies in the ruined nave of the cathedral.

Another, but not so famous, man lies in the nave of the cathedral. Curiously enough he lies beside William Cleland, and yet he was the grandson of the greatest Jacobite of them all, Charles Edward Stuart. The Prince's illegitimate daughter Charlotte had an affair with the Archbishop of Rouen, the result being **Count Rohenstart** (a name made up from "Rouen" and "Stuart"). On a trip to Scotland in 1854 he was killed in a carriage accident.

Most of the "little houses" in Dunkeld date from the early 18th century, as they were built to replace those that had been destroyed in the battle. Now the National Trust for Scotland looks after most of them. On the wall of one house in the square, the

Black Watch Inn

Bank Street, Aberfeldy, Perthshire PH15 2BB
Tel: 01887 820699 Fax: 01887 879532
e-mail: blackwatch@tesco.net

The small town of Aberfeldy, on the banks of the Tay, is where Scotland's senior regiment first paraded in 1740 under the Earl of Crawford. It had been formed from six independent regiments, raised to "watch" the Highlands for signs of Jacobite unrest. It was at that time called the 43rd Highland Regiment of Foot, and later changed its name to the Black Watch - undoubtedly the most famous of all Scottish regiments.

And in Bank Street, in the centre of this picturesque town, you will find a wonderful

inn that carries the same proud name - the **Black Watch Inn**. It is an elegant, stone-built hostelry that has recently been refurbished to an extremely high standard, yet retains all the period features that mark out an inn as something special. Owned and run by Chris Walls and Matt Mackie, it offers all that is best in genuine Scottish hospitality. It combines value for money with high standards of service, and at the same time is friendly and welcoming to both visitors and locals alike.

The bar carries a full range of drinks, from fine wines to whiskies (including a range of single malts), beers and liqueurs. If you are behind the wheel, then there is also a range of soft drinks on offer. The staff are friendly and knowledgeable, and can point you in the direction of all the historic sites in an area that is full of history and heritage.

This is an inn that is a favourite with the locals, which is always a good sign!

There is also a cosy yet spacious restaurant which serves mouth watering meals and bar snacks. The cuisine is Scottish with a few foreign influences, and the kitchens use only the finest and freshest of local produce wherever possible. The lunch/supper menu includes everything from haddock in a Belhaven Ale batter and chips to spaghetti carbonara with garlic bread. Plus you can order Scottish specialities such as mince and tatties (potatoes) with herb dumplings and herring in oatmeal with new tatties. And, of course, there is the ever popular sizzling fillet steak (from prime Scottish beef) with all the trimmings.

The bar snack menu includes sandwiches, filled baguettes and paninis, baked potatoes, stuffed Scotch pancakes, "lang tatties" (hand cut chips), Forfar bridies, Ayrshire ham and scampi in a basket. For the over 18s there is even a "pie and a pint"!

A three bedroom flat will be available from Spring 2005 for holiday let.

Ell Shop, is portrayed an old Scottish length of measurement called the "ell", which corresponds to 37 inches. Also in the square is the **Atholl Memorial Fountain**, erected in 1866 in memory of the 6th Duke of Atholl.

At the Birnam Institute is the **Beatrix Potter Gardens**, and within the Institute itself there is a small exhibition, which tells the story of the young Beatrix. She used to holiday in the area, and gained some of her inspiration from the surrounding countryside.

This is the heartland of the "big tree country", and it was in Dunkeld, in 1738, that the first larches were planted in Scotland.

Wade's Bridge, Aberfeldy

Aberfeldy

8 miles SW of Pitlochry on the A827

In 1787 Robert Burns wrote a song called *The Birks of Aberfeldy*, and made famous this small town and its surrounding area. "Birks" are simply birch trees, though some people claim that Burns was actually

writing about Abergeldie near Crathie in Aberdeenshire.

The village sits on the River Tay, and crossing it is **General Wade's Bridge**, built in 1733 by **Major-General George Wade**, Commander-in-Chief of North Britain from 1724 until 1740 ("Scotland" was not a name that was liked by the English establishment at the time). It was part of a road network so that the Highlands could be properly policed during the Jacobite unrest. At about the same time, six independent regiments were raised to "watch" the Highlands for signs of this unrest. These six regiments later amalgamated to form the 43rd Highland Regiment of Foot under the Earl of Crawford, and it paraded for the first time at Aberfeldy in May 1740. The regiment later became the Black Watch, and the **Black Watch Memorial**, built in 1887, near the bridge commemorates the event.

Right on the A827 is **Dewar's World of Whisky**. Here you will find out about one of Scotland's most famous whisky firms, located in the distillery where Aberfeldy Single Malt is made.

A mile or so north west of the village, near Weem is **Castle Menzies**, home to Clan Menzies (pronounced Ming -iz in Scotland). James Menzies of Menzies, son-in-law of the then Earl of Atholl, built it in the 16th century. The last member of the main line died in 1910, and it is now owned by the Menzies Charitable Trust. Parts of it are open to the public, and it houses a Clan Menzies museum. Charles Edward Stuart spent two nights within its walls in 1746 on his way to Culloden.

Kenmore

13 miles SW of Pitlochry on the A827

Kenmore sits at the eastern end of **Loch Tay**, and was founded in about 1540 by the Earls of Breadalbane. The loch is the source of the River Tay, one of the most

Fishing for Salmon, Kenmore

picturesque in Scotland. It is fourteen and a half miles long, less than a mile wide, and plunges to a maximum depth of over 500 feet. Overlooking it, on the northern shore, is **Ben Lawers** (4,033 feet), with the **Ben Lawers Mountain Visitor Centre** (National Trust for Scotland) on a minor road off the A827. There is a nature trail, and a booklet is available at the centre.

The Scottish Crannog Centre, run by the Scottish Trust for Underwater Archaeology, explains how people in the past lived in crannogs, which were dwelling houses situated in the shallow waters of a loch that offered defence against attack. They were either built on artificial islands or raised on stilts above the water, and were in use from about 2500 BC right up until the 17th century. Off the north shore of the loch is **Eilean nan Bannoamh** ("Isle of the Holy Women") where once stood a small nunnery founded in the 13th century.

Fortingall

15 miles SW of Pitlochry on a minor road off the B846

This little village has a unique claim to fame. It is said to be the birthplace of **Pontius Pilate**, the governor of Judea at the time of Christ's execution. It is said that his father, a Roman officer, was sent to Scotland by Augustus Caesar to command a unit, which kept the local Pictish clans in check. Whether Pontius was born of a union between Pontius and a local woman, or whether Pontius had brought a wife with him, isn't recorded. There is no proof that the story is true, but there was certainly a Roman camp nearby.

Sir Donald Currie laid out Fortingall as a model village in the 19th century, and it

has some picturesque thatched cottages that wouldn't look out of place in a South of England village. In the kirkyard of the early 20th century parish church is the **Fortingall Yew**, said to be the oldest living thing in Europe. The tree looks rather the worse for wear nowadays, but as it may be as much as 3,000 years old, perhaps this isn't surprising.

In a field next to the village is the 16th century **Cairn of the Dead**, which marks the mass grave of plague victims during the *galar mhor*, or great plague. It is said that one old woman, who was still sufficiently healthy, carried the bodies to the field on a horse-drawn sledge.

The village sits at the entrance to **Glen Lyon**, at 25 miles long, Scotland's longest, and perhaps loveliest, glen. Tumbling through it is the River Lyon, which rises at Loch Lyon, part of a massive hydroelectric scheme. At Bridge of Balgie a minor road strikes south, rising into some wild scenery and passing **Meall Luaidhe** (2,535 feet) before dropping down towards the Ben Lawers Mountain Visitor Centre (see Kenmore) and the shores of Loch Tay. Bridge of Balgie is also home to a gallery that houses prints and original paintings by renowned artist Alan Hayman.

On the B846 four miles north of Fortingall is the **Glengoulandie Deer Park**, with its herd of red deer, Highland cattle, goats and rare breeds of sheep.

Kinloch Rannoch

17 miles W of Pitlochry on the B846

This small village, laid out in the 18th century by James Small, a government factor, sits at the eastern end of **Loch Rannoch**, which has roads on both the northern and southern sides. It is overlooked by the conically shaped **Schiehallion** (3,547 feet), from the summit of which there is a wonderful view as far south as the Lowlands.

An obelisk in the centre of the village commemorates **Dugald Buchanan**, who died here in 1786. He was one of the Highland's greatest religious poets, and was buried at Balquidder.

Loch Rannoch

The B846 carries on westward past Kinloch Rannoch, and skirts the northern shores of Loch Rannoch. It eventually comes to an end at **Rannoch Station**. This station, on the Glasgow/Fort William line, is the loneliest railway station in Britain. Beyond it is **Rannoch Moor**, said to be the most desolate spot in Scotland, and "Europe's last great wilderness". In the winter, when snow covers it, it is treacherous, and no one should venture out onto it unless they're experienced. Even in summer, when it is hauntingly beautiful, it should still be treated with respect.

But the moor's landscape isn't a natural one. Even here, man has made his mark. The whole of the moor was once covered in the trees of the old Caledonian Forest, but man gradually cleared them to use as fuel and for building. The whole of the moor is littered with large boulders, debris carried by the glaciers that once covered this area.

Killiecrankie

3 miles N of Pitlochry off the A9

It was here, in 1689, that the **Battle of Killiecrankie** took place. The Pass of Killiecrankie is a narrow defile, and as government troops under General Mackay passed gingerly through it, they were attacked from above by Jacobite forces under Bonnie Dundee (see also Blair Atholl). It ended in a victory for the Jacobites, but Bonnie Dundee himself was killed. The **Killiecrankie Visitors Centre** (National Trust for Scotland) has displays explaining the battle.

At the north end of the pass is a spot known as the **Soldier's Leap**, high above the River Garry. It is said that, after the battle, a government trooper called Donald McBean leapt across the 18-foot wide gap to escape from some Jacobites who were chasing him.

Killiecrankie Visitor Centre

Blair Atholl

6 miles NW of Pitlochry off the A9

Blair Castle is one of the most famous castles in Scotland. It sits above the village, and with its whitewashed walls looks more like a great fortified mansion house than a castle. It is the ancestral home of the Murrays, Dukes of Atholl, and originally dates from 1269, though what you see nowadays is mainly from the 18th and 19th century refurbishments. About 30 furnished rooms are open to the public, with fine furniture, paintings, china and armour on display. The Duke of Atholl is the only person in Britain who is allowed to have a private army, the **Atholl Highlanders**, and a small museum has displays of uniforms, weapons and musical instruments.

In the kirkyard of **St Bride's Kirk** in Old Blair is the grave of John Graham, 1st Viscount Dundee, known as "Bonnie Dundee", who was killed at the Battle of Killiecrankie in 1689 (see also Killiecrankie). At Bruar, four miles north of Blair Atholl, is the **Clan Donnachaidh Museum**. Though the name translates into English as Donnachie, it traces the history of the Clan Robertson, and shows their place in local and Scottish history. **The Falls of Bruar** are close by, and fall through a picturesque ravine, with footbridges over them.

North East Scotland

North East Scotland is not what it seems. The area isn't really in the far north east of the country, which could be defined as the former county of Caithness, but centred on the city of Aberdeen, much further south.

The area abounds in scenery of all kinds. High mountains, wooded glens, cityscapes, beaches, rich farmland, towering cliffs and moorland - it's got the lot. And yet it is relatively unknown by those outside Scotland, apart from some areas in the Grampians and along Deeside. The beaches are quiet and uncrowded, the country lanes are a joy to drive in, and there is history and heritage aplenty.

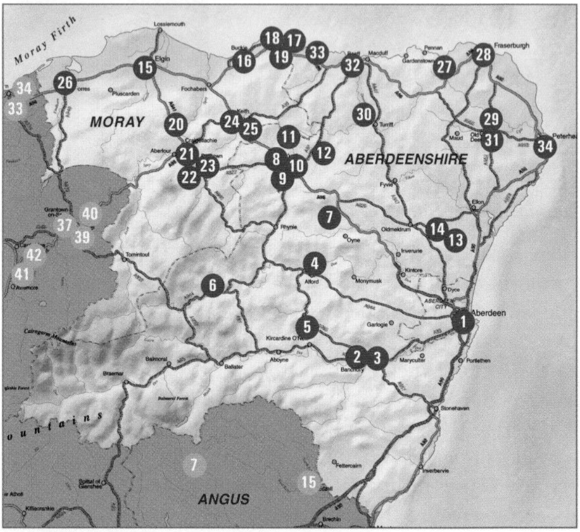

And always, in the background are the Grampians, which form a chain diagonally across Scotland, and which reach their highest peaks here. Queen Victoria

PLACES TO STAY, EAT AND DRINK

Gordon Highlanders Museum, Aberdeen	1	Visitor Attraction	p301
Burnett Arms Hotel, Banchory	2	Hotel	p305
Crathes Castle & Gardens, Banchory	3	Visitor Attraction	p305
Macbrae Lodge, Montgarrie	4	B&B	p306
Crossroads Hotel, Lumphanan	5	Pub, Restaurant & Accommodation	p307
Colquhonnie Hotel, Strathdon	6	Hotel	p307
The Mews at Drumrossie House, Insh	7	Self Catering	p310
Gordon Arms Hotel, Huntly	8	Hotel	p311
The Coffee House, Huntly	9	Café	p312
Dunedin Guest House, Huntly	10	Guest House	p313
Forbes Arms Hotel, Milltown of Rothiemay	11	Hotel	p313
Bognie Arms Hotel, Forgue	12	Hotel	p314
Udny Station Hotel, Udny Station	13	Pub with Restaurant	p314
Eat on the Green, Udny Green	14	Restaurant	p315
Royal Hotel, Elgin	15	Hotel	p316
The Old Coach House, Buckie	16	Hotel	p318
Three Kings, Cullen	17	Pub, Food and Accommodation	p319

● Denotes entries in other chapters

Heather on the Grouse Moors

popularised Deeside, a glen which goes deep into the heart of the mountains, and it has remained firmly on the tourist trail ever since. But as with many parts of Scotland, the tourist traps (such as Deeside and Aberdeen) swarm with people, while other places, equally as interesting and picturesque, are bypassed.

To go off the beaten track in the North East is to be rewarded with some wonderful discoveries. But who takes the time to find out about them? Who goes in search of the real Grampians? Who has explored the farmlands of Buchan, with their rich soil, which, even though they are above the Highland line, have more of a Lowland feel about them? How many people stop in Kincardineshire, with its fishing villages and its literary connections? It was here that Robert Burns's father was born. It was here that Lewis Grassic Gibbon, a local man, set his dark novels of country life - ones that had little to do with the couthy images of happy, rustic people that had prevailed up until then. And who, except those in the know, visit Elgin, a charming small city with the ruins of what was one of the largest and grandest cathedrals in Scotland?

Nowhere else in Europe is there such a concentration of historic castles - around 1,000 at the last count. The local tourist board has organised a Castle Trail, with a leaflet that explains their history and how you get to them. And then there are the

PLACES TO STAY, EAT AND DRINK

● Denotes entries in other chapters

Fisherman on the River

distilleries. The industry is centred mainly on Banffshire and Moray, where the streams are swift flowing and the water pure. It's amazing that two distilleries a mile or so apart can make whiskies that are totally different in character. The local tourist board has laid out a Whisky Trail, and like the Castle Trail there's a leaflet as well.

The inland villages are quiet and peaceful, and the market towns, such as Inverurie, Forres and Huntly, are packed with history and charm. The coastline is as dramatic as anywhere in Britain. Yet another trail, the Coastal Trail, takes you on a tour, from St Cyrus in the south to Findhorn in the west. The ruins of Dunnottar castle are perched dramatically above the sea, while the Ythan Estuary is a Site of Scientific Interest, rich in aquatic and bird life as well as having archaeological sites dating back to Neolithic times. Slains Castle, south of Peterhead, was one of the inspirations for Bram Stoker's *Dracula*, and the fishing port of Fraserburgh was, for a very short time, a university town.

For all its crowds (especially in late summer when the Queen is there), Deeside cannot be missed. This long glen, following the Dee, winds up into the heart of the Grampians, with Braemar, at its heart, being officially Britain's coldest place (though summer days can be balmy and long). But don't let the seeming remoteness put you off - the glen is green and wooded for most of its length. Balmoral - Crathie - Aboyne - the names are familiar to us all through news programmes, and yet the reality of seeing them makes you realise why Queen Victoria, and subsequent monarchs, fell in love with Royal Deeside in the first place.

Aberdeen is Scotland's third largest city, and Europe's oil capital. The name, which means "at the mouth of the Dee and the Don", sums up its location exactly, as the two rivers enter the North Sea here. The oil industry has brought money to the city, and it has also brought a cosmopolitan lifestyle that includes smart restaurants, boutiques, nightclubs and stylish pubs. But even here history is never far away. It was granted a royal charter by King William the Lion in 1175, and Old Aberdeen, which used to be a proud separate burgh, was granted its charter in 1489.

The other city in the region is Elgin, at one time one of the most important places in Scotland. It has lost some of that importance now, but hasn't lost any of its charm. It is still a busy place, the shopping and administrative centre for a large fertile area called the Laigh of Moray. Here too there are quiet country lanes and small villages to explore, while at Findhorn there is the Findhorn Foundation, where the emphasis is on spiritual living and alternative lifestyles.

Aberdeen

With a population of about 220,000, Aberdeen is Scotland's third largest city. Its nickname is the "Granite City" because of the predominant building material - one which has created a stylish and attractive place that seems to glisten in the sun. It prides itself on being Scotland's most prosperous city, due to the vast oil fields that lie beneath the North Sea. For this reason it is also known as the "Oil Capital of Europe", and the docks and harbours, which were once full of fishing boats, now pulse with supply ships ferrying men and machines out to the oil rigs.

River Dee Suspension Bridge, Aberdeen

But Aberdeen has yet two more nicknames - "Scotland's Garden City" and the "Flower of Scotland". Both derive from the many gardens and colourful open spaces that can be visited. It has won awards for its floral displays (including many "Britain in Bloom" awards), with **Johnston Gardens**, **Hazelhead Park**, **Union Terrace Gardens, Duthie Park** and the **Cruickshank Botanic Gardens** offering particularly fine examples. In 2003 Aberdeen took silver in the "Nations in Bloom" competition, beaten only by Seattle, USA, and Quanzhou, China.

It is also a centre of learning, administration, shopping and business. But it has never been scarred by industry in the way that some Central Belt towns have. It has managed to remain above such things, and its quality of life is among the best in Britain.

And for all its bustle and modern office blocks, it is an ancient city, having been granted a charter as a royal burgh in 1175. Even then it was an important and busy port, trading with the Baltic States as well as the Netherlands and France. During the Wars of Independence it was sacked three times by the English, and finally razed to the ground by Edward III in 1337. One unexpected early visitor to Aberdeen was William Shakespeare, who, with his troupe of actors, was sent by Elizabeth I to appear before James VI.

There are two Aberdeens - the original one, and Old Aberdeen, which was at one time a separate

Riverside, Aberdeen

burgh. Perversely Old Aberdeen was only granted its charter in 1489, and is a captivating area of old, elegant buildings and quiet cobbled streets.

The buildings you see throughout the city nowadays however, are mainly Georgian, Victorian and later, with some older buildings among them to add historical depth. The **Cathedral Church of St Machar's** in Old Aberdeen was founded in about 1131, and is dedicated to a saint who was a companion of St Columba. Legend states that he was sent by his companion to convert the Picts in the area, and had a vision from God to build a church at a point where a river bends in the shape of a bishop's crosier just before it enters the sea. As the Don bends in this way, he established his church here in about AD 580.

St Machar's as we see it today dates from the 14th century and later. The choir has completely disappeared, and what you see now was the nave of the original cathedral. In 1688 the central tower collapsed, leaving a rather truncated building with a beautiful west front with two towers. Perhaps its most famous bishop was **William Elphinstone**, Chancellor of Scotland and producer of the first book of liturgy in the country, the Aberdeen Breviary. It's heraldic ceiling is magnificent, the work of Bishop Gavin Dunbar, who succeeded Elphinstone in 1518. Dunbar also erected the two west towers.

The **Brig o' Balgownie** over the Don, near the cathedral, dates from the 14th century, and is reckoned to be the finest single arch structure in Scotland. Aberdeen's other old bridge, to the south of the city, is the **Bridge of Dee**, again built by Bishop Dunbar in the early 1500s.

At Bridge of Don is **Glover House,** the family home of Thomas Blake Glover, the Scotsman who, it is said, inspired Puccini's opera *Madame Butterfly*. Born in Fraserburgh in 1838, his family moved to Bridge of Don in 1851, when he was 13 years old. When he left school, he began working for a trading company, and got a taste for overseas travel.

When he first went to Japan at 21, he was entering a feudal society that had been closed to the west for over 300 years. However, within one year he was selling Scottish-built warships and arms to Japanese rebels during the country's civil war. At the same time he sent young Japanese men to Britain to be educated.

He was called the "Scottish Samurai", and helped found the Mitsubishi shipyards, the first step Japan took to becoming a great manufacturing power. He also helped found the famous Kirin Brewery, and his picture still appears on Kirin labels to this day. He was later presented with the Order of the Rising Sun, Japan's greatest honour. He later built himself a house at Nagasaki, and married a Japanese woman called Tsura, who invariably wore kimonos decorated with butterfly motifs. When Puccini came across a short story and subsequent play based on this relationship, it sowed the seeds of Madame Butterfly.

The **Church of St Nicholas** stands in St Nicholas Street. The first mention of a church on the site is a Papal Bull dated 1157, though there may have been a previous building, which was burned down during a great fire that swept through the city in 1153. At the Reformation it was divided into two churches, the East and the West. These were later united once more when the church was largely rebuilt in the 18th and 19th centuries. Of the original church only the transepts and the crypt survive. Its carillon of 48 bells is the largest of any church in Britain. There are six entrances to the kirkyard, the grandest being the granite colonnade in Union Street, built in 1830.

Union Street, Aberdeen's main thoroughfare, is over a mile long, and thronged with shops. It was laid out in the early 1800s to celebrate the union of Britain and Ireland. At one end, in Castle Street, is the city's 17th century **Mercat**

Cross, standing close to where Aberdeen's long gone medieval castle stood.

Provost Skene's House, off St Nicholas Street, dates from about 1545, and is named after a former lord provost of the city, Sir George Skene, who bought it in 1669. It is a tall, solid building of turrets and chimneys, and has wonderful painted ceilings and period furniture, as well as displays on modern history. **Provost Ross's House** is in Shiprow, said to be Aberdeen's oldest street still in use. The house was built in 1593, but is named after its most famous owner, John Ross, lord provost of Aberdeen in the 18th century. It now houses the **Aberdeen Maritime Museum**, with exhibits and displays on Aberdeen's maritime history, plus a re-created "helicopter ride" out to an offshore oilrig.

Aberdeen University was founded by Bishop Elphinstone in 1494. **King's College** stands in Old Aberdeen, and its chapel, built in 1505, forms one side of a quadrangle in the middle of which is a monument to its founder. The chapel's crown steeple was erected in honour of James VI in the early 17th century. When it was blown down in a great storm in 1633 there were dark rumblings from the people of Old Aberdeen that witchcraft was involved. The **King's College Centre** explains the college's history.

Marischal College, another university, was founded 99 years after King's College, which meant that the city had two universities - exactly the same number as the whole of England at the same time, as locals gleefully point out. It was founded by George Keith, Earl Marischal of Scotland, and the present imposing granite buildings in Broad Street date from the 19th century. In 1860 the two universities united to form Aberdeen University. The Marischal College Museum houses a collection of classical and Egyptian objects, as well as local collections.

The **Aberdeen Art Gallery and Museums** are at Schoolhill, near Robert Gordon's College. Apart from a fine collection of paintings and sculpture by such artists as Degas, Reynolds, and Epstein, it houses displays on Aberdeen's history, including finds made at various archaeological digs throughout the city.

James Dun's House, dating from the 18th century, forms part of the museum. The **Planetarium** at Aberdeen College in the Gallowgate Centre is a star dome, which shows the planets and stars as they "move" through the heavens. And the **Gordon Highlanders Museum** (see panel on page 301) on Viewfield Road tells the story of what Sir Winston Churchill called "the finest regiment in the world". There is an audiovisual theatre, gardens, a children's "handling area", a shop and a café. One of Aberdeen's newest attractions is **Satrosphere** in the Tramsheds in Justice Mill Lane, a hands-on science centre where children can explore all aspects of science, and watch a science show that explains things like colour and bubbles.

At one time there were well over 100 quarries in the city mining granite. **Rubislaw Quarry**, near the Gordon Highlanders Museum, was one of the biggest. It was still being worked right up until 1971, when it was about 480 feet deep and 900 feet across. Now it has been filled with water and fenced off. However, it can still partially be seen from Queen's Road.

At Blairs, on the outskirts of Aberdeen on the B9077, there was a catholic seminary, which closed in 1986. The **Blairs Museum** now holds the Scottish Catholic Heritage Collection, and is open to the public. There are objects connected with the Stuart line (including Mary Stuart and Charles Edward Stuart) on display, as well as a collection of rich vestments, church plate and paintings.

On the north bank of the Dee, where it enters the North Sea, is an area called **Footdee**, or, as it is known by Aberdonians, "Fittie". This is where Aberdeen's original fishing community lived, in rows of cottages that have now been renovated and smartened up.

Around Aberdeen

Stonehaven

16 miles S of Aberdeen off the A90

Stonehaven was once the county town of Kincardineshire. It is a fishing community, though the industry has gone into decline. Near the harbour stands the 18th century **Mercat Cross**, and the **Steeple**, from where James VII was proclaimed king in 1715. The Tolbooth is the town's oldest building, dating from the 16th century. It stands beside the harbour, and was formerly a storehouse belonging to the Earl Marischal of Scotland. Now it is the **Tolbooth Museum**, with displays and exhibits about the town's history and its fishing fleet on the ground floor.

Two miles south of the town is **Dunnottar Castle**. It is magnificently sited, as it stands on a promontory 160 feet above the sea and guarded on three sides by the North Sea and on the fourth by St Ninian's Den, a steep ravine. It dates from the 13th century and later, and has seen some gruesome episodes in Scotland's history. In

Stonehaven Harbour

1297 William Wallace torched it, burning to death every English soldier within its walls. In 1652 Cromwell's troops laid siege to it to capture Scotland's Crown Jewels. However, they were foiled by the wife of the minister of Kinneff Church, who smuggled them out (see also Inverbervie) under the very noses of the troops.

Each year at Hogmanay the traditional **Fireball Festival** is held in Stonehaven. It takes place in the "Auld Toon" area of the town, with men parading at midnight while swinging huge fireballs on the end of stout wires. The origins are rooted in paganism, with the light from the balls supposedly attracting the sun, ensuring its return after the dark days of winter.

Inverbervie

25 miles S of Aberdeen on the A92

Though no bigger than a village, Inverbervie is in fact a royal burgh, having been granted its charter in 1341 by David II, who was supposed to have been shipwrecked off the coast and "kindly received" by the people of the village. John Coutts, whose son **Thomas Coutts** founded the famous bank, was born here in 1699.

Three miles north, at Kinneff, is **Kinneff Church**. In 1651 the Scottish Crown Jewels were used at the coronation of Charles II at Scone, then hidden in Dunnottar Castle (see Stonehaven) so that Parliamentarian troops could not find them. But when their whereabouts became known, they were then smuggled out by the wife of Kinneff's minister, the Rev James Grainger, and placed within the church. There they lay for ten years, beneath the floor. Every three months the minister and his wife dug them up, cleaned them and aired them before a fire. With the Restoration of Charles II in 1660, they were taken to Edinburgh Castle. Though no longer used for worship, the church is still open to the public and under the care of the Kinneff Old Church Preservation Trust.

Arbuthnott

23 miles S of Aberdeen on the B967

The village of Arbuthnott lies in what is called The Mearns. **Arbuthnott Collegiate Church**, dedicated to St Ternan, a Pictish saint. The choir was consecrated in 1242, with the rest of the church being later. It was here that James Sibbald, priest of Arbuthnott, wrote the Arburthnott Missal in 1491. It laid out the form of service to be used at masses celebrated within the church, and can now be seen in Paisley Museum. The **Arbuthnott Aisle** contains the tomb of Hugo le Blond of Arbuthnott, whose effigy can be seen above it. Another tomb is of a later period, and is of James Arbuthnott of that Ilk.

The ashes of James Leslie Mitchell the author, otherwise known as **Lewis Grassic Gibbon**, lie within the kirkyard, and there is a memorial to him. He was born in the Mearns, and, when he had settled in Welwyn Garden City near London, wrote dark brooding novels about Mearns farm life, far removed from the couthy stories about simple Scottish country folk that had been published before. **The Lewis Grassic Gibbon Centre**, next to the parish hall, traces the life and works of a man who became one of the most important British writers of the 20th century.

The area has other literary associations. Robert Burn's father was born here before setting up home in Ayrshire, and in the kirkyard of the church at **Glenbervie** four miles to the northwest is the grave of Burns's great grandfather, James Burnes (the "e" in the name was dropped after Burns's father moved to Ayrshire).

Maryculter

6 miles SW of Aberdeen on the B9077

The land surrounding Maryculter were granted to the Knights Templar by William the Lion in the 12th century, and the order of monastic soldiers established a church and preceptory, dedicating it to St Mary. Pope Clement V suppressed the order in 1312, and at trials held at Edinburgh in 1319 the last Preceptor of the house at Maryculter was given as William de Middleton of the "tempill house of Culther". On the opposite bank of the Dee a church had been established and dedicated to St Peter, and this parish became known as Peterculter. It now lies within the City of Aberdeen, while Maryculter is in Kincardineshire.

Four miles west of the village is **Drum Castle** (National Trust for Scotland), built in the late 13th century, probably by the wonderfully named Richard Cemantarius, king's master mason and provost of Aberdeen. In 1323 it was given to William de Irwyn by Robert, and the Irvines lived in it right up until 1975. It was enlarged in 1619 by the creation of a grand Jacobean mansion.

Fettercairn

27 miles SW of Aberdeen on the B974

On the edge of the fertile Howe of the Mearns, Fettercairn is an attractive village with, at its heart, the **Mercat Cross** of 1670. In 1861 Queen Victoria and Prince Albert visited the village, and the **Fettercairn Arch** commemorates the event.

The B974 north to Strachar and Banchory on Royal Deeside has many fine views. Close to the road, about a mile north of the town, is **Fasque**, home of William Gladstone, prime minister in the late 19th century. It has a deer park, and is open for groups of more than 12 by prior arrangement.

Fettercairn Distillery sits to the northwest, and has guided tours (with a free dram at the end) and a visitor centre.

Daffodils at Fettercairn

Garlogie

10 miles W of Aberdeen on the B9119

The **Garlogie Mill Power House Museum** has a rare beam engine - the only one to have survived intact in its location -, which used to power this wauk mill, which finished off woven cloth. The mill is open to the public, and there are displays about its history and machinery.

The **Cullrelie Stone Circle**, close to the village just off the B9125, dates from the Bronze Age, and consists of eight stones placed in a 33 feet diameter circle.

Banchory

17 miles W of Aberdeen on the A93

This little 19th century burgh stands at the point where the River Freugh enters the Dee, and is often called the "Gateway to Royal Deeside". In Bridge Street is the **Banchory Museum**, which has collections explaining about tartans, royal commemorative china and the natural history of the area. The Scottish musician and composer **James Scott Skinner**, "the Strathspey King", was born in the town in 1843, and a further display in the museum is dedicated to his life. He now lies buried in Allenvale Cemetery in Aberdeen.

Three miles east of the town is **Crathes Castle** (National Trust for Scotland - see panel opposite). It dates

Burnett Arms Hotel

25 High street, Banchory,
Aberdeenshire AB31 5TD
Tel: 01330 824944 Fax: 01330 825553
e-mail: theburnett@totalise.co.uk
website: www.burnettarms.co.uk

For the last 160 years, the **Burnett Arms Hotel** has stood in the centre of Banchory, providing a focal point for locals and tourists alike. Now completely modernised, yet retaining many original features, it still offers the very best in Scottish hospitality. The building itself is elegant and well-proportioned, and offers 16 superb en suite rooms, each one with writing desk, hair dryer, direct dial telephone, tea/coffee making facilities and remote teletext TV with five Sky channels.

The hotel is the ideal base from which to explore Royal Deeside, as well as an overnight stay. Bar meals are served in its two bars, while its spacious dining room is the ideal place for a traditional high tea or a beautifully cooked three course dinner with coffee and mints. A selection of fine wines is available to complement your meal. Being a free house, the Burnett Arms is able to offer a wide range of beers, liqueurs and spirits, including a fine range of single malts. For the businessman, the hotel has everything. There are extra phone points in all the rooms for laptop modems, and the function suite can accommodate 120 people at conferences and seminars. Projection equipment, flipcharts and screens are readily available. For smaller meetings, the Red Lounge (which can accommodate up to 30 people) is the ideal venue. The hotel is owned and managed by Robert Melvin, and he looks forward to you visiting. You won't be disappointed!

from the 16th century, with some of the rooms retaining their original painted ceilings, which were only rediscovered in 1877. It was built by the Burnetts of Ley, who were granted the lands of Ley by Robert the Bruce in 1323. The ancient **Horn of Leys** hangs in the Great Hall. It is made of ivory and encrusted with jewels, and was presented to the Burnetts by Bruce at the time of the land grant. It remained

Crathes Castle and Gardens

Banchory, Aberdeenshire AB31 5QJ
Castle: Tel: 01330 844525
Fax: 01330 844797
Ranger service: Tel: 01330 844651
e-mail crathes@nts.org.uk
website: www.nts.org.uk

King Robert the Bruce granted the lands of Leys to the Burnett family in 1323: the ancient Horn of Leys, which can be seen today in the Great Hall, marks his gift. The castle, built in the second half of the 16th century, is a superb example of a tower house of the period. Some of the rooms retain their original painted ceilings and collections of family portraits and furniture.

A visit is enhanced by the walled garden, which incorporates herbaceous borders and many unusual plants, providing a wonderful display at all times of the year. The great yew hedges, fascinating examples of the art of topiary, date from as early as 1702. Explore the estate on the seven waymarked trails (including one suitable for wheelchairs) that lead through the mixed woodlands, along the Coy Bum and past the millpond.

with the family until 1951, when Sir James Burnett presented it to the National Trust for Scotland. Eight themed gardens have been laid out within the old walled garden, separated by yew hedges. There is also a shop and restaurant.

Kincardine O'Neill

23 miles W of Aberdeen on the A93

This little village claims to be the oldest village on Deeside. It is in fact a small burgh, which was granted its charter in 1511. It was here, in 1220, that the first bridge was constructed across the Dee beyond Aberdeen, so it became an important place. The ruins of the **Kirk of St Mary** date from the 14th century. It may have been the chapel for a hospital that stood here before the Reformation. It was thatched up until 1733, when someone shot at a pigeon perched in its roof and it caught fire. The **Old Smiddy Centre** explains the history of the area, and about the workings of a smithy.

Alford

26 miles W of Aberdeen on the A944

Alford is a pleasant village within a fertile area known as the Howe of Alford. The **Grampian Transport Museum** has displays and working exhibits about transport in the Grampian area. You can even clamber aboard some of the exhibits. The **Alford Valley Railway and Railroad Museum** is a two mile long narrow gauge passenger railway with steam and diesel locomotives that runs between the Transport Museum and **Haughton Country Park**, where there are woodland walks, a wildflower garden and a caravan park.

Four miles south of Alford, on the A980, is one of Aberdeenshire's finest castles, **Craigievar Castle**. With its many turrets and small windows, it looks like something from a fairy tale. It was built by William Forbes, who bought the land in 1610 and completed the castle in 1626. It has a fine collection of 17th and 18th century

furniture, as well as family portraits. William Forbes was also known as "Danzig Willie", and was a rich Aberdeen merchant who traded with the Baltic countries.

Lumphanan

24 miles W of Aberdeen on the A980

Lumphanan was founded when the Deeside railway was constructed, and was the highest point on the line. The **Peel Ring of Lumphanan** (Historic Scotland) is a huge motte and bailey where a castle built by the Durward family once stood.

Aboyne

27 miles W of Aberdeen off the A93

This small Royal Deeside town is famous for the **Aboyne Highland Games**, held in August each year. The village prospered with the coming of the railway in the 19th century, and is now a quiet settlement, popular with tourists. It is also the home of the **Royal Deeside Festival**, held in July and August, which features music, drama and art. There is a lovely, but in places difficult, walk up **Glen Tanar** two miles west of Aboyne.

Five miles north of Aboyne, and two miles north east of Tarland is the **Culsh Earth House**, a souterrain, or underground chamber, which is over 2000 years old. It is a long, doglegged tunnel, which was probably not used as a house, but as a store for foodstuffs. A torch is needed to explore it.

Ballater

34 miles W of Aberdeen on the A93

Set among the spectacular scenery of Royal Deeside, Ballater is surrounded by wooded hills of birch and pine, and makes an

excellent base for exploring an area of outstanding beauty. It is a comparatively modern settlement, and, like Aboyne, owes its growth to the coming of the railways in the 19th century. In fact, this was as far as the Deeside line came, as Prince Albert stopped a proposed extension as far as Braemar.

There is plenty of good walking country around the village, and **Glen Muick**, to the south of Ballater, has a narrow road that takes you up towards Loch Muick (the road ends before the loch is reached, so you have to walk part of the way), in the shadow of **Lochnagar**, which, notwithstanding its name, is a mountain rising to a height of 3,786 feet. It gave its name to Prince Charles's book, The *Old Man of Lochnagar*. The drive is a particularly fine one, and takes you past **Birkhall** (not open to the public) which was bought by Edward VII before he became king. It was formerly the Deeside home of the late Queen Mother.

Balmoral

42 miles W of Aberdeen off the A93

The Queen's private home in Scotland was purchased by Prince Albert in 1852. Four years previously, Queen Victoria had visited and fallen in love with the area. Though the castle as you see it today only dates from that time, a castle has stood here for centuries. The first recorded reference we have is in 1484, when it was called "Bouchmorale". The grounds are closed when the Royal Family is in residence. The present castle is in Scots Baronial style, and built from local granite.

A quarter of a mile east of the castle is the small **Crathie Church**, where the Royal Family worships while resident in Balmoral. It dates from 1895, and overlooks the remains of the 14th century kirk it replaced. Many of the fittings and furnishings have been donated over the years by members of the Royal Family. **John Brown**, the Queen's ghillie, lies in the adjoining cemetery. The **Royal Lochnagar Distillery**, established in 1845, is near the kirk, and has a visitors centre. It was given a Royal Warrant by Queen Victoria in 1864.

A **Victorian Heritage Trail** has been laid out (with distinctive brown signs) which traces the footsteps of Queen Victoria not just on Deeside, but throughout the area, and a leaflet is available from most tourism offices.

Braemar

50 miles W of Aberdeen on the A93

This little village high in the Cairngorms is officially Britain's coldest place. Between 1941 and 1970 its average temperature was only 6.4 degrees Celsius. On two occasions, in 1895 and 1982, it experienced the lowest temperature ever officially recorded in Britain - minus 28.2 degrees Celsius.

It sits at an altitude of 1,100 feet, and is famous for the **Braemar**

Balmoral Castle

Brig O'Dee, near Braemar

Highland Games, held every September, and visited by the Royal Family. **Braemar Castle** is the seat of the Farquharsons of Invercauld, and was built in 1628 by the Earl of Mar on the site of an older castle. It was used as a base by Hanovarian troops during the 1745 Rebellion. In the drawing room can be seen the world's largest Cairngorm (a semi-precious stone) which weights 52 pounds.

The 72,598 acre **Mar Lodge Estate** (National Trust for Scotland) lies five miles west of Braemar on a minor road, and is part of the **Cairngorms National Park**, which came into being in September 2003 (see Grantown on Spey). It has been described as the most important nature conservation landscape in Britain, and contains four out of its five highest mountains. It contains many features associated with Highland landscapes, and has a wealth of wildlife, plants and trees and archaeological sites. The estate is open daily, and the Lodge itself has special open days that are well advertised. To the south of Braemar, on the A93, is one of Scotland's most popular winter sports areas, **Glen Shee**. The snowfields stretch over three valleys and four Munros, with about 25 miles of marked pistes as well as off-piste skiing.

Kintore

10 miles NW of Aberdeen off the A96

Kintore is a small picturesque royal burgh four miles south east of Inverurie. **Kintore Tolbooth** dates from 1747, when the Earl of Kintore was the provost, and **Kintore Parish Church** was built in 1819. Incorporated into the west staircase is a piece of the sacrament house of the pre-Reformation Kirk of Kinkell.

To the west of the town stood a Roman Camp known as **Devona**. One of the likely locations for the **Battle of Mons Graupius** in AD 84 is the slopes of Bennachie (see also Inverurie), to the west of the town, and if this is so no doubt the camp played a major part. It was fought between a confederation of Caledonian tribes and the army of Agricola, though there was no clear victor.

Inverurie

15 miles NW of Aberdeen city centre off the A96

The royal burgh of Inverurie sits where the River Urie meets the Don. A legend tells of how a Roman soldier, when the Romans came to this area, exclaimed "urbi in rure!" (a city in the countryside) when he first saw the settlement. The town adopted the words as its motto, and it is on the coat of arms of the burgh. Mary Stuart visited the town in 1562, and stayed in the royal castle which once stood where the mound known as the **Bass** now stands. The **Battle of Harlaw** was fought near the town in 1411, and a monument now marks the spot. A Lowland army fought a Highland army under Donald, Lord of the Isles, and while the result was an honourable draw, it did stop the Highlanders from moving into the Lowlands and controlling them. It was one of the bloodiest battles ever fought on Scottish soil, which earned it the nickname of "Red Harlaw".

In 1805, the **Aberdeenshire Canal** was opened which linked Inverurie with Aberdeen. Designed by John Rennie, it was never a great success, and in 1845 it was sold to the Great North of Scotland Railway Company, who drained it and used part of its route to carry their railway lines. **Port Elphinstone**, to the south east of the town, recalls the canal, and part of it can still be seen there. It was the only canal in Britain to be closed down every winter in case of ice and snow. Within the **Carnegie Inverurie Museum** in the Square is a small display dedicated to the canal, as well as displays on local history.

To the west of the town is the area's best-known hill, Bennachie (see also Kintore). Though not particularly high (1,600 feet) it has a distinctive conical shape, and is sometimes called "Aberdeenshire's Mount Fuji", as it can be seen from all round the area. Near the Chapel of Garrioch is the **Bennachie Visitors Centre**, where the natural and social history of the hill is explained.

Six miles south of Inverurie is **Castle Fraser** (National Trust for Scotland). Work started on it in 1575 by Michael Fraser, the sixth laird, and was finished in 1636. It has a traditional "Z" plan, and contains many Fraser portraits, fine carpets, linen and curtains.

Monymusk

17 miles W of Aberdeen off the B993

Monymusk was once the site of an Augustinian priory, founded in 1170 by the Earl of Mar. The **Monymusk Reliquary**, in which was kept a bone of St Columba, was one of its treasures. It dates from the 8th century, and is a small wooden box covered in silver and bronze and decorated in semi-precious stones. It was paraded before Bruce's troops at the Battle of Bannockburn, and is now in the Museum of Scotland.

The **Parish Church of St Mary** dates from the early years of the 12th century. In 1929 it was restored to its original condition, and it is now one of the finest parish churches in Scotland. Inside it is the Monymusk Stone, on which is carved Pictish symbols.

Oyne

21 miles NW of Aberdeen on the B9002

Over 7000 ancient sites have been identified in Aberdeenshire, from Pictish carvings to stone circles, and these form the

basis for the **Archaeolink Prehistory Park,** which bridges the gap between ancient history and modern times by way of exhibits and hands-on displays, both indoor and out. It has some of the finest collections of ancient remains in Europe.

Fyvie

23 miles NW of Aberdeen city centre off the A947

The oldest part of **Fyvie Castle** (National Trust for Scotland) dates from the 13th century, and was once a royal stronghold. There are 17th century panelling and plaster ceilings, as well as a portrait collection that includes works by Raeburn, Romney and Gainsborough. One of the legends attached to the castle is that its five towers were built by the five great families in the northeast - the Gordons, the Leiths, the Meldrums, the Prestons and the Setons.

The Parish Church dates from the 19th century, and has a fine laird's pew and wine glass pulpit.

Fyvie Castle

Huntly

33 miles NW of Aberdeen on the A96

Huntly is an old burgh, which was granted its charter in 1488. It sits in an area called Strathbogie, and is famous for the ruins of **Huntly Castle** (Historic Scotland). It was originally called Strathbogie Castle, and was built by the Earl of Fife in the late 12th century. While in the area in the early 1300s, Robert the Bruce took ill, and spent some time in the castle, as the then Earl, David, was one of his supporters. However he changed sides and joined the English just before Bannockburn, and subsequently forfeited the lands of Strathbogie.

They were subsequently given to Sir Adam Gordon of Huntly, who lived in the

Huntly Town Square

Scottish Borders (see Gordon), and he moved north to claim them in 1376. In the 16th century the name of the castle was changed to Huntly, and in the early 1550s it was rebuilt by George, 4th Earl of Huntly.

During the Reformation, the Gordons of Huntly were one of the most important Catholic families in Scotland, and fought on the side of Mary Stuart. James VI, her son, had the castle demolished when the 6th Earl, George, was implicated in an uprising against him. George fled to France, but returned, made his peace with James, and had the castle rebuilt. During the turbulent Covenanting times, the castle changed hands many times until it finally fell into the hands of the Covenanters in the early 17th century.

From about the early 18th century the castle fell into decay. But even today you can see just how stately and comfortable the place must have been in its heyday. It

Dunedin Guest House

17/19 Bogie Street, Huntly AB54 8DX
Tel: 01466 794162
e-mail: dunedin_guest_house@btinternet.com
website: www.huntlyfloralfund.co.uk

With six fully en suite guest rooms, the **Dunedin Guest House** is one of the best B&Bs in Huntly. The rooms are spacious and comfortable, with a real home-from-home feel, and the dining room is welcoming and spacious. Owners Liz and Steve Woodhouse have spared no expense to create a family-friendly, cosy establishment that offers great service and value-for-money. In the morning, enjoy the full Scottish breakfasts, and in the warm summer evenings relax out of doors on the lovely wooden balcony, after a hard day sightseeing in an area of Scotland that is rich in history, heritage and scenery.

entertained many famous people, including Mary of Guise, mother of Mary Stuart, and Perkin Warbeck, pretender to the English throne.

The Brander Museum in the Square has collections dealing with local history, arms and armour and the works of local author **George MacDonald**, who died in 1905. His most popular stories were of fantasy and fairies, with a strong religious message.

Leith Hall, Near Huntly

Six miles south of Huntly, on the B9002 near Kennethmont, is **Leith Hall** (National Trust for Scotland). It was the home of the Leith (later Leith-Hay) family from 1650 onwards, and contains many of their possessions. The family had a tradition of military service, and its most

Forbes Arms Hotel

Milltown of Rothiemay, Huntly,
Aberdeenshire AB54 7LT
Tel: 01466 711248 Fax: 01466 711328

Dating from the 1760s, the **Forbes Arms Hotel** is a picturesque building, on the bank of the river Deveron, which offers the very best in Scottish hospitality. The hotel is an ideal base for guests on the Whisky Trail, the Castle Trail, fishing, golfing breaks or just sightseeing in the NE of Scotland. The cosy, comfortable bars are a favourite with locals and visitors alike. Home cooked meals are served every day in the lounge bar or in the restaurant. There are six en suite guest rooms, that are comfortable and spacious, and all have been furnished and decorated to a high standard. This is a place where friendly service and reasonable prices combine to give you the very best in Scottish hospitality.

Bognie Arms Hotel

Forgue, Huntly,
Aberdeenshire AB54 6BP
Tel: 01466 730204 Fax: 01466 730724

The **Bognie Arms Hotel** is an attractive, substantial, stone-built building in the small hamlet of Forgue, six miles from Huntly, that offers the very best in accommodation, food and drink. It also offers a warm Scottish welcome, and has three guest rooms, two of which are fully en suite. There is a cosy bar - just right for a relaxing drink! - a separate restaurant and a large function suite. The Bognie Arms serves good, honest, pub cuisine, all beautifully cooked from fresh, local produce, and all reasonably priced. It's the ideal base from which to explore the Castles trail, which takes you round the most beautiful and historic castles in Aberdeenshire and beyond.

famous member, Andrew Hay, fought for Charles Edward Stuart. After Culloden he became a fugitive, which was difficult for a man who was over seven feet tall. In an exhibition called "For King and Country: the Military Lairds of Leith Hall" you can see his hose, which measure over three feet from the knee to the heel.

Ellon

15 miles N of Aberdeen on the A920

Situated within an area known as the Formartine, Ellon is a small burgh of barony, which was granted its charter in 1707. It was one of the places burned down during what became known as the "Harrying of Buchan" in 1308 soon after Robert the Bruce defeated John Comyn, Earl of Buchan at Old Meldrum.

The town sits on the River Ythan, with a **Parish Church** that dates from 1777. It's hard to imagine nowadays that this little town, five miles from the coast, was once a port with a small steamer that took goods up and down the river. It is also one of the stops on the **Formartine Buchan Way**, based on disused railway tracks from Dyce, just outside of Aberdeen, to Fraserburgh. The **Moot Hill Monument** sits on Moot hill, from where justice was dispensed by the Earls of Buchan in the 13th and early 14th centuries.

Five miles west of the town, on the A920 is the **Pitmedden Garden** (National Trust for Scotland). The centrepiece is the Great

Udny Station Hotel

Udny Station, Ellon,
Aberdeenshire AB41 6QJ
Tel: 01651 842216 Fax: 01651 842182

The **Udny Station Hotel** is of warm stone, and very picturesque, with its hanging baskets that are a riot of colour in the summer months. Don't be fooled by the name - this isn't a hotel, but a first class, cosy pub with two restaurants, one of which is non smoking. It is owned and run by Eileen and Gordon Andrew, while their daughter Jane is the chef. Here you can get everything from a three-course dinner in the evening to bar lunches and quick snacks, all beautifully cooked and presented. There is also a function suite and a beer garden where you can relax in the sun. The Udney Station Hotel is the perfect example of a warm and welcoming country pub, with an atmosphere all its own.

Eat on the Green

Udny Green, Ellon, Aberdeenshire AB41 7RS
Tel: 01651 842337 Fax: 01651 843362
e-mail: enquiries@eatonthegreen.co.uk
website: www.eatonthegreen.co.uk

Eat on the Green brings a new dining experience to the picturesque village of Udny Green, tucked away in the green Aberdeenshire countryside between Oldmeldrum and Ellon. Owned and managed by husband and wife team Craig and Anne-Marie Wilson, it has earned a fine reputation for its imaginative range of contemporary and classic dishes using only the finest and freshest of specially selected local produce. Craig is an award-winning chef who brings a wealth of experience to the superb food served in the restaurant, and Anne-Marie looks after "front of house". She ensures that your dining experience takes place in a relaxed and informal atmosphere while still retaining all the hallmarks of a great restaurant - high standards of service coupled with value-for-money prices.

Eat on the Green seats up to 50 in absolute comfort, while the adjoining lounge bar offers fresh coffee and light snacks in a warm and inviting ambience. A sample menu might include Thai-style smoked haddock fishcakes, parsnip, honey and ginger soup, seared fillets of salmon, with lime Hollandaise and wok-fried greens, char-grilled sirloin of Aberdeen Angus beef with roasted shallots and homemade, chunky chips. Sweets might include caramelised lemon tart, banana and cinnamon Pavlova or iced terrine of white and dark chocolate. The restaurant is closed on Monday and Tuesday.

Garden, laid out by Sir Alexander Seton, 1st Baronet of Pitmedden, in 1675. In the 1950s the rest of the garden was re-created using elaborate floral designs. Four parterres were created, three of them being inspired by designs possibly used at the Palace of Holyrood in Edinburgh, and the fourth based on Sir Alexander's coat-of-arms. There is also a visitor centre and a Museum of Farming Life, which has a collection of old farming implements once used in this largely farming area.

Near the gardens are the substantial ruins of **Tolquhon Castle**, built by William Forbes, 7th Lord of Tolquhon in the 1580s. In 1589 James VI visited the house, and both his and the Forbes' coats-of-arms were carved over the doorway. William Forbes and his wife Elizabeth were buried in an elaborately carved tomb in the south aisle of the parish church at Tarves. The church has since been demolished, but the **Forbes Tomb** survives to this day.

Haddo House (National Trust for Scotland), one of the grandest stately homes in Aberdeenshire, lies 6 miles northwest of Ellon. It was designed by William Adam for the 2nd Earl of Aberdeen in the early 1730s, and restored in the 1880s. It is noted for its furniture, paintings and objets d'arts. It also has a terraced garden with rose beds and a fountain. In the grounds is **Kelly Lake**, one of the few natural (as opposed to man made) sheets of water called "lake" rather than "loch" in Scotland (see Lake of Menteith, Kirkcudbright and Stenton).

Elgin

Situated in the fertile Laigh of Moray, Elgin is a charming city with the ruins of what was one of the finest cathedrals in Scotland. Before the local government reforms in the mid 70s, there were only six towns in Scotland that were allowed to have lord provosts, and Elgin was one of them.

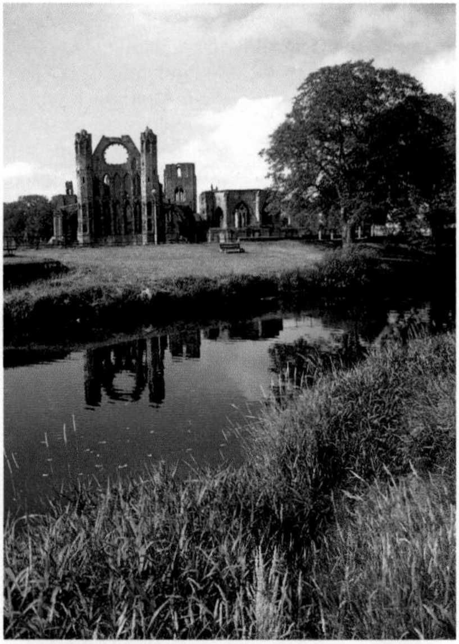

Elgin Cathedral

The city's layout is still essentially that of the medieval burgh, with a High Street that goes from where the royal castle once stood on Lady Hill to the cathedral. It widens in the middle into a market place called the **Plainstanes**, and close to it stands **St Giles Church**. It is in neoclassical style, and was built in 1828 to replace a medieval building.

Three 17th century arcaded merchants' houses are to be found in the High Street, one of which at one time housed the bank of William Duff, a member of the family which went on to become substantial landowners in the area. The award winning **Elgin Museum** is also in the High Street, and has many important collections, including natural history, archaeology and the social history of the area. Another museum worth visiting is the **Moray Motor Museum** in Bridge Street, with its collection of old cars and motorcycles.

Johnston's Cashmere Visitor Centre is

at Newmill. There are tours round the mill, an exhibition and audiovisual that explains the making of the luxury material. There is also a shop where Johnston products can be bought, and a coffee shop.

Work was started on **Elgin Cathedral**, or to give it its proper name, the Cathedral of the Holy Trinity, in about 1224. It was one of Scotland's grandest churches, and could compare to the great cathedrals of Europe. There had been three cathedrals in the dioceses before this one, at Birnie, Spynie and Kinneder, but the locations had all been unsuitable. By the end of the 13th century, building work was complete, though in 1390 the Wolf of Badenoch (see also Dunkeld and Fortrose), set fire to it after a violent quarrel with the Bishop of Moray, who had ordered him to give up his mistress and return to his wife, Euphemia Ross.

He did a lot of damage, and work on repairing it continued right up until the Reformation in 1560. After the Reformation, the cathedral became a quarry for the people of the town. In 1807 a keeper of the ruins was appointed, and from then on what was left was cared for and preserved. The east gate to the cathedral precincts, known as the **Panns Port**, still stands.

The **Old Mills** is the last remaining meal mill on the River Lossie. Its history goes back to the 13th century, when it was owned by Pluscarden Abbey.

North of the city are the impressive ruins of **Spynie Palace** (Historic Scotland), the home of the bishops of Moray. The palace sits on the shores of tiny Loch Spynie, and dates from the 14th century and later. David's Tower, the main part of the building, dates from the 16th century. Spynie Church, which stood nearby until 1736, was at one time the cathedral of the diocese.

Around Elgin

Duffus

5 miles NW of Elgin on the B9012

The ruins of the **Church of St Peter** (Historic Scotland) stand near the village. Though mainly 18th century, it incorporates work that is much older. Opposite the porch is the old **Parish Cross**.

Close by are the ruins of **Duffus Castle**, founded in the 12th century by Freskin, Lord of Strabrock, who later took the title and name of Lord of Duffus and Freskin or Moravia. He is the ancestor of the great Moray, or Murray, family, which has played such a prominent part in Scotland's history. The castle as we see it today dates from the 14th century onwards, and has the finest motte and bailey of any castle in the north of Scotland. **Gordonstoun School**, attended by both Prince Philip and Prince Charles is close to Duffus, housed in an 18th century mansion.

Lossiemouth

5 miles N of Elgin on the A941

This holiday resort sits at the mouth of the River Lossie, and was established as a small port for the city of Elgin in the 18th century. There are fine sandy beaches, and the **Lossiemouth Fisheries and Community Museum** near the marina traces the history of the town and its fishing industry. There is also a reconstruction of the study used by **James Ramsay Macdonald**, Britain's first Labour prime minister, who was born in a small cottage in the town in 1866.

Fochabers

8 miles E of Elgin on the A96

Fochabers dates from the 18th century, when the then Duke of Gordon decided that he didn't like the huddle of cottages that was old Fochabers within his parkland. He therefore built a new village with a large spacious square, and the present day Fochabers was the result. Within the former Pringle Church in the High Street is the **Fochabers Folk Museum**, and in the square is the elegant, porticoed **Bellie Church**. Its rather quaint name comes from the Gaelic "beul-aith", meaning "the

The Old Coach House

High street, Buckie, Moray AB56 1AR
Tel: 01542 836266 Fax: 01542 836361
e-mail: enquiries@oldcoachhouse.net
website: www.oldcoachhouse.net

Elegance, history and comfort all come together in **The Old Coach House** in Buckie. As its name implies, it is a former coaching inn dating from the mid 1800s which has now become a superb, family-run hotel dedicated to personal service and reasonable prices. All the 21 rooms are fully en suite, with colour TV, direct dial telephones, radio and full central heating. Being located just a short walk from the picturesque harbour in this old fishing port, it is only natural that seafood should have a special place in the hotel's menus. Whether it's lemon sole, prawns, crab, squid or Spey salmon, you can rely on the fact that the produce is always fresh. Of course, other dishes can be found as well, and here too the produce is always fresh and local wherever possible. The range of menus is extensive, and covers all tastes, whether it be for lunch, dinner or table d'hôte. Children are always welcome, and they have their own special menu.

In the stylish lounge you will find a great range of drinks, including (because you're not far from the Speyside Whisky Trail here) a fine selection of single malts. The hotel sits proudly in the centre of the town, and is a smart, graceful well-proportioned building of great character. There is ample car parking, and all the activities and attractions of the Moray Firth coastline are on your doorstep, as well as some great inland attractions, such as the small cathedral city of Elgin and its surrounding countryside.

mouth of the ford".

The imposing **Milne's High School** dates from 1844, and was built using money gifted by a native of the town who made his fortune in New Orleans.

West of the village centre is **Baxter's Highland Village**, home to one of the best-known food firms in Scotland. It all started in 1868, when George Baxter, who worked for the Duke of Gordon, opened a small grocery shop in Fochabers. This is one of the most fertile areas in Britain, famed for its fruit, vegetables and cattle, and soon George's wife was making jams and conserves in the back shop. Now the factory and associated shops, restaurants and kids' play areas are tourist attractions in their own right.

Fishing Boat at Buckie

Buckie

13 miles E of Elgin on the A990

Buckie is a major fishing port, and in the **Buckie District Fishing Heritage Museum** in Clunie Place and the **Buckie Drifter** in Freuchny Road are displays that tell the story of the fishing industry on the Morayshire coast. The **Peter Anson Gallery** is within the town's library, and has a collection of paintings from all over Scotland by the maritime artist Peter Anson.

Four miles west of the town is the mouth of the River Spey. It is half a mile wide, though no great port sits here. The village of **Kingston** dates from 1784, and was founded by Ralph Dodworth and William Osbourne. They came from Kingston-upon-Hull in Yorkshire, and named their village after it. It was near here that Charles II alighted after a trip from Holland on 23 June 1650. His ship grounded in shallow water, and he had to be taken ashore "piggyback" style on the back of a villager.

The small fishing communities round about, such as **Findochty** and **Portnockie**

Cullen Bay Hotel

Cullen, Morayshire AB56 4XA
Tel: 01542 840 432 Fax: 01542 840 900
e-mail: stay@cullenbayhotel.com
website: www.cullenbayhotel.com

Elegance - sophistication - comfort. You'll find them all at the **Cullen Bay Hotel,** overlooking the golden sands almost a quarter of a mile west of the small picturesque fishing port of Cullen. And that's not all - you will find great food, high standards of hospitality and superb value for money. The Hotel sits on a prominent headland, and from its commanding position you get great panoramic views out over the sandy Cullen Bay and the Moray Firth, where you may see dolphins, porpoises, seals and even whales.

Owned and managed by husband and wife team Marjory and Jim Tucker and their two sons Simon and Douglas, it offers efficient service and a real Scottish welcome to guests, who return year after year. The furnishings and décor are of the highest standard, the atmosphere is informal, the staff are friendly and approachable.

The elegant and imposing Verandah Restaurant looks out over this sweeping view of the sea, which offers much of the produce used in the hotel's kitchens. And the surrounding countryside also supplies fresh produce as well. Venison and lamb from the local hills; top quality beef from the plains of Moray and Aberdeenshire; and succulent vegetables from the rich Moray soil. All the ingredients are handled and cooked with respect, reflecting the traditional recipes of the area and culminating in dishes that are memorable and beautifully presented.

The hotel has fourteen beautifully decorated and furnished rooms, all of them fully en suite and all having TVs and hospitality trays. Many have wonderful views out over the bay. The hotel's policy is to charge per room rather than per guest, giving much better value for money. Of the fourteen rooms, ten are either doubles or twins, and four are family rooms sleeping two adults and one child, with a cot also being available if required.

There is so much to do and see in this part of Scotland. Apart from the wildlife in the Moray Firth (which is best viewed between June and September), you can also head inland to see deer and birds in their natural habitat. And you can also explore the Speyside Whisky Trail, which takes you around many distilleries in Strathspey, and where, if you're not driving, you can sample a dram or two! There is also the Grampian Castle Trail, with over 70 historic castles to view, and the Coastal Trail, which takes you round some wonderful coastal scenery and explains the area's fishing heritage.

The Tucker family look forward to welcoming you to their hotel, and to showing you some real Scottish hospitality.

Crannoch Hotel

Blantyre street, Cullen, Moray AB56 4RQ
Tel: 01542 840210 Fax: 01542 840223
website: www.crannoch,hotel.btinternet.co.uk

Situated on the A96 within easy reach of Buckie and Banff, the **Crannoch Hotel** makes the perfect base for exploring the beautiful Moray Firth coast. It has a homely atmosphere, yet offers high standards of service coupled with value for money. There are seven guest rooms on offer, three of which are fully en suite, and all are extremely comfortable and cosy. The dinners are beautifully cooked from good, fresh local produce wherever possible, or you can enjoy snacks and bar lunches in the welcoming bar.

Here you can enjoy a holiday that is relaxed or full of activity, among some of the finest coastal scenery in Scotland.

are very attractive, and well worth visiting. Five miles southwest of the town are the ruins of **Deskford Church**, within the village of the same name. It is noted for its ornately carved sacrament house. The 16th century **St Mary's Church** sits in the small fishing village of **Cullen**, to the north of Deskford, and was formerly collegiate. One of the most dramatically situated castles in the area is **Findlater Castle**, which sits on a small promontory jutting into the sea. The ruins you see now date from the 15th century, and were built by the Ogilvie family, though a castle may have stood here since at least the 13th century. Care should be taken when approaching or exploring it.

In the village of **Fordyce,** south east of Cullen, is the **Fordyce Joiner's Workshop and Visitor Centre**, dedicated to the skills and tools of carpentry in northeast Scotland. **Fordyce Castle** was built in the late 16th century by Sir Thomas Menzies of Durn. It is an L-plan tower, and is not open to the public.

Craigellachie

12 miles S of Elgin off the A95

The **Craigellachie Bridge** dates from 1814,

Ben Aigen Hotel

51 New Street, Rothes, Morayshire AB38 7BJ
Tel: 01340 831240 Fax: 01340 831921
e-mail: angelaswierczek@hotmail.com

The **Ben Aigen Hotel** is a handsome, stone-built building in the heart of the small town of Rothes. The watchwords here are high standards and value-for-money, and under the new ownership of Angela and Philip Swierczek, it is steadily gaining an enviable reputation among locals and visitor alike. There are 13 rooms, eight of which are fully en suite, a cosy lounge/bar and a spacious dining room that serves good, fresh home-cooked food as well as afternoon teas and coffees. Everything is spotlessly clean, and the whole place has a welcoming, family-friendly feel. It's the ideal base from which to explore the surrounding area,

Parkmore Holiday Cottages

Dufftown, Banffshire AB55 4DN
Tel: 01340 820072 Fax: 01340 821276
e-mail: enquiries@parkmorecottages.com
website: www.parkmorecottages.com

Set amid open countryside, **Parkmore Holiday Cottages** is a complex of self-catering holiday homes formed by the conversion of the farm steadings. They have been rebuilt to include many of the original features, such as exposed beams and other woodwork. Dufftown, with its shops, restaurants, pubs and supermarket, is just a mile and a half away. The cottages are right on the Speyside Whisky Trail, the Speyside Walk, a long distance footpath and the Castles Trail, which takes you round some of the most historic castles in Northeast Scotland.

There are seven self catering units that are the last word in luxury. One of these properties, Glenhead of Coachford, is between Keith and Huntly. All the cottages have payphones, barbecues, central heating, colour TV, double glazing, CD stereo, log fires and laundry facilities.

- **Sheaf End** sleeps eight in a double bedroom (with en suite toilet), two twins and a twin with bunk beds. There is a separate shower room, bathroom and toilet. A large lounge/dining area has stunning views, and the kitchen is well equipped, including a dishwasher.
- **Corn Loft** sleeps six in a double bedroom with en suite toilet and two twins. There is a separate bathroom with bath and shower, a large lounge/dining room and a fully fitted kitchen area with dishwasher.
- **The Stable** sleeps five in a double (with en suite toilet), a twin and a single, which has been adapted for occupation by an accompanied disabled person. There is a downstairs toilet, a large lounge and a dining/kitchen area that has retained the effect of the original stable.
- **Straw End** is a small, picturesque cottage that sleeps four in a double and a twin bedroom. There is a lounge/dining room, a fully fitted kitchen area and separate shower and toilet.
- **The Bothy** is the smallest of the cottages, and has been converted from a traditional single-room farm worker's cottage. It sleeps two in a double bedroom, with a lounge, well-equipped kitchen and shower plus separate toilet. There is extensive wood panelling, giving a cosy, attractive atmosphere and it has its own private garden.
- **The Farmhouse** itself sleeps ten in five bedrooms, and has a lounge with satellite TV, DVD, CD and radio. There is also a private garden. The kitchen is well-equipped, and has a table that seats ten.
- **The Neep Shed** is a new facility and has been converted to exacting standards. For a nominal fee it allows groups of visitors to more than one cottage to have somewhere they can meet and eat and still retain the privacy of their own cottage.
- **Glenhead of Coachford** sits in a 40-acre farm between Keith and Huntly, and sleeps six in two doubles (one of which is en suite) and a twin. There is a lounge, a dining room with beautiful views, a large cottage kitchen, utility room and bathroom. This is the perfect base for various sporting activities, such as golf, fishing, mountain biking, hill walking and climbing, as there is a lockable store attached to the house where equipment can be locked away. There is ample parking for two vehicles.

and is Scotland's oldest iron bridge. It was designed by Thomas Telford, and has one single graceful arch, which spans the Spey. The village sits in the heart of the **Malt Whisky Trail**, and most of the distilleries organise tours round the premises, with a tasting at the end. The **Speyside Cooperage**, on the Dufftown road, has a visitor centre where you can learn about the skills involved in making and repairing whisky casks.

Craigellachie Distillery lies within the village, as does the **Macallan Distillery**, and four miles north is the **Glen Grant Distillery**. The **Glenfarclas Distillery** is seven miles southwest, near **Ballindalloch Castle.** The castle dates from the 16th century, and is the home of the McPherson-Grant family, who have lived here continuously since it was built. It is open to the public during the summer months. About four miles south of Ballindalloch is the **Glenlivit Distillery**, which again has organised tours.

Glen Fiddich Distillery, Dufftown

Dufftown

16 miles S of Elgin on the A941

Dufftown is the world capital of malt whisky and was founded in 1817 by James Duff, the 4th Earl of Fife. Built to provide employment after the Napoleonic wars, it is based around seven stills, including the world famous **Glenfiddich Distillery**. The most prominent feature is the **Clock Tower**, originally built in 1839 as the town jail. The clock itself came from Banff, where it was known as the "Clock That Hanged MacPherson". McPherson of Kingussie had been sentenced to death in 1700, but was later pardoned. While the pardon was on its way to Banff, Lord Braco put the clock forward to ensure that MacPherson would hang.

Mason Arms

22 Conval Street, Dufftown,
Banffshire AB55 4AE
Tel/Fax: 01340 820302
e-mail: themasonarms1@aol.com

Dufftown is the "whisky capital of the world", and it is here that you will find the small, friendly, family-run village inn called the **Mason Arms**. It's exterior is colourful and picturesque, with baskets of flowers brightening up the street. It has four lovely and comfortable guest rooms on offer, and makes the ideal base for exploring the Speyside Whisky Trail. Home-cooked food is served all day, with the specialities being local game and steaks. The lively bar serves a fine range of beers, wines and liqueurs, along with, naturally enough, a great selection of fine single malts.

Mortlach Church, which is a Scottish Heritage site, was founded on a much earlier church, thought to have stood here since the community began in AD 566 and to have been in regular use as a place of worship ever since. Although much of the church was reconstructed in the 19th century, parts of the original building still survive. In the graveyard is an old Pictish cross, and inside the church is the **Elephant Stone**, again with Pictish associations. **Balvenie Castle** (Historic Scotland), lies a mile north, and was once home to the Comyns and later the Stewarts and the Douglases.

The **Keith and Dufftown Railway** connects Dufftown to the market town of Keith, eleven miles away. It was reopened in 2000/2001 by a group of enthusiasts, and runs services between the two towns.

The 18 hole Dufftown Golf Club boasts the highest hole in the UK. Besides golf, the town caters for all types of outdoor activities including walking, fishing, shooting and cycling.

Keith

15 miles SE of Elgin on the A96

Keith is home to the **Glenisla Distillery**, which is open to the public. The old **Packhorse Bridge** dates from 1609, though the town's oldest building is **Milton Tower**, dating from the 15th century. It was a stronghold of the Ogilvie family, whose most famous member was John Ogilvie. Raised a Protestant, he later converted to Roman Catholocism on the Continent and was sent back to Scotland to promote the faith, posing as a horse dealer and soldier called John Watson. He was

Royal Hotel

Church Road, Keith,
Morayshire AB55 5BR
Tel: 01542 886978
Fax: 01542 889919

With ten fully en suite rooms, the **Royal Hotel** is one of the best hotels in the small country town of Keith. The whole place has recently been refurbished to an extremely high standard, with a modern but relaxing bar/lounge and a spacious second-floor restaurant that serves wonderful, home-cooked food. The atmosphere is relaxed and informal, with a real "family feel" to the place. The prices are reasonable, the service is outstanding and the place is comfortable yet stylish. It makes the ideal base from which to explore Morayshire and the Speyside Whisky Trail.

eventually hanged in Glasgow in 1615, and was made a saint in 1976. There is a **Scottish Tartans Museum** in Keith's Institute Hall. The town is the eastern terminus of the Keith and Dufftown Railway (see Dufftown)

Tomintoul

27 miles S of Elgin on the A939

Tomintoul, situated at a height of 1,160 feet, is the highest village in the Highlands (but not in Scotland). The A939 southwest to Cockbridge is called "**The Lecht**", and is notorious for being blocked by snow in winter. The ski area of the same name lies six miles from Tomintoul. The small **Tomintoul Museum**, in the village square, has displays on local history and wildlife.

View over Tomintoul

Pluscarden

6 miles SW of Elgin on a minor road

Pluscarden Priory was founded in 1230 by Alexander II and settled firstly by the Valliscaulian and then the Benedictine monks. In the 19th century the Bute family acquired the ruined buildings, and in 1943 presented them to the monks of Prinknash in England, who took up residence in 1948. At first it was a priory, but became an abbey in its own right in 1974. Since then the monks have been restoring the buildings so that nowadays it is the only medieval abbey in Britain with monks still living and worshipping in it. It is open to the public, and has a small gift shop.

Forres

12 miles W of Elgin on the A96

This small royal burgh, which was granted its charter in the 13th century, was once one of the most important places in Scotland, and is mentioned in Shakespeare's Macbeth. The ground plan of the medieval settlement still forms the basis of the town today, though it is much more open and green than it was then, thanks to some large areas of parkland.

The 20 feet high **Sueno's Stone** (Historic Scotland) dates from the 9th century, and is the largest known stone with Pictish carvings in Scotland. One side shows a cross, while the other shows scenes of battle. It is now floodlit, and under glass to protect it from the weather. **The Falconer Museum** in Tolbooth Street was founded in 1871, and highlights the history and heritage of the town and its surroundings. It was founded using money from a bequest left by Hugh Falconer, who left Forres to work in India as a botanist and geologist in the Sewalik Hills.

Dominating the town is the **Nelson Tower**, opened in 1812 in Grant Park to commemorate Nelson's victory at Trafalgar, the first such building to do so in Britain. If you're fit enough to climb its 96 steps, you'll get spectacular views over the surrounding countryside and the Moray Firth.

Brodie Castle (National Trust for Scotland) lies four miles west of the town. It is a 16th century tower house with later additions, which give it the look of a comfortable mansion. It dates back at least to the time of Malcolm, Thane of Brodie, who died in 1285, and possibly earlier. It contains major collections of paintings, furniture and ceramics, and sits in 175 acres of ground. Within the grounds is Rodney's Stone, with Pictish carvings.

Floral Sculptures in Forres

A couple of miles northeast of Forres is **Kinloss**, with an RAF base and the scant remains of an old abbey. It was founded in about 1150 by David I, and colonised by

Cistercian monks from Melrose. It is said that David founded it in thanks after being guided to safety by a dove after losing his way in a dense forest. Before the Reformation, it was one of the wealthiest and most powerful abbeys in Scotland.

On the coast north of Forres is perhaps Scotland's most unusual landscape, the **Culbin Sands**. In 1694 a storm blew great drifts of sand - some as high as 100 feet - over an area that had once been green and fertile, causing people to flee their homes. They covered cottages and fields, and eventually created eight square miles of what became known as "Scotland's Sahara". Occasionally, further storms would uncover the foundations of old cottages, which were then covered back up again by succeeding storms. The sands continued to shift and expand until the 1920s, when trees were planted to stabilise the area.

At **Findhorn**, on the Moray Firth coast, is the **Findhorn Foundation**, one of the most successful centres in Britain for exploring alternative lifestyles and spiritual living. It was founded by Dorothy Maclean and Peter and Eileen Caddy in 1962 in a caravan park. The **Findhorn Heritage Centre and Museum** has displays on the history and heritage of the village.

Dallas Dhu Distillery (Historic Scotland) sits to the south of Forres, and explains the making of whisky. It was built between 1898 and 1899.

Fraserburgh

Fraserburgh sits on the coastline just at that point where the Moray Firth becomes the North Sea. It is one of the main fishing ports in northeast Scotland, and the largest shellfish port in Europe. It was founded in the 16th century by Alexander Fraser, eighth laird of Philorth. In 1546 he built the first harbour, used by the seamen of Broadsea, an old settlement that stands near Kinnaird Head. The **Old Kirk** in Saltoun Square isn't as old as its name would suggest. It was built in 1803 to replace the original church built by Alexander between 1570 and 1571. Beside it is the **Fraser Burial Aisle**.

One of Alexander's grander schemes was the founding of a university in the town, and he even went so far as to obtain James VI's permission to do so. The Scots Parliament gave it a grant, and the Rev Charles Ferme became its first principal. Unfortunately, the Rev'd Ferme was later arrested for attending a general assembly of the Church of Scotland in defiance of the king. The embryonic university subsequently collapsed, though one street in the town, College Bounds, still commemorates the scheme.

Kinnaird Lighthouse (Historic Scotland) must be the most unusual lighthouse in Scotland, as it is built onto a castle founded by Alexander Fraser in 1572 as his main residence after founding the town. It is now a museum dedicated to

The Royal Hotel

63 Broad treet, Fraserburgh,
Aberdeenshire AB43 9AU
Tel: 01346 518524 Fax: 01346 515774
e-mail: balant@hotmail.com

The elegant, stone-built **Royal Hotel** sits at the heart of the historic town of Fraserburgh, close to all the town's amenities and tourist attractions. It is a historic building, dating from the early 1830s, and has recently come under new management. A huge restoration scheme will transform it into one of the best hostelries in the area - though it has always had a good reputation as a comfortable place to stay while in that part of the northeast of Scotland known as Buchan. Both outside and inside will be upgraded to take into account all the modern standards of convenience and value for money.

As you would expect from such a hotel, the

fifteen spacious yet cosy rooms are fully en suite, and also boast colour satellite TVs and hospitality trays with tea, coffee, hot chocolate and biscuits. They have been furnished and individually decorated to an exceptionally high standard, and planned improvements will increase their comfort even further so that your stay is pleasant and enjoyable. But for all these improvements, the hotel's atmosphere will stay friendly and informal. The staff are efficient and knowledgeable about what to do and see in this magnificent part of the country, and will always give you a warm Scottish welcome and a cheery smile!

The lounge bar is a popular meeting place for locals and visitors alike, and here you can meet the friendly people of Fraserburgh as you enjoy a quiet drink. There is a wide range of beers, wines, spirits, liqueurs and soft drinks, and with the carpeted floor and warm wood of the furniture, you can relax after a hard day sightseeing.

The non-smoking *Alexander's Restaurant*, part of the hotel, will also be benefiting from a complete refurbishment. It's resident chef has put together a menu that is imaginative yet traditional, blending fresh local produce with new, innovative, but always tasty ideas. It can seat up to 50 diners, and with its tartan theme, you'll always remember that you're in Scotland, which is famous for its Aberdeen Angus beef, venison, vegetables, lamb and seafood. The speciality is fresh seafood, though this isn't surprising as it is a major fishing port. Superb lunches are served between 12 noon and 2 pm, and dinner is served between 6 pm and 9 pm, with all major credit cards being taken.

Fraserburgh makes the ideal base when exploring Aberdeenshire and Northeast Scotland. The country roads are surprisingly quiet, the views are stunning and the beaches are invariably clean and uncrowded.

Scotland's lighthouses. In Quarry Road is the **Fraserburgh Heritage Centre**, which has exhibits about the history of the town, including some haute couture dresses designed by the late Bill Gibb, who hailed from Fraserburgh. The most unusual building in Fraserburgh is the **Wine Tower**, next to the lighthouse. It too was built by Alexander Fraser, possibly as a chapel. It has three floors, but no connecting stairways. At Sandhead, to the west of the town, is the **Sandhaven Meal Mill**, dating from the 19th century. Guided tours and models show how oatmeal used to be ground in Scotland. At Memsie, three miles south of Fraserburgh on the B9032, is the **Memsie Burial Cairn**, dating from about 1500 BC.

Fraserburgh Beach

Around Fraserburgh

Old Deer

12 miles S of Fraserburgh on the B9030

In a beautiful position on the banks of the River South Ugie are the ruins of **Deer Abbey** (Historic Scotland), founded in 1219 by William Comyn, Earl of Buchan, for the Cistercian order of monks. Little remains of the abbey church, but the walls of some of the other buildings are fairly well preserved. It is said that it was built on the site of a Celtic monastery founded by St Columba and his companion St Drostan in the 6th century.

Close by is the village of **Mintlaw**, where you'll find the 230 acre **Aden Farming**

Forglen Country Cottages

Home Farm Office, Forglen Estate, Turriff,
Aberdeenshire AB53 4JP
Tel: 01888 562918/518
e-mail: forglen.estate@tiscali.co.uk
website: www.forglen.co.uk

Set deep in rolling farmland beyond the Grampian mountains lies the Deveron Valley, a place of quiet and entrancing beauty. The River Deveron flows northwards through it, and on its wooded slopes lies the ancient **Forglen Estate**, extending to 1000 acres, with forestry, farm, and walled and wild gardens. The estate also contains many old, stone cottages that are now available to let on a self catering basis. They are all cosy and warm in winter and cool and welcoming in summer, and make the ideal base from which to explore this beautiful area. Guests are free to wander the miles of estate roads and

paths between ancient broadleaf woodland, mixed conifers and fields. There's a wild glen garden to explore also, with its tumbling stream and ponds, specimen trees and magnificent azaleas. The whole place is a haven for wildlife, and you may encounter red squirrels, deer, badgers, foxes and a variety of birds.

There are six cottages available, each one fully furnished and equipped to give you the holiday of a lifetime away from the bustle and stress of life, while still retaining all the modern conveniences that make a holiday so special and worry-free. Electricity is included in the price of the hire, and water is from springs. Each cottage has a bathroom, heating, colour TV, and there is ample parking and a grassed garden with bench table for sunny days.

The Ivy sleeps up to six in one double and two twin rooms and has a kitchen/dinette, while the Smiddy sleeps eight in one double room and three twin and has a living/dining room. The Pheasantry is the largest cottage, sleeping nine in two double rooms, two twin and a single, and in addition has a separate dining room. The Garden sleeps up to six people in a double and two twins and has a living/dining room, while the Kennels sleeps six in two doubles and a twin and has a living/dining room. Meadowhead is a bungalow that sleeps up to six in two double rooms and one twin, with kitchen/dinette and a separate lounge. Some cottages have dishwashers, microwave, cafetiere, hair dryer, second toilet and shower and open fireplace.

The cottages are open all year round and in high summer, the nights never really get dark. In spring the azaleas put on a fine display of colour, while autumn brings a riot of orange and bronze foliage.

Salmon fishing is available from mid February to mid May, and there is free brown trout fishing from March to early October, (fishing by arrangement). The Forglen Estate is a special place, and gives you a true flavour of the richness, diversity and friendliness of Scotland!

Museum, which sits within a country park. It traces the history of farming in this rich area of Aberdeenshire through three separate themes - the Aden Estate Story, the Weel Vrocht Grun ("well worked ground") and the country park itself.

Maud

12 miles S of Fraserburgh on the B9029

Maud grew up around the railway line that once connected Aberdeen to Fraserburgh, and in the **Maud Railway Museum**, in the village's former station, you can relive the days of the Great North of Scotland Railway through exhibits, photographs, artefacts and displays.

Turriff

20 miles SW of Fraserburgh on the A947

Set in the heart of the Buchan farmlands, Turriff is an ancient burgh that was given its charter in 1512. The Knights Templar once owned land in the area, and a Templar chapel stood here. **Turriff Parish Church** was built in 1794, and there are some good carvings on its belfry and walls from the previous kirk that stood on the site. Seven miles south west of Turriff along the B9024 is the **Glendronach Distillery**, situated on the banks of the Dronach Burn. Tours are available, and there is a visitor centre and shop.

Delgatie Castle, close to the town, was founded in about 1050, though the castle as you see it today dates from the 16th century. It is the ancestral home of Clan Hay, and has been in the hay family for over 650 years.

Turriff was the scene of a famous incident concerning the **Turra Coo** ("Turriff Cow") which received widespread publicity throughout Britain. New National Insurance Acts were passed in 1911 and 1913 which required employers to pay 3d per week for each of their employees. The farmers of Aberdeenshire, in common with others all over Britain, didn't want to pay, as they reckoned that farm workers had a healthy lifestyle, and wouldn't need much medical treatment. Curiously enough, the farm workers themselves supported the farmers on this issue.

One Turriff farmer in particular, Robert Paterson, refused to pay, so one of his cows was taken to be sold at auction to pay off his arrears. However the auction, held in Turriff, turned into a fiasco, as the cow, which had slogans painted all over its body, took fright and bolted through the streets of the town. Meanwhile, the auctioneer was pelted with raw eggs and bags of soot. Three days later the cow was taken to Aberdeen, where it was sold for £7.00.

It was a hollow victory for the authorities, which had spent nearly £12 in recovering the sum. And they were further annoyed to hear that Paterson's neighbours had clubbed together and bought the cow so that it could be returned to him. So, while the authorities were out of pocket

over the whole affair, it hadn't cost Robert Paterson a penny.

Pennan

9 miles W of Fraserburgh on the B9031

Pennan is possibly the most spectacular of the little fishing villages on the northern coast of Aberdeenshire. It is strung out along the base of a high cliff, with many of the cottages having their gable ends to the sea for protection. It is a conservation village, and is famous as being the setting, in 1983, for the film *Local Hero*. The red telephone box, famously used in the film, was a prop. However, Pennan's real telephone box, about 15 yards away from where the prop stood, is still a favourite place for photographs.

Banff

20 miles W of Fraserburgh on the A98

Banff was once the county town of Banffshire, and is a small fishing port close to the mouth of the River Deveron. It is an ancient royal burgh, having been granted its charter in 1163 by Malcolm IV. The **Banff Museum** in the High Street is one of Scotland's oldest, having been founded in 1828. It has a nationally important collection of Banff silver.

Duff House (Historic Scotland) was designed by William Adam and built between 1735 and 1740 for William Duff of Braco, who later became Earl Fife. After a bitter wrangle with Adam, William Duff abandoned it, and it was left to James, the 2nd Earl Fife, to complete the grand plan, including the grounds. Over the years it has had a chequered career, having been a hotel, a sanatorium, a prisoner-of-war camp and the scene of an attempted murder, when a luckless Countess Fife tried to do away with her husband. It is now a satellite

of the National Gallery of Scotland, with fine collections of paintings by such artists as Raeburn and El Greco, as well as furniture and tapestries.

The small town of **Macduff** sits on the opposite shores of the small bay where the Deveron enters the Moray Firth. It was founded by the 2nd Earl Fife in 1783, and contains the **Macduff Marine Aquarium** at High Shore, which is essentially a central tank surrounded by viewing areas so that you get a good view of fish and marine mammals from all angles. The aquarium has a wave-making machine which adds to the experience of seeing underwater life in its true condition. Six miles west of Banff, on the A98, is the attractive little fishing port of **Portsoy**, which is well worth visiting if only to soak in the atmosphere. At one time it was famous for its marble, which was used in the Palace of Versailles in France.

Peterhead

16 miles SE of Fraserburgh on the A982

Peterhead is the largest town (as opposed to city) in Aberdeenshire, and one of the chief fishing ports in the northeast. It was founded by George Keith, the 5th Earl Marischal of Scotland in 1593, and is Scotland's most easterly burgh. Now that fishing has declined, it benefits from being one of the ports that services the offshore gas industry. The **Arbuthnot Museum** in St Peter Street tells the story of the town and its industries, and has a large collection of Inuit, or Eskimo, artefacts. It was given to the town of Peterhead in 1850 by Adam Arbuthnot, a local man who had acquired a huge collection of antiquities.

Set by the harbour of refuge to the south of the town, in a purpose-built building, is **Peterhead Maritime Heritage Museum**. This tells of the town's connections with the sea over the years, from its fishing fleet (which went as far as the Arctic in search of fish) to its whaling fleet and finally to the modern offshore gas and oil industries. The building was shaped to resemble a "scaffy", a kind of fishing boat once used in the area.

A few miles south of the town, at Cruden Bay, are the ruins of **Slains Castle**, built by the ninth Earl of Errol in 1597 to replace an earlier castle. It has been rebuilt and refurbished several times since then, and the ruins you see now date from the early 19th century. It has literary associations of an unusual kind. While staying at the nearby village of Cruden Bay in 1895, Bram Stoker began writing Dracula, and based the vampire's Transylvanian castle on Slains. In an early draft of the novel he even has the Count coming ashore at Slains rather than Whitby.

If you want to explore the area round Slains, great care must be take, as it sits close to a cliff top above the sea.

The Highlands

When people talk of Scottish scenery, they inevitably mean the scenery of the Highlands - mountains, deep glens and dark, brooding lochs. And though other areas also have these features, this is the one that has them in abundance.

The Highlands area has no set boundaries, and some places described in earlier chapters, such as Aberdeen & Grampian, Argyllshire and parts of Perthshire, can lay

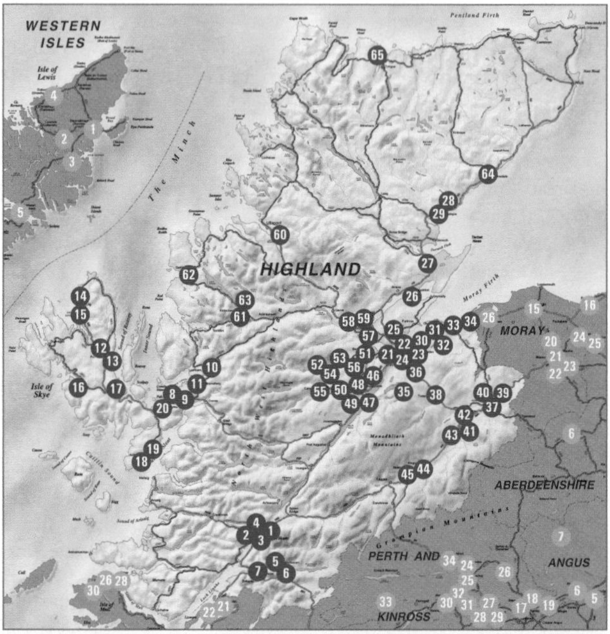

PLACES TO STAY, EAT AND DRINK

Kismet Villa B&B, Fort William	1	B&B	p338
Crolinnhe, Fort William	2	Guest House	p339
Ashburn House, Fort William	3	Hotel	p340
Rhiw Goch, Banavie	4	B&B	p341
Macdonald Hotel Kinlochleven, Kinlochleven	5	Hotel	p342
Highland Getaway, Kinlochleven	6	Accommodation and Restaurant	p343
An Darag B&B, Upper Carnoch	7	B&B	p344
Gateway Restaurant, Kyle of Lochalsh	8	Restaurant	p347
Balmacara Estate & Garden, Balmacara	9	Visitor Attraction	p347
Rockvilla Hotel, Lochcarron	10	Hotel	p348
Soluis Mu Thuath Guest House, Achmore	11	Guest House	p349
The Pier Hotel, Portree	12	Hotel	p352
Greenacres Guest House, Portree	13	Guest House	p352
The Pub at the Pier, Uig	14	Pub with Restaurant	p353
Uig Hotel, Uig	15	Hotel	p354
Old Inn & Waterfront Bunkhouse, Carbost	16	Pub, Food and Accommodation	p355
Sconser Lodge Hotel, Sconser	17	Hotel	p356

Denotes entries in other chapters

PLACES TO STAY, EAT AND DRINK

Sleat Holiday Homes, Ardvasar	18	Self Catering	p357
Ardvasar Hotel, Sleat	19	Hotel	p358
Castle Moil Restaurant & Bar, Kyleakin	20	Bar & Restaurant	p359
Trafford Bank Guest House, Inverness	21	Guest House	p360
Crown Guest House, Inverness	22	Guest House	p361
Smithton Hotel, Smithton	23	Hotel	p362
Loch Ness House Hotel, Inverness	24	Hotel	p363
Munlochy Hotel, Munlochy	25	Hotel	p364
Craigaron, Invergordon	26	B&B	p366
Carnegie Lodge Hotel, Tain	27	Hotel	p366
Dunrobin Castle & Gardens, Golspie	28	Visitor Attraction	p367
Ben Bhraggie Hotel, Golspie	29	Hotel	p368
Easter Dalziel Farm B&B /Cottages, Dalcross	30	B&B and Self Catering	p368
Gun Lodge Hotel, Ardersier	31	Hotel	p369
Cawdor Cottages, Cawdor	32	Self Catering	p370
Aurora Hotel, Nairn	33	Hotel	p371
Boath Stables, Auldearn	34	Self Catering	p371
The Steadings Hotel, Flichity	35	Hotel	p372
Westhill House, Westhill	36	B&B	p373
Culdearn House, Grantown-on-Spey	37	Hotel	p374
Tomatin Inn, Tomatin	38	Pub with Restaurant	p375
Grant Arms Hotel, Grantown-on-Spey	39	Hotel	p375
Haugh Hotel, Cromdale	40	Pub, Food and Accommodation	p376
Steornabhagh Guest House, Boat of Garten	41	Guest House	p376
Strathspey Mountain Lodges, Boat of Garten	42	Self Catering	p376
Cairngorm Mountain Railway, Aviemore	43	Mountain Railway	p377
Ruthven Farmhouse & Cottages, Kingussie	44	B&B and Self Catering	p378
Mains Hotel, Newtonmore	45	Hotel	p379
Loch Ness Clansman Hotel, Brackla	46	Hotel	p380
Castle View B&B, Drumnadrochit	47	B&B	p381
Benleva Hotel, Drumnadrochit	48	Hotel	p381
Glen Rowan Guest House, Lewiston	49	Guest House	p382
Glenurquhart House Hotel/Lodges, Marchfield	50	Hotel and Self Catering	p382
Beauly Coffee & Gift Shop, Beauly	51	Café and Gifts	p383
Glass Restaurant at the Struy Inn, Struy	52	Restaurant	p384
Cnoc Hotel, Struy	53	Hotel	p385
Culligran Cottages, Struy	54	Self Catering	p386
Slaters Arms, Cannich	55	Pub with Restaurant	p386
Brockie's Lodge Hotel, Kiltarlity	56	Hotel	p387
Ord House, Muir of Ord	57	Hotel	p388
Fir Lodges, Blackmuir Wood	58	Self Catering	p389
Richmond Hotel, Church Brae	59	Hotel	p390
Leckmelm Holiday Cottages, Loch Broom	60	Self Catering	p391
Kinlochewe Hotel, Kinlochewe	61	Hotel	p392
Steading Restaurant, Achtercairn	62	Restaurant	p393
Cromasaig, Kinlochewe	63	B&B	p394
Bannockburn Inn, Helmsdale	64	Pub with Food	p397
The Craggan Hotel, Melness	65	Pub, Food and Accommodation	p398

Denotes entries in other chapters

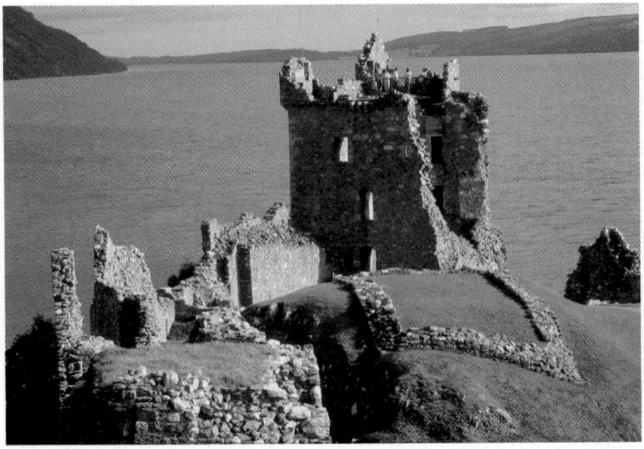

Urquhart Castle, Loch Ness

claim to being in the Highlands as well. But the area described in this chapter can legitimately be called the heart of the Highlands. It stretches from the northernmost coast of the mainland down to Perthshire, and from the rugged west coast to the borders of Aberdeenshire and Moray, taking in one or two of the Inner Hebridean islands on the way.

It is mostly wild country, with few roads compared to other parts of Scotland. Some areas are totally inaccessible unless you go by foot over difficult terrain, and if you do decide to take to the hills, remember that Highland weather can be unpredictable, even in summer. Take the correct clothing, and always leave word with someone about your intended route and your estimated times of arrival at various stages.

The capital of the Highlands is Inverness. It is a thriving city, and reckoned to be the place with the most rapid growth in Britain (if not Europe), with an enviable quality of life. Seen from the A9 as you head over the Kessock Bridge, it has all the appearance of a large metropolis, with suburbs that sprawl along the Moray and Beauly Firths. But in fact its population is no more than 50,000, though this is growing almost daily. And some of the countryside surrounding it looks more like the Lowlands than the Highlands, though this notion is soon dispelled if you head southwest along the A82 towards Loch Ness.

Within the Highlands you'll find Scotland's most famous features. Ben Nevis, Scotland's highest mountain, is here, as is Loch Morar, the country's deepest loch. Loch Ness, undoubtedly the most famous stretch of water in Europe, is a few miles from Inverness, and the last full battle on British soil was fought at Culloden. Here too is Glencoe, scene of the famous massacre, as well as John O' Groats, Aviemore, Skye, Fort William, Cape Wrath

Scots Piper

Glencoe

and Plockton, the setting for *Hamish Macbeth*.

The west coast is rugged, with sea lochs that penetrate deep into the mountains. Settlements are few and far between, and most of them are to be found on the coast. Some visitors to the west coast of the Highlands are amazed at the sub tropical plants, such as palm trees, that seem to thrive here. It's all down to the Gulf Stream, which warms the shores and makes sure that snow is not as common as you would imagine.

The east coast, from Nairn to Inverness then north to John O' Groats, is gentler, with many more settlements. Dornoch, though small, has a medieval cathedral, so is more of a city than a town, and at Fortrose there are the remains of another cathedral. Strathpeffer was once a thriving spa town, with regular trains connecting it to Edinburgh and London.

And in the middle are the mountains, the lochs and the glens. The scenery can be austere and gaunt, but never anything less than beautiful. No Gulf Stream here, and in some sheltered corners, snow lies well into the year. Glencoe/Nevis and Aviemore take advantage of this by being skiing centres.

In Caithness and Sutherland - Scotland's two northernmost counties - you'll find the Flow Country, mile upon mile of low peaks, high moorland and small lochans. This isn't the dramatic scenery of the West Highlands where mountain seems to pile on mountain, but it has a ruggedness and grandeur of its own.

The Highlands is an area that amazes at every turn. The grandeur of the scenery takes the breath away, there are areas where all is mountains, lochs and glens, and there are areas that are as intensely cultivated as the Lowlands. There are lonely places, where another human being is likely to be miles away, and there is Inverness, which is busy and cosmopolitan. All these qualities make sure that the Highlands is one of the most rewarding places in Britain to visit.

Fort William

The small town of Fort William lies at the western end of Glen Mor (meaning "the Great Glen"), in an area known as Lochaber. It is the northern "terminus" of the 95-mile long West Highland Way, which snakes its way through Western Scotland from Milngavie on the outskirts of Glasgow. The fort referred to in the town's name was built by General Monk in the 1650s, then rebuilt during the reign of William III to house a garrison of 600 troops to keep the Highland clans in order, and renamed Maryburgh, after William's queen. Only parts of the wall survive, as the rest was dismantled in the 19th century to make way for the West Highland Railway.

It was the coming of the railway that established Fort William as one of the Highland's main centres for tourism, and it has remained so to this day. A few miles east of the town is **Ben Nevis**, at 4,406 feet, Britain's highest mountain. The five-mile climb to the top, along a well-trodden path, is fairly easy if you're reasonably fit. It is reached by way of **Glen Nevis**, often called Scotland's most beautiful glen, though there are other contenders for the title. If you do decide to climb Ben Nevis, let people know, and dress appropriately. While it may be warm and sunny at sea level, the weather on the mountain's slopes can be changeable. The rewards for the climb are immense. The Cairngorms can be seen, as can the Cuillin range on Skye and the peaks of Argyllshire. On an exceptionally clear day even the coast of Northern Ireland can be glimpsed through binoculars. At the **Glen Nevis Visitors Centre** there are exhibits about local heritage and wildlife, and, importantly, information about the weather on the mountain.

At 4,006 feet high, **Aonach Mor** is Ben Nevis's little brother, lying a mile to the east. In the winter this is a skiing area, but

Kismet Villa B&B

Heathercroft, Fort William,
Inverness-shire PH33 6RE
Tel: 01397 703654
e-mail: warmwelcome@kismetvilla.com
website: www.kismetvilla.com

Set above the picturesque town of Fort William, the two-star **Kismet Villa B&B** enjoys fantastic views out over Loch Linnhe. As it's in a quiet cul de sac, it can offer you all the peace and quiet you need for a relaxing holiday in welcoming, cosy surroundings. Or you can use it as a base for a variety of activities, such as hill walking, mountaineering, golf, sailing, fishing or watching wildlife. Kismet Villa is run by the Thacker family, who are committed to providing the very best in accommodation at affordable prices. It boasts three spacious and extremely comfortable rooms - a double, a twin and a king-sized. All the bedding is comfortable soft cotton, though satin bedding is available on request for those special romantic weekends.

All the rooms are on the ground floor, and come with a wash hand basin, TV/VHS/DVD entertainment systems, hospitality tray with tea, coffee, hot chocolate and mineral water, plus a little treat! There is plenty of storage space, and complimentary toiletries as well as face clothes and so on. There is a garden and well-behaved children and pets are more than welcome. Occasional barbecues are held in the Kismet Villa garden - great occasions for children and adults alike. This area of Scotland is truly beautiful, and deserves to be explored. Kismet can supply a packed lunch at a small extra cost. It's the perfect place to stay in Fort William!

Caledonian Canal, Fort William

it is equally popular in the summer. Britain's only mountain gondola takes you half way up the mountain to a restaurant and bar, and there are several walks to enjoy when you reach them.

Within the town, in Cameron Square, is the **West Highland Museum**, with exhibits and displays about the area. The most famous exhibit is the 18th century "Secret Portrait of Prince Charles Edward Stuart". It is a meaningless swirl of colours which, when reflected onto a polished cylinder, gives a likeness of the Prince. There are also some pieces of eight brought up from the Spanish galleon, which sank in Tobermory Bay (see also Tobermory). On the A830 at Corpach, northwest of the town, is the award winning Treasures of the Earth, one of Europe's finest collections of crystals and gemstones.

Fort William's newest attraction is

Crolinnhe

Grange Road, Fort William
Inverness-shire PH33 6JF
Tel: 01397 702709 Fax: 01397 700506
e-mail: crolinnhe@yahoo.com
website: www.crolinne.co.uk

A warm welcome awaits you at **Crolinnhe**, a superb guest house overlooking the waters of Loch Linnhe in Fort William. This grand Victorian villa has been totally refurbished so that it is now one of the most tasteful and elegant guest houses in Fort William, with three beautifully furnished and decorated guest rooms. All have colour TV, tea and coffee making facilities, hair dryers etc. All are double and have king-sized beds, and one even boasts a Jacuzzi in the bathroom. Crolinnhe is a mere ten minutes walk from the shops, restaurants, bars and other attractions of Fort William town centre, and makes an excellent base from which to explore an area that is rich in history, heritage and wildlife. There is also so much to do in the area, from golf and hill walking (Ben Nevis, Britain's highest mountain, lies close to Fort William) to fishing, sailing and mountain biking.

The full Scottish breakfasts are hearty and filling, with all the produce used being sourced locally wherever possible. Lighter options are available if required, and there is also delicious home baking and preserves. The proprietor is Flora MacKenzie, who is committed to maintaining the extremely high standards she has set over the years, and who is equally committed to offering you a warm Highland welcome. The attention to detail at this establishment means that you can enjoy a holiday that is as active or as peaceful as you like. The atmosphere is calm and tranquil, with a homely feel to it. Pay a visit and you're sure to agree!

Ocean Frontier on the banks of Loch Linnhe, which features marine life (including over 42 species of fish) and diving shows in a large aquarium. You can even take dives yourself and get guided tours round the adjacent diver training centre.

The impressive ruins of 13th century **Inverlochy Castle** (Historic Scotland) sit one and a half miles north east of Fort William. It was built by the Comyn family in the 13th century, though the ruins you see now date from much later. It was here that Montrose had an important victory over the Campbells, who were Covenanters, in 1645. It sits close to the 73-mile Great Glen Way, a long distance footpath that connects Fort William to Inverness.

Not far away, on the A82, is the 174-year-old **Ben Nevis Distillery and Whisky Centre**, which has conducted tours. One of its products is a blend of whiskies called The Dew of Ben Nevis.

Being at the southern end of the Great Glen, Fort William is where the **Caledonian Canal** begins (see also Inverness). It is not one uninterrupted canal, but a series connecting Loch Lochy, Loch Oich and Loch Ness (see Drumnadrochit for details of Loch Ness). **Neptune's Staircase** at Banavie, near Fort William, was designed and built by Thomas Telford in the early 1800s, and takes the canal through a series of eight locks while raising it over 60 feet.

Spean Bridge sits eight miles north east of Fort William. It was around here that commandos trained during World War II, and they are remembered by the **Commando Memorial**. It was designed by

Ashburn House

Achintore Road, Fort William,
Inverness-shire PH33 6RQ
Tel: 01397 706000 Fax: 01397 702024
e-mail: christine@no-1.fsworld.co.uk
website: www.highland5star.co.uk

On the shores of picturesque Loch Linnhe, and overlooking the Ardgour Hills, you will find one of the best hostelries in Fort William. **Ashburn House** sits only five minutes away from the centre of Fort William, and is an elegant Victorian building that has been tastefully converted to create an establishment that combines great standards of service with realistic prices.

A magnificent "barley-twist" pine staircase leads up to five spacious and extremely comfortable bedrooms on the first floor, while two further bedrooms are on the ground floor. All are fully en suite, with TV, tea/coffee making facilities, hair dryer, radio alarm and various other touches of luxury that make a stay enjoyable. A truly authentic and imaginative Highland breakfast is served in the Victorian-corniced dining room, along with "melt in the mouth" scones that are baked daily in Ashburn House's own Aga oven. Adjacent is the conservatory lounge, where you can relax in the evening over a book or a newspaper. It has views out over Loch Linnhe's shimmering waters to the hills beyond, and the sunsets must be seen to be believed.

Ashburn House makes the perfect base from which to explore the area, which is rich in Jacobite history. Loch Ness is a few miles to the north east, and you can take trips on the famous West Highland Line. Ashburn House is owned and managed by Christine and William MacDonald, who look forward to welcoming you to their excellent establishment.

Ben Nevis

the sculptor Scott Sutherland, and depicts three commando soldiers. It was unveiled by the late Queen Mother (at that time consort of King George) in 1952. **The Spean Bridge Mill,** which is nearby, has demonstrations of tartan weaving as well as a clan tartan centre.

In the summer months, the **Jacobite Steam Train** travels the famous Fort William to Mallaig line. It passes along the northern shores of Loch Eil - a continuation of Loch Linnhe after it turns westward - on a 45-mile journey that has some of the most beautiful scenery in Britain.

Around Fort William

Achnacarry

9 miles NE of Fort William on a minor road off the B8005

Since 1665 Achnacarry Castle had been the home of Cameron of Locheil, known as "Gentle Locheil", one of Charles Edward

Stuart's most ardent supporters. After 1745 it was burned down by Hanoverian troops. Locheil's family was banished from the country, but they were allowed to return in 1784, when they built a new home nearby. A building close to where Achnacarry once stood now houses the **Clan Cameron Museum**, which has displays, charts and exhibits relating to the history of the clan and to the commandos who trained here during the Second World War. A minor road takes you past the museum and along the lovely banks of **Loch Arkaig,** finally petering out near its western end.

Fort Augustus

28 miles NE of Fort William on the A82

Fort Augustus Abbey, on the shores of Loch Ness, was founded in 1876 for Benedictine monks. It was established on the site of a fort (named after George II's son) built on the orders of General Wade between 1729 and 1742 to keep Jacobite sympathisers in check. However, this it failed to do, and was actually taken by the Jacobite army in 1745. The abbey eventually closed in 1998, due to a decline in the number of monks. Many of the valuable books and manuscripts that were in the abbey library are now owned by the National Library of Scotland

The **Caledonian Canal Heritage Centre** is located in a converted lock keeper's cottage near the locks that take boats up into Loch Ness, and explains the history and uses of the canal.

The **Highland and Rare Breeds Croft** is on Auchterawe Road, and you can see Highland cattle, red deer and rare breeds of sheep, and at the **Clansman Centre** there are presentations on ancient Highland life.

Kinlochleven

10 miles SE of Fort William on the B863

This little town sits at the head of Loch Leven, and is on the West Highland Way.

Macdonald Hotel Kinlochleven

Fort William Road, Kinlochleven,
Argyll PH50 4QL
Tel: 01855 831539 Fax: 01855 831416
website: www.macdonaldhotel.co.uk

The **Macdonald Hotel** is situated beneath the Mamore Mountains and beside a tidal creek at the head of Loch Leven on Scotland's west coast, surrounded by mountains of breathtaking grandeur. The hotel is modern, yet built in traditional West Highland style, and offers high standards of service and a warm Scottish welcome. It has ten fully en suite bedrooms - four double, five twin and one family room. The doubles and twins can accommodate a third, folding bed if required, and a cot is available on request. All rooms have independently controlled heating, colour TV and tea/coffee making facilities.

The Macdonald Hotel makes the ideal base for touring the West Highlands, being handy for Oban, Fort William, Ben Nevis and historic Glencoe, and there are many fine walks in the area including the West Highland Way, a long distance footpath. A small campsite adjacent to the hotel caters for walkers who are walking the footpath, and it has showers and toilet facilities. There are also nine all-season timber cabins, with four bunks in each. They are warm and comfortable, with double glazing and plenty of storage space.

The Bothy Bar is comfortable and cosy, and occasionally features traditional music. There are over 40 single malts on offer. And if you're looking for that special meal, make your way to the spacious, elegant restaurant, which serves a range of meals, from bar lunches to set dinners. The cuisine is based on local produce, such as salmon, venison, beef and game.

Highland Getaway

28 Leven Road, Kinlochleven,
Argyll PH50 4RP
Tel: 01855 831258 Fax: 01855 831717
e-mail: info@highlandgetaway.co.uk
website: www.highlandgetaway.co.uk

Billed as a "restaurant with rooms", **Highland Getaway** is situated in the scenic village of Kinlochleven at the head of Loch Leven. The premises started life as a co-operative store, and was built about 1923. It was here that the present owner, Hugh Dailly, started his working life as a grocery boy, progressing on to be grocery manager. He then worked in the local aluminium smelters and ran a bakery before returning full circle to where he started.

In the main building is a superb licensed restaurant that serves the very best in food, using locally sourced, fresh produce wherever possible. It advertises itself as "café-bar by day, restaurant by night, our stylish fully licensed eatery is where you can begin your day with a hearty breakfast and end it with an excellent meal and fine wine". The ambience is relaxed and informal, and the décor and furnishing have recently been fully refurbished. The accommodation consists of four fully en suite rooms that are available all year round. There is a sitting area in each room, and they come equipped with colour TV, tea/coffee making facilities, vanity units, hair dryers and video. In a building adjacent to the Highland Getaway are shared facility apartments, with spacious TV room where you can relax over tea or coffee. Groups of up to seven can be accommodated. Kinlochleven is within easy reach of Oban or Fort William and the surrounding countryside offers great opportunities for hill walking, mountain biking, fishing and observing wildlife.

The **Aluminium Story Visitor Centre** on Linnhe Road at the library tells how hydroelectric power from the Blackwater Reservoir, high on the hills behind the town, was harnessed by the great aluminium smelting works that stood here up until the year 2000. Outside the centre is a giant sundial designed by blacksmith Robert Hutcheson that takes its inspiration from the area's history and scenery.

The **Ice Factor** on Leven Road is Britain's premier indoor mountaineering centre, and features the world's largest indoor ice climbing wall as well as Britain's largest articulated rock climbing wall. There is also a children's activity zone, audiovisual lecture theatre, steam room, plunge pool and hot tub and a cafeteria and restaurant.

Ballachulish

10 miles S of Fort William on the A82

The area surrounding Ballachulish ("settlement near the narrows") was once famous for its slate quarries. There are actually two villages separated by the waters of Loch Leven - North Ballachulish and Ballachulish itself, and they were once connected by ferry, which stopped running in 1975 when a bridge was built.

Ballachulish straggles along the southern shore of Loch Leven. To the west of the village a cairn marks the spot where Jacobite sympathiser **James of the Glen** was hanged for a crime he did not commit. He was found guilty of the murder of **Colin Campbell**, known as the "Red Fox", a government agent, by a Campbell judge and jury. Robert Louis Stevenson used the incident in his book *Kidnapped*. Another cairn marks the site of the murder. The **Slate Interpretive Centre** in the village has displays on the once prosperous slate quarrying industry.

To the east of Ballachulish, on the A82, is one of the most evocative places in Scotland - **Glencoe**. It was here, in 1691,

Loch Linnhe, Ballachulish

that the infamous Massacre of Glencoe took place. Because of bad weather, McIan of Clan MacDonald had failed to take the oath of allegiance to William III in time, and a party of Campbell troops were sent to Glencoe to massacre his people. They pretended at first to come in peace, and were offered hospitality. But in the early hours of February 13 they set about systematically killing McIan's people - men, women and children - with few escaping. A monument in the shape of a tall Celtic cross commemorates the event.

Glencoe, further east than the village, is a wild, beautiful place, though it does get crowded in summer months with hikers and climbers. On the north side is **Aonach Eagach**, a long ridge, and on the south side three peaks of Beinn Fhada, Gearr Aonach and Aonach Dhu, known as the **Three Sisters**. About 14,000 acres within Glencoe are now owned by the National Trust for Scotland,

and it has set up the **Glencoe Visitor Centre**, which tells the story of the massacre. In Glencoe village itself is the **Glencoe Folk Museum**, which has exhibits about the history of the area and its people.

About nine miles east of Glencoe, on a minor road off the A82, is the Glencoe skiing area with a chair lift that is open in the summer months, and gives wonderful views over Glencoe and Rannoch Moor.

Ardnamurchan

30 miles W of Fort William

The B8007 leaves the A861 at **Salen** (where a small inlet of Loch Sunart is usually crowded with picturesque yachts) and takes you westwards onto the Ardnamurchan Peninsula. It is single track all the way, so great care should be taken. It heads for Ardnamurchan Point and its lighthouse, the most westerly point of the British mainland, and in doing so passes some wonderful scenery.

At Glenborrodale you can glimpse the late Victorian **Glenborrodale Castle**, once the home of Jesse Boot, founder of the chain of chemists. At Kilchoan there are the ruins of **Mingary Castle**, a stronghold of the MacIan clan before passing to the Campbells. It was visited by James IV in the 1490s. It was briefly used in the 2002 movie *Highlander: Endgame*. Kilchoan is Britain's most westerly mainland village, and up until 1900, when the B8007 was constructed, it was also Britain's most inaccessible, as it could only be reached by boat. Nowadays, in summer, a ferry connects it to Tobermory on Mull.

A few miles North of Salen, on the edge of the area known as Moidart, are the ruins of **Castle Tioram** (pronounced "Chirrum"). The castle sits on a small island and was originally built in about 1353 by Lady Anne MacRuari, whose son Ranald gave his name to Clan Ranald. It was burnt by the Jacobites in 1715 to prevent it being used by Hanovarian forces, and has been a ruin ever since. At the head of Loch Moidart is a line of five beech trees. Originally there were seven, and were known as the **Seven Men of Moidart**. They commemorate the seven men who landed with Charles Edward Stuart and sailed with him up Loch Shiel, and were originally planted in the early 19th century (see Glenfinnan).

Strontian

20 miles SW of Fort William on the A861

Strontian (pronounced "Stron - teeh - an") sits in an area known as Sunart, which lies to the south of Loch Shiel. The village gave its name to the metal strontium, which was discovered in 1791 in the local lead mines by a chemist called Adair Crawford. A few years later Sir Humphrey Davie gave it its name.

Morvern

24 miles SW of Fort William

Morvern is that area of the mainland that sits immediately north of the island of Mull. The A884 leaves the A861 east of Strontian and travels down through it as far as Lochaline, on the Sound of Mull. **Kinlochaline Castle** sits at the head of Loch Aline, and was once the ancestral home of Clan MacInnes. The clan takes a special pride in being one of the few clans in Scotland without a chief. The last one, and all his family, was butchered by John, Lord of the Isles, in 1354.

The narrow B849 from Lochaline (with passing places) follows the shores of the Sound of Mull as far as Drimmin, and makes a wonderful drive.

Glenfinnan

13 miles W of Fort William on the A830

It was here, at the northern tip of **Loch Shiel**, that Charles Edward Stuart raised his standard in 1745, watched by 1,200 Highland followers. He had been rowed a short distance up the loch from the house of MacDonald of Glenaladale on the western shores. The **Charles Edward Stuart Monument** (National Trust for Scotland)

Re-enactment of Bonnie Prince Charlie's Arrival, Glenfinnan

was erected in 1815 by Alexander MacDonald of Glenaladale to commemorate the event, and a small visitors centre nearby tells the story.

The **Glenfinnan Station Museum**, which lies on the Fort William - Mallaig line, and tells of the building of the line by Robert McAlpine (known as "Concrete Bob") in the late 19th and early 20th centuries.

Arisaig

29 miles W of Fort William on the A830

The tiny village of Arisaig has wonderful views across to the islands of Rum and Eigg. Southeast of the village is **Loch nan Uamh**, where, on July 25 1745, Charles Edward Stuart first set foot on the Scottish mainland. After his campaign to restore the Stuart dynasty failed, he left for France from the same shore. A cairn now marks the spot. The **Land, Sea and Islands Centre** in the village has exhibits and displays about the history and wildlife of the area.

Mallaig

31 miles NW of Fort William on the A830

Mallaig, Britain's most westerly mainland port, is a busy fishing port and the ferry terminal for Skye. It is also the western terminus for the Jacobite Steam Train (see Fort William). The **Mallaig Heritage Centre** on Station Road has displays and exhibits that tell the story of the districts of Morar, Knoydart and Arisaig. The **Mallaig Marine World Aquarium and Fishing Exhibition** sits beside the harbour, and tells the story of Mallaig's fishing industry and the marine life found in the waters of Western Scotland. Most of the live exhibits were caught by local fishermen.

Southeast of the town is water of another sort - **Loch Morar**, which is Britain's deepest fresh water loch. It plunges to a depth of 1,077 feet, and if you were to stand the Eiffel Tower on the bottom, its top would still be 90 feet below the surface. A minor road near Morar village, south of Mallaig, takes you to its shores.

Kyle of Lochalsh

40 miles NW of Fort William on the A87

Kyle of Lochalsh was once the mainland terminus of a ferry that made a short

Ben Nevis from Mallaig

crossing across Loch Alsh to Skye. Now the graceful Skye Bridge has superseded the ferry. Three miles east of the village on the A87 is the **Balmacara Estate and Lochalsh Woodland Garden** (see panel below), with sheltered walks beside the shores of Loch Alsh, as well as mature woodlands and a variety of shrubs, such as rhododendrons, bamboo, ferns, fuchsias and hydrangeas. There is a small visitors centre at the square in Balmacara, just off the A87. Also centred on Kyle of Lochalsh is **Seaprobe Atlantis**, a glass-bottomed boat that takes you out into the Marine Special Area of Conservation and shows you the rich diversity of marine life in the waters surrounding Scotland..

Six miles east of the village is one of the

Gateway Restaurant

Station Road, Kyle of Lochalsh
Inverness-shire IV40 8AB
Tel/Fax: 01599 530258
e-mail: oorrestaurant@aol.com

For a lunch, dinner or light snack in Kyle of Lochalsh, make sure you visit the **Gateway Restaurant**, one of the best establishments in town. It serves great food, and is fully licensed, so you can also enjoy a drink with your meal if required. The premises are light, modern and airy, with colourful prints on the wall and huge windows. Try the tower of haggis, neeps and tatties, or the pan-seared Lochalsh scallops! There is also a children's menu which contains many favourites such as macaroni cheese with chips or pasta. The food is good, the service is efficient and friendly, and the prices are very reasonable!

Balmacara Estate & Lochalsh Woodland Garden

Lochalsh House (INITS), Balmacara, Kyle, Ross shire IV40 8DN
Tel: 01599 566325 Fax: 01599 566359
e-mail balmacara@nts.org.uk
Ranger/naturalist: Tel: 01599 511231 Fax: 01599 511417

A crofting estate of 2,750 ha (6,795 a), it has outstanding views of Skye and Applecross, and also the village of Plockton, an Outstanding Conservation Area. The estate also includes the Coille Mhor oakwood Special Area of Conservation (SAC) and the neighbouring Loch Alsh is part of the Loch Alsh & Loch Duish marine SAC. Visitors can discover more about this secluded, fascinating area at the small Visitor Centre at Balmacara Square, where an interactive CD ROM is available. Guides to the extensive footpath network and other local information can also be found here.

The Visitor Centre is located within the recently restored farm steadings beside the old millpond. There are craft workshops and a small delicatessen within the Square complex, which makes an excellent spot for a picnic. Lochalsh Woodland Garden offers quiet sheltered walks by the lochside among mature Scots pine, oaks and beeches with developing collections of rhododendrons, fuchsias, bamboos, hydrangeas and ferns. Interpretation can be provided at the reception kiosk in the garden.

Rockvilla Hotel

Main Street, Lochcarron,
Wester Ross IV54 8XB
Tel: 01520 722379 Fax: 01520 722844
e-mail: richardmunro@rockvilla-hotel.co.uk
website: www.rockvilla-hotel.co.uk

The Rockvilla Hotel sits in the centre of the village of Lochcarron, one of the loveliest areas of the Western Highlands, and has absolutely stunning views out over the loch and the mountains. It is a small, three-star, family run hotel offering personal service, high standards and great value for money, and is owned by Elspeth and Richard Munro, who take a genuine interest in the comfort of each of their guests.

The bedrooms are all attractively furnished and decorated, and all have colour television,

tea/coffee making facilities, en suite or private toilet and shower, and most have superb sea views. And the views here are wonderful, taking in Loch Carron itself and the glorious mountains on the other shore.

The comfortable lounge bar is fully licensed, and offers a wide selection of traditional cask ales, beers, wines, liqueurs and spirits, including, of course, a fine range of single malts. Here you can also enjoy a bar lunch or dinner, with the menu containing many beautifully cooked dishes that are both tasty and keenly priced. Accompanied children are welcome for bar meals up until 8pm, and a separate children's menu, and children's portions, are always available. The hotel's restaurant is recommended by "Taste of Scotland", and makes full use of fine, fresh local produce, such as Aberdeen Angus beef, local venison, game and lamb. Being on the coast, seafood is a speciality. The menu includes salmon, tasty prawns, plump scallops, mussels, lobsters and crab, all from the cold waters of the Western Highlands. The daily 'specials' change according to the availability of the produce, and there is also a small but carefully selected wine list. You're sure to find something that will complement the meal perfectly! Traditional Scottish music is promoted in the lounge bar where regular traditional live open music sessions take place.

The hotel nestles beside a deep sea loch and between the rugged Torridon and Kintail mountain ranges, and is ideally placed as a base from which to explore the surrounding area. You can cross over to Skye, or head for Eileen Donan Castle - surely the most romantic of the Scottish castles, being on a small island in Loch Duart. Or you could catch the train from Strathcarron and travel the Kyle line, reckoned to be the most beautiful in Scotland. Or there's Inverewe Gardens, owned by the National Trust for Scotland, and the remote, early Christian sanctuary at Applecross, reached by the Bealach na Ba', meaning the "Pass of the Cattle", which climbs from sea level to over 2000 feet in three miles. Plus there are miles and miles of white, deserted sandy beaches for picnicking or just relaxing in.

most photographed castles in Scotland, **Eilean Donan Castle**, which sits on a small island connected to the mainland by a bridge. Parts of it date back to 1220, when it was built by Alexander II. It is now the ancestral home of Clan MacRae, and has a small clan museum. It has also featured in many films, most notably *The World is Not Enough* and *Highlander*.

Kyle of Lochalsh

If you continue eastwards along the A87 you will eventually arrive at **Shiel Bridge**, at the head of Loch Duich. To the southeast is Glen Shiel, where the **Five Sisters of Kintail** (National Trust for Scotland) overlook the picturesque glen. Close by is the site of the **Battle of Glen Shiel**, fought in 1719 between a Hanovarian Army and a force of Jacobite (which included 300 Spaniards), and the last battle fought on British soil between British and foreign soldiers. There is a **Countryside Centre** at Morvich Farm, off the A87, and it makes a good starting point for walking on some of the surrounding hills and mountains.

Northeast of Kyle of Lochalsh is the village of **Plockton**, with its palm trees and idyllic location. This was the Lochdubh of

Hamish Macbeth fame, as it was here that the TV series was filmed. It sits on Loch Carron, and on the opposite bank, a few miles inland off a minor road, are the ruins of **Strome Castle** (National Trust for Scotland). It was built in the 15th century, and was a stronghold of the MacDonalds, Lords of the Isles. It later belonged to the MacDonnells of Glengarry. On **Craig Highland Farm**, near the village, you can view rare breeds, as well as feed the farmyard animals

Eigg

Kyle of Lochalsh is the western terminus for the famous Dingwall - Kyle of Lochalsh railway line (see Dingwall).

Canna

57 miles NW of Fort William

Canna means the "porpoise island", and has been owned by the National Trust for Scotland since 1981. It is about five miles long by just over a mile wide at its widest, and is usually sunny and mild. The remains of **St Columba's Chapel**, dating from the 7th or 8th centuries, with an accompanying Celtic cross, stand opposite the small island of Sanday, and have been excavated. **An Corghan**, on the east coast, is all that is left of a small tower house where a Clanranald chief imprisoned his wife, who was having an affair with a MacLeod clansman. The island is reached by ferry from Mallaig.

Eigg

40 miles W of Fort William

In 1997 the island of Eigg was bought on behalf of its inhabitants by the Isle of Eigg Heritage Trust. Its most famous feature is the 1,277 feet high **An Sgurr**, which slopes gently up to a peak on one side, and dramatically plunges on the other.

Southwest of the main pier is St Francis's Cave, also known as the **Massacre Cave**. It got its name from a gruesome event in 1577, when nearly 400 MacDonalds took refuge there when pursued by a force of MacLeods. The MacLeods lit fires at the entrance, and every one of the MacDonalds was suffocated to death. A nearby cave, MacDonald's Cave, is also known as the **Cathedral Cave**, as it was used for secret Catholic church services following 1745.

At **Kildonnan,** on the west coast, are the ruins of a 14th century church, built on the site of an ancient Celtic monastery founded by St Donnan. The saint and his 52 monks were massacred in AD 617 by a band of pirates.

Muck

46 miles W of Fort William

The tiny island of Muck's improbable name comes from eilean nam muc, meaning "island of pigs", though in this case the pigs may be porpoises, which are called "sea pigs" in Gaelic. It is reached by ferry from Mallaig, and is a low-lying island with good beaches. **Port Mor** is the main settlement and harbour, and on the south side of the Port Mor inlet are the scant remains of **Dun Ban**, a prehistoric fort. Northwest of the settlement are the ruins of an old ruined chapel surrounded by a graveyard.

Hebridean Princess off the Coast of Muck

The highest point, at 445 feet, is **Beinn Airein**, and from the top there is a good view of the whole of the island.

Rum

47 miles W of Fort William

When Sir John Bullough bought the island of Rum in 1888 he arrogantly changed its name to "Rhum", as he didn't like the associations it had with strong drink. However, when the Nature Conservancy Council took over the island in 1957 they changed the name back to the more correct "Rum", and it has been that ever since. Nowadays it is a Special Site of Scientific Interest and a Specially Protected Area, as its plant life has remained almost unchanged since the Ice Age.

The main settlement is Kinloch, on the east coast. **Kinloch Castle** was built by Sir George Bullough, John's son, as his main home on the island between 1901 and 1902. The **Bullough Mausoleum** in Glen Harris, to the south of the island, was built to take the bodies of Sir George, his father John and his wife Monica.

Kilmory, on the north coast of the island, has a fine beach and an old burial ground.

Skye

40 miles NW of Fort William

The new **Skye Road Bridge**, opened in 1995, has robbed Skye of its island status. However, it still remains one of the most beautiful and haunting of the Inner Hebrides, and the place has beauty and history aplenty. At Kyleakin, near the bridge, is the **Bright Water Visitor Centre**, with tours to the island nature reserve of Eilean Ban ("White Island") beneath the bridge. Perhaps the most famous features on the island are the **Cuillins** (or more properly, Cuillin), a range of mountains in the south east of the island. Though not the highest, they are perhaps the most spectacular mountains in Scotland, and present a challenge to any climber. The highest peak is **Sgurr Alasdair**, at 3,309 feet.

The A87 leaves the Skye Bridge and

Castle Moil, Skye

The Pier Hotel

Quay street, Portree, Isle of Skye,
Inverness-shire IV 51 9DE
Tel: 01478 612094 Fax: 01478 612810
e-mail: enquiries@pier-hotel.co.uk
website: www.pier-hotel.co.uk

Portree is the capital of Skye, and looks west towards the island of Raasay. It's name comes from "port-an-righ", means the "king's port", due to a visit in 1540 by James V. And in this picturesque place you'll find **The Pier Hotel**. It sits in the heart of the town by the harbour, and offers a warm Highland welcome. This is a place where tradition meets the modern concepts of great service and value-for-money. The atmosphere is informal and the staff are friendly and knowledgeable.

The rooms are all comfortable and fully en suite, with TV and tea/coffee making facilities and all have views out over Portree Harbour. During the summer season, the hotel's excellent restaurant serves superb food and uses only the finest and freshest of local produce wherever possible. Seafood is a speciality, and there is a daily specials board to choose from as well as the printed menus. The hotel's bar has a great range of ales, wines, spirits and liqueurs. Here you can meet and chat with the people of Portree, who will regale you with tales of the sea and the island. So if you're looking for good food, good accommodation and good drink, head for the Pier Hotel!

Greenacres Guest House

Viewfield road, Portree, Isle of Skye,
Inverness-shire IV51 9EU
Tel: 01478 612605 Fax: 01478 613175
e-mail: greenacreskyle@aol.com
website: www.greenacres-skye.co.uk

Situated on a scenic promontory 15 minutes walk away from the centre of Portree, Skye's capital, the **Greenacres Guest House** is owned and run by Marie and Ewan MacRae, who are determined to bring old-fashioned standards of great service coupled with value for money to their guest house. It is a modern building surrounded by wonderfully landscaped and immaculate gardens, and from the patio there are great views out over Portree Bay and the Cuillins. There are seven beautifully furnished and decorated guest rooms at Greenacres, each one comfortable and spacious. Three are on the ground floor, and four are on the first, and they all have colour TVs, hair dryers and tea and coffee making facilities.

Breakfasts are served in the pleasant dining room, and you can choose from a full Scottish - which is hearty and filling - to a lighter Continental option. Vegetarian dishes are also available. All the produce used is sourced locally, and is as fresh as possible. The lounge and conservatory are attractively furnished and also command outstanding views. Well behaved children aged over ten are very welcome, and there is plenty of overnight parking.

In nearby Portree you will find shops, a library, a swimming pool, bars and restaurants. At the Aros Heritage Centre, five minutes from Greenacres, there is also a gift shop, a restaurant and cinema. Skye has wonderful scenery and great wildlife and there are plenty of activities to take part in.

Uig Ferry, Skye

heads west along the northern shore of the island, passing through **Broadford**, one of its main settlements. Here, at Harrapool you will find the **Skye Environmental Centre**, which explains the island's wildlife. Also at Harrapool is the **Skye Serpentarium Reptile World**, an award winning reptile exhibition, and **World of Wood**, with an arboretum containing trees native to Scotland. The road then passes through Sconser, the southern terminus of a ferry linking Skye to the smaller island of **Raasay** (once visited by Boswell and Johnson), before reaching the island's main settlement of **Portree**. Its name (*port righ*, meaning "king's port") comes from a visit made to the place in 1540 by James V. Before that it was called Kiltragleann ("the glen church of St Talarican"). The town is the gateway to the Trotternish Peninsula, which juts out for 20 miles into the Minch, that sea channel separating the Outer Hebrides from the

Uig Hotel

Uig, Isle of Skye, Inverness-shire IV51 9YE
Tel: 01470 542205 Fax: 01470 542308
e-mail: manager@uighotel.com
website: www.uighotel.com

Owned and managed by Wendy and Bill Pearce, the **Uig Hotel** is a picturesque, whitewashed former coaching inn that overlooks Uig Bay and Loch Snizort. It is one of the most popular hotels on the magical island of Skye, and is the perfect base from which to explore its many attractions. Not only that - Uig has ferry connections with both Tarbert on Harris and Lochmaddy on North Uist, so you can travel even further afield than Skye! Wendy and Bill took over the hotel in 2003, and have managed to create something special - a place that

combines old fashioned values such as a warm Scottish welcome and great service with the modern ones of value for money and efficiency.

It boasts eighteen full en suite rooms ranging from comfortable singles to a lovely family suite with double bedroom, second bedroom with three single beds and a Jacuzzi. Several of them are in "Sobhraig House", the converted steading that adjoins the hotel. All are beautifully furnished and decorated, and all have colour TV, a phone and tea/ coffee making facilities. Most of the rooms have superb views across bay and loch, while the remainder look out onto wooded slopes, a picturesque church and the steading behind the hotel.

The cuisine at the Uig Hotel is excellent, using only the finest and freshest local produce wherever possible. The menu in the restaurant ranges from freshly caught local seafood to the exotic, such as crocodile tail or Springbok fillet. But beware - the food is so good here that you are advised to book well in advance! Full Scottish or Continental breakfasts are served in the restaurant between 8 am and 9 am Monday - Saturday, and 8.30 am - 9.30 am on Sunday.

The hotel bar has a cocktail/lounge bar with sun lounge, and serves a wide range of drinks, from ales and beers to spirits, wines, liqueurs and soft drinks. The famous Isle of Skye cask-conditioned ales are served, and there is a good selection of single malts, including Talisker, Skye's own malt whisky. It is open Monday - Saturday 11 am - 12 midnight and 12.30 pm to 11 pm on Sundays. Delicious and mouth-watering bar lunches are served in the hotel's sun lounge from 12 noon to 2 pm every day. And in the winter months, coal and wood fires are constantly burning in the bar to add warmth and cheeriness to an already welcoming ambience.

The Uig Hotel is a friendly, family-run hotel that offers a warm welcome to everyone. Wendy and Bill - and all the staff - are knowledgeable about what to do and see while on Skye, and are always on hand to offer advice and help. It is open all day, and serves morning coffees and light lunches. There is plenty of parking space, and all around there are opportunities for observing wildlife or taking part in many activities and sports, such as golf, fishing (both sea and fresh water), sailing and cycling. Or if you just want to relax and watch the world go by, where better to do it than at the Uig Hotel on Skye?

The Old Inn & Waterfront Bunkhouse

Carbost, Isle of Skye,
Inverness-shire IV47 8RS
Tel: 01478 640205
e-mail: reservations@oldinn.f9.co.uk
website: www.carbost.f9.co.uk

Standing on the shores of Loch Harport, the **Old Inn & Waterfront Bunkhouse** has splendid views of the Cuillin Hills and is the ideal base for hill walkers, climbers or sightseers. This is a free house, and the complex consists of the inn itself, a chalet or lodge with self-contained rooms and a bunkhouse-style hostel which has been expanded and modernised to provide a high degree of style and comfort.

It stands no more that twenty feet from the shores of beautiful Loch Harport, with the inn patio having splendid views. The atmosphere is relaxed and informal, and the

owners are determined to keep the place as traditional and welcoming as possible. The stone walls and bare boarded floors add to the "olde worlde" ambience. It is a favourite meeting place for the locals, so you could spend many a happy night meeting the true people of Skye and listening to their tales.

All the B&B rooms in the separate lodge are fully en suite, and all have been furnished and decorated to an extremely high standard so that guests can be assured of a good night's sleep. They have colour TV, tea/coffee making facilities and a hair dryer. In addition, there is a 24-bunk waterfront bunkhouse where the accommodation is still comfortable and warm, with all bedding and amenities provided. It's just right for hill walkers or climbers. Of the five rooms one is fully en suite, and all have views towards the loch or the Cuillins. There is a well-equipped kitchen and common room upstairs, with a balcony overlooking the loch. Shower facilities are available which can be used by visiting yachtsmen.

You can enjoy meals and drinks on the patio of the Old Inn. If you are a climber or a hill walker, the inn makes an ideal location, as it is central to all the attractions of the island, including the Talisker distillery, which is in the village, and is Skye's only whisky distillery. The food is simple and beautifully cooked, with hearty portions. Daily specials are available, with most of the produce used in the kitchen being extremely fresh and sourced locally wherever possible. And there is a great range of drinks at the bar, from ales, ciders and beers to wines, spirits (including Talisker!) and liqueurs.

The range of activities on Skye is impressive - climbing, hill walking, fishing, golf, sailing, cycling, or exploring the many historic sites and attractions. And the wildlife is staggering, from seals and otters to deer, buzzards, eagles and a multitude of other birds.

SCONSER LODGE HOTEL

Sconser, Isle of Skye,
Inverness-shire IV48 8TD
Tel: 01478 650333 Fax: 01478 650386
e-mail: skye@sconserlodge.co.uk
website: www.sconserlodge.co.uk

The **Sconser Lodge Hotel** sits in the picturesque hamlet of Sconser, close to the Skye terminal of the Raasay ferry. This magnificent stone building, with its distinctive turret, was built in 1881 as a hunters' haven in one of the most panoramic and central locations on Skye, and still retains many of its original features. It shelters beneath Glamaig, one of the "Red Cuillin" mountains, and overlooks The Braes on the northern shore, where a famous battle took place in 1882 between crofters and their landlord. It is owned and managed by Debra and Philip Grice, who have created a warm, friendly family atmosphere within a country house hotel - one that brings guests back again and again.

It boasts eight spacious bedrooms, all fully en suite and all immaculately furnished and decorated and having a colour television, hair dryers and tea/coffee making facilities. After a great night's sleep start the day with a full Scottish breakfast in the delightful dining room.

The hotel sits right on the shore, with its own jetty, and its Waterside Bar and Restaurant makes a great "19th hole" for the Isle of Skye golf course, which is nearby. It serves a superb range of local beers, ales, spirits (including a range of single malts), wines and liqueurs.

Why not enjoy a pre-dinner drink as you relish the thought of dinner in the restaurant? The food is outstanding, as you would expect, with the kitchens using only the finest and freshest of local produce wherever possible. The menu is imaginative while still retaining all the traditions of true Scottish cuisine. Salmon - Aberdeen Angus beef - venison - locally grown vegetables - all feature on the menu, as does freshly caught seafood. An interesting wine list is available, and you are sure to find something that complements the food exactly.

This part of Skye is rich in history and heritage, and deserves to be explored. The short ferry crossing to Raasay will take you to an island that is quiet and picturesque. Plus there are so many activities to take part in. Skye's golf course is close by, and there are ample opportunities to fish, golf, go hill waking, riding or cycling, (cycle hire available). You can even fish from the hotel's own jetty! If you are lucky you might see otters, seals or even dolphins from the hotel windows during your stay.

Time seems to move more slowly on Skye. It is an idyllic place, and if you fancy just relaxing and doing very little, then the Sconser Lodge Hotel is also the place for you! Put your feet up in one of the lounges with a drink and read the papers or a book. Or just gaze out the window at all the magnificent scenery. The hotel has got it all, and people seem to come back here year after year!

Sleat Holiday Homes

4 Calligarry, Ardvasar, Isle of Skye,
Inverness-shire IV45 8FU
Tel: 01471 844471 Fax: 01471 844278
e-mail: shonestag@supanet.com

Sleat has often been called the "garden of Skye", and this is no idle boast. It is a pleasant and fertile part of the island lying opposite Mallaig and sheltered by the bulk of the Cuillins, Skye's own mountain range. **Sleat Holiday Homes** is in the small village of Ardvasar, and offers some of the best self-catering accommodation in the island for those discerning tourists who appreciate quiet surroundings, comfort and convenience.

Eoin Mhara is a cottage that sleeps four adults in two extremely comfortable

bedrooms, a double and a twin, and is furnished and decorated to a high standard. Heating, lighting and cooking are all supplied through a coin-in-the-slot meter, and off-peak is supplied at no cost.

There is a spacious, open plan sitting room/kitchen with patio doors that look out over the Sound of Sleat to the high hills of Knoydart and Lochabar on the mainland, and from here you can see the ferry ply back and forth between Mallaig and Armadale, a mile or so away. The cottage is well equipped for a holiday that can be as relaxing or as hectic as you wish, and boasts a colour TV, cooker, microwave, washer/dryer, fridge, dishwasher, kettle and toaster, as well as all cutlery, crockery and cooking utensils. The bathroom has a shower fitted over the bath, and all the other usual fitments.

The owner, Grace Shone, is determined that your stay will be as enjoyable as possible, and strives to maintain exceptional standards while at the same time offering prices that are as keen as possible. And she also leaves a "welcome" food pack for your arrival - just one of the nice touches that make you realise you are in the midst of good, Highland hospitality. All linen is provided, and a cot and high chair is available on request. There is a small fenced garden - just right for those long, mild summer evenings you get in Skye - and ample car parking. Well-behaved dogs are also welcome at no extra cost. The village of Ardvasar, which is within walking distance, has a general store, a post office and a hotel with a friendly bar (popular with the locals) and good food.

There is so much to do and see in Sleat. Boat trips and fishing are popular pastimes, and can be laid on by prior arrangement. There is also golf, fishing (both fresh and sea), climbing, hill walking and trekking, cycling, and the study of the area's superb wildlife. Seals and otters can be seen on the coast, and inland there are deer, eagles and a host of other birds. You can also visit the many historical sites of the island.

Ardvasar Hotel

Sleat, Isle of Skye, Inverness-shire IV45 8RS
Tel: 01471 844223 Fax: 01471 844495
e-mail: Richard@ardvasar-hotel.demon.co.uk
website: www.ardvasarhotel.com

A visit to the **Ardvasar Hotel** is a truly memorable experience. It was built in the early 1800s, making it one of the earliest hotels on Skye. The ten en suite rooms are comfortable and elegant, each having colour TV, clock radio, telephone, hospitality tray and hair dryer. Three of the rooms are very spacious, and one boasts a four poster bed. Several rooms are also suitable for families. Well behaved dogs are more than welcome in the rooms, but not, unfortunately, in any of the public rooms. On the landing, guests will find a trouser press as well as ironing facilities. The cosy lounge has superb views across the Sound of Sleat towards Knoydart and Mallaig on the mainland, and there is an excellent selection of books and games for those days when the weather isn't quite to your liking!

The lounge bar has a convivial and friendly atmosphere, and is the perfect place to enjoy that pre-dinner drink, whether it be a warm, rounded single malt, a liqueur, a glass of wine or a refreshing beer. Or you could choose the small public bar, which is a great favourite with the locals (always a good sign!). This is where you can meet and talk to real Skye people, and enjoy a lively bit of *craik* or a pint. In the summer months when the sun is shining, why not have afternoon tea in the hotel's private garden? The views are breathtaking, and you will feel yourself relaxing almost immediately away from the hurry and scurry of modern life.

The Ardvasar Hotel is renowned for its food, and has a reputation second to none. It uses only the finest and freshest of local produce wherever possible, such as locally caught lobster, langoustine, crab and salmon. Local venison and Aberdeen Angus beef also feature on the menu, as well as locally grown vegetables. The award-winning chef combines flair and imagination to create memorable dishes that meld traditional Scottish cooking and ingredients with carefully selected foreign influences. In addition, there is a fine selection of good wines, and you are sure to find one that will be a wonderful complement to your meal.

There's so much to do on Skye. Your holiday can be as relaxed or active as you want. The roads are quiet, so exploring by car is a real pleasure. History is all around, and wherever you go the views are truly stunning. Activities include sailing, golf, fishing and hill walking and climbing, with the Cuillin range being particularly challenging. Or you can study wildlife. The waters round Skye are a haven for seals and otters, and inland you can see golden eagles, buzzards and deer. Spring is spectacular, with bluebells, primroses and wood anemones.

Castle Moil Restaurant And King Haakon Bar

Kyleakin, Isle of Skye,
Inverness-shire IV41 8PL
Tel: 01599 534164

Kyleakin is a small, picturesque village that was once the terminal for a small ferry that ran from Skye to the mainland and now sits in the shadow of the Skye Bridge, opened in 1995. Within the village you will find the **Castle Moil Restaurant and King Haakon Bar**, one of the best places in the area to eat. This modern, smart establishment is family-run and friendly, and has earned an enviable reputation for its food and drink, making it popular with both visitors and locals alike.

The restaurant and bar menus each have a wide range of delicious dishes to choose from, including starters and light bites such as haggis, neeps and tatties, breaded mushrooms and home-made soups. There is also a wide range of salads, and of course seafood, as well as the famous Castle Moil steak pie and a range of vegetarian dishes. All the produce is sourced locally, and is as fresh as possible!

Throughout the season there are regular traditional and contemporary music sessions, which bring a real touch of Scotland in the King Haakon Bar. And if you want to take a souvenir home with you, drop in at the gift shop. It sells a wide range of goods and crafts that are authentically Scottish, from ceramics and postcards to flags, books and tea towels.

Kyleakin is the gateway to Skye, surely the most romantic of the Inner Hebrides. Why not visit the **Bright Water Visitor Centre**, with tours to the island nature reserve of Eilean Ban beneath the bridge? Kyleakin is one of Skye's prettiest village, with so much to do and see, and a perfect base from which to explore the rest of this mystical island.

mainland. A road from Portree follows its coastline right round until it arrives back at the town.

Fifteen miles west of Portree along the A850 is Dunvegan, famous for **Dunvegan Castle**, perched above the waters of Loch Dunvegan. It has been the home of Clan MacLeod for eight hundred years, and though much of it is Victorian, parts date back to the 13th century. In the drawing room is the famous Fairy Flag, revered by members of Clan MacLeod, which was supposed to bring success in battle.

Across the loch, and reached by the B884, is the **Colbost Croft Museum**, based on a "black house" (a small traditional cottage of turf or stone, topped with a thatched roof). It shows the living conditions of islanders in the past, and features an illicit still.

To the southeast of the island, on the Sleat Peninsula at Armadale, is the **Armadale Castle Gardens and Museum of the Isles**. It sits within a 20,000 acre Highland estate, once owned by the MacDonalds of Sleat, and was purchased by the Clan Donald Land Trust in 1971. The earliest parts of the castle date from the 1790s, when it was built by the first Lord MacDonald on the site of a farm and gardens, where Flora MacDonald married in 1750.

Dunscaith Castle, the ruins of which lie on the western side of the peninsula, was abandoned by the MacDonalds of Sleat in the 18th century. Legend says that the castle was built by fairies in one night, and subsequently protected by a pit full of snakes. It was the home, the legend continues, of the Queen of Skye, who taught the arts of war.

Inverness

Inverness is the capital of the Highlands. It is said to be the most rapidly expanding place in Britain, and though it only has a

Trafford Bank Guest House

96 Fairfield Road, Inverness,
Inverness-shire IV3 5LL
Tel: 01463 241414 Fax: 01463 241421
e-mail: info@traffordbankhotel.co.uk
website: www.traffordbankguesthouse.co.uk

Inverness, "Capital of the Highlands", is one of the most historic cities in Scotland. With its great shopping (including the stunning Eastgate Centre and the more traditional Market Hall), its restaurants, pubs and clubs; it is also one of the country's most popular holiday destinations.

Here you will find the perfect place to stay - the non-smoking **Trafford Bank Guest House**, which has been awarded five coveted red diamonds from the AA, meaning that the service and facilities are "flawless". Owned and personally managed by Lorraine and her partner Koshal, it was formerly the home of the Bishop of Moray and Ross, and is only ten minutes walk from the city centre. The building is of warm, local stone, with a mature garden where you can walk and admire the flowers in the long summer evenings. Lorraine and Koshal have retained many of the building's original features, marrying them to the modern concepts of high standards of service and outstanding value for money. This is a place where you can experience luxury and pampering in a friendly, informal atmosphere!

The guest house has five rooms, each one individually furnished and decorated to an exceptionally high standard. All are en suite, and the furnishings and fittings are a mixture of antique and modern. The Trafford Suite, with its king-size bed and day bed, and the Green Room with its wrought iron double and single beds, can be used as family rooms, and are at the front of the house. The Floral is a double or twin room, the Tartan Room is a double, and the Blue Room is a twin room. All have hospitality trays, colour TVs (the Trafford and the Floral have flat screen TVs), DVD players, flowers and fruit, a decanter of port or sherry and a hair dryer. Being a supporter of Highland industries, the rooms have Arran Aromatic or Skye soaps.

Trafford Bank boasts two comfortable and elegant guest lounges, one with cable TV and a DVD player. These are the perfect places to relax or plan your next trip to one of the many scenic areas in the Highlands. Culloden, the Moray Firth dolphins, Loch Ness, Cawdor Castle, Nairn, skiing at Aviemore and Elgin are all within easy reach. Lorraine and Koshel between them speak Italian, French, Hindi and Swahili, and can advise you on what to see in the area.

Breakfasts are served in a spacious and airy conservatory overlooking the gardens. You can choose from a hearty full Scottish breakfast or a lighter option. Everything will be prepared from fresh, local produce, and served on stylish Anta Pottery, which is manufactured at Fearn, just north of Inverness. The facilities and the luxurious extras here make Trafford Bank very special.

St. Andrews Cathedral, Inverness

The city sits at the northeastern end of the Great Glen, at a point where the River Ness enters a short channel connecting the Beauly and Moray Firths. It was once the capital of the Northern Picts, and it was to Inverness that St Columba came in the 6th century to confront King Brude MacMaelcon and convert him and his kingdom to Christianity. The doors of Brude's stronghold were

population of about 50,000, its hinterland supports a further 20,000. But for all its size, it still has all the feel and bustle of a much larger place, and its shopping - especially in the pedestrianised High Street, where the Eastgate Shopping Centre is located - is superb.

firmly closed, but Columba marked them with the sign of the cross and they flew open of their own accord.

No one knows where this stronghold stood, though some people have suggested Craig Phadraig, two miles west of the mouth of the Ness, and others have

Crown Guest House

19 Ardconnel Street, Inverness,
Inverness-shire IV2 3FU
Tel: 01463 231135
e-mail: reservations@crownhotel-inverness.co.uk
website: www.crownhotel-inverness.co.uk

With six comfortable and well-furnished rooms (four of which are en suite) the three-star **Crown Guest House** is one of the best establishments of its kind in the city of Inverness. All the rooms have tea/coffee making facilities, colour TV, radio alarm, hair dryer and central heating.

The guest house is situated close to the city centre in a traditional sandstone Victorian terrace built in 1890, and though it offers high standards of service and all modern conveniences, it still retains many of its original features. Owned and run by locals Catriona and Gordon Barbour, it is a place that combines great comfort and style with informality and real customer service.

The residents' lounge is spacious, warm and comfortable and has television, chess set, book swap and games console - though often the kids have to fight with parents to play! Breakfasts are served in the elegant pastel blue and white dining room, where guests can choose from a full Scottish or a Continental option. You can come and go as you please, with your own personal pass key, and both Catriona and Gordon are extremely knowledgeable about what to do and see in the area, from Loch Ness, Culloden battlefield, the Moray Firth dolphins and Fort George. In each room you will find an eating out guide for the city. This is an establishment that puts service and value for money first. Pay a visit and you won't be disappointed!

SMITHTON HOTEL

Smithton, Inverness, Inverness-shire !V2 7NL
Tel: 01463 791999
Fax: 01463 794559
e-mail: reservations@lakeforth.com
website: www.smithtonhotel.co.uk

Sitting to the east of Inverness's city centre, the **Smithton Hotel** has been owned and managed since October 2003 by Sarah and Norry Thom, who are local to the area. This is a family run hotel which was built in 1980, with the top storey added seven years later, and it has a friendly, warm and informal atmosphere while still retaining all the high standards of service and value for money you would expect from a hotel of this quality. It has 16 fully en suite rooms on offer to discerning guests, and each one has a colour TV, direct dial telephone, tea/coffee making facilities, internet access and trouser press.

The hotel bar is open all day and every day

for the sale of keg ales, beers, wines, spirits, liqueurs and soft drinks. It is both spacious and smart, with comfortable fixtures and fittings so that you can relax over a welcoming drink after a hard day's sightseeing or other activity. This is the place to meet the local people, and enjoy a gossip with them! Or you can make use of the games room, with its multiple pool tables and a 5 foot wide television to view all the top sporting events. The large and comfortable lounge bar provides daily bar meals and suppers, and is a popular venue for local people. There is also a smaller, more intimate TV lounge. The cosy yet spacious dining room offers excellent home cooked food together with a select wine list. The food is all prepared from good, fresh, local produce wherever possible, and no use whatsoever is made of "bought in" frozen ingredients that merely need heating up before being served. In this way, guests are assured of a great eating experience that they will remember for all the right reasons. The menu includes many dishes that marry traditional Scottish fare, such as prime beef, salmon and locally grown vegetables with imagination and a hint of the Continent.

The hotel has that homely, friendly atmosphere that people are looking for, and it is a place where children are more than welcome. It makes a great base from which to explore the area, and is no more than a mile and a half from Inverness city centre and five miles from the airport.

Culloden battlefield is two miles away, and from Smithton you get a great view of the Moray Firth, the distant mountains and the Kessock Bridge. The bottle-nosed dolphins of the Firth can be seen at Chanonry Point on the Black Isle, and the skiing area at Aviemore is no more than half an hour south by car. Plus, of course, there's Loch ness, with romantic Urquhart Castle and Nessie - the local name for the Loch Ness monster.

Bridge over the River Ness

suggested Torvean, just outside the town.

The present **Inverness Castle** dates from 1835, and houses the local courthouse. Castles have stood on the site since at least the 12th century. However, Macbeth's castle, where Shakespeare set the murder of Duncan, stood some distance away. General Wade enlarged Inverness Castle after the uprising of 1715, and its garrison surrendered to Charles Edward Stuart when he occupied the town in 1745. He then ordered the castle to be blown up. Close to the castle is a statue of **Flora MacDonald**, who helped Charles Edward Stuart evade capture.

Near the castle, in Bridge Street, is the **Town House**, which was completed in

1882. It was here, in 1921, that the only cabinet meeting ever held outside London took place when Lloyd George was prime minister. Across from it is the **Tolbooth Steeple**, dating from the late 18th century. It was once part of a complex of buildings that contained a courthouse and jail. In Castle Wynd is **Inverness Museum and Art Gallery**, which has a large collection relating to the history of the Highlands and the town in particular.

The oldest secular building in the city is **Abertaff House** in Church Street (National Trust for Scotland), which dates from 1593. It was built as a town house for the Frasers of Lovat, and is now a craft shop. **Dunbar's Hospital** is also on Church Street, and dates from 1668. It was founded by Provost Alexander Dunbar as a hospital for the poor. It has now been divided into flats.

Balnain House (National Trust for Scotland), on Huntly Street on the opposite bank of the River Ness, was built in 1726 and is now the Trust's regional HQ. It is not open to the public. Also on the opposite

MUNLOCHY HOTEL

54 Millbank Road, Munlochy,
Ross-shire IV8 8NL
Tel: 10463 811494 Fax: 01463 811803
e-mail: info@munlochyhotel.com
website: www.munlochyhotel.com

Judith and Ronnie welcome you to the top rated **Munlochy Hotel**, which is situated in the small village of Munlochy on Munlochy Bay in the Black Isle, on the Moray Firth. Ever since it was built in the late 18th century, it has always been called the Munlochy Inn, and is a picturesque, white washed building that retains many period features while still offering modern standards of service and value for money. It is an informal, friendly place, with plenty of car parking and set right in the heart of the village.

It boasts six exceedingly comfortable guest rooms, three of which are fully en suite and on the first floor. There is a good choice of differing sizes, and children are most welcome. The décor and furnishings in each one are of the highest standard, and the beds are all comfortable ensuring a good night's sleep. The B&B tariff includes a hearty, Scottish breakfast, though lighter options are available. The hotel opens during the winter months at 5pm on Monday and Tuesday, and closes between 2 pm and 5 pm from Wednesday to Friday. It opens all day seven days a week in the summer months. When open, good food is available from 12 noon until 2 pm and from 5.30 pm until 8.30 pm on weekdays and until 9 pm at weekends. In fact, so good is the food that you are advised to book at weekends.

Judith is an excellent cook, and uses only the finest and freshest of local produce wherever possible, including locally caught seafood, Scotch beef, lamb, poultry, salmon and locally grown vegetables. The cuisine is Scottish with Continental influences, and the menu includes many imaginative dishes that are sure to please. There is also a select wine list which is sure to contain something that suits the food exactly.

The bar is popular with both visitors and locals alike, which is always a good sign. There is a great selection of beers and ales - including real ales - as well as ciders, wines, liqueurs and spirits. Why not try one of the hotel's single malts?

The Munlochy Hotel is the perfect base from which to explore the surrounding area. The bustling city of Inverness is only five miles south, and Chanonry Point, a few miles east, is one of the best vantage points to see the famous bottle-nosed dolphins of the Moray Firth. There is skiing at Aviemore, south of Inverness, and Loch Ness is almost on the doorstep.

Judith and Ronnie want to welcome you to their establishment and with years of being in the catering trade know a thing or two about making people feel welcome!

bank is **Inverness Cathedral,** dedicated to St Andrew, a gem of a building designed by Alexander Ross and consecrated in 1874. It was supposed to have had two large spires, but these were never built.

The Old High Church in Church Street, dedicated to St Mary, is Inverness's parish church and was built in 1770, though parts of the tower may date from medieval times. After the battle of Culloden, the church was used as a jail for Jacobite soldiers, some of whom were executed in the kirkyard. It is said to be built on a site where St Columba once preached. The **Old Gaelic Church** was originally built in 1649, though the present building dates from a rebuilding of 1792.

Inverness is one of the few Scottish towns to have retained its traditional market, and the indoor **Victorian Market** in Academy Street building dates from 1890, when it was rebuilt after a disastrous fire.

The magnificent **Kessock Bridge** carries the A9 over the narrows between the Moray and Beauly Firths and connects Inverness to the Black Isle. At North Kessock is the **Dolphins and Seals of the Moray Firth Visitor and Research Centre**. The Moray Firth is famous for its bottlenose dolphins, and boats leave from many small ports so that you can observe them. This visitor centre gives you one of the best opportunities in Europe to learn about the creatures, and to listen to them through underwater microphones.

Around Inverness

Cromarty

16 miles NE of Inverness on the A832

This picturesque small royal burgh, which received its charter in the 13th century, sits on a small headland at the start of the Cromarty Firth. It is probably the best-preserved eighteenth century town in Scotland, and was where many Highlanders embarked for Canada during the Clearances of the early 19th century.

It was the birthplace, in 1802, of Hugh Miller, writer and the father of geology. **Hugh Miller's Cottage** (National Trust for Scotland), where he was born, is open to the public. It has a collection of fossils and rock specimens, as well as some of his personal possessions such as his geological hammer and microscope.

The **Cromarty Courthouse Museum**, as its name suggests, is housed within the old courthouse. There is a reconstruction of an 18th century trial in the courtroom itself, plus you can see the old cells, children's costumes, a video presentation giving 800 years of Cromarty history and an audio tape tour of the old part of the town.

The Cromarty Firth has always been a safe anchorage for British ships. On 30 December 1915 *H.M.S. Natal* mysteriously blew up here, with the loss of 421 lives. Many of those killed lie in the kirkyard of the **Gaelic Chapel**.

Fortrose

8 miles NE of Inverness on the A832

Fortrose Cathedral (Historic Scotland) was founded by David I as the mother church of the diocese of Ross. Building began in the 1200s, though the scant remains you see nowadays date from the 14th century. One of the three fine canopied tombs is of Euphemia Ross, wife of the Wolf of Badenoch (see also Dunkeld and Elgin). The other two are of bishops, possibly Robert Cairncross and John Fraser.

Nearby **Chanonry Point** is one of the best places to observed the Moray Firth dolphins. Here, where the firth is at its narrowest, you can sometimes see up to 40 of these graceful creatures glide through the waters or put on a fine display of jumping and diving.

In nearby **Rosemarkie** is the **Groam House Museum,** with exhibits and displays that explain the culture of the Picts, those mysterious people who inhabited this part of Scotland in the Dark Ages. The cathedral for the diocese of Ross was established here before moving to Fortrose, the site now being occupied by the parish church of 1819.

Craigaron

17 Saltburn, Invergordon,
Ross-shire IV18 0JX
Tel:01349 853640 Fax: 01349 853619
e-mail: jobrown@craigaron.freeserve.co.uk
website: www.craigaron-invergordon.co.uk

The two star **Craigaron** is housed in a picturesque, friendly, 19th century cottage that has been tastefully converted to offer the best in reasonably-priced accommodation. Owned and managed by Mrs Jo Brown, it is located on a sunny seafront a short walk from the centre of town, and has superb views south towards the Cromarty Firth and the Black Isle. There are five extremely comfortable and well-furnished rooms on offer - a single and four twins, two of which are fully en suite and have security locks.

The breakfasts are hearty and filling. All the produce is sourced locally, and is as fresh as possible.

Mrs Brown has a wealth of information about attractions in the area, including news of the many cruise liners (including the QE2) that sail past the house to call in at the Cromarty Firth. John O'Groats and the ferry to Orkney is a two hour drive away. Inverness, Loch Ness, the Moray Firth dolphins and Culloden battlefield are an hour south, as is Inverness Airport. Skye can be reached in two hours, and there are 20 or more superb and challenging golf courses all within an hour's drive. Mrs Jo Brown has run the guest house since 1988, and in that time it has earned a reputation which is second to none. It has a genuine home-from-home atmosphere.

Carnegie Lodge Hotel

Viewfield Road, Tain, Ross-shire IV19 1NR
Tel: 01862 894039 Fax: 01862 894907
e-mail: Carnegielodge@hotmail.com
website: www.carnegielodge.com

Carnegie Lodge is a small, comfortable hotel set on the outskirts of the small royal burgh of Tain, on Scotland's north east coast. It is owned and managed by Scott McLean, who brings a wealth of experience to the job. He sets very high standards in accommodation, food and drink, all at prices that are as keen as possible. The hotel has six modern, en suite rooms on offer, all extremely comfortable, and all well decorated and furnished. Food is important here, and the dining room/conservatory has a menu that marries traditional Scottish produce with a touch of imagination and flare. All the ingredients, such as prime beef, salmon, poultry and seafood, are sourced locally, and are as fresh as possible. Main courses include rack of lamb, king scallops, salmon, seafood platter, sizzling steaks and pork, all beautifully cooked and presented. The chef is John Dyer, former head chef at the Café Royal, Traverse Theatre and Raffaelli in Edinburgh. Vegetarian options are available, and there is a good wine list. In the country-style bar you can order tasty bar meals and suppers as well as beers, wines, spirits and soft drinks. The facilities are available for private functions and parties, and there are frequent entertainment nights with the focus on live entertainment from local musicians. Tain itself is a picturesque town that is well worth exploring and in addition, Dunrobin castle, the ancestral home of the Dukes of Sutherland, is close by, as is Skibo Castle, once owned by Andrew Carnegie. Royal Dornoch golf course is a few miles away, and there are opportunities for sailing, shooting, fishing and walking.

Tain

23 miles N of Inverness on the A9

In medieval times, Tain was a place of pilgrimage, drawing pilgrims from all over Europe to the shrine of St Duthus within **St Duthus Collegiate Church**. Now an exhibition and visitors centre called **Tain Through Time** explains about St Duthus himself, the pilgrimage, and the people who made it. The museum, which is part of the centre, also has displays about Clan Ross. A ruined church near the mouth of the river was built, it is said, on the site of St Duthac's birthplace.

Half a mile north of the town is the **Glenmorangie Distillery**, which has guided tours and a museum, with a tasting at the end of the tour.

Dornoch

30 miles N of Inverness on the A949

Dornoch Cathedral dates originally from the early 13th century. However, the church as we see it today is largely a rebuilding of the early 19th century, though there are some old features still to be seen, mostly in the chancel and crossing. Sixteen Earls of Sutherland are said to be buried within it. It was also where, in December 2000, the pop star Madonna married Guy Ritchie.

Dornoch was the scene, in 1722 (or 1727), of Scotland's last execution for witchcraft, when an old woman called Janet Horne was burned for supposedly turning her daughter into a pony. The judge at the trial was later reprimanded for his handling of the case. The **Witch's Stone**, within a garden in Littletown, marks the spot where Janet was executed.

Brora

45 miles NE of Inverness on the A9

Brora is a picturesque coastal village at the mouth of the River Brora. The **Brora Heritage Centre** has a hands-on guide to the history and wildlife of the area. At one time it was the location of the Highland's only coal mine, with the coal being shipped out from the local harbour until the railways took over.

Golspie

40 miles NE of Inverness on the A9

A steep hill path takes you to the summit of **Ben Bhraggie**, on which there is a

Ben Bhraggie Hotel

Old Bank Road, Golspie,
Sutherland KW10 6RS
Tel: 01408 633242
e-mail: myra@theben.co.uk
website: www.the-ben.co.uk

The small, picturesque town of Golspie can be summed up as "great golf, beautiful beaches and a fairytale castle". And it is here that you will find the **Ben Bhraggie Hotel**. It was built in 1829 of warm, local stone and has the added attraction of having it's own spring well. It boasts seven rooms, all comfortable and furnished to an extremely high standard. There are two twin, two single, two double and a spacious family room that can sleep up to five. Each room has a wash hand basin, colour TV, tea/coffee making facilities, hair dryer and iron.

The hotel kitchen specialises in good, old-fashioned home cooking, using only the finest and freshest of local produce where available. The menus are put together with imagination and flair. Choose from the bar menu, the daily specials board or à la carte. A children's menu is also available. There is also a children's play area. The lounge bar is a great favourite with local people, and here you can enjoy a quiet drink away from the hustle and bustle of modern life. It has plenty of atmosphere and retaines many original features. Golspie itself is well worth exploring. Dunrobin castle - looking more like a French chateau than a Scottish castle - is the ancestral home of the Dukes of Sutherland, and on Ben Bhraggie is a statue of the 1st duke, who became notorious during the Highland Clearances. Close by is Royal Dornoch golf Course, and Golspie has its own challenging 18-hole course.

Easter Dalziel Farm B&B & Cottages

Dalcross, Near Inverness IV2 7JL
Tel/Fax: 01667 462213
e-mail: hp@easterdalzielfarm.co.uk

Set within a seventeenth century farmhouse which was partially rebuilt in the 19th century, the four star **Easter Dalziel Farmhouse** house B & B offers three superbly furnished and decorated guest rooms to discerning tourists. There are two double rooms and one twin room each with hospitality tray, duvet and washbasin. The full Scottish breakfasts are filling and hearty, though lighter options are available if required. Breakfast times can be arranged to suit your individual requirements, and are served in the spacious dining room.

The gardens are awash with colour in the summer months, and a stroll round them is sure to set you up for a good night's sleep in the comfortable beds!

Also on the farm are the three Self Catering Cottages graded from three to four star by VisitScotland. All are extremely well appointed, and are furnished and decorated to a high standard. Birch and Pine sleep six and Rowan four. All the cottages are heated and have a comfortable lounge/dining area, bathroom and fully equipped kitchen. A large grassy area and attractive flowerbeds surround them. Fresh linen (sheets and pillowcases) and towels are supplied and changed weekly.

statute by Chantry of the first Duke of Sutherland, who died in 1833. Locally, it is known as the "Mannie", it was erected in 1834 by "a mourning and grateful tenantry to a judicious, kind and liberal landlord". The words ring hollow, however, as the Duke was one of the instigators of the hated Clearances of the early 19th century, and there have been continued calls to have the statue removed, and in some cases blown up. Others have argued that the statue should stay as a reminder of those terrible times.

Dunrobin Castle (see panel on page 367), the seat of the Dukes of Sutherland, is the most northerly of Scotland's stately homes and one of the largest in the Highlands. Though the core is 14th century, it resembles a huge French chateau, thanks to a remodelling in 1840 by Sir Charles Barry, designer of the Houses of Parliament. Some of the castle's 189 rooms are open to the public, and there is a museum in the summerhouse.

Lairg

40 miles N of Inverness on the A836

Lairg is an old village that sits at the southeastern tip of **Loch Shin**, which has been harnessed for hydroelectricity. The loch, which is famous for its fishing, is over 18 miles long by no more than a mile at its widest, with the A838 following its northern shoreline for part of the way. The village became important because it sits at the meeting point of various Highland roads that head off in all directions. Five miles south are the picturesque **Falls of Shin**, which has a visitor centre and a Harrod's shop. **Ord Hill**, west of the town, has an archaeological trail, which takes you round a landscape rich in ancient sites. **Ferrycroft Countryside Centre** explains land use in this part of Sutherland since the end of the last Ice Age.

Fort George

10 miles NE of Inverness on the B9006

Fort George (Historic Scotland) was named

Cawdor Cottages

Cawdor Estate Office, Cawdor,
by Nairn IV12 5RE
Tel: 01667 402402 Fax: 01667 404787
e-mail: helen@cawdor.com
website: www.cawdor.com

Cawdor Cottages are situated on the Cawdor Estate and are surrounded by some 60,000 acres of natural beauty. Inverness airport is only a 10 minute drive from Cawdor village and offers quick and easy access to London. Inverness, the capital of the Highlands, with its many historical and leisure attractions, is just 12 miles away, whilst Nairn with its long sandy stretches of beach and renowned golf courses is a mere 4 miles away. There are excellent road and rail connections to the North and South.

Cawdor Estate offers many forms of relaxation such as fishing, cycling, walking and shooting and is an excellent base for touring and sight-seeing. Many guests simply stroll along the lanes and enjoy the scenery or walk along to Cawdor Castle. The castle, still in use as a private residence, is immortalised in Shakespeare's *Macbeth*, and is open to the public during the summer months. Nature lovers will particularly appreciate the ancient woodlands surrounding the Castle and the spectacular Drynachan Valley.

The seven cottages have all been personally decorated and refurbished by Isabella Cawdor. They are fully equipped with wonderful thick towels, central heating, log fires/stoves, comfortable beds and modern kitchens and bathrooms. A stay at Cawdor Cottages offers the guest an opportunity to engage in many healthy outdoor pursuits, whilst experiencing the tranquillity and luxury that a visit to this part of the world affords. Additional services such as massage, home-cooked meals, guided walks and many others can easily be arranged. Guests are sent a list of local food suppliers to assist them with catering, and there are some excellent restaurants in the area.

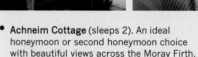

- **Achneim Cottage** (sleeps 2). An ideal honeymoon or second honeymoon choice with beautiful views across the Moray Firth.
- **Rose Cottage** (sleeps 2). A wonderfully comfortable, secluded cottage overlooking open pastureland. Ideal for romantic breaks.
- **Pinewood Cottage** (sleeps 4). Victorian cottage with spacious gardens, within walking distance of Cawdor Castle and the famous conservation village.
- **Ivy Cottage** (sleeps 6). Victorian property with a traditional cottage garden in Cawdor village, within walking distance of all village amenities.
- **Gardener's Cottage** (sleeps 6). Traditional Highland cottage, situated on the banks of the River Findhorn, in the spectacular Drynachan Valley, offering guests the chance to experience the great outdoors.
- **Fisherman's Cottage** (sleeps 6). A contemporary property offering deluxe, spacious accommodation. The wood panelled sitting room has fabulous views over the River Findhorn. Ideal for family holidays.
- **Lochanshelloch Cottage** (sleeps 6). A bright blue cottage - exceptionally popular with families and groups of friends.

after George II, and sits on a headland that guards the inner waters of the Moray Firth near Ardersier. Work started on building it in 1748 as a direct result of the Jacobite Uprising of 1745, and it was subsequently manned by Government troops. It covers 42 acres, has walls a mile long, and the whole thing cost over £1bn to build at today's prices. It has been called the finest 18th century fortification in Europe, and has survived almost intact from that time. The **Queen's Own Highlanders Museum** is within the fort.

Nairn

16 miles NE of Inverness on the A96

Nairn is a small, picturesque holiday and golfing resort on the Moray Firth. Local people there will tell you that the name is a shortened version of "no rain", and indeed this area is one of the driest in Britain. It has a fine, clean beach and a large caravan park. The River Nairn, which flows through the town, is supposed to mark the boundary between the English speaking areas to the east and the Gaelic speaking areas to the west. A great royal castle stood here, built by William the Lion in 1179, but it is long gone. The **Nairn Museum** on Viewfield Drive has collections on local history, archaeology and wildlife.

At Auldearn, two miles east of the town (now bypassed), is the **Boath Doocot** (National Trust for Scotland), which sits within what was a small medieval castle. A battle was fought here in 1645 between the Royalist troops of the Marquis of Montrose and a Covenanting army under Sir John

The Steadings Hotel

Flichity, Farr, Inverness-shire IV2 6XD
Tel/Fax: 01808 521314
e-mail: stay@thesteadings.com
website: www.thesteadings.com

The Steadings Hotel is in the small, picturesque village of Farr, a few miles south of Inverness and only five miles from the southern shores of Loch Ness. This is Upper Strathnairn, an area of deep lochs and fine heather slopes - once the lands of ancient Clan McGillivray, which fought alongside Charles Edward Stuart at Culloden. The hotel is owned and managed by the husband and wife team of Caroline and Andrew Pavitt, who are committed to making their guests' stay at the hotel a special and memorable one. Built in 1860, the building was once a farm steading, and formed part of the original Flichity Hotel. It still retains many of its original features, which have been

incorporated into an establishment that offers fine, modern standards of hospitality and a warm, informal atmosphere where you will feel completely at home.

There are ten rooms on offer, each one having colour TV, tea/coffee making facilities and private bathroom/shower. They have been furnished and decorated to an exceptional standard, and each one has a unique atmosphere of is own to ensure a relaxing stay and a good night's sleep!

The Clach an' Airm restaurant within the hotel is a favourite place among tourists and visitors alike. Though relaxed and informal, it is spacious and comfortable, serving great food and the best wines. The cuisine is Scottish with Continental influences, with the kitchen only using fresh Scottish and Highland produce in its dishes. Why not try the hotel's famous cullen skink - a great Highland delicacy - a tasty fish soup using locally caught seafish? Or collops of beef fillet on Cockburn's haggis and stovied potatoes? The menu is varied and imaginative, and also makes great use of local lamb, salmon, chicken and fish. For the sweet, you could try iced cranachan, a traditional Scottish desert of oats and fresh cream? The Steadings goes one step further, and adds just a hint of Drambuie, creating a dish that you will remember for many a long day. Finish it all off with good, Scottish shortbread and coffee, and you'll be ready to enjoy a quiet drink in the hotel's lounge. But be warned - so well known is the Clach an' Airm that you are well advised to book in advance!

The Steadings Hotel is located in a quiet area of magnificent Scottish scenery, yet it is ideally placed to explore the area. Loch Ness only a short distance away, and bustling Inverness - now one of the most rapidly expanding cities in Britain - is only about twenty minutes north. Here you will find great shopping, fine restaurants, pubs and clubs, as well as many historical attractions to explore.

Hurry. The army was routed, and some of the dead were buried in the kirkyard of **Auldearn Parish Church** built in 1757.

Cawdor Castle sits a few miles south west of the town off a minor road. It was made famous by Shakespeare in his play *Macbeth*, though the core of the present castle was built in the 14th century by the then Thane of Cawdor, who was sheriff and hereditary constable of the royal castle at Nairn. With its fairy tale looks and its turrets, it is said to be one of the most romantic castles in Scotland.

Leanach Cottage, Culloden

Culloden

5 miles E of Inverness on the B9006

The Battle of Culloden was fought in 1746, and was the last major battle to take place on British soil. The hopes of the Jacobites to return a Stuart king to the British throne were dashed on that cold, April day and the clan system was smashed forever. The battlefield is on Drumossie Moor, which, in the 18th century, was a lonely, wild place.

Culdearn House

Woodlands Terrace, Grantown-on-Spey
Morayshire PH26 3JU
Tel: 01479 872106 Fax: 01479 873641
e-mail: enquiries@culdearn.com
website: www.culdearn.com

Culdearn House is a fine granite Victorian villa dating from 1860 which has beautiful corniced ceilings, wood panelling and original marble fireplaces. It is owned and personally managed by William and Sonia Marshall, who have recently refurbished it making it one of the best small hotels in Speyside. Situated on the edge of Grantown-on-Spey, yet still within walking distance of the town, the house sits in its own grounds surrounded by mature trees.

With just seven bedrooms, all en suite, the house is more of a country house than a hotel, offering luxury accommodation, comfort and excellent hospitality. There is no smoking in the house.

Culdearn is renowned for its fine dining, excellent wines and selection of malt whiskies, some rare cask strengths. Accolades for the food include an AA red rosette, RAC Fine Dining Award, 3 medallions Taste of Scotland and the hotel is also a member of the Scotch Beef Club. The menu changes daily and offers a selection of locally produced food using the finest ingredients, including Morayshire lamb, Highland Beef and some of the freshest and finest fish from the West Coast of Scotland, all prepared and cooked to perfection by Feona, the chef. Special diets can be catered for.

The Hotel has also won numerous awards including 'Scotland's Hotel of Year' and 'The Best Small Hotel in Speyside'.

Situated within the heart of Speyside, and in the National Park, Culdearn House is the perfect base for the many attractions in the area as well as being on the whisky and castle trails. Be it fishing on the Spey, playing golf at some of the most spectacular courses in Scotland, walking in the Cairngorms Mountains or visiting the many bird sanctuaries in the area (including the Osprey at nearby Boat of Garten), or just for sheer relaxation, this is the ideal place to stay.

Open from March to December, the Hotel offers dinner, bed and breakfast either on a daily or weekly basis. Once you have stayed at this excellent country hotel you will certainly wish to return again and again.

Tomatin Inn

Tomatin, Inverness-shire IV13 7YV
Tel: 01808 511791 Fax: 01808 511245

Dating from the 1800s, the **Tomatin Inn** has all the charm of a typical Scottish country inn. It is popular with visitors and locals alike, and has a small, cosy bar lounge where you can relax over a drink after a hard day sightseeing. The place also serves home-cooked food made from fresh, local produce in its 80-seat restaurant. You can choose from a menu that includes fresh fish, steak pie and a host of other tasty dishes and snacks. There is a children's play area, a delightful beer garden and plenty of car parking. So if you're in the Tomatin area, the Tomatin Inn is the place for you!

Now it has been drained and cultivated, though the battlefield itself has been returned to the way it was. There is still a sadness about the battlefield, and it was once said that no birds ever sang here. That's not quite true, but no one who visits can fail to be moved by the place. You can still see the stones that mark the graves of various clans, and there is a huge memorial cairn at the centre of the battlefield. **Leanach Cottage**, which survived the battle, has been restored, and the **Culloden Visitors Centre** (National Trust for Scotland) has displays and exhibits which explain the battle. The **Cumberland Stone** is where the Duke of Cumberland, third son of George II, and commander of the Royalist troops, watched the battle. He earned the nickname "Butcher Cumberland" for his unspeakable acts of cruelty after the battle.

Not far from the battlefield are the **Clava Cairns** (Historic Scotland), a fascinating group of burial cairns of the early Bronze Age.

Tomatin

13 miles SE of Inverness off the A9

Tomatin sits on the River Findhorn, just off the A9. The **Tomatin Distillery**, north of the village, is one of the highest in Scotland, and was founded in 1897. Now owned by a Japanese company, it has 23 stills, and draws its water from the Alt-na-Frithe burn. It has tours, a visitor centre and tastings.

Grant Arms Hotel

The Square, Grantown-on-Spey,
Morayshire PH26 3HF
Tel: 01479 872526 Fax: 01479 873589
e-mail: info@grantarmshotel.com
website: www.grantarmshotel.com

If you're looking for luxury combined with comfort and value for money, then look no further than the **Grant Arms Hotel**, right in the heart of Grantown-on-Spey. This magnificent establishment - housed in a grand house dating from 1776 - offers the very best in hospitality, whether you're having a holiday or just passing through. The food, as you would imagine in such a place, is superb, as are the 56 en suite rooms. Queen Victoria stayed here in 1860, and many of the period features she saw then have been retained by the present owner. Scottish entertainment is offered on some evenings.

HAUGH HOTEL

Cromdale, Granton-on-Spey,
Morayshire PH26 3LW
Tel/Fax: 01479 872583

The **Haugh Hotel** is an excellent family-run establishment that offers the very best in Scottish hospitality. Once an old coaching inn, with parts dating from the 15th century, it has 7 extremely comfortable bedrooms (six of them en-suite) that have been furnished and decorated to an extremely high standard and include a TV and hospitality tray among the facilities. The pubic bar/lounge is cosy and warm, and the food is all home-cooked using fresh, local ingredients wherever possible. Be sure to call in - you'll get a warm welcome from hosts Kerry and Graham Lee!

Grantown-on-Spey

26 miles SE of Inverness off the A939

This beautiful and elegant tourist centre is situated in the heart of Strathspey (never, ever the "Spey Valley"), and sits at a height of 700 feet above sea level. It was built by James Grant of Grantcastle in the late 18th century and laid out in a grid plan. The

STEORNABHAGH GUEST HOUSE

12 Deshar Road, Boat of Garten,
Inverness-shire PH24 3BN
Tel: 01479 831371
e-mail: val.inglis@virgin.net

There are four extremely comfortable en suite bedrooms in the **Steornabhagh Guest House**, situated in the small village of Boat of Garten, south of Inverness. This modern yet picturesque bungalow stands off the road, with neat gardens and plenty of parking, and has a self-catering cottage that can sleep up to six people. Breakfasts are served in the attractive and spacious dining room, next to which is a conservatory with good views, where you can relax in the evening with either TV or books, magazines, games and holiday brochures of the local area. The whole place has a real "home from home" feeling, and if you visit, you're sure to come back!

STRATHSPEY MOUNTAIN LODGES

Mains of Garten Farmhouse, Boat of Garten,
Inverness-shire PH24 3BY
Tel: 01479 831551 Fax: 01479 831445
website: www.strathspeymountainlodges.co.uk

Right in the heart of beautiful Strathspey, you'll find the **Strathspey Mountain Lodges**, owned and managed by William Grant, who has farmed here for many years.

Five self-catering lodges are on offer, each one built to full housing standard with double glazing, three bedooms, a spacious lounge, a well-appointed kitchen, bathroom and patio for the fine summer evenings.

There is ample car parking beside each lodge, and linen can be supplied at a small extra cost.

Inverallan Parish Church in Mossie Road was completed in 1856, and commemorates the 7th and 8th Earls of Seaforth.

The 15,000-acre **Revack Country Estate** is to the south of the town, on the B970 to Nethy Bridge. It has gardens, woodland trails and an adventure playground. Revack Lodge was built as a shooting lodge in 1860

Carrbridge

21 miles SE of Inverness on the A938

The arch of the original packhorse bridge still stands, and dates from 1717, when it was built by Brigadier-General Sir Alexander Grant of Grant. It also carried funeral processions to Duthil Church, and for this reason was given the nickname of the "Coffin Bridge".

South of the village is the **Landmark Forest Heritage Park**. It is carved out of woodland, and has such attractions as a Red Squirrel Trail, Microworld (where you can explore the world of tiny insects) and the Fire Tower, the tallest timber tower in the country. It gives amazing views over the surrounding countryside. At Dulnain Bridge, six miles east of the village on the A95 is the **Speyside Heather Garden and Visitor Centre**, which explains all about a plant, which has become synonymous with Scotland.

Aviemore

24 miles SE of Inverness off the A9

Once a quiet Inverness-shire village,

CairnGorm Mountain Railway

Aviemore, Inverness-shire PH22 1RB
Tel: 01479 861261 Fax: 01479 861207
website: www.CairnGormMountain.com

Almost 2km long, CairnGorm's funicular railway is the highest railway in the United Kingdom and takes you up the slopes of CairnGorm, the UK's fifth highest mountain at 1245metres and one of Scotland's most extreme arctic wilderness environments, valued for its landscape and rare habitats. Travelling up the wind scoured slopes gives a close up view of the northern Cairngorms, created and moulded by over 400 million years of geological drama while, rising above, CairnGorm itself provides a majestic backdrop.

Down in the valley below, in Glen More, the panorama is no less dramatic with the ancient Caledonian pine forest and Loch Mortich creating a gentler landscape setting. The CairnGorm Mountain Experience provides an unrivalled opportunity for visitors of all ages and physical ability to relax and enjoy one of Britain's most spectacular mountain areas in safety and comfort.

Nestled just below the summit of CairnGorm the brand new Ptarmigan Station offers spectacular views and is home to the Mountain Exhibition.The story of how the mountains have evolved and how wildlife has adapted to survive in such extreme conditions, climate change, folklore and the human impact on the mountain landscape are all explored. Visitors who want to explore the mountain on foot are encouraged to make use of two, specially created, clearly marked footpaths within the ski area boundary. Both paths start from the railway Base Station. Along each route you'll find information points highlighting topics of interest.

The highest shop in the land features an interesting range of gifts to buy and the Ptarmigan Restaurant, with its viewing terrace, offers a menu of wholesome traditional local ingredients. The railway and restaurant are available for private functions - phone for details.

Winter in Aviemore

Aviemore has now expanded into one of the main winter sports centres in the Highlands. The skiing area and chair lifts lie about seven miles east of the village, high in the Cairngorms. This is also the starting point of controversial **Cairngorm Funicular Railway** (see panel on page 377), which carries passengers during winter and summer to the Ptarmigan Station, within 400 feet of the summit of the 4,084 feet high Cairngorm itself. On the road to the skiing area is the **Cairngorm Reindeer Centre**, where Britain's only permanent herd of reindeer can be seen.

The **Rothiemurchus Highland Estate** is a magnificent area with spectacular views, deep forests and woodland trails. You can try hill walking and mountain biking, and there are guided walks and safari tours in Land Rovers. The estate contains some of the last remnants of the great, natural **Caledonian Pine Forest**, which once covered all of the Highlands. Details of all the activities are available from the Visitor Centre on the B970 south east of the village.

Aviemore is one of the termini of the **Strathspey Steam Railway,** which runs to **Boat of Garten**, five miles away. It was once part of the Aviemore to Forres line, which was closed, in the early 1960s.

Kingussie

28 miles S of Inverness off the A9

Kingussie (pronounced "King - yoosy") sits in Strathspey, with good views of the Cairngorms to the east, while to the west lie the **Monadhliath Mountains**, rising to over 3,000 feet. In Duke Street sits the **Highland Folk Museum**, which gives an insight into the history and lifestyle of the ordinary people of the Highlands throughout the years.

Mains Hotel

Laggan Road, Newtonmore,
Invernesshire PH20 1DF
Tel: 01540 673206 Fax: 01540 673881
website: www.mainshotel@yahoo.co.uk

With 31 fully en-suite rooms, the **Mains Hotel** is a value for money hotel set among some beautiful Scottish countryside. Newtonmore sits just off the A9, so the hotel makes a superb overnight stop when heading north or south. The rooms all have colour TVs and tea/coffee making facilities, and are comfortable and stylish. Beautifully cooked bar snacks and pub lunches are available in the cosy dining room, with evening suppers also available until 9pm. A wide range of drinks are available in the lounge bar.

At **Newtonmore**, four miles south of the village, is another **Highland Folk Museum**, where there is a reconstruction of an 18th century Highland township. Also in the village is the **Clan MacPherson House and Museum**, which, as its name implies, recounts the history of the MacPhersons.

The ruins of **Ruthven Barracks** (Historic Scotland) lie to the west of Kingussie, on the other side of the A9. They were built in 1719 on the site of a Stewart castle dating from the 14th century to house government troops when Jacobite sympathies were strong in the area. Charles Edward Stuart's army captured them in 1746 and burnt them. After the Jacobite defeat at Culloden, over 3,000 Jacobite troops mustered here to continue the fight. However, Charles Edward Stuart saw that further fighting was useless, and sent a message saying that each man should return home. Four miles north of Kingussie is the **Highland Wildlife Park**, which has an array of Scottish wildlife, plus some

Urquhart Castle, Loch Ness

Loch Ness Clansman Hotel

Brackla, Loch Ness-side,
Inverness-shire IV3 8LA
Tel: 01456 450326
Fax: 01456 450845
e-mail: lochnessclansman@aol.com
website: www.lochnessview.com

The **Loch Ness Clansman Hotel** is the only hotel that stands on the shores of the beautiful and mysterious Loch Ness. Situated with ten acres of woodland, it has three coveted Visit Scotland stars, and has breathtaking views out over the loch, and is a comfortable, relaxed family-run establishment that has been refurbished with a typically Scottish theme so that as soon as you step over the threshold you get a warm, Highland welcome.

There are 24 fully en suite bedrooms plus a further four bedrooms in the Lodge. All have colour TVs, tea/coffee making facilities and direct-dial telephones. The unique design

of the hotel means that most rooms have views of Loch Ness and the hills beyond. The Deluxe Loch View bedrooms have large showers with marble effect walls and are generally larger rooms, with high quality furnishings. Most of the deluxe rooms have king-size beds, rooms on the first floor give the best views. Some have private balconies - just right for enjoying that romantic bottle of wine or after-dinner liqueur on the long, summer evenings as you gaze out over the loch searching for Nessie! There is a passenger lift to the first floor.

But even if you don't manage to book a loch view room, the hotel's public areas are all strategically placed to offer unique views out over the waters. In the Observation Lounge or no-smoking Loch View Dining Room you can enjoy snacks, afternoon teas or bar meals, for instance. The Dining Room also serves superb dinners, with the menus featuring many dishes that feature traditional Scottish produce. This means that the cuisine is imaginative and innovative, while still retaining the very best of Scottish cooking traditions. There is a fine wine list, and there is sure to be something that complements your meal exactly. The bar is open to non residents, and sells a wide range of beers, ales, ciders, wines, spirits (including single malts) and liqueurs. And if you're driving, there is also a selection of soft drinks.

Within the hotel you will find the wonderful Loch Ness Nessie Gift Shop, which offers a wide range of good quality gifts and souvenirs. It also sells a wide range of single malt whiskies, preserves, confectionary, woollens, crystal, shortbread, clothes and novelties.

Boat trips run to Urquhart Castle from the adjacent harbour hourly and all year round. There is a beautiful woodland walk to Abriachan from the hotel grounds maintained by the Woodlands trust, linking near to the "Great glen Way", a long distance footpath.

Castle View B&B

Drumnadrochit, Inverness-shire IV63 6XL
Tel: 01456 450460
e-mail: valronlochness@talk21.com
website: www.castleviewbandb.com

Castle View, so called because it overlooks the romantic ruins of Urquhart Castle, is right on the shores of Loch Ness. It is owned and managed by Val and Ron Moffat and Val even claims to have seen the Loch Ness Monster - twice! There are three rooms, one of which is en suite. All are extremely comfortable and beautifully decorated and each has a view of the loch. Val is noted for her breakfasts and you can choose from the full Scottish or a lighter option if required. Castle View represents great value for money and both Val and Ron look forward to welcoming you!

animals that used to roam the Highlands but have now died out.

A few miles south west of Kingussie, along the A86, is **Loch Laggan**, where the BBC series *Monarch of the Glen* was filmed. The Adverikie Estate, with its large house, played the part of Glenbogle.

Drumnadrochit

16 miles SW of Inverness on the A82

Drumnadrochit sits on the shores of **Loch Ness**, at Drumnadrochit Bay. The loch is famous as the home of the Loch Ness Monster, commonly called "Nessie". Whether a monster actually exists or not has never been proved, but the crowds still

Benleva Hotel

Drumnadrochit, Inverness-shire 1V63 6UH
Tel: 01456 450080
e-mail: enquiry@benleva.co.uk
website: www.benleva.co.uk

The **Benleva Hotel** is housed in a former church manse which is over 300 years old. It was converted in 1950, and locals believe that the ghost of a former minister still haunts the premises! It is set in an acre of ground just outside the village of Drumnadrochit, on the shores of loch Ness, and has six guest rooms that are completely en suite, including a family room and one with a four poster. They are all well furnished and decorated, and offer comfortable yet affordable accommodation. In the driveway leading up to the hotel is an old hanging tree, which is over 400 years old, and it was here that justice was meted out to murderers in days gone by. The place was bought and fully refurbished to an extremely high standard in the year 2001, and now it is one of the best hotels in the area, having been voted the best Highland Country Pub of the Year in 2003. It also came 3rd in the Pub of the Year for Scotland and Northern Ireland in the same year.

The main aim of the hotel is to sell real ale and good food, and it has achieved this admirably. Three real ales are on offer, as well as a range of beers, wines and spirits. And the food is superb, and uses good quality, locally sourced produce such as salmon, venison, lamb and beef. There is a small beer garden which is a sun trap, and dogs and children are more than welcome. Drumnadrochit is on the shores of Loch Ness, and the place makes an ideal overnight stop or a base from which to explore the area. The shops, bars and restaurants of Inverness is a short drive away, as is the Moray Firth and the battlefield at Culloden.

Glen Rowan Guest House

Lewiston, Drumnadrochit,
Inverness-shire IV63 6UW
Tel: 01456 450235 Fax: 01456 450817
e-mail: info@glenrowan.co.uk
website: www.glenrowan.co.uk

Karen and Jamie Hookham welcome you to their Highland home in Lewiston, less than a mile from the picturesque village of Drumnadrochit on the shores of Loch Ness. The AA four-diamond **Glen Rowan Guest House** offers superior accommodation and is set in a peaceful location. The fully en suite guest rooms are tastefully furnished and decorated to an extremely high standard, each one having colour TV, tea/coffee making facilities, bedside lamps, radio alarm, heated towel rails and individual heating control.

There is a choice of comfortable lounges and a smart dining room where delicious home cooked fare is served at individual tables. The Scottish breakfasts are hearty and filling, though lighter options are available if required. Surrounding the house are large, neat gardens and the rooms at the back of the house overlook the delightful River Coiltie and the hills beyond.

Jamie and Karen are very knowledgeable about the area, and can recommend restaurants and cafés where you can enjoy a meal in the evening. Glen Rowan is a no-smoking establishment, and for the comfort of guests, only guide or assist dogs are allowed. There is plenty of off street parking, and the whole place has a relaxing, friendly atmosphere that is sure to enhance your Highland holiday. The area is full of history, and within a few minutes you can be on the shores of Loch Ness, keeping your eyes peeled for Nessie, or exploring the romantic ruins of Urquhart Castle.

Glenurquhart House Hotel And Lodges

Marchfield, Drumnadrochit,
Inverness-shire IV3 6TJ
Tel: 01456 476234 Fax: 01456 476286
e-mail: carol@glenurquhartlodges.co.uk

Less than five miles from Loch Ness, and on a hillside near Loch Meikle within beautiful Glen Urquhart, you will find the **Glenurquhart Hotel and Lodges**, one of the best establishments of its kind in Inverness-shire. It nestles in a 6-acre estate amid some of the most spectacular scenery in Scotland, and offers first class accommodation. There are seven comfortable, fully en suite guest rooms, all having remote control TVs and tea/coffee making facilities. The hotel's restaurant, which is open to non-residents, serves superb food, and only the finest and freshest of local produce goes into its preparation. You can chose from such dishes as Scottish salmon in a lemon butter sauce, braised lamb shank in red wine and rosemary, Glenurquhart fillet steak in whisky sauce, or those old favourites, battered cod and chips or a sizzling steak with all the trimmings.

The hotel also offers magnificent, fully furnished wood-built lodges, each one sleeping six in absolute comfort. They have a double and a twin room, a room with large bunk beds (cot available), lounge area with colour TV and electric fire, well equipped kitchen and bathroom. Towels, bed linen and duvets are also supplied. Electricity is by coin meter. The Glenurquhart makes the ideal base from which to explore this area of Scotland including Loch Ness, Drumnadrochit and the romantic ruins of Urquhart Castle. Inverness is only half an hour away by car as is the Black Isle.

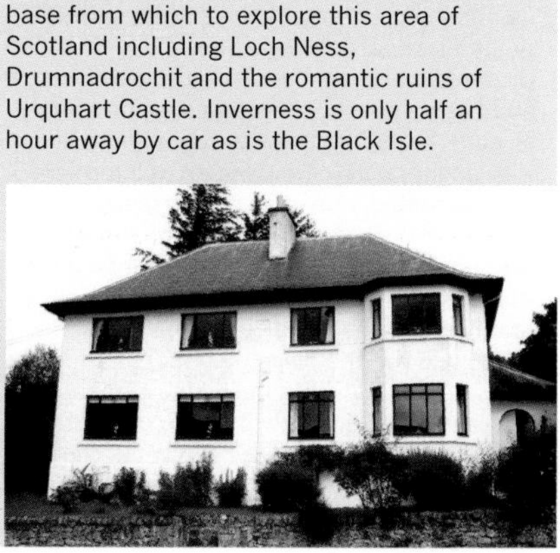

flock here in the hope of seeing something. The loch measures just less than 23 miles long by a mile wide, and contains more water than any other loch in Britain.

The first mention we have of a monster - though in this case it was in the River Ness and not in the loch - occurs in Adamnan's *Life of St Columba*, written in the 7th century. In the year AD 565 St Columba was heading up the Great Glen towards Inverness, when he encountered a monster attacking a man in the River Ness at the point where it enters the loch. He drove it back by prayer, and the man's companions fell on their knees and were converted to Christianity.

Nowadays the monster is a bit more timid. Most sightings have been made at **Urquhart Castle** (Historic Scotland), about a mile from Drumnadrochit, and curiously enough, this is where the loch is at its deepest at 754 feet. The castle is one of the largest in Scotland, and sits on a promontory that juts out into the water. A fortification has stood here for centuries, but the present ruins date from the 16th century, when the Grants occupied it. Though it may have had early links with the area, Urquhart Castle has nothing to do with Clan Urquhart, whose homeland was on the Black Isle, north of Inverness. After the Jacobite Uprising of 1689 the castle was blown up and never rebuilt. A visitor centre contains a model of the castle, which shows what it was like in its heyday.

Two exhibitions in the village, **Loch Ness 2000** and the **Original Loch Ness Exhibition** have displays about the Loch Ness Monster.

Beauly

7 miles W of Inverness on the A862

Within this picturesque village are the ruins of **Beauly Priory** (Historic Scotland),

Beauly Coffee And Gift Shop

11 High Street, Beauly,
Inverness-shire IV4 7BY
Tel: 01463 783379 (Coffee Shop)
01463 783709 (Gift Shop)

The **Beauly Coffee and Gift Shop** sits right in the heart of the picturesque village of Beauly, and is the ideal place to buy a souvenir of your holiday or to have a refreshing cup of tea or coffee. It is popular with both tourists and locals alike, with the coffee shop being owned and managed by Margaret Geddes, who is determined to maintain the high standards she has set and the value for money prices. The food is delicious, ranging from filled baguettes and sandwiches to hot rolls, baked potatoes and specials. The produce used in the kitchen is sourced locally, meaning that you can have a genuine taste of the Highlands. Of course, you could just relax over a warming cup of tea or coffee.

The gift shop is run by Eileen MacDonald, who has a wide range of gifts and souvenirs on display. There is something for everyone here, from local crafts to cards, pottery, glassware, framed prints, candles (in all shapes, colours and sizes!), woodwork, costume jewellery and wind chimes. The shelves and display areas are crammed with great gift ideas, though there is plenty of floor space for you to browse at your leisure. Take your time - the whole place is full of colour and wonderful ideas, and there's no doubt you'll be spoiled for choice! The staff are very knowledgeable about the gifts on offer, and can help you choose something that is just right. They are also knowledgeable about what to see in and around Beauly, and if you ask nicely, they might also tell you the story of how Mary Queen of Scots gave the name "Beauly" to the village!

Glass Restaurant At The Struy Inn

Struy,By Beauly, Inverness-shire IV4 7JS
Tel & Fax: 01463 761219
e-mail: glassrest@supanet.com
website: www.glassrestaurant.supanet.com

The Struy Inn is a picturesque, stone-built building located in one of the most beautiful parts of the Highlands - Strathglass, west of Inverness. It is close to both Glen Strathfarrar and a short distance from Glen Cannich and the National Nature Reserve at Glen Affric.

Here you will find the **Glass Restaurant at the Struy Inn.** Proprietor, Douglas Brown and Front of House manager Kerry, invite you to join them there to enjoy superb food served in a wonderful ambience. Only the finest and freshest of produce is used in the kitchens wherever possible, and the menus make imaginative use of salmon, venison, seafood, Scotch beef and locally grown vegetables. The inn is over 120 years old, and is of warm stone. The place retains many period features, adding to the enjoyment of eating here. The restaurant itself, which is just off the cosy lounge area, is spacious spotlessly clean, and with its crisp linen, sparkling glasses and polished cutlery, you are assured of a wonderful eating experience. If you prefer, you can eat in the lounge, where meals are served at lunchtime and between 6 and 7 pm. There is also a choice of 50 Malt Whiskies on offer at the Inn.

The Struy Inn offers superior accommodation for the discerning tourist. It has four double bedrooms, with three sharing bathroom facilities (shower, bath and toilet) and the fourth, which is on the ground floor, having en suite facilities. All the rooms have central heating, colour TV, DVD players (with free movies) and tea/coffee making facilities. Guests can have a hearty and filling full Scottish breakfast or a lighter Continental option.

The inn is set amidst some of the most spectacular scenery in Scotland. It is on the A831, which takes you along Strathglass into the heart of the Highlands. You can turn off east of the village and make for remote Glen Strathfarrar, or you can leave the main road at Cannich and head west along Glen Cannich's narrow, single track road to Glen Cannich. This is Scotland at its best - high mountains and deep, brooding lochs. Most of the rivers and lochs offer superb salmon and trout fishing, with tackle and boats being available for hire.

Climbers and walkers will find the surrounding area a paradise, and there are a number of way-marked walks There is a nine-hole golf course at Aigas, and there are also many splendid opportunities for mountain biking.

But for all this, Inverness, with its shops and bustling streets, is only an hour away by car, and the ski slopes at Aviemore are with an easy 90 minute's drive. Or you could spend a day watching the Moray Firth dolphins.

Cnoc Hotel

Struy, By Beauly, Inverness-shire IV4 7JU
Tel:01463 761264 Fax: 01463 761207
e-mail: cnochotel@talk21.com
website: www.thecnochotel.co.uk

Welcome to a Highland country house hotel nestling in the picturesque countryside of Strathglass, at the foot of Glen Strathfarrar. Welcome to a hotel where the high standards of service, the attention to detail and the excellent value for money have given it a reputation second to none and a 3 star rating from the STB. Welcome to the **Cnoc Hotel**!

Under the personal supervision of its owner, Joanne Dixon, it has become one of the best and most respected hotels in the area, offering superb, comfortable accommodation, good food and drink, and a warm Scottish welcome to guests from all over the world. The Cnoc (meaning "small hill" or "hillock") is a warm, stone-built building of great character, and was converted from four cottages which were once part of the Erchless Castle Estate, ancestral home of Clan Chisholm. It boasts seven fully en suite rooms which are beautifully decorated and furnished, and have central heating, colour television sets, tea/coffee making facilities, radio alarm and hair dryer. Two of the rooms are family rooms, and sleep at least four, with cots available if required. In time for the 2004 season, five bedrooms and the lounge were fully refurbished to a very high standard.

The hotel prides itself on its cuisine, and its award winning restaurant is open to non-residents. All the produce used in the kitchen is fresh and local wherever possible, with venison and game being a speciality. Another speciality is seafood, with shellfish being plentiful and always fresh from the cold Scottish waters. Lobster can be served by prior arrangement. Reservations can be made for table d'hôte dinner from 6.30pm until 8.45pm in the luxurious dining room. Superb, tasty bar meals are available from noon onwards. For those who like to enjoy a full day of outdoor activities, a packed lunch can be ordered in advance. Fine wines, beverages and a superb range of single malt whiskies are always available.

All around the Cnoc Hotel there is so much to do and see. Salmon and trout fishing is available on the Beauly, Farrar and Glass rivers, or on one of the many lochs in the area. Shooting and stalking is also available in the season, and the hotel can supply details. Four miles away at Aigas is a wonderful and challenging nine-hole golf course on the banks of the River Beauly. Walkers will enjoy Glen Affric, Glen Cannich or Glen Strathfarrar, which runs up to the Monar dam, through large areas of the Caledonian pine forest. And there is plenty of climbing and "Munro-bagging" on the doorstep.

Culligran Cottages

Glen Strathfarrar,Struy,Near Beauly,
Inverness-shire IV47JX
Tel: 01463 761285 Fax: 01463 761285
e-mail: juliet@culligran.demon.co.uk

Culligran Cottages are situated west of Beauly at Struy, where beautiful Glen Strathfarrar strikes off westwards from the equally beautiful Strathglass. The scenery is among the most majestic and beautiful in Scotland, and the cottages make the ideal base from which to explore the area. They are owned and managed by Juliet and Frank Spencer-Nairn, and sit snugly amid some stunning scenery in Strathfarrar National Nature Reserve. The pinewoods here are a remnant of the ancient "Forest of Caledon", which, according to the Greek geographer Ptolemy in the 2nd century, stretched from Beauly to the coast of Argyll. The accommodation comprises a traditional stone-built cottage and four Norwegian-style chalets within a wooded area, and all are comfortable and well-appointed. The cottage sleeps up to seven, and has three double bedrooms, a spacious sitting room, a large kitchen, bathroom and shower room.

The chalets boast an open plan living room with kitchen/dining area, a bathroom and either two or three bedrooms. A sofa bed in the living area means that they can sleep five or seven depending on size. All are furnished to an extremely high standard, and all have double glazing, electric heaters, cooker and fridge. Frank offers regular guided tours of Culligran Deer Farm by Landrover, and you can watch the deer or feed them by hand. A daily permit allows you to fish for salmon and trout on five beats spread over five miles on both banks of the Rivers Farrar and Glass, the main tributaries of the River Beauly. The cottages are open between mid March and mid-November each year.

Slaters Arms

Cannich, Strathglass, Inverness-shire IV4 7LP
Tel: 01456 415215
Fax: 01456 4145323

Within the village of Cannich, on the A831, you will find the **Slaters Arms**, a modern, smart inn and restaurant that offers the very best in Scottish hospitality. It is owned and managed by Angela and Scott Muir, who between them have a wealth of experience in the catering trade. The non smoking restaurant area seats 50 in absolute comfort, and serves good food between 9 am until 9.45 pm each day. The décor is modern, with the dining area being spacious and light, and the food is prepared using fresh local ingredients wherever possible. For dinner, you can choose from such dishes as Aberdeen Angus sirloin steak with all the trimmings, baked trout, salmon steak, salads, home made steak pie, deep fried haddock, and so on. Plus there is a range of vegetarian dishes. Lunches are served from 12 noon until 5 pm, with the dishes including baked potatoes, sandwiches and salads. From the ever popular Sunday lunch menu you can choose roasts with all the trimmings, including Yorkshire puddings and roast potatoes. A children's menu is also available. Breakfasts are served from 9 am until 11.30 pm. So popular is the place that during the summer months you are well advised to book a table in advance. The whole place is spotless, and the prices are as keen as possible. You can enjoy a drink with your meal, or just relax over a single malt or one of the two real ales available from the bar. There is a bouncy castle for kids in the summer months, and plenty of car parking. Children are more than welcome at this family-friendly establishment. Most credit cards (except Diners) are accepted.

founded by the Bisset family in 1230 for monks of the Valliscaulian order, though what can be seen nowadays dates from between the 14th and 16th centuries, when the Frasers of Lovat were the dominant family. The north transept is the burial place of the MacKenzies of Kintail.

It is said that the village got its name when Mary Stuart stayed in the priory in 1564 on her way to Dingwall and declared it to be a "beau lieu", or beautiful place. However, it was called Beauly long before she arrived, though the name may indeed come from the Latin for "beautiful place".

The **Beauly Centre**, next to the priory, has displays about the history of the area. There is also a reconstructed village store, a weaving centre and a Clan Fraser Exhibition.

To the southwest is **Strathglass**, one of the most beautiful glens in the area. It was here that the Sobieski Stuarts once lived, claiming to be the legitimate grandsons of Charles Edward Stuart. Their claims were believed by many people, notably the Earl of Moray, Lord Lovat and the Earl of Dumfries. There is no doubt, however, that they were charlatans.

The **Wardlaw Mausoleum**, at Kirkhill Parish church to the east of the village, is one of the burial places of Clan Fraser. In 1988 it was restored by Historic Scotland. Two miles south of the village is Moniack Castle, home of the **Moniack Winery**, which makes country wines from locally grown fruits.

Dingwall

11 miles NW of Inverness on the A862

Dingwall's name derives from the Norse thing vollr, meaning "the place of the parliament", which shows that even in ancient times it was an important settlement. It is a royal burgh, and received its charter from Alexander II in 1227. Its castle, now long gone, was the birthplace of Macbeth in 1010. Another famous son is **Sir Hector MacDonald**, a crofter's son who was born in 1853 and joined the army as a private, rising through the ranks to become a major general and national hero. He was known as "Fighting Mac", and eventually committed suicide in 1903 after unproved accusations of homosexuality from those who objected to his lowly birth. A monument to him, known as the **Mitchell Tower**, stands on a hill to the south of the town.

Within the old Tolbooth of 1730 is the **Dingwall Museum**, where the town's history is explained by way of displays and exhibits. Dingwall is the eastern terminus for the famous Dingwall - Kyle of Lochalsh railway line, which runs through some of the most beautiful scenery in Scotland as it crosses the country. The **Dingwall Canal** (now closed) is Britain's most northerly canal, and was designed by Thomas Telford in 1817. At the end of the canal is the **Ferry Point,** which has a picnic area.

Ord House

Muir of Ord,
Ross & Cromarty IV6 7UH
Tel/Fax: 01463 870492
e-mail: admin@ord-house.co.uk
website: www.ord-house.co.uk

Ord House dates from 1637, and is both elegant and attractive, with a well proportioned front and a host of original features that will take your breath away. It sits close to the village of Muir of Ord, which has its own railway station just a couple of stops from the bustling city of Inverness, and therefore offers all the convenience of a country retreat with the amenities of a city close at hand. This makes it the perfect base from which to explore an area that is particularly rich in history and heritage.

The hotel is owned and managed by John and Eliza Allen, who have lived here for 16

years, and who are determined to maintain the high standards they have set over the years. The hotel is well-known even beyond the Scottish shores, and because of this, people return again and again for the peace and tranquillity. There are twelve fully en suite bedrooms, each one being individually furnished and decorated to an exceptional standard. One room even has a four poster bed, and three are on the ground floor for the less energetic guest.

The public rooms are also spacious and relaxing, and most have roaring, open fires when the weather turns chilly. The lounges are just right for reading the paper over a cup of coffee, or for discussing the day's events. The dining room has a host of warm wood, sparkling glasses and cutlery and crisp linen.

As you would expect, the food is outstanding, and the hotel has an AA rosette for its cuisine. The produce used in the kitchen is sourced locally wherever possible, and is always fresh. Game, fish and local beef and lamb is put to good effect, producing a menu that marries tradition with innovation. This guarantees a culinary experience that will long be remembered for all the right reasons! Plus there is a fine selection of wines to accompany your meal.

Ord House is the perfect base for the enthusiastic sportsman. The Conon and Beauly rivers, famed for their salmon, are only a couple of miles away, and within 30 minutes drive there are at least 12 golf courses, including Nairn and Royal Dornoch, and Muir of Ord has its own 18-hole course, where special rates apply for Ord House guests. The hotel can also arrange stalking for deer and grouse shooting in season.

Surrounding the house is 40 acres of mature grounds. There are walled, formal and vegetable gardens, plus park and woodland which Guests are encouraged to stroll round.

Ord House is closed November - February.

Fir Lodges

Blackmuir Wood, Strathpeffer,
Ross-shire IV14 9BT
Tel: 01997 421682
e-mail: bookings@firlodges.co.uk
website: www.firlodges.co.uk

Fir Lodges, on the edge of Blackmuir Wood, which is owned and managed by the Forestry Commission, are an ideal base for touring the area. The West coast is less than an hours drive where you can cruise around the Summer Isles and the Isle of Skye. The East coast is six miles away at Dingwall and from there you can go North to John O'Groats or even take a trip to the Orkneys.

Wildlife enthusiasts may wish to take a boat trip from Inverness to see seals and dolphins or head into the glens to see red deer or, in the Cairngorms, reindeer. Bird life is plentiful, from golden eagles to crested tits and red squirrels come into the grounds to feed. The golfer is well catered for with the local course just a mile away, and the more celebrated ones at Dornoch. Fishing is readily available from river to sea and freshwater lochs and can be arranged for you on a daily or weekly basis. The hill walkers should be in their element starting with Ben Wyvis which overshadows Strathpeffer. There are also many interesting and varied walks.

There are, of course, many distilleries to visit and together with a castle or two, you can enjoy the breathtaking scenery of the Highlands. Inverness is only 20 miles away with its excellent retail and leisure facilities.

The log cabins are within walking distance of the village where there is a shop and Post Office. They are constructed of solid logs to a very high standard and are well maintained. They have been completely renovated and modernised to provide spacious, warm accommodation for a holiday or short break anytime of the year as they have full central heating. Furnishings and fittings are of a high quality and they have a bright, comfortable, welcoming atmosphere. The verandas and patios have furniture to sit out on and enjoy the peaceful setting. All bed linen, towels etc. are included (there are no £1 coin machines).

The main cabin has five bedrooms and two bathrooms, together with a rayburn in the kitchen, woodburner in the sitting room and a separate dining room.The other cabins each have a double and twin bedded rooms, with a combined living/dining and kitchen area. A double sofa bed is also included. There is an electric shower over the bath and the utility room has a freezer, washer/dryer, hair dryer and the sitting room has a colour TV. All the cabins have a fully fitted kitchen including microwave ovens.

For those not wishing to drive up to the Highlands, there are very good air and rail links into Inverness and vehicle hire can be arranged. Pick ups are available for those on a short break and then car tours to suit your requirements each day thus giving you a complete break.There are plenty of good hotels and restaurants within easy reach offering first class food, mostly from local sources.

There are ample walks for dogs which are welcome by prior arrangement. There is a no smoking policy (woods!)

Please contact the phone number above to discuss your holiday/ break requirements so that at the end of the day you will have a break to remember!

Richmond Hotel

Church Brae, Strathpeffer,
Ross-shire IV14 9AW
Tel & Fax: 01997 421300

The **Richmond Hotel**, an elegant, granite built hotel dating from 1885, a time when Strathpeffer was one of the leading spa towns in Europe. It has a mature, well tended garden where birds are actively encouraged by the careful placing of birdbaths, feeders and nest boxes. To complete the picture, there are hanging baskets, roses, rockeries, fruit bushes and herbs, as well as a pathway up an incline alongside a lawn and flower beds to a patio seating area.

The hotel is owned and managed by Marian Grubb and Heinz Nagler, and offers superb hospitality. The interior retains many original features whilst still offering modern standards of service. A cosy bar leads off

from the hallway, and has two fireplaces and prints and photographs of the hotel and village in days gone by. It is warm and welcoming - the ideal place to enjoy a quiet pre dinner drink or a refreshing pint after a hard day sightseeing. The spacious, no-smoking dining room has a beautiful marble fireplace and a wood panelled bay window.

There are five fully en suite bedrooms, all on the first floor. The ones at the front of the hotel are wood-panelled round the windows and have four poster beds. All the bedrooms, however, are extremely comfortable, and are furnished and decorated to a high standard, with colour TVs, hair dryers and tea and coffee making facilities. One of the rooms can be used as a family room.

The Richmond Hotel offers both fine dining in the restaurant - with an imaginative menu that changes weekly - to tasty and keenly priced bar meals. All the produce used in the kitchens is as fresh as possible, with most being sourced locally. Locally caught salmon - prime Scotch beef - succulent venison - all are cooked to perfection. There is also a fine wine list, as well as brandies and liqueurs to make your meal complete. The breakfasts too are prepared from only the finest ingredients, and are hearty and filling. Of course, lighter options are also available. Heinz is a fine chef, and has received several accolades for his food at previous establishments, including a Michelin star and AA Rosettes.

Strathpeffer is only a few miles north of the bustling city of Inverness with its restaurants, bars, pubs and clubs. Loch Ness is also a short drive away, as is the Moray Firth with its dolphins. It makes a perfect base for such activities as shooting, fishing, observing wildlife, playing golf and mountain biking. In the village itself there are occasional clan gatherings, Highland games and ceilidhs, and even performances in the village square by the Strathpeffer Pipe Band and Dancers.

Eight miles west of the town, off the A835, are the **Rogie Falls** on the Blackwater, reached by a footpath from a car park on the main road. A fish ladder has been built to assist salmon to swim upriver.

Strathpeffer

14 miles NW of Inverness on the A834

At one time, this small village was one of the most famous spa resorts in Britain, and trains used to leave London regularly carrying people who wanted to "take its waters". For this reason, it is full of hotels, B&Bs and genteel guesthouses. So fashionable was it that the local paper used to publish a weekly list of the crowned heads and aristocratic families who were "in town".

The spa days are over now, though the **Spa Pump Room** has been refurbished and re-creates the halcyon days of the village when the cream of society flocked here to "take the waters". You can even sample the curative waters yourself. The adjacent Victorian gardens, where Victorian society used to promenade and play croquet, have also been restored.

Within the disused railway station is the **Highland Museum of Childhood,** with dolls, photographs, toys, games and videos. On the eastern outskirts of the village is the **Eagle Stone**, with Pictish symbols. Scotland's own Nostradamus, the Brahan Seer (Kenneth Mackenzie, born in the early 17th century) predicted that if the stone fell over three times, the waters of the Cromarty Firth, five miles to the east, would rise so that ships could drop anchor near where the stone stood. The stone has fallen over twice so far, and as some of the Seer's other predictions have come true, it is now embedded in concrete to be on the safe side.

Kinlochewe Hotel

Kinlochewe, By Achnasheen,
Wester Ross IV22 2PA
Tel: 01445 760253
e-mail: kinlochewehotel@tinyworld.co.uk
website: www.kinlochewehotel.co.uk

Set on the edge of Europe's last great wilderness, amidst the towering peaks of the Torridon mountains, and close to the famously scenic Loch Maree, **Kinlochewe Hotel** is ideally placed for walkers and climbers or as a base for touring the Western Highlands by car. For climbers, there are over 20 Munros within 20 miles of the hotel. For tourers, the Inverewe Gardens, owned by the National Trust for Scotland, the spectacular Applecross Peninsula and the misty Isle of Skye are all within easy reach, while Beinn Eighe National Nature Reserve, the first of its kind in Britain, is on the

doorstep.

The hotel has nine comfortable guest rooms, seven with en suite facilities and two with private facilities. Each one has tea/coffee making facilities, and is beautifully furnished and decorated to make your stay enjoyable. The food is outstanding. Everything is home-cooked and uses only the finest and freshest of local produce wherever possible. Local fresh fish, venison and beef feature on the imaginative menu, and there is a small but select range of fine wines to accompany your meal. Packed lunches can also be ordered in advance. The bar is well stocked with a range of ales, beers, spirits, liqueurs and soft drinks. There are over 50 single malts to choose from, as well as real ale from the Isle of Skye Brewery. Why not relax here after a hard day exploring with a pre dinner drink or relax in the resident's TV lounge.

The adjacent bunkhouse offers modest self-catering accommodation for climbers and walkers. There is one spacious dormitory sleeping twelve people, as well as a well-equipped kitchen with a commercial cooker. There is also a microwave, toaster, fridge, and all the cooking utensils required. There is a drying room, electric showers and toilets, and the place has central heating throughout, with constant hot water. Sleeping bags and towels are not provided. The facilities of the hotel, such as the dining room and bar are available to people using the bunkhouse. You are well advised to book in advance, especially parties .

Kinlochewe Hotel sits among some of the finest scenery in Scotland, in an area that is rich in history and heritage. If climbers feel the need, the hotel can even arrange for guides to be laid on if booked well in advance. The wildlife in this part of Scotland is spectacular, with eagles, sea eagles, pine martens and otters being regularly sighted. And the area is renowned for its dragon flies and beetles.

The hotel also prides itself in its high standards of service, its friendliness and its value for money. People return year after year. If you visit, you're sure to return as well.

Ullapool

Beach at Gairloch

This fishing port and ferry terminal on Loch Broom was founded by the British Fisheries Society in 1788 and laid out in a grid plan. By 1792 much of the work on the port buildings and some houses was completed, settlers having been given a plot of land, free stone to build a home, and land for a garden. Over the years the fortunes of the village fluctuated as the fishing industry prospered or went into recession, though it has always managed to survive.

Now the town is a tourist resort, and a centre for hill walking, sightseeing, wildlife study and fishing. It is also the mainland terminus for the Stornoway ferry, and can be a busy place during the summer months. The award winning **Ullapool Museum and Visitor Centre** is housed in a former church in West Argyll Street designed by Thomas Telford - one of the so-called "parliamentary churches". In 1773, before the town was established, the very first settlers bound for Nova Scotia left Loch Broom in the *Hector*, and there is a scale model of the ship within the museum.

One of the hidden jewels of the West Highlands are the **Leckmelm Gardens**, three miles south of the town just off the A835. They were planted in about 1870, but by 1985 had become overgrown. In that year work began in re-establishing them and revealing the beauty that had been lost for so long. The area surrounding Ullapool is famous for its golden beaches, the best ones being at **Achnahaird**, **Gruinard Bay** and **Achmelvich**.

Around Ullapool

Gairloch

22 miles SW of Ullapool on the A832

This little village, on the shores of Loch Gairloch, has one of the loveliest settings in Scotland. The **Gairloch Heritage Museum,** housed in old farm buildings, has an "illicit" still, village shop, lighthouse interior and other displays that explain how life was lived in northwest Scotland in the past.

Cromasaig

Kinlochewe, Ross-shire IV22 2PE
Tel: 01445 760234
e-mail: cromasaig@msn.com
website: www.cromasaig.com

Cromasaig is a small, family-run B&B owned and managed by keen climbers and hill walkers who are always available to give advice about the area. There are three guest rooms, a twin on the ground floor and a double and a family room sleeping four on the first floor. Adjacent to each room is a private toilet and shower facility. The lounge is comfortable and cosy, the ideal place to relax after a day exploring. Or why not relax in Cromasaig's sauna? Drying facilities are available, and there is ample car parking.

Five miles northeast, on the banks of Loch Ewe are the famous **Inverewe Gardens** (National Trust for Scotland). It has plant collections from all over the world, which thrive in these northern latitudes due to the Gulf Stream. The gardens were founded by Sir Osgood Mackenzie.

Sixteen miles south east of Gairloch, and beyond beautiful Loch Maree, is the quiet village of **Kinlochewe**. It is in the heart of what is recognised to be some of the finest mountain scenery in Scotland. The **Beinn Eighe Nature Reserve**, Britain's first, has a visitor centre and nature reserve. It sits just west of Kinlochewe, along the A832

Lochinver

17 miles N of Ullapool on the A837

This small fishing port sits on Loch Inver, at the end of the A837. A few miles east is Loch Assynt, on whose shores you will find the ruins of **Ardvreck Castle**, built in the 1490s by the MacLeods. It was here, in 1650, that Montrose was kept prisoner before being taken to Edinburgh to be executed. The **Assynt Visitor Centre** has small displays and exhibits about local history.

Four miles south east of the village is what has been called "the most beautiful mountain in Scotland" - **Suilven**. At a mere 2,389 feet, it is not even a Munro, nor is it the highest in the area. Seen from Lochinver, it appears to be a solitary mountain that rises sheer on all

Kyle of Durness

sides. However, it is the western end of a high ridge, and makes for some superb walking and climbing country.

At Achiltibuie, 10 miles south of Lochinver, and reached by a narrow road, is the **Hydroponicum**, a "garden" where plants grow without soil. It calls itself the "garden of the future" and kits are available so that you too can start growing plants without soil. It was set up in the mid 1980s to show that some of the problems found in this part of Scotland -- poor soil, a short growing season and high winds - could be overcome. It now provides high quality produce (from lettuces to bananas) for homes and businesses in the area.

Durness

50 miles N of Ullapool on the A838

Durness, in Sutherland, is one of the most northerly villages in Scotland, and sits close to **Cape Wrath** - one of only two "capes" in Great Britain, the other being Cape Cornwall. To reach it, you have to cross the Kyle of Durness from Durness itself on a small ferry and walk or take a minibus to the cape itself, ten miles away. The peculiarly named **Smoo Cave** is in the cliffs a mile and a half west of the village. It consists of three chambers, and goes underneath the coast road. The name may come from the Old Norse smjugga, meaning "rock". A walkway with railings takes you down to the cave, which has had lights fitted.

There are many clean, golden beaches in the area, most of them uncrowded. The best ones are **Balnakeil**, **Ceann na Beinne**, **Sango Beag** and **Sango Mor**.

The village has associations with John Lennon of the *Beatles*, who used to spend holidays here with his family when he was young. There is a memorial to him.

The **Choraidh Croft Farm Park** is on the shores of Loch Eriboll, off the A838 a few miles south west of Durness.

Wick

Wick is a an ancient royal burgh on the North Sea coast, and was once the leading herring port in Europe, but these times have long gone. The name comes from the Old Norse word vik meaning "bay", and this whole area owes more to Norse culture than it does to the culture of the Gaels. **Parliament Square** near the Market place recalls the fact that James V held a parliament at Wick as he made a royal progress through the kingdom in 1540.

The award-winning **Wick Heritage Centre** in Bank Row has exhibits and displays about life in Wick and Caithness. The **Northlands Viking Centre** at Auckengill, a mile north of the town, tells the story of the Vikings and Norsemen in the area, as well as recounting the life of John Nicolson, a local artist and mason.

The **Old Parish Kirk**, dedicated to St Fergus, dates from 1830, though a church has stood

Wick

here since medieval times. In the kirkyard is the **Sinclair Aisle**, burial place of the old Earls of Caithness.

An old story featuring George Sinclair, the 4th Earl, explains just how bloodthirsty times were in the 16th century. He was suspected of murdering the Earl and Countess of Sutherland so that he could marry off his daughter to their heir, and thus claim the Sutherland lands. However, in 1576, the heir left the country, and Sinclair's plans were thwarted. In revenge, he ordered his son John to lay waste to the Sutherland lands, but when he refused Sinclair had him thrown into a dungeon.

With the help of his gaoler, John hatched a plot to escape. John's brother William found out about this and told his father, who executed the jailer. When William went down to the dungeon to goad his brother, John killed him with his chains. For this, his father punished him by denying him food for five days, then feeding him salt beef without giving him anything to drink. John died in agony, his tongue swollen through lack of water. His father had him buried in the predecessor to the present church, and years later, just before he too died, full of remorse for what he had done, he asked that his heart be buried beside his son.

One mile south of the town, on a cliff top, are the ruins of the **Castle of Old Wick** (Historic Scotland), built by Harald Maddadson, Earl of Caithness, in the 12th century. It was later held by Sir Reginald de Cheyne, and then the Sinclairs, Oliphants, Campbells and Dunbars. Care should be taken when exploring the ruins.

On a hill to the south of Wick Bay is a memorial to the engineer **James Bremner**, who was born in Wick and who died in 1856. He collaborated with Brunel, and salvaged the SS Great Britain when it ran aground off Ireland.

North of Wick, the two castles of **Girnigoe** and **Sinclair** stand above Sinclair Bay. They were strongholds of the Earls of Caithness. Girnigoe is the older of the two, dating from the end of the 15th century, and it was in its dungeons that George Sinclair had his son incarcerated. Sinclair Castle dates from about 1606.

On the northern edge of the town is **Wick Airport**, Scotland's most northerly mainland commercial airport. It has flights to and from Teeside, Norwich, Aberdeen and Kirkwall.

Around Wick

Latheron

15 miles S of Wick on the A9

Within the old church of Latheron, which dates from 1735, is the **Clan Gunn Heritage Centre**. It traces the history of the clan from its Norse origins right through to the present day. At Dunbeath, three miles south of Latheron, is the **Laidhay Caithness Croft Museum**, which shows a typical Highland house, with living quarters, byre and stable all under the one roof. And in the old schoolhouse at Dunbeath is the **Dunbeath Heritage Centre**.

Neil Gunn, one of Scotland's finest writers (author of *The Silver Darlings*), was born in Dunbeath and attended the very school in which the Heritage Centre is located.

Helmsdale

30 miles SW of Wick on the A9

Within this little fishing port is **Timespan**, a visitor centre that tells the story of Helmsdale and its surrounding communities. There are exhibits about the Clearances, Picts, Norse raids, witches and so much more.

The **Strath of Kildonan**, through which flows the River Helmsdale, was the scene of a famous gold rush in 1868. A local man called Robert Gilchrist, who had been a prospector in Australia, began searching for gold in the river. He eventually found some, and once his secret was out, the Duke of Sutherland began parcelling off small plots of land to speculators. At its height, over 500 men were prospecting in the area, and a shantytown soon sprung up. But in 1870, when sportsmen complained that the prospectors were interfering with their fishing and hunting, the Duke put a stop to it all, and the gold rush was over. There is still gold there today, and it is a favourite spot for amateur gold panners.

Tongue

50 miles W of Wick off the A838

Tongue is a small village situated near the shallow Kyle of Tongue. In 1972 a causeway was built across it to take the A838 westwards towards Loch Eribol and Durness. On a promontory to the west of the village are the ruins of the small **Castle Varrich** ("Caisteal Bharraigh in Gaelic), which once belonged to Clan Mackay.

The 16th century **House of Tongue,** overlooking the Kyle of Tongue, was also a Mackay stronghold. It was destroyed in the 17th century, with the Mackays building a new house sometime in the 18th century. The gardens are open to the public.

In 1746 a ship carrying gold coinage for Charles Edward Stuart's Jacobite army tried to take shelter in the Kyle of Tongue to escape government ships. The crew took the coinage ashore for safekeeping, but were followed and captured by some Mackay clansmen, who were supporters of the government. The crewmen threw the coins into a loch, but they were later recovered.

Nine miles northeast of the village, within the old St Columba's Church at Farr, is the **Strathnaver Museum**, with exhibits about local history, most notably the Clearances and Clan Mackay. Strathnaver was probably the most notorious area in the Highlands for the eviction of tenants so that they could be replaced with the more profitable sheep. The whole area abounds with prehistoric archaeological sites, and within the kirkyard of the museum is a burial stone dating to the 8th or 9th

The Craggan Hotel

Melness, Sutherland IV27 4YP
Tel: 01847 601278

The **Craggan Hotel** is a place that has a warm and inviting atmosphere, ensuring that people call by regularly, whether by car, yacht or even helicopter! It is a family run inn, with the present owner, James McKay, having been mine host for 33 years. This means that he has a vast amount of experience in running an establishment that offers the very best in food, drink and accommodation. It is popular with visitors, who return again and again, and with locals, which is always a good sign. Come in and sit by a cosy peat fire while enjoying a malt whisky from the fine range that is available. Hamish or Lynn will be behind the bar to offer you a warm Highland welcome, and, if

you like, guide you to a malt that is exactly to your taste! The atmosphere is friendly and informal, with occasional entertainment evenings and impromptu music nights where you can enjoy the local folk music and musicians.

The Craggan Hotel is renowned throughout the north of Scotland for its excellent cuisine, served in the spacious, comfortable dining room, with its furniture of dark, warm wood, its sparkling glass and cutlery and its bright napkins. It combines fresh local produce, such as venison, salmon, seafood and beef, with Continental or Oriental influences. Starters include Cullen skink, a hearty, traditional fish soup, Graggan gateau, a trio of black and white puddings and haggis, served with game jus, Carpaccio of wild smoked salmon with a chilli olive oil, or Loch Eribol mussels in a sauce of your choice, caught on a local loch. There is also a fine

selection of fish dishes, including monkfish, wild sea trout, haddock and lobster. Also on the menu is a wide selection of meats, including sizzling steaks stuffed with oysters, steak and Guinness pie, stuffed breast of pheasant, and venison with red onion marmalade. There are also occasional food nights, when you can try various cuisines, such as Chinese.

The hotel also offers superior accommodation to discerning tourists. It has four extremely comfortable and spacious rooms (both double and twin), each one beautifully decorated and furnished. Each one has its own colour TV, washbasin, central heating and tea and coffee making facilities.

The Craggan sits in the small village of Melness, on the Kyle of Tongue on Scotland's northern coast. The village overlooks the quaintly named Rabbit Islands, at the entrance to the bay, where a French sloop once ran aground in 1745 while carrying gold for Bonnie Prince Charlie's attempt to regain the British throne for the Stuarts. At Whiten Head, some miles west, and not accessible by car, there are numerous caves. The whole area is rich in history and heritage, and there are many opportunities for hill walking, climbing, fishing, golf, sailing and exploring. The wildlife is spectacular, with deer, foxes and a host of bird life regularly seen.

centuries. The £190,000 **Strathnaver Trail** opened in May 2003 and takes you round 16 sites, which date from 5000 BC to the 20th century.

Altnaharra

51 miles W of Wick on the A836

Sitting close to the western tip of **Loch Naver**, Altnaharra is a small village famous as a centre for game fishing. Loch Naver is the source of the River Naver, one of the best salmon rivers in Sutherland, which flows northwards through Strathnaver to the sea (see also Tongue).

On a narrow, unclassified road from Altnaharra to Loch Hope are the remains of the **Dun Dornaigil Broch**. Some of its walls rise to 22 feet, and over the entrance is a strange triangular lintel. A few miles beyond the broch is **Ben Hope**, at 3,041 feet Scotland's most northerly Munro.

The B873 goes along Strathnaver, following the loch and then the river, until it joins the B871, which joins the A836 south of Bettyhill. It is a superb run, with magnificent scenery.

Thurso

19 miles NW of Wick on the A9

Thurso is a former fishing port on Caithness's northern coast, and is the most northerly town on mainland Britain. It was once a Norse settlement, with its name meaning "river of the god Thor". The ruins of **St Peter's Church** sit in the old part of the town, and date from the 16th century, though a church has stood here since at least the 13th century. It was once the private chapel of the Bishop of Caithness, whose summer retreat was **Scrabster Castle**, of which only scant ruins survive. The **Thurso Heritage Museum** is located within an old cottage, and has displays and mementos relating to the town's past. It is open during the summer.

Eight miles west of the town, on the A836, is Dounreay, where Scotland's first operational nuclear reactor was built. The **Dounreay Visitor Centre** explains about nuclear power and the history of the site.

John O'Groats

13 miles N of Wick on the A99

John O' Groats is 873 miles by road from Land's End in Cornwall, and 290 miles from Kirkmaiden in Wigtownshire, Scotland's most southerly parish. It is supposed to be named after a Dutchman called Jan de Groot, who, to settle an argument about precedence within his family, built an eight sided house with eight doors which gave onto an eight-sided table. This house has now gone, though a mound marks its site. The **Last House in Scotland Museum** contains displays and artefacts about the area.

To the west is **Dunnet Head**, the most northerly point on the British mainland. Between the two is the **Castle of Mey**, the late Queen Mother's Scottish home. It is an ancient castle of the Earls of Caithness, and was built in the 16th century by the 4th Earl. **Mary-Ann's Cottage** at Westside shows how successive generations of one crofting family lived and worked over the last 150 years.

John O'Groats

The Western Isles

The Western Isles look like a huge kite with a long tail streaming out behind it. The kite itself is the island of Lewis and Harris, and the tail consists mainly of the smaller islands of North Uist, Benbecula, South Uist and Barra. The whole length between Barra in the south and the Butt of Lewis in the north is about 130 miles, and they are separated from the mainland by a stretch of water called The Minch.

These islands are the last bastion of true Gaeldom in Scotland, and in some places English, though spoken and understood perfectly, is still a second language. Some are also bastions of Free Presbyterianism, where the Sabbath is strictly observed, and work or leisure activities of any kind on a Sunday is frowned upon. Visitors should, of course, respect these Sabbath customs. Unfortunately, they have given the islanders the reputation of being dour and strict, frowning on anything that smacks of pleasure. Nothing could be further from the truth. They are fun loving, friendly and always helpful.

For all that, the Western Isles are full of contradictions. They may be where Gaelic culture is cherished and preserved, but there are just as many Norse influences here as Celtic, and many of the place

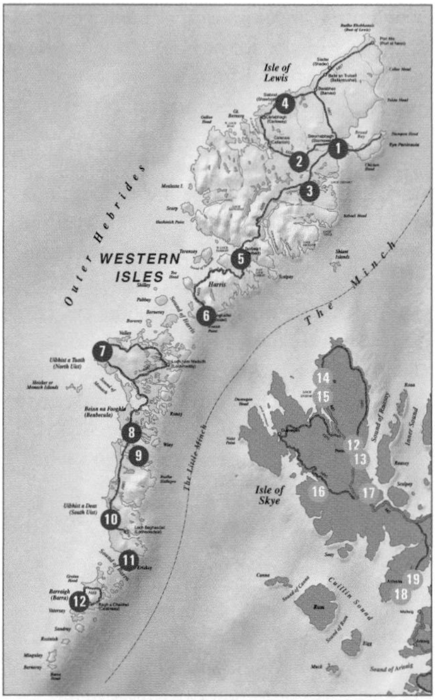

PLACES TO STAY, EAT AND DRINK

Hebridean Guest House, Stornoway	1	Guest House	p402
Cleascro Guest House, Achmore	2	Guest House	p404
Glengravir Cottage, South Lochs	3	Self Catering	p405
Shawbost Inn & Restaurant, North Shawbost	4	Pub, Restaurant & Accommodation	p406
Kirklee Terrace Cottages & Motel, Tarbert	5	Motel and Self Catering	p408
The Rodel Hotel, Rodel	6	Hotel	p410
Baleloch House, Tigharry	7	Self Catering	p411
Isle of Benbecula House Hotel, Creagorry	8	Hotel	p413
Orosay Inn, Lochcarron	9	Hotel	p414
Borrodale Hotel, Daliburgh	10	Hotel	p415
AM Politician, Eriskay	11	Pub with Food	p416
Isle of Barra Hotel, Tangasdale Beach	12	Hotel	p417

● Denotes entries in other chapters

The Western Isles

are home to dolphins, basking sharks, whales and seals. In fact, some people claim that the waters surrounding the Western Isles are the most "fertile" in Britain.

The main island is divided into two parts, Lewis and Harris, an ancient arrangement going back as far as the 13th century. Though joined geographically, they are usually considered to be two separate islands, and indeed the differences between them are marked. Lewis is the northern, and larger part, and up until the mid 1970s was within the county of Ross and Cromarty. Harris (and the smaller islands to the south) came under Inverness-shire. A natural boundary of mountains and high moorland ran between Loch Resort on the west and Loch Seaforth on the east. Now they all form one administrative area, with the capital being at Stornoway.

The underlying rock of Lewis is gneiss, one of the oldest in the world. It is largely impermeable, so doesn't absorb water. For this reason the interior of the island is a large, empty peat moorland dotted with shallow lochs, while most of the settlements are on the coast. Harris is more

names (especially in the north) have Norse origins. Up until the Treaty of Perth in 1266 the Western Isles were ruled by Norway, but in that year Magnus IV surrendered all of his Scottish possessions, with the exception of Orkney and Shetland, to Alexander III of Scotland.

And though Free Presbyterianism dominates Lewis and Harris, some of the other islands are largely Roman Catholic, not through Irish immigration, but because the Scottish Reformation of 1560 never fully penetrated this far.

The weather in the Western Isles, especially in winter, can be harsh, though there are occasions where it can be astonishingly mild and sunny. Snow is rare because of the Gulf Stream, but there are between 45 and 50 inches of rain a year, and the winds blowing in from the Atlantic are invariably strong. The compensations, however, are enormous. The long summer evenings can be still and warm, and at midnight in the north of Lewis it is still possible to read a newspaper out of doors.

And the wildlife is astounding. Deer and otters abound, and the machair (the meadows bordering the sandy beaches) are full of flowers in summer. And the seas

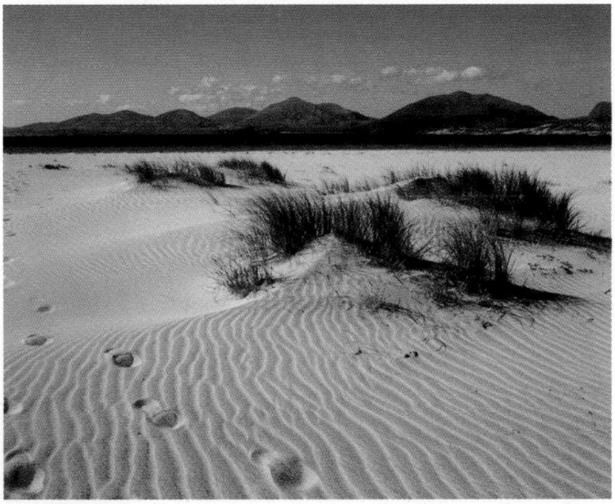

Beach on South Harris

Hebridean Guest House

61 Bayhead Street, Stornoway,
Isle of Lewis HS1 2BZ
Tel: 01851 702268 Fax: 01851 701791
e-mail: hebgh@sol.co.uk
website: www.hebrideanguesthouse.co.uk

The **Hebridean Guest House** sits in the historic royal burgh of Stornoway on the Isle of Lewis, close to the town centre and all its amenities, and overlooking the castle and golf course. It is a welcoming and friendly establishment dating from the beginning of the 20th century, and combines great service with prices and facilities sure to please.

It is owned and managed personally by Linda Johnson, who is determined to maintain the high standards she has achieved. As well as the friendly service, she ensures there is the informal atmosphere

that contributes so much to a relaxing and enjoyable holiday. Over the years the guest house has earned itself a fine reputation, which is reflected in its coveted VisitScotland three-star status. There are two extremely comfortable living rooms for the exclusive use of the clientele, one smoking and one non-smoking. The dining room, where breakfasts are served, is spacious and light, just right for one of the hearty Scottish breakfasts that are the Hebridean's speciality. Only the freshest of local produce is used in their preparation, setting up guests for a day exploring an island that some say has a mystical quality all of its own. Lighter options are, of course, also available.

The guest house is centrally heated throughout and boasts 12 bedrooms over two floors, all are fully en suite and decorated and furnished to a high standard, with extremely comfortable beds. The rooms are a mixture of single-bedded, twin-bedded and double-bedded. There is colour television and tea and coffee making facilities in each one.

The Hebridean Guest House sits on the outskirts of Stornoway, yet within easy walking distance of its shops, pubs, clubs and restaurants, and makes the ideal base from which to explore the islands of Lewis and Harris. And you won't be disappointed by their history and heritage. You'll be drawn to the Callanish Standing Stones (Scotland's Stonehenge) which have an air of wonder that is both compelling and mysterious. And there are other ancient landscapes to explore as well, such as the many standing stones, cairns and stone circles that date back thousands of years.

If it's something a bit more hectic you're after, there is golf, sea and fresh water fishing, walking, climbing and biking. In fact, the place has got something for everyone!

mountainous, and has peaks reaching 2,500 feet. It is also an area where the underlying rocks break through to the surface like bones, giving an essentially bleak but never less than attractive landscape. It too is divided into two parts, North and South Harris, with the narrow ithsmus between West Loch Tarbert and East Loch Tarbert being the boundary.

Of the main southern islands, Berneray, North Uist, Benbecula, South Uist and Eriskay are joined by causeways. North Uist connects to Harris by a ferry between An t-Obbe and Berneray, and Barra has a ferry connection with Eriskay. Each island in the chain has its own flavour, and all are noted for their quality of light, especially in summer.

The Western Isles sit on the farthest edge of Europe, with North America being the next stop. But for all their seeming isolation, they have a long history. The standing stones at Callanish - the second largest stone circle in Britain - are over 4,000 years old, and were built for pagan ritual and possibly to record the passing of the seasons so that crops could be sown and harvested. And there are individual stones, duns, brochs and old forts dotted all over the landscape. The local people are proud of their history, and on your travels, look out for small, village-based museums which seem to be everywhere.

And during the Dark Ages the Western Isles were at the crossroads of trade. To the south were the Lowlands of Scotland, as well as England, Ireland and the Isle of Man. To the east, beyond Scotland, were the Norse countries. This made for a mixture of cultural influences that enriches the islands - influences that can still be seen today.

Norse invasions began in earnest in the 8th century, and by about AD 850 Norsemen ruled all of the Outer Hebrides. In 1266 they came into Scottish hands, even though the local leaders acted almost independently of the crown. For this reason there was much friction between the Scottish kings and the Lords of the Isles, though the kings gradually imposed their authority. The islands eventually accepted this and became fully integrated into Scotland. Some historians claim, however, that the Norse language only died out in the late 16th century.

Various attempts have been made over the years to encourage industry, most notably when Lord Leverhulme bought both Lewis and Harris in 1918 and tried to promote fishing. Today the islands rely on fishing, crofting and tourism, with the weaving of Harris Tweed being an important industry on Lewis and Harris. The weaving is a cottage industry, with the weavers working at home or in sheds at the back of the house. Some weavers will welcome you into their weaving rooms and explain the processes involved in turning wool into fine cloth.

Ferries for Stornoway leave from Ullapool, and there is also a ferry connection between Oban, South Uist and Barra, as well as one from Uig on Skye to Lochmaddy and Tarbert.

Stornoway

With a population of about 6,000, Stornoway (from the Old Norse stjorna, meaning "anchor bay") is the only town of any size in the Western Isles. It is their administrative, educational and shopping centre, and is a surprisingly cosmopolitan place, with a sizable Asian population.

It was founded in the middle ages round an old MacLeod castle, and has a fine natural harbour and an airport. On Lewis Street is **The Parish Church of St Columba**, dating from 1794, and in **St Peter's Episcopal Church** (1839) is David Livingstone's Bible and an old font from the Flannan Isles, about 33 miles west of Lewis. It's bell, which was made in 1631, was once the town bell that summoned townspeople to important meetings. The **Free Church** in Kenneth Street has the

Stornoway Harbour

distinction of being the best attended church in all of Britain, with the Sunday evening congregation regularly exceeding 1,500.

Lews Castle, now a college surrounded by public gardens, was built in the 1840s and 50s by James Matheson, a businessman who earned a fortune in the Far East trading in tea and opium. In 1843 he bought Lewis, and began a series of improvements in what was then an isolated and inward looking island. He built new roads, improved the housing and brought running water and gas to the town.

One of his pet projects was a plant to extract oil from the peat that blanketed the island, and in 1861 the Lewis Chemical

Works began production. But problems beset the setting up of the plant, and it actually blew up, putting the citizens of Stornoway into a state of fear and alarm. The venture finally folded in 1874.

The **Museum nan Eilean** on Francis Street has artefacts and exhibits highlighting the history of both the island of Lewis and Stornoway itself, as well as displays about archaeology on the islands. It makes a good starting point if you want to explore the area. A new **An Lanntair Arts Centre** is currently being built across from the ferry terminal. There will be contemporary and traditional exhibitions, as well as varied programmes of music and drama highlighting the Gaelic culture.

One of Stornoway's most famous sons was the 18th century explorer Sir Alexander Mackenzie, who gave his name to the Mackenzie River in Canada. In Francis Street, on the site of his house, is **Martins Memorial**, built in 1885.

The Western Isles are synonymous with Harris Tweed, and at the **Loom Centre** on Bayhead you can find out about its history and about how it is woven. To attain the "orb" symbol of genuine Harris Tweed, the cloth needs to be woven from "virgin wool produced in Scotland", then spun, dyed and hand woven in the Outer Hebrides.

West of Stornoway, on the Eye Peninsula, are the ruins of **St Columba's Church**, built in the 14th century. It is said that nineteen MacLeod chiefs are buried here within carved tombs.

Around Stornoway

Callanish

16 miles W of Stornoway on the A858

Dating back at least 4,000 years, the **Callanish Stone Circle** (Historic Scotland) is second only to Stonehenge in

Shawbost Inn & Raebhat Restaurant

North Shawbost, Isle of Lewis HS2 9BD
Tel/Fax: 01851 710632
e-mail: shawbostinn@btinternet.com

Shawbost is an attractive village on the west coast of the Isle of Lewis, and it is here that you will find the **Shawbost Inn & Raebhat Restaurant**, which offers superior food and accommodation to tourists and visitors. Under the ownership and personal management of Gordon Keppie, it has an enviable reputation as an establishment that offers only the very best at keen prices. The rooms are comfortable and spacious, and are offered on a B&B basis, along with full board packages and packed lunches on request.

The lounge and public bars are popular

with the locals, and here you can enjoy a quiet drink, choosing from a wide range of beers (including Hebridean ales), wines, spirits, liqueurs and soft drinks. There is regular live music, with the emphasis being on the traditional, and these are always lively, fun-filled affairs that set your toes tapping.

The whole place makes an ideal base from which to explore Lewis and Harris, where scenery combines with history, creating the perfect get away from it all holiday experience. The roads are empty, the people are friendly, and here you can fish, cycle, sail, go bird watching, indulge in nature study, visit places that are steeped in Celtic heritage and culture, or just relax with a good book and let the world go by.

The 40-seat Raebhat Restaurant is famous throughout the island (and beyond!) for its good food and wine. It has a cosy, relaxed atmosphere with a traditional theme, attentive staff, and a menu that makes imaginative use of produce that is sourced locally, and is always as fresh as possible. Seafood · fresh salmon · juicy steaks · succulent vegetables · these are the stock-in-trade of Gordon, who does most of the cooking himself. Trained in Edinburgh, he worked in Aviemore before coming to Shawbost, where he managed the place before finally buying it. Try his signature dish, smoked salmon fettucine, or the prime 8oz Scotch fillet steak with all the trimmings. Or there's the roast loin of Lewis lamb, pan fried monkfish, whole king prawns, and fillet of cod. You can also try one of his bar snacks or takeaway dishes, and he does a fine range of pizzas with different toppings. On Sundays the menu changes, and you are well advised to book in advance. There is also a fine selection of wines that will complement any meal, and the lounge bar is the ideal place to enjoy a brandy after experiencing some of the best cooking on Lewis.

Gordon and his staff are enthusiastic about what they do, and if you visit the premises, they will offer you a great welcome!

importance in Britain. It is more than just a mere circle of upright stones, however. Four great arms made up of monoliths radiate from it to the north, south east and west, with the northern arm (which veers slightly to the east) having a double row of stones as if enclosing an approach way. And in the middle of the circle is the tallest stone of them all, measuring over 15 feet in height.

Standing Stones, Callanish

It is a mysterious place, and has attracted many stories and myths over the years. One story tells of a race of giants who met to discuss how to defeat the new religion of Christianity that was spreading throughout the islands. This so incensed St Kieran, a Celtic monk and missionary, that he turned them all to stone. Another says that the stones were brought to Lewis by a great priest king who employed "black men" to erect them. The men who died building the circle were buried within it.

Plus there are the more modern, and unfortunately predictable, theories that the stones were erected by mysterious beings from outer space as a means of guiding their spacecraft, though why people with such technology should need a guidance system made of Lewisian gneiss stones seems equally as mysterious.

A visitors centre next to the stones tries to uncover the truth behind them, which may have something to do with primitive ritual and predicting the seasons for agricultural purposes.

Carloway

17 miles W of Stornoway on the A858

The 1,500-year-old **Dun Carloway Broch,** overlooking Loch Roag, is one of the best-preserved brochs in Scotland. It is over 47 feet in diameter, and its walls are 22 feet high in places. Some of the galleries and internal stairways are still intact. The Doune Broch Centre has displays explaining what life must have been like within a broch.

Shader

16 miles NW of Stornoway on the A857

The **Steinacleit Stone Circle and Standing Stones** sit on a low hill, and date from between 2000 and 3000 BC. The stones are more in the shape of an oval than a circle.

Shawbost

16 miles W of Stornoway on the A858

Housed within a former church, the **Shawbost School Museum** has artefacts and objects collected by school pupils 30 years ago as part of a project that illustrate the way people used to live in Lewis. Near it is the **Norse Mill and Kiln**, a restored water mill of the type used in Lewis up until the mid 20th century.

Barvas

13 miles NW of Stornoway on the A858

At one time, most of the population of Lewis lived in small cottages known as blackhouses. On the west coast at Arnol, the **Arnol Blackhouse** (Historic Scotland) shows what life was like in one of them.

Kirklea Terrace Cottages And Macleod Motel

Tarbert, Isle of Harris HS3 3DG
Tel: 01859 502364 & 502138
Fax: 01859 502578
e-mail: angus@macleodmotel.com
website: www.macleodmotel.com

The small ferry port of Tarbert lies sheltered in a green valley on a narrow isthmus between East and West Loch Tarbert. Macleod Motel, situated in the heart of the village, is a modern building, designed to provide great accommodation at reasonable prices. Accommodation is on a bed and breakfast basis with hearty and filling full

Scottish breakfasts. Lighter options are also available. For lunch and dinner, the motel incorporates the Clisham Keel Bar & Restaurant, where locally caught langoustine and scallops are a speciality. Traditional live music can be heard regularly in the bar.

If it is self-catering you are after, we also have Kirklea Cottages. They are in an elevated position overlooking the hub of the village and ferry terminal. Faced in Harris stone, these modern cottages are tastefully furnished and full of character. Decorated to an exacting standard, each one can sleep four to six people in warmth and comfort. There is a large sitting/dining room with radio, TV and video. Also, a fully equipped kitchen, utility room with washing machine and tumble dryer and a spacious shower room. Upstairs, there are two twin bedrooms with wash hand basins. Natural pinewood is a feature of the cottages and each one is heated by electric storage heaters throughout. There is private parking, as well as a garden and patio where you can relax on those long summer evenings.

The cottages are just a short walk from the local shops, bus and ferry terminal and the amenities at the Motel.

The Isle of Harris is very beautiful and has some of the best beaches in the world. The machair (the softly grassed areas inland from the shoreline) is a riot of wild flowers in the summer months. This is where the world famous Harris Tweed is produced, and you can visit some weavers in their homes and watch the cloth being woven.

People and animals lived under the one roof, separated by thin walls, with the roof usually being of thatch and turf. They had tiny windows because of the seasonal gales and rain (plus the fact that glass was very expensive) and its thick, dry stone walls (with a central core of clay and earth) kept it cool in summer and warm in winter.

The Arnol house has been furnished in typical fashion, and it has a clay floor. There is no fireplace, the fire being placed centrally, with no chimney. The houses got their name in the mid 19th century to distinguish them from the more modern white houses, which had mortar binding the stones.

There is also an interpretation centre in a nearby cottage, which has a model of a typical blackhouse showing how they were made.

Ballantrushal

15 miles NW of Stornoway on the B857

The **Clach an Trushal** (Historic Scotland), at 18 feet high, is the tallest standing stone in Scotland, and is said to mark the site of an ancient battle, though this is unlikely. In the 19th century several feet of peat were cut away from around its base, revealing the true height.

Great Bernera

18 miles W of Stornoway off the B8059

The small island of Great Bernera measures only six miles long by three miles wide at it's widest. It is connected to the mainland by the **Great Bernera Bridge**, which was the first bridge in the country made from pre-stressed concrete girders. The **Community Centre and Museum** has displays about the island, and also sells tea, coffee and cakes. On the lovely beach at **Bostadh** an Iron Age village has been excavated, and a reconstruction of an Iron Age house built. A cairn commemorates those men who took part in the **Bernera Riot** of 1874, when crofters stood up for their right of tenure. Three of them eventually stood trial, though a later Act of Parliament gave them the rights they were fighting for.

Tarbert

33 miles S of Stornoway on the A859

The small village of Tarbert has a ferry connection with Uig on Skye. This is the starting point of South Harris, and an isthmus no more that half a mile wide separates East Loch Tarbert, which is an arm of the Minch, from West Loch Tarbert, which is an arm of the Atlantic. In fact, *Tairbeart* in Gaelic means "isthmus" or "place of portage", where boats were dragged across land from one stretch of water to another. **Amhuinnsuidhe Castle** was built in 1868 by the Earl of Dunsmore, who owned Harris. It was the Earl's wife who introduced the weaving of Harris Tweed to the island. The castle was subsequently owned by the Bulmer family, which founded the cider firm. It was here that J.M. Barrie wrote his play *Mary Rose*. It is now used as an upmarket conference centre.

Scalpay

33 miles S of Stornoway

The tiny island of Scalpay, off Harris's east coast, is connected to the mainland by the £7m **Scalpay Bridge**, the biggest civil engineering project ever undertaken in the Western Isles. It was opened in 1998 by Tony Blair, the first serving prime minister ever to visit the Western Isles. The visit is also remembered because of the biting criticism he received from one of the island's more militant inhabitants - *culiciodes impunctatus*, more commonly known as the midge.

Rodel

48 miles S of Stornoway on the A859

Rodel sits near the southern tip of Harris, and is famous for **St Clement's Church**, burial place of the MacLeods. It was built in 1500 by Alasdair Crotach McLeod, who lived in the church's tower from 1540 to

The Rodel Hotel

Rodel, Isle of Harris HS5 3TW
Tel: 01859 520210
Fax: 01859 520219
e-mail: reservations@rodelhotel.co.uk
website: www.rodelhotel.co.uk

A warm Hebridean welcome awaits you at **The Rodel Hotel** on the beautiful Isle of Harris. It sits at the southernmost tip of the island, half an hour's drive from the ferry port at Tarbert, and is a place with a unique history, as it was built in 1781 for captain Alexander MacLeod of Berneray. In 2000 and 2001 it underwent a refurbishment that turned it into one of the most comfortable hotels on the island, offering modern standards of service and value for money while still retaining many of the original features that add so much to its unique ambience.

The four guest rooms are spacious and comfortable, each being individually furnished and decorated to an exceedingly high standard. All are completely en suite, and three have king sized beds (one being a four poster) while the fourth has twin beds. Each one has tea/coffee making facilities, a telephone, radio alarm and hair dryer. Jessie's Room is so called because it was from here that Jessie of Balranald eloped with her lover in 1850.

Food is important in the Rodel Hotel and only the freshest of local produce is used in the kitchens. Seafood from Western Isles ports, local venison, prime Scotch beef, Harris lamb and locally grown vegetables are used to create dishes that combine imagination and flair with old-fashioned tradition. The menu changes daily according to the produce that is in season. As well as superb dinners, lunches are also served between 12 noon and 2.30 pm. And from then until 5.30 pm you can order sandwiches and delicious home baking. If you have special dietary needs, the chef can accommodate them as well if given notice. Before the meal you can enjoy a pre-dinner drink in the spacious lounge, choosing from a wide range of local ales, single malts, brandies and liqueurs. The wine list is extensive, including some fine examples from the New World. If it's the local *craic* you're after, why not head for the public bar? You'll be made royally welcome!

The Rodel Hotel is the perfect place to stay while exploring the Western Isles. There are so many stunning landscapes to see and historic sites to explore. Plus you can take part in such activities as sailing, fishing, studying wildlife and biking on the quiet roads.

Adjoining the hotel are self catering flats which are comfortable and cosy, and come fully equipped for a great holiday. The weekly tariff includes electricity and linen, and guests can still enjoy the hotel's amenities.

Rodel Church, Harris

his death in 1547. He is still within the church, in a magnificent tomb that shows carvings of his home at Dunvegan on Skye. By 1787 the church was ruinous, but in that year Alexander MacLeod, a captain with the East India Company, restored it.

Other Western Isles

North Uist

59 miles SW of Stornoway

Like most of the Western Isles, North Uist is low lying, with more water than land making up its total area of 74,884 acres. **Loch Scadavay** is the biggest of the lochs, and though it only has an area of eight square miles, it has a coastline measuring 51 miles in length. The highest point on the island, at 1,127 feet, is **Eaval**, near the southeast corner. The island has a ferry service to An t-Obbe in Harris from Berneray, and one to Skye from **Lochmaddy**, the island's capital, and where

Baleloch House

Post Office House, Tigharry, Lochmaddy, North Uist HS6 5DG
Tel/Fax: 01876 510247

Baleloch House is a traditional, stone-built dwelling on the west side of the island of North Uist. It is approximately 18 miles from from Lochmaddy along the A867 road, with a ½ mile long track leading off up to the house, which is located in grounds of over one acre and enclosed by a walled garden. It is an idyllic setting, nestling in a quiet, private location in an Area of Outstanding Natural Beauty. There are views of hills, of open moorland and of the beautiful machair pasturelands, famous for their flowers, butterflies and birds.

The silvery, sandy beaches of Hosta are only ¾ of a mile away, and Loch Hosta, excellent for brown trout fishing, stretches out below the grounds. The house is well maintained, spacious and warm, and provides comfortable accommodation. Bed linen and towels are provided.

Downstairs is a spacious lounge with open fire and colour TV, a large family kitchen with dining table, a shower room with toilet and a pay phone which is situated in the hall. Upstairs there are three double bedrooms, a single bedroom and bathroom. There is an additional single bed in one of the double rooms, and in the kitchen is a fridge, chest freezer, automatic washing machine with tumble drier and microwave. Cooking and hot water is by electricity, and heating is by electricity and open peat or coal fires. Well behaved pets are more than welcome. The house sits approximately one mile from the RSPB nature reserve at Hougharry.

most of the hotels and B&Bs are to be found. **Taigh Chearsabhagh**, a museum and arts centre is housed in an old inn dating from the early 18th century.

Teampull na Trionad ("Trinity Temple"), on the south west shore, was once a great place of learning in the Western Isles. Indeed some people claim that it was actually Scotland's first university, with scholars and students making their way here from all over the country, one being Duns Scotus (see also Duns).

North Uist

It was founded in the early 13th century by one Beathag, a prioress from the priory on Iona and daughter of Somerled, Lord of the Isles. By the end of the 15th century, however, its influence began to fade, and during the Reformation it was attacked. Valuable books, manuscripts and works of art were tossed into the sea, and so much of the island's heritage was lost. The other building on the site is **Teampull MacBhiocair**, (MacVicar's Temple), where the teachers were buried.

It was in this area, in 1601, that the **Battle of Carinish** took place, the last battle on British soil not to have involved firearms. A troop of MacLeods from Harris was raiding the island, and took shelter in the Trinity Temple buildings when attacked by the MacDonalds. But the MacDonalds ignored the status of the temple, and slaughtered every MacLeod clansman except two, who escaped.

On the island's west coast, off the A865, is the **Balranald Nature Reserve**, where you can see waders and seabirds on various habitats.

Benbecula

80 miles SW of Stornoway

Benbecula is Beinn bheag a' bh-faodhla in Gaelic, meaning mountain of the fords. It is sandwiched between North and South Uist, with a landscape that is low and flat and dotted with shallow lochans, though **Rueval**, its highest peak, soars to all of 403 feet. The island marks the boundary between the Protestant islands to the north and the Roman Catholic islands to the south. There is no ferry terminal on the island, as it is connected to South Uist and North Uist by causeways.

The main settlement is **Balivanich**, or Baile na Mhanaich, meaning "Monk's Town". It sits on the west coast, and beside it is a small airstrip. The scant ruins of **Teampall Chaluim Cille**, founded by St Torranan, lie close to the village. The monks who lived here are supposed to have given the village its name.

To the south of the village, on the B892, are the ruins of **Nunton Chapel**, supposed

Isle Of Benbecula House Hotel

Creagory, Benbecula,
Hebrides of Scotland HS7 5PG
Tel: 01870 602024 Fax: 01870 603108
e-mail: reservations@iobhh.co.uk
website: www.isleshotelgroup.co.uk

History · wonderful landscapes · wildlife · romantic sunsets · invigorating seascapes · art and craft galleries · museums · the island of Benbecula has the lot. It also has the Isle of Benbecula House Hotel, surely one of the finest establishments in the Western Isles. Overlooking the Atlantic Ocean and the romantic hills of South Uist, it boasts 20 comfortable and spacious en suite rooms. The hotel is open all year to enjoy a relaxing time within a welcoming and informal atmosphere. The staff speak Gaelic and English, ensuring a genuine taste of the Western Isles.

The dining room seats up to 30 and serves delicious food prepared from only the finest and freshest of local produce. The cuisine is traditional Scottish, with a menu that combines flair and imagination. With prior notice special dietary needs can also be accommodated. There is a comprehensive wine list, so you are sure to find something that complements your meal.

The tastefully furnished lounge is cosy and relaxing, and here you can have a pre or after dinner drink in absolute comfort. The friendly bar serves a wide range of drinks, including over 60 single malts, gins and vodkas from Shetland and fine ales from Lewis and Skye. There is also a function suite for special celebrations, be it a wedding reception or party, or more formal occasions such as seminars and conferences.

The hotel prides itself on being family-friendly, with children and well-behaved dogs being more than welcome.

to have been a nunnery built in the 14th century. It was Lady Clanranald from nearby Nunton House (built from the stones of Nunton Chapel) who gave Charles Edward Stuart his disguise as a serving girl when he escaped from Benbecula to Skye in 1746.

Borve Castle, about three miles south of Balivanich, was owned by Ranald, son of John of Islay, in the 14th century. The ruins show a typical tower house of the period. Within the school at **Lionacleit**, three miles south of Balivanich, is a small museum.

South Uist

87 miles SW of Stornoway

Running down the east side of South Uist is a range of low mountains, with **Beinn Mhor** being the highest at 2,034 feet. The west side of the island is gentler, with fine white sandy beaches. **Lochboisdale**, in the southeast corner, is the largest village on the island, and has a ferry connection to Mallaig, Oban and Castlebay on Barra.

The island is one of the few places in Scotland never to have embraced the Reformation, and is predominantly Roman Catholic. To the northwest of the island is the famous statute of **Our Lady of the Isles**, overlooking Loch Bee. It was erected in 1957. It stands 30 feet high and was sculpted by Hew Lorimer. At the **Loch Druidibeag Nature Reserve**, which is close by, many birds such as greylag geese and mute swans, can be observed.

It was in South Uist, near **Milton** on Loch Kildonan, that Flora MacDonald was born in 1722. Her house is now completely ruinous, though it can still be seen. She was no simple Gaelic lass, but the daughter of a prosperous landowning farmer who died when she was young. Her mother then married Hugh MacDonald, a member of the great MacDonald of Sleat family. She was brought up in Skye and went to school in

Orasay Inn

Lochcarnan, Isle of South Uist HS8 5PD
Tel: 01870 610298
Fax: 01870 610267
e-mail: orasayinn@btinternet.com
website: www.witb.co.uk/links/orasayinn.htm

Owned and personally managed by Isobel and Alan Graham, the **Orasay Inn** is one of the best and friendliest small hotels on the beautiful island of South Uist. It is a modern building that blends beautifully into the surrounding landscapes, and offers the very best in Scottish hospitality. Isobel and Alan are committed to offering high standards at surprisingly keen prices, which means that the hotel is also one of the most popular.

There are nine rooms on offer, all fully en suite and all having colour TV, tea/coffee making facilities, central heating, hair dryer and telephone. The beds are extremely comfortable and the furnishings and decoration are of the highest standard possible. Deluxe rooms have sofas and patio doors to a decked area where guests can relax on those long, lazy evenings for which the Western Isles are justly famous.

However, it's the food that makes the Orasay Inn so special. Isobel is a "Natural Cooking of Scotland" trainer, and was even one of the team picked to prepare the gala dinner for the grand opening of Scotland's new parliament in 1999. Her philosophy when it comes to cooking is use fresh, local produce and keep the dishes simple while still offering imagination and flair. In this she has succeeded admirably, and now the inn has a reputation far beyond the Western Isles for it cuisine. A quote from the Sunday Times travel section on the Western Isles read "Finally don't forget to eat some seafood. The scallops, in particular are enormous and one of the best ways to enjoy them is as part of a seafood platter at the Orasay Inn on South Uist. Clean, functional and home to one of the best chefs in the highlands". The menu includes dishes based on locally caught seafood, such as seared Isle of Uist scallops, baked fillet of Orasay halibut and a gratin of seafood that includes local prawns, cockles, mussels and crab. There's also chicken wrapped haggis, Hebridean venison, local lamb chops, duck and prime Scotch beef. All are served in the spacious dining room, which has superb views of sea and mountain. There is also a daily changing specials board, and you might find delightful surprises on it such as deep fried squid or Thai red curry! The inn also offers snacks, and just as much care is taken with their preparation as with the dishes in the dining room. The assistant chef is also a qualified baker, and produces mouth watering fresh bread, scones and a selection of desserts.

There is a fine selection of wines from around the world to choose from, and in the cosy lounge bar you can choose from a wide range of beers, lagers, spirits (including single malts), liqueurs and soft drinks.

South Uist is one of the loveliest of the Western Isles, and full of history and romance. It can be reached by ferry from Oban, or by causeway from Benbecula, and any visit is sure to be rewarding and enjoyable. You can also indulge in golf, sailing, fishing, walking and a host of other outdoor activities.

South Uist

Sleat and Edinburgh.

Kildonan Museum, north of Lochboisdale on the A865, has displays and exhibits on local history, as well as a tearoom and shop. Further north along the A865 are the ruins of **Ormiclate Castle**, built between 1701 and 1708 as a sumptuous residence for the chief of Clanranald. Alas, the chief's stay there was short lived, as it burnt down in 1715 after a rowdy Jacobite party.

Off the south coast of South Uist is the small island of **Eriskay** (from the Norse for "Eric's Island"), which is joined to South Uist by a causeway. It is noted for one of the most beautiful of Gaelic songs, the *Eriskay Love Lilt*. It was here, on 23 July 1745, that Charles Edward Stuart first set foot on Scottish soil when he stepped off a French ship to reclaim the British throne for the Stuarts. The beach where he landed is now called Prince's Beach, and legend says that his first action was to plant the sea convolvulus, which now thrives here today.

It was in February 1941 that another

Beach at Eriskay

event took place, which was to make Eriskay famous. **The SS. Politician** was heading towards the United States from Liverpool with a cargo of 260,000 bottles of whisky when it was wrecked on the Sound of Eriskay. Legend has it that as soon as the seamen were removed from the ship to safety, work began on "removing" the cargo, and this lasted for a few weeks. Eventually Customs and Excise men appeared on the island, but by this time the bottles had been spirited away into peat bogs and other hidey-holes. Only 19 people were charged with illegal possession.

Sir Compton Mackenzie used the incident as the basis for his novel *Whisky Galore*, made into a film in 1948. The

AM Politician

3, The Village, Eriskay HS8 5JL
Tel: 01878 720246
website: www.ampolitician.co.uk

The **AM Politician** is the only public house on the small but beautiful island of Eriskay, off the southern tip of South Uist. It is named after the famous S.S. Politician, which ran aground off the coast of the island in 1942, carrying a cargo of whisky bound for the United States. Sir Compton Mackenzie later based his novel *Whisky Galore* on the incident, and the bar area contains memorabilia from the original SS Politician, which includes portholes, a machete, an anchor chain link, a bottle of whisky and a Jamaican ten shilling note.The pub originally opened in 1988 and was bought by the new owners, sisters Morag MacKinnon and

Margaret Campbell from South Uist, in 2003.

It is now one of the best hostelries in the whole of the Western Isles, and has been refurbished to an extremely high standard. It serves a wide range of beers, spirits (including single malts), wines and liqueurs, and you are sure to find something to your taste as you relax after a hard day's sightseeing.

The island is connected to South Uist by causeway, so many of the islands, such as North Uist, and South Uist can be explored at your leisure.

The pub is open seven days a week, serving good, honest pub food, such as soup of the day with crusty bread, home made lasagne with side salad, juicy sirloin steaks and local breaded haddock. The whole place has a homely yet spacious feel to it, and if you visit, you won't be disappointed!

wreckage can still sometimes be seen at exceptionally low tide. In the late 1980s an attempt was made to get at the rest of the cargo, but this proved unsuccessful.

The highest point on the island is **Ben Scrien**, at 609 feet. It is an easy climb, and gives magnificent views. The island's native pony, the grey and black Eriskay pony, was at one time used to carry seaweed and peat on panniers slung across their back. In the 1950s they nearly died out, but now are on the increase again.

Barra

105 miles S of Stornoway

Barra ("Barr's Island") is the southernmost of the Western Isles, separated from South Uist by the Sound of Barra. To the south is a string of tiny islands, including Sanday, Rosinish, Mingulay and Berneray.

The island's airstrip is to the north of the island, and is the fine sandy beach at **Cockle Bay**, a name which is richly deserved as cockles are still collected there today. The main settlement is to the south at Castlebay, the terminal for the Oban ferry.

On an island in the bay itself is **Kisimul Castle** (Historic Scotland), the largest fortification in the Western Isles. It was the home of the Macneils of Barra, chiefs of clan Macneill, who were granted the island in the 15th century, first by the Lord of the Isles and then by James VI. Others say, however, that the Macneils have been associated with the island since at least the 11th century.

Isle Of Barra Hotel

Tangasdale Beach, Isle of Barra HS9 5XW
Tel: 01871 810383 Fax: 01871 810385
e-mail: Barrahotel@aol.com
website: www.isleofbarra.com/iob.html

Overlooking a beautiful white, sandy bay washed by the Atlantic Ocean, the **Isle of Barra Hotel** is a family-run, seventies-style establishment offering an oasis of calm in the modern world. It has a truly wonderful, almost magical, atmosphere, and is warm and inviting, thanks to its friendly local staff. The spacious lounge is the place to have a relaxing drink as you look out over Halaman Bay, with Ben Tangaval rising in the distance. The bedrooms are all fully en suite, and have colour TV and hospitality tray. They are furnished and decorated to a high standard in keeping with the overall style, and most have splendid views out over the bay.

The hotel is noted for the excellence of its cuisine which is served in the dining room, with its stunning westerly outlook. It specialises in fresh, local seafood, Barra lamb and beef, and the menu is put together with imagination and flair while still retaining all the traditions of fine Scottish cooking. There is an extensive wine list which contains wines from around the world, so you are sure to find something to complement your meal. Before dinner, why not have a drink in the fabulous cocktail bar with its seashell pictures, or stroll out onto the patio after dinner with a coffee or single malt, and admire the sunsets over the Atlantic.

Barra is easily reached by air or sea. Either way, you will be enthralled by an island rich in history and heritage.

Cottage on the Isle of Barra

The castle was originally built in about 1030, though the present building dates from the 15th century. In 1838 the island was sold to Gordon of Cluny, who proceeded to remove the islanders from the land and ship them off to the New World. In 1937 the island was bought back by the 45th Chief of Clan Macneil, an American called Robert Lister Macneil. The 15th century castle had been burnt down in the late 1700s, and he set about restoring it.

The old chiefs of Clan Macneil had the reputation of being haughty and proud. A story is told of a Macneil chief at the time of Noah, who was invited aboard the Ark to escape the flood. He is supposed to have arrogantly replied, "Macneil already has a boat." And in later times, after Macneil had dinner, one of his servants would go up to the ramparts of Kisimul Castle and announce to the world: "as the Macneil has dined, the other kings and princes of the world may now also dine."

The ruined **Cille-bharraidh** (Church of St Barr) is located at the north end of the island, and was the burial place of the Macneils. Also buried here is **Sir Compton Mackenzie**, who wrote *Whisky Galore* (see also Eriskay). The island is predominantly Catholic, and at Heaval, a mile north east of Castlebay, is a marble statue of the Madonna and Child called **Our Lady of the Sea**.

Orkney & Shetland

In 1469 James III married Margaret, the young daughter of Christian I of Denmark and Norway. Her father pledged Orkney and Shetland to the Scottish crown until such time as the dowry was settled in full. As he was crippled with debts, the dowry was never paid, and in 1472, the islands became part of Scotland, creating the kingdom as we know it today.

The Norse influences are still strong. Gaelic was never spoken here, and the place names (and many family names) all have Norse derivations. Both sets of islands are nearer Oslo than they are London, and there have even been occasional calls for the islands to be independent of Scotland.

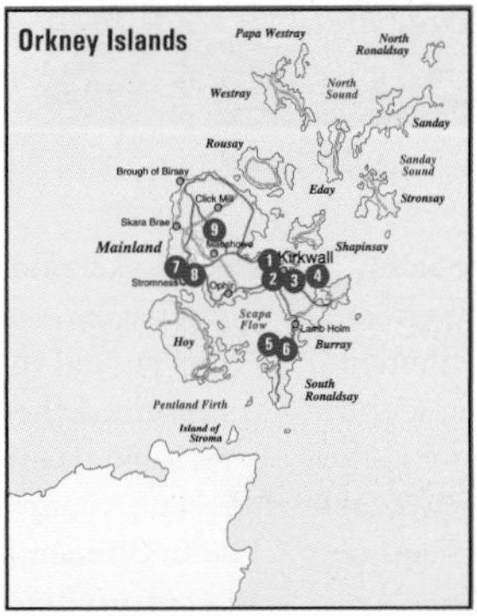

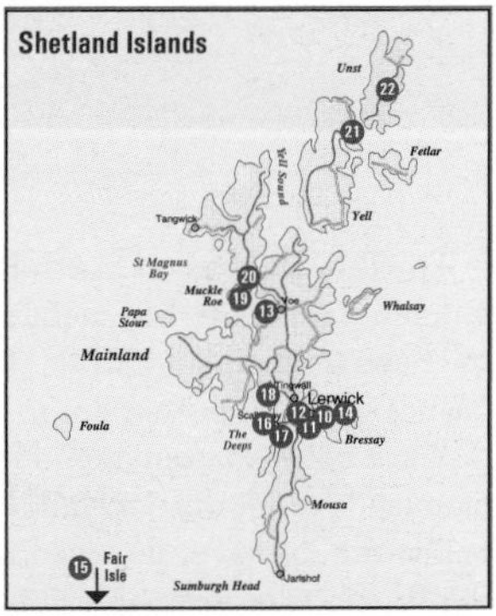

PLACES TO STAY, EAT AND DRINK

The Albert Hotel, Kirkwall	1	Hotel	p421
West End Hotel, Kirkwall	2	Hotel	p422
Kirkwall Hotel, Kirkwall	3	Hotel	p422
Quoyburray Inn, Tankerness	4	Pub with Restaurant	p424
Murray Arms Hotel, St Margaret's Hope	5	Hotel	p425
Galley Inn & Restaurant, St Margaret's Hope	6	Pub, Restaurant & Accommodation	p426
Plainstones, Stromness	7	B&B	p426
Howe Holiday Homes, Stromness	8	Self Catering	p427
Rickla, Harray	9	B&B	p427
Monty's Bistro, Lerwick	10	Bistro	p429
Shetland Fudge, Lerwick	11	Confectioners	p430
Self Catering Shetland, Lerwick	12	Self Catering	p430
Pierhead Tavern & Bar, Lower Voe	13	Restaurant	p431
Maryfield House Hotel, Bressay	14	Hotel	p432
Fair Isle, Fair Isle	15	Visitor Attraction	p433
Kiln Bar & Café, Scalloway	16	Bar & Café	p433
Easterhoull Chalets, East Voe	17	Self Catering	p434
The Westings Inn, Whiteness	18	Pub, Restaurant & Accommodation	p435
Westayre, Muckle Roe	19	B&B	p435
Busta House Hotel, Busta	20	Hotel	p436
Gutcher Post Office and B&B, Gutcher	21	B&B	p436
Buness House, Baltasound	22	B&B	p437

Denotes entries in other chapters

Cliffs on the West Coast

The Brough Ness on South Ronaldsay in Orkney is no more than eight miles from the Scottish mainland, while the Shetland Islands sit much further out to sea, with the distance between Sumburgh Head and the mainland being over 100 miles. Few people realise the distances involved, as maps of the British Isles invariably put the Shetlands in a convenient box off Scotland's north east coast. However, fast ferries and air services put the islands within easy reach of the mainland nowadays.

In olden times they were at a major communications crossroads, and gained an importance that far outweighed their size. They were on the main route from Scandinavia to Scotland, England, Ireland and the Isle of Man, and seafarers invariably stopped off there, some eventually settling. They are rich in historical sites and remains (far too many to mention them all in this book), which show a continued occupation for thousands of years. Indeed, there are about 120 confirmed broch sites in the Shetlands alone. And because the landscape has never been intensely farmed or cultivated, many of these sites have remained relatively undisturbed.

The main difference between the two archipelagos can be summed up in the old saying that an Orcadian (an inhabitant of Orkney) is a crofter with a boat, whereas a Shetlander is a fisherman with a croft. Orkney is therefore the more fertile of the two, though this is relative, as the landscape is nothing like the fertile areas of the Scottish mainland, and trees are the exception rather than the rule. One thing has brought prosperity to the islands, however, and that is North Sea oil. It has transformed their economies, but at the same time has remained remarkably unobtrusive, apart from places like Sullom Voe in Shetland, the largest oil terminal and port in Europe.

The Orkney archipelago consists of about 70 islands, only 19 of which are inhabited. The largest island is Mainland, where the islands' capital, Kirkwall, is located. It is a small city as well as a royal burgh, as it has its own medieval cathedral, the most northerly in Britain and the most complete in Scotland. Most of the islands are connected by ferry, and the best way to appreciate the smaller ones is on foot rather

Crofters Drying Hay at Netherdale, Shetlands

than by car. Some of the sites, such as Skara Brae, are world famous and must not be missed.

The Shetland Islands has about 100 islands, with less than 20 being inhabited. Its largest island is again called Mainland, and it is here that Lerwick is situated. It is the islands' capital, and the most northerly town in Britain. Every year in January the ancient "Up Helly Aa" festival is held, where a Viking ship is paraded through the streets of the town before being ceremonially burnt. Its origins go back to pagan times, when the turn of the year meant that the days started getting longer again

Kirkwall Harbour

Kirkwall

The capital of Orkney has a population of about 4,800, and was granted its charter as a royal burgh in 1486. It sits almost in the centre of Mainland, and divides the island into East Mainland and West Mainland. It is a lively, busy place of old stone buildings and streets paved in flagstones, with a shopping centre that serves all of the islands.

St Magnus Cathedral was founded in 1137 by Saint Magnus's nephew Rognvald, though the cathedral as you see it today dates from between the 12th and 16th centuries. The story goes that Magnus was the son of Erlend, one of two earls who ruled Orkney. The King of Norway had them removed, and then appointed his own son Sigurd as Overlord. The King and his son then set out on a raiding party for Wales, taking Magnus with them. However, Magnus refused to take part in the usual rape and pillage, deciding instead to sing psalms. The Norwegian king was displeased, and young Magnus had to flee.

After the king's death, he returned to Orkney, and in 1117 arranged to meet with Haakon, the new ruler of the islands, to

West End Hotel

Main Street, Kirkwall, Orkney KW15 1BU
Tel: 01856 872368 Fax: 01856 876181
e-mail: west-end@orkney.com

Within the small cathedral city of Kirkwall you will find one of the best privately-run hotels in the whole of Orkney - the **West End Hotel**. You'll get a warm welcome at this comfortable and charming establishment, which is renowned for its high standards and realistic prices. Set in a quiet area of the city, yet within easy walking distance of the main attractions, it was built in 1824 as a town house and later became a hospital. Now a popular hotel it offers ten comfortable rooms within the hotel itself and a further six in the nearby annexe, all fully en suite. They are cosy yet spacious, and are furnished and decorated to a high standard. All have colour televisions, hospitality trays and direct-dial phones.

Excellent food is served in the restaurant, all made from fresh local produce, you are assured of quality every time. Of course, seafood and the best Orkney beef is on a menu that combines the traditional and modern, and there is also a fine selection of wines to accompany your meal.

Why not have a quiet pre dinner drink in the friendly atmosphere of the lounge bar? You can choose from a wide range of ales, beers, wines, spirits and liqueurs, not forgetting soft drinks if you're driving. There is ample parking at the rear, plus a garden which is just right for those long summer evenings you get in Orkney.

claim his inheritance. However, Haakon had him murdered by an axe blow to the skull. At first, Magnus was buried in a small church on Birsay, but his remains were later taken to the new cathedral at Lerwick when it was consecrated. Some people regarded this story as more of a legend than historical fact, but in 1919, during some restoration work, a casket containing human bones was found embedded high up in one of the cathedral's pillars. The skull had been split open with an axe.

The ruined **Bishop's Palace** (Historic Scotland) dates mainly from the 12th century, when it was built for Bishop William the Old. The Round Tower, however, was built by Bishop Reid between 1541 and 1548. It was within the palace, in

Kirkwall Hotel

Harbour Street, Kirkwall, Orkney KW15 1LF
Tel: 01856 872232 Fax: 01856 872812
e-mail: enquiries@kirkwallhotel.com
website: www.kirkwallhotel.com

Overlooking Kirkwall's picturesque harbour, the **Kirkwall Hotel** is one of the town's most prominent landmarks. It is owned by local couple Debra and Colin Low, who take great pride in the warm family atmosphere of the hotel and the high standards they maintain. It has 38 en suite rooms, all featuring a TV, telephone and hospitality tray to make your stay as comfortable and enjoyable as possible. The hotel also features two bars and one of Orkney's most spacious and highly regarded restaurants, as well as two function rooms ideal for accommodating small parties, weddings or business meetings.

1263, that King Haakon IV of Norway died, having just been defeated at the Battle of Largs (see also Largs). He was buried in Lerwick Cathedral, but his body was later taken back to Bergen in Norway.

The notorious Patrick Stewart, Earl of Orkney and grandson of James V, built the adjacent **Earl's Palace** (Historic Scotland) between 1600 and 1607. The Stewart earls were hated in the islands because they exploited the people and bled them dry. Patrick himself was arrested by James VI and executed for treason in 1615.

All that is left of the medieval **St Olaf's Church**, after which Kirkwall (kirkjuvagr, meaning "church bay") was named, is a doorway in St Olaf's Wynd. Within Tankerness House, built as a merchant's house in the 16th century, is the **Orkney Museum**, which contains artefacts and exhibits about the island. The wooden box that contained St Magnus's bones, discovered within a pillar in the cathedral, is one of the exhibits. The **Orkney Wireless Museum** is at Kiln Corner, and has examples of wartime and domestic wireless sets used on the islands. It was founded by local man Jim MacDonald, who had a lifetime's fascination with wireless and radio sets, and amassed a huge collection.

On a building in Castle Street is a plaque commemorating **Kirkwall Castle**, which was dismantled in 1615 and finally demolished in 1865. It had been built in the 14th century by the Sinclairs of Roslin, who had been created Earls of Orkney by Haakon of Norway in 1379, long before the islands became part of Scotland.

Around Kirkwall

Lamb Holm

7 miles S of Kirkwall on the A961

After the sinking of the Royal Oak by a U-boat in 1939 a string of islands to the south of Mainland were joined by causeways to prevent submarines from slipping through again. On Lamb Holm, one of the islands, is the ornate **Italian Chapel**. It was made by Italian prisoners-of-war captured in North Africa in 1942 that were working on the causeways. The work is remarkable considering its basis is two Nissen huts and various pieces of cast off metal and wood. In 1960 some of the ex-POWs were invited to return to the island to restore it.

Maeshowe

8 miles W of Kirkwall off the A965

Maeshowe (Historic Scotland) is Britain's largest chambered cairn. The name comes from the Old Norse and means "great mound". It is a great, grassy hill, 36 feet high and 300 feet in circumference, and was built about 2,700 BC. A long, narrow passage leads into a central chamber with smaller side chambers, which are roofed and floored, with massive slabs. It stands beside the A 965 between Kirkwall and Stromness.

Also looked after by

Italian Chapel, Lamb Holm

Quoyburray Inn

Tankerness,
Orkney KW17 2QU
Tel: 01856 861255
e-mail: texasthehorse@hotmail.com

The **Quoyburray Inn**, on Orkney's Mainland island, is a picturesque, stone built inn that offers a warm, Orcadian welcome to everyone. It sits on the A960, in the village of Tankerness, only a few miles from both Kirkwall and its airport. It is owned and personally managed by Angela and Craig Burns, with Craig having many year's experience in the licensing trade.

This is the perfect place to enjoy a quiet drink as you explore the beautiful Orkneys. It serves a great range of beers, wines and spirits, as well as a fine range of soft drinks. Red MacGregor, Dark Island, Northern Light and Ravel Ale are all local ales from the renowned Orkney Brewery, and all are

available in bottle form. In addition, there is a wide range of single malts from all over Northern Scotland. There is a public bar (a favourite place for both locals and visitors) and here you can join in the "craic" and enjoy the kind of hospitality for which the islands are famous. The spacious yet cosy Kiln Bar, with its large wooden bar, is both comfortable and welcoming, with plush banquette seating and soft carpeting. The décor and furnishing are tasteful and practical, with prints adorning the walls and antiques and nicknacks strategically placed on shelves. The overall ambience of the place creates an atmosphere that is redolent of the beauty of the Orkneys. In the colder months, a roaring open fire adds a touch of warmth.

And yet, up until 1975, the building was no more that a "tatty" (potato) shed! Tasteful renovations have turned it into a delightful hostelry combining the modern concepts of value for money and high standards of service with an "olde worlde" feeling.

Upstairs is the Rafters Restaurant, which serves superb pub food at extremely competitive prices. The raftered ceiling, in old dark wood, adds a certain warmth to the place, as do the green table covers and the whitewashed walls. There are different menus for lunch and dinner, but in each one the dishes are both imaginative and tasty, using only the finest and freshest local produce wherever possible. At lunchtime Craig is the chef, and in the evenings two special chefs take over to make your meal here one to remember! There is also a daily specials board, and diners can be assured that all the desserts are freshly prepared. Why not try Scotland's traditional dish, haggis, with a Drambuie and onion sauce? Or deep-fried golden scampi? Or even herring in oatmeal? Plus there is chicken, juicy steaks, salads and vegetarian dishes to suit all.

Orkney is full of places to see and visit, such as Mine Howe, excavated in 1946 revealing a two-storey structure sunk into the bowels of the earth. It was covered over, and painstakingly reopened in 1999, revealing once again the "29 steps" that take you down into it. No one knows its purpose or when it was dug out of the earth.

Ring of Brodgar

Historic Scotland are the four **Stenness Standing Stones**, the largest such stones in Orkney. They are all that are left of a huge stone circle, and date from about the same time as Maeshowe. To the north of the stones is the **Barnhouse Settlement**, a Neolithic village discovered in 1984. The **Ring of Brodgar**, also dating from about 2700 BC, still has 27 of its original 67 stones. They are smaller than the Stenness Stones, and stand on a strip of land between two small lochs.

Orphir

9 miles W of Kirkwall off the A964

During early Norse rule, Orphir was one of the main Orcadian settlements. **Orphir Church** was built in the 11th or 12 century, some say by Haakon, who murdered St Magnus in the 12th century, possibly as an act or penance after a pilgrimage to Jerusalem. It was a circular church about 18 feet in diameter, with a small apse at its eastern end, and was the only such medieval church in Scotland. Nothing now remains apart from the apse and some of the east wall. **Bu Interpretation Centre**, next to the church, explains the ruins.

Murray Arms Hotel

Back Road, St Margaret's Hope,
Orkney KW17 2SP
Tel/Fax: 01856 831205
e-mail: murrayarms@freeuk.com
website: www.murrayarmshotel.com

The warm stone of the **Murray Arms Hotel** in the pleasant village of St Margaret's Hope on South Ronaldsay is the first indication you have that this is a special place. It combines all the traditional qualities of a popular village inn with first class, value-for-money accommodation in one of the most beautiful parts of Scotland. Five guest rooms are available - two single, two double and a twin, and all have recently been redecorated and upgraded to an exceedingly high standard. All are fully en suite, with radio alarms, TVs, and tea/coffee making facilities. There is also a residents' lounge with TV and video recorder. Breakfasts, either a full Scottish or a full Continental, can be ordered for guests catching the early morning ferry from the village.

The hotel is popular with the locals, and has a public bar with pool table, darts board and other games, as well as a separate no-smoking lounge bar/restaurant. This offers tempting hot or cold snacks and meals throughout the day and a full evening menu, using fresh and local produce whenever possible.

On sunny days guests can sit outside in the beer garden for a meal or a quiet drink while enjoying the slower pace of life that is found on Orkney. Or you can join the locals in the public bar and enjoy the usual friendly atmosphere.

Orkney, often called a "bird watchers' paradise", is ideal for walking and golf and there are numerous museums, old churches, prehistoric cairns, craft studios and mysterious standing stones to be seen.

The Galley Inn & Shore Restaurant

Front Road, St Margaret's Hope,
Orkney KW17 2SL
Tel: 01856 831526
e-mail: info@galleyinn.co.uk
website: www.galleyinn.co.uk

You should never visit the Orkneys without visiting **The Galley Inn and Shore Restaurant** in the picturesque village of St Margaret's Hope. Its patio overlooks the quayside, and is the perfect place to relax over a quiet drink as you take in the slower pace of life on these lovely islands. Galley Inn has a relaxed, informal atmosphere, and serves a wide range of beers (including locally brewed bottled beers), wines, spirits and soft drinks, being a popular place for visitors and locals to mingle and chat. Hanging on the walls are works by local artists, and all are for sale. The B&B accommodation (which is non-smoking) has recently been completely refurbished to an extremely high standard, and consists of three spacious rooms, a twin and two doubles, all fully en suite and all having TV and hospitality tray. They offer comfortable accommodation and great value for money.

The Shore Restaurant is open seven days a week and serves home cooked meals that are prepared from fresh, local produce such as Orkney beef and lamb, vegetables and fish. Everything from a simple bar meal to a lunch or dinner is available, and there's sure to be a wine in the small but comprehensive wine list that complements each dish perfectly. The restaurant is non-smoking for your comfort and convenience, and the service is quick, efficient and friendly.

Stromness

15 miles W of Kirkwall on the A965

This little burgh faces Orkney's second largest island, Hoy. Though it looks old and quaint, it only received its burgh charter in 1817, and was founded in the 17th century. The **Stromness Museum** in Alfred Street has displays on **Scapa Flow**, whaling, lighthouses and the Hudson's Bay Company (which had a base here, and employed many Orcadians). Scapa Flow, between Hoy and Mainland, is one of the best natural harbours in the world. After World War I the German fleet was brought to Scapa Flow while a decision was made about it's future. However, the German officers decided the fleet's future themselves

Plainstones

130 Victoria Street, Stromness,
Orkney KW16 3BU
Tel: 01856 851566
e-mail: k.grieve@ukonline.co.uk

Plainstones B&B is one of the best establishments of its kind in the picturesque old town of Stromness. Centrally situated with only a short walk from the ferry terminal, this listed mid 1800s house retains many original features. It has a friendly, relaxed atmosphere and offers three rooms, two of which have superb views over Scapa Flow. All rooms - two with twin beds and a single - have hospitality trays and hand basins and there are two shower rooms/toilets. Plainstones is renowned for its breakfasts produced from traditional island produce where possible. Vegetarian and special dietary requirements can be catered for.

Howe Holiday Homes

Howe Farm, Stromness,
Orkney KW16 3JU
Tel: 01856 850302
e-mail: e.h.reid@btinternet.com

The three-star **Howe Holiday Homes** offers great self-catering accommodation for those wishing to holiday in Orkney. There are five beautifully appointed cottages on offer, all situated within a dairy farm close to the picturesque town of Stromness. The lounges (each one having a TV) are spacious, kitchens are all well equipped, and the bedrooms are cosy and comfortable. The cottages sleep between three and five people, and there is plenty of car parking and public transport to and from Stromness. They make the ideal base from which to explore the beautiful Orkney Islands, which are rich in scenery and legend.

- they scuttled the ships, and most still lie at the bottom of the sea, a constant attraction for divers.

Golf by the Loch, Stromness

Hoy

17 miles W of Kirkwall

Hoy is Orkney's second largest island, and sits off the west coast of Mainland. The **Old Man of Hoy** is a famous sandstone stack over 445 feet high off its north west coast, and a constant challenge to climbers. The first successful climb was in 1966, and TV cameras were there to record it. At the southwest end of the island is a **Martello Tower**, erected between 1813 and 1815 to protect the island from the French.

The **Dwarfie Stone** is unique in the

Rickla

Harray, Orkney KW17 2JT
Tel/Fax: 01856 761575
e-mail: jacky@rickla.com
website: www.rickla.com

Established in 1996 by Jacky and Stewart Anderson, **Rickla** is a superior five star B&B situated off the A986 and close to Loch Harray. It has 3 sumptuous rooms on offer, two of them being suites of bedroom and lounge with magnificent views. This is luxury on the grand scale, and people come back here year after year because of the informal atmosphere and high standards. There is a comprehensive breakfast menu featuring locally sourced produce wherever possible, and the establishment even has a small library of books and maps on the Orkneys.

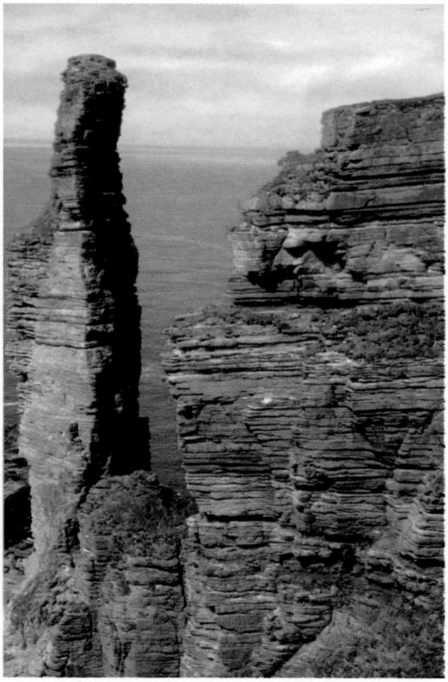

Old Man of Hoy

United Kingdom - a burial chamber dating from at least 3000 BC cut into a great block of sandstone. Some people claim, however, that it was not a tomb, but an ancient dwelling.

Click Mill

13 miles NW of Kirkwall on the B9057

Click Mill (Historic Scotland) is the islands' last surviving example of a horizontal watermill, and got its name from the clicking sound it made when turning. They were once common throughout Scandinavia.

At Harray, a couple of miles south of the mill, is the Corrigall Farm Museum, housed in an old 18th century farmhouse. Exhibits include a working barn with grain kiln.

Skara Brae

17 miles NW of Kirkwall on the B9056

In 1850 at the Bay of Skaill a storm uncovered the remains of a village, which was at least 5,500 years old - older even than the Pyramids. It is the oldest known prehistoric village in Europe, and the remains are now looked after by Historic Scotland. They show that the people who built it from stone were sophisticated and ingenious, and that the houses were comfortable and well appointed, with beds, dressers and cupboards made of stone, as wood was hard to come by. Archaeological evidence tells us that it was built by Neolithic people who farmed, hunted and fished.

Close by is **Skaill House**, the finest mansion in Orkney. The main part of the house was originally built in 1620 for George Graham, Bishop of Orkney, though it has been extended over the years. It houses a fine collection of furniture, including Bishop Graham's bed, on which are carved the words *GEO. GRAHAM ME FIERI FECIT* ("George Graham caused me to be made").

The house was built on the site of an ancient burial mound, which may account for the many ghosts that allegedly haunt it.

Skara Brae

Brough of Birsay

21 miles NW of Kirkwall off the A966

This little island, which is connected to the mainland at low tide by a narrow causeway, has the remains of a Norse settlement and an early medieval chapel (once the cathedral of the diocese of Orkney), built on the foundations of a chapel that may date back to the 7th or 8th centuries. After he was killed, St Magnus was buried here until such time as his body could be taken to the newly built St Magnus Cathedral in Kirkwall. When visiting the island, the times of tides must be taken into account. The tourism office at Kirkwall can advise.

Earls Palace, Birsay

The ruins of **Earl Stewart's Palace** overlook the island. This was one of the castles owned by the unpopular Stewarts, Earls of Orkney. The **Kirbuster Farm Museum** has examples of farm implements used on Orkney over the years, and a Victorian garden.

South of the island, at Marwick Head, is a squat tower - the **Kitchener Memorial**. It was erected in memory of Kitchener of Khartoum, who was killed when *HMS Hampshire*, on which he was travelling to Russia to discuss the progress of the war, struck a German mine near here in 1916. Only twelve people survived the sinking of the ship.

Lerwick

The capital of the Shetland Islands was granted its burgh charter in 1818. However, its history goes much further back than that, and it was originally developed by the Dutch in the 17th century to service their fishing fleet. It is the most northerly town in Britain, and, with a population of about 7,000, sits on the island of Mainland. The town is so far north that during June, there is little or no darkness.

Every year, on the last Tuesday in January, the festival of **Up Helly Aa** is held. After being hauled through the streets

Shetland Fudge

11 Harbour Street, Lerwick,
Shetland ZE1 0LR
Tel: 01595 694324 Fax: 01595 697300
e-mail: enquiries@shetlandfudge.com
website: www.shetlandfudge.com

For a taste of that wonderful, sweet and creamy fudge that you remember from your childhood, make your way to **Shetland Fudge** when you're in Lerwick. It, and the other wonderful confectionery sold here, are all hand-made to carefully devised recipes from pure ingredients with no artificial colourings, preservatives or sweeteners added.

The family-run business produces confectionery in small, carefully controlled batches using as many local ingredients as possible, and only the finest spirits, liqueurs and extracts. Even the nuts are organic! Rich and creamy Belgian chocolate · the finest stem ginger · Tia Maria · Baileys · Stewart's Rum · fat, juicy raisins · truffle fudge · traditional Scottish tablet · mandarins · pecan nuts · all are used to create a mouth-watering selection of confectionery. The "olde-worlde" shop is bursting with character and flavour, and you'll be amazed at the range of goodies on display. As well as confectionery, you can buy beers, wines and spirits, hand made ice cream, Shetland hampers, smoked salmon, Jago (a local drink made from vodka, cream and Shetland water) and even salmon cured in gin!

Upstairs a surprise awaits you, for here you will find an art and craft gallery that stocks a great selection of prints, paintings, artists' supplies, pottery, cards and craft goods. It's the perfect place to buy that special souvenir of the Shetlands!

Self Catering Shetland

Inches, Bell Road, Lerwick,
Shetland ZE1 0QB
Tel: 01595 692793 Fax: 01595 692476
e-mail: info@selfcateringshetland.com
website: www.selfcateringshetland.com

Shetland, with its many islands, its long summer evenings and its spectacular sunsets, is the ideal location for a get-away-from-it-all holiday. Whether you want to walk, fish, cycle, play golf, study wildlife or just relax, it offers unrivalled facilities. It also offers **Self Catering Shetland**, a company offering excellent holiday accommodation that is comfortable and always reasonably priced. If you are coming by ferry or bus, arrangements can be made to pick you up and bring you to any of the properties.

Situated just outside Lerwick, The Decca is a substantial property with two comfortable and well-appointed self catering houses, each with three bedrooms, kitchen, living room with TV and video, and a utility room with washing machine and tumble dryer. It is only five minutes from a bus stop that takes you into Lerwick, and there is ample car parking. A mobile phone is available (£60 deposit) that has been programmed with useful numbers. This will be refunded (minus the cost of calls) when you leave.

63 Burgh Road sits in the heart of Lerwick, with all the amenities of this charming town right on your doorstep. It comprises a sitting room, kitchen/dining room, family bedroom and double bedroom. The large shared garden at the back is a sun trap during the summer months, and here you can relax and let the world go by. Again, a mobile phone is available with a £60 deposit.

Lerwick

of the town accompanied by men carrying torches and dressed as Vikings, a Viking longboat is set on fire. Though an enjoyable and spectacular sight, it is a ritual, which is thought to date back to pagan times, when darkest days of winter were feared. It was thought that the light from celebrations of this kind attracted the light of the sun, which would then gradually return, lengthening the days. The introduction of a Viking ship, however, was a Victorian idea. Before that tar barrels were used.

Like Orkney, all the islands are rich in ancient remains. There are also many small interpretation centres and museums - too many for all of them to be mentioned in this book.

The number of days in the year when the temperatures rise above 75 degrees are few in Shetland (though the last few summers have been excellent!), but there are compensations, not least of which is the quality of light and the almost 24 hours of daylight at the height of summer. And there is less rain here than in Fort William or even North Devon.

Fort Charlotte, named after George III's wife, was built in the 1780s on the site of 17th century fortifications, which protected the town from the Dutch. **Shetland Museum** in Lower Hillhead gives an insight into the history of the islands and its people, and has some marvellous displays on archaeology.

The wonderfully named **Böd of Gremista** is located north of the town, and was the birthplace in 1792 of **Arthur Anderson**, co-founder of the P&O line. He joined the Royal Navy, and subsequently fought in the Napoleonic wars. In 1833 he co-founded the Peninsular Steam Navigation Company, which, in 1937, became the Peninsular and Oriental Steam Navigation Company. The 18th century building has been restored as a small museum and interpretation centre about the island's maritime history.

Around Lerwick

Bressay

1 mile E of Lerwick

Sandwick, Mousa

The island of Bressay sits opposite Lerwick, and shelters its harbour. The **Bressay Heritage Centre**, close to the ferry terminal, illustrates through displays and exhibits what life was like on the island in former times. The tiny island of **Noss**, off its west coast, is a nature reserve. Boat trips to the island are available. Bressay has some fine walks, notably on its east coast. Its highest point is **Ward Hill**, at 742 feet.

Mousa

13 miles S of Lerwick

There are about 70 confirmed broch (a round, fortified tower) sites in Shetland, and one of the best preserved is at Sandwick on this tiny island off the east coast of Mainland. The **Broch of Mousa** (Historic Scotland) was built sometime between the 1st and 3rd centuries from local stone, and is over 40 feet high and 49 feet in diameter. It has lost its uppermost courses, but is still in a remarkable state of preservation, and shows the typical layout of these curious buildings, which are found nowhere else but in Scotland. The double walls slope inwards as they get higher, and embedded in them are staircases (which you can use to climb to the top) and defensive galleries.

Jarlshof

25 miles S of Lerwick on the A970

Lying close to Sumburgh Airport on Mainland, Jarlshof is one of the most important historical sites in Europe, and has been continuously occupied from the Bronze Age right up until the 17th century. There are Bronze Age huts, Iron Age earth houses, brochs, wheelhouses from the Dark Ages, Norse longhouses and medieval houses. It is managed by Historic Scotland, and there is a small museum and interpretation centre.

At **Old Scatness**, close to Jarlshof, is an archaeological site centred on a number of ancient brochs, wheelhouses and dwellings. There is a living history area with demonstrations that reproduce ancient

technologies using authentic materials. It was discovered in 1975 when a road was cut through what was thought to be a natural mound. Old walls were discovered, and work began on excavating the site in 1995.

The **Ness of Burgi**, a small promontory jutting out into the sea, lies to the west of Jarlshof, and has an Iron Age fort.

Fair Isle

46 miles S of Lerwick

The most southerly of the Shetland Islands lies almost half way between Shetland and Orkney. It is owned by the National Trust for Scotland, and is one of the remotest inhabited islands in the country, with a population of about 70. It was originally called Fridarey, meaning "island of peace", by Norse settlers.

The island was once owned by George Waterston, who was the Scottish Director of the Royal Society for the Protection of Birds, and who founded a bird observatory in 1948. **The George Waterston Memorial Centre and Museum** has displays about the history and wildlife of the island.

The **Feely Dyke**, a turf wall separating common land from modern crofting land, may date from prehistoric times.

Scalloway

6 miles W of Lerwick on the A970

Though only six miles from Lerwick, this small village sits on the Atlantic coast while its larger neighbour sits on the coast

of the North Sea. Its name comes from the Norse "Scola Voe", which means the "Huts by the Bay".

Up until 1708 it was once Shetland's capital, but as Lerwick expanded so the centre of power shifted eastwards. **Scalloway Castle** dates from around 1600, and was built by Patrick Stewart, who was executed 15 years later in Edinburgh (see also Kirkwall).

During World War II the village was a secret Norwegian base, and from here Norwegians used to be ferried across to their country in fishing boats (nicknamed "Shetland buses") to mount sabotage operations and bring back resistance fighters who were on the run from German troops. The small **Scalloway Museum** in Main Street tells the story of these men, as well as the story of Scalloway itself.

Tingwall

6 miles NW of Lerwick on the A970

Law Ting Holm near Tingwall was where the ancient Shetland Islands parliament, or Althing, used to meet. It sits on a small promontory (which in Norse times was an island) jutting out into the Loch of Tingwall.

Just off the Scalloway - Tingwall Road is the **Murder Stone**, a prehistoric standing stone. It got its name from a local legend, which states that murderers were made to run between Law Ting Holm and the stone pursued by relatives of the murdered person. If the murderer made it to the stone unscathed, he wasn't executed, if he didn't, his pursuers killed him.

Tangwick

33 miles NW of Lerwick on the B9078

The **Tangwick Haa Museum**, based in Tangwick Haa, has displays and artefacts about the local history of the northern part of Mainland. The haa ("hall") itself dates from the 17th century, and was built by the Cheyne family, the local landowners. It was restored and opened as a museum in 1988.

Boddam

20 miles S of Lerwick on the A970

The **Crofthouse Museum** comprises a thatched house, steading and water mill, and illustrates what life was like in a 19th century Shetland Islands croft. It would have housed an extended family of children, parents and grandparents, and the men would have earned their living from the sea while the women worked the land. In the summer months it hosts a programme of traditional music, songs and stories.

Whalsay

18 miles NW of Lerwick

This small island, no more than six miles

The Westings Inn

Wormadale, Whiteness, Shetland ZE2 9LJ
Tel: 01595 840242 Fax: 01595 691029
e-mail; enquiries@westings.shetland.co.uk
website: www.westings.shetland.co.uk

Situated ten miles from Lerwick, **The Westings Inn** has been given three coveted stars from Visit Scotland, and is a roomy and comfortable hostelry offering six en suite rooms, two of which can be family suites. All have TV, hair dryer and hospitality tray. There is also a camp site in the gardens which can accommodate tents, caravans and campervans. The countryside surrounding the hotel is stunning, and it is ideal for walkers, cyclists and anglers, as some of the best fishing on Shetland is available close by. It's also the ideal place to "switch off" from the hustle and bustle of modern life, as things move at a slower pace here - just right for the discerning tourist!

long by two miles wide, is connected to Mainland by a ferry from Dury Voe. There are superb coastal walks and many ancient remains. **Symbister House**, in the island's ferry port, is the finest Georgian house in Shetland. It was built by the Bruce family, who nearly bankrupted themselves in doing so, something that did not trouble the people of the island, as the family had oppressed them for years. It now forms part of the local school.

Fetlar

40 miles NE of Lerwick

The small island of Fetlar is no more than seven miles long by five miles wide at its widest, and sits off the east coast of Yell, to which it is connected by ferry. **The Fetlar**

Westayre

Muckle Roe, Brae, Shetland ZE2 9QW
Tel: 01806 522368
e-mail: westayre@ukonline.co.uk

Bed and breakfast accommodation doesn't come any better than the four-star **Westayre**, a modern, smart family home on the small island of Muckle Roe. The island is connected to Shetland's Mainland by a short bridge, making the house only four and a half miles from the village of Brae, with its two hotels, swimming pool and shop.

The B&B is owned and managed by Mrs Elsie Wood, who has created a warm and welcoming establishment with high standards and is great value-for-money. Westayre has four extremely comfortable rooms - a double, a twin and two singles. Two are fully en suite, and all have TV, hospitality tray and hair dryer. There is a visitors' lounge/dining room that overlooks Magnus Bay, with wonderful views of the rolling Atlantic Ocean. It has a TV and in chillier months there is a roaring open fire. The B&B also boasts washing and ironing facilities, and there is ample parking.

The full Scottish breakfasts will set you up for a day exploring the Shetlands. Lighter options are also available, with the speciality of the house being smoked kippers when available. The fish is caught by Elsie's husband Ivor, who personally smokes them in his own smoking shed behind the house. Fresh fruit is always available, and packed lunches and evening emails can also be made available by prior arrangement.

Westayre sits 30 miles north of Lerwick, and makes the perfect base for walkers, or those interested in archaeology, history and wildlife. And, of course, if you just want to relax and get away from it all, then Westayre is also the place for you!

Busta House Hotel

Busta, Brae, Shetland ZE2 9GN
Tel: 01806 522506 Fax: 01806 522588
e-mail: reservations@bustahouse.com
website: www.bustahouse.com

Parts of **Busta House Hotel** date back to 1588 when it was built by the Gifford family who were prominent members of Shetland society. Nowadays it is an elegant and welcoming hotel that boasts three coveted VisitScotland stars. The present owners, Veronica and Joe Rocks, are determined to maintain the high standards they have set since buying the hotel in 2000.

There are 22 en suite rooms, each one named after a Shetland island, and all having a modem port, direct dial telephone and hospitality tray. They offer discerning guests comfort combined with tradition, always a winning combination, and the furnishings and decoration reflect this.

You can dine in the elegant Pitcairn Room, where the four course à la carte menu makes imaginative use of fresh local produce. You can also eat in more informal surroundings in the bar, where another à la carte menu offers many tempting dishes that are beautifully cooked and presented. And why not have a pre or after dinner drink in the relaxing atmosphere of the 20 metre long Long Room, with its comfortable seating and open peat fire in the cooler months?

Conferences and social functions are a speciality of the hotel. The library, on the first floor, offers glorious views and can accommodate seminars of up to 18 people. The studio, on the second floor, retains its original wood panelling, and can accommodate up to 25 people. It also has OHP, data projector, flip charts and TV video.

Interpretive Centre at Beach of Houbie has displays on the island's history, wildlife, history and folklore, as well as genealogical archives. There is also an archive of over 3000 photographs.

Yell

30 miles N of Lerwick

The second largest island in Shetland is about 20 miles long by seven miles wide at its widest, and is connected to Mainland. Though its population is close to 1000, it still has lonely moorland and a varied coast that lend themselves to hill walking and bird watching.

The **Old Haa of Burravoe** ("Old Hall of Burravoe"), at the island's south east corner, is the oldest complete building on the

Gutcher Post Office & B&B

Gutcher, Yell, Shetland ZE2 9DF
Tel: 01957 744201 Fax: 01957 744366
e-mail: margaret.tulloch@btopenworld.com

Owned and managed by Margaret Tulloch, the three star **Gutcher Post Office & B&B** is undoubtedly the best establishment of its kind on the island of Yell. Set within a picturesque 19th century building of mellow stone, it offers accommodation for six people in four rooms, all with TV, radio and hospitality tray. The traditional Scottish breakfasts are hearty and filling, and

beautifully cooked evening meals are also available by prior arrangement. Gutcher lies close to the short ferry crossing to Unst, Britain's most northerly isle, and makes the ideal base from which to explore Shetland.

Croft on Unst

Unst

46 miles N of Lerwick

Unst is the most northerly of the Shetland Isles, and **Hermaness** is the most northerly point in the United Kingdom that can be reached on foot. Offshore is **Muckle Flugga**, with its Outer Stack being the most northerly point in the United Kingdom. At the southeast corner of the island are the gaunt ruins of **Muness Castle**, said to be the most northerly castle in Britain. The castle dates from 1598, and was built by Lawrence Bruce, a relative of the wayward Stewart dynasty that ruled the islands, and a man every bit as cruel and despotic as they were. He was appointed sheriff of Shetland, and when Patrick Stewart succeeded his father Robert as the Earl of Orkney, Lawrence felt so threatened that he built the castle as a place of safety. In 1608 Patrick came to Unst with 36 men to destroy it, but retreated before he had a chance to do so for some reason. In about 1627 a party of French raiders attacked and burnt the castle, and it was never rebuilt.

At **Harnoldswick** is Britain's most northerly church. The Methodist church was built between 1990 and 1993, and has a simple design based on a traditional Norwegian church

island, and dates from 1637. It now houses a small museum and interpretation centre, and has a digital recording studio. The **Lumbister RSPB Reserve** sits almost in the middle of the island, between Whale Firth (said to be the smallest "firth" in Scotland) and the A968, the island's main road. Here you can see the red-throated diver, eider, dunlin, great and Arctic skua, dunlin, wheatear, curlew, merlin and snipe.

TOURIST INFORMATION CENTRES

ABERDEEN, ABERDEEN
Address: 23 Union Street, Aberdeen, Aberdeen, Scotland, AB11 5BP
Tel: 01224 288828
Fax: 01224 252219
e-mail: info@agtb.org
website: www.aberdeen-grampian.com

ABERFELDY, PERTH & KINROSS
Address: The Square, Aberfeldy, Perth & Kinross, Scotland, PH15 2DD
Tel: 01887 820276
Fax: 01887 829495
e-mail: aberfeldytic@perthshire.co.uk
website: www.perthshire.co.uk

ABERFOYLE, STIRLINGSHIRE
Address: Trossachs Discovery Centre, Main Street, Aberfoyle, Stirlingshire, Scotland, FK8 0TH
Tel: 08707 200 604
Fax: 01877 382153
e-mail: info@aberfoyle.visitscotland.com
website: www.visitscottishheartlands.org

ALFORD, ABERDEENSHIRE
Address: Old Station Yard, Main Street, Alford, Aberdeenshire, Scotland, AB33 8FD
Tel: 019755 62052
e-mail: info@agtb.org
website: www.aberdeen-grampian.com

ALVA, STIRLINGSHIRE
Address: Mill Trail Visitor Centre, West Stirling Street, Alva, Stirlingshire, Scotland, FK12 5EN
Tel: 08707 200 605
Fax: 01259 763100
e-mail: info@alva.visitscotland.com
website: www.visitscottishheartlands.org

ANSTRUTHER, FIFE
Address: c/o Scottish Fisheries Museum, Harbourhead, Anstruther, Fife, Scotland, KY10 3AB
Tel: 01333 311073
Fax: 01333 312996
e-mail: anstruther@visitfife.com
website: www.standrews.co.uk

ARBROATH, ANGUS
Address: Market Place, Arbroath, Angus, Scotland, DD11 1HR
Tel: 01241 872609
Fax: 01241 878550
e-mail: arbroath@angusanddundee.co.uk
website: www.angusanddundee.co.uk

ARDGARTAN, DUNBARTONSHIRE
Address: Forestry Car Park, Glen Croe, Ardgartan, by Arrochar, Dunbartonshire, Scotland, G83 7AR
Tel: 08707 200 606
Fax: 01301 702432
e-mail: info@ardgartan.visitscotland.com
website: www.visitscottishheartlands.org

AUCHTERARDER, PERTH & KINROSS
Address: 90 High Street, Auchterarder, Perth & Kinross, Scotland, PH3 1BJ
Tel: 01764 663450
Fax: 01764 664235
e-mail: auchterardertic@perthshire.co.uk
website: www.perthshire.co.uk

AVIEMORE, INVERNESS-SHIRE
Address: Grampian Road, Aviemore, Inverness-shire, Scotland, PH22 1PP
Tel: 0845 22 55 121
e-mail: info@visitscotland.com
website: www.visithighlands.com

AYR, AYRSHIRE
Address: 22 Sandgate, Ayr, Ayrshire, Scotland, KA7 1BW
Tel: 00845 22 55 121
e-mail: info@ayrshire-arran.com
website: www.ayrshire-arran.com

BALLACHULISH, ARGYLL & BUTE
Address: Albert Road, Ballachulish, Argyll & Bute, Scotland, PH39 4JR
Tel: 0845 22 55 121
e-mail: info@visitscotland.com
website: www.visithighlands.com

BALLATER, ABERDEENSHIRE
Address: The Old Royal Station, Station Square, Ballater, Aberdeenshire, Scotland, AB35 5RB
Tel: 013397 55306
Fax: 013397 54088
e-mail: info@agtb.org
website: www.aberdeen-grampian.com

BALLOCH, DUNBARTONSHIRE
Address: Balloch Road, Balloch, Dunbartonshire, Scotland, G83 8LQ
Tel: 008707 200 607
Fax: 01389 751704
e-mail: info@balloch.visitscotland.com
website: www.visitscottishheartlands.org

BANCHORY, ABERDEENSHIRE
Address: Bridge Street, Banchory, Aberdeenshire, Scotland, AB31 5SX
Tel: 01330 822000
e-mail: info@agtb.org
website: www.aberdeen-grampian.com

BANFF, ABERDEENSHIRE
Address: Collie Lodge, Banff, Aberdeenshire, Scotland, AB45 1AU
Tel: 01261 812419
e-mail: info@agtb.org
website: www.aberdeen-grampian.com

BETTYHILL, SUTHERLAND
Address: Clachan, Bettyhill, by Thurso, Sutherland, Scotland, KW14 7SS
Tel: 0845 22 55 121
e-mail: info@visitscotland.com
website: www.visithighlands.com

BIGGAR, SOUTH LANARKSHIRE
Address: 155 High Street, Biggar, South Lanarkshire, Scotland, ML12 6DL
Tel: 01899 221066
Fax: 01899 221066
website: www.seeglasgow.com

BLAIRGOWRIE, PERTH & KINROSS
Address: 26 Wellmeadow, Blairgowrie, Perth & Kinross, Scotland, PH10 6AS
Tel: 01250 872960
Fax: 01250 873701
e-mail: blairgowrietic@perthshire.co.uk
website: www.perthshire.co.uk

BO'NESS, WEST LOTHIAN
Address: Car Park, Seafield Place, Bo'ness, West Lothian, Scotland, EH51 0AJ
Tel: 08707 200 608
Fax: 08707 200 608
website: www.visitscottishheartlands.org

BRAEMAR, ABERDEENSHIRE
Address: The Mews, Mar Road, Braemar, Aberdeenshire, Scotland, AB35 5YP
Tel: 013397 41600
Fax: 013397 41643
e-mail: info@agtb.org
website: www.aberdeen-grampian.com

BRECHIN, ANGUS
Address: Brechin Castle Centre, Haughmuir, Brechin, Angus, Scotland, DD9 6RL
Tel: 01356 623050
e-mail: brechin@angusanddundee.co.uk
website: www.angusanddundee.co.uk

BROADFORD, ISLE OF SKYE
Address: The Car Park, Broadford, Isle of Skye, Scotland, IV49 9AB
Tel: 0845 22 55 121
e-mail: info@visitscotland.com
website: www.visithighlands.com

BRODICK, ISLE OF ARRAN
Address: The Pier, Brodick, Isle of Arran, Scotland, KA27 8AU
Tel: 0845 22 55 121
e-mail: info@ayrshire-arran.com
website: www.ayrshire-arran.com

CALLANDER, STIRLINGSHIRE
Address: Rob Roy and Trossachs Visitor Centre, Ancaster Square, Callander, Stirlingshire, Scotland, FK17 8ED
Tel: 08707 200 628
Fax: 01877 330784
e-mail: info@callander.visitscotland.com
website: www.visitscottishheartlands.org

CAMPBELTOWN, KINTYRE
Address: MacKinnon House, The Pier, Campbeltown, Kintyre, Scotland, PA28 6EF
Tel: 08707 200 609
Fax: 01586 553291
e-mail: info@campbeltown.visitscotland.com
website: www.visitscottishheartlands.org

CARNOUSTIE, ANGUS
Address: 1b High Street, Carnoustie, Angus, Scotland, DD7 6AN
Tel: 01241 852258
e-mail: carnoustie@angusanddundee.co.uk
website: www.angusanddundee.co.uk

CASTLE DOUGLAS, DUMFRIES & GALLOWAY
Address: Market Hill, Castle Douglas, Dumfries & Galloway, Scotland, DG7 1AE
Tel: 01556 502611
e-mail: castledouglas@dgtb.visitscotland.com
website: www.visitdumfriesandgalloway.co.uk

CASTLEBAY, WESTERN ISLES
Address: Main Street, Castlebay, Isle of Barra, Western Isles, Scotland, HS9 5XD
Tel: 01871 810336
Fax: 01871 810336
e-mail: castlebay@visithebrides.com
website: www.visithebrides.com

CRAIGNURE, ARGYLL & BUTE
Address: The Pier, Craignure, Isle of Mull, Argyll & Bute, Scotland, PA65 6AY
Tel: 08707 200 610
Fax: 01680 812497
e-mail: info@mull.visitscotland.com
website: www.visitscottishheartlands.org

CRAIL, FIFE
Address: c/o Museum & Heritage Centre, Marketgate, Crail, Fife, Scotland, KY10 3TL
Tel: 01333 450869
Fax: 01333 450869
e-mail: crail@visitfife.com
website: www.standrews.co.uk

CRATHIE, ABERDEENSHIRE
Address: The Car Park, Crathie, Ballater, Aberdeenshire, Scotland, AB35 5UL
Tel: 013397 42414
e-mail: info@agtb.org
website: www.aberdeen-grampian.com

CRIEFF, PERTH & KINROSS
Address: Town Hall, High Street, Crieff, Perth & Kinross, Scotland, PH7 3HU
Tel: 01764 652578
Fax: 01764 655422
e-mail: criefftic@perthshire.co.uk
website: www.perthshire.co.uk

DAVIOT WOOD, INVERNESS-SHIRE
Address: Picnic Area (A9), Daviot Wood, by Inverness, Inverness-shire, Scotland, IV1 2ER
Tel: 0845 22 55 121
e-mail: info@visitscotland.com
website: www.visithighlands.com

DORNOCH, SUTHERLAND
Address: The Coffee Shop, The Square, Dornoch, Sutherland, Scotland, IV25 3SD
Tel: 0845 22 55 121
e-mail: info@visitscotland.com
website: www.visithighlands.com

DRUMNADROCHIT, INVERNESS-SHIRE
Address: The Car Park, Drumnadrochit, Inverness-shire, Scotland, IV63 6TX
Tel: 0845 22 55 121
e-mail: info@visitscotland.com
website: www.visithighlands.com

DRYMEN, DUNBARTONSHIRE
Address: Drymen Library, The Square, Drymen, Dunbartonshire, Scotland, G63 0BD
Tel: 08707 200 611
Fax: 01360 660751
website: www.visitscottishheartlands.org

DUFFTOWN, ABERDEENSHIRE
Address: The Clock Tower, The Square, Dufftown, Aberdeenshire, Scotland, AB55 4AD
Tel: 01340 820501
e-mail: info@agtb.org
website: www.aberdeen-grampian.com

DUMBARTON, DUNBARTONSHIRE
Address: Road Chef Service Area, A82 Northbound, Milton, Dunbartonshire, Scotland, G82 2TZ
Tel: 08707 200 612
Fax: 001389 371164
e-mail: info@milton.visitscotland.com
website: www.visitscottishheartlands.org

DUMFRIES, DUMFRIES & GALLOWAY
Address: 64 Whitesands, Dumfries, Dumfries & Galloway, Scotland, DG1 2RS
Tel: 01387 253862
Fax: 01387 245555
e-mail: info@dgtb.visitscotland.com
website: www.visitdumfriesandgalloway.co.uk

DUNBAR, EAST LOTHIAN
Address: 143a High Street, Dunbar, East Lothian, Scotland, EH42 1ES
Tel: 0845 22 55 121
e-mail: info@visitscotland.com
website: www.edinburgh.org

DUNBLANE, STIRLINGSHIRE
Address: Stirling Road, Dunblane, Stirlingshire, Scotland, FK15 9EP
Tel: 08707 200 613
Fax: 008707 200 613
website: www.visitscottishheartlands.org

DUNDEE, TAYSIDE
Address: 21 Castle Street, Dundee, Tayside, Scotland, DD1 3AA
Tel: 01382 527527
Fax: 01382 527551
e-mail: enquiries@angusanddundee.co.uk
website: www.angusanddundee.co.uk

DUNFERMLINE, FIFE
Address: 1 High Street, Dunfermline, Fife, Scotland, KY12 7DL
Tel: 01383 720999
Fax: 01383 625807
e-mail: dunfermline@visitfife.com
website: www.standrews.co.uk

DUNKELD, PERTH & KINROSS
Address: The Cross, Dunkeld, Perth & Kinross, Scotland, PH8 0AN
Tel: 01350 727688
Fax: 01350 727688
e-mail: dunkeldtic@perthshire.co.uk
website: www.perthshire.co.uk

DUNOON, ARGYLL & BUTE
Address: 7 Alexandra Parade, Dunoon, Argyll & Bute, Scotland, PA23 8AB
Tel: 08707 200 629
Fax: 01369 706085
e-mail: info@dunoon.visitscotland.com
website: www.visitscottishheartlands.org

DUNVEGAN, ISLE OF SKYE
Address: 2 Lochside, Dunvegan, Isle of Skye, Scotland, IV55 8WB
Tel: 0845 22 55 121
e-mail: info@visitscotland.com
website: www.visithighlands.com

DURNESS, SUTHERLAND
Address: Durine, Durness, by Lairg, Sutherland, Scotland, IV27 4PN
Tel: 0845 22 55 121
e-mail: info@visitscotland.com
website: www.visithighlands.com

EDINBURGH AIRPORT, CITY OF EDINBURGH
Address: Airport Information/Tourist Info Desk, Edinburgh International Airport, Turnhouse, City of Edinburgh, Scotland, EH12 9DN
Tel: 0845 22 55 121
e-mail: info@visitscotland.com
website: www.edinburgh.org

EDINBURGH AND SCOTLAND INFORMATION CENTRE, CITY OF EDINBURGH
Address: 3 Princes Street, Edinburgh, City of Edinburgh, Scotland, EH2 2QP
Tel: 0845 22 55 121
e-mail: info@visitscotland.com
website: www.edinburgh.org

ELGIN, MORAY
Address: 17 High Street, Elgin, Moray, Scotland, IV30 1EG
Tel: 01343 542666/543388
Fax: 01343 552982
e-mail: info@agtb.org
website: www.aberdeen-grampian.com

EYEMOUTH, SCOTTISH BORDERS
Address: Auld Kirk, Manse Road, Eyemouth, Scottish Borders, Scotland, TD14 5JE
Tel: 0870 608 0404
Fax: 01750 21886
e-mail: info@scot-borders.co.uk
website: www.visitscottishborders.com

FALKIRK
Address: 2-4 Glebe Street, Falkirk, Scotland, FK1 1HX
Tel: 08707 200 614
Fax: 01324 638440
e-mail: info@falkirk.visitscotland.com
website: www.visitscottishheartlands.org

FORFAR, ANGUS
Address: East High Street, Forfar, Angus, Scotland, DD8 2EG
Tel: 01307 467876
e-mail: forfar@angusanddundee.co.uk
website: www.angusanddundee.co.uk

FORRES, MORAY
Address: 116 High Street, Forres, Moray, Scotland, IV36 0NP
Tel: 01309 672938
e-mail: info@agtb.org
website: www.aberdeen-grampian.com

FORT AUGUSTUS, INVERNESS-SHIRE
Address: Car Park, Fort Augustus, Inverness-shire, Scotland, PH32 4DD
Tel: 0845 22 55 121
e-mail: info@visitscotland.com
website: www.visithighlands.com

FORT WILLIAM, INVERNESS-SHIRE
Address: Cameron Centre, Cameron Square, Fort William, Inverness-shire, Scotland, PH33 6AJ
Tel: 0845 22 55 121
e-mail: info@visitscotland.com
website: www.visithighlands.com

FORTH BRIDGES, FIFE
Address: c/o Corus Hotel, St Margaret's Head, North Queensferry, Fife, Scotland, KY11 1HP
Tel: 01383 417759
Fax: 01383 410802
e-mail: forthbridges@visitfife.com
website: www.standrews.co.uk

FRASERBURGH, ABERDEENSHIRE
Address: 3 Saltoun Square, Fraserburgh, Aberdeenshire, Scotland, AB43 9DA
Tel: 01346 518315
e-mail: info@agtb.org
website: www.aberdeen-grampian.com

GAIRLOCH, ROSS-SHIRE
Address: Achtercairn, Gairloch, Ross-shire, Scotland, IV22 2DN
Tel: 0845 22 55 121
e-mail: info@visitscotland.com
website: www.visithighlands.com

GATEHOUSE OF FLEET, DUMFRIES & GALLOWAY
Address: Car Park, Gatehouse of Fleet, Dumfries & Galloway, Scotland, DG7 5EA
Tel: 01557 814212
e-mail: gatehouseoffleet@dgtb.visitscotland.com
website: www.visitdumfriesandgalloway.co.uk

GLASGOW
Address: 11 George Square, Glasgow, Scotland, G2 1DY
Tel: 0141 204 4400
Fax: 0141 221 3524
e-mail: enquiries@seeglasgow.com
website: www.seeglasgow.com

GLASGOW AIRPORT, RENFREWSHIRE
Address: International Arrivals, Glasgow International Airport, Paisley, Renfrewshire, Scotland, PA3 2ST
Tel: 0141 848 4440
Fax: 0141 849 1444
e-mail: airport@seeglasgow.com
website: www.seeglasgow.com

GRANTOWN ON SPEY, INVERNESS-SHIRE
Address: 54 High Street, Grantown on Spey, Inverness-shire, Scotland, PH26 3EH
Tel: 0845 22 55 121
e-mail: info@visitscotland.com
website: www.visithighlands.com

GRETNA, DUMFRIES & GALLOWAY
Address: Unit 10, Gretna Gateway Outlet Village, Gretna, Dumfries & Galloway, Scotland, DG16 5GG
Tel: 01461 337834
e-mail: gretna@dgtb.visitscotland.com
website: www.visitdumfriesandgalloway.co.uk

HAMILTON, SOUTH LANARKSHIRE
Address: Road Chef Services, M74 Northbound, Hamilton, South Lanarkshire, Scotland, ML3 6JW
Tel: 01698 285590
Fax: 01698 891494
e-mail: hamilton@seeglasgow.com
website: www.seeglasgow.com

HAWICK, SCOTTISH BORDERS
Address: Drumlanrig's Tower, Tower Knowe, Hawick, Scottish Borders, Scotland, TD9 9EN
Tel: 0870 608 0404
Fax: 01750 21886
e-mail: info@scot-borders.co.uk
website: www.visitscottishborders.com

HELENSBURGH, DUNBARTONSHIRE
Address: Clock Tower, The Pier, Helensburgh, Dunbartonshire, Scotland, G84 7NY
Tel: 08707 200 615
Fax: 01436 672642
e-mail: info@helensburgh.visitscotland.com
website: www.visitscottishheartlands.org

HUNTLY, ABERDEENSHIRE
Address: 9a The Square, Huntly, Aberdeenshire, Scotland, AB54 8BR
Tel: 01466 792255
e-mail: info@agtb.org
website: www.aberdeen-grampian.com

INVERARAY, ARGYLL & BUTE
Address: Front Street, Inveraray, Argyll & Bute, Scotland, PA32 8UY
Tel: 08707 200 616
Fax: 01499 302269
e-mail: info@inveraray.visitscotland.com
website: www.visitscottishheartlands.org

INVERNESS, INVERNESS-SHIRE
Address: Castle Wynd, Inverness, Inverness-shire, Scotland, IV2 3BJ
Tel: 0845 22 55 121
e-mail: info@visitscotland.com
website: www.visithighlands.com

INVERURIE, ABERDEENSHIRE
Address: Bookstore, 18 High Street, Inverurie, Aberdeenshire, Scotland, AB51 3XQ
Tel: 01467 625800
Fax: 01467 625800
e-mail: info@agtb.org
website: www.aberdeen-grampian.com

ISLAY, ISLE OF ISLAY
Address: The Square, Main Street, Bowmore, Isle of Islay, Scotland, PA43 7JP
Tel: 08707 200 617
Fax: 01496 810363
e-mail: info@islay.visitscotland.com
website: www.visitscottishheartlands.org

JEDBURGH, SCOTTISH BORDERS
Address: Murray's Green, Jedburgh, Scottish Borders, Scotland, TD8 6BE
Tel: 0870 608 0404
Fax: 01750 21886
e-mail: info@scot-borders.co.uk
website: www.visitscottishborders.com

JOHN O'GROATS, CAITHNESS
Address: County Road, John O'Groats, Caithness, Scotland, KW1 4YR
Tel: 0845 22 55 121
e-mail: info@visitscotland.com
website: www.visithighlands.com

KELSO, SCOTTISH BORDERS
Address: Town House, The Square, Kelso, Scottish Borders, Scotland, TD5 7HF
Tel: 0870 608 0404
Fax: 01750 21886
e-mail: info@scot-borders.co.uk
website: www.visitscottishborders.com

KILCHOAN, ARGYLL & BUTE
Address: Kilchoan Community Centre, Pier Road, Kilchoan, Acharacle, Argyll & Bute, Scotland, PH36 4LJ
Tel: 0845 22 55 121
e-mail: info@visitscotland.com
website: www.visithighlands.com

KILLIN, STIRLINGSHIRE
Address: Breadalbane Folklore Centre, The Old Mill, Falls of Dochart, Killin, Stirlingshire, Scotland, FK21 8XE
Tel: 08707 200 627
Fax: 01567 820764
e-mail: info@killin.visitscotland.com
website: www.visitscottishheartlands.org

KINGUSSIE, INVERNESS-SHIRE
Address: c/o Highland Folk Museum, Duke Street, Kingussie, Inverness-shire, Scotland, PH21 1JG
Tel: 0845 22 55 121
e-mail: info@visitscotland.com
website: www.visithighlands.com

KINROSS, PERTH & KINROSS
Address: Heart of Scotland Visitor Centre, adjacent to Service Area J6, M90, Kinross, Perth & Kinross, Scotland, KY13 7NQ
Tel: 01577 863680
Fax: 01577 863370
e-mail: kinrosstic@perthshire.co.uk
website: www.perthshire.co.uk

KIRKCALDY, FIFE
Address: 19 Whytescauseway, Kirkcaldy, Fife, Scotland, KY1 1XF
Tel: 01592 267775
Fax: 01592 203154
e-mail: kirkcaldy@visitfife.com
website: www.standrews.co.uk

KIRKCUDBRIGHT, DUMFRIES & GALLOWAY
Address: Harbour Square, Kirkcudbright, Dumfries & Galloway, Scotland, DG6 4HY
Tel: 01557 330494
Fax: 01557 332416
e-mail: kirkcudbright@dgtb.visitscotland.com
website: www.visitdumfriesandgalloway.co.uk

KIRKWALL, ORKNEY
Address: 6 Broad Street, Kirkwall, Orkney, Scotland, KW15 1NX
Tel: 01856 872856
Fax: 01856 875056
e-mail: info@visitorkney.com
website: www.visitorkney.com

KIRRIEMUIR, ANGUS
Address: Cumberland Close, Kirriemuir, Angus, Scotland, DD8 4EF
Tel: 01575 574097
e-mail: kirriemuir@angusanddundee.co.uk
website: www.angusanddundee.co.uk

KYLE OF LOCHALSH, ROSS-SHIRE
Address: Car Park, Kyle of Lochalsh, Ross-shire, Scotland, IV40 8AQ
Tel: 0845 22 55 121
e-mail: info@visitscotland.com
website: www.visithighlands.com

LAIRG, SUTHERLAND
Address: Ferrycroft Countryside Centre, Lairg, Sutherland, Scotland, IV27 4AZ
Tel: 0845 22 55 121
e-mail: info@visitscotland.com
website: www.visithighlands.com

LANARK, SOUTH LANARKSHIRE
Address: Horsemarket, Ladyacre Road, Lanark, South Lanarkshire, Scotland, ML11 7LQ
Tel: 01555 661661
Fax: 01555 666143
e-mail: lanark@seeglasgow.com
website: www.seeglasgow.com

LARGS, AYRSHIRE
Address: The Railway Station, Main Street, Largs, Ayrshire, Scotland, KA30 8AN
Tel: 0845 22 55 121
e-mail: info@ayrshire-arran.com
website: www.ayrshire-arran.com

LERWICK, SHETLAND ISLANDS
Address: The Market Cross, Lerwick, Shetland Islands, Scotland, ZE1 0LU
Tel: 01595 693434
Fax: 01595 695807
e-mail: info@visitshetland.com
website: www.visitshetland.com

LINLITHGOW, WEST LOTHIAN
Address: Burgh Hall, The Cross, Linlithgow, West Lothian, Scotland, EH49 8RE
Tel: 0845 22 55 121
e-mail: info@visitscotland.com
website: www.edinburgh.org

LOCHBOISDALE, WESTERN ISLES
Address: Pier Road, Lochboisdale, Isle of South Uist, Western Isles, Scotland, HS8 5TH
Tel: 01878 700286
Fax: 01878 700286
e-mail: lochboisdale@visithebrides.com
website: www.visithebrides.com

LOCHGILPHEAD, ARGYLL & BUTE
Address: Lochnell Street, Lochgilphead, Argyll & Bute, Scotland, PA30 8JN
Tel: 08707 200 618
Fax: 01546 606254
e-mail: info@lochgilphead.visitscotland.com
website: www.visitscottishheartlands.org

LOCHINVER, SUTHERLAND
Address: Assynt Visitor Centre, Main Street, Lochinver, by Lairg, Sutherland, Scotland, IV27 4LX
Tel: 0845 22 55 121
e-mail: info@visitscotland.com
website: www.visithighlands.com

LOCHMADDY, WESTERN ISLES
Address: Pier Road, Lochmaddy, Isle of North Uist, Western Isles, Scotland, HS6 5AA
Tel: 01876 500321
Fax: 01876 500321

MALLAIG, INVERNESS-SHIRE
Address: The Pier, Mallaig, Inverness-shire, Scotland, PH41 4SQ
Tel: 0845 22 55 121
e-mail: info@visitscotland.com
website: www.visithighlands.com

MELROSE, SCOTTISH BORDERS
Address: Abbey House, Abbey Street, Melrose, Scottish Borders, Scotland, TD6 9LG
Tel: 0870 608 0404
Fax: 01750 21886
e-mail: info@scot-borders.co.uk
website: www.visitscottishborders.com

MOFFAT, DUMFRIES & GALLOWAY
Address: Churchgate, Moffat, Dumfries & Galloway, Scotland, DG10 9EG
Tel: 01683 220620
e-mail: moffat@dgtb.visitscotland.com
website: www.visitdumfriesandgalloway.co.uk

MONTROSE, ANGUS
Address: Bridge Street, Montrose, Angus, Scotland, DD10 8AB
Tel: 01674 672000
e-mail: montrose@angusanddundee.co.uk
website: www.angusanddundee.co.uk

NAIRN, INVERNESS-SHIRE
Address: The Library, 68 High Street, Nairn, Inverness-shire, Scotland, IV12 4AU
Tel: 0845 22 55 121
e-mail: info@visitscotland.com
website: www.visithighlands.com

NEWTON STEWART, DUMFRIES & GALLOWAY
Address: Dashwood Square, Newton Stewart, Dumfries & Galloway, Scotland, DG8 6EQ
Tel: 01671 402431
e-mail: newtonstewart@dgtb.visitscotland.com
website: www.visitdumfriesandgalloway.co.uk

NEWTONGRANGE, MIDLOTHIAN
Address: Scottish Mining Museum, Newtongrange, Midlothian, Scotland, EH26 8HB
Tel: 0845 22 55 121
e-mail: info@visitscotland.com
website: www.edinburgh.org

NORTH BERWICK, EAST LOTHIAN
Address: Quality Street, North Berwick, East Lothian, Scotland, EH39 4HJ
Tel: 0845 22 55 121
e-mail: info@visitscotland.com
website: www.edinburgh.org

NORTH KESSOCK, ROSS-SHIRE
Address: Picnic Site, North Kessock, Ross-shire, Scotland, IV1 1XB
Tel: 0845 22 55 121
e-mail: info@visitscotland.com
website: www.visithighlands.com

OBAN, ARGYLL & BUTE
Address: Church Building, Argyll Square, Oban, Argyll & Bute, Scotland, PA34 4AR
Tel: 08707 200 630
Fax: 01631 564273
e-mail: info@oban.visitscotland.com
website: www.visitscottishheartlands.org

OLD CRAIGHALL, EAST LOTHIAN
Address: Old Craighall Service Area (A1), by Musselburgh, East Lothian, Scotland, EH21 8RE
Tel: 0845 22 55 121
e-mail: info@visitscotland.com
website: www.edinburgh.org

PAISLEY, RENFREWSHIRE
Address: 9a Gilmour Street, Paisley, Renfrewshire, Scotland, PA1 1DD
Tel: 0141 889 0711
Fax: 0141 848 1363
e-mail: paisley@seeglasgow.com
website: www.seeglasgow.com

PEEBLES, SCOTTISH BORDERS
Address: High Street, Peebles, Scottish Borders, Scotland, EH45 8AG
Tel: 0870 608 0404
Fax: 01750 21886
e-mail: info@scot-borders.co.uk
website: www.visitscottishborders.com

PERTH, PERTH & KINROSS
Address: Lower City Mills, West Mill Street, Perth, Perth & Kinross, Scotland, PH1 5QP
Tel: 01738 450600
Fax: 01738 444863
e-mail: perthtic@perthshire.co.uk
website: www.perthshire.co.uk

PITLOCHRY, PERTH & KINROSS
Address: 22 Atholl Road, Pitlochry, Perth & Kinross, Scotland, PH16 5BX
Tel: 01796 472215/472751
Fax: 01796 474046
e-mail: pitlochrytic@perthshire.co.uk
website: www.perthshire.co.uk

PORTREE, ISLE OF SKYE
Address: Bayfield House, Bayfield Road, Portree, Isle of Skye, Scotland, IV51 9EL
Tel: 0845 22 55 121
e-mail: info@visitscotland.com
website: www.visithighlands.com

ROTHESAY, ARGYLL & BUTE
Address: Isle of Bute Discovery Centre, Winter Garden, Rothesay, Isle of Bute, Argyll & Bute, Scotland, PA20 0AT
Tel: 08707 200 619
Fax: 01700 505156
e-mail: info@rothesay.visitscotland.com
website: www.visitscottishheartlands.org

SELKIRK, SCOTTISH BORDERS
Address: Halliwells House, Selkirk, Scottish Borders, Scotland, TD7 4BL
Tel: 0870 608 0404
Fax: 01750 21886
e-mail: info@scot-borders.co.uk
website: www.visitscottishborders.com

SPEAN BRIDGE, INVERNESS-SHIRE
Address: The Kingdom of Scotland, Spean Bridge, by Fort William, Inverness-shire, Scotland, PH34 4EP
Tel: 0845 22 55 121
e-mail: info@visitscotland.com
website: www.visithighlands.com

ST ANDREWS, FIFE
Address: 70 Market Street, St Andrews, Fife, Scotland, KY16 9NU
Tel: 01334 472021
Fax: 01334 478422
e-mail: standrews@visitfife.com
website: www.standrews.co.uk

STIRLING (DUMBARTON ROAD), STIRLINGSHIRE
Address: 41 Dumbarton Road, Stirling, Stirlingshire, Scotland, FK8 2QQ
Tel: 08707 200 620
Fax: 01786 450039
e-mail: stirlingtic@aillst.ossian.net
website: www.visitscottishheartlands.org

STIRLING (PIRNHALL), STIRLINGSHIRE
Address: Motorway Service Area, Junction 9 M9/M80, Pirnhall, Stirling, Stirlingshire, Scotland, FK7 8ET
Tel: 08707 200 621
Fax: 01786 810879
e-mail: info@pirnhall.visitscotland.com
website: www.visitscottishheartlands.org

STIRLING (ROYAL BURGH), STIRLINGSHIRE
Address: Royal Burgh of Stirling Visitor Centre, Castle Esplanade, Stirling, Stirlingshire, Scotland, FK9 5LF
Tel: 08707 200 622
Fax: 01786 451881
e-mail: info@rbsvc.visitscotland.com
website: www.visitscottishheartlands.org

STONEHAVEN, ABERDEENSHIRE
Address: 66 Allardice Street, Stonehaven, Aberdeenshire, Scotland, AB39 2AA
Tel: 01569 762806
e-mail: info@agtb.org
website: www.aberdeen-grampian.com

STORNOWAY, WESTERN ISLES
Address: 26 Cromwell Street, Stornoway, Isle of Lewis, Western Isles, Scotland, HS1 2DD
Tel: 01851 703088
Fax: 01851 705244
e-mail: stornoway@visithebrides.com
website: www.visithebrides.com

STRANRAER, DUMFRIES & GALLOWAY
Address: 28 Harbour Street, Stranraer, Dumfries & Galloway, Scotland, DG9 7RA
Tel: 01776 702595
Fax: 01776 889156
e-mail: stranraer@dgtb.visitscotland.com
website: www.visitdumfriesandgalloway.co.uk

STRATHPEFFER, ROSS-SHIRE
Address: Square Wheels, The Square, Strathpeffer, Ross-shire, Scotland, IV14 9DW
Tel: 0845 22 55 121
e-mail: info@visitscotland.com
website: www.visithighlands.com

STROMNESS, ORKNEY
Address: Ferry Terminal Building, Pier Head, Stromness, Orkney, Scotland, KW16 3BH
Tel: 01856 850716
Fax: 01856 850777
e-mail: info@visitorkney.com
website: www.visitorkney.com

STRONTIAN, ARGYLL & BUTE
Address: Strontian, Acharacle, Argyll & Bute, Scotland, PH36 4HZ
Tel: 0845 22 55 121
e-mail: info@visitscotland.com
website: www.visithighlands.com

TARBERT (HARRIS), WESTERN ISLES
Address: Pier Road, Tarbert, Isle of Harris, Western Isles, Scotland, HS3 3DG
Tel: 01859 502011
Fax: 01859 502011
e-mail: tarbert@visithebrides.com
website: www.visithebrides.com

TARBERT (LOCH FYNE), ARGYLL & BUTE
Address: Harbour Street, Tarbert, Argyll & Bute, Scotland, PA29 6UD
Tel: 08707 200 624
Fax: 01880 820082
e-mail: info@tarbert.visitscotland.com
website: www.visitscottishheartlands.org

TARBET (LOCH LOMOND), ARGYLL & BUTE
Address: Main Street, Tarbet, Loch Lomond, Argyll & Bute, Scotland, G83 7DE
Tel: 08707 200 623
Fax: 01301 702224
e-mail: info@tarbet.visitscotland.com
website: www.visitscottishheartlands.org

THURSO, CAITHNESS
Address: Riverside, Thurso, Caithness, Scotland, KW14 8BU
Tel: 0845 22 55 121
e-mail: info@visitscotland.com
website: www.visithighlands.com

TOBERMORY, ISLE OF MULL
Address: Main Street, Tobermory, Isle of Mull, Scotland, PA75 6NU
Tel: 08707 200 625
Fax: 01688 302145
e-mail: info@tobermory.visitscotland.com
website: www.visitscottishheartlands.org

TOMINTOUL, ABERDEENSHIRE
Address: The Square, Tomintoul, Aberdeenshire, Scotland, AB37 9ET
Tel: 01807 580285
Fax: 01807 580285
e-mail: info@agtb.org
website: www.aberdeen-grampian.com

TYNDRUM, STIRLINGSHIRE
Address: Main Street, Tyndrum, Stirlingshire, Scotland, FK20 8RY
Tel: 08707 200 626
Fax: 01838 400530
e-mail: info@tyndrum.visitscotland.com
website: www.visitscottishheartlands.org

ULLAPOOL, ROSS-SHIRE
Address: Argyle Street, Ullapool, Ross-shire, Scotland, IV26 2UB
Tel: 0845 22 55 121
e-mail: info@visitscotland.com
website: www.visithighlands.com

WICK, CAITHNESS
Address: Norseman Hotel, Riverside, Wick, Caithness, Scotland, KW1 4NL
Tel: 0845 22 55 121
e-mail: info@visitscotland.com
website: www.visithighlands.com

LIST OF ADVERTISERS

A

B

C

G

H

I

J

O

P

Q

R

INDEX OF TOWNS, VILLAGES AND PLACES OF INTEREST

A

B

C

D

E

H

I

L

M

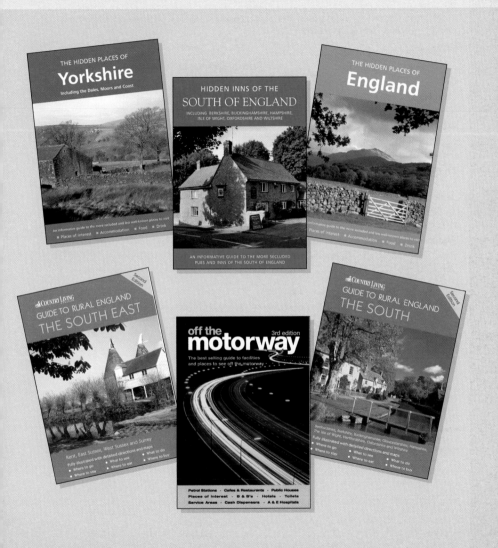

HIDDEN PLACES ORDER FORM

To order any of our publications just fill in the payment details below and complete the order form. For orders of less than 4 copies please add £1 per book for postage and packing. Orders over 4 copies are P & P free.

Please Complete Either:

I enclose a cheque for £ ______ made payable to Travel Publishing Ltd

Or:

Card No: ______ Expiry Date: ______

Signature: ______

Name: ______

Address: ______

Tel no: ______

Please either send, telephone, fax or e-mail your order to:

Travel Publishing Ltd, 7a Apollo House, Calleva Park, Aldermaston, Berkshire RG7 8TN

Tel: 0118 981 7777 Fax: 0118 982 0077 e-mail: karen@travelpublishing.co.uk

	Price	Quantity
Hidden Places Regional Titles		
Cambs & Lincolnshire	£7.99	....
Chilterns	£7.99	....
Cornwall	£8.99	....
Derbyshire	£8.99	....
Devon	£8.99	....
Dorset, Hants & Isle of Wight	£8.99	....
East Anglia	£8.99	....
Gloucs, Wiltshire & Somerset	£8.99	....
Heart of England	£7.99	....
Hereford, Worcs & Shropshire	£7.99	....
Highlands & Islands	£7.99	....
Kent	£8.99	....
Lake District & Cumbria	£8.99	....
Lancashire & Cheshire	£8.99	....
Lincolnshire & Notts	£8.99	....
Northumberland & Durham	£8.99	....
Sussex	£8.99	....
Yorkshire	£8.99	....
Hidden Places National Titles		
England	£11.99	....
Ireland	£11.99	....
Scotland	£11.99	....
Wales	£11.99	....

	Price	Quantity
Hidden Inns Titles		
East Anglia	£7.99	....
Heart of England	£7.99	....
Lancashire & Cheshire	£7.99	....
North of England	£7.99	....
South	£7.99	....
South East	£7.99	....
South and Central Scotland	£7.99	....
Wales	£7.99	....
Welsh Borders	£7.99	....
West Country	£7.99	....
Yorkshire	£7.99	....
Country Living Rural Guides		
East Anglia	£10.99	....
Heart of England	£10.99	....
Ireland	£11.99	....
North East of England	£10.99	....
North West of England	£10.99	....
Scotland	£10.99	....
South of England	£10.99	....
South East of England	£10.99	....
Wales	£11.99	....
West Country	£10.99	....

Total Quantity ______

Post & Packing ______

Total Value ______

READER REACTION FORM

The *Travel Publishing* research team would like to receive readers' comments on any visitor attractions or places reviewed in the book and also recommendations for suitab le entries to be included in the next edition. This will help ensure that the *Hidden Places* series of guides continues to provide its readers with useful information on the more interesting, unusual or unique features of each attraction or place ensuring that their visit to the local area is an enjoyable and stimulating experience. To provide your comments or recommendations would you please complete the forms below and overleaf as indicated and send to:

The Research Department, Travel Publishing Ltd,
7a Apollo House, Calleva Park, Aldermaston, Reading, RG7 8TN.

Your Name:

Your Address:

Your Telephone Number:

Please tick as appropriate:

Comments ☐ Recommendation ☐

Name of Establishment:

Address:

Telephone Number:

Name of Contact:

READER REACTION FORM

Comment or Reason for Recommendation:

READER REACTION FORM

The *Travel Publishing* research team would like to receive readers' comments on any visitor attractions or places reviewed in the book and also recommendations for suitab le entries to be included in the next edition. This will help ensure that the *Hidden Places* series of guides continues to provide its readers with useful information on the more interesting, unusual or unique features of each attraction or place ensuring that their visit to the local area is an enjoyable and stimulating experience. To provide your comments or recommendations would you please complete the forms below and overleaf as indicated and send to:

The Research Department, Travel Publishing Ltd,
7a Apollo House, Calleva Park, Aldermaston, Reading, RG7 8TN.

Your Name:

Your Address:

Your Telephone Number:

Please tick as appropriate:

Comments ☐ Recommendation ☐

Name of Establishment:

Address:

Telephone Number:

Name of Contact:

READER REACTION FORM

Comment or Reason for Recommendation:

....
....
....
....
....
....
....
....
....
....
....
....